CW01455989

FAITH AND THE CRISIS OF A NATION

FAITH AND THE CRISIS OF A NATION

Wales 1890–1914

R. Tudur Jones

Translated by Sylvia Prys Jones

edited by

ROBERT POPE

UNIVERSITY OF WALES PRESS
CARDIFF
2004

© Editor's Preface Robert Pope, 2004

Translated from Welsh by Sylvia Prys Jones

British Library Cataloguing-in-Publication Data.
A catalogue for this book is available from the British Library.

ISBN 0-7083-1909-2

**Published with the financial support of the Arts and Humanities
Research Board**

Printed in Great Britain by Dinefwr Press, Llandybïe

Contents

General Editor's Foreword

As Christians in many parts of the world celebrate the centenary of the 1904–5 Revival, the Centre for the Advanced Study of Religion in Wales offers its contribution to the study, interpretation and understanding of that event through the publication of this book.

Established in 1998, one of the main aims of the Centre was to encourage scholarly research. Sometimes this can be done through opening new avenues of study; at other times it can be achieved by disseminating to a wider readership knowledge already gained but formerly limited in its distribution.

Such is the case here. When R. Tudur Jones's work first appeared in Welsh in 1981 and 1982, it was immediately apparent that this was a major contribution to the study of the history, religion and culture of Wales. It can only be a matter of regret that it has taken over twenty years for it to be made available to English readers.

This translation is the sixth volume in the present series published by the Centre, and it records and analyses the spiritual throes of the late nineteenth and early twentieth centuries which were such a great part of the story of modern Wales. Now, a much wider readership can read about the events that impacted in such a significant way upon the lives of people both in Wales and beyond, and it is our hope within the Centre, not only that a better understanding of the period will be achieved but also that further studies of it will be undertaken as scholars attempt to gain even deeper insights into what happened in those heady days.

We are grateful to Dr Robert Pope for supervising the task of translating and undertaking the editing of the text. It is a task that has been done with great sensitivity and a discernible measure of respect for the author's memory, and that is something which is very much appreciated.

Geraint Tudur
The Centre for the Advanced Study of Religion in Wales,
University of Wales, Bangor

Editor's Preface

During the twentieth century, considerable research was undertaken into Wales's social and religious history and was published in the Welsh language. The result has been that Wales and the subtle nuances of its history have remained something of a mystery to those unable to read the ancient language. R. Tudur Jones contributed much to this historiography and, in order to make his conclusions more widely available, a project was launched in 2000 by the Centre for the Advanced Study of Religion in Wales, University of Wales, Bangor, to translate some of his work into English. This volume is the fruit of that project.

R. Tudur Jones (1921–98) was the most prolific and most important of all the church historians produced in Wales during the twentieth century. Though ordained an Independent (Congregational) minister, he spent most of his life as professor of church history and then principal of the Bala–Bangor Theological College in Bangor. He wrote numerous books and articles, all of which were both scholarly and erudite, matching a skill for conveying complex detail with a homely and readable style which proved to be accessible to professional and popular audiences alike. It is widely considered that his two-volume work *Ffydd ac Argyfwng Cenedl*, originally published in 1981 and 1982, was his magnum opus. Based on thirty years and more of teaching, research and publication, *Ffydd ac Argyfwng Cenedl* considers in detail Wales during the period 1890 to 1914 and treats the interaction of religion, language, culture and national identity in what he believed was a fateful period in the nation's history. It combines an interest in the history of institutions and characters with Tudur Jones's specialism in the history of Christian thought, the subject which he taught in the University of Wales, Bangor, from 1966 to 1997.

Tudur Jones was convinced that many of the problems facing Wales in the late twentieth century stemmed from events and the shaping of attitudes which occurred during the quarter century before the First World War. He identified what could be considered to be a sustained attack on Welshness, particularly on the Welsh language, which occurred simultaneously with a loss of identity within Wales itself. This produced a crisis of faith because the churches were caught up in this loss of identity. In their haste to become 'British', they forgot that there was a tradition of Welsh Christianity and of Welsh theology, while the lack of Welsh-language education and institutions meant that the churches ultimately became cultural centres which people attended because they conducted their affairs in Welsh rather than through faith in Jesus Christ. It is his eye for detail and his critical analysis of those events – all consciously and unapologetically presented from within a Christian, theological understanding – which make the work of enduring value, even though much changed in education and in politics in Wales between 1982 and 2002 to put a different slant on his conclusions.

Although originally published in two volumes, the opportunity was taken to produce a single volume which nevertheless maintained the shape of the original. Many of the chapters originated as lectures, though much of the conversational style of the original has, by and large, been edited here. Dr Tudur's impeccable and idiomatic Welsh, which is a delight to read, has somewhat complicated the task of translation. We have striven to ensure that the original meaning is consistently conveyed, even when we have had to stray from a literal rendering of the text. In this I am grateful to the translator, Dr Sylvia Prys Jones, for the care with which she approached the work. She produced a text which was fluent and accurate and did so with great speed which kept the project to timetable. The result is, I am sure, as accurate and as readable as is possible.

There are some points in the text where the Welsh has had to be retained. These include references to forms of Welsh verse and to the *sedd fawr* (the diaconal pew which surrounded the pulpit in many Welsh chapels), and to the *seiat* (referring to the Welsh Methodists' class meeting). There is no meaningful translation of the Welsh *eisteddfod* when referring to the various local and national literary and musical festivals. Having considered this, and the word's familiarity to a non-Welsh readership, it was decided to leave the Welsh word in the text. References in the original text to bardic names alone have been amended here. A Welsh readership may well be familiar with these men; their unfamiliarity to an English-language readership suggested that the authors' proper names should be used with bardic names in parentheses. Perhaps the most perplexing question was how to translate references to 'Annibynwyr'. In English, these particular Christians are referred to as 'Congregationalists'; in Welsh they have been known as 'Independents'. Some would maintain that there is a degree of detail separating the two forms, though, on the whole, they are the same. However, it seemed inappropriate to translate all references as 'Congregational' or 'Congregationalist', especially when the 'Union of Welsh Independents' is a familiar name. It has proved impossible to maintain consistency, particularly as, at some points, stylistic concerns deserved consideration. In the main, where references are clearly to Welsh chapels or organizations, 'Independent' has been used. References which include English and Welsh churches, and most references to individuals, have been rendered as 'Congregational' and 'Congregationalist' simply because reference in English to someone as an 'Independent' may possess unintended connotations.

Where the original text used a quotation which Tudur Jones had translated into Welsh, every effort has been made to locate and utilize the original. In a minority of cases, it has proved impossible to find the original and so the version included here is a translation of a Welsh translation of the English original. Where this has occurred, a note to that effect has been made. Where the original quotation was in Welsh, no attempt has been made to phrase it in antiquated English. On the whole, biblical quotations are from the King James Version unless otherwise stated.

The dust jacket includes a drawing of Siloam Congregational Chapel, Pentre Estyll, Swansea. It depicts the chapel in the condition in which it could be found in 2003, namely having fallen into ruin. As such, it seems to represent the crisis which R. Tudur Jones's work identified. The church was in its zenith in the period reviewed here. It retained a vibrancy through to the 1960s and early 1970s when it continued to reflect the area's Welsh-language culture and was able to retain its own full-time minister. By the mid 1980s the congregation had declined and, by the turn of the twenty-first century, the building was derelict. If R. Tudur Jones was correct, then to some extent even the roots of Siloam's ruin can be found buried in the period of its apparent success. I am grateful to Margery Stephenson for producing the drawing and in so doing encapsulating in image form the thesis of this book.

There are many people who have been involved in the production of this volume, all of whom deserve sincere thanks. The work would have been impossible without a substantial grant from the Arts and Humanities Research Board. To those who supported and commended the application, I am grateful for their faith in the venture and their conviction that the work should see the light of day. I would particularly like to thank Professor R. Geraint Gruffydd, Aberystwyth and Dr Matthew Cragoe of the University of Hertfordshire for their support of the project, and Professor Emeritus Gwilym H. Jones who read through part of the work and suggested many improvements in expression and style. I am grateful to them for their work which has saved the final version of the text from many errors and improved it greatly. Dr Geraint Tudur, director of the Centre for the Advanced Study of Religion in Wales, has also been generous in support of the project. Dr D. Densil Morgan read the final typescript and made many valuable suggestions for improvements. Without his assistance, this book would not have seen the light of day. All these people have helped to produce the volume and without their assistance the project doubtless would never have reached a successful conclusion. Nevertheless, I alone am responsible for any errors or infelicities which remain. I am also grateful to the officers of the University of Wales Press for their support and their careful production of a fine volume in the Bangor History of Religion Series.

This book is offered to its readership as a fascinating and enlightening contribution to the analysis of Welsh religious history, and in the hope that it will make that history better-known among an English-speaking readership. It will do so under R. Tudur Jones's conviction that each crisis that a nation or society faces is fundamentally a crisis of faith. This thesis will, no doubt, be accepted by some and rejected by others. Nevertheless, it is passionately and expertly argued and it retains the ability to teach us much in the early twenty-first century as it taught its original readership in the late twentieth and, as such, it ensures that Dr Tudur's name and legacy will live on in a way that would have pleased him.

Author's Preface

At the beginning of the twentieth century, Wales was remarkable among the nations of Europe for its religiosity. Within three-quarters of a century the majority of its people had deserted the Christian faith. In 1890 Wales was rediscovering its national confidence and beginning to realize the riches of its cultural inheritance. By 1979 its culture was under siege and its national confidence was about to expire. Is there a connection between the retreat from Christianity and that seismic cultural shift? This work considers what was happening in these fields between 1890 and the outbreak of the Great War. To do justice to the subject would require a discussion of every aspect of the nation's life, economics, society and politics as well as culture and religion. That was more than can be expected of a single author. We must make do with discussing part of the field. Justice cannot be done to great national changes without considering the faith which is the source of all human activity. The enormous amount of material, and the paucity of scholars working in the field, makes it difficult to offer straightforward answers (or, often, any answers) to the complicated questions which arise. But perhaps asking questions is itself no bad thing. One obvious conclusion is that the years between 1890 and 1914 were fateful in Wales's history. That is what makes studying them a fascinating venture and, at the same time, difficult work.

Much of the substance of this volume was delivered as the D. Owen Evans Memorial Lectures in the University of Wales, Aberystwyth, in November 1977. Sir Goronwy Daniel, the principal, and his wife, Lady Valerie, were particularly gracious in their hospitality to the lecturer, and keen to discuss some of his ideas until the early hours of the morning. Other parts of the book were delivered as the annual Welsh Lectures in the University of Wales,

Bangor, in January 1978. On that occasion Professor J. Gwynn Williams, the vice-principal, was a particularly considerate chairman. I am indebted to both institutions for the great privilege of being invited to deliver these lectures.

I bothered many people in gathering the materials for this book. They were exceptionally patient in answering enquiries by letter and in conversation. Among them are Bishop Daniel Mullins; former-Chancellor J. W. James; Archdeacon Owain W. Jones; Archdeacon D. Eifion Evans; the Revds Walford Jones; W. J. Edwards; Dr G. F. Nuttall; Dr Arvel H. Steece, Lynn, Massachusetts; Dr R. Geraint Gruffydd; Mary Ellis; Dr R. M. Jones; Emyr Humphreys; Ernest Roberts; the late Aneirin Talfan Davies; and Father O. J. Murphy.

My son, Geraint Tudur, was tireless in confirming references in the libraries of Oxford, and the willingness of D. Eirwyn Morgan, principal of the Bangor Baptist College, to permit me to use that institution's library unhindered was a great help. Indeed, I consider it difficult to measure my dependence on the advice and the scholarship of my colleagues in Bangor. Conversations with scholars in different fields throughout the years cause one to realize how poor one's personal resources are. And as one who is a particularly poor mathematician, I am grateful to Thomas G. Edwards of the Normal College for casting a critical eye over the statistics in this book. In the same way my wife, Gwenllian, ensured that I did not do too much injustice to the French authors whose work I discuss. I had the opportunity daily to discuss many points with E. Stanley John, especially points of doctrine. I depended heavily, as I have over the years, on the kindness of Derwyn Jones, the Welsh Librarian in the University of Wales, Bangor. I admire not only his ability to solve problems in the library but his encyclopaedic knowedge of nineteenth-century Welsh literature. Every researcher weighs heavily on the experience and knowledge of the officers of libraries and the ready kindness of the staff of the National Library, Cardiff Library and the University Library in Bangor has been enough of a marvel over the years. My gratitude is immense to all these friends and I would be pleased if this book was worthy of their kindness.

I spent many hours discussing aspects of this book with my colleague, Professor J. Alwyn Charles. He died when the work was half completed and our life in Bangor is poorer and emptier after his passing. I would be very pleased if his wife, Pegi, would permit me to dedicate this book to her as a thank-offering for his work and service.

R. Tudur Jones
Coleg Bala–Bangor
12 October 1979

Abbreviations

Bywg. (1941–50)	R. T. Jenkins and E. D. Jones (eds), Y *Bywgraffiadur Cymreig, 1941–1950* (London, 1970)
Bywg. (1951–70)	E. D. Jones and Brynley F. Roberts (eds), Y *Bywgraffiadur Cymreig, 1951–1970* (London, 1997)
DNB	*Dictionary of National Biography*
DWB	J. E. Lloyd and R. T. Jenkins (eds), *Dictionary of Welsh Biography down to 1940* (London, 1959)
GPC	*Geiriadur Prifysgol Cymru*
Report of the Royal Commission on Disestablishment	Disestablishment Commission, *The Royal Commission on the Church of England and Other Religious Bodies in Wales and Monmouthshire* (London, 1910)
SWDN	*South Wales Daily News*

~ 1 ~

Wales, 1890

Wales, in 1890, was a Christian country, and the eyes of the nation were fixed on the dawn of a bright future. In the deepest recesses of its history, when Roman soldiers encamped in Segontium and Caerleon, the Christian faith began to shape the nation. Although it often wavered, this influence never failed during the succeeding centuries, and it gave a remarkable uniformity to the nation's life. The pattern of integration changed from age to age as first the Celtic church held sway, then the Catholic Church in the Middle Ages, then the Church of England and latterly Protestant Nonconformity. Whatever the differences between these traditions, their common Christianity endowed the life and culture of Wales with a certain symmetry and unity. We recognize the same accent in St David's last sermon, in Siôn Cent's *cywyddau*,[1] in Edmund Prys's psalms,[2] in Charles Edwards's prose,[3] in Williams Pantycelyn's hymns,[4] in the autobiography of Thomas Jones, Denbigh,[5] in the homilies of Robert Ambrose Jones (Emrys ap Iwan)[6] and in hymns by H. Elvet Lewis (Elfed).[7] In short:

Pridd ac isbridd wedi eu troi a'u trafod
Trwy'r canrifoedd yng Nghymru gan yr aradwyr Efengylaidd
A'u herydr teircwys, eu hogedi a'u ffydd.[8]

Soil and subsoil turned and treated
Through the centuries in Wales by the Evangelical ploughmen,
With their three furrow ploughs, their harrows and their faith.

As a result, Christianity and the national culture became intertwined in complex and subtle ways. The influence of faith was felt in the remotest corners of society. Christian theology and beliefs

1

moulded people's deepest preconceptions and gave substance to their hopes. Echoes of the liturgy were heard in the various local dialects. The nation's calendar was defined by Christian festivals. Poets celebrated the story of salvation and God's glory, and authors wrote books explaining the mysteries of biblical teaching. In 1890, many Welsh people believed that a more glorious dawn was nigh. Were the achievements of the nineteenth century not a sign that more splendid things were yet to come? 'There has not been a single century since the days of the Apostles', said Lewis Jones, Ty'n-y-coed, 'in which religion had such a prominent place as in this century'.[9] Thomas Rees, of the Congregational Memorial College in Brecon, agreed: 'No children of any century will be prouder of their flag nor louder in their praise to Him who ordains their times and seasons, than those of the nineteenth century', and he felt confident enough to prophesy, 'but the twentieth century will be yet more privileged'.[10] This prophecy was not realized. By 1965 Christianity in Wales was in serious retreat and the nation was fighting for its very existence.

The departure from Christianity in the modern world has occupied the thoughts of historians and sociologists for many years, and has been a matter of concern for Christians.[11] It is generally agreed that the relationship between Christianity and the life of Western nations underwent a transformation during the eighteenth and nineteenth centuries. The faith that was once a formative influence on European culture has been driven to a small sliver of ground on the fringes while the creed that was once confessed by powerful societies in their public rituals has become a leisure-time hobby for minorities. If the Word of God was for Morgan Llwyd a mighty 'tumult' reverberating throughout all creation, for Matthew Arnold it was nothing more than the 'melancholy, long, withdrawing roar' of the ebbtide on a lonely beach.[12] And that which the critic sensed at the zenith of the Victorian age in England, the Welsh nation was to experience a century later.

How did such a transformation happen? Why should a powerful and vibrant faith lose its grip on a nation? These are the kind of questions that this study will attempt to answer. Wales will be its focus and, generally speaking, the discussion will be historical. The historian's chief concern is with the ways in which human beings exercise their ability to shape a culture out of the raw materials of their world and their different personalities. In some eras they fulfil their cultural task in masterly fashion, expressing their genius in artistic, scientific, scholarly or social achievements which arouse delight and satisfaction at the time and admiration later. At other times they fail in their task and create a disjointed, ugly culture which is oppressive and meaningless. Thus human generations have their ebb and flow, their dawn and dusk. In tracing these changes, the historian cannot but inquire as to the nature of the faith that provided such a significant stimulus for cultural development. There is a strong case for presuming that the quarter century between 1890 and 1914 was a more critical juncture in the history of modern Wales than people supposed at the time. During those years many influences came to bear on Welsh life and culture which threatened the national character and its religion in a new way, and as Christians attempted to respond, their faith began to falter. Not every aspect of Welsh life was under threat at the same time or to the same degree during those years, but it is a fascinating task to try to understand and interpret people's reactions to the perils that surrounded them. The period abounded with energy, the nation tackling with gusto some of the most complex problems facing the modern world. However, during this period enthusiasm was often stronger than wisdom and understanding weaker than confidence. As a result, the years between 1890 and 1914 witnessed a dizzy mixture of achievement and chaos, greatness and pettiness, faith and superstition, liberality and reaction, emotionalism and reason, success and failure. This puzzling complexity is at the heart of the crisis which is the subject of this work.

This complexity was the inevitable consequence of the intertwining of faith and culture. By 1890, Christianity and Welsh-language culture were joined so closely that not even a wizard could discern the seam. The classics of Welsh literature were, more often than not, Christian classics too. Throughout the centuries, many of the nation's heroes had also been Christian heroes. Under the churches' influence people came to exalt values which they regarded as Christian. The Bible provided them with their convictions concerning human relations and their ideals about the nature of society, with virtues such as veracity, kindness, temperance, thrift and care for the poor and needy. There was no doubt in their minds that their emphasis on sexual purity and the value of family life, that their respect for the written and spoken word, that their rejection of violence and oppression were rooted in the Christian faith.

Above all they were certain that their whole life was under God's sovereignty and rule and that there was no future for them as individuals or as a nation were they arrogantly to refuse salvation in Christ. Whether the values of the generation of 1890 were truly Christian or not is a question which will be considered shortly. Whether that generation was faithful to its avowedly Christian ideals is another question which will be discussed. What needs to be emphasized now is that by 1890 to be a Welshman and a Christian meant more or less the same thing. Since the overwhelming majority of Welsh people at that time shared the same understanding of the meaning of life and of its essential values, they were conscious of a spiritual unity that reinforced their national unity. It seemed to them that there was a common core around which the whole varied richness of their life revolved. Society impressed the demands of the faith on every Welsh citizen in various ways. By ordaining patterns of behaviour and by reinforcing 'Christian' values by means of countless social influences, the nation itself was an ambassador for Christ. As the theologian Karl Rahner said of Catholic Germany in the twentieth century, it can be said of Wales at the end of the nineteenth that Welsh life exalted, and expedited, the decision of faith.[13] For a Welsh person in 1890 there was little difference between accepting Christ as Saviour within the fellowship of the church and accepting the standards and values of the society within which he or she had been raised.

There is no doubt, then, that the close marriage between Christian faith and Welsh culture benefited Christianity. It was no small feat to create a nation whose overall culture bore witness to the vital importance of Christian truths. However there were also great dangers. When storms buffet society, the churches also feel the keen wind. The earthquake that brings cultural upheaval can also crack the foundations of faith. An economic crisis inevitably becomes a spiritual crisis too. A huge transformation in the social or industrial or political or economic life of a nation – in short, a major cultural transformation – sends icy shivers through the whole structure of its religious life as well. Faith expresses itself in culture. If the culture is healthy then faith is strengthened. If the culture crumbles then faith is undermined. From 1890 these dangers were increasingly recognized in Welsh life. The threat did not reach its climax until 1914, but it is easy to see it gathering momentum. It will also become obvious that there is no simple answer to the question why Christian Wales was so badly ravaged in the three-quarters of a century between 1890 and 1965. It would be so easy to focus on one aspect and make that an explanation for the whole. Yielding to that temptation in itself is proof that the most prominent characteristic of the transformation, namely the complexity of its causes, has escaped our observation. Some insist on exaggerating the significance of the churches' chilly indifference to the aspirations of the proletariat, while others see modern science as the problem, while yet others blame creeping Anglicization or the influence of middle-class morality, or the higher criticism, or the failure of teetotalism, or lifeless church services. To pursue such partial notions would be foolish. For those people who lived through the heat of battle, what weighed most heavily on them was the fact that their enemies were so numerous and their attacks so varied. All this will become very clear in the following pages. From 1890 the relative uniformity of Welsh society and its robust and homogeneous Welsh-language culture was beginning to yield to pluralism, and the complexity of the ensuing change forms the background of this discussion.

An extraordinary social revolution took place in the life of Wales during Queen Victoria's reign. Industry began to change the face of the country. Between 1850 and 1880 aggressive capitalism was at the helm and money was poured like water on any venture that promised a profit. During this period the railway network penetrated every corner of Wales. Heavy industries saw rapid expansion. The Gwent and Aberdare valleys switched from iron to coal, and after 1870 the work of sinking the coal mines of the Rhondda began. The coal industry continued to expand until 1914 when it employed more workers than all the other industries put together.[14] Similarly the tin industry was expanding in the Tawe and Amman valleys, and around centres such as Llanelli, Pontarddulais and Neath. In 1850 there were only eighteen tin works in Wales but by 1889 there were ninety-six, employing 16,000 workers.[15] It was the same story with the slate quarries. In Gwynedd by 1890 the Blaenau Ffestiniog, Bethesda, Llanberis and Dyffryn Nantlle areas all had populations of more than 11,000.[16] The rapid and unstructured growth of these industrial communities created a host of social, spiritual and moral problems that the churches had to deal with, as we shall see. But the first effect of industrialization was to create a mobile population. Between 1801 and 1891 the population of

Glamorgan increased almost tenfold, from 70,897 to 693,001. In the same period the population of Gwent increased sixfold, from 45,568 to 275,085. Despite the aridity of statistics, we would do well to take a closer look at the information revealed in the 1891 census. The population of Wales in that year was 1,771,174 compared with 587,000 in 1801. By 1911 it was to reach 2,420,921. Thus 1891 was the midpoint of a period of massive expansion in the population: between 1871 and 1911 it increased by a little over one million. This means that we are not looking at a static society but rather a society that required rapidly produced and extensive facilities for its new members, not least within the religious sphere. Other considerations apart, a million people will fill a huge number of chapels and churches and require the service of a veritable army of ministers and priests.

By 1891, one in seven of the inhabitants of Wales had arrived from England and other countries. This non-native element was more pronounced in some places than others, for example in Glamorgan where non-Welsh-speaking immigrants numbered 139,031 compared with 121,653 who had migrated to the county from other parts of Wales. The ratio was even less favourable to the Welsh language in Gwent with 61,061 foreign immigrants and only 30,504 Welsh people. In Flintshire there were 13,744 immigrants, while 16,847 of the inhabitants of Denbighshire had been born outside Wales. One consequence of the increase in population was an increase in the number of Welsh-speakers. There were 898,914 of them in 1891, when statistics for the language were included for the first time in the government census, but the number continued to increase until 1911 when it reached 977,366, the highest total ever in the history of the language. This was no cause for celebration, however, because the percentage in relation to the population as a whole was steadily declining; 54.4 per cent of the population could speak Welsh in 1891, 49.9 per cent in 1901, 43.5 per cent in 1911 and 37.2 per cent in 1921.[17]

This movement of people had a very noticeable effect on rural areas. By 1891 56 per cent of the population was living in urban areas; that is, more than half. According to the census of that year, of the people born in Anglesey, Merionethshire, Cardiganshire, Pembrokeshire and Radnorshire, 80,356 had moved to other parts of Wales and 53,259 had moved to England. The loss of 133,615 people from these rural counties was equivalent to the disappearance of sixteen towns the size of Aberystwyth, which in 1901 had a population of 8,014. Thomas E. Ellis spoke of the countryside as the place where 'those who lead the causes that are dear to us and those who discovered the light which we live by were raised'.[18] If this description is correct, by the 1890s the rural areas were facing a particularly grievous crisis. William Thomas, Congregational minister of Gwynfe, Carmarthenshire, said that he issued letters of dismissal to more than 1,000 of his members between 1860 and 1899. Despite this, the membership of his churches remained fairly constant at around 400 because, during the same period, he had admitted over 900 into membership.[19] William Thomas was obviously a very effective minister and succeeded in maintaining high pastoral standards. However it is evident from his testimony that even rural areas had not remained static. The day would soon arrive when this ceaseless migration would deplete the rural population to such a degree that the consequent shortfall in congregations could not be met by making new members from the same area. The truth is that the rural community which had been immersed in Christian values was being robbed of its population on a vast scale. It is no wonder that the counties of Anglesey, Cardigan, Merioneth, Montgomery, Pembroke and Radnor saw a drop in population between 1871 and 1911.

Wales also exported its people. By 1891, 21 per cent of Welsh people lived outside Wales. One in eight Welsh people – 228,616 – lived in England. It was estimated that 31,292 Welsh people lived in the Registration District of London and that 29,454 of them could speak Welsh. The majority of them swiftly lost contact with their roots for no more than 8,000 of them were members of Welsh-language churches.[20] According to the 1891 census there were 21,379 Welsh people in Cheshire and 60,819 in Lancashire,[21] but these soon ceased to be Welsh. Thomas Gray of Birkenhead, described the situation vividly: 'No more than ten per cent of the children of our church members, and only two per cent of the second generation, stay with our [Calvinistic Methodist] Connexion in our big cities, such as Liverpool, Birkenhead, Manchester, Birmingham and London'.[22] By 1891, one in sixteen Welsh people lived in the United States of America, a total of around 100,000.[23] So we are talking about a nation that was in the midst of enormous changes in 1890, with the whole quality and pattern of its life being disrupted and weakened. Its leaders did not immediately realize what was happening. The farm hand jumped at the chance to leave the countryside where labourers aged between 18 and 20 were earning between £15 and £20 a year, and move to the coal mines where he could earn between £5 and £8 a month.[24] Even though the lack of sewerage, poor accommodation and brutal working conditions aroused the righteous anger of social reformers in the industrial valleys, thousands were glad enough to turn their backs on the poverty and social bondage of rural areas and journey into the midst of the smoke and dust of the pits. For them the train was more than just a convenient vehicle to transport them from Bryncir to Merthyr, or from Llanbryn-mair to Liverpool: it was a door to freedom leading them to a new world. The uniformity and stability of traditional society were for them a kind of bondage, while ambition, romance and opportunity offered a different kind of life in the heterogeneous societies that were springing up in the Merthyr valley, in Liverpool, Ohio, Cape Town and Melbourne.[25] The romance of progress continued to mesmerize those people who remembered Wales as a wholly agricultural society. After all, it was that kind of age. It was just as if the wheels of history had begun to turn more quickly.[26] Amazing inventions followed hot on one another's heels: Graham Bell invented the telephone in 1875; Forest put the finishing touches to the self-kindling engine in 1888; Gramme and others perfected hydroelectricity in 1889; the motorcar appeared in about 1890; Lumière's *cinematograph* in 1894, the telegraph in 1895 and, around 1900, the aeroplane. The infants that were to grow into the twentieth century's industrial giants were born more or less at the same time. Could the people of the 1890s be blamed for feeling that humankind was faced with incredible possibilities? Is it any wonder that Wales, now with its command of English and its new education system, was feeling the same excitement that was electrifying the whole of Europe and America? No doubt the people of Wales at the time derived considerable pleasure from the minor products of the new industries, those objects that transformed everyday life, such as plenty of cheap coal for the fires in kitchen and parlour, cheap newspapers, colourful heavy curtains, the fruit of mass-production methods and the chemical discoveries of the dyeing industry, and the sewing machine.

In what other age could a match have inspired such lyrical enthusiasm? David Griffith, Bethel, was nearly 80 when he reminisced about the long-gone past: 'Indeed,' he said, 'the Lucifer match has a splendid majesty . . . such as man cannot fully express. I remember well the time when these matches came to be used first; it was the year 1833.' He bought a box in Caernarfon and knew immediately that a new age in the history of humankind had dawned. 'From the beginning of the world until the time of the Reform Bill' human beings had only two ways to light a fire, rubbing sticks together or 'by means of the firestone and the tinder box, two extremely tedious methods'. But as for the match, 'the improvement is incomparable'.[27] The old man's enthusiasm is significant. Here was a man who, despite his years, faced the future full of energy and verve. Wales, in his opinion, was 'travelling forward untrammeled along the path of culture' as demonstrated by 'the increase of its trade, its wealth, its inhabitants, and its literature during the sunny period' that was the immediate past. It all went to show that Providence was smiling on Wales. 'Since the hand of the Almighty rests on us in this way for good, let us consider our obligations, and be thankful to Him.' Alas, not everyone shared his confidence. Different and more sorrowful voices could be heard mingled with the noise of industrial machinery. In his autobiography, *Ecce Homo*, Friedrich Nietzsche asked 'Where is God?' And he answered his own question, 'I shall tell you: we have killed him, you and I! . . . God is dead! God is dead! And we killed him!' Nietzsche died in Weimar on 25 August 1900. At that time a great distance separated Weimar from Bethel but the machines that brought them to within hailing distance of one another had already been invented.

The Wales of 1965 was taking shape in the womb of the Wales of 1890.

~ 2 ~

Church and Chapel

By the turn of the twentieth century the Christian faith in Wales seemed to be in an impregnable position. To all appearances the nation possessed no stronger institutions than the churches, and all the signs were that their grip on people's lives was about to tighten. Historians of the period have at their disposal the most comprehensive and accurate statistical analysis ever undertaken in relation to religion in Wales. It was published by the Disestablishment Commission in 1910 in its report *The Royal Commission on the Church of England and Other Religious Bodies in Wales and Monmouthshire*. There was some ill-tempered squabbling among the commissioners, and among the public following the publication of the report, concerning the accuracy of the statistics. The main bone of contention was the statistical relationship between the Church in Wales and the Nonconformist denominations. It was quite natural for this to be a matter for debate at the time since one subject of compelling interest concerned how to decide as precisely as possible what percentage of the population supported one camp or the other. But for the historian whose interest is in the situation of Christianity generally in Wales in 1905 – the year most fully reported in the statistics – the fruit of the Commission's investigation is invaluable. The report cautions against placing too much emphasis on the statistics given for 'adherents', in other words, those people who attended services but were not communicants or full members. On the other hand, the statistics for full members, namely those who had been formally received into the communion of the various churches, are safe and reliable.[1]

We can begin with the general pattern. In 1905 two in five Welsh people were church members, namely 743,361 out of a population of 1,864,696.[2] Of this number, 25.9 per cent (193,081) were communicants in the Anglican Church in Wales; 23.5 per cent (175,147) were Congregationalists; 23 per cent (170,617) were Calvinistic Methodists; 19.2 per cent (143,835) were Baptists and 5.4 per cent (40,811) were Wesleyan Methodists. Three per cent (19,870) belonged to smaller denominations, not including Roman Catholics.[3] Although the report noted that the figures it gave for 'adherents' were 'of little, if any, value for statistical purposes', perhaps they should not be completely disregarded since they indicate quite a significant social pattern. At the turn of the century the church service was not a private meeting for church members but rather a public meeting that anyone who so wished might attend. Consequently, every service had people in attendance who were not members of the chapel or church where the service was being held, although they might be members of other churches and this is one of the reasons, of course, why one cannot place too much reliance on these statistics. However, this social trend can be demonstrated by looking at the two extremes of the country. According to the statistics for Anglesey Congregationalists, there were 21,251 full members and 33,098 adherents. In Glamorganshire there were 202,648 full members in the chapels, and 187,979 adherents. To be on the safe side statistically, it is sufficient to conclude that the influence of church services reached a wide circle beyond those in full membership.

The ratio of church membership to the population as a whole varied somewhat from area to area. Since historians have taken considerable interest in the influence of migration to towns and industrial areas on the retreat from Christianity in the modern world, it is worth seeing whether the statistics of the Disestablishment Commission can enlighten us on the matter. What about the rural areas to start with? In every county that bordered on the Irish Sea, namely, Anglesey, Caernarfonshire, Merioneth, Cardiganshire, Carmarthenshire and Pembrokeshire, over half the population of the rural areas were communicants, Cardiganshire being in first place with 61.8 per cent and Pembroke at the bottom of the list with 51 per cent. In every other county less than half the population of rural areas were communicants, with Montgomeryshire on top with 45.2 per cent and Flintshire in last place with 27.7 per cent. In only three counties, namely, Merioneth, Cardiganshire and Carmarthenshire, more than half the population of the urban areas were communicants.[4]

Let us now compare the statistics for the rural areas in these counties with the statistics for the urban areas. In the counties of Denbighshire, Flintshire, Merioneth, Glamorganshire and Monmouthshire, the proportion of the population who were communicants was higher in urban areas than in rural areas. This is rather unexpected and would seem initially to indicate that the churches were stronger in the towns in those very counties where there had been the most industrialization. The obvious exception is Merioneth with 60 per cent of the population of its urban areas communicants and only 58 per cent of its rural population, but, after all, the slate industry was a substantial part of that county's economy. The first conclusion we must draw is that it is unwise to link industrialization and urbanization with the incipient crisis of faith in Wales – at least during the period until 1905. It is important not to apply uncritically any conclusions that might be true in that period of England to Wales. In a sentence that has been quoted countless times, A. F. Winnington-Ingram, later the bishop of London, said of England in 1895, 'it is not that the Church of God has lost the great towns; it has never had them'.[5] When Winnington-Ingram began his ministry as rector of Bethnal Green in 1895, he claimed that only 1 per cent of the population attended a place of worship of any kind. The pattern in Wales was very different. Even in Cardiff 16.8 per cent of the population were communicants, and the percentages in other industrial and urban areas were Aberdare, 27.1; Merthyr, 29.3; Rhondda, 34.9; Neath, 40.3; Maesteg, 47.5; Llanelli, 52.8 and Ammanford, 67.9. These bare statistics only reinforce claims such as those made by a reporter after the tragic explosion at the Cilfynydd pit in 1894 when he wrote, 'Workers are the strength of our churches in the industrial areas' and he went on to report that the Congregational church there had lost forty members and adherents in the explosion.[6]

Nevertheless the difference between urban and rural areas gives rise to another question which might be significant. The statistics for Pembrokeshire show a large gap between the proportion of the rural population who were church members and the proportion that were members in urban areas – a gap of 21 per cent, the largest in Wales. In rural areas, 51 per cent of the inhabitants were communicants but only 30 per cent were in towns. This difference can hardly be attributed to industrialization. However, when we recollect that the urban areas of the county at that time were

Haverfordwest, Neyland, Milford Haven, Pembroke and Tenby, we see that these towns were all part of 'Little England'. It would be reasonable to interpret the statistics as illustrating the difference between Welsh-language culture and English-language culture rather than the difference between town and country.

According to the 1901 census, virtually half the population of Wales spoke Welsh – 49.9 per cent of them. Linguistically Wales had reached a crucial period in its history when the Welsh language was finally ceasing to be the language of the majority of its population. By 1911 only 43.5 per cent of the population would be able to speak Welsh. Among the Welsh-speakers in 1901, 15.1 per cent were monoglot. However these statistics do not give any indication of the geographical distribution of the language. The excellent colour maps placed by the Disestablishment Commissioners at the back of the first volume of their report can enlighten us on the subject. In studying them, it becomes apparent that Wales contained three linguistic corridors, each one extending from north to south. In the western corridor the majority of the population were monoglot Welsh-speakers. This corridor extended from Anglesey, through Caernarfonshire, Merioneth (except for the area around Tywyn), through Cardiganshire down as far as the district councils of Llanfyrnach and Newcastle Emlyn. This corridor also contained the areas where Welsh was the language of the majority and monoglot Welsh-speakers were more numerous than monoglot English-speakers, areas such as the district councils of Conwy, St Asaph, Ruthin, Edeyrnion, Llansilin, Tywyn (Merioneth), Cardigan, St Dogmaels, the whole of Carmarthenshire, (apart from the areas surrounding the Town Councils of Carmarthen, Llandeilo, Llandovery and Llanelli), and the areas comprising the district councils of Ystradgynlais and Ystradfellte in Breconshire, and Llangyfelach and Pontardawe in Glamorgan.

Welsh-speakers were also in the majority in the second corridor, but it contained more monoglot English-speakers than monoglot Welsh-speakers. This second corridor extended from north Flintshire, through the districts of Llanfyllin and Newtown and then (avoiding Radnorshire) down through most of Breconshire, to mid-Glamorgan, including the valleys of the Gelli-gaer district, to the districts of Neath, Margam and Bridgend. The district of Haverfordwest in Pembrokeshire also belonged to this linguistic pattern.

The third corridor, where the majority of the population did not speak Welsh, extended along the border (apart from the rural district of Wrexham). Similar pockets where the majority were monoglot English were found along the south coast, in Cardiff, Cowbridge, Aberafan, Swansea, the Gower Coast, Narberth and Pembroke, and also in Rhyl, Colwyn Bay and Llandudno along the north coast.

In other words, Welsh was the language of the majority of people across most of the length and breadth of Wales.

How does this analysis correspond to the life of the churches? It is interesting to compare it with the statistics on church membership contained in the report of the Disestablishment Commission. To begin with the western corridor. In the territories of the councils bordered by the west coast 95.2 per cent of the population could speak Welsh. In the same areas 63.4 per cent of the population were church members.[7] In the middle corridor, 59.4 per cent of the population could speak Welsh and 48.7 per cent of the population were members of churches.[8] As for the third corridor, where non-Welsh-speakers were in the majority and only 13.9 per cent spoke Welsh, 30.3 per cent were church members.[9] A clear statistical pattern emerges. In areas where monoglot Welsh-speakers were in the majority, there was a high proportion of church members, or to put it in another way, as the proportion of monoglot English-speakers increased, so the proportion of church members in the population decreased.

Language is only one influence among many, of course, and thus there are variations here and there. For instance, in the rural district of Holywell, in Flintshire, 78 per cent spoke Welsh and only 33.3 per cent were church members, and yet, in Bangor, with 79.9 per cent speaking Welsh, 59.6 were church members. In Rhondda, where 64.3 per cent spoke Welsh, only 38.3 per cent were church members. This is not dissimilar to the pattern in Aberdare where 71.2 per cent spoke Welsh and 41 per cent were church members. It is obvious that the influence of the Welsh language in attracting people to formal membership in the churches was qualified by the influence of industrial or urban society, because in Merthyr Tudful 57.1 per cent spoke Welsh and 32.7 per cent were church members, and in the town of Swansea where 32.3 per cent spoke Welsh, 31.8 per cent were members of churches. Allowing for exceptions, the general rule was that if more than 60 per cent of the population could speak Welsh, then about half the population were church members but if less than 30 per cent were Welsh-speakers, it was rare for more than a third of the population to be church members. What, then, of the churches' officials? The total number of ministers and clergy in Wales in 1905 was 4,123, quite a substantial increase since 1891 when the Census reported that 3,739 were engaged in church work. Of the 1905 total, 1,597 were in the service of the Anglican Church in Wales, 968 of them in parochial offices. It is interesting to note that the proportion of ministers to the general population varied according to the proportion of non-Welsh-speakers therein. Where less than 10 per cent of the population were non-Welsh-speakers, ministers comprised 0.32 per cent; where non-Welsh-speakers accounted for over 10 per cent but less than 51 per cent of the population, 0.27 per cent were ministers. Where the non-Welsh-speaking element comprised over 51 per cent of the population 0.17 per cent were ministers. There is nothing remarkable in this, because wherever there was a high proportion of members more ministers were required. But this analysis indicates that the influence of the ministry was much greater in those areas where monoglot Welsh-speakers were in the majority than in those areas where non-Welsh-speakers were in the majority.

In Nonconformist churches ministers were not the only preachers. In the tradition of John Wesley, the Methodists of Wales were heavily dependent on assistant preachers. It is remarkable to note that the Wesleyan denomination had as many as 953 assistant preachers in Wales in 1905. The Baptists also made considerable use of assistant preachers, but to a lesser extent. They had 416 while the Congregationalists had 331 and the Calvinistic Methodists had 316. The total number of assistant preachers in the denominations was 1,863, not to mention 452 college students.[10] Counting ministers, assistant preachers and students, the chapels of Wales could draw on the services of 4,841 preachers. Not all of them could preach at one time, because the Nonconformist denominations had only 4,526 chapels and schoolhouses, but it is certain that there were preaching meetings where more than one preacher was in attendance and that this was a help to reduce the number of the unemployed! The Anglican Church was more hard pressed because it had 1,546 churches and 318 mission rooms but only 1,597 clergymen to fulfil its needs.

Another category of leaders who played a key role in religious and public life were the deacons or elders, those leaders who were not ordained to carry out the work of the ministry but nevertheless accomplished much of it. In Wales in 1905 there were at least 22,730 Nonconformist deacons.[11] Although there is a tendency to speak of them informally as a 'class', such a description is inappropriate. For instance, there were 482 in Aberdare, but they never used to meet together for any reason outside the confines of their own denomination – assuming of course that they met within it – and we can say the same about the seventy who were in Aberystwyth, or the 154 in Ffestiniog. However, their talents as leaders in their own congregations equipped them to lead in a wider sphere, as evinced in town or county councils, trade unions and similar bodies.

I shall turn our attention now from the statistics to the people they represented. In the period between 1890 and 1914 the Christians of Wales were not one institutional body but rather were distributed among a number of different bodies – the denominations. By 1905 there were thirty denominations with churches or branches in Wales[12] and the number increased as a result of the 1904–5 Revival. For the sake of convenience, one can think of these various denominations as the product of four waves that washed across the life of the nation to a greater or lesser degree over the centuries. The first of these was represented by the Roman Catholic Church. Next the Protestant Reformation gave rise first to the Church of England, and then as a result of dissatisfaction with that Reformation the Puritan denominations appeared, including the Independents (Congregationalists) and the Baptists. The third wave was the Evangelical Revival of the eighteenth century that produced the Methodist churches. Lastly, as the result of the upheavals of the nineteenth century, movements such as the Plymouth Brethren and the Salvation Army came into being. Although these bodies jealously guarded their 'distinguishing principles' as they called them, and were very anxious about their identity, the relationship between them was complex. As we shall see, they were often extremely prickly towards one another concerning issues which, in fact, they had in common.

In spite of these organizational differences, common convictions served to bind together a great number of the Christians of Wales across denominational boundaries. Thus it is possible to speak of an Evangelical Accord that by the end of the century had a profound influence on the life of the nation. The integration between Christianity and the national culture was determined, not completely but to a very great degree, by this cluster of beliefs, institutions and values that were held in common by evangelical Anglicans, Congregationalists, Baptists, Calvinistic Methodists and Wesleyan Methodists. Although they disagreed quite fundamentally with some of the theological tenets of the evangelical faith, some of the smaller churches, and especially the Unitarians, supported many practical and social aspects of the Accord. Because of its strength and Welsh character, the development of the national and spiritual crisis in Wales would hinge to a very great extent in the next years on what became of this Evangelical Accord.

One of the most heroic chapters in the history of Welsh Christianity is that of the endeavours of Welsh Catholics to safeguard their heritage. The advent of the Protestant Reformation brought years of cruel persecution, and the flight into exile by the generation of Morris Clynnog, Gruffydd Robert and Owen Lewis.[13] Men such as Richard Gwyn, the schoolmaster, William Davies, the priest, and John Roberts, the monk from Trawsfynydd, testified to their faith by forfeiting their lives.[14] Before long Welsh Catholicism was no more than a smoking flax. By 1773 there were only 750 communicants and nine missionaries throughout the whole of Wales.[15] The faithful remnant continued to meet in a few centres such as Abergavenny, Brecon, Usk, Newport and Holywell and enjoyed the patronage of a handful of aristocratic families such as the Mostyns of Talacre in Flintshire, the Vaughans of Courtfield in Welsh Bicknor on the border and the Herberts of Llanarth in Gwent. There is some justification for regarding the Herberts as the last of the old aristocratic patrons of Welsh-language Catholicism because when Augusta, the daughter of Gwenynen Gwent, married John Arthur Herbert, the Welsh lineage of Llanofer Manor continued uninterrupted. In truth, though, Catholicism's foothold in Wales was very tenuous and almost disappeared. At the beginning of the nineteenth century, the outlook for Welsh Catholicism was very bleak with about 1,000 communicants throughout the whole country.[16]

A change in fortunes came with the beginning of the Industrial Revolution, and particularly the migration from Ireland. Before 1822, as far as we know there was only one Catholic in Cardiff; by 1861 there were about 10,800 – all of whom were Irish.[17] Mass began to be celebrated again in places such as Cardiff (about 1825),

17

Pontypool, Newport (1809), Merthyr Tudful (1824), Porthcawl and Bridgend in the south, and Bangor (1827), Caernarfon and Wrexham in the north. The oppression of the Penal Laws came to an end in 1829 with Catholic Emancipation but the resources of Welsh Catholics were too scarce for them to profit overly from their new freedom. Demand grew because by 1838 the number of their communicants in Wales had risen to 6,250, with more than half of them in Gwent.[18]

From 1688 to 1849 the Catholics of Wales were part of the Western District, one of four apostolic vicariates in Wales and England. The system changed in 1840 when Pope Gregory XVI created eight new districts to replace them. Wales and Hereford became one of the eight new vicariates. Thomas Joseph Brown, the former prior of Downside, who died in 1880, was appointed vicar apostolic.[19] This appointment was part of the preparation for the restoration of the Catholic hierarchy, and was thus short-lived. In his apostolic letter, *Universalis Ecclesiae*, 9 September 1850, Pope Pius IX restored the hierarchy in England and Wales.[20] The metropolitan, or archbishop's, diocese of Westminster was created, containing twelve suffragan dioceses. The unity of Wales was ignored, and its Catholics split between two dioceses, both of them containing parts of England. The six counties of north Wales were to form part of the diocese of Shrewsbury and the seven counties of the south were to be joined with Hereford to make up the diocese of Newport and Menevia. The apostolic vicar, T. J. Brown, was elevated to the post of first bishop of Newport. The new bishop of Shrewsbury was James Brown. With his superior abilities T. J. Brown accomplished great work in Newport and Menevia and there was a substantial increase in the Catholic provision in this diocese. However he began to suffer under the workload and in 1873 John Cuthbert Hedley was appointed as his assistant. When T. J. Brown began his work in Wales in 1840 there were sixteen stations and eighteen priests in the whole country; by the time of his death in 1880, there were forty stations and the same number of priests in his diocese alone.[21] His brother in Shrewsbury, James Brown, died not long after him in 1881. Thus both dioceses had new bishops almost at the same time. John Cuthbert Hedley[22] was appointed bishop of Newport and was inducted on St David's Day 1881, and Edmund Knight became the bishop of Shrewsbury exactly one year later. Hedley gave faithful service in Newport and Menevia, and did his best to learn more about Wales's national characteristics, but with little success.

Before the end of the century the Catholic Church in Wales saw a new organizational development. Under Pope Leo XIII's apostolic brief, *De Antimarum Salute*, 4 March 1895, the counties of north Wales were detached from the diocese of Shrewsbury and were joined to the counties of Cardiganshire, Pembrokeshire, Carmarthenshire, Radnorshire and Breconshire to form a new apostolic vicariate. It was given the name Menevia when it was elevated to the status of a diocese on 12 May 1898. At the same time 'Menevia' ceased to be a part of the title of the diocese of Newport. Hedley continued as bishop there until his death in 1915 and Edmund Knight, the bishop of Shrewsbury, ceased to bear responsibility for north Wales when the apostolic vicariate was formed in 1895.

Although he was only 35 years old, the man who was appointed vicar apostolic under the new regime was Francis Mostyn (1860–1939), and when the diocese of Menevia was created, he became its first bishop, holding that post until March 1921 when he moved to Cardiff and became archbishop. He came from a family who knew some Welsh, and that, together with his ability and energy, commended him to Catholics and Protestants alike.[23]

Indeed, the appointment of Francis Mostyn served to remind the Catholic Church that it must be involved with the life and culture of Wales. The majority of Catholics in Wales were Irish and a man like Cuthbert Hedley, for perfectly valid pastoral reasons, tended to see his diocese as being not unlike a church for Irish exiles.[24] Not that Hedley was unmindful of Wales and its culture. He occasionally attended the eisteddfod and helped to establish the University College of South Wales and Monmouthshire in Cardiff. He also lent his support to the establishment of the Society of St Teilo in 1889, a society for the publication of Catholic literature in Welsh. But Francis Mostyn had an advantage over him because he knew Wales as a Welshman. Cardinal Herbert Vaughan (1832–1903), the archbishop of Westminster and a member of the old Catholic family of Courtfield, was one of the chief supporters of the movement to create the diocese of Menevia because he believed that 'Wales ought to be treated as an independent state rather than as a mere appendage of England'. He approved of the appointment of Francis Mostyn because he was a Welshman who would represent the Catholic Church among the Welsh 'by kindness, sympathy and consideration'.[25] Thus, although the Catholic Church is on the fringes of our story, as it were, as we cast a glance over the life of the churches of Wales in 1890, it was preparing to take a more prominent role in the life of the nation. By 1905 it had seventy-one centres of worship (not counting mission rooms and schools) which were frequented by 64,800 worshippers, including children, with 142 resident priests serving them. There were also twenty-nine orders for women working in Wales, and twenty-eight for men.[26]

To turn now to the Anglican Church in Wales. Gladstone said in 1891, 'Without a doubt, the Church in Wales is a church on the increase, a hardworking church, a lively church and, I truly believe, a church which is always rising higher'.[27] It is easy to understand why the old man could strike such a confident note. The church enjoyed a mighty revival during the nineteenth century. In 1899, Richard Lewis, the bishop of Llandaff, wrote that 'the church in Wales at the beginning of the present [nineteenth] century showed all the signs and characteristics of a church that was decaying and dying'.[28] By 1890 the picture was very different. Although it possessed undisputed advantages because of its social pre-eminence and its connection with the state, these were to no avail without spiritual vitality. Indeed as the century marched on and the common folk flocked in their thousands to the Nonconformist churches, these advantages were rapidly turning into disadvantages as the people of Wales began increasingly to regard it as the church of the privileged classes and one of the main routes for foreign and English domination. Despite all this, it underwent a great transformation between 1800 and 1900.[29]

This change can be attributed to four influences: first, improvements in the administrative and financial arrangements of the church; secondly, the passion of the evangelical wing; thirdly, the dedication of the disciples of the Oxford Movement, and lastly a more lively awareness of the nationhood of Wales. These influences did not, of course, always pull in the same direction and the Church in Wales, like all the denominations, had its share of fractious quarrels between those holding different viewpoints.

The Church in Wales benefited from the general reform of the Church of England as a consequence of the recommendations of the Church Commission appointed by Sir Robert Peel in 1835. The tithe was transformed into a cash payment, and the estates of the bishops and their salaries became the responsibility of the permanent

Church Commission which was established in 1836. As a result, there was no longer any financial need for the bishops of Wales to hold additional posts and livings in order to make ends meet. A series of reforms made the pastoral and administrative work of the church easier; these included the appointment of resident canons in the cathedrals, deacons for Llandaff and St Davids, the restoration of the former post of archdeacon, the reorganization of diocesan boundaries and rural deaneries and so on.[30] All things considered, these improvements, in the opinion of Chancellor J. W. James, deserved to be called a reformation second only to the Protestant Reformation itself.[31]

These reforms were an appropriate accompaniment to the new vitality linked with the names of leaders such as Thomas Burgess, bishop of St Davids from 1803 to 1825. He tackled the work of publishing and distributing literature, establishing libraries, day schools and Sunday schools, increasing the number of applicants for holy orders and establishing St David's College, Lampeter (1822–5).[32] Far higher standards were set for clergymen and the work expected of them. One prominent aspect of this activity was the restoration of church buildings. When David Owen James arrived to begin his ministry in two parishes in Pembrokeshire, he found that one church was in ruins and the other almost completely overrun by thistles, thorns and brambles and that the communion chalice was sitting in the middle of a refuse tip on a nearby farm. His first task was to restore both buildings and make them fitting centres of worship.[33] This was a parable of what was happening to the church itself in many places.

The evangelical movement within the Church in Wales has received harsh treatment from historians.[34] During the battle for Disestablishment, Nonconformist historians tended to portray everyone in the church as a fanatical ritualist, and the tendency of the high church commentators by contrast was to disparage the evangelicals and ignore their contribution. But, according to Archdeacon D. Eifion Evans, '*both* movements made a great contribution for good to the religious revival'.[35] In the diocese of Llandaff, under the leadership of Alfred Ollivant, the champions of the evangelical position were seen to concentrate their energies on the Church Extension Society.[36] With the support of influential laity such as Henry Austin Bruce and Edward Priest Richards,[37] they began to evangelize in earnest within the diocese, especially among the new industrial population. The number of clergy rose from fifty in 1850 to 170 in 1870 and the new curates were 'soldiers in the Evangelical crusade'.[38] During the same period Ollivant licensed at least sixty rooms for worship, as well as building thirty-two new churches.[39] By 1870, the tide of evangelicalism was ebbing from the diocese,[40] but the missionary spirit did not cease, as William Lewis, the vicar of Llandyfodwg, testified. He saw the three parishes in the Rhondda in 1869 grow into twelve by 1907 and the five churches grow into fifty-one, including mission rooms, in the same period.[41]

As D. Eifion Evans commented, 'The Welsh Evangelicals placed great emphasis on preaching. For them preaching the Gospel was the only way to awaken the Church from its apathy'.[42] And there was among them a history of mighty preachers. The stream of evangelical tradition did not run dry, although the Methodists finally left the church in 1811. As an example of the link with the great men of the eighteenth century, I shall mention the mighty dynasty of Thomas Richards (Darowen).

Thomas Richards (1754–1837) was one of Daniel Rowland's most enthusiastic followers and a close friend of Thomas Jones, Creaton. Of his five sons, all of whom became clergymen, the eldest, Richard Richards, Caerwys (1780–1860), could be counted among the giants of the pulpit in his generation, and he did not hesitate to share the stage with John Elias from time to time.[43] Another of those who could hold his audience spellbound was John Hughes, the archdeacon of Cardigan.[44] From the beginning of his ministry at Rhos on Sea, Denbighshire, in 1811, people flocked to listen to him. It was ironic that he was invited to preach at the consecration of the Tractarian church of Llangorwen near Aberystwyth in 1841, but he probably could not be denied this privilege since the church was in his parish of Llanbadarn-fawr. However he did not refrain from taunting the high church faction on that occasion by maintaining that 'preaching was the instrument used by God to save sinners'.[45] Not for nothing was David Parry nicknamed the 'Silver Bell' because of the incomparable quality of his voice and the magic of his evangelical preaching in his own church in Llywel, Brecknockshire, where he was vicar from 1821 to 1862, and in many other churches the length and breadth of the country.[46] His father-in-law, David Herbert, was not so well known as a preacher, but he had held *seiadau*, prayer meetings and preaching meetings ever since he began his ministry in Llansanffraid and Llanrhystud in

Cardiganshire.[47] John Griffith, the vicar of Aberdare from 1846 to 1859 and the rector of Merthyr Tudful from then until his death in 1885, belonged to the band of evangelicals that enjoyed the patronage of Bishop Ollivant. Indeed there was no more militant defender of the evangelical position. He succeeded in attracting the wrath of the church hierarchy and also in attracting the crowds to church to listen to him. This was hardly surprising because he was the 'most colourful, aggressive, controversial, entertaining, terrifying and popular preacher in the diocese'.[48] He should not be confused with another imposing figure in the movement, Archdeacon John Griffiths, rector of Neath from 1855 to 1896.[49] If his eloquence in the pulpit was like a flood, his stand for his principles was completely uncompromising. He set his face like flint against ritualism and believed that there was no significant difference in doctrine between the evangelicals within the church and the orthodox Nonconformists.[50] During the golden age of the evangelical party in the Llandaff diocese under Ollivant, there were other noteworthy preachers, such as John Tinson Wrenford in Newport, Evan Jenkins in Dowlais, Richard Pendrill Llywelyn, whose acerbic preaching terrified the inhabitants of Llangynwyd, Lodwick Edwards and his successor, William Evans, in Rhymney.[51] Canon Leigh Morgan turned his three-decker pulpit in the church of St Mary's Cardiff, into an influential preaching station. William Rees Thomas was possessed of the same temperament as the popular preachers of the Nonconformist churches. He served as curate with John Griffith in Aberdare and later became the parson of Abersychan. He would leave his parish for five or six weeks at a time to go on preaching tours. It is said that he preached in 668 churches in Wales and England during his career, and not the least of his talents was his ability to hold common folk and scholars alike enthralled.[52]

Although Llandaff was the stronghold of the evangelical cause between 1850 and 1870, the evangelical voice could be heard in other dioceses also. Mention has already been made of David Parry, Llywel, and David Herbert in the diocese of St Davids. By 1850 Lampeter College was a stronghold of the evangelical position, a natural enough consequence of Ollivant's work as principal there from 1827 to 1843.[53] 'Hughes, Llandovery' would in time become a renowned figure. He was vicar of Llandovery from 1845 until he was appointed bishop of St Asaph by Gladstone[54] in 1870.

His appointment made history in that he was the first Welshman to hold the post of bishop in Wales since John Wynne moved from St Asaph in 1727 to become bishop of Bath and Wells.[55] He was a popular preacher and a champion of evangelicals in his diocese. There were no more solicitous guardians of the evangelical faith than the two canons, Robert Williams, Llanfaelog, and Eleazer Williams, Llangefni.[56] They were even wary of David Howell (Llawdden) when the three of them were ministering in the Llŷn peninsula and took him to task on the soundness of his doctrine.[57] They need not have worried. The tradition of Griffith Jones, Llanddowror, Thomas Richards, Darowen, and David Parry, Llywel, was safe enough in the hands of Llawdden, David Howell (1831–1903). He was the son of a Calvinistic Methodist elder, from the parish of Llan-gan. John Griffiths, later of Neath, encouraged him to consider holy orders. It would be difficult for a lad brought up in such an atmosphere to embrace any standpoint but the evangelical one. He was vicar of Pwllheli (1861–4), vicar of St John's Cardiff (1864–75), vicar of Wrexham (1875–91) and vicar of Gresford until he was appointed dean of St Davids in 1897. 'He was a man of conviction,' said Mary Ellis, 'and the flame burned within him. He could see how poor and pitiful was the preaching within the church and he made a deliberate effort to perfect his craft'.[58] Like Richard Richards, John Griffiths and Joshua Hughes, he had many friends among Nonconformists and there is no greater proof of that than when the radical Dissenting *Celt* – of all the papers in Wales! – called him 'a man of the nation'.[59]

But the evangelical party was beginning to weaken during the last quarter of the century and one sign of the change was that Canon Eleazar Williams was the last of the evangelical wing to be a member of the chapter of Bangor cathedral.[60]

By that time, the high church faction that stemmed from the Oxford Movement had become a power within the church, and in the Bangor diocese more than anywhere.[61] However, it was in St Davids that the movement's first memorial was built, the church of Llangorwen. This church was the fruit of the enthusiasm and generosity of Matthew Williams (the brother of Isaac Williams), and his family, and was consecrated by Bishop Thirlwall on 16 December 1841. The chancel has remained as a true expression of Tractarian architectural ideals, with three steps – a symbol of the Holy Trinity – ascending towards the first stone altar built in an

Anglican church in Wales since the Protestant Reformation.[62] However the early Tractarians were concerned with doctrinal reform rather than ritual, and some of them, including Pusey, were quite indifferent to the liturgical minutiae that occupied the attention of their disciples. To them, the 'Church, the Body of Christ and the holy Society, was God's instrument for salvation' and the best way to create a religious revival was to build up Anglicans in the true faith, and incorporate them into the life of the holy society, that holy society being the Catholic Church.[63]

Although the first Tractarian church in Wales was built in the diocese of St Davids, Connop Thirlwall knew of only one other supporter of the Oxford Movement in his diocese in 1854, apart from the main benefactor of the church in Llangorwen, Matthew Williams. That man was Robert Raikes, Treberfydd, of the same family as the famous Sunday school pioneer and whose lasting contribution was to rebuild the church of Langasty, Brecknockshire.[64] The only bishop who showed some sympathy with his views in the middle of century was Christopher Bethell, bishop of Bangor from 1830 to 1859. Thus it is no wonder that it was in the diocese of Bangor that the movement first grew and 'became most deeply rooted'.[65] In 1853 a lay society was formed in the diocese to promote these new church principles with Robert Isaac Jones (Alltud Eifion) and Robert Roberts (Y Sgolor Mawr) as joint secretaries.[66] Meetings were held here and there, with addresses by people such as Owen Wynne Jones (Glasynys) and John Williams, Llanllechid.[67] The society's principles were outlined in the magazine, *Baner y Groes* (The Banner of the Cross). It was short-lived; its publication ceased in 1857 and by that time the society itself had run out of steam.[68]

A number of Welshmen came under the influence of the Oxford Movement while they were university students. The most well-known of these was Morris Williams (Nicander),[69] the pioneer of the movement in the diocese of Bangor, and a vigorous apologist for its principles in periodicals, as well as a translator of devotional books. One who had a more profound influence on his parishes and on young people who came into contact with him was Evan Lewis.[70] As curate in Llanllechid (1847–59), vicar of Aberdare (1859–66) and rector of Dolgellau (1866–84), he undertook to restore the Gregorian chants[71] and to raise the standard of the liturgy, to make the buildings more beautiful and to hold retreats and other devotional meetings. In Llanfairfechan, where he was rector from 1862 until his death in 1900, Philip Constable Ellis accomplished his greatest work.[72] He built Christchurch in 1863 and made his parish an example of what a high church parish should be. He was particularly enthusiastic in his support for the work of the church schools and was also a tenacious defender of his principles, incurring the displeasure of his bishop and angering Nonconformists, with whom he wished to have no contact at all.[73] Although he cherished the same ideals for the church, Griffith Arthur Jones was a man of very different temperament. As vicar of Llanegryn, Merioneth, from 1857 to 1872 he enthusiastically immersed his people in Catholic principles, with a particular emphasis on appropriate rituals and robes in the services.[74] By 1858, every member of the choir wore a surplice, Gregorian chants were used in every service, and before he left the parish, Jones himself had begun to wear the eucharistic vestments and adorn the altar with candles at the eucharist.[75] At first Jones was a lonely pioneer and he would occasionally become impatient as he saw how slowly these principles were taking root. As late as 1887 he complained that the Catholic faith and customs had not had a fair chance in Wales. 'An outspoken teaching of the Sacramental system alone can meet the needs of fallen man,' he said, 'be he a Welshman or of any other nationality.'[76] Thus in the diocese of Bangor, the revival started during the years between 1859 and 1869 and these were the kind of men who were in the vanguard, with a band of followers that grew with every succeeding year.[77]

A. G. Edwards maintained that it was between 1846 and 1870, while Thomas Vowler Short was bishop, that St Asaph enjoyed 'the greatest awakening' experienced by the diocese.[78] If this is true, the Oxford Movement made little contribution to it. The movement could hardly be expected to make rapid strides during the time of Joshua Hughes, a willing patron of the evangelical party, but even then it did have some fervent supporters. One of them was William Walsham How, rector of Whittington, 1851, and chancellor of the cathedral from 1869 until he moved to England in 1879.[79] As well as carrying out reforms within his parish, he frequently arranged quiet days and retreats and became well-known as a devotional writer and popular hymnist. He was succeeded in Whittington by Henry Powel Foulkes, a man eager to follow in his footsteps.[80] Others of the same persuasion were Richard Pughe of

Rhuddlan, Mostyn and Llanycil;[81] Bulkeley Owen Jones, the warden of Ruthin; Robert Roberts (Y Sgolor Mawr); Lewis Lewis, Denbigh; Thomas Richard Lloyd (Yr Estyn);[82] Howell Evans, Oswestry; Stephen Gladstone, Hawarden; and Rowland Ellis, Mold.[83]

The Catholic revival in the diocese of St Davids had little vitality in the period before 1890. George Huntingdon made his parish in Tenby a stronghold of high church principles, but he had few imitators. However there was no more striking figure in the whole movement than Joseph Leycester Lyne, the nearest thing to a Catholic Nonconformist that Wales had ever seen. He combined very disparate talents. He was the means by which monastic discipline returned to the Church of England which is why he became much better known throughout the country as Father Ignatius than by his given name. He accomplished this by founding a house of the Order of Saint Benedict in Nanthonddu. However, he was a thorn in the side of the ecclesiastical authorities and was banned from preaching in churches. This did not restrain him one whit because he filled the public halls with crowds who were eager to listen to his enthralling eloquence. And to top it all, he was 'Dewi Honddu' of the 'Guild of the Bards of the Island of Britain'.[84]

The spread of the Oxford Movement in the diocese of Llandaff resulted in the storming of the chief citadels of the evangelical party there. If Aberdare was a centre of evangelicalism under John Griffith, it soon became a high church stronghold under his successor Evan Lewis, the incumbent from 1859 to 1866. It was the same story in Cardiff with the installation of Griffith Arthur Jones in St Mary's in 1872. He swiftly transformed the evangelical parish of Leigh Morgan into a high church parish, repeating there what he had already done in Llanegryn. Like Jones, Griffith Roberts moved from Llanegryn to south Wales. He arrived in Dowlais in 1880 and was appointed diocesan missionary in 1889, taking his Catholic principles and practices with him everywhere. In the parish of St German's, Roath, Cardiff, Tractarianism flourished under a succession of vicars, none other than Frederick William Puller (1872–80), Charles Alan Smythies (1880–7) and Robert James Ives (1887–1920). Among the laity there was Christopher Rice Mansel Talbot, the politician and squire of Penrice and Margam, whose family were generous patrons of the high church movement. They built the church of St Theodore, Port Talbot – a splendid example of the movement's architectural style.[85]

Until 1890, the story of the Oxford Movement in Wales was one of expansion and increase. It was a minority movement, but its uncompromising approach to doctrine and worship and its emphasis on spirituality brought new vigour into the life of the church, far beyond the confines of the movement's direct disciples.

Henry Thomas Edwards, the dean of Bangor, believed that the weakness of the Church in Wales, compared with the Nonconformist churches, could be attributed to the disparagement of the Welsh language by foreign bishops and by the aristocracy and the consequent lack of understanding of the culture and aspirations of common folk. 'The regeneration of the Church of the Cymry, by the restoration of the masses into her fold', he said in his letter to Gladstone in January 1870, 'can only be effected by none other than native bishops and native clergy.'[86] He believed that the Church had been used as a stooge in the hands of people who had adopted a deliberate policy to eradicate the Welsh language,[87] and that the social leaders of Wales were party to this conspiracy. 'The aristocracy and the higher middle classes are almost without exception attached to the Church', and yet 'there is not a single nobleman in Wales who can converse in the language', and 'it would be difficult to find half a dozen squires in the whole of Wales who can write a Welsh letter or deliver a Welsh speech'.[88] And what is the result? 'Many of the Welsh people are unable to think of the Church except as "Yr Eglwys Wladol", a State Church using religion as an instrument for fulfilling the purposes of a short-sighted statecraft.'[89] Whatever impression his letter 'The Church of the Cymry' made on Gladstone's mind, it is a fact that not one non-Welsh-speaking bishop was appointed between that time and Disestablishment. But H. T. Edwards's letter expressed, in impassioned terms, the impasse in which the church found itself by the second half of the nineteenth century. On the one hand, it claimed to be a national church, and yet the majority of the Christians of Wales were not within its fold and the national language had little status within its parishes. It is remarkable, nevertheless, that such an able and influential leader as H. T. Edwards could challenge the church and the people who appointed its bishops and clergy to consider much more seriously their duty towards the nation and its culture.

Members of the church continued to contribute significantly to the national culture in many ways. The contribution of the 'literary clerics' to the regional societies and their eisteddfodau is now well-documented, starting with the Carmarthen Eisteddfod in 1819 under the patronage of the Dyfed Society. A place of honour in this story is reserved for men such as John Jenkins (Ifor Ceri), David Richards (Dewi Silin), William Jenkin Rees of Casgob, Bishop Thomas Burgess and their contemporaries.[90] Among the poets of the eisteddfod a substantial contribution was made by people such as Walter Jenkins (Gwallter Mechain), Daniel Evans (Daniel Ddu) of Cardigan, Evan Evans (Ieuan Glan Geirionydd), John Blackwell (Alun) and Morris Williams (Nicander).[91] The interest in eisteddfodau continued for the rest of the century, with prominent clergymen such as John Griffiths, Neath, helping to reform the eisteddfod and to establish the National Eisteddfod in its present form.

Similarly, members of the Anglican Church in Wales contributed to the growth of scholarship. If John Williams (Ab Ithel) was, in the words of Sir Thomas Parry, a 'gullible fool' and a 'deceitful pretender',[92] others of his fellow clergymen had an important contribution to make. The Society for Welsh Language Manuscripts, founded in 1836, was responsible for publishing a series of ancient and important texts. Thomas Price (Carnhuanawc), as well as being a fervent supporter of the eisteddfod, was a historian who made a substantial contribution in his *Hanes Cymru* (History of Wales, 1842) and a linguist who inspired fresh interest in Brittany and its language.[93] John Jenkins (Ifor Ceri), David Richards (Dewi Silin) and his sister Mair Richards – in truth the entire Darowen family – took a lively interest in chronicling old melodies, reviving old dances and copying literature. Daniel Silvan Evans, the first professor of Welsh in the colleges of the University of Wales, stood firmly in this scholarly and church tradition.[94]

Despite this, the church in the nineteenth century was not a comfortable home for patriotic Welsh people. Its Anglicized officialdom was an affront to many. By 1800, there was hardly anyone alive who remembered a Welsh-speaking bishop in Wales. As H. T. Edwards said much later, a Welshman had little hope of being promoted to an important position within his church, however great his talent or his dedication. And neither Thomas Burgess's interest in the eisteddfod, nor Connop Thirlwall's clumsy Welsh, much less the wholly unintelligible Welsh of James Colquhoun Campbell in Bangor, was sufficient to make amends for the injustice done to the language.[95] It is true that the storm that followed the abolition of the Court of Great Session and the national declarations made at that time gave rise to the 1835 Act which made it mandatory for every clergyman serving in a Welsh-speaking parish to know the language, but it was not difficult for those who so wished to get past the requirements of the Act.[96] However there was a surge in national sentiment towards the middle of the century. The foolish scheme contained in the 1840 Act to merge the dioceses of Llandaff and Bristol and St Asaph and Bangor served to inflame emotions. Mercifully both plans had run aground by 1846. In this fight, as in the constant battles against appointing foreigners to livings in Wales, clergymen living outside Wales were particularly vocal, especially the Society of Welsh Clergymen of West Yorkshire under the leadership of men such as Joseph Hughes (Carn Ingli), David James (Dewi o Ddyfed) and his brother Thomas James (Llallawg).[97] These expatriate clergymen made a very significant contribution to the growth of modern Welsh nationalism. David James (Dewi o Ddyfed) was not only expressing his own opinion when he said in the Newcastle Emlyn Eisteddfod in 1859: 'The policy of the English government with regard to the people of Wales is to eradicate them'.[98] What worried those of like mind was that the church itself frequently behaved as if that was also its intention. In 1886, the Anglican periodical *Yr Haul* announced:

> The diocese of St Asaph is much more Anglicized than its sister diocese of Bangor . . . the Bishop is a Welshman, the two archdeacons are Welsh, the resident Canons are Welsh, and yet, very little that is popular and involving the laity and concerned with the Welsh language or culture goes on in the Annual Conference . . . all the work is carried on in English.[99]

The supporters of the language were facing a hard battle. T. Edwin Davies, the vicar of St Mary's church, Bangor, complained bitterly in 1893 because no Welsh services were held in any of the cathedrals, except for the parish services in Bangor and St Davids.[100] And clergymen, just like others outside the church, were capable of airing very ignorant opinions. Robert Williams, Dolwyddelan, argued that the National Eisteddfod should help nurture poets to compose in English, and 'thus enrich the literature of the world with the fruit of Welsh inspiration' – whatever that was supposed to mean![101] On the other hand there was criticism of Bishop A. G. Edwards for his lack of sympathy for the Welsh language and culture, particularly since he breached the terms of the deeds of Llandovery College when he was warden there, attempting to drive the Welsh language out.[102] Although Bishop John Owen was a prominent figure on the national eisteddfod field, the radical journal *Young Wales* announced that the patriots within the church could expect nothing from him, because he was so anti-Welsh.[103] It was possible by 1898 to speak of patriots, nationalists – even 'the national party' – within the church.

In short, between 1800 and 1890, the Church in Wales saw a substantial increase in its effectiveness, its dignity and its spirituality and a lesser, but perceptible, increase in its awareness of its duty towards the national culture.[104]

I turn attention now to the Nonconformist churches. In Wales, the Independents (Congregationalists), the Baptists and the Quakers had their roots in the spiritual soil of the seventeenth century. The Calvinistic Methodists and the Wesleyan Methodists, on the other hand, as well as the Unitarians and the Scotch Baptists, were the product of the eighteenth century. Thus their backgrounds contained different influences, but with the passage of time they were changing, as they influenced one another, or reacted against one another. Independent and the Baptist secession from the established church became part of Methodist tradition too by the nineteenth century. On the other hand, the Evangelical Revival had such a profound influence on the Independents and the Baptists that the warmth and missionary spirit of the early revivalists became typical of the life of the older Dissent as well as the new denominations created through their ministry. And the Unitarians and the Scotch Baptists represented two different reactions to this very thing. With their militant spirit and the increasing effectiveness of their missionary methods the Independents, Calvinistic Methodists, Baptists and Wesleyan Methodists grew into large denominations during the nineteenth century, transforming the religious face of Wales as a result.

Neither the Unitarians nor the Quakers were missionary minded. In 1851 the Unitarians had twenty-seven churches in Wales and on the day of the Census, 2,130 worshippers were present in their morning services, 703 in the afternoon and 979 in the evening.[105] They remained fairly stable for the rest of the century with twenty-eight churches in 1905 and 1,735 members,[106] while the Society of

Friends had dwindled. In 1851 they had eight meeting houses with 102 morning worshippers and 43 in the evening. By 1905 they had only six meeting houses and the total number of Quakers in Wales was 271.[107]

The statistical progression of the Independents, the Baptists, the Calvinistic Methodists and the Wesleyan Methodists was very different. Welsh Independents had 225 churches in 1812[108] and by 1851, according to the Census, they had 640 gathered churches and 700 chapel buildings.[109] This increase continued in the second half of the century and by 1905 they had 1,078 churches.[110] On Census Sunday in 1851 87,237 people worshipped in Independent chapels in the morning, 32,465 in the afternoon, and 96,527 in the evening. By 1905 their membership totalled 175,147.[111] The Baptists also saw a large increase during the century. In 1812 they had 176 churches[112] but by 1900 the Particular Baptists had 854 churches and 108,990 members.[113] By 1905 the total membership of the Baptists of Wales, including the Scotch Baptists and the Disciples of Christ, was 144,918 in 901 churches.[114]

There was no official Methodist 'denomination' in Wales in 1800, although the Calvinistic Methodists were rapidly growing apart from the Church of England. The final separation came in 1811 with the ordination of ministers. When the deeds of the new denomination were registered in 1826–7, it was noted that they had 437 chapels and fifty-six ministers but the membership is not recorded. By 1851 they had 807 chapels and the number of worshippers in the three Sunday services on the day of the Census, 30 March 1851, was 76,274, 57,747 and 120,734 respectively. In 1855 they had 226 ministers and 60,455 members. By 1905 their churches numbered 1,411 and their membership was 170,617.[115] This denomination should not be confused with the Presbyterian Church of England, although the two denominations preserved fraternal links. In Wales, the Presbyterian Church of England had only four churches, with 1,206 members.[116]

One of the most remarkable events in the history of religion in the nineteenth century was the rapid expansion of the Wesleyan Methodists. Welsh Wesleyanism officially came into being on 6 August 1800[117] and initially it had only one chapel and forty-five members. By 1810, however, the denomination had ninety-two chapels and 5,700 members.[118] By 1851 the original Wesleyans (not counting the breakaway denominations) had 499 chapels and the attendance in the three services on the Sunday of the Census was 30,302, 19,534 and 53,730.[119] By 1905 they had 661 chapels and 40,811 members.[120]

The lesser denominations also had their place in the pattern. John Richard Jones, Ramoth, Merioneth, was the father of the Scotch Baptists in Wales. Their twelve congregations were in north Wales and they had 414 members.[121] In the late 1830s some of these churches came under the influence of the teaching of the American, Alexander Campbell, and broke away from the Scotch Baptists. This denomination went by the name of the Disciples of Christ and had twelve congregations in Wales in 1905 and 669 members.[122]

The first forty years of the century were a turbulent period in the history of Wesleyanism in England and echoes of the debates heard there also reverberated throughout Wales. Discipline rather than doctrine was at the root of the upheavals in the Methodist body as people rebelled against the autocracy of the system bequeathed by John Wesley to his followers. William O'Bryan, a preacher in Devon and Cornwall, left in 1815 and formed the Bible Christians. Alexander Kilham had previously departed with his followers in 1797 to form the Methodist New Connexion. The United Methodist Free Churches combined three factions which had seceded, namely the Protestant Methodists who broke away in 1827, the Wesleyan Methodist Association, formed in 1835 and the Wesleyan Reformers who seceded in 1849. The three movements merged in 1857.[123] These movements had branches in Wales by the middle of the century: the 1851 Census records that the Bible Christians had fourteen congregations, the Methodist New Connexion had ten, the Wesleyan Methodist Association had ten and the Wesleyan Reformers had eight. By 1905 the congregations of the Bible Christians numbered thirty-five, with 2,501 members, all of them in Glamorgan and Gwent.[124] The Methodist New Connexion had nine congregations, eight in Flintshire and one in Denbighshire, and 468 members,[125] The United Methodist Free Churches are particularly interesting because of their Welsh-language connections. By 1905 the denomination had twenty chapels and 1,195 members.[126] Among them were the remainder of the 'Wesle Bach' (Little Wesleyans), the breakaway Wesleyan movement that began in Anglesey on 6 October 1831.[127] Now there were only four chapels left and they were in fellowship with the United Methodist Free Churches. In September 1907, the three denominations, namely the Bible Christians, the United Methodist Free Churches and the Methodist New Connexion, joined together to form the United Methodist Church giving this new denomination sixty-five chapels and 4,164 members. In Wales, however, the largest of the denominations with roots in Wesleyanism were the Primitive Methodists. This denomination came into being as a result of the evangelical campaigns of Hugh Bourne in Staffordshire and the work of the American, Lorenzo Dow, who held open-air preaching festivals. Both were excommunicated by the Wesleyan Conference in 1810 and this signalled the beginning of the formation of a separate denomination. By 1905 they had 147 chapels in Wales and 8,306 members, making them the fifth largest Nonconformist denomination in Wales.[128]

The Brethren have always caused statisticians a headache. The movement was founded in Ireland in about 1828 and the first branch was established in Plymouth, England, by the Anglican clergyman J. N. Darby. Thus the movement came to be known as the Plymouth Brethren. One of their basic tenets has been to try to undermine denominationalism and thus they have been unwilling to be called a denomination or to proffer information about themselves as if they were a denomination. Thus the statisticians of the 1851 Census and the Disestablishment Commission had some difficulty in obtaining any information about them at all. They had two congregations in Wales in 1851 with somewhere between one hundred and two hundred members. One of their officials agreed to give evidence to the Disestablishment Commission and said they had about three dozen congregations in south Wales and two in the north. Cardiff was their stronghold however, with around 1,000 members in the eight congregations there.[129] As for the other small denominations – fourteen in all – the only one which claimed to have more than 1,000 members was the Salvation Army.[130]

To summarize, and to show the general pattern of development; the Anglican body had 1,180 parish churches in 1851; by 1905 it had 1,546 (not counting mission stations). During the same period the number of Nonconformist houses of worship increased from 2,760 to 4,280, and those of the Catholic Church from twenty-one to seventy-one. It is not possible to make such precise comparisons with regard to church membership. The best that can be done is to compare attendance in the services on Census Sunday, 30 March 1851, with church membership in 1905. The problem, though, is that this comparison disregards the people who attended church services although they were not members. In 1851, there were 100,953 in attendance at the morning services in Anglican churches, and 39,662 in the evening. The number of communicants in the church in 1905 was 193,081. It would not be far from the truth to say that the number of those attending the Anglican Church had doubled in half a century. Attendance at Catholic churches in 1851 was 5,742 in the morning and 1,326 in the evening. The number of worshippers in 1905 was approximately 64,800. Would it be correct to say that their membership had increased elevenfold in half a century? Taking the Nonconformist churches as a whole, 268,512 of their members attended the morning services in March 1851, and 369,494 the evening. By 1905 their membership was 550,280. When we try to guess the extent of the increase, we run into difficulty. How many of those attending chapel in 1851 were members? In 1905 the Nonconformist statisticians claimed that there were as many as 470,594 'adherents' – people who were not members – attending their chapels.[131] The commissioners refused to make any use of this figure because a large number of people could move from chapel to chapel, which was a common practice at that time, and be counted twice or three times. So we must follow the Commission's advice in its report and refrain from making statistical use of the figure. But, if we look at the statistics generally, we see the huge shift in the balance that had occurred during the century and how the Evangelical Accord (that encompassed many Anglicans as well as Nonconformists) had become the position of the overwhelming majority of Christians in Wales.

The large increase in the strength of the Nonconformist churches had given rise to many changes. To begin with, changes had occurred within the 'major' denominations themselves. The Independents, Baptists, Calvinistic Methodists and Wesleyans had grown into national denominations in the sense that they had branches throughout the whole of Wales. This is reflected in the development of their organization. In 1864 the Calvinistic Methodists formed their general assembly and although it had no legal status, it was an expression of the sentiment that the work of the two regional associations (of north and south Wales) and the monthly meetings were a service to the whole of Wales. Two years later the Baptists established their union, with the Independents following suit in 1871.[132] These unions did not have any authority to govern the churches in either denomination. They were wholly voluntary bodies. However their annual meetings soon became a platform for the discussion of issues that were of national significance, as well as denominational matters. Lastly, the Welsh Methodists were given their national body when the Conference of Welsh Wesleyan Methodists was established in 1898.[133] Although the Independent firebrand Michael D. Jones was wholly convinced that the Union of Welsh Independents was part of the conspiracy to Anglicize Wales, it is difficult not to see the formation of these institutions as part of the tendency within the Nonconformist churches to extend their responsibility to the nation as such.[134]

The appearance of these institutions is significant for another reason. One of the characteristics of the Victorian age in Britain was the proliferation of organizations of all kinds. The regimentation of social life proceeded apace. An effort was made in many spheres to turn activities that were formally voluntary and sporadic into established regimes. This happened with the police, the postal service, transport, business and education, and the churches only reflected the fashion of the age. Of course, some churches were already more organized than others so the change did not strike them as out of the ordinary. Nevertheless, the increasing pressure of the centralist and bureaucratic yoke caused some protest and controversy. We have already seen that the Wesleyans had their fair share of protest movements and breakaway denominations. One of the bitterest controversies of the century occurred among the Independents, in the shape of the 'Battle of the Constitutions' between 1879 and 1892, and although the constitution of Bala Independent Theological College was the bone of contention, the supporters of the Old Constitution were campaigning mainly against the regimentation and centralization of the denomination.[135] The Calvinistic Methodists had their share of rebels and schismatics as well as we shall see when I discuss Eglwys Rydd y Cymry (the Free Church of the Welsh). Irrespective of the success or otherwise of individual attempts at regimentation, there was a visible trend away from the emphasis formerly placed on the spiritual well-being of the individual believer and the close fellowship of the local congregation or *seiat* (fellowship meeting) to the glorification of the denominational institution, its policies and its accolades. In a word, the Nonconformist churches were busy shedding the characteristics of 'sects' and growing into 'denominations' and adopting more and more of the sentiment and spirit of established churches.[136] The subsequent clash between them and the Church in Wales was inevitable.

Nevertheless, these churches could not lightly disregard the anti-institutional elements within their own background. Mention has already been made of protest movements within the denominations. These gave rise to breakaway movements and the formation of new sects that operated, as it were, on the fringes of the major denominations. It is worth pointing out that sectarian activity of this kind was a characteristic of certain parts of the country more than others. In 1905, it did not exist in Gwynedd. There the major denominations had the field to themselves. This was true of Cardiganshire also because the Unitarians represented an old tradition in the religious life of the county. There was a little sectarian activity in Carmarthenshire, but it was so negligible in 1905 – only four congregations[137] – that it made little difference to the general pattern. There was not much more in Radnorshire, Breconshire and Pembrokeshire. The minor denominations had more congregations in Denbighshire and Flintshire but in Gwent and Glamorgan they flourished with a vengeance. The overall pattern tends to confirm the presupposition that sects prosper more in a heterogeneous and changing society.

Of more significance than this activity, however, as we consider the growth of institutionalism, were the pentecostal manifestations that became characteristic of Nonconformist churches throughout the nineteenth century. Although certainly by 1900 spokesmen for the various denominations were very jealous of the purity of their lineage, the truth was that Nonconformity in Wales was of mixed parentage. Of the various antecedents, two are now of interest, namely the Reformed strand, which can be traced back to Calvin's Geneva, and the revivalist and charismatic strand. The meshing of these two created the particular character of Welsh Nonconformity. The desire of the former was to remain faithful to the concept of the church as a manifestation of believers' obedience to biblical revelation, while the latter maintained that the church could not exist without the direct anointing of the Holy Spirit. When these two aspects were balanced, church life combined strength of doctrine and warmth of experience, organizational stability and dynamic spirituality. However it was difficult to maintain this equilibrium and the two influences often worked against each other. It was difficult to reconcile the desire to be a national institution with the conviction that the church is a colony of heaven. It was not easy to marry the wild enthusiasm of a sect and the sober demeanour of a denomination. It is possible that this tension became a basic paradox which by the twentieth century had mortally weakened all the churches. We shall see! Certainly, one of the chief characteristics of Welsh Nonconformity in the nineteenth century was the series of revivals that it experienced. Some of them were fleeting and localized, others, like the Beddgelert Revival (1817–21) and the 'Temperance' Revival (1839), extended over large portions of the country and had a profound influence. The greatest of this series was the 1859 Revival connected especially in Wales with the name of Dafydd Morgan, Ysbyty Ystwyth, whose memory lingered like a fragrance in people's souls for half a century. Indeed, people began to think of revivals not as rare and unexpected visitations, but as a part of the rhythm of spiritual life. This was perhaps a result of the teaching of the American revivalist Charles Finney.[138] One revival had hardly ceased when pentecostal expectations were being fired up for another. It was quite generally believed that one could expect a revival every ten years and people began to speak of Wales as the 'Land of Revivals'. In short, it would not be a disservice to the evidence to say that revivals were enthroned as part of the institutionalism of the denominations long before the end of the nineteenth century. The mania for regimentation had almost sucked the charismatic forces dry – but not quite.

As the Nonconformist churches grew in numbers, they became the churches of the 'common folk and the masses', to quote Samuel Roberts (S.R.). It would be an exaggeration to say that their evangelism had brought Christianity within reach of sections of the population hitherto untouched. But these churches created an opportunity for common folk to organize their religious life in an unprecedented way. The churches nurtured for themselves many thousands of leaders from among people who throughout the centuries had been voiceless and powerless. Procedures were put in place to train these leaders and give them the kind of education that would equip them to hold responsibility within their fellowships. The Sunday school, the *seiat* (Methodist class meeting) and the religious periodical were key means in this process. New denominational colleges were established to prepare the chief leaders, namely the ministers. This development was revolutionary, to say the least.

Now the former leaders of society, the squire and the parson, were forced to share their kingdom with new princes who had risen from the land.[139]

Since this new common class was gaining confidence apace, it was inevitable that it would turn its attention to politics as a means of securing a different kind of freedom for itself and curtailing the privileges of the old ruling class. Under the leadership of Nonconformist ministers such as Roger Edwards, William Rees (Gwilym Hiraethog), David Rees, S.R. and others, these political aspirations fuelled their radicalism.[140] The Nonconformist leaders fought the battles of their congregations to a great extent and, naturally, in doing so they strengthened the tie between them. But the marriage was not all sweetness and light, as was increasingly evident as the century drew to a close. To what extent was Christian content altered by the demands of the political battle? Which was the main motivation by 1890, the desire to lead Welsh politics along paths that would be acceptable to Christians or the desire to ensure that the denominations supported policies that were acceptable to politicians? Or, to phrase the question in a more modern idiom, to what extent was Christianity being politicized? These are questions we will have to revisit.

Another difficulty was emerging as the denominations grew to become the homes of 'the common folk and the masses'. As Wales became more thoroughly Christianized, it was becoming more difficult for the churches to continue to exist as societies of believers who had consecrated themselves to total obedience to their saviour. They were developing into institutions whose purpose was to contribute spiritual resources to the whole of society. A core transformation was taking place in the moral presuppositions of Welsh church leaders. Previously, morality had depended on the pre-eminence and unquestioned authority of the divine revelation and the example of Jesus Christ in his life, his atoning sacrifice and the power of his resurrection. Now there was a growing temptation to consider morality in light of what would be acceptable and practical from the perspective of the whole of society. We shall see how this transformation created grave crises in Welsh Christianity between 1890 and 1914.

Finally, as the Nonconformist denominations grew they came to share with the Church in Wales the problems that arose from the clash between two cultures, the ancient Welsh culture and the aggressive English culture. The Anglican Church in Wales was, from its inception, a bilingual church which endeavoured to accommodate both cultures and languages within the same organization and in the same buildings. The arguments, fairly acrimonious at times, concerning the equity of this provision, particularly with regard to Welsh-speakers, show that this policy had its share of difficulties. The Nonconformist churches generally adopted a different plan. Their preference was not to separate services within the same organization but to divide local churches according to language. We have become so used to studying those churches that have throughout the years existed and worshipped in Welsh that we do not realize how many English-language churches there are in Wales. In 1905, 39.5 per cent of the chapels of Wales were English-language chapels.[141] The denominations arranged for these English chapels to link together in unions, or presbyteries or festivals or circuits separate from the corresponding bodies for Welsh-language churches, but this arrangement also had its share of critics. Although they agreed that it was right and proper for those Christians who wished to worship in English to do this in their own chapels, and to form any denominational organization that they felt would be appropriate for themselves, strong voices were raised against plans for Welsh-speakers to build chapels for non-Welsh-speakers. This was what led to the conflict of the 'Inglis côs' (English cause) among the Calvinistic Methodists, with Robert Ambrose Jones (Emrys ap Iwan) in the front line of battle. And among the Independents Michael D. Jones argued that 'establishing English chapels to take away the Welsh culture' of the nation was part of the conspiracy to eradicate Wales's national identity.[142]

Such was Christian Wales in 1890. The leading actors have been introduced, and we can now watch the drama in which they were involved between then and 1914.

~ 3 ~

Stoking the Denominational Fires

In Wales, during the 1890s, there was a striking contrast between a destructive, divisive and contentious spirit and a longing for peace and unity. While religious and social divisions had people at one another's throats, patriotism and the ecumenical spirit made a fervent appeal for those divisions to be healed.

Over many years, the monthly journal *Y Geninen* (The Leek) sounded the alarm about the dangers of denominational sectarianism.[1] One of the most talented satirists of the period, W. R. Jones (Goleufryn), had the opportunity to castigate the denominations for their narrow-mindedness.[2] Under the nom-de-plume 'Silurian' he wrote scathingly about Wales's 'denominational philistinism':

> Calvinistic Methodists look down with a degree of contempt upon everybody, as befits the John Bull of the denominations! The Independents are envious of everybody – of the Baptists in Gwent and Glamorgan, and of the Methodists in Gwynedd. The Baptists are prejudiced against everybody; the Wesleyans try to win everybody; and the Established Church is arrogant towards everybody. The main concern is the aggrandizement of the denomination, not the conversion of the world.[3]

This article was published in 1887. Three years later, in a piece bearing the same title, he tackled philistinism within the denominations once more, claiming that 'the greatest and most dreadful tyranny that exists within most of the religious organizations in Wales these days is what is known as cliquism'.[4] Despite all the talk of unity within the Church of England, all its members, he said, are either 'high church, or low church or mid church; they are all broad or narrow'. Nor did the Nonconformists get off scot-free. He

41

launched a bruising attack on the hypocrisy and bogus respectability of the Calvinistic Methodists, describing with gusto characters such as the Revd Epaphroditus Fflach (Flash) Rhys who succeeded in persuading the general assembly to promote his 'immortal book', *Fflach yn y Badell* (A Flash in the Pan). But he reserved the harshest treatment for the Independents for having staged the 'Great Battle of Catterick'[5] between the armies of the Revd Uthr Bendragon and the Revd Gwgan Farfdrwch ('Wogan the Bearded') – in other words the Battle of the Constitutions with John Thomas of Liverpool, and Michael D. Jones of Bala, wittily depicted as generals of the opposing forces. It is no surprise that John Thomas was deeply wounded by the essay, which was easily (he claimed) the most 'bilious and venomous' piece that he had ever read.[6] But not even John Thomas's silver-tongued talent could hide the incontrovertible fact that much of what Silurian wrote was true.[7]

Sectarianism reigned supreme. R. Gwylfa Roberts, for instance, wrote of the expansion of the Congregational cause in Tabernacle, Ffair-fach, Carmarthenshire, just as the denomination's elegant New Chapel was being built in the neighbouring town of Llandeilo. 'It would not be worthy of Tabernacle or of the denomination if it were not made into a spacious and beautiful chapel.'[8] One of the most noticeable effects of this concern for denominational dignity was the building of many hundreds of chapels that were far too large for their congregations even at the time. Each denomination insisted that it should have its own chapel in virtually every village throughout the land. How many examples are there in the whole of Wales of two denominations agreeing to build a single chapel between them? If the Catholics and Protestants in many parishes of French Alsace could share the same church without falling out, why was not the same thing possible in Victorian Wales? The answer was 'denominational pride'. The same was true elsewhere. One only needs to turn the pages of the periodicals to realize the extent that denominational allegiance was such an omnipresent force. Those who won eisteddfod competitions, or who were appointed to public office as councillors or Members of Parliament, or gained local renown in their profession as teachers or physicians were all congratulated for 'bringing honour to our denomination'.[9] This is how the magazine Y *Greal* (The Grail) fanned the flames of Baptist praise:

It brings us great joy as a denomination, that the three most popular men in the great town of Cardiff today are Dr. William Edwards B.A, D.D., E. Thomas (Cochfarf) and Sir Alfred Thomas M.P . . . There is not a single denomination in the town to rival us for power and influence.[10]

The last sentence is extremely revealing; each of the denominations saw itself as the centre of 'power and influence' in some sphere or other. The Calvinistic Methodists' *Y Drysorfa* (The Treasury) swelled with denominational pride: '[Our Connexion] has the honour of having created nearly every scheme for deepening the influence of religion on the nation's soul: and the other denominations show quite an aptitude for imitating us, and following in our footsteps'.[11] The Independents were no better. After sniping at the Baptists for harping on continually about their 'distinctive characteristics', *Y Celt* declared smugly, 'No other denomination has done so much – yes, so much, remember – to win for our people national and religious freedom, as the Independents.'[12] This overwhelming mania for self-praise was the result of the social power that the various denominations had recently acquired, and they took great pride in using it whenever they could. One of the places where a denomination's power could be felt was the school board which meant that every school board election became a fierce sectarian battle. The Pen-y-Bryn school board near Cardigan in Dyfed had a Baptist majority. In March 1891 the school was closed for a day for the local Baptists' annual singing festival. The singing festivals of the village's Anglican church or the Independent chapel gained no such civic favour.[13]

The 'spirit of narrow-mindedness, bigotry and oppression' that was implicit in this militant denominationalism elicited a heavy price.[14] The Anglican D. Ambrose Jones wrote of current sectarianism 'as one of the plagues of Egypt, which has gripped the whole nation without exception'. He demonstrated how members of the different denominations confined their reading to the literary output of their own denomination.[15] Such narrow-mindedness led to bitterness, as another conciliatory Anglican, David Howell (Llawdden) commented: 'Even our professed religious publications are marred by the most bitter personal references, and the most base insinuations. Such intolerance causes me to tremble when I think of my country's future.'[16] The denominational walls were very high indeed. One of the main leaders of the campaign to separate church from state was John Thomas, Liverpool. Early in 1890 he heard the leading evangelical cleric, Llawdden, preaching and confessed that it was only the second time he had ever heard a clergyman preach. The first time was as far back as 1843 in Abernant church where he heard David Parry, Llywel. 'I have never sat through an entire religious service in the Anglican Church', he added nonchalantly.[17] This did not prevent him from holding forth with supreme authority on the foibles and weaknesses of that body. The situation was no different among Anglican leaders, as is patent to anyone who has ever read *Memories*, the autobiography of Bishop A. G. Edwards; the book is wholly bereft of any insight into the true characteristics of Nonconformity. The bishop of St Asaph was very different from his brother, Henry Thomas Edwards, dean of Bangor, who, in spite of his Anglican zeal, could well appreciate the particular characteristics of Nonconformity. (His first wife, Mary, was the daughter of David Davies, Maes-y-ffynnon, Aberdare, a coal-owner and entrepreneur, and a fervent Congregationalist from the school of Michael D. Jones![18])

On the whole, however, denominational divisions were entrenched and there was very little crossing of boundaries, although paradoxically social tradition dictated that a woman upon marrying should join her husband's denomination. These divisions frequently gave rise to a contentious spirit. 'In North Wales, there is not only fierce hatred towards the Church, but bitter rivalry between the sects', one observer remarked.[19] R. Iwan Jenkyn agreed, claiming that 'sectarianism is one of the strongest forces in Wales'.[20] The denominational journals did not tire of bludgeoning one another. Towards the end of the century *Y Drysorfa* suffered from a bad bout. It boasted of the denominational achievements of the Calvinistic Methodists, and then found fault with others for doing likewise. It agreed that the tone of the Wesleyans' *Eurgrawn* (Treasure-trove) was 'evangelical and respectable', but hastened to say that 'it scarcely sees any good outside its own denomination'.[21] If this was inconsistent, then the way *Y Drysorfa* treated the Anglican *Haul* (The Sun) was cruel: 'We found it pathetically – we could almost say sinfully – lacking in talent; it has not a spark of genius between its covers'.[22] It may have been true that *Yr Haul* was not at its best at the time, but it was denominational bitterness and not honest criticism that lay behind that nasty jibe.

At times it is difficult to know how seriously to take these contentious skirmishes. The vast majority of the religious leaders of the period were sons of the soil, or of the common folk at least, and the mantle of bourgeois Victorian courtesy rested lightly enough on their shoulders. They needed little provocation to cast reserve to the wind and revel in a glorious quarrel. When Michael D. Jones heard that agreement had at last been reached between the two factions in the Battle of the Constitutions, he is said to have retorted: 'Well, there goes the end of some splendid fun!' Whether the anecdote is factually true or not, one is tempted to believe that it was typical of the reaction of many an uncouth protagonist at the end of a skirmish. Even so, not all denominational conflicts could be considered an entertaining way of whiling away an idle hour. More often than not, laughter turned to tears. There were many at that time who deplored the ugly spectre of denominational sectarianism. It is easy to understand why one anonymous writer claimed that Wales's new god was 'the Great Denomination'. There were sectarians, he said, who in their desire to make their own denomination into the Great Denomination, were happy to besmirch the very nation's life.

> It is the Great Denomination that is responsible for the baseness of the press, for the deceit of the Eisteddfod, for the servility of our fellow workers, for the persecution of good men, for the decline of religion and the lethargy of our denominational festivals and for the malice and envy that defile our national character.[23]

The question to ask is, what spawned the bitterness which so often poisoned the denominational relations? A glance at the newspapers and magazines of the period reveals an amazingly comprehensive picture of contemporary life. There is scarcely any aspect of the nation's life about which these periodicals cannot teach us something. This was the inevitable result of the conviction that Christianity should infuse all aspects of human life. This basic motivation was wholly laudable. Alas the reader also knows that he is seeing Welsh life from a very narrow perspective for the simple reason that the periodicals viewed everything in denominational terms. To take one instance, John Thomas (Eifionydd) published a series of articles in Y Geninen on the contribution of the various denominations to Welsh literature. The series gives the impression that the sole talent that an author needed to possess was membership in an

Anglican or a Baptist church, and if any success came his way then the glory accrued to the denomination to which he belonged.

At the root of the malady was a theological error that was to cause increasing confusion in the way that the churches viewed the nation's life. A church or denomination is directly accountable to God. No one emphasized this conviction more stubbornly than the Independents. It was to this that they referred when they spoke of the 'crowned rights of the Redeemer'. This was at the root of their theological opposition to an established church which, in their opinion, allowed the state to come between it and God. However it is only fair to add that, by the end of the century, many Anglicans – especially among those of the high church persuasion – shared the same fundamental conviction, although their reasons for so doing were different. In Wales, where several denominations shared the same Protestant, evangelical and moral convictions, and yet could hardly agree amongst themselves, there was no alternative but to overemphasize these denominational differences. Ironically the result was that each denomination was free to organize its own structure according to the light of conscience. Christian fraternity could permit no other solution, and this denominational pattern was an important and conciliatory solution to the problem of inter-denominational relationships.[24] Though not wholly successful, it nevertheless combined passion for principle with civil freedom. As such, it has been to date the most successful attempt to alleviate denominational rivalry.

By the end of the nineteenth century, there was a tendency to insist that the cultural and social life of the nation be brought under the authority of the denominations, forgetting that the secular sphere was directly accountable to God just as the churches were. The individual believer does not answer to God through his church or denomination – that was the costly mistake of the medieval church – but rather directly. Thus each sphere within the nation's life was responsible for its own well-being before God, and in consequence was free from ecclesiastical tyranny. This basic Christian principle was hardly understood. The denominations fragmented the nation's life by usurping the legitimate autonomy of its various activities before God, and insisting on bringing them instead directly into its own realm. The irony, of course, was that the Independent churches were unwittingly adopting an extreme Anglican standpoint. 'Secular' existence could not be permitted any significance except as an aspect of life as a member of a denomination. It was indeed a position that the medieval papacy would have understood – and applauded!

Nevertheless it took more than intellectual confusion to create bitterness. There is little doubt that the hunger for power and worldly ambition soured the relationships between denominations – an age-old malady which has caused much unpleasantness in Christian church life ever since the days of Constantine the Great. The Church of England had the edge because of its connection with the state and its alliance with the privileged class. But following the results of the 1851 Census, the Nonconformist denominations realized that together they already had a larger total membership than the Anglicans in Wales and they saw that they could wrest the reins of social and political influence from the church. During the following years, the Nonconformist denominations gradually translated their statistical superiority into election majorities. Soon the struggle for influence became a vital part of denominational life. They needed to compete with one another in building chapels in order to 'take possession' of areas – the very expression is suggestive! The emphasis was now on refining the organization of the denominations, and in the wake of this they came to think of important posts as 'honours' rather than as an opportunity for service. Since it was still uncertain who held the reins of power, it was inevitable that envy developed between leaders and feelings were wounded. Denominationalism was turning into denominational sectarianism. According to Thomas Roberts, in his address to the Union of Welsh Independents in 1892, religious and social life had degenerated into 'naked rivalry – an unseemly battle for supremacy'. This phenomenon at its worst, he claimed, could be seen 'in our elections – our parliamentary, county and board elections. We see it in the insatiable desire to seize every advantageous post and position for the denomination.'[25]

Nevertheless there was a general feeling that this was an unsatisfactory state of affairs. Strangely enough, although John Thomas confessed that he had never sat through an entire Anglican service, within two months he had changed his tune. 'Those who have listened most to other denominations are always the most liberated men,' he said. 'We should know a lot more about the movements of other denominations, their literature and publications.'[26] In fact, there was a palpable surge in ecumenical fervour. In 1890, Griffith

Ellis, Calvinistic Methodist minister at Bootle, Liverpool, said: 'In whatever direction we look, we see these days a certain longing for religious unity.'[27] William James, a Congregationalist from Swansea, agreed. 'Such a desire for unity between the different Nonconformist denominations in Wales as is apparent today has never before been manifested.'[28]

Much was written on this subject between 1890 and 1900. It was quite natural for the Free Churches to warm to this subject because their own evangelical tradition had formerly made a substantial contribution to the growth of the ecumenical cause.[29] One of the most ambitious organizations founded to promote ecumenism was the Evangelical Alliance, which was established during a conference in London in August 1846 attended by 800 representatives from fifty-two countries. The Alliance's proposal, to hold prayer meetings for Christian unity during the first week of the year, became common practice in Welsh chapels. The express purpose, however, was soon forgotten in Wales, and the meetings became an opportunity to greet the New Year.[30]

One reason for the decline of the Alliance's influence in Wales was its reluctance to declare an opinion on the issue of disestablishment. This was understandable in view of the fact that it included many members of established churches. Radical Nonconformists were hardly pleased. John Thomas deemed it 'nothing but an alliance to shut the mouths of Nonconformists'.[31] In his view, no serious discussion of religious unity could be engaged in 'except on the basis of the absolute equality of all parties in the eyes of the law'.[32] David Griffith of Bethel expressed the classical evangelical viewpoint when he addressed the Union of Welsh Independents on 'Christian Unity' in 1890. The fundamental unity is the union of Christians with Christ. The members of the true church are those who believe in eternal life, 'to whatever church or denomination they may belong'. Differences of opinion existed, he maintained, and they must be respected but they should not give rise to bitterness for God has his elect among all the denominations. He discussed the invitation of the Lambeth Conference (1888) to unite on the basis of the faith and order of the early church, and he believed that discussion was possible, though more with the Church of England than with the Catholics, the Unitarians and the Swedenborgians. There was plenty of room for discussion with the Nonconformist denominations too. In Griffith's opinion, though, the time was not ripe for formal unity but for brotherly love, co-operation and mutual understanding.[33]

David Griffith's reference to the Lambeth Conference showed how world-wide denominational institutions were influencing discussion in Wales. The world-wide Anglican communion had a focus in the episcopal conference in Lambeth. The first was held in 1867, the next in 1878, and in 1888 the issue of church unity was specifically discussed for the first time. At this time the Lambeth Quadrelateral was agreed upon as the basis for the discussion of unity with other churches. Its four indispensable points were: (i) the acceptance of the Bible as the rule and ultimate standard of faith; (ii) the acceptance of the Apostles' Creed as a baptismal declaration and the Nicene Creed as a sufficient declaration of the Christian faith; (iii) the acceptance of the two sacraments, Baptism and the Lord's Supper; and (iv) the acceptance of the 'historical episcopate, with its administrative methods locally adapted to the needs of the nations and people whom God calls to the unity of his Church'.[34] Given the situation that existed in Wales in the 1890s, these guidelines were hardly likely to lead to any sort of dialogue between church and chapel. However the Declaration was important, even in Wales, because it modified Anglican attitudes to the question of unity with other churches.

Following the 1888 conference, Griffith Roberts, the dean of Bangor, expressed the hope that a united church might some time be seen in Wales, but that would only be possible on the basis of the 'four principles' of Lambeth.[35] This note would be heard frequently in the declarations of Anglicans thereafter. It was unity only according to specific conditions. For those who wrote concerning this matter around the turn of the century, the only version of unity that Anglicans could envisage was one in which Nonconformists yielded fully to the church.

It might be thought that the first of the Lambeth principles at least opened a promising door to discussion since both Nonconformists and Anglicans accepted the unquestioned authority of the Bible. However Robert Williams, the vicar of Dolwyddelan, posed one of the thorniest of ecclesiastical questions. On the subject of 'Episcopalianism', he wrote, 'The constitution of the Church is independent [of the Bible] because it antedates Scripture'. In other words, as the episcopal system existed before the New Testament it could hardly be judged in light of the New Testament.

Indeed the three-fold ministry – bishop, elders and deacons – is impervious to criticism from the New Testament because, according to Williams, 'This is the divine order – the order established by the holy apostles according to the instructions of our Saviour and under the guidance of the Holy Spirit. We cannot dispense with this.'[36] Maurice Jones, latterly principal of St David's College, Lampeter, agreed. He said of the church, 'It is the Catholic Church of Wales because historically it is linked to the Apostolic Ministry, the Christian Sacraments, and the Divine Creeds'.[37] Henry Thomas Edwards was willing to consider how uniting with the Nonconformists might enrich the life and organization of the church. He recognized the value of the elders in the chapels and he felt the need to give the laity a more prominent role.[38] Nevertheless by the 1890s even this spirit had disappeared. 'The union of the Church in the apostolic era was a union from the top downwards – the apostles governed and led, and the people allowed themselves to be led by them.' The Nonconformist denominations held to a diametrically opposite view, because for them 'the congregations rule'.[39] It is hardly likely that these men seriously believed that a debate on unity on such terms would lead anywhere. As high church people they simply could not abide Nonconformists.

This chilly attitude towards pan-Christian cooperation is demonstrated by attitudes common among some of the dignitaries of the Church. During the sitting of the Disestablishment Commission, 15 June 1908, important evidence was given by Watkin Herbert Williams, the bishop of Bangor. In response to a question by the chairman, Sir Roland Vaughan Williams, the bishop explained that no cooperation occurred between the church and Nonconformists in religious services because none was possible. 'We cannot entirely support that', he said. Later on, the Congregationalist J. Morgan Gibbon, one of the commissioners, asked him whether he would be willing to acknowledge that both Anglicans and Nonconformists were partakers of the Christianity that they held in common. The bishop prevaricated, explaining that he would have to find out, for instance, whether any Nonconformist who wished to be recognized as a Christian believed the clauses of the Apostles' Creed. He was unwilling to give a clear answer.[40] The bishop's hesitation suggests that such questions were very difficult to answer by 1908. He was not prepared to state categorically that people outside the Anglican fold were not Christians and yet he was a bishop in a church that was now waging a fierce battle to safeguard its position as the established national church. If he wished to adhere strictly to the conditions of the Lambeth Conference and insist that the doctrine of the creeds must be embraced, then how could he avoid defining the church as a denomination, and moreover the denomination of a minority of the population? His policy was to forbid cooperation as far as possible. How could he then support the movement of the Lambeth Conference towards reunification of the churches? Could he do this at all without acknowledging that these other religious bodies were in some sense churches? In this discussion, the bishop found himself between a rock and a hard place.

Edward Latham Bevan, the vicar of Brecon, took a similar stance in his evidence before the Commission. Since he was not burdened with wider episcopal cares he could give more clear and categorical answers than Watkin Williams. He did not believe that any co-operation with the Nonconformists was legitimate, even in the case of social issues such as temperance. Cooperation would mean sac-rificing the truth by ignoring basic credal differences. On the other hand, he welcomed every opportunity to discuss these differences and to remove any obstacles that hindered Nonconformists who wished to draw near to the church.[41]

For those who shared Bevan's view, the movement for unity was a form of missionary activity, and their opinion was quite logical. When a high church clergyman came to a parish, his instinct would be to prevent any contact between Anglicans and others. From his perspective, it would be a betrayal of Catholic principles to follow the example of William Herbert, the evangelical vicar of Llansantffraid, who scolded the Methodist elders in Llannon, Cardiganshire, for not ensuring that the children were at their lessons in the chapel Sunday school but rather leaving them to play on the main road.[42] On the other hand, he would be very much in favour of the new system that Robert Williams instituted in Clynnog. Before he went there as rector, there was a very close bond between the Calvinistic Methodists and the Anglican Church. The service on Sunday morning in the chapel was at 9.30, and the church service at 11.00 and the congregation would move en masse from one to the other. Richard 'Waterloo' Jones (who was 92 years old in 1907) led the singing in both services. But with the arrival of Robert Williams things changed. The church service was moved to 10.00 and soon the chapel moved its service to the same time and the old arrangement ceased to exist.[43]

However this did not happen everywhere. In many parishes there was friendly interaction and collaboration. In the parish of Llanfihangel-ar-arth, Carmarthenshire, disagreements between Anglicans and chapel-goers were very rare, it was said.[44] And in Botwnnog, according to the rector, T. E. Owen, both parties joined forces quite happily to arrange a tea party to celebrate the coronation of Edward VII, or to hold a bazaar whose proceeds would go towards the Grammar School, and even to launch the Farmers' Alliance, a local cooperative enterprise.[45] John Roland Pryce, the rector of Gladestry in Radnorshire, testified that the relationship between his flock and the Nonconformists was a very happy one. Indeed he counted it as part of his duty to pastor all in the same manner.[46] We obtain yet another perspective on the relationship between church and chapel in the lively diary of David Griffith, the curate of Pentraeth, Anglesey. The poor man wrote in the midst of his troubles with 'her imperial highness . . . Charlotte, the Pope-Queen and Rectoress of Pentraeth with Llanbedrgoch'. Because the rector's wife insisted on laying down the law on liturgical matters, David Griffith sank into melancholy, and to whom did he turn for consolation? 'Kindly received and entertained by these Nonconformist families. So kind and respectful to the "Curate" ' – different, of course, from the parson's wife!'[47]

There were many within the church who attempted to ease the bitter relationship between church and chapel, and many who desired to prepare the way for some form of union with other churches, in accordance with the guidelines laid down by the Lambeth Conference. David Howell (Llawdden), like other supporters of the evangelical position, was very much in favour of cooperation, fostering contact and the discussion of unity. Those who supported this position were given great encouragement by 'A Pastoral Letter from the Archbishops and Bishops at the end of the century'. It said that the greatest obstacles to the furtherance of Christ's kingdom lay within the bosom of the Christian world itself. Next to the inappropriate lifestyles and irreligious spirit of many professing Christians, perhaps the main hindrance was to be found in the sinful divisions within the Church of Christ.[48] This conviction is echoed throughout succeeding years in the periodicals of the Anglican Church in Wales. The first step towards uniting all the churches of Christendom, said one of the correspondents of *Yr Haul*, is 'to bring back to the Mother Church all the denominations that have seceded from it during recent centuries'.[49] Canon William Williams of St Davids argued tenaciously that the church was the only body that could provide a fitting spiritual home for the various Christians of Wales,[50] and his numerous contributions to the discussion throughout the years were characterized by their graciousness as well as by their faithfulness to the deepest convictions which Anglicans held.

There was a willingness to consider different schemes for unity,[51] but the only one that recommended itself was for organic union on the basis of the Lambeth conditions. After the meetings of the Anglican Congress in Rhyl in October 1891, one observer was convinced that it was no use contemplating any kind of bargaining between denominations, that there was no possibility of 'a corporate unification of Christianity on any foundations that one branch or denomination of the church might offer another'.[52] The majority of church leaders held similar views until the end of the First World War. Indeed, many of them would have agreed with the verdict that it would be 'a vain attempt to try to unite the various Christian denominations in one body'.[53] A few believed that the schisms could only be healed by divine intervention.[54] Indeed the first hesitant attempt to hold any kind of joint conference between the Anglican Church and Nonconformists was a miserable failure. A measure of cooperation was attempted through a scheme to celebrate the tercentenary of William Morgan's Bible by building a memorial to the translators outside St Asaph cathedral. This venture was a success and when the memorial was unveiled, on 22 April 1892, representatives of the Nonconformist denominations, as well as Anglican dignitaries, addressed the meeting.[55] After the first meeting of the committee in 1888, the members had begun to enjoy one another's company and they decided that it would be a splendid idea for A. G. Edwards and Thomas Charles Edwards, principal of the Calvinistic Methodists' Bala College, to organize a conference for July 1889. However the idea elicited so much public and personal criticism that it was abandoned forthwith. A cross was placed on the altar, the banns were not called, and the courtship was over before it had even begun.[56]

If the Lambeth Conference of 1888 was significant for the Church in Wales as an incentive to foster ecumenical discussion, the same could hardly be said of the international bodies formed by the other denominations. In 1875 the World Alliance of Reformed and Presbyterian Churches was formed and held its first conference in Edinburgh two years later. In September 1881 the first meetings of the Ecumenical Methodist Conference were held in London with delegates from twenty-eight Wesleyan churches from twenty countries in attendance. Also in London the World Congregational Council met for the first time in 1891. Some years went by before the Baptists followed this pattern. In 1905 the World Baptist Alliance met for the first time, once again in London.[57] Welsh Nonconformists took considerable interest in these developments but if these new bodies had any influence at all in Wales, they tended to intensify denominational pride.

Another international movement that attracted some interest in Wales was the series of Grindelwald conferences, organized between 1892 and 1895 by Henry Lunn, Methodist, minister, doctor, journalist and organizer of holiday excursions. His idea was to bring people of various religious convictions together under the same roof where they could combine holidays amidst the glories of Switzerland with open discussion on ecumenical matters. It was a bargain for those who signed up – ten guineas for thirteen days.[58] After the Grindelwald conference of 1892, there were the Lucerne conferences in July and September 1893. Thomas Charles Edwards attended from Wales and T. Edwin Jones, the vicar of St Mary's Church, Bangor, published a Welsh translation of an address delivered in one of these conferences by Canon Joseph Hammon, *Aml-Eglwysyddiaeth* ('Multi-ecclesiasticism', 1894).[59]

How did the Nonconformists view the movement for denominational unity? W. R. Jones (Silurian) wrote waspishly in 1887, 'There is more *talk* of union and brotherhood among the various religious parties in Wales, than hardly any other subject, and less *action* than in any country under the sun'.[60] In 1893 the Congregationalist and academic Edward Anwyl took a different tone when he claimed that Calvinistic Methodists, Independents and Baptists, and even Wesleyans, would realize 'before long' that there is little difference between them and that 'it would be better for them to join forces. This, we believe, is much nearer than we are willing at times to think.'[61]

It is clear that, in retrospect, Silurian was nearer the mark than Anwyl; nevertheless, in many circles there was a desire to create a different spirit among the denominations. Evan Aeron Jones, Manordeilo, turned his address from the chair of the Baptist Union

in 1893 into an apologia for denominationalism while at the same
time emphasizing that it was necessary to foster a compassionate
spirit in order to ensure the fullest cooperation.[62] Thomas Rees,
Merthyr, from the chair of the Calvinistic Methodist General
Assembly did likewise. For him 'divisions are a plague and a great
curse' and the denominations needed to unite in order to overcome
them. Nevertheless, the union he argued for was 'the union of
hearts with the Head of the Church, one faith, one Lord, one baptism'.[63] Some writers argued that the variety of denominations and
the rivalry between them had proved a blessing for Wales, by
ensuring a much more thorough evangelization of the country.[64]
There was great desire, therefore, for better relationships between
the denominations, but little desire for organic union. This
point of view was summed up in Towyn Jones's motto: 'Denominationalism is of God, if sectarianism is of the devil.'[65]

One of the chief promoters of fuller cooperation between the
denominations was Owen Owen (1850–1920),[66] headmaster of the
Oswestry High School and chief examiner for the Mid Wales Board
from 1897 to 1915. Although he was a first cousin to Bishop John
Owen, he was a fervent supporter of disestablishment and believed
passionately that the Nonconformist churches needed to draw closer
together. In 1889 he corresponded with no less than 200 denominational leaders and succeeded in persuading them that it would be
a good idea to discuss plans for unity. Some twenty-six of them met
at Tabernacle, the Welsh Independent chapel at Shrewsbury, on 22
and 23 April 1890 to discuss the possibilities. Among them were the
Baptists, Abel J. Parry, David Powell and Gethin Davies; the
Calvinistic Methodists, N. Cynhafal Jones, Evan Jones, Caernarfon,
and Griffith Ellis, Bootle; the Wesleyans sent John Evans, Eglwys-
bach, Robert Jones, of the North Wales District, and Hugh Jones,
Liverpool, the secretary and Thomas C. Lewis, Bangor; and from
among the Congregationalists, Robert Thomas, Landore, Swansea,
J. Machreth Rees, Penygroes, Arfon, C. R. Jones, Llanfyllin, and
Beriah Gwynfe Evans.

After a hearty tea at the expense of Owen Owen in the Raven
Hotel, a private discussion was held on the Tuesday night and
continued the next morning and then a public meeting was held at
ten o'clock. Robert Jones, the chairman of the North Wales
Wesleyan District, was elected chairman of the meetings, the Baptist
J. A. Morris, Aberystwyth, and Owen Owen were appointed

secretaries, and the Congregationalist, C. R. Jones, was elected treasurer. It was decided to recommend to the denominations the 'appropriateness' of forming a Union of Welsh Nonconformists in order to ensure more effective cooperation 'with regard to social, moral and spiritual questions'. Then, in a second motion, each of the four denominations was asked to appoint six individuals to form a Council of Welsh Nonconformists to act as a committee and to organize a general conference.[67]

This conference in Shrewsbury filled Griffith Ellis with great enthusiasm and he hoped that 'it was the beginning of a new era in the religious history of our country'.[68] David Powell was equally in favour because he maintained that 'denominational prejudice' was abating and he approved of the movement precisely because 'it did not make any attempt to make one denomination out of four'.[69] The issue of political cooperation was raised, but, according to Griffith Ellis, 'every member of the conference was deeply concerned that spiritual objectives should be given precedence'.[70] This conviction was short-lived. The general conference was held in Swansea, 29 October 1891. The committee met under the leadership of the Calvinistic Methodist minister David Saunders, and two public meetings were held, one in Capel Gomer Baptist chapel led by Thomas Davies, Llanelli, and the other in the more worldly surroundings of the Albert Hall in the evening under the chairmanship of the elder Thomas Freeman of Swansea. The addresses showed that Griffith Ellis's 'spiritual' considerations were being edged out by political enthusiasm as the huge audiences most audibly applauded the quick jibes against the church. The main subject of the hour, after all, was disestablishment. The union continued to meet but made little contribution to permanent cooperation between the denominations.[71]

The specifically Welsh Nonconformist Union lost some of its appeal because of interest in the corresponding movement in the whole United Kingdom. After its Manchester congress in 1892 the National Free Church Council was established and immediately began to set up local councils throughout Britain, each containing representatives from local evangelical churches. The National Council was not comprised of official representatives from the denominations, but rather by committed and interested individuals. Those who had enjoyed such close fellowship at Grindelwald during these years led the campaign to bring the churches closer together; it was they who wanted the movement to be organized much more tightly. As a result, on 10 March 1896 in Nottingham the National Council of the Evangelical Free Churches was formed, with the Carmarthen-born Methodist Hugh Price Hughes as its first president.

Now the movement was on a more official footing with regard to its relationship with the denominations, since the council included delegates nominated by the local councils, and it was also recognized by the denominational authorities and governing bodies.[72] There was considerable enthusiasm for the council in Wales and by 1908 167 local councils had been established.[73] The objective of these institutions was to create an opportunity for Nonconformists to get to know one another, to promote cooperation, to enrich their spiritual life, to explain and defend the common principles of the Free Churches and oppose ritualism in religion and sectarianism in education.

About a dozen denominations belonged to the council in 1908. The most prominent exceptions were the Strict Baptists, for whom communion was the stumbling block. In the Cardiff meetings, 12–14 March 1901, for instance, the 'Alliance' (as it was called in the Welsh-language press) arranged for communion to be administered in one of the meetings.[74] This naturally offended the Strict Baptists because it violated their conviction that the only ones who should partake of communion were those who had been baptized on their confession of faith. The Welsh Baptists tried many times to explain their position to the authorities. The Anglesey Assembly, for instance, passed a strong motion in June 1899 stating 'that it would be a great error for us to join the Alliance of the Free Churches' because that would be contrary to their principles and would 'endanger our honesty and consistency'.[75] The Baptist Union also corresponded with officials of the council in London, and in Rhymney (1899) the union declared its willingness to collaborate on condition that no branch of the Alliance was permitted to celebrate communion.[76] However the officials in London were unyielding. The Baptist Union could not approve the answer it received from them and subsequently it had no choice but to withdraw from the Alliance.[77]

Nevertheless, there was an attempt to maintain some kind of contact between the various local councils in Wales and the National Council of Wales met for the first time in 1907 in Aberystwyth.[78]

During these years the Independents and the Calvinistic Methodists attempted to strengthen the relationship between them. Representatives from both sides were appointed and met in Liverpool, 24 June 1897. Some practical details were agreed upon, such as exchanging pulpits, holding joint meetings, getting delegations from the Monthly Meetings to visit the Quarterly Meetings (and vice versa) and helping one another in elections. However the discussion was uninspired and in 1901 the joint committee was abruptly disbanded, leaving the local councils that had been created under the auspices of the Free Church Council to organize all further collaboration.[79]

Throughout it all they succeeded in inspiring considerable interdenominational cooperation. The council decided to celebrate the arrival of a new century with a major evangelization campaign – 'The Timely Mission', as it was called. It was to conclude officially on 4 February 1901, but some local campaigns were held after that. It made little impression in Wales outside the churches.[80] After the revival the Alliance was responsible for considerable evangelistic activity. Its three evangelists, Gypsy Smith, the Revd J. Tolefree Parr and Mr W. R. Lane, held over a dozen ten-day missions in Wales during 1907 alone, and scores of similar campaigns were also held under the auspices of the local church councils – thirty-four of them in the South-Eastern Federation area alone.[81] National conferences were also held 'to deepen spiritual life', in 1907 in Aberystwyth and in 1908 in Bridgend.[82] Local councils similarly worked hard to encourage interdenominational activity on social and temperance issues. All this went some way towards diminishing the envy and bad feeling that existed between denominations.[83]

The discussion continued on the unification of the denominations. The Revival was a blow to denominational sectarianism – but only temporarily. After the heat of the Revival had cooled, the denominations in many areas were once more at loggerheads,[84] but the issue of unity was not dropped during these years.[85] In 1910 the international and interdenominational mission conference was held in Edinburgh – one of the most significant events of the modern ecumenical movement. Many Welsh people were inspired by the vision of that conference and they believed that the unification of churches was a practical goal for which to aim.[86] Among the Independents there was a renewed desire to engage in discussions with the Methodists and the general assembly agreed that it would be a good thing to give it another try. This time the two Wesleyan districts in north Wales wanted to join in the discussions and in 1914 they began to nominate representatives to form a joint committee.

The War put an end to this plan[87] but the debate on the movement filled the pages of *Y Beirniad* (The Critic). D. Tecwyn Evans attempted to weigh up the advantages and disadvantages of denominationalism, but the real basis of his hope of unifying the denominations was the spread of the principles of liberal theology.[88] John Williams, Brynsiencyn, disagreed, arguing that every denomination had its particular contribution to make and that the way forward was to support the efforts of the Alliance of Free Churches to promote cooperation.[89] There was little prospect of any unification according to Joseph Jones, Brecon, and he did not believe that there was much enthusiasm even for the attempts at cooperation but he felt that the scheme for a single syllabus for Welsh Sunday schools could be pursued – and as it happened, this was successfully achieved after the War.[90] For Herbert Morgan,[91] one of the basic needs was to get each denomination to recognize the other denominations, but D. Morgan Lewis, Aberystwyth, was passionately in favour of denominationalism and weighed in against the position of Tecwyn Evans and others.[92] Similar discussions were brewing in the other periodicals too.

To conclude, the relationship between the denominations was not a dead issue between 1890 and 1914. There was a general feeling that inexcusable and unjust things were being said and done under the cloak of denominational loyalty, and that this shameful state of affairs should be banished, but there was no general sentiment in favour of any kind of unity. The Disestablishment Commission's conclusion in 1910 was that there was plenty of cooperation between evangelical churches regarding every aspect of their lives, but 'although there has been some increase in co-operation between the Church of England and Nonconformists in matters regarding the improvement of the social and moral condition of the people', in 'wholly religious matters there is no cooperation whatsoever'.[93]

~ 4 ~
Anxieties

As the nineteenth century drew to a close there appeared to be a storm brewing on the horizon. The outlook was no longer as bright as it had previously been. The chill breeze of doubt touched some, others longed for the warmth of their long-gone childhood, and everyone stirred uneasily because they did not know what turmoil would face them in the future.

Most agreed that an age was coming to an end. Between 1890 and 1900 some of the most prominent figures of the former age disappeared from the stage. It was exactly as if Providence was lowering the curtain on a great act in the drama and clearing the stage for a new act. The year 1891 saw the death of Owen Thomas, the biographer of John Jones, Tal-sarn, and the most able leader of the Calvinistic Methodists following the death of Lewis Edwards in 1887. The following year, his brother, John Thomas, died. He had been the most artful of Congregationalists, an editor, preacher and statesman. Some of the most eloquent preachers of the age fell silent during these years; Edward Matthews in 1892, Hugh 'Cefni' Parry in 1895, Herber Evans in 1896, John Evans, Eglwys-bach, in 1897 and John Rhys Morgan, Lleurwg, in 1900. Scholars such as David Charles Davies, the principal of Trefecca, passed away in 1891, Gethin Davies, the principal of Bangor Baptist College, in 1896 and Thomas Charles Edwards in 1900. From among the political leaders, John Roberts MP died in 1894, Sir George Osborne Morgan and Thomas Lewis, Bangor, in 1897, Thomas Gee and Michael D. Jones in 1898, and Thomas Edward Ellis in 1899. Richard Parry (Gwalchmai), John Hughes, Liverpool and Caernarfon, Robert Jones, Llanllyfni, David Roberts (Dewi Ogwen), Goleufryn, Morgan Lloyd, R. D. Roberts, Llwynhendy and Henry Jones, Maenordeilo – all slipped away into silence during these years.

But perhaps the one death more than any other that convinced people that an unparalleled era had drawn to a close was that of Queen Victoria on 22 January 1901. Although radicals such as Samuel Roberts (S.R.) and John Roberts (J.R.) had written in very harsh terms about the royal family and the cost of maintaining it, by the turn of the century public opinion had turned strongly in favour of the crown. Wales joined more and more enthusiastically in the paeon of praise. When Victoria visited Pale, Llandderfel, in 1885, the Nonconformist ministers of Denbighshire, Flintshire and Merioneth chose David Roberts (Dewi Ogwen) to deliver a loyal address to her on their behalf. His meeting with the Queen sufficed to inspire Roberts to publish a volume of sermons in English, *A Letter from Heaven* (1890), and he begged the Queen's permission to dedicate the book formally to her. Permission was granted and after the Queen wrote to him to express her pleasure at seeing the flowery dedication in the printed volume, Roberts framed her letter and hung it on his study wall.[1]

For Michael D. Jones, on the other hand, a royal visit to Merioneth did nothing but feed 'the servility that is so strong among conquered nations'[2] and he was not among those who added their names to David Roberts's address. 'There was never so much fat in the pig troughs of Pale as when Victoria was there', he remarked scornfully, but after the Queen's Golden Jubilee in 1887, this kind of talk became rare. The imperialist spirit was swiftly consuming Wales and the adulation of the Queen reached a climax at the time of her death. The Baptist periodical *Y Greal* noted, 'in almost every meeting house belonging to our denomination throughout Wales and England, mention has been made of this mournful circumstance'.[3] It continued, 'her sober and godly demeanour won the affection of all'. The periodicals united in singing her praises. 'In her court and in her family virtue was her main aim', was the view of *Y Cenad Hedd* (The Missionary of Peace).[4]

In his Welsh-language biography of the Queen, Griffith Ellis summed up the nation's adulation when he wrote: 'Her character and her history showed an indissoluble marriage of greatness and goodness'.[5] The poets also joined in the mourning and it is estimated that 3,000 elegies were published after her death in the United Kingdom and the Commonwealth.[6] As Griffith Ellis's biography demonstrated, by the end of her life Victoria had grown to become a kind of Universal Mother. Occasionally this image was developed 'into a kind of Victoriolatory, and the Queen-Mother becomes the Queen of Heaven'.[7] Despite these sentimental excesses, people were not far from the mark when they supposed that her death represented the end of an era. 'We mourn', said Arthur Balfour, in his memorial address to the House of Commons, 'not only because we have lost a great personality, but because of our feeling that the end of a great age has overtaken us.'[8]

This sentiment was felt strongly in Wales. The heavy odour of decline hung over everything. This was not confined to Wales, of course. This was the period of the French *fin-de-siècle* and the English naughty nineties, with their frivolous delight in decadence. And as the century drew to a close, the people of Wales complained increasingly that everything was getting worse. This was not false pessimism. Those who live in a society that suffers from rapid changes experience considerable inner turmoil. Their loyalty and dedication find a focus in the institutions which give their lives significance. The weave of their personality is determined by the social contacts which provided them with values and cultural stability. Respect for these values is passed on from one generation to the next. The people of Wales had been raised and disciplined to extol a rich cluster of values. Kindness, good deeds, thrift, hospitality, generosity towards the poor, and diligence – all these had a place of honour in the pattern. Family life was to be respected and although unchastity among young unmarried folk was tolerated, and while the illegitimate child was usually treated with great kindness, adultery was considered inexcusable. Mothers were given unprecedented respect and children were increasingly treated with tenderness.[9] Eloquence was admired as was music and craftsmanship. Snobbery was despised and no one was more scorned than those who forgot their Welsh after being away in college for a fortnight. Those who succeeded in bettering themselves through their own abilities were applauded; the old working-class prejudice against reading and scholarship was dwindling, and interest in ideas and debate were on the increase. Church and chapel were to be respected and their office holders extolled. Swearing could be tolerated, but blasphemy was abhorrent. The mighty in society deserved respect, but that respect should never turn into servility and flattery. Much more could be said to illustrate these values.

All of these values came under threat as soon as the social institutions that reinforced them lost their stability. Economic and social upheavals shook families, districts, chapels, churches, cultural societies, schools and eisteddfodau. From about 1870 industrial production began to slow down in Britain while overseas countries, particularly America, overtook her in producing equipment for the new technology, electrical equipment and tools for making machinery and machines generally.[10] After 1880 agriculture went into recession. However it would be a mistake to see the crisis solely in economic terms; it also had social, philosophical, literary and spiritual ramifications. A substantial proportion of the people of Wales had been cast into a completely new pattern of society in the industrial valleys where the old rural institutions were no longer available, or where they had to adapt rapidly to meet new requirements. The rural, extended family was becoming fragmented by mass emigration, English-medium culture was pouring like a river into the country and British politics, as it penetrated the consciousness of the Welsh rural dweller, shook age-old beliefs and raised profound doubts about the significance of the values in which country-folk were raised. Did thrift mean the same thing in Liverpool as in Tregaron? How could cooperative principles be transplanted from the farms of Eifionydd to the iron works of Dowlais? Was temperance as important in Birmingham as in Caernarfon? And what use was the Welsh language in London – or India?

Of course, the people of the 1890s felt only the lightest of showers; another generation and a half was to pass before the deluge came. In 1890, people were on the brink of huge changes. The forces that would shake the nation's life to its foundations were starting to gather momentum. At the same time, many different attempts were being made to halt, or to alleviate, or to change the direction of these forces and this is one reason why so many people felt perplexed and confused. Griffith Parry, Carno, expressed this aptly in a discussion of the signs of the times in 1892:

> They [that is, the signs] point in different directions . . . This is the most practical and the most imaginative age, the most stubborn and the most softhearted, the most pedantic and the most doubtful, the most despondent and the keenest, the most independent and the most gullible of all the ages the world has seen. This is, of course, because it is an age of transition. It has to a great extent broken adrift from what has gone before, and does not rightly understand the time that is to come.[11]

That which was felt most acutely in 1890 was a vague threat, an intangible fear. Thomas Charles Edwards spoke in 1888 about people's activity and energy, and yet beneath these there was something more difficult to define. 'After lengthy consideration, it must be acknowledged that it is anxiety that occupies the minds of the most reflective and thoughtful men, and those with the most penetrating insight.' Yet this apprehension had no definite object. 'It is anxiety, but such that those who are anxious do not know exactly why. This anxiety has no definite form, but instead of alleviating it this makes it worse.' He sensed that people's faith was fading. 'It is not impossible for Wales again to become religionless and faithless . . . and if Wales loses its faith in the gospel . . . it is certain that our country will be more irreligious and more ungodly, than it has ever been before.'[12] The next three-quarters of a century was to prove beyond doubt how penetrating this analysis was.

Religious leaders are renowned for flagellating their own age and comparing it unfavourably with some previous era, and those of the 1890s were no exception. Nevertheless, one cannot capture the spirit of these years without looking carefully at their complaints. One concern that was voiced time and time again by religious leaders was that Christian Wales was rapidly losing its grasp of the divine. John Thomas, Liverpool, may have been the first to use the word 'secularization' in the sense that became common after the Second World War. In 1890 he expressed the fear that 'spiritual religion' in the chapels was being endangered because of the 'secularization of the Gospel'.[13] His fear was echoed four years later by an Anglican observer who remarked, 'current Nonconformity has been over-secularized'.[14] Throughout the years Thomas had devoted considerable time to politics, but towards the end of his pilgrimage he felt that interest in public matters had displaced all concern for the spiritual life.[15] 'Can anything be done to ensure that our Assemblies are more of a spiritual force in our country?' he asked impatiently.[16] It was he who said that 'there would be more blessing upon our conferences if we knew better how to pray'.[17]

This weakness was not confined to the Independents. The council of the Baptist Union complained that spiritual matters were not given enough attention in the denomination's various conferences: all the time was swallowed up by deliberations on political, social and current affairs.[18] Another aspect of the decline was emphasized by Thomas Rees, Merthyr, in 1894 as he addressed the Calvinistic

Methodist General Assembly on 'the need for the church to possess a more exalted Christian spirit'. He condemned the obsession with statistics and collections as 'an unhealthy, base contagion'. He was equally scathing in his attack on the accompanying 'lowly, unworthy, attempt' to gain popularity. 'A chapel or church can be full of men and women and children . . . and empty of religion . . . But is it not as important, if not more important, to improve the quality of religion, making it purer, more scriptural and worthier, as to swell the number of communicants?'[19] Indeed, one correspondent in *Y Drysorfa* saw a clear pattern in the decline among the Calvinistic Methodists during the century. He remembered an earlier period when people such as John Elias, Richard Jones of Wern and Michael Roberts provided stalwart leadership and a later generation including such men as Henry Lewis and Lewis Edwards, and he ventured the opinion 'that this was the period in which the *Hen Gorff*[20] had the most spiritual influence in my lifetime'. Owen Thomas, Thomas Charles Edwards and John Hughes were the leaders during the third era, and, although the *Hen Gorff* had by then broadened its horizons, it was also true that 'many unspiritual elements found their way in'. 'But', he said, 'of all these periods, the present is the most grave. Yes, indeed, I could almost say that my heart trembles as I observe it.'[21]

This is a very significant analysis because it applies to Wales a pattern traced by English and American scholars in the development of culture during the Victorian era. According to this pattern, English Christian culture reached an equilibrium during the period between 1850 and 1870 and then began to disintegrate.[22] In the case of Wales, John Hughes concurred that a great decline had occurred since the beginning of the century. In his opinion, the rewards of culture were displacing spiritual realities in people's minds. 'Our spiritual vision is not as clear as that of our fathers, and the spiritual world is not as close and tangible as it was to religious people at the turn of the century.' The main reason for that, he said, was 'the pursuit of new loves; culture, civilization, mammon!'[23] Yes, mammon! Others besides John Hughes were aware of the temptations that came in the wake of the gradual improvement in standards of living.

'Miserliness and love of money is the great sin of this age', said E. H. Davies, Pentre, to the Union of Welsh Independents. 'Gold is the idol of the age, and it is adulated.'[24] Indeed, Robert Ambrose

Jones (Emrys ap Iwan) had warned years before – in 1877 – against making a god of the golden calf. 'This is a god who is not despised by any nation on the earth, but only the Welsh, the English and the Americans love him with all their strength and with all their minds.'[25] In 1893–4 John Morris Jones composed his *Salm i Famon* (Psalm to Mammon):

> Yn gyfrwys i'w eglwysi,
> Yn ddistaw iawn treiddiaist ti;
> Ni thynnaist yn wrthwyneb,
> Ond yn gu, na wybu neb,
> Cynhyddaist, gan ei oddef,
> Onis di-feddiennaist Ef.[26]

> Cunningly, into their churches,
> And very silently you penetrated:
> You did not rise in opposition,
> But sweetly, so that no one knew,
> You increased, tolerating Him,
> Until you dispossessed Him.

Naturally, the challenge posed by worldliness to the lordship of Christ in his churches weighed heavily upon religious leaders too.

There was a continual desire among the Christians of Wales in the last quarter of the nineteenth century to give concrete expression to their social and denominational pride in magnificent chapels and churches. Many leaders realized that it was an easy matter for mammon to take the form of a chapel architect. This is what worried David Powell, Liverpool, when he wrote: 'Is it not the highest religious ideal of many of those who profess religion to have a beautiful chapel, a large organ, a very respectable church in a worldly sense, and a popular preacher . . . while ignoring the spiritual and eternal dimension?'[27] Respectability and affectation were a constant target for satirists. If common folk earlier in the century sighed that their poverty did not permit them to build anything more costly than the most austere chapels or to wear anything but the roughest clothes, the times were changing and people tried to broadcast their new-found affluence in their buildings and their attire. This fuelled the provocative remarks of sharp-tongued critics.

Go to any large religious meeting and the zeal has dissipated, the godly uprightness has gone; now the most prominent feature of every religious festival is frivolity and affectation . . . When the festival has passed, everyone talks, not about the presence of God, but about so-and-so trumpeting a great, well-executed, polished, profound, eloquent, theological, poetic, philosophical, sermon . . . and about so-and-so and her new feathers, and her frills and her fancy clothes, worthy of the Great Denomination, and so on and so forth. Religious gatherings and prayer meetings in Wales are smaller than previously; people absent themselves from communion, without embarrassment . . . people go from the chapel to the public house, and back, without any shame; they harass their ministers, slander one another, are as hypocritical as apes, from one Sunday to another, from one religious festival to another . . .[28]

But neither mammon nor affectation nor respectability were the only reasons for the decline. Commentators differed in the selection of vices. Some lamented the popularity of sports, while others bewailed increasing Anglicization. Yet others wished to emphasize the younger generation's irresponsibility and young men's unwillingness to take a public role in meetings.[29] One of the bleakest portraits of the spiritual condition of Wales was that painted by Rees Rees, Allt-wen, in 1893 in his address 'Aspects of our National Decline'.[30] Such was his catalogue: an increase in pride, with people desperate to acquire lush carpets and costly houses; lavish food with 'haughtiness and affected politeness in social intercourse'; the craze for summer holidays; the building of elaborate chapels; the disappearance of family devotions; increasing disrespect for authority in every sphere; political meetings in chapels; decline in biblical knowledge and the sanctity of the Sabbath being trampled underfoot with people going on Sunday excursions on bicycles or trains. This was the uncompromising voice of early Puritanism that was rapidly disappearing from the land. Like many similar declarations during the period, there was a tendency to regard every social change as a moral decline, and there was little attempt to weed out serious matters from those of little import. Rees Rees evidently had a very low opinion of the effects of this new luxury, the colourful carpets and expensive houses. He thundered against the new forms of politeness and 'bourgeois' formality (as it came to be described later on) in such matters as table manners. However not every religious leader agreed with him. Twenty-one years previously John Thomas, Liverpool, had spoken in a different vein:

No one now supposes that there is any danger of missing out on heaven by having expensive furniture, multicoloured carpets, lavish delicacies, and the luxuries of life, and indeed there is no danger, provided that men do not make such things their main aim in life.[31]

One must exercise caution when trying to weigh up these various statements. Was Rees Rees, for instance, really sufficiently familiar with what was happening throughout Wales to be able to declare that biblical knowledge was everywhere decreasing? Nevertheless these statements shed much light on the sentiments of their authors. It is evident that the changing times caused uncertainty, if not real confusion. In light of people's ability to buy furniture and carpets and other luxuries, John Thomas's response in Liverpool in 1872 was fundamentally different from Rees Rees's response in Allt-wen in 1893. It is possible that the attitude of religious Welsh people in Liverpool, where the influence of middle-class standards was strong, was different from the attitude of the chapel-goers of the Swansea valley, where the congregations were largely composed of industrial workers. Was it not also true that this huge social change was confusing people's standards and principles? After all, the poor common folk were instructed in their churches to work out the principle 'in all things give thanks' in the midst of hardship, while suffering privation bravely and even cheerfully, and practising thrift. When thrift and a simple lifestyle, as well as a modest rise in the standard of living, meant that they had a little money to spend on things other than bare necessities – things such as more comfortable chairs, a sewing machine, heavy and colourful curtains and carpets – were they, perhaps, transgressing against the fundamental principles of their former life? Rees Rees and those like him suggested they were; John Thomas's conviction was that they were not. Who was right?

Not everyone was willing to engage in blanket condemnation. To give one example, Edward Parry, Aberdulais, included a scathing paragraph in his book on revivals claiming that 'dishonesty, deceit and worldliness' were widespread in society, that 'immorality, drunkenness, malice, and jealousy, were boundless, that the play-houses were full every night in Wales, and the chapels more than half empty'.[32] There was one reviewer, however, who could not agree. Parry, he said, was 'unreasonably excessive'. Wales was in 'a sorry enough state, but is it not true to say that Wales is in a better and purer condition, than it has ever been before?'[33] Neither should we ignore the opinion of the Calvinistic Methodist General Assembly meeting in Rhyl in 1897: 'the review of the general state of the cause throughout the Connexion . . . produces a quiet, but certain, conviction that the Lord dwells and remains with us'.[34] Nor should one ignore the spirited optimism that existed around the turn of the century. For Thomas Rees, latterly principal of the Bala–Bangor theological college, the nineteenth century was not a century of decline because 'the children of no other century will be prouder of their flag or louder in their praise to Him who ordains the times' than the children of that century.[35] Richard Davies (Tafolog) said of his own age that, 'since Christianity was established in the world', no other age had come nearer to realizing 'the great tenet of Christianity which places the proper value upon man'.[36] But we should look carefully at the very things that won the enthusiasm of those who acclaimed the century as it drew to a close. The increase in freedom, trade, industry and education struck wonder in their hearts. Scientific achievements had people straining 'to look forward to the future . . . towards yet greater things'.[37] The use of such standards to measure human progress was proof in itself that there was a great change afoot. In the opinion of Lewis Jones, Ty'n-y-coed, 'there has been no century since the days of the apostles when religion has had such a prominent position as this century'.[38] The lengthy chapter on religion in the volume *Trem ar y Ganrif* (View of the Century, ed. J. Morgan Jones) told of the achievements and progress of the denominations – and in fairness to the authors, they were achievements of which any church in any century could be proud.

Despite giving its rightful place to the optimism that flourished at the turn of the new century, the confusion and concern about the spiritual life of Wales cannot be concealed. One of the issues that caused the most unease was entertainment. It would be easy to dismiss the whole debate as one of little importance, but this would be a mistake. Not only do we have to think historically and allow the people of the past to tell us what their problems were, but it is quite obvious also that here we have a painful confluence between the old and new.

One of the consequences of the improvement in working conditions was the creation of more leisure time. The progress of technology and business meant that new and interesting ways were available for people to entertain themselves in their leisure hours. 'Is this the age of sports?' This question was asked by the secretary of the Baptist Union in 1890. The answer was an unequivocal 'yes'. There were frequent speeches on this issue in denominational meetings[39] and it was the subject of many discussions and motions in conferences.[40] Some condemned all sports without exception, as did M. C. Morris, Ton Pentre, as he criticized the 'athletic sports, the football clubs, the lawn tennis clubs, the dancing clubs, the singing saloons, and the chess tournaments'.[41] John Davies, Cadle, spoke in similar vein, keeping his sharpest arrows for football.[42] His hatred of the game was so intense that he resigned from the school board when it arranged football lessons for the pupils.[43] This fierce hatred of football was quite common. 'It would be very amusing', said one author, 'to read of the apostle Paul, or Peter, that he was captain of the football match in Corinth or Athens.'[44] The purpose of such an argument was to put a stop to the protestations of all who kicked a ball, but it is strange that the author had not considered Paul's willingness to use imagery from the world of athletics. As for Peter, what lessons, I wonder, would the author recommend to the respectable people of Llandudno or Porthcawl on the basis of the fact that the apostle publicly swam naked (John 21)? The religious institutions had a harsh attitude towards sports. The North Wales Association of the Calvinistic Methodist Connexion lamented 'the extremes to which many young people go with sports, such as football, public dances, and similar practices'.[45] The Baptists of Caernarfonshire mourned 'the harmful tendency of present-day sports, especially football'.[46]

Sports were not the only type of entertainment that caused problems. Holidays and excursions were the subject of condemnation too. Some believed that going on summer holidays to the seaside or to the spas of Llandrindod and Llanwrtyd was a matter for reproach.[47] Others believed that the cheap excursions offered by the railways enticed young people into wayward behaviour. In an address to the Union of Welsh Independents, 'The Perils of Excursions for Young People', David Roberts (Dewi Ogwen) did not take the matter too seriously. Indeed, one gains the impression that he was in favour of the occasional trip, and contented himself with warning travellers against swearing, bad company and drinking alcohol.[48] However not everyone shared Dewi Ogwen's lightness of heart. For instance, W. Oscar Owen complained bitterly about the increasing popularity of the bicycle. 'Our young people cannot go to hell too swiftly on their feet.'[49] Many frowned upon this new invention. The vicar of St Peter's parish in Llanelli tried to take advantage of the situation in 1894 by arranging a special service and inviting bikers to ride en masse to the church. The Independents and Baptists of Llanelli were furious at such 'sinful madness' and the clergyman had to give up his plan.[50]

Other types of entertainment that caused concern were concerts, plays, musical evenings and the like. At the request of the singer Megan Watts Hughes the Defynnog Calvinistic Methodist Association (1896) passed a motion calling the attention of young musicians in the churches 'in the most serious manner to the impropriety of them taking part in concerts that would be held in indecent places, such as music halls, and singing coarse and bawdy songs'.[51] Ever since the seventeenth century the Puritans and their successors had been opposed to the theatre but towards the end of the Victorian era attitudes within the churches began to change. Nonconformists had already changed their attitudes towards literary and musical competitions and the eisteddfodau. This development paved the way for a similar sea-change in attitudes towards entertainment and their attitude to the novel had changed once chapel writers realized that the novel could be harnessed to the evangelical cause. Now it was the turn of drama.

At the beginning of the 1880s, we hear of church members being rebuked, and some being excommunicated for taking part in plays.[52] As late as 1890, John Thomas was furious after seeing a performance of *The History of Joseph*, saying 'that I never before saw anything so degrading'.[53] But this was a minority opinion by this time because these little 'dialogues' had become extremely popular in temperance meetings and children's meetings in churches. By 1894, the young people of Caersalem, Dowlais, were performing *Jac y Bachgen Drwg* (Jack the Naughty Boy) in the Oddfellows Hall and giving a second performance in Merthyr Vale at the invitation of Calfaria church.[54] According to T. Hudson-Williams, drama was considered a sinful activity in Caernarfon, although this condemnation did not extend to performances of *Macbeth* and *Hamlet* in Liverpool. According to Hudson-Williams the turning point came when the stage version of Daniel Owen's *Rhys Lewis* went on tour.[55] This evidence is interesting because on 4 April 1887 the Flintshire Monthly Meeting passed a motion 'wholly disapproving the work of a company which is touring with *Rhys Lewis*'. The motion was sent as a message to the Calvinistic Methodist Association and in consequence the Corwen Association prepared a lengthy motion quoting the rule of the Confession of Faith on 'Sports' and urging church officials to insist that young people 'cultivate the serious and sober demeanour which befits those professing godliness, and to seek after the pleasure to be found in dedication to religious life and labour'. There is no mention of drama, or of *Rhys Lewis*, or of the company that offended the people of Flintshire.[56] It is evident that the climate was already changing and that the Calvinistic Methodist Association was quite willing to condemn any immorality linked with the performance of plays, but not drama as such. In any case how could it condemn material first published on the pages of their own periodical *Y Drysorfa*?

According to Hudson-Williams, as he reminisced about the Caernarfon of his childhood, the fierce criticism of more frivolous pursuits was abating. The August regatta was widely condemned until a boat belonging to two church elders won a race! Similarly horse racing was severely frowned upon until Ladas, a horse belonging to Lord Rosebery, the Liberal prime minister, won the Derby.[57] Strangely enough, there was more ambiguity in the chapels' attitude towards gambling. There are many examples of chapels clearing their debts by holding raffles, but there is little mention of betting until the turn of the century. The old objection was that gambling was tantamount to blasphemy. In other words it was seen as a spurious form of the biblical practice of 'casting lots', which appealed for a direct declaration from God. That is why John Roberts, Corris, condemned the custom in the 1890s because it 'did away with God'.[58] Nevertheless, one observer commented in 1908 that gambling 'had spread with frightening rapidity during the last twenty or thirty years'.[59]

Enough has been said to show that the churches and their leaders were sorely exercised on the question of entertainment. Why this discomfort? It would be foolishly unhistorical to conclude that these people were sour faced puritans eager to trample on every pleasure. For one thing, they were too close to the era when folk pastimes would regularly turn into skirmishes that were much more savage than the vandalism that was to plague the world of soccer during the second half of the twentieth century. They did not wish to see the improvements that had come about during the century as a result of the churches' work being sacrificed but they were facing an even more intractable problem. According to their understanding of Christian faith, work gave human beings dignity and idleness was a curse. This was one of the motives behind the radicals' attacks on the privileged classes, and especially on the royal family whom they considered to be worthless layabouts, living off other people's labour. The Welsh hardly needed Karl Marx to teach them that lesson; Samuel Roberts, the Independent, and his like had already done so years before. More moderate Nonconformists than Roberts still aspired to give the high and mighty a few lessons on this matter. We find the Cil-y-Cwm Calvinistic Methodist Association, for instance, discussing the scandal of cheating at the baccarat table in Tranby Croft in September 1890, when the prince of Wales came under censure. A motion was passed greatly regretting that 'gentlemen of the very highest social rank' had played such a game and set a bad example to ordinary people, and it added 'conduct such as this detracts considerably from the dignity of the Royal House'.[60]

However reprehensible were the vices of the privileged class, the truth was that social progress was enabling more of the common folk to imitate the idle pursuits of the aristocracy. The older emphasis on the dignity of work had blended quite felicitously with the Industrial Revolution's demand for ever increasing production. Towards the end of the century, however, that same revolution had begun to create numerous new leisure opportunities, as well as the wealth which enabled ordinary people to take advantage of them. In addition, the churches' moralistic emphasis on thrift had put more money in the pockets of the common folk, not to mention the fact that the humanitarianism of the trade union was sounding the death knell for the old order that demanded that workers should labour daily from dawn to dusk. In that context, the increasing leisure time enjoyed by workers was not idleness to be condemned but legitimate recreation to be claimed as a right. It was evident not only that a new social era was dawning, but that moral principles would have to be revised in order to meet the challenge of this new age.

What were the churches to do? In the case of some leisure-time activities, it was not impossible for the churches to make a direct contribution. Ever since the middle of the century the churches had provided a certain amount of entertainment for their members by way of cultural societies, literary meetings, penny readings, popular lectures, concerts, teas, banquets and so on. While members' leisure hours were scarce and entertainment spasmodic and voluntary, this type of provision fulfilled the requirements adequately. However, one of the characteristics of the Victorian age was the desire to regiment everything and entertainment was no exception. With the increasing interest of capitalists in the field, and the formation of sports leagues of all sorts, great strides were being made towards turning entertainment into an industry. In due course the things that people used to do in order to forget about their work would, in turn, become a form of work, giving rise to the paradox of the 'professional player'. Should the churches take this organizational challenge seriously?

Forward-thinking ministers in America and England argued that churches should provide for all the leisure activities of their members by forming guild churches which offered not only classes, lectures and concerts, but also football and hockey facilities and anything else that the members wanted. This was more than the religious leaders of Wales could stomach. John Thomas spoke scathingly on the subject. 'I would prefer', he said, 'to see the young people in the church under my care pursuing sports in the most godforsaken places, than see sports being linked with the house of God.'[61] In 1901, another minister made a forthright declaration on this basic principle: 'It is not the church's work to form clubs or guilds . . . It is not our job to provide entertainment for men.'[62] In practical terms, this is where the chapels finally drew the line. They continued to sponsor 'cultural' activities, whether competitive, literary or musical, but it was exceptional for a church to sponsor sports of any kind. Nevertheless, the attempt to deal with these dilemmas had, intriguingly, an architectural consequence. Were Nonconformist chapels to be consecrated buildings? According to the Anglicans, the churches were. Nonconformists were criticized for holding 'all sorts of meetings in their chapels, such as political meetings, lectures, eisteddfodau, concerts, and entertainment meetings'. The Anglicans, for their part, 'have too great a respect for their temples to hold anything in them except for that for which they were prepared and consecrated'.[63] Little did this critic realize that when Christians overemphasize the sanctity of their buildings, the totality of their vision is growing dim.[64] If an activity – whether literary, musical or entertainment – is Christian outside the place of worship, surely it is equally Christian within it. Nevertheless it was already a custom in parish churches to hold entertainment activities in rooms or halls separate from the church, and the chapels discovered that they could do likewise. During the last years of the century numerous schoolrooms and vestries were built alongside chapels in order to allow non-worship activities to be held. It was yet another proof that double standards were beginning to drive a wedge between sacred and secular.

It became clear towards the end of the century that the churches lacked a rounded and balanced doctrine which would enable them to assess the customs and institutions that resulted from the new social changes. The ethical framework constructed to embrace the activities of those brought up in rural society was coming apart. Nevertheless, there were religious leaders who were conscious of the problem.[65] According to one correspondent, 'we look to the Church for a way to solve the important question of the relationship between religion and the people's means of entertainment'.[66] Churches were still expected to give moral guidance, but this was no easy task. The churches should be careful not to 'condemn without reserve' as they discussed entertainment, said David Rowlands, Bangor, but to distinguish between diversions that were essentially immoral, such as gambling, dancing and the theatre, and pursuits that were essentially innocuous, such as chess, quoits and ball games. However, it is obvious that this particular division was not entirely satisfactory.[67] The suggestion of H. Elvet Lewis (Elfed) was more circumspect. 'Many current sports are innocent in themselves, though they had been undertaken in an evil manner. This is true, for instance, of football.' Sports which should be condemned, he claimed, promoted savagery, gambling or carousing, as well as those games which tempted their players to neglect the claims of home and religion.[68] It was an important step in the discussion but it can hardly be said that anything approaching a consensus on the subject appeared in the period up to 1914.

This discussion indicated concern among religious leaders that interest in sports created 'excessive frivolity and levity' that destroyed the spiritual life.[69] It was felt that other developments had the same effect. Occasionally people claimed that the Nonconformist churches were nothing more than political institutions.[70] There was a keen awareness, especially among young people, that theology had become a dry academic discipline which failed to nourish devotion and the spiritual life. There was a general consensus that spirituality had deteriorated due to the decline of the 'family altar' – the name given to religious exercises held in the home. As paterfamilias, the father was expected to take responsibility for family worship. By the end of the century there were constant complaints that this custom was dying out.[71] A sign of the concern about this decline was Thomas Gee's publication of *Yr Allor Deuluaidd* (The Family Altar) in 1892, a substantial volume of prayers to be used in the home. In his preface Thomas Gee said that the book had been prepared for three categories of people: those who were too shy to exercise their gift for extempore prayer, mothers who wished to lead devotions in the absence of their husbands and 'the elderly devout, who will have had a surfeit of the monotony of their own prayers'.

In the wake of such spiritual lethargy, there was growing interest in the person and work of the Holy Spirit. There was a longing in many hearts to experience a movement of the Spirit once more. 'The great need of Wales', said R. P. Williams of Holyhead, in 1890, 'is an outpouring of the Holy Spirit to create a spiritual revival.'[72] The Cil-y-cwm Calvinistic Methodist Association set aside one session in June 1891 for a 'serious discussion of the great need for an outpouring of the Holy Spirit on the church and the country generally'.[73] Remembering the Victorian obsession with organizing everything, it is significant that, in 1890, the Independents in Liverpool discussed 'the need for the Holy Spirit in order to keep the Church from stooping to schemes of men to ensure success'.[74] This was in response to the decision of the Congregational Union of England and Wales to set aside Sunday 28 September 1890 to pray for a special outpouring of the Holy Spirit. In this respect Wales shared in a world-wide interest in the subject. In England, Scotland, America and on the continent, there was a wealth of books, articles and movements concerned with the spiritual life and expressing the longing for revival.[75] The Baptists took a particular interest in the matter and Y *Greal* in 1896 and 1897 carried a series of articles by different authors on 'The present awakening with regard to the place of the Holy Spirit in the success of the Gospel'. The various periodicals contained discussions on the work of the Holy Spirit generally,[76] his particular relationship with believers,[77] and the characteristics of his role in revival.[78] Practical considerations were not far from the minds of those involved in the discussion. They felt certain that the only hope for revival was through the intervention of the Holy Spirit. E. T. Jones, Meinciau, expressed this in his booklet, *Yn Eisiau – Beth? 'Amser Nodedig', sef adfywiad crefyddol ar eglwysi Cymru* (Wanted – What? 'A Special Time', that is, a religious awakening in the churches of Wales). One important source for the concept of revival in these years was A. J. Gordon's book, *The Ministry of the Spirit* (1895).[79] One of Gordon's central themes was that the church should be thought of as a body designed for the Holy Spirit. This was an aspect of the doctrine in which Western theologians had shown little interest, preferring to concentrate on the relationship of the Spirit with the other persons of the Trinity and the nature of his work in the life of the individual.[80] Gordon's emphasis was echoed in a book by W. H. Evans, Rhyl, *Yr Ysbryd Glân yn yr Eglwys* (The Holy Spirit in the Church, 1895). This debate continued amongst theologians until 1904 when the Revival made it an experiential reality for all.

In the heat of the debate the longing for a mighty outpouring of the Holy Spirit deepened. Proof of this was the way the spirit of prayer took hold of people. In 1897 church members were urged to join the 'General Circle', which was established with the aim of getting 'every Christian throughout the world to pray at specific times on the first day of every month for more explicit manifestations of the presence of the Holy Spirit'.[81] This supplication for revival was not a new phenomenon. In 1748 Jonathan Edwards published his influential book, *A humble attempt to promote explicit agreement and visible union of God's people in extraordinary prayer, for the revival of religion and the advancement of Christ's kingdom on earth*.[82] The influence of this book was broadened when it was reprinted in the nineteenth century and was reinforced by James Haldane Stewart's *Hints for a General Union of Christians for the Outpouring of the Holy Spirit* (1821). By 1855 the Tractarian Society had sold 332,137 copies.[83] These appeals and others like them were evidently a spur to the spiritual efforts of Christians in Wales. For instance, we find the Wesleyans in north Wales setting aside the week 19 to 25 November 1893 'to pray for a revival of the Lord's work in the region'.[84] In June 1900 the Baptist Association of Anglesey called upon the churches to set aside the first Sunday in August to pray for 'the influences of the Holy Spirit'[85] and the Baptist Union of Deeside, 22 October 1900, backed the decision of the Baptist Union of Wales, meeting in Bangor, to hold special meetings as 'a means of religious awakening and revival at the beginning of the new century'.[86] The Calvinistic Methodists did not lag behind either, setting aside the preachers' meeting in the Llanwrtyd Association (1900) to discuss 'The need for an outpouring of the Holy Spirit'.[87]

These entreaties were not in vain. Although in 1904 people insisted that Wales had not seen revival since 1859, this was hardly correct. For some reason, people were not willing to call an awakening a 'full-blown' revival if it did not touch the whole of Wales, but a revival is a revival whether it happens in one congregation, or one county, or throughout the land. Quite a mighty revival occurred under the ministry of Richard Owen of Anglesey from 1873.[88] The visits of Dwight L. Moody and Ira D. Sankey made a considerable impression in Wales, and through the book *Swî n Y Jiwbili* (The Sound of the Jubilee, 1874), by John Roberts (Ieuan Gwyllt),[89] their tunes and the Welsh-language versions of their hymns became very popular. There was a revival in Bangor under the ministry of John Evans, Eglwys-bach, in 1887,[90] and a similar awakening in the same year in Landeilo-fawr.[91] These outpourings continued in the 1890s. In 1890–1 there was a vigorous revival in Caersalem, Dowlais, and a particularly powerful one in Newbridge, Gwent, in August 1892 with 165 being converted within three months.[92] During the winter of 1892–3 Trefeglwys was shaken by a mighty awakening. By the beginning of March 1893 there were 143 converts there and the churches of the Wesleyans and the Calvinistic Methodists were worshipping together. When the two ministers, H. Pritchard (W) and D. Jones (CM) went to hold meetings in Llandinam, the revival spread there as well.[93] In 1894 the chapels began to hold meetings for an awakening in Merthyr Vale and on 27 November 1896 revival broke out in Aberfan.[94] The following year, it was noted that the prayers of the people of Landeilo-fawr were 'quite extraordinary in their passion' and soon it became evident that the cause was being revived.[95] The same passion was felt in Pontycymer Calvinistic Methodist Association in May 1898. It was like 'the old associations of yesteryear'. When the sermon ended, the crowd made no attempt to leave, but stayed to sing hymns over and over again. The correspondent could not help but ask 'is there some promise in this, or some prophecy, that the Lord wishes to visit his people again?'[96] He asked the same question as he was telling the story of the Llwynypia Association the following year because there had not been so much anointing or such exaltation in any association in the south since 1859.[97] As happens so frequently in the history of revivals, these local awakenings were just like the first drops of a shower before a mighty and general downpour.

If devotion to prayer was one solution to the concern about the spiritual condition of Wales in the 1890s, evangelism was another. Wales had of course long been used to the travelling preacher holding his personal evangelical campaigns, but as the travelling preachers were increasingly assimilated into the stable organization of the *cyrddau mawr* (literally 'great meetings') and the denominational assemblies, there was a tendency to preach chiefly to believers. However, the duty to the unconverted was not long forgotten. The 1890s was a decade when concern for communicating the Christian message to people on the periphery of the church was once more evident.

One of the interesting features of this type of evangelism was that it combined traditional Welsh practices with American techniques and one of its most brilliant exponents was John Evans, Eglwys-bach. He worked within the Wesleyan structures, but his attention was always focused on those outside and he never finished a service without inviting those under conviction to come forward and confess Christ publicly. 'Drawing in the net' was the name for this custom that came to Wales from America at the time of the 1859 Revival, and the older generation did not approve of it. John Elias and his generation would invite converts to attend a *seiat* or church meeting a few days after coming under conviction in a service.[98] By that time they would have had an opportunity to mull things over and there was less danger of them making a false profession in the heat of the moment. John Evans rejected this practice. Moreover, it was his custom to pray before a service asking for a specific number of converts and he would repeat his invitation to the congregation at the end until he had obtained that number.[99] He had been converted during the 1859 Revival and he retained much of its inspired passion throughout his life. It was said that his preaching had brought about the conversion of thousands.[100]

Evans was in his element holding revival campaigns and his favourite slogan was 'Wales for Christ'.[101] He made an unwise move in 1890 when he left Wales to serve an English circuit in London. His admirers in Wales longed to see him return and their wish was granted in 1893 when Evans was appointed to start a mission in south Wales with its headquarters in Pontypridd. This was an attempt to imitate what Hugh Price Hughes had done in the West London Mission. The pattern of John Evans's work was as follows: he would preach on Sundays in the hall in Pontypridd, hold meetings on Saturday nights on the 'Tumble' amidst the tumult and drunkenness of the fair and make daily forays into nearby villages to preach. He also organized processions to draw attention to the meetings and other varied activities. However, the mission was not a success; it was expensive to maintain and the success of its early days could be attributed to the presence of members of other chapels. When they returned to their own folds, the congregation at the hall declined. Also John Evans's second wife, who was English, was not much help since she had little idea of how to handle the people of Pontypridd. Ill health began to hinder his work and eventually he was overcome by the strain and to Wales's great loss he died aged only 57 on 23 October 1897.[102]

Another, more successful movement to evangelize from within a denominational structure was the Forward Movement of the Calvinistic Methodist Connexion, which grew out of one man's missionary zeal. He was John Pugh from New Mills, Montgomeryshire, where he had followed his father's craft as a builder and undertaker. He cut a striking figure as he strutted in his coloured waistcoat and his tall, white hat. He was converted, partly under the influence of Thomas Charles Edwards when the latter served as a missionary among the navvies at the time the railway was laid in Pembrokeshire. When Pugh began his ministry in Tredegar in 1872, he discovered his calling as a preacher with a particular appeal to those outside the chapels. Soon the fifteen who had called him increased to 400. He enjoyed similar success during his ministry in Pontypridd (1881–9). When he moved to Clifton Street, Cardiff, in 1889 he became aware of the misery and immorality of the poorest parts of the city and commenced his efforts to help the inhabitants. Passing Cardiff Prison in June 1890 he was astonished when he realized that there was no arrangement with any minister or church to look after the inmates. He immediately set up the 'Society for the Aid of Freed Prisoners', and by July 1891 it had given a free breakfast and the consolation of the gospel to more than 1,000 prisoners.

Early in 1891, Dwight L. Moody held a campaign in Cardiff and filled the huge Wood Street chapel to overflowing, even at seven in the morning. Pugh insisted on going to see Moody in Richard Cory's house, where he was staying. He made quite an impression on the American who tried to persuade Pugh to go and work with him in Chicago. 'No,' said Pugh, 'Cardiff is the Chicago of Wales.' But he had learnt some lessons from Moody and in May 1891 he inaugurated the Cardiff Evangelical Movement near East Moors steelworks. He remembered that a man called Seth Joshua, who had been converted under his preaching in Pontypridd, had a large tent and he asked Joshua to come to Cardiff and bring his tent with him. The campaign in East Moors began in that tent on the first Sunday of May 1891. It was not without hardship, including physical abuse, that he and his helpers succeeded in distributing tickets for the meetings, but success ensued. As Seth Joshua said, if the district were to close its doors to the gospel, it would come in through the keyholes! Following this success Pugh decided to instigate a second Cardiff mission, this time in Canton. One obvious advantage for Pugh was Seth Joshua's ready tongue. As Joshua hammered the pegs into the ground, one local character asked 'What is this – a boxing contest?' 'Yes,' replied Seth. 'Who is going to box?' 'I'm taking the first round.' 'Against whom?' 'Some chap called Beelzebub, he's a great boxer,' said Seth. The first to hit the canvas in the following day's sparring was the witty interrogator. Tales like these soon became part of the mythology of the revival campaigns led by John Pugh and Seth Joshua.

Meanwhile, during its meetings in Liverpool in 1890, the general assembly of the Calvinistic Methodist church considered a report by the Conference of English-language churches which highlighted the immorality that was widespread in Glamorgan and Monmouthshire. A decision was made to begin a mission and appoint someone to lead it. John Pugh spoke on the motion but his patience ran out when the assembly set about electing a committee to make further arrangements. He approached Edward Davies, Llandinam,[103] directly. 'What do you want me to do?' asked Davies, and Pugh's answer was 'to be the treasurer of the new movement I intend to start'. The matter was discussed in the associations and at the general assembly at Morriston, in June 1891, it was finally decided to launch a 'Society for the Establishment of new and missionary causes' otherwise known as 'the Forward Movement'. Though Pugh's organization became an official branch of the church and he was invited to dedicate his time fully to it, David Saunders was its first president. Saunders died on 14 October 1892, and Owen Prys, principal of Trefecca college, was elected in his place.[104] This story shows how the impatient enthusiasm of one dedicated individual could be combined with the unwieldy machinery of a denomination. It is true that there was subsequent tension in many committees because Pugh's adventurousness seemed like foolhardiness to more timid souls, but the work continued. He set up the *Christian Standard* as the movement's periodical and he did not miss an opportunity to establish new causes not only in Cardiff, but also in Newport, Barry, Swansea, Rhondda, Maesteg, Aberdare Vale, the Monmouth valleys, north Wales and London. By the day of his death, 24 March 1907, he and his fellow workers had established fifty mission halls. There was no doubt that John Pugh was one of the great figures of the period.[105]

Mention has already been made of Seth Joshua. Seth and Frank Joshua[106] had been brought up in the Welsh Baptist chapel at Trosnant, Pontypool, and after their father moved to work at the furnaces in Treforest, Frank became a pupil teacher and Seth a carrier in the iron works. Seth was the main attraction at the musical evenings at the Rickett Arms Hotel, with his wonderful voice, his ready tongue and his nimble fingers on the piano. Frank was converted during one of the Salvation Army campaigns and it was not long before Seth had the same experience in a revival meeting in Pontypridd. When he passed the Rickett Arms the day after his conversion, his old friends hailed him, 'Seth, come and have a drink!' 'Lads,' replied Seth, 'I have found a better well: come and have a drink of that!' He spent the rest of his days telling people about that well, and he never lost his common touch. He went to help his brother, Frank, in the Free Mission in Blaenafon and when Frank moved to Neath, Seth accompanied him. Between 1882 and 1891 they laid the foundations of a flourishing mission that made a lasting impact on the town. Afterwards, as we have seen, he joined John Pugh.

For people like John Pugh and Seth Joshua, the main aim of their work was to bring the Christian message to those outside the chapels and bring about their conversion. It was the responsibility of the Forward Movement to gather the converts together into congregations that became, in due course, churches in their own right.[107] It was not always easy to distinguish between evangelization among unbelievers and the building of new chapels in areas where the denomination had none. Evangelism and denominational expansion often blended into one another. The Anglican Church in Wales, for instance, counted the various societies that contributed to the expansion of churches as sponsoring mission among the faithless and unbelievers. However, the Anglican Church also had its own forward movement in the Church Army set up in London in 1882 by Wilson Carlisle to work among the poor. More important, however, in the overall life of the Church in Wales were the campaigns held in individual parishes. Scores of these parish missions were held throughout the length and breadth of the country during the period in question.[108] A clergyman from another area would be invited to visit a parish and hold a series of meetings which combined public evangelism with strengthening the spiritual life of the parishioners. For instance, the Tractarian Griffith Arthur Jones, 'Father Jones', held a Welsh-language mission in 1888 in one of the national schools of Cardiff. The missionaries were William Hughes, the vicar of Gelli-gaer, assisted by J. Wynne Jones, the vicar of Aberdare. Before long Eglwys Dewi Sant (St David's church) would be founded in this part of the city.[109] It was not only those of a high church persuasion who held such campaigns; evangelical priests could also be depended on for support.

The other denominations also tried to incorporate evangelism into their established machinery. In 1895, in its meetings in Rhyl, the Baptist Union founded the Home Missionary Society, with Owen Waldo James as secretary and overseer. Unfortunately the work had little success and by 1904 the society had huge debts and James resigned. Within a year all the ministers who were serving as missionaries under its patronage retired and the arrangements had to be thoroughly revised.[110] In 1895, the Union of Welsh Independents founded a movement to collect a fund of £20,000 for the establishment of new causes and to help struggling churches. The response during the first four years was slow but by 1902 £24,000 had been collected and was available for missionary work. In 1904, in order to underline the missionary aims of the fund, Rosina Davies was appointed as evangelist to hold meetings and campaigns, and in 1906 Josiah Towyn Jones was appointed missionary under its auspices.[111]

The conviction that extending the church establishment was the best way of evangelizing was strongest in the Catholic Church. Of all the churches during this period, it was the Catholic Church that used the word 'mission' most often. Indeed, ever since the hierarchy was restored in 1850, England and Wales were both missionary territories. In other words the dioceses were under the control of the Missionary Congregation de Propaganda Fide rather than the general rule of the Western church. This arrangement was terminated by the *Spienti Consilio* of Pope Pius X in 1908.[112] Nevertheless the usual term for work in a new area was 'mission'. Bearing this in mind, the host of new centres set up by the Catholics of Wales between 1890 and 1914 must be counted as an expression of their missionary zeal. This happened regularly throughout the years. First, mass was celebrated in a conveniently situated venue, such as the town hall, Beaumaris, in 1898. Then, after the congregation increased and proved that the work had a future, they would venture to build a church, as in Penmaenmawr in 1906. As part of this development, it was usually arranged that a resident priest would come to serve the faithful.

The pioneers in many such missions were the religious orders. A few examples will serve to illustrate the pattern. In 1889 the Passionists[113] took over the mission in Carmarthen and in 1903 the Sisters of the Holy Spirit came over from Brittany to assist them, their black and white habit becoming a very familiar sight in Wales thereafter. The French Jesuits from St David's College in Mold were responsible for reopening the mission in Ruthin in 1882. In 1893, we find them building a church in Buckley, and, when they left soon after, the work was continued by the Sisters of Charity from Caen. One of the most well-known Catholic centres in Wales is Pantasaph. When Lord Feilding and his wife converted to Rome in 1851, they decided that the Anglican church that they were building on their estate near Holywell would become a Catholic one instead. In 1852, they invited the Capuchins of the Order of St Francis to settle there. Their new buildings were opened in 1865 and they added a new wing by 1899. With its striking stations of the cross and its splendid Calvary, Pantasaph soon became a destination for pilgrims. It became well-known to lovers of literature because of the connection with Francis Thompson and Coventry Patmore, just as the Jesuit College of St Beuno in nearby Tremeirchion became famous years later because it was there in 1875 that Gerard Manley Hopkins composed his poem 'The Wreck of the Deutschland'. The Capuchins diligently set about strengthening the missions along the north Wales coast. Much more could be said about the missionary activity of various religious orders.

The Catholic Church's aim was to win the Christians of Wales – and especially the Nonconformists – back to the 'Old Faith'. This aspect of its work infuriated church leaders, particularly the Calvinistic Methodists.[114] It is no wonder that the 'Old Father' (as the people of the Llŷn peninsula called him) complained that 'the Methodists had tried to rouse the country against me when I arrived'. Henry Bailey Hughes was born and bred in Caernarfon, the son of an Anglican curate, and joined the Catholic Church in 1850. After serving in many countries, he decided to establish a monastery on Tudwal Island off Aber-soch, and evangelize the mainland. In 1886, he celebrated mass at Aber-soch for the first time since the Protestant Reformation. Life on the island was extremely hard, his missionary work bore no fruit and his fellow Catholics were quite contemptuous of his efforts. He died in December 1887.[115]

Henry Hughes believed that missionaries from Brittany were the most likely to win over the Welsh-speaking Welsh to Catholicism. Many years after his death, in August 1900, two Oblates of Mary the Immaculate from Quimper in Brittany, Father Trébaol and Father Mérour, landed in Holyhead. One missionary settled in Llanrwst and the other in Blaenau Ffestiniog. It would not be true to say that their mission was an undivided success, although the congregation in Llanrwst increased from one to 120 during Trébaol's stay. The opposition to Mérour was so great in Ffestiniog that he moved to Pwllheli and there he saw his congregation grow, though they were mostly visitors rather than local inhabitants. When war broke out in 1914, both men were recalled to Brittany. In 1910 Trébaol launched his magazine *Cennad Catholig Cymru* (The Welsh Catholic Herald) and he continued to publish it until he left the country.

There were other Catholics who realized that the only way to make progress in Wales was through the medium of Welsh. In October 1904 St Mary's College was founded on the tiny estate of Y Fron in Holywell and Paul Edward Hook was appointed principal, with Denis Joseph Quigley assisting. Both of them had learnt Welsh, Hook becoming a militant Welshman who insisted that Welsh should be the normal medium of communication in the college. He retired from the post in 1921 and the college was moved to Aberystwyth.[116] Its aim was to train priests specifically to evangelize in Wales. The need was also felt for Catholic literature in Welsh and in order to help to accomplish this the bishop, J. Cuthbert Hedley, gave his patronage in 1889 to the scheme to set up St Teilo's Society. One of the contributors to the society's work was John Hugh Jones who was a priest in Caernarfon from 1872 to 1903 and tutor in Welsh at St Mary's College, Holywell, from 1908 until his death in 1910.[117] He translated the historian John Hobson Matthews's book, *The Old Religion and the New Religion* for the Society,[118] but his prayer book published in 1899 was even more significant. Generally speaking therefore, the Catholic Church worked hard at evangelism in Wales between 1890 and 1914.[119]

The Salvation Army certainly shared many of the characteristics of the religious orders, with its 'uniform', its emphasis on obedience, its self-denying and militant spirit. It was established by William Booth in 1865 but it was in 1878 that it acquired its famous form and title. It began its work in Wales early on and had its first successes in the valleys of the south. By 1879 it had 'attacked' Merthyr Tudful, Dowlais, Aberdare, Newport and Cardiff. However, the first Welsh-language corps established by the Army was the one in Caernarfon and by 1892 it comprised four companies. One of the Army's well-known methods of evangelism was to sell the *War Cry* in public houses. On 9 April 1887 the first issue of its Welsh-language paper, *Y Gad-lef*, appeared, some six months after the 'battle' in Gwynedd began. Initially it was quite successful and sold well, but the situation worsened and in December 1890 an abbreviated version appeared, published with the *War Cry*. The last issue appeared on 19 November 1892. On the whole the Army found it hard to gain ground in Wales, although its presence cannot be ignored as a significant evangelical and humanitarian influence, especially in the industrial valleys.[120]

I cannot close this chapter without referring to individual evangelists who were active during these years. Perhaps two of them can be taken to represent the rest. Rosina Davies was born in Treherbert in the Rhondda valley and brought up in Carmel Independent Chapel. She realized that religion was in decline in the Rhondda in 1879 but the arrival of the Salvation Army rekindled the flame and she felt the call to evangelize under its banner. She was sent to Maesteg where she attracted great attention with her captivating voice, her talent for public speaking and her youth – she was only 13 years old. When General Booth visited the valley and wished to make her an officer, she refused, saying that she wanted to stay in Wales. Over the years she held campaigns in Wales and America. In 1895, for instance, she held 180 services and gained eighty converts and in 1896, 173 meetings. Because she travelled so extensively during the 1890s, her observations on the state of the country towards the end of the century carry considerable weight. At the end of 1899, she declared: 'People came to listen, but my heart ached, because the decline was so disheartening. I realized that the ninety-nine were growing cold, that their church membership was more of a badge than anything else . . . Religion has become easy and respectable, while we lost sight of the highways and fields.'[121]

Of these individual missionaries, perhaps the most brilliantly talented was Hugh Hughes (Y Braich), born in Braich-talog, Tregarth, Bangor, in March 1842, and converted under the preaching of John Evans, Eglwys-bach. When he began to travel as a Wesleyan minister, people realized that his preaching had very remarkable effects. While serving on the Caernarfon circuit from 1895 to 1898, he held an evangelistic campaign in the pavilion and filled it to overflowing every night for five weeks. The railway company ran special trains to the meetings and over 500 were converted. In 1898 he was appointed as a travelling evangelist, so that he could dedicate himself to this kind of work. He died in Trawsfynydd on 1 May 1933. D. Tecwyn Evans said that he believed that Hughes 'preached more often than any other preacher, not only in Wales, but in the world, during his time'.[122] According to T. Jones-Humphreys, he was 'one of the most popular preachers raised up in Wales during the last hundred years'.[123] It is strange that he has been so completely forgotten by Christians in Wales because there is no doubt about the significance of his contribution.

To summarize, it is evident that the 1890s was a decade of growing concern about the spiritual condition of Wales, and indeed there was cause for anxiety because there is no doubt that religion was in decline. However this concern did not lead to flippancy. If there was decline, there were also dedicated pioneers who tried to eradicate its causes, without succeeding as well as they had hoped.

~ 5 ~

'And Here are the Announcements!'

The position of 'announcer' (*cyhoeddwr*) in a Welsh-language chapel was taken very seriously. He would rise to his feet in the *sedd fawr*[1] – this was a job for a deacon or elder – either after the long prayer or before the blessing was pronounced at the end of a service, in order to list the meetings held during the week and the arrangements for the following Sunday. In the English-language chapels, the Anglican Church in Wales and the Catholic Church the person leading the service would usually deliver the announcements.

It would be fair to say that virtually every church in the period between 1890 and 1914 was a hive of activity. Membership of a church meant devoting a large portion of time to activities held in addition to the usual Sunday services. As a result, belonging to a church meant membership of a warm and intimate social unit, which offered education and entertainment as well as spiritual edification.

In the course of its investigations, the Disestablishment Commission did not seek detailed information about this aspect of church life. Consequently, the statistics available vary somewhat from place to place, and more abundant information is available for some areas of the country. In Anglesey, for instance, the Nonconformist churches gave statistics for the weekly meetings. Some kind of meeting was held on weekdays in every single one of the 184 chapels on the list. In Ebeneser Calvinistic Methodist chapel, Holyhead, there were as many as fifteen; Hebron Baptist chapel, Holyhead, and Moriah Calvinistic Methodist chapel, Llangefni, had thirteen and Hyfrydle Calvinistic Methodist chapel, Holyhead, twelve. Only two churches out of the total were content with just one meeting during the week.[2]

Evidence from the other end of the country tells us not only about the number of meetings but about their nature. The forms sent from Swansea borough listed in detail what meetings were held and on what evenings. The answers are not complete, but they suffice to give a very lively picture of chapel activity in that town. Of the 114 chapels on the list, four admitted that they had no musical instrument at all, and only thirty-four said that they had an organ, while seven had a harmonium. Sixty-seven of these chapels had a choir, and five had two choirs. Only one stated categorically that it had no choir, and that was the English Calvinistic Methodist chapel at Port Tennant. With resources such as these, it is hardly surprising that the borough boasted a flourishing musical culture. One column was set aside for the chapels to note how many cantatas or oratorios they had performed in the five years until 1905. Mount Calvary, the English Baptist church at Dan-y-graig, with its two choirs, performed three whole works every year, while the English Congregational chapel on Walter Road had a similar programme. Several of the churches noted that they did a 'book' every year. The choice of works was fairly eclectic – 'Paradise', 'David the Shepherd Boy', 'Queen of the Year', 'Daniel', 'Messiah', 'Jesus of Nazareth', 'Cloud and Sunshine'. Tabernacle chapel, Morriston, the Welsh-language Congregational church, with its 1,080 members and 550 adherents, chose to perform 'Stabat Mater', 'Hymn of Praise', 'Hiawatha', 'Messiah' and 'Galatea'. Forty churches had held a concert to perform works of this kind during the previous five years, and of course, the preparation meant weekly choir practices.

The overwhelming majority of the churches held meetings every evening. To give one example, Libanus (Welsh-language Baptists) held the following meetings: Monday night, prayer meeting and temperance meeting; Tuesday night, Band of Hope and Christian Endeavour; Wednesday night, *seiat*; Thursday night, sisterhood prayer meeting, and choir; Friday night, Bible class; and Saturday night, men's prayer meeting. This was the usual pattern of the Calvinistic and Wesleyan Methodists, the Independents, Baptists and Unitarians. Interestingly enough, the Quakers in their meeting houses observed the same pattern, the difference being that they set aside Thursday nights to hold evangelistic meetings on the streets or in houses. The Brethren, in the Gospel Hall in George Street, preferred to emphasize the devotional life with prayer meetings every night, but they also held separate meetings for mothers, young people and children. As one might expect, the Salvation Army concentrated on public witnessing on every weeknight, although they held a religious meeting on one day a week at their headquarters in Richardson Street.

The nature of the meetings varied considerably. General movements, such as the Rechabites and the Independent Order of the Good Templars, had their branches in the chapels, as did Christian Endeavour, and these were divided into senior and junior sections. Some of the churches also had branches of the Boys' Brigade and Girls' Brigade.[3] It is remarkable how many churches made provision for physical exercise and dance. The choir and its activities occupied the place of honour of course, but there was a sewing meeting, a Dorcas or a Zenana society in many churches.

The Congregational chapel at Rhyddings held ambulance lessons and the Wesleyan chapel at Brunswick organized cycling and walking trips, as well as sports such as tennis, cricket and football, and the church had a team for each of these. But not one of the churches of Swansea had followed the example of Noddfa Baptist chapel, Merthyr Tudful, which held a physical exercise class.[4]

In one sense, all the churches were involved in social work to some extent, if only to hold temperance meetings and Bands of Hope, but quite a few churches engaged in more specialized social work. The two Gospel Missions, one in the Albert Hall and the other in Orchard Street distributed free meals to poor people. The English-language Congregational chapel at Dan-y-graig organized visits to hospitals and to ships docked in port. The members of the new Calvinistic Methodist chapel, Central Hall, worked in the slums while Rhyddings Park Calvinistic Methodist chapel held a 'social' every month. Indeed the social was a popular institution in many churches throughout Wales. It was a combination of a meal and a concert or eisteddfod. It was considered an acceptable way of giving a meal to people for whom such a feast would be quite a rare event. Nor should we forget the Savings Bank found in many churches. Children and adults would bring their halfpennies and their pennies regularly every week and then just before Christmas or the summer holidays, or when they needed a suit or a pair of shoes, they would get their savings back. The Disestablishment Report gives scraps of information about humanitarian activity in other areas. Soar Independent chapel, Aber-nant, Hermon Calvinistic Methodist chapel, Penrhiwceiber, Ynys-lwyd Baptist chapel, Aberdare, organized regular visits to poor people, and the English-language Congregational church in Bridgend took up a monthly collection for the poor.[5]

To return to Swansea, most of the Welsh-language chapels had a literary society – or a cultural society, as it was called in many places – and it was not unheard of in the English-language chapels either. The Unitarians in the High Street held educational activities, with classes in philosophy and languages, and Soar Independent chapel held a Welsh class every Monday night. Bethlehem Calvinistic Methodist chapel held an eisteddfod on Christmas Day and there was an annual eisteddfod at Mount Calvary, the English-language Baptist chapel, and also at Hermon, the Welsh-language Congregational chapel. There was a very narrow dividing line between education and entertainment in this area. The competitive meetings – the penny readings – the informal concerts or *noson lawen*, the debates and the lantern lecture were as much fun as they were instruction.[6]

Such was the pattern of activity of the various meetings in a big town and the industrial area surrounding it. The pattern was not fundamentally different in the rural areas of Wales, although in the west and north, there tended to be more emphasis on oral activities, on debate and on literature. There was great enthusiasm for 'reading papers', the subject of every paper being set by the society, or chosen by the reader himself. The Cultural Meeting at Seilo chapel, Corris, listened to papers on the 'Destruction of Jerusalem', 'An Exposition on the Parable of the Ten Maidens', and 'The Main Events of 1901'[7] and at the Memorial Chapel Society at Porthmadog papers were delivered on 'Oliver Cromwell' and 'Ioan Madog'.[8] The popular lecture continued to flourish. The society at Hyfrydle chapel, Holyhead, held a lecture on 'Islwyn' and the Methodists of Bryncir on 'The Best Way to Spend Leisure Hours'.[9] The people of Ffestiniog leaned towards philosophy with the society at Bowydd chapel hosting a lecture on 'Genius' in the same week as Siloh chapel held a lecture on 'The Relationship between Mind and Body'.[10] It was always possible to have an evening of impassioned debate. 'The Freedom of the Will' was the subject one evening in the Fan Society in Llanidloes and during the same week the society at Ebeneser chapel, Caernarfon, wrangled over the subject 'Is it the Work of the Church of Christ to Provide Entertainment?'[11] In Moreia, Llithfaen, members enjoyed debating the question 'Which is the Most Influential – Wealth or Character?'[12] And it is not surprising to find Bethesda's United Literary Society, even in 1903, debating the question 'Individualism or Socialism?'[13]

Although all such activities were extremely popular, local news columns in the various papers leave the impression that competitive meetings of all kinds aroused the most enthusiasm. One example of the competitive meetings – or 'penny readings' – from thousands of possibilities will suffice, held by the Independents at the Old Chapel, Rhodiad, on 16 January 1895. 'The meeting, was lively, entertaining and edifying, and lasted for over two hours.' In the essay competition, there were three essays on 'The Second Journey of the Apostle Paul' and one on 'The Birth of Christ' – and these were from children under 15 years of age. Afterwards came the 'requests' competition. A box was situated at the entrance to the chapel for which the minister held the key. People were invited to place questions in the box to be answered in the following meeting. On that evening there were twenty-two questions and satisfactory answers were given to almost all of them. There was a competition to compose a piece of poetry on the subject of 'The Sea'. There was only one entry because the poet that used to win in every competition of this kind had been excluded – by dint of appointing himself as adjudicator! Mr Owen, Trefadog, had offered a copy of *Yr Holwyddoreg Ymneilltuol* (The Nonconformist Catechism) to the boy who gave the best reading of an unseen piece. Then the five minute speech competition was held with 'Jezebel' as the subject. All three contestants delivered 'fiery and lively speeches'. Then came the solos and a piece by St David's Sunday school choir. By this time it was getting late and the meeting had to be drawn to a close without holding the competition on the delivery of an impromptu speech.[14] This was only a small meeting. There were many eisteddfodau with open competitions, for instance the Congregational Christmas eisteddfod at Ffestiniog.[15]

These examples are like drops in the ocean. They gave pleasure to many thousands of people, providing them with knowledge and edification at the same time, as Kate Roberts described in reminiscences about the period: 'I remember that once they advertised in a children's meeting that there would be a competition in the next meeting to collect the names of birds of the area, just collect all the names, that was all, and recite them publicly in the meeting'. Her brother Richard enthusiastically set about collecting names, with the rest of the family helping him.

Anyway, the evening of the children's meeting arrived, and we were all very excited . . . Willie, the brother of Richard Hughes Williams, the story-teller, was the adjudicator, and after two or three contestants had said their piece, and had named about half a dozen or a dozen birds, it was my brother's turn. He stepped forward and began before anybody could draw breath, and since he had learned them by heart, he rattled them off as if he were 'charming a sty on the eyelid'.[16] Willie raised his hands in the air and shouted, 'Stop, stop, give me a chance to write them down!'[17]

The contestant had completely floored the adjudicator!

In similar fashion the Church in Wales provided the means of education and entertainment for its communicants. One only needs to turn the pages of the magazine *Y Llan* (The [Parish] Church) to see that the Anglican contribution in this area was very similar in quantity and quality to the contribution of the chapel, although the atmosphere was inevitably somewhat different. For instance the Revd J. Gallagher, Clwyd Hall, visited the National School in Llanychan to present a gift from Miss Williams of Herne Hill in London, the gift being 'cosy cloaks' for the little girls.[18] It is easy to conjure up the scene with the children bowing politely to the rich people and the visitors quite sincere in their belief that charity of this kind was perfectly acceptable. Before long, incidents such as these that underscored the dependence of the ordinary people on the aristocracy would be part of the past. But for children visits like these were memorable occasions.[19]

There was little to choose between the nature of the entertainment offered by chapel and church. Eisteddfodau were held in all parts of the country, for instance, the St David's Day eisteddfod held at St James's parish church, Cymer, in the Rhondda valley[20] or the eisteddfod held in the Welsh Anglican church at Dowlais[21] and the Iron Church eisteddfod held in Ferndale.[22] Competition was the main element in the 'entertainment meeting' at the parish church of Llanbadarn Trefeglwys[23] or those held in Ffestiniog by the Literary and Debating Society of St Martha, Tyddyn-gwyn,[24] and by Glanogwen church, Bethesda.[25]

The cultural society flourished all over the country in the parish churches as in the chapels. In Pwllheli, the Literary and Debating Society of St Peter's church was extremely active. In February 1903, for instance, we find them listening to T. E. Owen, the rector of Botwnnog, lecturing on 'Plygain' (matins), and the following week holding a debate on the subject 'Who is the Most Contented, the Worker or the Master?'[26] A month previously the St Martha society at Tyddyn-gwyn passed, after a lively debate, that the 'proliferation of religious sects in the country was not beneficial'.[27] By 1903, the magic lantern had arrived[28] because we hear of it being used in Llan-gors in that year by L. H. O. Pryce, the curate of Brecon, in a lecture on 'The Dawn of Christianity in Wales'.[29] Similar societies existed all over Wales, with debates, lectures and competitive meetings brightening the winter evenings. There was also a place for drama. In Trefor, Llanaelhaearn, the Uwchllifon Dramatic Society from Penygroes gave a memorable performance. They performed two plays, first 'An Attempt to Murder the Welsh Language', with the company acting with great aplomb, according to the correspondent, and the farce, 'The Adventures of Deio and Polly Jones', which had everyone in fits of laughter.[30] At almost the same time, the Anglicans of Meidrim had great pleasure in watching a performance by the 'Bankyfelin Dramatic Society'.[31]

All sorts of feasts were very popular. The impression given from reading the local news in *Y Llan* is that they were held very frequently. The annual church choir tea or supper was a long-established institution. In Porthmadog it had grown into an event to which all were invited: in 1903, 103 people sat at the laden tables in the church hall.[32] The provision was not so generous in Henllan and Llanfairorllwyn in Cardigan, because they only had 'tea and currant bread', but even so, all church members could partake.[33] The vicar of Cardigan who held a feast for all his Sunday school members was just one example of a generous parish priest, and there were similar happy annual events in hundreds of parishes.[34] All such feasts finished with entertainment.

Another type of activity that became very popular in church and chapel in the Victorian age was the bazaar. The main aim of the bazaar was to sell goods made or donated by the people, in order to raise money for some purpose connected with the work of the parish or chapel. The 'sale of work' was a very close relative, with the emphasis very much on the sewing work which had kept the ladies busy throughout the winter. Jumble sales are not often mentioned in the columns of religious papers, but that institution also had its social value. It was one way for poor people to buy clothes, shoes, hats and similar items without anyone wounding their pride by suggesting that they were objects of charity. Of course the

Anglican Church in Wales contained branches of general societies, such as the Mothers' Union. There was also the Girls' Friendly Society, which even in 1886 had forty-nine branches in Wales and 4,086 members.[35]

Only scattered individuals spoke Welsh in the Catholic Church, so there was no demand among its communicants for the Welsh-language cultural activities that were found in other churches. Nevertheless, any Welsh person, especially a Welsh-speaker, could appreciate the nature of the social activities organized for the Catholics, particularly those in Glamorgan and Gwent. What is striking is the strongly Irish nature of these activities. The following are the churches in Cardiff that were centres of social activity: in 1887 St David's in Charles Street was consecrated (it later became the city's cathedral); in 1893 St Paul's was opened and St Mary of the Angels in 1907. St Peter's Church in Roath had been established in 1861. There were drum and pipe bands, plays were performed and concerts held. Much of this industriousness was linked with the temperance movement. Many of the communicants were poor Irish people who had emigrated to Wales and the priests tried to teach them thrift, for instance by means of the Penny Bank set up in 1868. In order to help to provide assistance in the face of sickness and unemployment, branches of the St Vincent de Paul Society were set up in St David's in 1889 and St Peter's in 1890. Branches of several Catholic societies were gradually established and most of them combined entertainment with humanitarian objectives or religious and educational activity. Among these various societies one of the most helpful was the Ancient Order of Hibernians, a long established society in Cardiff, dating back to the 1840s. By 1874 it had grown strong enough to establish the Hibernian Benefit Building Society which lent its members money to buy their houses. The society's name explains why it had a prominent place in the processions and feasts held to celebrate St Patrick's Day every year. All this activity created a very close-knit unit of Catholics in Cardiff.[36] Indeed the social effect was in some ways very similar to that found in any Welsh-language Nonconformist church in England or overseas.

The Catholicism of Cardiff did not reflect that of all other parts of Wales, but the Irish element was also very strong in such places as Merthyr Tudful, Swansea, Newport, Wrexham and Bangor[37] and, consequently, several of the features of the Catholicism of

Cardiff were manifest in the social life of Catholic congregations in those towns. The Catholic tradition had a more liberal attitude towards folk pursuits than did the Nonconformist tradition, and thus was more disposed to approve of moderation in all forms of entertainment rather than condemning some totally. However many entertainment activities held under the auspices of the priest had quite a serious aim, to raise money to meet the costs of building churches, maintaining schools and strengthening the various movements and religious orders that undertook to care for the poor and vulnerable.

What was the significance of this aspect of the churches' work? As far as the English-language churches were concerned, the various entertainments and social activities fulfilled a valuable pastoral function, bringing people together, facilitating and deepening personal relationships between them, bonding them in a close-knit unit by meeting their manifest practical and cultural needs. This was also true of the churches where Welsh was the natural means of communication, but there is more to say about this latter group. As we study the culture of the Band of Hope, the cultural meeting, the choir and concert we cannot fail to realize how different it was from the culture offered by the contemporary educational system. The first major difference to be noted is that this culture was conducted in the Welsh language, while the culture of school and college was English. Another striking feature in the Welsh culture of church meetings was that it was a culture for all, not just for children, not just for young people, and certainly not just for clever people. It was a comprehensive culture in the fullest meaning of the phrase.[38] It served as a means of awakening the interest of thousands in their national culture and heritage. This is how Ben Davies, minister and poet, described the beginnings of his literary career in the Cwmllynfell area: 'I received my first prize in "Beulah fach" chapel in a literary meeting, for verses to "The Night", the judge was Arianglawdd. The adjudicator praised them, he read the last verse with *hwyl* [enthusiasm]. This gave me *hwyl* too'.[39] Many others also learnt to compose in metre and in prose in these meetings. Thousands also learnt something of the nation's history and of its great figures, at a time when the history of Wales had no place in the day schools. For others, taking part in these meetings made speakers and public leaders of them, because great importance was placed on the spoken word and expressing one's opinion clearly and convincingly. All things considered, these meetings were a means of strengthening the Welshness of many of the participants. W. C. Elvet Thomas summarized the influence of his upbringing in the chapel in Cardiff as follows:

> Yes, I am greatly indebted to the church at Severn Road. There I learnt many hymns, those ancient hymns that have no equal, I'm sure, in any language . . . In Severn Road I also learnt to take part in public religious meetings of all kinds, in singing festivals and prayer meetings, in concerts and plays. In Severn Road I came to realize that I could only worship in Welsh.[40]

The scale of these activities was immense. In 1900 many more people were under the influence of church or chapel culture than were affected by the day schools, colleges and English-language newspapers. It was a huge power in the land and Welshness would have perished long before were it not for the churches' contribution to the survival of its culture.

However, one should not romanticize this period. Even when we take into account the contribution of these meetings in literature and song, their standards were arbitrary and inconsistent. The highest possible standards were juxtaposed with the most dismal failings. Activities were geared towards helping the weak and creating confidence in those who had been given few opportunities. This is always a laudable aim, but it is very easy for sentimental people to encourage the weak at the expense of strict discipline and content themselves with what those of little talent could produce. Their labours were always in danger of becoming nothing more than a means of amusement. Not for nothing did some leaders worry about permitting all types of meetings in places of worship. On many occasions they only encouraged frivolity. If they did much good, they also did much harm. In many areas the competitive spirit was like a cancer, poisoning personal relationships and debasing the production of literature to the level of unhealthy ambition and fostering a spirit that could in no way be reconciled with Christian morality. Even more ominous was the fact that many people began to identify Christianity with this kind of activity. To such people the Christian faith was merely one facet of the Welsh-language entertainment culture, and when a mighty tempest came to batter Welsh Christianity, they had not the strength to withstand its force.

In brief, the overemphasis on literary, musical and entertainment activities in the churches was one of the surest indications that a considerable degree of secularization had occurred well before 1900. An increasing number of people began to lose interest in the devotional activities of the churches, and yet they upheld their membership because of the pleasure they derived from the secular meetings, the Sunday school trips and other such activities.[41] When such activities could be maintained outside the churches, they let their membership lapse.

To return to the meetings in chapels and churches, devotional meetings had a place of honour among the weekly activities. Every Nonconformist church held a prayer meeting, usually once a week, and in some churches more often than that. A few were satisfied with one every fortnight.[42] This was the pattern: one person would be invited to open the meeting by reading a passage from the Bible and praying, then three or four others would come forward to pray, usually at the minister's invitation. The *seiat* (society), as the Calvinistic Methodists called it, or the *cyfeillach* (fellowship meeting), as the Independents and the Baptists called it, was a different kind of meeting.[43] The *seiat* had an honourable and vital place in the history of the Calvinistic Methodist churches. It was an opportunity to share members' experiences, to consider doctrinal matters and, when the need arose, it was a chance to discuss business. The *cyfeillach* or fellowship meeting was based on the Methodist *seiat* but concerned itself less with experience and more with doctrinal or scriptural matters. Because the *seiat* and the Sunday school gave sufficient opportunity to discuss the Bible, the 'Bible class', an American invention, had little appeal in Welsh chapels.

The pattern of religious meetings on weekdays was different in the Church in Wales and the Catholic Church, and both patterns derived from the same root. Although liturgical historians have long discussed the details of Christian worship, there is no doubt that from the earliest times Christians prayed at specific times of the day, especially at the beginning and end. By the end of the fifth century in the West, this custom had evolved into an established liturgical form in the *canonicae horae*, the canonical hours or the daily services, as they came subsequently to be called. It was the custom at that time to hold services seven times a day, namely matins and lauds, and then prime, terce, sext, nones, vespers and compline. Although the services have undergone expansion and revision throughout the centuries, the principle has remained the same – namely that the day's labour be punctuated with prayer and praise at set hours. Naturally enough, the services were a prominent part of the discipline of religious orders throughout the centuries. It was not so easy for lay Catholics to practise this discipline, even in private. In any case, recent liturgical scholarship agrees that the custom in the early church was to pray in the morning and evening. This is why the Second Vatican Council declared in its 'Constitution on the Sacred Liturgy' that matins or morning prayer and vespers or evening prayer are the two axes on which the daily services turn. It is striking that the discipline of the Nonconformist churches in its most exacting form affirmed the same emphasis by supporting the 'family altar' in the morning and evening. This was solely domestic worship, however, whereas the Catholic ideal was to ensure that the faithful should, if possible, join in a public service to keep at least some of the canonical hours.

By the sixteenth century there were widespread calls in the Catholic Church for the breviary to be revised because the services had become so complicated. The fruit of these various efforts was the publication of the *Breviarum Romanum*, a new and authoritative breviary, by Pope Pius V in 1568. By that time the Protestant Reformers had attempted to revise it, among them Melanchthon, Martin Bucer and Osiander, who was the uncle of Thomas Cranmer's wife. Cranmer knew of these revisions and, in a manuscript dating from about 1538, he drew up two services which were obviously inspired by the Lutheran revisions but which also lean heavily on the Sarum rite, that is, those forms of service that derived from the diocese of Salisbury but which were generally used in Wales, England and Ireland by 1457. When the opportunity arose to compile the Book of Common Prayer, the old canonical hours were represented by two services, morning and evening prayer. The ideal was to restore the two basic services found in the early church period, and to ensure full lay participation. Thus the Prayer Book instructs that 'every priest and deacon is bound to say daily the Morning and Evening Prayer, either specifically, or in public' – not just on Sundays, then, but 'daily'.[44]

The ideals of theologians and liturgists are one thing, it is quite another to realize these ideals in everyday church life. In his testimony to the Disestablishment Commission the bishop of Llandaff said that daily services were available in towns and populous areas but not necessarily in every parish church. The Royal Commission on Ecclesiastical Discipline had noted that there were 263 churches in the diocese and that 175 of them had no daily service while 130 had no service on feast days and holy days.[45]

St Asaph was the only diocese that submitted statistics for weekday meetings to the Disestablishment Commission. There were daily services in forty-five parishes,[46] one service a week in forty-six parishes, and between two and five in twenty-nine parishes. Fifty-nine parishes held services at particular times of the year, mainly during Lent and Advent. There were 209 parishes in the diocese (191 of them in Wales) and some fifty (about a quarter of the total), had no service at all between Sundays. Taking the Anglican Church in Wales as a whole, in 1905 it had 1,546 churches in 990 parishes, and 318 schoolhouses or mission rooms. In 278 of these there were services on feast days, and daily services were held in 193.[47] As for non-liturgical services, these were very rare. When Archdeacon Albert Owen Evans was asked whether prayer meetings were held in the diocese of Bangor, he explained that the Anglican Church's liturgy forbade such meetings, nevertheless he admitted that certain parishes did hold them.[48] Indeed the Commission had already heard evidence from Canon David Jones describing the prayer meeting that he held at Penmaenmawr. Apart from including a section of biblical exposition during the service, it followed the same pattern as the Nonconformist prayer meetings.[49] And these were not rare events in the diocese of St Davids because the bishop gave evidence that prayer meetings were held in many places there.[50]

However, Sunday was the most important day of the week and there was no lack of services on that day in Wales. The Protestant Nonconformists had 4,669 places of worship while the Catholics had seventy-eight churches and held services on Sundays in sixteen other places of worship. The Church in Wales provided the Disestablishment Commission with a detailed account of its services. In 389 churches one service was held, in 1,139 there were two services and in 216 there were more than two. The church therefore held 3,300 services every Sunday. The Catholics provided about one hundred. Assuming that there were two services in four out of every five Nonconformist places of worship, that makes a total of 8,406 services. It would be no exaggeration to say that about 11,800 Christian services were held every Sunday in Wales in 1905, not to mention the Sunday schools, which increased the total by about

5,243. That makes a total of 17,043 services every Sunday, which does not include such meetings as the young people's prayer meeting, choir practice or 'singing school', and other such ancillary activities.

The churches' weekly activities fitted into the overall pattern of the year's work. In the Catholic Church and the Church in Wales this pattern was governed by the liturgical year, starting with the first Sunday in Advent, and reaching its climax with the two most important Christian festivals, Christmas and Easter. The proper feast days for the saints and the Virgin Mary were woven into the pattern of the calendar as well, although these had a much more prominent place in the devotion and liturgy of the Catholics than the Anglicans, until the influence of the Oxford Movement began to be felt. As good an example as any of the new eagerness to celebrate these feast days in a devout manner in the Church in Wales was the practice of Charles Green as the vicar of Aberdare from 1893 to 1914. As well as being a zealous promoter of the Oxford Movement, Green, as one might expect from one of the most learned clergymen of his generation, had something approaching an obsession for drawing up detailed rules for his own work and that of his six curates. The following is a description of his methods.

> Before every high feast day, at Christmas, Easter, Ascension day, Whitsun, the vicar would visit each Church in turn to lead a service to prepare the communicants for the feast. He personally fulfilled this duty and never delegated this task. It is no wonder that he regularly had 1,200 communicants at Easter.[51]

As well as preparing the hearts and minds of the communicants, he made sure that these important services were dignified and orderly down to the smallest detail. Christmas of course had long since become part of the traditional life of the nation and the 'Plygain' or carol-singing service on Christmas morning was held in many parishes.[52] But in the Church in Wales Easter had a place of honour among the festivals and attracted the biggest congregations. By the end of the century preparations for Easter were given increasing attention. If Shrove Tuesday and its pancakes were celebrated enthusiastically throughout Wales, the solemnity of Lent which followed it was emphasized by special services in numerous churches. In some of them there were special series of Lenten sermons on

Sundays and the atmosphere of devotion deepened as Palm Sunday approached, and then daily services in the following week reached a climax during the great festival of the resurrection, Easter Sunday.[53] Of course the Catholic Church continued in its traditional manner to celebrate these festivals with appropriate devotion and rituals.

The Nonconformists rejected the traditional church year, and then promptly proceeded to draw up a new one of their own. One way of accomplishing this was to reinstate some of the traditional festivals. By the end of the Victorian era, the old Puritanical conviction that the Sabbath was the only festival that could be justified on biblical grounds was beginning to wear thin. The old rebellion or intractability continued here and there of course. In south Wales the tendency to hold secular activities during the major festivals was stronger than in the north. In many areas an eisteddfod or concert was held on Christmas Day or Good Friday, but there was some unease at this practice. For instance, in Bethel Independent chapel, Caerphilly, on Christmas Day 1889, devotion and entertainment were combined. At 5.30 in the morning there was a 'Plygain' service, with prayer, singing and recitation by the children. At 10.30, there was a worship meeting with more recitation by the children and at 7.00 in the evening, a concert was held with the 'great chapel choir' singing 'Belshazzar's feast'. Thus you had a combination of catholicism and puritanism! In the Old Chapel, Maenclochog, on the same day, there were three meetings: a Sunday schools' meeting in the morning; a banquet for the Band of Hope in the afternoon and a temperance meeting in the evening.[54] On Good Friday, 'mainly literary meetings are held . . . in the South', where the holy day was commemorated at all, 'but in the North, preaching meetings take precedence'.[55] Similarly, there were preaching meetings on Easter Sunday and Whitsun in many places, again more so in north Wales than the south.

Thus, one way of creating a new church year was by celebrating some of the traditional festivals, particularly those which were Christ-centred. Another way was by creating new festivals. One of the great Wesleyan holidays was the new year. Of course, since the earliest times common folk had devised exciting ways of celebrating the new year in style,[56] but it was the Wesleyans who created the 'watch nights'. The first was held in London, on the 9 April 1742. John Wesley approved of this practice because he believed that it followed the pattern of the watch nights of the early church. Initially they were held every month, at full moon, but long before the end of Wesley's life, the monthly watch night had disappeared though the annual watch night remained as an opportunity to welcome the new year and for members to renew their covenants.[57] In most Wesleyan churches at the turn of the twentieth century the watch night service contained a sermon. It was common practice to spend the first evenings of the new year in prayer meetings. These meetings were the idea of the Evangelical Alliance and they had an ecumenical aim, namely to pray for unity among Christians. Each year the Alliance would announce an appropriate message to set the tone of the meetings.[58] However, the meetings in Wales soon lost their particular connection with the Evangelical Alliance and its mission.

By the Victorian age, the thanksgiving meetings for the harvest had become a part of both the Anglican and the Nonconformist calendar. Although there had long been occasional meetings of this kind, the new brand of harvest thanksgiving that became popular in Wales was devised by Robert Stephen Hawker, the vicar of Morwenstowe, and often brought together worshippers from all denominations, as well as those who would not darken the doors of church or chapel for the rest of the year. However, the most characteristic Nonconformist festivals were preaching meetings which will be dealt with in the following chapter.

Despite all these incidental activities, worship was still central to the work of the churches and Sunday was the most important day. By 1890, great changes had occurred in the methods, spirit and content of the services of the Anglican Church in Wales. For one thing, the old careless attitude towards church buildings was beginning to yield to a fresh interest in ecclesiastical architecture and liturgical renewal. When Thomas Davies became vicar of Trawsfynydd in 1850, the wood in the gallery was rotting, the walls were covered with both memorial plaques and spiders' webs, and there were great holes in the ground between the collapsed gravestones. The only musical instrument was the bass violin belonging to Cadwaladr Jones, the grandfather of Principal Maurice Jones of St David's College, Lampeter, and the congregation did not participate in the service at all.[59] But if Thomas Davies's arrival in the parish was 'like the arrival of Nehemiah from Babylon to Jerusalem', he was only one among scores of priests who were determined to rebuild the old sanctuaries.[60] The second half of the nineteenth century was an unparalleled period of building, renewing and transforming churches, with the disciples of the Oxford Movement leading the way. Deeply influenced by the teaching of *The Ecclesiologist*, the periodical of the Ecclesiological Society founded in 1845, it was not the Tractarians alone who believed that the only style of ecclesiastical architecture for which there was a scholarly justification was the 'second pointed method', the decorative Gothic style popular between 1300 and 1375.[61] The fashion spread even among Nonconformists and the chapels of the 'English Cause' were not the only ones which tried to imitate this pattern. Although this weakness for Gothic churches had driven people to disregard the old, plain, homely church buildings that were an integral part of the history and landscape of Wales,[62] and make quite tasteless alterations to some of them, destroying valuable furniture and screens, the desire for dignity and devotion inspired Anglicans throughout the country to clean, tidy up, weatherproof and restore their buildings. This work had made such progress by the end of the century that in 1891 Dean John Owen could declare confidently that the church's zeal for decorum in the sanctuary was a valuable example to all the Christians of Wales.[63] A short time later a visitor to Anglesey was able to express delight and wonder at so many renovated churches; the surplices were white and clean and the worship was devout. 'There were clear signs in every direction that the harsh winter had passed and that pleasant springtime had arrived.'[64]

Under the influence of the Oxford Movement, a new emphasis came to be placed on the spiritual and symbolic meaning of the liturgy, the vestments of the clergy, the furniture in the sanctuary and the building itself. Gradually the often rickety communion tables of the previous era were replaced by heavy altars which began to be adorned with crosses and candles. The three-decker pulpit disappeared and the lectern, now in the form of a brass eagle, took its place alongside the reading desk. The altar was the focus of the services and it was vital that all the worshippers could see it from their pews in the body of the church. In order to ensure sufficient room for a more elaborate ritualism, many chancels were widened. The church choir – each member clothed in a surplice – began to supplant Cadwaladr Jones, Trawsfynydd, and his like. The clergyman's vestments changed. It was said that Beaumaris, during the time of Hugh Davies Owen, was the first parish in the diocese of Bangor where the black preaching gown was replaced by the surplice, and that the instigator of the change was the curate, John Jones Brown.[65] At the same time there occurred a restoration of daily service in the diocese.[66] It was from such beginnings that the new spirit spread and, as well as valuing propriety in small details, it also restored the fullness and dignity of the Prayer Book services. By the end of the century probing questions were being asked – particularly in evangelical circles and among Nonconformists – concerning how to reconcile the new enthusiasm for ritual with the provisions of the Book of Common Prayer. One of the consequences of this disquiet was that a Royal Commission was set up to study the matter. We are given lively and detailed portraits of the liturgical practices of those churches in Wales that were most zealous for ritualism. In his evidence to the Commission, the Revd Z. Paynter Williamson described a service in the church at Margam Abbey on 5 June 1904, and the liturgical ritualism of its incumbent.

> On that occasion he wore a biretta, chasuble, alb, stole, maniple, girdle and amice. On this occasion he did not burn incense, but I have previously seen it used during the procession. He burned six candles when not required for the purpose of giving light, and seven oil lamps continuously of a ruby colour. He used wafers instead of bread. He mixed water with the Communion wine during the service. He elevated the consecrated elements. He genuflected or knelt after pronouncing the words of institution in the Prayer of Consecration. He washed his hands before the Prayer of Consecration. The manual acts were not visible to the congregation. There is in the church one cross over the Communion Table, also a crucifix. He made the sign of the Cross over the head of each communicant before presenting the wafer.[67]

Of course, churches where such extreme ritualism as this existed were very few indeed.

For Nonconformists, the Catholic awakening in the Anglican Church in Wales was a subject of alarm and lamentation. Periodicals bristle with articles deploring 'ritualism' and 'Puseyism'. Such careful analyses as that proposed by Griffith Ellis, Bootle, were very rare. On the basis of articles published by the English Church Union, he gave information about Catholic ritual in the parish churches of Wales in 1898. Eight churches used incense, six of them in Cardiff. Eucharistic vestments were worn in fifty-two churches, thirty-one of them in Glamorgan. Wine mixed with water was used in eighty-six churches, forty-three of them in Glamorgan and seventeen in Monmouthshire. Candles were lit during communion in 110 churches, forty-seven of them in Glamorgan and twenty-one in Monmouthshire.[68] The priests adopted the 'eastern position' in 187 churches, seventy-two of them in Glamorgan and twenty-seven in Monmouthshire. Evan Jones, the Nonconformist firebrand from Caernarfon, maintained that there were 200 ritualistic churches in Wales, with three dozen of them in the diocese of St Asaph. But in his triennial exhortation, on 25 November 1898, the bishop insisted that there were no extremes of ritualism in St Asaph.[69] If these statistics are to be believed, Glamorgan and Gwent contained the strongest concentration of high church ritualism, the county least affected was Carmarthenshire and next on the list were Cardiganshire, Merioneth and Anglesey. This evidence hardly justifies the claim made by many contemporary critics that ritualism had carried all before it in the Anglican Church in Wales.

One common complaint by Nonconformists was that this increase in ritualism meant a corresponding decline in spirituality.[70] 'There is no doubt that ritualism and similar pompous forms of conducting public worship are responsible for a strong anti-spiritual influence,' said Cynffig Davies.[71] However, the leaders of the high church movement can hardly be accused of neglecting spirituality and the devotional life. In their view, the symbolism of the rituals served to make spiritual realities more profound. In fact, some of the leaders set extremely high standards for the governance of devotion and discipline. The 'Roath system' and its asceticism, as it was applied by F. W. Puller to his priests, was so harsh that it was beyond endurance.[72] Some Nonconformists realized that the ritualists were men acting from conviction. John Adams, Barmouth, warned that there was more to the movement than 'this *millinery* that blinds the eyes of the foolish and numbs the ears of young girls who are often clad in trousers as well as in petticoats'. The ritualists were serious men, he said, 'ready to become martyrs for their convictions'.[73] Evan Jones, Caernarfon – one of their harshest critics – acknowledged that the ritualists were sincere men, 'ready if need be to face prison and death' for their beliefs.[74] The truth was that these critics saw ritualism as a perilous step in the direction of Romanism. John Adams believed that it was part of a conspiracy 'to overthrow completely the British Episcopalian church and bring it in line with the traditions and doctrines of the Catholic Church'.[75] Another commentator claimed that the church that had so long professed to be a rampart against Romanism had now become 'the chief breeding ground of Popery in our country'.[76] In the same vein Francis Jones of Abergele, chairing the Calvinistic Methodist Association in Holyhead in April 1899, attacked Romanism 'whether under its own name or under another name', the other name of course being ritualism.[77] This debate in Wales coincided with the debates in the House of Commons and through the United Kingdom generally at this time concerning ritualism.[78]

One aspect of liturgy that won the enthusiasm of Anglicans and chapel-goers alike, although not in exactly the same way, was congregational singing. In the second half of the nineteenth century, and with extraordinary energy, Wales turned itself into a musical nation. In the first place, this was the golden age of the singing festival. The first ever festival was held in Aberystwyth in 1830 and others were held here and there until John Roberts (Ieuan Gwyllt) took to the field and held his historic singing festival in the Temperance Hall in Aberdare on 4 April 1859.[79] It was a historic occasion because it was the direct predecessor of the popular festivals that followed.[80] He and his contemporaries took it upon themselves to organize festivals in every part of the country and did so on a denominational basis. The most popular arrangement was to set aside a day for the festival, with three services, the one in the morning being especially for children.[81] By the end of the century, each denomination held its own festival in almost every area, although a great number of individual churches held their own independent festivals. The festival programme would be published with the tunes usually in tonic sol-fa but occasionally in both notations. It is certain that the work of Eleazar Roberts and others in popularizing the tonic sol-fa system was an effective means of disseminating musical knowledge. This system spread very quickly and, by 1870, almost every single Welsh chapel held a sol-fa class while mastering this system became as much a part of a child's education as reciting a Bible verse in chapel. In 1893, Davies persuaded the Tonic Sol-fa Council that the handbooks and examinations in Wales should be in Welsh.[82] It comes as no surprise that Wales developed into the main centre for this system in the United Kingdom. Indeed, Wales provided 83 per cent of candidates for higher certificates in the Tonic Sol-fa College between 1892 and 1896, and 80 per cent between 1901 and 1906.[83]

Soon the singing festival developed into a national institution. Moses Owen Jones estimated that in 1895 the Nonconformist denominations held 280 festivals with 134,550 singers, almost 9 per cent of the population, taking part.[84] This estimate is almost certainly too low, especially since it does not include Anglicans. According to Thomas Thomas of Cardiff, the Calvinistic Methodists held 115 festivals, representing 988 churches, with 61,500 singers.[85] Alas, increasing popularity did not necessarily mean that high standards were preserved. There was an obvious tendency for the festivals to lose the atmosphere of worship and the temptation arose to overdo emotional singing. John Roberts (Ieuan Gwyllt) emphasized accuracy of tempo and tonality and, despite being impatient and irritable, he would persist until the singers were completely obedient to his rules.[86] When he died in 1877 the men upon whom his mantle fell were John Thomas, Llanwrtyd, D. Emlyn Evans and David Jenkins. John Thomas and David Jenkins were at the forefront of the tendency to relax strict discipline in order to allow for rejoicing and dramatic emphasis in the singing. For instance, when the choristers in one festival were singing 'on the banks of the deep Jordan River' to the tune *Moab*, John Thomas stopped them at the end of the line 'remembering the might of the water' and ordered them to emphasize the word 'dŵr' (water). He said, 'There is something very suggestive in it. Can you hear the sound of the water and the rushing waves?'[87] Although all this kind of variation of tempo and emphasis could create a memorable effect, nevertheless the disregard for the composer's instructions meant that the singing often degenerated into a display of unbridled emotion. As in other areas, sincerity was endangered by sentimentality and too much emphasis was placed on subjective pleasure.

On the whole, Anglicans were more aware of this danger than Nonconformists. Because of this their festivals had a different feel from those of the chapels. Even the title 'singing festival' offended them and they preferred the term 'choral festival'.[88] The festivals were based on individual church choirs and consequently the choral festival was a collection of 'choirs joining together after much practice, to hold a musical service – a devotional service – such as afternoon prayers or some other similar service'.[89] The Nonconformist festivals were a gathering together of congregations and singers.

Nevertheless it would be a mistake to differentiate too rigidly between them, as did Moses Owen Jones when he said that the singing of the choral festivals was 'correct but mechanical' while the singing in the Nonconformist festivals was 'majestic, impressive and devotional'.[90] Such a view denotes the prejudice of the age.

The Glanogwen parish in Carmarthenshire was said to be the first rural parish to hold a major choral festival in 1850 during the time of Evan Lewis's curacy there.[91] But within about twenty years the work of organization began in earnest, pioneered by John Owen (Owain Alaw) and Owen Humphrey Davies (Eos Llechid),[92] and the festivals became widely popular. For instance, one was held on the coast of Flintshire on 10 November 1885 in Trinity Church, Rhyl, with seven choirs of 200 voices.[93] W. Farren, an Englishman who had learnt Welsh and was the precentor in St Mary's church, Caernarfon, established a choral festival for the area and the first was held in the abbey church at Clynnog on 2 October 1885, with 470 singers from seventeen churches in attendance. The service was sung in plainsong and a sermon was given by the Revd E. T. Davies, Aberdovey.[94] At the other end of the country, the Carmarthen choral festival was held on 29 June 1886, with 516 singers representing thirteen parishes.[95]

Before long a choral festival was being held in every rural deanery and, if traffic was inconvenient or the deanery was large, two were held instead. A book would be printed for every area and the choirs would use it to practise during the winter for the festival which was usually held between the two harvests.[96] In some deaneries a music specialist was employed to train the choirs, and every festival cost between £30 and £50. Throughout the diocese of Bangor – apart from the Arwystli rural deanery – Welsh was the language of the festival. In the cathedral, however, the festivals were held in English and Welsh alternately and there were separate festivals for children. The festivals held in Bangor cathedral were renowned for their size; in the Welsh festival held on 20 June 1904 the choristers numbered 1,600 and in the English festival held on 3 August 1905 there were 600. The children's festival was held on 29 June 1906 with 2,000 singers in attendance, as at the adults' festival on 13 June 1907.[97] In the archdeaconry of Carmarthen, the festival was held alternately in Welsh and English after the first one in 1866.[98] In 1906, thirty-five choirs belonged to the Choral Union and 1,500 programmes were printed for the singers and this was still insufficient to meet the demand. Arrangements were made for trained musicians to instruct the choirs during the winter and the singing festivals were held in three centres, with one each year in Swansea.[99]

Thus the emphasis of the singing festivals within the Anglican Church was on discipline and thorough training, and on the day the singing was invariably placed within the framework of the service so that the reading of scripture and prayers had their rightful place. This protected the festivals from the temptation that was so ready to corrupt the chapel festivals – in other words divorcing the singing from its proper context within the service of worship itself.

By the 1890s, the battle against having musical instruments in either chapel or church was to all intents and purposes over. People such as Dafydd Williams, an elder in Aberthin Calvinistic Methodist church in the Vale of Glamorgan, were the exception to the rule. He continued to campaign fiercely against having an organ in the chapel when J. J. Morgan began his ministry in Cowbridge.[100] In the last quarter of the nineteenth century, the organ came to be one of the indispensable items of the grand chapel.[101] In some areas the chapel orchestra became quite famous. Some chapels (such as Bethel, Arfon, or Jerusalem, Bethesda) were designed to provide a place for the musicians immediately in front of the *sedd fawr*. In Capel Als, Llanelli, too, there were as many as twenty-eight musicians in the orchestra.[102]

The result of all this activity was that congregational singing was revolutionized in the churches in Wales. The era when books were not used and when the preacher would lead by singing each couplet of the hymn in turn had long gone. Rejoicing no longer meant that each one would 'seize his favourite verse and shout it out, while throwing his arms around with the soles of his feet leaving the ground'.[103] People could now rejoice in unison because the training during the singing festivals had created a musical medium suitable even for the passion of a revival, as would be seen in 1904. The same was true of the Anglican Church. Evan Jones recalled his period as curate at Llanfihangel-ar-arth when the church did not possess any hymn books. Instead, Morris the bellringer acted as precentor, but only for verses he happened to remember![104] That age had now gone and in the churches, as in the chapels, there had been a huge improvement in the quality of the singing.

In the wake of this musical enthusiasm came a demand for new hymn books which would include both words and music. Also, since music lovers tended to cross denominational boundaries to enjoy the festivals, there was a demand for more uniformity in the hymns and the tunes, since the various churches used many different books.[105]

The Church in Wales was hesitant to sing hymns in its services in the first half of the century and, as we have seen, the singing of psalms was not very memorable. Nevertheless, it is obvious that *Casgliad o Psalmau o Hymnau* (A Collection of Psalms and Hymns) published by the Tract Society in the diocese of Bangor was very popular, since the sixth edition was published in 1856.[106] In south Wales, the greatest influence was the work of Daniel Rees, the permanent curate of Aberystwyth. In Llandovery in 1831, at the request of the bishop of Llandaff, he published his book, *Casgliad o Psalmau a Hymnau* (A Collection of Psalms and Hymns) which reached its sixth edition in 1860. Indeed 'that which Ieuan Gwyllt [John Roberts] did for the Nonconformists, Daniel Rees did for the Anglicans'.[107] But a new era began with the publication of *Hymnau a Thonau er Gwasanaeth yr Eglwys yng Nghymru* (Hymns and Tunes for the Service of the Church in Wales) published by Daniel Evans (1832–88), Corris, in 1865. It was a pioneering work among Welsh-language hymn books inasmuch as it contained tunes as well as hymns. *Hymnau hen a diweddar* (Old and recent hymns), edited by Owen Jones, Pentrefoelas, and Shadrach Pryce, the dean of St Asaph, was even more popular, with the twelfth edition published in 1891.[108] Then, in 1892, Elis Wyn of Gwyrfai published *Hymnau yr Eglwys* (Church Hymns) with a second edition, containing hymn tunes, following a year later, edited by J. H. Roberts (Pencerdd Gwalia) and F. S. Garston, the organist of St David's cathedral.[109] And then, in 1897, *Emyniadur yr Eglwys yng Nghymru* (The Hymnal of the Church in Wales) was published under the editorship of Daniel Lewis Lloyd, the bishop of Bangor, with the second edition in 1898 containing music as well as words.[110] The Tractarians also contributed to these developments. G. A. Jones published *Y Gwasanaeth Dwyfol ar Gân* (The Divine Service set to Music), and then *Y Psallwyr neu Psalmau Dafydd ynghyd â'r caniadau a Chredo Sant Athanasius* (The Psalter or the psalms of David together with the songs and the Creed of St Athanasius, 1854). He later joined forces with Evan Lewis and J. Wilberforce Doran to publish *Hyfforddwr ar y Gân Eglwysig i'r côr a'r gynulleidfa* (An Instruction Manual on the Ecclesiastical Song for

111

the choir and congregation, 1884). In this way the Tractarians insisted on communicating to Welsh-language congregations their enthusiasm for restoring the traditional Catholic singing of the Western church.

The Calvinistic Methodists decided in their first general assembly in Swansea in 1864 that it would be 'very desirable to have one Hymn Book for the whole Denomination',[111] and a committee was elected to prepare it under the chairmanship of Henry Rees.[112] The result of its work was the publication of *Llyfr Hymnau y Methodistiaid Calfinaidd* (The Hymn Book of the Calvinistic Methodists) by Gwasg Gee in 1869.[113] Despite some sloppy proof reading, before long there were very few congregations that did not use the book.[114] Some of the connexion's churches still used *Llyfr Tonau Cynulleidfaol* (A Book of Congregational Tunes) compiled by John Roberts (Ieuan Gwyllt) and the *Ychwanegiad* (Appendix) to it of 1870. A combined edition of these two volumes was first published in 1876 and as late as 1890 there was a new edition. In 1883, David Jenkins published *Tonau, Salmau ac Anthemau* (Tunes, Psalms and Anthems) adding an appendix in 1894 bearing the title, *Gemau Mawl* (Jewels of Praise). But the age of variety was drawing to a close and, in 1897, the Calvinistic Methodists published *Llyfr Hymnau a Thonau y Methodistiaid Calfinaidd ynghyd â salmdonau ac anthemau, cyhoeddedig gan y Gymanfa Gyffredinol* (The Book of Hymns and Tunes of the Calvinistic Methodists together with psalm tunes and anthems, published by the General Assembly).[115]

In the 1890s, the Independents too began to demand a single hymn book for their denomination. In October 1890, the matter was first raised in the Merioneth Quarterly Meeting by Lewis J. Davies (1853–1919), Llanuwchllyn. The task was entrusted to a committee, whose members had been nominated by the various quarterly meetings and it began to meet on 31 May 1892.[116] Joseph Parry refused to cooperate with the committee so the book's musical editors were William Emlyn Jones, David Emlyn Evans, David William Lewis and Moses Owen Jones.[117] The hymn editors were David Roberts (Dewi Ogwen), David Rowlands (Dewi Môn), H. Elvet Lewis (Elfed) and David Adams.[118] Y *Caniedydd Cynulleidfaol* (The Congregational Hymnary) came off the press in late August 1895. It became immediately popular and, by 1911, over a quarter of a million copies had been sold. In order to promote sales, the committee attempted to buy the copyright on other similar volumes. The owners of E. Stephen and J. D. Jones's book *Llyfr Tonau ac Emynau* (The Book of Hymns and Tunes, 1868) and the *Ail Lyfr* (Second Book) refused to enter into any discussions with the committee but they succeeded in buying *Aberth Moliant* (A Sacrifice of Praise, 1873) for £185 and the *Salmydd* (Psalmist, 1892) for £250. Following Joseph Parry's death, an agreement was reached with his widow to buy the copyright of his musical products and thus his *Llyfr Tonau Cynulleidfaol Cymru* (Book of Congregational Tunes of Wales, 1887) came into the possession of the *Caniedydd* committee.

David Evans and Rowland Hughes's book, *Casgliad o Emynau* (A Collection of Hymns) was published in 1844 and the Wesleyans used it for over half a century. The denomination had no music book until the publication of *Casgliad o Donau ac Emynau, cyfaddas i Lyfr Hymnau y Wesleyaid Cymraeg* (A Collection of Tunes and Hymns, suitable for the Wesleyan Methodist Hymn Book) in 1872, by a Congregational musician brought up as a Wesleyan, J. D. Jones of Ruthin. In 1880 the *Casgliad o Salm-donau at wasanaeth cynulleidfaoedd y Wesleyaid Cymreig* (Collection of Psalm tunes for the service of the Welsh Wesleyan congregations) was published and in 1887 John Richards (Isalaw)[119] edited *Atodiad i Lyfr Tonau y Trefnyddion Wesleyaidd* (An Appendix to the Wesleyan Methodists' Tune Book). Then, in 1876, John Evans (Iota Eta) published *Odlau Moliant* (Rhymes of Praise) and, in order to find tunes to go with these hymns, in 1881 the Wesleyan Press in Bangor published *Sain Cân, sef casgliad o donau . . . cyfansoddol i'r hymnau a geir yn 'Odlau Moliant'* (The Sound of Song, a compilation of tunes . . . composed for the hymns found in 'Rhymes of Praise'). By the 1890s, however, it was felt that a new book was needed and, in 1897, the Circuit Meeting at Porthmadog decided to make arrangements for one to be compiled. The circuits elected a committee, with John Hughes (Glanystwyth) as president, to select the hymns. The fruit of their undertaking was *Llyfr Emynau y Methodistiaid Wesleyaidd* (The Wesleyan Methodist Hymn Book, 1899). It received an enthusiastic welcome and there were soon calls for a second edition. But there was great demand within the churches for a book that combined tunes and words. Work was soon under way to meet this demand and, in 1902, *Llyfr Tonau ac Emynau y Wesleyaid* (The Wesleyan Tune and Hymn

Book) appeared. The hymns were selected by John Hughes (Glanystwyth), John Cadvan Davies, T. J. Pritchard, John Price Roberts and John Humphreys.[120] The tunes were edited by D. Emlyn Evans, Wilfred Jones, J. M. Harris and Maengwyn Davies.

Many Baptist churches relied on the compilation of hymns published by Lewis Jones, Treherbert, in 1867 and the volume of tunes published to accompany it, bearing the title *Llwybrau Moliant* (Paths of Praise, 1872). Soon afterwards came *Llyfr Hymnau at Wasanaeth Enwad y Bedyddwyr Cymreig* (A Hymn Book for the Use of the Welsh Baptists, 1878). However, these were soon overshadowed by the decision of the Arfon Baptist Association to prepare a volume containing tunes and hymns. The volume appeared in 1880 under the title *Llawlyfr Moliant* (A Handbook of Praise). Such was the enthusiasm for the book that when the churches were asked whether an expanded edition of it should be published, the vast majority of them were in favour and it appeared in 1890. This hymn book became the possession of the Baptist Union of Wales and thus superseded all other collections in the denomination's churches and formed the basis for later collections of the same name.[121] In 1899, *The Baptist Book of Praise* was published for the English-language congregations.

The smaller denominations had their own hymn books too. In 1896 the Unitarians published *Perlau Moliant* (Pearls of Praise) and the Scotch Baptists published *Gwisg Moliant* (A Garment of Praise) in 1903. One of the signs of the times was the preparation of special hymn books for children, such as the compilation by Thomas Jones, Coed-poeth, *Hymnau a Thonau* (Hymns and Tunes, 1891) for the children of the Wesleyan churches, *Llawlyfr Moliant yr Ysgol Sabbothol* (The Handbook of Praise of the Sabbath School, 1897) by the Arfon Baptist Association for the children of Baptist churches, *Caniedydd yr Ysgol Sul* (The Sunday School Songbook, 1899) for the children of Congregational churches, and *Hymnau a Thonau ar gyfer yr Ysgol Sabbothol* (Hymns and Tunes for the Sabbath School, 1904) for the children in Calvinistic Methodist churches.

All things considered, it seems that the wide-ranging activities of the churches in this period touched all aspects of the social and cultural life of their members.

~ 6 ~

The Demise of the Great Preacher

Within the pattern of activity established by Welsh Christians by 1900, the sermon held the place of honour. Each Sunday some 11,000 sermons were preached, not to mention the host of sermons delivered on various occasions on other days of the week.

Nonconformist chapels held preaching services on Sunday morning and evening. They were so-called because the other parts of the service, prayers, Bible reading and singing, were organized in accordance with the conviction that the climax of a service consisted in listening to the minister expounding and applying the Word of God. This is why the liturgy leading up to the sermon came to be known as the 'introductory parts'. Chapel architecture symbolized and affirmed the Bible's importance by placing it on the front lintel of the pulpit, which occupied an elevated and central position.

Since the Nonconformist tradition had rejected the liturgical year of the Catholic tradition there was a tendency to punctuate the year with preaching meetings. It became natural to speak of them as 'festivals' and an elaborate tradition grew up around them. The majority of chapels held a 'preaching meeting' every year and in south Wales they went a step further and organized twice-yearly meetings. In some towns, where there were several chapels belonging to the same denomination, 'preaching assemblies' were held. Each church would invite two preachers and they would move from chapel to chapel, with the services being held in succession. Festivals of this kind were held in places such as Liverpool, London, Bethesda, Ffestiniog and Merthyr Tudful. With such a system in place, it is easy to see how it was possible for as many as sixty sermons to be preached on a single weekend during the Merthyr Festival organized by the Independents.

County festivals were also held, with sermons in the open air. A roofed stage would be erected for the preacher in a field, with sufficient room for people to sit behind him. One onlooker wrote mockingly of the 'ministers and budding preachers' and the ladies 'in their newest silks' sitting on the stage as if 'seeking a safe haven from the arrows of the ministry'.[1] D. Morgan Lewis, on the other hand, found pleasure in looking at them because 'those on the stage are not critical listeners. They are there feeling that the one who preaches is speaking on their behalf'.[2] The main reason for holding open-air meetings was that the congregations were too large for any chapel. There were very few buildings in Wales of the size of Caernarfon Pavilion which could hold 10,000 or more. In the towns, too, every chapel had its appointed date for its preaching meeting so that there were a series of meetings for local people lasting throughout the winter. Sermons were also delivered on special occasions and harvest thanksgiving, new year, the Cymanfa Bwnc[3] in the south-west, funerals, and during the denominations' administrative meetings such as the monthly and quarterly meetings, the associations and local unions.

In the midst of this complex system stood the 'Pregethwr Mawr' (literally, 'Great Preacher'). The Great Preacher was a product of the Victorian age. Influential and inspired preachers were to be found at other periods of history of course, but this age, more than any other in Wales, made heroes and idols of them. Their classic panegyric is found in Owen Thomas's *Cofiant John Jones, Talsarn* (The Biography of John Jones, Talsarn), chapter 16. It does not take much imagination to visualize Owen Thomas relaxing between services in a convivial household and drawing on his limitless fund of remarkable anecdotes about past giants of the pulpit while the assembled company listened in awe. The chapter is memorable as a piece of powerful prose, but also because it is infused with national pride. According to Owen Thomas, an analysis of the virtues of Welsh preaching would explain that 'the pulpit is accorded superior status in our nation, and its influence on our nation's thought, we would claim, is stronger and has lasted longer than in any other country in the entire history of the Christian church'.[4] Strong words indeed! The truth is that it was Thomas's generation who became enamoured of the talents of preachers and who treasured the minutiae of their characters, their sayings and their feats of eloquence in pulpits and open-air festivals. A substantial

116

body of literature grew up around them. Each Great Preacher's enduring memorial was his biography (*Cofiant*), but immeasurable articles and books were also produced, each adding to the store of serious and humorous stories about their lives.[5]

The preaching meetings and festivals became the showcases for the talents of these 'masters of the congregations'. It became possible to measure a preacher's stature not only by the frequency of his preaching engagements but also by his position in the hierarchy of preachers. There was no doubt that such a hierarchy existed and that one Great Preacher differed from another in reputation. The festival preacher was higher on the scale than the one who preached at ordinary services, and the man who preached at association meetings and local unions belonged to a privileged class among festival preachers. This order developed into an independent cultural and social microcosm. Preachers would travel between the various lodgings that became famous throughout the country for the wealth of their hospitality to the Great Preacher.[6] They knew how to attend to the comfort of their visitors and there was much agreeable conversation and sharing of religious experiences between services. All Great Preachers were authorities on the geography of Wales, particularly the geography of their own denomination, and they were cognizant of the mysteries of the transport system. They had no need to study a map or timetable to tell the best way to travel from Bodorgan to Bedwas, or from Cynwyl Elfed to Coed-llai. And with this nationwide traffic in preachers, Chester or Pontypool Road station on a Saturday morning was like a festival field, with the preachers impeccably turned-out in their silk hats and tailcoats, each with his Gladstone bag in his hand and his umbrella under his arm.

The preaching system had cultivated congregations that were a match for the preachers. They knew precisely what to watch and listen for, and not a gesture or intonation escaped their notice. They paid close attention to the preacher's preamble, to the way he set out his subject and developed it. The standards were very high and it is no wonder that during this period public speaking in the Welsh language attained a polish and fluency that was quite exceptional. The congregations were not placid, stoical listeners either. They wanted the preacher to go into *hwyl*, in other words to speak in an inspired and influential manner. Consequently they saw nothing wrong in responding aloud and with fervour. Weeping was quite a common reaction. Reporters did not stray far from the truth when they reported of a service that 'there was not a dry eye in the place'. 'Feeding' (*porthi*) a preacher was very common during this period. In other words, listeners would utter an 'Amen' or 'Diolch iddo!' ('Thanks be to him!') or 'Felly!' ('So!') in response to his words. 'Rejoicing', which involved expressing joy by standing or even jumping, and chanting a verse or singing a hymn, was not uncommon. A less emotional way of expressing interest was to make notes as the sermon progressed – a practice which dated from Puritan times. Children in many places were brought up to do this, as well as to learn the sermon headings, in order to recite them in the *seiat*.

Preaching had become part of the social and cultural life of the nation and it would not be an overstatement to claim that it had become a cultural ritual, operating according to rules as strict as those governing medieval Welsh verse. It is yet another example of the tendency towards regimentation in the Wales of that era. Despite a stubborn adherence to the charismatic conviction that a sermon was dependent upon direct inspiration from the Holy Spirit, the weight of the system and the expectations of audiences placed restraints upon preachers. Of course there were many services where the preacher broke loose from his fetters and delivered a truly gripping message, just as a poet of genius can transcend the confines of the strictest measures of traditional Welsh verse and create something truly new.

The death of a number of eminent preachers in the years between 1890 and 1900 indicated that an era was drawing to a close. Owen Thomas died on 2 August 1891, and he, more than any other preacher of his generation, reminded older listeners of the oratorical powers of John Elias. His brother, John Thomas died within a year, on 14 July 1892. Although they spent their lives in different denominations, the same Methodist influences shaped their preaching and John Thomas himself had experienced extraordinary unction, such as when he delivered his address from the chair of the Union of Welsh Independents in Llandeilo (1878) and the congregation responded by bursting into hymns of praise.[7] However, by 1890 he felt that a new age had dawned and he could not come to terms with the new 'grandiloquence' of the pulpit.[8]

Edward Matthews, Ewenni, represented a different tradition in Welsh preaching.[9] He was a complex, even tangled, character, combining a sweet nature with intemperate outbursts which bordered on rudeness. For thousands, he was an idol, but others found him irritating, particularly people like Thomas Charles Edwards and Thomas Levi who valued sobriety more than anything.[10] The truth is that Matthews combined genuine evangelistic zeal with the techniques of redneck folk preaching which had been castigated so mercilessly by David Owen (Brutus)[11] towards the middle of the century. This explains the histrionic gestures that offended the more sober brethren: tearing up a Bible during his sermon, bending backwards over the edge of the pulpit or pulling his coat tails over his head like a hood. On the other hand there was no one in his generation who could transmit so effectively to a congregation of common folk the emotional and existential force of Christ's saving grace. With his death on 26 November 1892, a unique tradition in Welsh preaching came to an end.[12]

As regards his personality and his style of preaching, Robert Davies Roberts, Llwynhendy, was at the opposite end of the spectrum from Matthews. He was upright, courteous and wholly without malice. Although he was endowed with a deep, melodious voice, and a fluency of expression that rose by degrees until it reached a sweeping climax towards the end of his sermon, he would not have dreamt of unseemly behaviour in the pulpit. During his childhood in the village of Dinorwig in the shadow of Snowdon, he came under the spell of Christmas Evans's rhetoric and he became quite his equal in his use of extended and flowing illustrations.[13] Nevertheless his sermons were full of doctrine. He adhered closely to the Bible and refrained from quoting any other authors. His services were in great demand over the years and when he died on 15 May 1893 Wales in general and the Baptists in particular lost a preacher of exceptional talent and influence.[14]

But perhaps the greatest specialist in preaching doctrine was John Hughes (1827–1893) of Liverpool and Carmarthen. In Crosshall Street chapel, Liverpool, he would lead a class each winter term working through such substantial tomes as Mansell's *Metaphysics* and Martensen's *Christian Dogmatics*.[15] He clearly believed in exercising his listeners' mental faculties to the full. 'Among the Calvinistic Methodists there was no more excellent doctrinal preacher than John Hughes',[16] and according to T. Hudson Williams, who was brought up under his ministry, he was 'one of the greatest men in Wales'.[17] Despite all this, because of his mastery of his subject, his expert phrasing and his humour, he held congregations in the palm of his hand. He died on 23 October 1893.[18] David Charles Davies, the principal of Trefecca College, did not share John Hughes's popularity but he was a more able scholar and his sermons were always robustly doctrinal. In the opinion of many of his listeners, he held a place among the finest preachers. He died on 26 September 1891.[19]

Archdeacon John Griffiths of Neath was one of the last representatives of the golden age of evangelical preaching in the Anglican Church in Wales. 'As a pulpit orator he deserves to be listed as one of the great preachers of Wales.'[20] He was certainly a preacher who could attract audiences, both Nonconformists and Anglicans. His doctrine was rooted in the theology of the Protestant reformers and their evangelical successors, and free grace was central in his preaching. He was endowed with a striking voice and presence and unerring fluency in the pulpit. He died on 1 September 1897[21] leaving David Howell (Llawdden) to continue the tradition. Just as Llawdden's preaching retained the Methodist flavour of his youth, so also Henry Jones of Maenordeifi, Cardiganshire, was true to his background among the Independents. The son of Thomas Jones, the Independent minister of Llangeler, he was ordained in 1852 as minister of the Independent church at Rhyd-y-bont. In 1860 he joined the Anglican Church and served as curate to Llawdden in Pwllheli. He obtained the living of Maenordeifi in 1877. He had no sympathy with the Catholic emphases of the Tractarians and he considered the gospel above all to be a message of salvation to individuals. He became a very prominent preacher in the Church in Wales and his evangelical fervour was in much demand. He passed away at Whitsun 1893.[22]

Three preachers who died during this period cannot be neatly pigeonholed within the various Welsh preaching traditions because they came under foreign influences. The trio were John Evans, Eglwysbach, Herber Evans and Thomas Charles Edwards. The easiest to place is John Evans. He could count his converts in thousands, a fact that indicated the thrust of his preaching. He excelled in presenting the gospel to unbelievers and heedless listeners. Many noted the incomparable magic of his tenor voice and the sincerity which he conveyed through his lively imagery and gracious movements.[23] He travelled the country with no thought for his own welfare and placed a terrible strain upon himself when he founded the mission in Pontypridd.[24] It was this labour that contributed towards his early death on 23 October 1897.[25] It is difficult to avoid grouping Herber Evans with John Evans because there was an obvious similarity between their oratorical talents. Herber filled the pulpit with his presence and there was a sense of excitement in his clear voice. On the other hand he had little of John Evans's evangelical zeal. The characteristics of both, and the pitfalls of their preaching styles, can be inferred from a remark made by one who listened to them preaching in the same service in Cardigan. His comment was that he had never been in a better 'theological concert'.[26] Some maintained that there was nothing particularly Welsh about Herber Evans's style and perhaps it was significant that he preached as effectively in English as in his native tongue.[27] Certainly he was heavily influenced during his last years by D. L. Moody, the American evangelist.[28] His sermons were not noted for their biblical exposition or for the richness of their doctrine. His strength was in his ability to reach the hearts of his listeners with memorable clarity and sweeping rhetoric and his congregations often responded in unexpected and emotional ways. A Cardiganshire Unitarian wept as he listened to him preaching in the Three Counties' Festival in 1874 and said after the service, 'I do not believe a word he says, but the man is totally overwhelming'.[29] When those listening concurred with his message, however, the inspiration of his services remained as a fragrant recollection for years afterwards.[30]

Like John Evans and Herber Evans, Thomas Charles Edwards was one of the many ministers who were profoundly influenced by the 1859 Revival, and neither his administrative work as the first principal of the University College of Wales, Aberystwyth, nor his scholarly labours succeeded in quenching the flame kindled at that time.[31] But he was also steeped in the new scholarship that began to influence Welsh Nonconformity in the second half of the nineteenth century as men took their degrees in the University of London and the ancient English universities. In his preaching, Edwards straddled two eras. As the son of Lewis Edwards and great grandson of Thomas Charles of Bala, he could not fail to be deeply aware of the mighty tradition of Methodist preaching, and as a graduate from the universities of London and Oxford he inherited scholarship that was to revolutionize the theological world. In his preaching, he succeeded in combining both scholarship and passion.[32]

No doubt those familiar with the period would choose individuals other than those already mentioned as examples of the giants of the age. It is clear, however, that by the 1890s an era was drawing to a close. The last quarter of the Victorian age produced a generation of preachers who left a profound impression on the life and memory of the Welsh nation. Thousands were convicted and comforted and enriched by their preaching. Yet, before very long it became fashionable to mock them, to speak scornfully of them and to deride their memory. Whether justified or not, it became obvious that the age of the Great Preacher was drawing to a close. The public praise that was part of the heritage of the Great Preacher was turning into scorn. Why was it that this class of men would be so vilified?

It would be unwise to accept all the criticism as truth. Much of it was based on ignoring facts, much of it was clearly prejudiced, and some of it was frankly ridiculous. Nevertheless this carping was significant. One of the main sources of criticism was the influential monthly magazine Y Geninen. Its editor, John Thomas (Eifionydd),[33] who was a brilliant journalist, had realized the value of religious debates to broaden the appeal of his journal. It is significant that many of the critics and satirists wrote under pseudonyms, owing to the fact that no tradition of reviewing sermons had ever developed in Wales. There was some objective assessment in a few biographies, written after the death of the preacher in question, but since the presentation of measured, balanced, objective comment on preaching was not a feature of the age, the denominational periodicals resorted to flattery. By contrast the critics felt that there was safety in hiding behind a pseudonym. Consequently, there was a temptation to write in an irresponsible fashion and this in turn caused readers to doubt the validity of the criticism.

In October 1892, Charles Davies, the Baptist minister of Tabernacle church, Cardiff, could state quite confidently 'that the influence of the Pulpit is healthier and stronger than ever'.[34] Within a few months, however, another writer claimed that it was generally assumed that preachers did not live to preach but preached to live and that they suffered from 'clichéd formality; self aggrandising officiousness; and an insatiable desire for money'.[35] Some critics went on incessantly about the avarice of preachers. 'The curse of Nonconformist Wales today', said Richard Mills, 'is that men make the ministry into a trade and preach for gain'.[36] The preachers of Wales were characterized by 'a passionate striving for profit and praise – the profit helps the praise and the praise helps the profit'.[37] Others hit out against the desire to make preaching popular at any cost. One observer maintained that it was 'as clear as the noonday sun that preachers in Wales today think more of "*hwyl*" than anything else'.[38] Soon afterwards, in his address from the chair of the Calvinistic Methodist General Assembly, Thomas Rees, Cefn-coed, saw fit to launch a scathing attack on popular preaching. 'The careless, unrestrained, mocking tone that is widespread among preachers is not a good sign', he said.[39] The editor of *Y Tyst* also weighed in heavily against the failings of preachers and especially against the tendency to turn preaching into a performance.[40] The temptations common to the Independents and Methodists also affected the Baptists. Their preachers were afflicted by a 'thirst for popularity'. '*Hwyl* is the temptation of some of the brethren. They will do anything to achieve it.'[41] Bearing in mind the tendency of the complex system of preaching meetings and festivals to give prominence to some preachers and ignore others, it is easy to understand the ferocity of E. Garmon Roberts. He said that 'the insatiable desire for publicity, the endless self-proclamation in the newspapers, the painful envy one of another, the attempt to undermine one another secretly – all these things and their like are destroying the influence of ministers with young men'.[42]

Although later generations thought of the Victorian era as a heavy, solemn and humourless period, there is quite substantial evidence that, towards the end of the era, flippancy penetrated even into the holiest sanctuary. We have already seen this in connection with the growing readiness of churches to provide entertainment for their members. There is no doubt that the same danger threatened preaching. 'The most popular man is the one who can captivate the congregation with his melodious voice', said Cynddylan Jones,[43] and such 'melodious voices' most often gave out their range of notes as they went into *hwyl*. By now there was suspicion that this sing-song delivery did not stem from true charismatic passion. 'Believe me,' said Thomas Charles Edwards, 'in far too many cases it is only an affectation, not true anointing.'[44] One observer complained that one of the ready weaknesses of the Baptists as a denomination was that they resorted to artificial *hwyl*.[45] This was another example of the stranglehold of institutionalism on the Christianity of the time. The *hwyl* ceased to be a means of expressing passionate emotion and became degenerated into an oratorical ritual. Not everyone had mastered the *hwyl*, but everyone could try to be entertaining if they so wished. Thomas Roberts, Mold, said that 'entertaining preaching is the most popular. This is the kind of preaching generally found in our great meetings'.[46] David Rowlands (Dewi Môn), a fellow Congregationalist and principal of the Memorial College, Brecon, agreed, saying 'That which is great, refined and serious has no chance in some Welsh congregations beside that which is petty, witty and impressive'.[47] Keri Evans knew what answer to expect when he asked the question 'Is there no urge for popularity – an attempt to make witty remarks although they are often cheap, and a desire to preach in "great" meetings, as they are called'.[48] Owen Evans agreed that there was 'too much effort to make witty remarks'.[49] It is no coincidence that an Independent made this comment because witty preaching spread first and fastest in their midst. The entertaining preaching, however, soon spread to other denominations. These, for instance, are the remarks of David Williams (1877–1927) in his diary on the preaching of the all-too-popular Philip Jones of Porthcawl – 'very clever, but without a frisson of spontaneity or ethical passion'; and again, 'P. J.'s preaching appears to me to demoralize the congregation'.[50] There was a time when preaching was reckoned to be too serious a work to allow congregations to laugh during a service, but times were changing. Anthony Davies the diarist heard David Emrys James (Dewi Emrys)[51] preaching in 1913, and his comment was 'I gained very little from his sermon: too many stories that kept on making the congregation laugh out loud'.[52]

This mania for titillating congregations and turning the preaching meeting into a form of entertainment was perilous in the extreme. It eroded preachers' ideals and the religious character of their congregations. Truly great preaching can combine substance and excitement, it can be serious and interesting, but when entertainment becomes the main motive, a preacher's sincerity and dedication become beleaguered.

'A certain ambition to be popular, as one might say, is quite commonly found, but how much self-sacrifice is there in all this?' one observer asked.[53] This question is relevant because, in the world of entertainment, the self is king. For instance, W. E. Watkins, Pembrey, preached in the same meeting in Ffynnonhenri, Carmarthenshire, as E. T. Jones, Llanelli. On the first evening, Jones preached after

Watkins. Both were supposed to preach in the service on the following evening but Watkins went home. When he was asked the reason why he replied 'He killed me last night; and just in case he buried me tonight I went home.'[54] This was only one instance among many of the prevalence of envy and childishness.[55] It did not only affect the preachers; their congregations were similarly corrupted. For one thing the style of expression often became more important than the message itself. When Griffith Hughes said at the end of his sermon, 'Well my dear friends, I am drawing to a close', one man in the congregation rose to his feet and said 'One more shout, if you please, Mr Hughes'.[56] From 1797 until his death in 1839, Hughes was minister in Groes-wen, where this incident occurred. Perhaps such a request could be attributed to naiveté, but naiveté cannot explain an odious practice that emerged during the 1870s. In the concert held to mark the opening of a school in 1875, Owen Jones, Plas Gwyn, Four Crosses, imitated preachers.[57] What makes this practice particularly objectionable is that it happened not among satirists and religious critics but among ministers and church members.

Imitating a famous preacher explaining some profound aspect of the crucifixion or the salvation of a sinner was a shining example of the tasteless philistinism that betrayed the underlying flippancy of the period. Even a preacher of the stature of John Jones, Blaenannerch (1807–75), could succumb to the temptation of being jocular about such a serious matter. Preaching on heaven, he asked: 'Will there be Wesleyans in heaven? Yes, *some*. Will there be Congregationalists in heaven. Yes, *some*. Will there be Methodists? Yes: a great multitude that no one can number.'[58] Y *Cymro* plumbed the depths when it organized a lottery with a prize of £5 for the person who could guess correctly which five preachers came top of the list in a postal vote among readers.[59] Ten years later the *British Weekly* announced that the five most popular preachers in Wales were John Williams (Brynsiencyn), E. T. Jones, Thomas Charles Williams, Principal William Edwards and H. Elvet Lewis (Elfed).[60] In such an atmosphere, is it any wonder that a spiritual cancer developed? Certain sensitive souls were deeply troubled by such matters. David Williams struck a painful note in his diary which shows how the pressure to compete could become an onerous burden. After preaching in Siloh, Llanelli, on 8 November 1908, he wrote: 'These meetings give too much glory to the preacher who takes part in them. In spite of myself, I worry about my reputation as a preacher. Is it possible to let go of all this and think only of the glory of the Kingdom?'[61]

In 1894, in the midst of these discussions, a book was published which caused a great controversy. The authors of *The Welsh Pulpit* hid behind the pseudonyms 'A Scribe, A Pharisee and A Lawyer' but it soon became common knowledge that they were Robert Arthur Griffith (Elphin), John Owen Jones (Ap Ffarmwr) and David Edwards, the manager of the *Nottingham Express*.[62] The authors adopted the satirical idiom that was popular at the time (and subsequently) among Welsh people who tried to please the English public.

> You know the Congregationalist at once by his operatic airs, his crescendos and diminuendos, his pianissimos and fortissimos. No less recognizable is the sedate, solemn, almost funereal manner of the Calvinistic Methodist, swelling out in moments of passion into an angry roar. The Wesleyan prides in a jaunty, flippant, somewhat artificial style of elocution, while the Baptist is remarkable for a certain homeliness and geniality of address, which not seldom generates into uncouthness.[63]

However, the authors wished to do more than provoke their readers and some of their jibes are perceptive and well made. They maintained that the most prominent failings of preachers were envy, ambition and quarrelling.[64] Many preachers were really thwarted writers who, since literature was a hard mistress, had turned to the pulpit as a means of earning a living.[65] Their main accusation, however, was that the pulpit was old-fashioned, its inhabitants preaching doctrines that were wholly incompatible with contemporary thinking. Welsh youth, they wrote, was embracing the doctrines of contemporary scientists and secular thinking and even inside the churches there were thousands who were no more than unitarians and materialists. The pulpit was wholly incapable of allaying the fears of young people who were coming under the influence of the great revolution in ideas that was sweeping across Wales. 'I urge preachers to lay aside completely their medieval theology . . . and bring their dogmas into closer contact with the spirit of the age, and into harmony with modern ideas'.[66] In reality, the book is a plea for the adoption of theological liberalism. It provoked a strident response,[67] and it is evident that what had caused offence was its critique of the ministry and not its doctrinal stance. There is no doubt that some of the barbs had penetrated very deep.

By 1890 the Welsh pulpit was in dire straits, though not everyone was willing to acknowledge this. Some believed that the change afoot was beneficial. According to one observer, 'the virtues of the pulpit these days are orderly composition, good exposition, the fruit of good knowledge and culture'. The weakness of the 'old preaching', he said, was that little attention was paid to human beings, their lives and experiences, but now things were changing and there was a place for 'the analysis of the life of man in its different aspects'. Thus *entertaining*, philosophical preaching is most common now, enriched with simplicity, sympathy, naturalness, beauty and poetry'. He believed that the increase in this kind of preaching could be attributed to the influence of novels because they were more widely read now than ever before and 'by no-one more than by preachers'.[68] It is obvious that *entertaining* preaching' in this context did not mean preaching with *hwyl*, but something completely different. The younger generation were turning their backs on the passionate, rhetorical tradition of the former age. One wrote, 'we believe that lively, conversational style will be the style of the age to come. The influence of this style is already evident in some places'.[69]

On the whole, the denominational periodicals were reluctant to discuss the crisis in preaching. One spokesman for the Church in Wales felt that 'the prospects for its pulpit were currently very bright and heartening'.[70] In 1907, another commentator felt, with regard to the pulpit in Wales generally, that 'it had retained its glory and increased its usefulness'.[71] The Baptist David Powell of Liverpool waxed lyrical: 'the pulpit in Wales is more optimistic than ever',[72] and another, unnamed, Baptist acknowledged some shortcomings in the pulpit of his denomination but nevertheless declared that it was faithful to the old biblical and Puritanical method of preaching, was a Welsh pulpit, faithful to its doctrine, while also being a missionary and Liberal pulpit – in the sense of being broadminded no doubt.[73]

There is some justification for these kinds of statements from a man who lived long enough to see great changes take place. T. Hudson Williams was brought up in Engedi, Caernarfon, and he remembered gratefully what he had received there. He said 'in Engedi the pulpit was a means of culture as well as a means of grace, broadening our knowledge of the literature and history of Wales and the world'. This was not to say that the standard of preaching was invariable. His mature opinion was that 'there were more experts among the preachers of Wales in that era', 'and there were also more dimwits'.[74]

What is more remarkable is how much debate there was concerning this matter, and this is the justification for discussing it at such length. All sorts of people were worried – and deeply worried – about the state of the pulpit. Preaching was becoming less powerful, 'and the press had played its part', according to one commentator.[75] Some declared that the effectiveness and authority of the pulpit had faded by 1907.[76] Preaching had become 'frail and grey' it was said in 1908.[77] Whatever the exact truth was, said David Rowlands (Dewi Môn),[78] there were general complaints that preaching was meaningless and useless.[79] In 1911, Francis Jones, Abergele, declared from the chair of the Calvinistic Methodist General Assembly, 'the sermons may be better, but preaching is poorer'. Why? 'Because we are inferior to the fathers in strength and because we are not as convinced as them of the importance of our message.'[80] It is no wonder, therefore, that from the beginning of the twentieth century, preaching appeared to become irrelevant and 'did not come into vital contact with the spirit of the times'.[81]

As Robert Arthur Griffith (Elphin) said, the preacher was one of the 'false gods' of Wales and in that respect it is appropriate to speak of him as the Great Preacher. In days past, he had fertilized the roots of the nation's faith which in turn expressed itself in dynamic cultural activity. But now he was swiftly becoming a prisoner of the institution which he had helped to create. Elphin was not far from the truth when he said of the preacher who did not wish to see 'that his denomination had become an established church. There had never been a bishop as autocratic as the "Great Preacher." ' Instead of the Great Preacher holding the culture of Wales up to the light of the Eternal, Wales began to regard him as one of the products of its culture. It made him into a star in its world of entertainment, but now the period of his glory was at an end. The preacher's only hope was to rediscover the eternal and thereby rediscover his own lowly function as his servant. However, as we shall see, doctrinal developments would hinder that discovery for more than a generation.

~ 7 ~

The Word Once Spoken

To gain some insight into the social environment of the pulpit, we would have to listen to contemporary observers discussing the virtues and weaknesses of the preaching of the period. However, it is safer and more enlightening to turn to the sermons themselves; safer because they give us a far more balanced picture of what preachers actually said, and more enlightening because it is like discovering an old forgotten continent. Within two generations, this literature has been cast aside, although scholars have diligently studied much poorer material.

The primary characteristic of a sermon is that it is based on a verse or verses from scripture, so let us look first at what portions of the Bible appealed most to preachers at the beginning of the twentieth century. The overwhelming majority of their texts – about 71 per cent – came from the New Testament.[1] This in itself is significant because it shows how the influence of the Old Testament on Welsh thought was in decline. One consequence of this is that people's vision of the link between their faith and culture becomes dimmer. It is in the Old Testament, in the doctrine of creation and the vibrant portrayal of the covenantal and providential relationship between God and Israel in history that some of the most important principles for appreciating the relationship between human beings and culture are to be found, and as will become clear in retrospect, it was in this area that great confusion developed in the minds of Welsh Christians at the end of the nineteenth century.

The Pauline Epistles, including Hebrews, were by far the most popular portions of the New Testament among preachers during the period between 1890 and 1914. Indeed, they took exactly the same percentage of subjects from these Epistles (29 per cent) as they took from the whole of the Old Testament. The Synoptic Gospels were second to the Pauline Epistles with about 18 per cent of sermons based on texts from them. The Johannine literature, including the Gospel, Epistles, and Revelation, accounted for about 14 per cent. To return to the Old Testament, about 11 per cent of the texts came from the Psalms and the Wisdom literature and 9 per cent from the prophets. Considering the growing interest in social matters, it is surprising that there was not a greater proportion from the prophets.

Perhaps one of the most remarkable aspects of the analysis is that it shows what areas the preachers avoided. Very little use was made of the historical portions of the Bible. About 9 per cent of the sermons discuss material from the historical books of the Old Testament and no more than 5 per cent were based on the events of the Gospels.

Before I analyse the hundreds of sermons published during the period in question, a little must be said about the background. It will be sufficient to note that preachers in the Protestant tradition perceived three possible connections between the various parts of the Bible, namely the doctrinal connection, the historical connection, and the experiential connection, each of which gave rise to a different kind of sermon. Of the three, doctrinal preaching was by far the most important. A quotation from the work of John Calvin will suffice to explain its characteristics: 'Now, in order that true religion may shine upon us, we ought to hold that it must take its beginning from heavenly doctrine and that no-one can get even the slightest taste of right and sound doctrine unless he be a pupil of Scripture.'[2] Calvin worked within the conviction that scripture contains a wealth of doctrine, or truths, that can be expressed in an orderly pattern. This is why people like George Lewis[3] came to speak of 'a body of theology'. This same conviction served as the basis for the development of doctrinal preaching among the Protestant Fathers and the Puritans. The aim of such preaching was to show what doctrine might be found in the portion of the Bible being studied, to explain it, show its implications, and apply it to the lives of the listeners. The basis for this type of preaching was the belief that the Bible not only bore witness to God's revelation of himself in history, but was itself part of the revelation. God reveals himself in a book as well as in his Son, in key historical events and in the world of nature. For this reason preachers maintained that the

Bible had one divine author although it had many human authors, and in the work of a single author it is fair to expect unity and consistency.

When we turn to the volumes of sermons by men such as Henry Rees, Edward Morgan or David Jones, Treborth, we realize that what we are reading are very like theological essays, though in fact they are considerably more entertaining than many of the theological essays which were published during the period. They yield a clear and comprehensive idea of the richness of the Christian faith. The convictions of preachers were reflected in the shape of their sermons, with a preface introducing the subject and the 'truths' or 'doctrine' contained therein, then the 'headings' expounding the doctrine, and the 'application' linking it to the lives of those listening. To take one example, the theme of David Saunders's sermon on Job 33: 13–14 was 'that it is folly for man to strive against God in the face of his tribulations, however dark they may happen to be'.[4] In a sermon on Job 23: 8–10 David Jones, Treborth, discussed almost the same subject as Saunders though he had not one subject but two, namely 'The dark perspective which Job held of God's oversight of him in his providence' and secondly, 'The strong trust that Job had in the Lord in the midst of his sorrows'.[5]

These two sermons were evidently neither remote nor abstract. On the contrary, the 'doctrine' touched closely upon any listener who had experienced trials or affliction. There was a danger that sermons of this type could sometimes become over-intellectualized and descend into arid speculation. Nevertheless this kind of preaching was so influential that its format was used even when the content of the sermon was anything but doctrinal, which is why nineteenth-century sermons all look so similar on paper. If we look carefully at their content, or if we read about how they were delivered, we realize that even historical and ethical sermons were composed according to the format of a doctrinal sermon.

In considering sermons on historical themes, it is clear that the preachers believed that God was active through the medium of world history. It is apparent to all that the Bible contains a narrative, but Christian tradition has interpreted this narrative in a remarkable way. The historical portions of the Bible do not contain a series of stories but rather a world portrayed through the medium of history, drama, dialogue and chronicle. In one sense, it is a strange way to portray the world. It could be said that a philosophical analysis, or a scientific description, or a social essay, would be more appropriate in order to do justice to the reality of a transcendent God, while the style of the Bible is even more foreign to modern people because of the development of a literary medium, namely the novel, or more specifically, the realistic novel, that tries to do the same thing as the Bible. The realistic novelist tries to convey a world by means of dialogue, story and context, and by reading the events as they unfold, the reader is led into the author's world. It is no accident that literary critics speak of 'the world of Dickens' or 'the world of Daniel Owen'.

The narrative portions of the Bible lead the believer into God's world as they relate the story of Adam and Abraham, Moses and David, Jesus Christ and Paul and, in order to appreciate the Bible as a portrayal of a world, it must be read as history, not as a parable, illustration or allegory. This perspective on the Bible is most evident in the work of St Augustine, the Protestant Fathers and the Puritans. There was a single world with a history spanning the entire period from creation to consummation with the Second Coming of Christ. It was not a static world, like Plato's world of ideas, but rather a dynamic world, the world of the living God. The story told of ebb and flow, increase and decline, rebellion and obedience, sin and repentance, with the individual stories therein linked together by means of such devices as shadow and substance, promise and fulfilment, prophecy and realization. Human history, even that of the sixteenth century, or the eighteenth century, is neatly encompassed by the world of the Bible and only within this real world can we see the significance of our contemporary world. This historical understanding was taken for granted until it was undermined by the humanistic developments of the Enlightenment in the eighteenth century.

This was the vision that illuminated the history of Wales for Gildas and John Penry. Charles Edwards discussed Welsh history with the same conviction:

> After the war of Owen Glyndŵr, this onerous slavery continued upon our nation throughout the reign of five English kings; and it was sufficient to bring terrible poverty and ignorance upon it. And to inhibit or extinguish any generosity, skill, art, faith and good morals, previously found in their midst. In this condition it found cause to mourn before God, like Zion afflicted, 'we have transgressed and have rebelled: thou

hast not pardoned . . .' (Lamentations 3: 42) because God's threat to it was fulfilled quite rightly, 'Because thou servedst not the Lord thy God with joyfulness . . . therefore shalt thou serve thine enemies . . . in hunger' (Deuteronomy 28: 47, 48).[6]

It would be superficial to assume that Edwards tried to force the biblical quotations into the discussion in an unnatural manner. For him, it was the biblical narrative that portrayed the true relationship of God with a nation in history, and Wales's history is a reflection of the basic history contained in that narrative.

The classical document which conveys this understanding of the significance of biblical history is *Golwg ar Deyrnas Crist* (A View of Christ's Kingdom) by William Williams Pantycelyn. The unifying theme which undergirds this great poem is the fact of Christ's covenant with his people. It shows how the culture and history of humankind in general connects with the real history found in the Bible.

This conviction continued to influence preaching throughout the nineteenth century, although it became visibly weaker towards its close. We find it, for instance, in Christmas Evans's sermon, 'Preaching the Gospel in Sinai'. Worded thus, the subject immediately suggests the unity of biblical history.[7] It links Sinai with Calvary and the listener is drawn into the story by the bonds of the covenant which he or she affirms. The same conviction can be seen in the dynamic historical images in Christmas Evans's sermon, 'God as the First Cause Operating through the Whole'.[8] He described judgement and mercy as chariots driven by God:

In their opinion the old world, and Sodom were safe; but when God rode the chariots of judgement, the outpouring came like the chariots of judgement upon them . . . Sodom was on fire before midday. Pharaoh thought that he was safe like a crocodile and a mighty long dragon in the middle of the sea . . . But God sent chariots of judgements down there to meet him . . .

After describing God riding the chariots of judgement against Babylon, he moved seamlessly into the New Testament to describe the chariot of mercy:

Satan thought that he had the whole world in the castle of death . . . but the son of Mary sent the chariots of salvation up through the trenches of death, until the earth trembled, and rocks split, towards Calvary and on the morning of the third day, he had stolen from the devil's hand the power of death.

Even during the late nineteenth century there were some who still professed this classic vision. John Hughes's idiom was very different from that of Christmas Evans, but in his sermon 'An Eternal Covenant',[9] he dealt with the unity of history in light of the covenant. 'This covenant is the revelation of God's grace and salvation to a lost world and is seen in some form or another in every dispensation, but which was given to David in connection with the kingdom.' Hughes interpreted his text, 2 Samuel 23: 5, as real history. For unless he is like David, unless God has made a covenant with him, the whole construct of his theme will collapse. However, assuming that the covenant with David was a historical fact, he could commend this message to his listeners precisely because the covenant which God made with David was steadfast and eternal. The world of the congregation of Engedi, Caernarfon, in 1890 was of a part with the biblical history which included Moses, David and the apostle Paul. This conviction was set out clearly and concisely by one of John Hughes's most able contemporaries. In 'Advice to Preachers' in 1880 David Saunders (1831–92) combined an emphasis on the unity of the Bible with the importance of the history chronicled within it. According to Saunders:

> Notice carefully the gradual development of the way of salvation, as it is revealed in scripture. The Bible is not a collection of unconnected parts but one great, divine volume composed of different parts, with each part complementing the others and all of them together creating one complete revelation of the mind of God, through the history of the way of salvation.[10]

During the half century after he uttered these words in 1880 the unity of this vision would be shattered, with far-reaching consequences for Welsh spiritual and cultural life. But before I turn to that subject, I must consider a third method used to express the unity of the Bible in preaching.

The first method, as we have seen, was to trace the doctrinal connections which linked various parts of the Bible, and the second method was to pursue the historical links. The third method became prominent in the preaching of the Puritans and it experienced a mighty resurgence in the preaching of the Evangelical Revival of the eighteenth century. The silver thread that linked different parts of the Bible with one another and linked the modern listener to the Bible was the experience of the soul. The journey of the believer from sin to paradise was the meaningful pattern that made the Bible intelligible and relevant. One of the obvious consequences of this method of interpreting the Bible was the use of allegory that has flourished in the church ever since the time of Origen, namely that the words of scripture convey several meanings, all concealed within one another.[11]

The most famous example of this allegorization during the Puritan period was found in *The Pilgrim's Progress* by John Bunyan, while the classical expression of this vision in the literature of the Evangelical Revival was *Theomemphus* by Williams Pantycelyn. However the very names of these two authors warn us not to suggest that their emphasis on the experience of believers supplanted the objective emphasis. Neither was a Romanticist who transformed the substance of Christianity into a subjective and individual experience. Bunyan was a Calvinistic realist rooted in God's objective self-revelation in scripture while Williams wrote not only *Theomemphus* but also *Golwg ar Deyrnas Crist* (A View of Christ's Kingdom) which expresses so powerfully the awareness of the objectivity of salvation history and the unity of the biblical teaching which bears witness to it. In his hymns, too, Williams Pantycelyn interweaves objectivity and subjectivity. It is worth noting the power of the word 'Dacw' (See yonder) in the following verse:

> Dacw'r nefoedd fawr ei hunan
> Nawr yn dioddef angau loes;
> Dacw obaith yr holl ddaear
> Heddiw'n hongian ar y groes:
> Dacw Noddfa pechaduriaid,
> Dacw'r Meddyg, dacw'r fan
> Y caf wella'r holl archollion
> Dyfnion sydd ar enaid gwan.

> See yonder the great heavens himself
> now suffering the pain of death;
> See yonder the hope of all the earth
> Hanging today on the cross:

> See yonder the Refuge for sinners,
> See yonder the Physician, see yonder the place
> Where I may heal all the deep
> Wounds of a weak soul.

Worshippers are invited to concentrate their attention on something that happened outside themselves – 'see yonder' – and on a specific time – 'one afternoon'. Of course this objective event is connected with the subjective experience of the believer, but Pantycelyn places the 'deep wounds' of the soul within the compass of the objectivity of the divine act. The work of Bunyan and Pantycelyn safeguards the balance between the objective work of God and the subjective experience of the believer.

As we move into the twentieth century we see that balance being destroyed. It is not that preachers in Wales went as far as to deny the existence or significance of an objective saviour but there was an increasing trend towards linking various parts of the Bible with the experience of the soul. Once this trend had gained momentum the preaching it inspired became increasingly detached from the classical Christian conviction that we have been placed in a temporal and spiritual world that is an objective home for us and that there is a great history that encompasses the history of all human beings. The consequence of this type of trend is that preaching becomes psychological, introspective and fanciful, and eventually, as the decline becomes entrenched, irrelevant. It cannot speak purposefully to human beings in the midst of their cultural, social and political activities and it inevitably becomes private, individualistic and uninspired.

Before considering what happened to these three ways of interpreting the Bible and evaluating the changes that occurred in the preaching based on them, I shall cast a glance over the sermons published between 1890 and 1914.

Since the belief in the doctrinal unity of the Bible was the strongest influence on the pulpit until 1890, it is appropriate to begin with doctrinal preaching. H. Ivor Jones maintained that 'we must preach God's truth, and not the opinions of men' and his advice as a result was that 'the aim should be to make the sermon rich in beneficial truths, and laden with valuable thoughts'.[12] This continued the heavy emphasis of the previous era on ideas – or ideals (*meddylddrychau*) to use the customary word of that age.

Poets and writers were expected to offer their readers dramatic or beautiful reflections and H. Ivor Jones applied this to preaching, as did preachers in the vast majority of sermons published between 1890 and 1914. In other words, the backbone of their preaching was doctrine and there was a continued emphasis on delivering ideas that were consistent with the Bible. In an address to students of the Bangor Baptist College, Edward Parry encouraged young preachers to preach orthodox doctrine, namely the infallibility of scripture, the divinity of Christ, his miraculous birth, his atoning death, his resurrection, his ascension and his intercession.[13] Where this emphasis was found, the sermons had a substantial intellectual content but, as we shall soon see, one of the characteristics of the age was the separation of the 'reflections' from orthodox doctrine and their use for their aesthetic attractiveness or their emotional impact.

In the sermons published at the beginning of the 1890s, we find that a prominent position was given to the 'order of salvation'. An important aspect of the Calvinistic inheritance was the belief that God was a God of order in providence and grace. R. D. Roberts, Llwynhendy, for instance, preached on the 'clarity of the order of the gospel' and explained that the 'order of the gospel'[14] was God's plan for the salvation of a sinner. There is nothing arbitrary or accidental in salvation; rather the various elements within it join together in a clear plan that the weakest intellect can comprehend. In the words of another preacher: 'The great plan of salvation is characterized by order. Every part of it, although it stretches like a single excellent line from eternity to eternity, is where it should be. Predestination, calling, justification and glorification are in their rightful place'.[15] God's various actions formed a single unity for the purpose of salvation,[16] and it all worked so effectively that even the most wretched could trust it and the least in intellectual capacity could see its purpose. 'We are forgiven for failing to understand many things in the scriptures, but no one is excused for failing to understand the order of the gospel', said William Evans, Aberaeron.[17] John Hughes (1827–93) gave a typically clear and powerful explanation of this order in his sermon, 'Peace and God in Justification'.[18] In the first stage of his introduction he showed that the whole of humanity is under the condemnation of God's law. The second stage explained that there is hope nevertheless because God extends righteousness to unrighteous men. The two features of this righteousness are that it has been secured 'through the redemption in Christ Jesus', and that it is a righteousness 'that comes through faith'. 'Through this order all the faithful throughout the ages are justified.' It is an objective order, as Hughes goes on to explain. To begin with, 'justification is a legal change'. Thus it is 'a perfect and whole work, and not a gradual work dependent on the growth of any virtue in the believer'. The peace between God and humankind does not rest 'on the work of grace within . . . but on the work of Christ without, and that work is perfect'. So the believer's security before God depends not on the qualifications of the believer, or on morals, or on feelings, but on the completeness of the saving work of the Redeemer. As a result, there are no 'degrees in justification' because it is 'the work of a court', which declares that the perfect righteousness of Christ has been accounted to a sinner. Sinners personally connect with this objective work by 'approaching Christ and his merit' in order to be justified by faith.

According to Hughes, this involves maintaining a clear distinction between justification and sanctification. God's order of salvation does not imperil sanctification; on the contrary, it is a means of endorsing God's eternal call for sanctification, but the position he adopted meant disagreeing with the Catholic doctrine which 'teaches sound doctrine on the objective or divine side of salvation, but which is misleading and confusing on the method of its application'. He proceeded to summarize correctly and carefully the doctrine of the Church of Rome concerning imputed righteousness which understands justification not as a legal declaration counting the merit of Christ in place of the sinner, but as an inner alteration in the character of a person which makes him or her justified and which means that a person's merit is added to the merit of Christ in order ultimately to obtain salvation.

It is worth lingering with this remarkable sermon for two reasons. It is in itself a splendid expression of the classical Protestant doctrine concerning justification through faith alone (*sola fide*) on the basis of Christ's merits. Also this doctrine must be understood in order to appreciate the crucial significance of the departure from it that occurred increasingly among Welsh Protestants after 1890. Luther described the doctrine as *articulus stantis vel cadentis ecclesiae* – the article upon which the church would either stand or fall. Once the Welsh preachers and theologians began to vacillate on this matter, the survival of Welsh Christianity in its historical evangelical form came under threat.

Some sermons show evidence of concern about some aspects of the way the order of salvation had been presented in the past. It was believed that this order was part of God's eternal purpose and that it was an aspect of the election of grace. By this time, however, not even such a stalwart Calvinist as Samuel Owen, Tanygrisiau, professed the doctrine of reprobation,[19] while David Charles Davies felt that a difficulty which troubled many needed to be addressed, namely how to reconcile the doctrine of election, even the election of grace, with the moral freedom of humankind.[20]

Although some difficulties of this kind emerged, justification, the cross and faith in the salvation wrought by Christ's death remained the staple doctrinal fare for the majority of preachers in that period, with Pauline theology well to the fore. This is not to say that the victory and conquest of Christ – the theme of Christus Victor – was not celebrated at times. D. O. Jones (1856–1903) expressed it thus:

> God, through the cross, has won a total victory over your enemies, so, if you believe in Christ, they can no longer harm you . . . without a sword or mighty weapons, the Lamb tramples the dragons underfoot, and weakens the head of the great Dragon – their Prince. He himself fights against all the forces, and conquers them.[21]

In presenting Christianity to their contemporaries, it was inevitable that preachers should focus much of their attention on the blessings that came from Christ's saving work. The main blessing, as Benjamin Davies, Tre-lech, explained, was salvation, the new life in all its fullness.[22] Christ died not only to redeem sinners from the condemnation of the law, and thus from spiritual death, but to secure for them a full life, to create them anew and ensure for them the fruits of his lordship.[23] But the gospel is like a 'box in which Jehovah's most precious jewels and pearls are kept, to make the sinner eternally rich',[24] meaning that all the wealth of Christ comes into the possession of the Christian.[25] The most glorious of these blessings was the Holy Spirit[26] and the first fruit of the Holy Spirit's work was rebirth, namely the 'alteration of the governing element in man's character' and the 'creation of a clean heart'. He considered this to be 'one of the fundamental doctrines of the Christian religion' because only this alteration under the influence of the Holy Spirit can enable the mind to 'give a hearty welcome to the other great doctrines', such as 'the divinity of Christ's person, redemption, and salvation by grace through faith'.[27] It was through the Holy Spirit also that union with Christ,[28] reconciliation with God and full communion with him[29] were obtained, and from that numerous other blessings flowed.

One priceless blessing in a turbulent world was the assurance that God is on the side of his people.[30] They no longer need to fear the condemnation of the law because justification also involves forgiveness. 'Redemption is forgiveness, the payment is grace . . . God forgives . . . but pays for doing so', said William James.[31] Other blessings follow in its wake, such as peace[32] and comfort,[33] and a quiet conscience.[34] The future – the 'world to come' – begins to penetrate the present because the Christian enjoys a foretaste of the rest that still remains for the people of God.[35] It follows from this that the Christian is sustained by a lively hope[36] and his or her life is comforted by joy.[37] In a word, believers are assured of the more 'abundant life' that Christ promised his followers.[38] In spite of their insignificance, men and women can take possession of everything of God in Christ, in the words of Robert Ambrose Jones (Emrys ap Iwan):

> What is the order of salvation? An order which gives to the great possession of the small, and to the small possession of the great. What takes place when man believes and God saves? The small gives himself to the great and the great gives himself to the small.[39]

The wealth of content in these sermons on the blessings of the Christian life show that the accusation that Welsh Christianity at the threshold of the twentieth century was affected and hypocritical was quite groundless. To discount all the sermons as being empty rhetoric is little short of ignorant cynicism. Indeed as one reads them one realizes the source of the psychological health and quiet strength that characterized so many Welsh people in that period. The warmth and unmistakable sincerity of the sermons show that the preachers spoke out of the fullness of their hearts.

In one respect it is remarkable that there were not many more sermons on the subject of the person of Jesus Christ. After all, it is he and his work which constitute the substance of justifying faith, but it is comparatively rare to find whole sermons devoted to Christ. One possible reason for this was the tendency towards Sabellianism which emerged towards the end of the nineteenth century. There was a considerable emphasis on the divinity of Christ and consequently preachers no doubt felt that the references in their sermons to God the Father could be directly applied to God the Son. A striking example of this emphasis was the mighty sermon by the Baptist Charles Davies, minister of Tabernacle church, Cardiff, on 'The Immutability of Our Lord'.[40] He described the unchanging greatness of Christ on the basis of the words, 'But thou art the same' from Hebrews 1: 12, which itself is a quotation from Psalm 102: 27. It was almost inevitable, based on this text, that he should analyse the characteristics of Christ in words that would be appropriate to describe the Father. He scarcely touched upon the humanity of Christ and the sermon barely avoids Sabellianism.[41] However, by the 1890s there was a healthy reaction to this inasmuch as Jesus Christ's humanity began to be taken more seriously. Thus we find sermons that try to safeguard the classical balance of the Chalcedonian definition. William Davies (1843–1922) of Llandeilo, in his sermon on 'Christ Fulfilling Everything'[42] spoke of the Word becoming united with flesh; a 'divine person took upon himself a human nature, and thus two natures made one immortal person, without either becoming lost in the other; differentiated, but not separated'. Here we have a clear echo of the words of the Chalcedonian definition. In similar vein T. Lloyd Jones, Pencader, in his sermon on 'The Son of Man', underlined the humanity of the Redeemer,[43] and Cynddylan Jones did likewise in his sermon on 'The Man Christ Jesus',[44] as he discussed the subject 'A man of men'. He emphasized that Jesus was truly human in his body, his physical weaknesses and all his characteristics.

However, the drive to do full justice to Christ's humanity led some forward-thinking minds to embrace the doctrine that Christ in his incarnation shed some of his divine attributes. This was the doctrine of *kenosis*, or the self-emptying of God the Son. Few preachers were willing to embrace this doctrine because of their fear that it could detract from the full divinity of the Redeemer. The clear tendency among the preachers of this period was to adhere to the traditional doctrine that the Word made flesh emptied himself of his divine glory but nothing else. This was the standpoint of S. T. Jones who believed that such a view did not in any way compromise Christ's humanity,[45] and of William Morris (1843–1922), Treorchy, who agreed that the Word, in becoming incarnate, divested himself of his heavenly glory.[46] Nevertheless, there was a growing desire to embrace some form of the doctrine of *kenosis*, as we shall see when I come to discuss doctrine generally. Thomas Charles Williams opposed the tendency not to take the incarnation seriously when he criticized those who, in attempting to safeguard the glory of the Redeemer's person, were tempted to 'make the incarnation nothing'.[47] At the same time he was not prepared to compromise at all on the full divinity of Christ.[48]

The impression given by the sermons generally is that there was a strong tendency in the pulpit towards exalting Christ's divinity at the expense of taking his humanity seriously. In historical terms, the trend was towards the Alexandrian rather than the Antiochian tradition in the interpretation of the person of Christ. It did not augur well because the danger was to make Jesus Christ a divine visitor wearing some kind of robe of flesh. This served to make his earthly pilgrimage unreal and made him irrelevant and remote from humankind.

In a discussion of the sermons of John Williams, Brynsiencyn, his biographer, R. R. Hughes, said that the 'governing idea' of his doctrinal preaching from 1879 onwards was 'man's need for revelation and God's answer to him in Christ'. This emphasis was an unexpected development in Nonconformity because it contrasted with the older doctrine that humankind's prime need was to be redeemed from sin. According to Hughes, John Williams maintained that 'Jesus Christ revealed God because he had always held the place of a Revealer within the Godhead. He revealed God to God himself throughout eternity.' He continued, 'this was a thoroughly Welsh development in the history of preaching', and that during the 1880s it took the place of the atonement in the development of Welsh theology.[49]

It is difficult to understand some of these claims. John Williams's ideas echoed the lively discussion in England at the time on the significance of the incarnation as some kind of covenant between God and man. Thinkers such as F. D. Maurice, Bishop Westcott, Charles Gore and R. W. Dale had contributed in their various ways to the restoration of the former Alexandrian emphasis on Jesus Christ as the Logos, the Revealer, who would have become incarnate, sin or no sin, in order fully to reveal God to humankind.

John Williams represented this emphasis in the Welsh pulpit.[50] At its simplest, it stated that 'the Lord Jesus Christ had come into the world in order to reveal and show the Father to men'.[51] But even such a simple statement indicated in what direction the doctrine was likely to develop. Jesus Christ could easily be seen as the mediator of truths about God; subsequently it was not he but the truths he proclaimed that would be at the centre of the picture. This would lead to a doctrine of the Word which was not dissimilar to the doctrine of the second-century Apologists.

D. Stanley Jones took a big step in that direction when he defined faith as 'spiritual intuition' – the faculty which enabled human beings to internalize revelation – rather than the possession of a lively trust in the Redeemer. We can actually see the change in emphasis occurring during this particular sermon. At the beginning, Stanley Jones said that the purpose of Christ's coming into the world was to seek and to save the lost but the essence of his sermon is an explanation of the work of Christ in revealing spiritual realities.[52] David Adams's sermon, 'Jesus as the Interpreter of Life', clearly emphasized Jesus' role as a revealer of philosophical truths.[53] However not all preachers of this kind focused on the truths revealed by Jesus. Towards the turn of the twentieth century there was evidence of a growing desire to see Jesus as the revealer of 'life' or the 'more abundant life', or the 'higher life'.[54] There is no doubt that these sermons echoed the teaching of the Keswick Movement.

By the turn of the century it was apparent that the focus of Welsh preaching was shifting from the atonement to the incarnation, to Bethlehem rather than Calvary. There was also a trend towards emphasizing the humanity of Christ and the content of his message rather than the uniqueness of his person. Before long preachers would speak of the 'faith of Jesus' rather than of a faith centred upon Jesus.

Preachers continued to include references to the 'Last Things' in their sermons. Many sermons remind us that a healthy other-worldliness is essential to Christianity. In his sermon, 'The Life and Death of the Christian as Glory to Christ', William Roberts (1845–96) of Llanrwst, said of the Christian's death:

> The house of clay must be scattered into dust, in order to obtain a new house suitable for a land without sin. As death entered through sin, so sin must go out through death . . . Death is gain also, since it is a movement to a state which is far better than the present: to have heaven

instead of death, a throne instead of a prison, to be with Christ instead of being away from home from the Lord, and to see him as he is instead of seeing him through a glass darkly and though parables.[55]

Humankind's true home is beyond this mortal world and beyond time. Their earthly pilgrimage involves preparing for another world, thus it is essential to keep the realities of that world continually in view. 'It is not possible', said Principal Thomas Lewis, 'for the Church to place its affection too much on those things that are above.'[56] 'We are pilgrims', said Robert Ambrose Jones (Emrys ap Iwan). 'We have left the pleasures of Egypt and the world avers from this that we have exchanged bad for worse, have fled from the smoke into the fire, have escaped from the river Clwyd only to be drowned in the river Conwy.' But it is not thus because 'we are passing through this to a land of rivers, wells and depths springing out in the valley and in the mountain' and we have already tasted the grapes of the promised land. 'It is true that man will not experience as much of heaven in this world as in the world to come; but he can have as much of heaven now as he can receive.'[57] Emrys ap Iwan addressed his congregation in the Vale of Clwyd on the glories of heaven with unique passion:

> Now God, as he offers men heavenly glory and honour, also offers them incorruptibility. They will be immortal; for that reason they will live eternally to enjoy eternal blessings; moreover, they will live incorruptibly, without deteriorating, or aging. They will live for ever young and lissom; and thus they will be able to enjoy the good things of the other world with all the passion and pleasure of young people.[58]

Emrys ap Iwan was no doubt perfectly familiar with the medieval belief that every one would be 30 years old on the morning of the resurrection! However there are signs that people by the end of the period were growing indifferent to this dimension because we find John Hughes (1850–1932) of Liverpool, saying, 'Our great need in these days is to move closer to the other world and open the windows of our dwellings to let in the breezes.'[59]

Nor were these preachers shy of warning their listeners of the consequences of sin. H. M. Hughes, the Independent minister in Cardiff, was not averse to reminding his congregation of the reality of damnation:

Indeed, it is terrible to think of losing a soul. But although it is so terrible, it is sometimes our duty to dwell upon this matter. It is frivolous and unhealthy not to reproach those who refuse the Gospel by showing the terrifying consequences of so doing.[60]

John Williams, Brynsiencyn, heartily agreed. In his disturbing sermon 'The Stone', he said: 'Seldom is the word hell heard in a pulpit. The lightning is extinguished and the thunder is silenced.' He went on, 'I am afraid that the root of this is a shallow conviction of sin, and that the ears of a superficial age are becoming dull.'[61] Dull or not, John Roberts (Iolo Caernarfon) announced forthrightly that 'the shame and sorrow of the ungodly will be dreadful and terrible, wholly inexpressible and incomprehensible to those of us present here'.[62] D. O. Jones did not hesitate to conclude a sermon on the 'Inadequacy of a Profession of Faith on the Day of Judgement', with a description of the final sifting. 'And while the pure multitude is being led to the land of light, the multitude on the left are sinking into the utmost darkness.'[63] It is evident that death, judgement, heaven and hell still had a place in the sermons of this period. Few now attempted to include references to hell and the Day of Judgement in every sermon, as did John Jones (Yr Hen Gloddwr – 'The Old Digger').[64] However, some of the older preachers tried to safeguard the consistency of the faith by dealing with each theological doctrine in turn.[65]

It is part of Christian belief that God judges humankind constantly through the vicissitudes of history as well as in the Great Judgement at the end of the world. Indeed the preaching of the gospel itself reveals God's righteousness and his call for holiness. As a result there were some preachers whose message brought their listeners under a deep conviction of sin. Among early twentieth-century preachers, no one did this more regularly than R. B. Jones, Porth. In October 1905, he preached for five nights in Siloh, Tredegar, and one present said:

We were whipped mercilessly by him for a week. We were held throughout this time at the foot of Mount Sinai, and in the presence of the fire and the smoke, the lightning and the thunder, [and] most of us felt like the children of Israel long ago about whom was said, 'And all the people saw the thunder and lightning . . . and when the people saw this, they retreated and stood afar' . . . And no doubt everyone will confess that it was impossible to listen to Mr Jones without feeling our imperfection and the need to strive to live a more holy life and closer to Christ . . .[66]

R. B. Jones's harshness arose from his characteristic and passionate emphasis on God's call for sanctity among his people, but he certainly succeeded in bringing his listeners to the crisis of judgement. William Jones, Morriston, had a different style of delivery but according to witnesses hundreds were converted by the sermon which he delivered in the Calvinistic Methodist Association on Anglesey in 1893. For Jones there was no distance at all between 1893 and the Day of Judgement:

> Are things right between you and the Counsel for the Defence? Has the quarrel been settled yet? 'Well, no indeed' said someone. 'I am afraid in my heart; I am terrified of facing the Judge. Cold shivers crawl over me as I think of the Judgement. What shall I do?' Do not despair, my friend; if you are on the way to Judgement, Forgiveness is on its way too! The Chalice and the Blood are on their way. Atonement is on its way! The Righteousness of the Surety *is* on its way . . . Place your case in the hand of the Counsel – you know who he is. And then when the Judge comes to your case, you will be able to shout out within earshot of all the people, *Settled out of Court.*[67]

The doctrinal premises of the sermon are clear: there will be a final judgement one day and all those who have faith in the Redeemer will be pronounced not guilty. However, by the end of the nineteenth century these two convictions, characteristic as they were of the classic Protestant scheme, were beginning to wane. A sermon on 'God's Judgments' by the Congregational poet-preacher J. J. Williams interpreted judgement in terms of the mechanical effects of transgressing the moral law rather than in terms of a personal clash between sinners and their God. For Williams, moral wickedness had social and political effects that are equivalent to punishment.[68] As yet it was a matter of emphasis, that the personal God revealed in Christ was also governor of the moral order. Robert Ambrose Jones (Emrys ap Iwan) also gave an unexpected twist to the concept of divine judgement in his comments on the demise of the Welsh language:

God punishes the people who neglect the language of their country; and because of this the Welsh people of Radnorshire and Breconshire and the borders are so much inferior in understanding, in morals and in religion to the Welsh people of the most Welsh parts of the Principality.

But he safeguarded the link between faith and culture, between transgressing a moral order and angering God, when he added 'that the same God who gave his Son to save the world gave every nation a suitable language to speak of that Son'.[69]

The fact that the classic Protestant doctrine of justification by faith alone was losing its grip on the Welsh religious imagination was apparent in the tendency of some preachers to alter the second premiss mentioned in connection with William Jones's sermon above. Morris D. Jones of Mountain Ash expressed the old belief succinctly. Christians, he said, will appear before the judgement throne of God, but when the books are opened there will be nothing there to condemn them because of 'their having believed in the Son of God, who died for them, and buried their sins in the depths of his merit'.[70] William James, Aberdare, expressed a different understanding which revealed how the traditional belief was being transformed. Love, 'like the love that brought Jesus to Calvary, and that feeling in its fullness, and sanctified through the blood of the cross, will give them confidence on the day of judgement'. This love, according to James, included believing. In other words, it meant faith.[71] Although anti-papism was still strong at the turn of the twentieth century, it is striking how James and others show a definite movement away from the Protestant reformers' *sola fide* (faith alone) towards the *fide caritate formata* (faith working through love) of the Catholics. Speaking of Catholicism, it is worth noticing that a change was occurring in the place given to Catholicism in the eschatology of Welsh Nonconformists in the period under scrutiny. In his *Cyfrol o Bregethau* (Volume of Sermons, 1893) William Evans, Aberaeron, had an essay on 'The Man of Sin'. He identified him with the 'Antichrist' of John's Epistle and with the 'Beast' of the Book of Revelation and explained it as the 'Papist religion'. This aspect of traditional Protestant eschatology was rapidly disappearing by the end of the nineteenth century. Not that Catholicism did not come under sharp criticism from time to time, especially in connection with ritualism,[72] but a sermon such as that by Evan Roberts, Dolgellau, on 'The Foolish Maids', which is nothing more than an extended attack on Catholicism, was quite a rare event.[73]

To summarize the discussion thus far, it can be maintained that doctrinal preaching was still popular and that a majority of these sermons adhered to the standards of orthodoxy expected by the various denominations. This means, of course, that the vast majority of sermons professed some form of Calvinistic–evangelical theology. However, there was a clear change of emphasis, sometimes with regard to pivotal subjects, and prejudice against doctrinal preaching was increasing. 'Between 1875 and 1900', said Puleston Jones, 'the essay sermon disappeared almost completely'.[74] He was speaking of the style rather than the content. This was 'the abstract, essay' style, 'remote from the people' where the preacher developed his subject in an academic way without once addressing his congregation directly and reserving any application until the end. Preachers increasingly adopted the 'conversational style that is in keeping with the age'[75] but until 1914 in most sermons the doctrinal content remained. Puleston Jones himself was an example of this. Although he was a master of the conversational style and of clear and robust Welsh, his interest lay in the doctrinal substance, as his volume of sermons *Gair y Deyrnas* (The Word of the Kingdom) shows.

At the same time, strangely enough, expositional preaching was not popular. In September 1859, as a young minister in the Calvinistic Methodist church at Jewin Crescent, London, David Charles Davies began a series of expositional sermons on the Epistle to the Ephesians. The series continued for thirteen years until his congregation was heartily sick of it.[76] Preachers and congregations preferred sermons with a strong structure rather than the moving back and forth from subject to subject which is inevitable in expositional preaching.

We can see the change to which Puleston Jones referred when we compare different sermons on the same subject. In his sermon on the 'Unsearchable Riches', Owen Evans adhered to the essay style, taking great care for sound doctrine and qualifying the discussion with appropriate references to the Bible.[77] This was a fine example of the old style. On the other hand, W. Matthias Griffith, who began to preach in 1880, confined himself to three simple points, delivered in a poetic style without any biblical references and quoting an *englyn*[78] and a poetic verse and adding a few interesting anecdotes.[79] This exemplified the new style. It is interesting that

Thomas Charles Williams, who began to preach in 1887, combined elements of the two previous styles in a sermon on the same text. His interest in doctrine is evident and, like the old preachers, he was also prepared to use subheadings. But he betrayed his allegiance to the new fashion when he adopted alliteration in his main headings. He discussed the 'unsearchable riches', (1) 'Yn ei gynnwys' (In its content), (2) 'Yn ei gyflawnder' (In its completeness), (3) 'Yn ei gyfaddaster' (In its convenience). By now Welsh preachers were moving into the golden age of fancy headings.[80]

The volume that was most influential in establishing the new fashion in preaching was *Planu Coed* (Planting Trees) by H. Elvet Lewis (Elfed), published in 1898. Elfed wrote a sensitive and discerning prose and respected the difference between oral and written style – which few preachers or their biographers did when they prepared their sermons for publication. Like Puleston Jones and Robert Ambrose Jones (Emrys ap Iwan), Elfed deliberately set out to fashion a fluent and uncomplicated speaking style. In the 'Preface' *to Planu Coed*, he wrote 'I do not usually write a sermon down before preaching it' and consequently the sermons in the volume are very similar to literary essays. The sermon that gives its title to the volume is an excellent example of this style. Abraham 'planted a grove in Beersheba, and called there on the name of Lord, the everlasting God' (Gen. 21: 33). After outlining the background to the verse, Elfed made various inferences. The first was that Abraham planted trees, not in his youth, but in his old age, when he would not live to enjoy their blessings, thus it is a privilege for us also to prepare blessings for those that come after us. Secondly, Abraham planted the trees when he was only a pilgrim in Beersheba, thus the fact that we live in a mobile age when we are forced to move from place to place is no excuse to be idle in Christ's work. Next, Abraham planted trees and not flowers and in this respect Abraham is a picture of Christ because he gave people permanent shelter and not transient adornments. Lastly, 'Abraham planted trees, and was given a new verse' – 'and he called on the name of the Lord, the everlasting God'. Elfed summarized the message in his last paragraph:

This is the work and blessing of our most sacred religion – to plant trees to be a shelter for others. Let us take care not to curtail the blessings for our children. There are those who are constantly engaged in cutting the trees down. Will you do that, reader? Parents' advice – gone: verses and prayers – gone: sermons and appeals – gone. There is already precious little shade for the soul. Let one tree stay, at least. Do not take your axe to the Cross![81]

All this was delivered in the deep, melodious voice that would keep its vigour until the middle of the twentieth century. The style is discerning, the expression concise. The manner is quiet and restrained, always focusing upon the inferences arising from the text. This style of preaching became extremely fashionable, spreading throughout all the denominations. Elfed was well-known as a leader of the eisteddfod movement and with him many felt that the golden age of the poet-preacher had arrived. However not all poet-preachers were like Elfed. His simplicity was deceptive because it was rooted in stern self-discipline, unerring taste and an extraordinary breadth of culture. Something resembling poetic preaching had existed for many years – what John Davies (Sion Gymro)[82] called 'the preaching of fancies (*dychmygion*)'.[83] Such preaching might certainly gain inspiration in the delivery, but on paper it reads like a parody. There was no preacher held in higher respect and with a greater talent for oratory than William Jones of Fishguard, who died on 24 March 1895, and yet he would launch into a feast of unbridled allegories and puns, which are virtually meaningless.

> *Great angels* are famous for their *little books*. Homer was a great angel; and he was a great angel who was famous for his little books. Milton was a great angel and his 'Paradise Lost' is a little book. Bunyan was a great angel, and 'The Pilgrim's Progress' is a little book. They are all little books, but great books in the realm of the mind. A great angel is needed to write a great little book.[84]

This is all very different from the restrained, unerring preaching of Elfed. Nevertheless, *Planu Coed* gave a new impetus to this style of delivery. Furthermore, it also led to a substantial increase in 'poetic' preaching. T. Gwernogle Evans edited two bulky tomes of sermons with the significant title, *Pwlpud y Beirdd* (The Pulpit of the Poets).[85] The seventy preachers who contributed came from all denominations and few of them were poets, although most of them wrote poetry! These volumes show how the new fashion took hold. R. Gwylfa Roberts chose to contribute a sermon on three events, the disciples singing a hymn in the upper room, the disciples sleeping in Gethsemane, and the disciples fleeing. The headings used alliteration (1) 'Canu yn ymyl bwrdd yr Iesu' (singing near Jesus' table), (2) 'Cysgu yn swn gweddi'r Iesu' (sleeping to the sound of Jesus' prayer) (3) 'Cilio o flaen ystorm yr Iesu' (fleeing before the storm of Jesus). These volumes contain many other similar examples. Sometimes the headings led to a climax rather than concentrating on alliteration. William Morris of Treorchy preached on 'I will sing with the spirit, and I will sing with the understanding also' based on 1 Corinthians 14: 15. The sermon's three headings were (1) 'Man under the government of nature', (2) 'Nature under the government of understanding', (3) 'Understanding under the government of the spirit'.[86] The problem with clever little headings like these is that they squeeze the biblical text into a preconceived framework, instead of allowing the sermon to elucidate the text. Far too often it became an excuse for the preacher to draw attention to his own talents.

Worse still was the desire to turn the content of sermons into poetry. If the poet-preachers turned poetry into religion, they also turned religion into poetry. One of the strangest sermons in *Pwlpud y Beirdd* is that by the editor, T. Gwernogle Evans, on the subject, 'And he carved all the walls of the house round about with carved figures of cherubims and palm trees and open flowers, within and without' (1 Kings 6: 29). The sermon is one long extravaganza of unfounded exposition, unrestrained allegorization and the drawing of frivolous conclusions. He claimed that the pictures on the walls of the Temple 'were the basis for the custom of papering and hanging pictures on the walls of our houses'. Then he turned to the decorations in the Temple hypothesizing that their purpose was to reveal God. The 'open flowers' reveal God's beauty, the palm tree reveals God's riches and generosity, 'and the cherub shows that God is strong and brave – active – that he moves swiftly, that he is also intelligent'.[87] There is not a scrap of scholarly justification for interpreting the Temple decorations in this way.

Gwernogle Evans's sermon is an extreme example but there were many others which exhibited the same trend. T. Talwyn Phillips of Bala published a book of sermons in 1903 bearing the title *Angel y Nos* (The Angel of the Night). Phillips was more securely grounded in scholarship than Gwernogle and had more discerning taste. He possessed an undisputed talent for creating memorable sayings such as 'The God of Elijah defends a nation in danger, but the God of Elisha defends a family in distress.'[88] However, he indulged considerably in the dubious practice that was growing in popularity, namely taking a meaningful phrase and constructing an edifice that was far too heavy for the foundation. To give one example, in a sermon on 'The Hymn of the Last Supper' based on Matthew 26. 30, Phillips said (1) 'that the Christian comes into possession of the song very slowly'; (2) 'that Jesus has a song for the night'; (3) 'that sacrifice and song dwell side by side'; (4) 'that the church of Jesus Christ is to walk down the centuries singing'. The first heading delineates a pure fantasy, as the first sentences of the exposition show: 'When the end was near, and Calvary was in sight, Jesus was heard singing for the first time in our world. This was for him a Vesper hymn. We must run the race for years before religion becomes a song and a pleasure.'[89] It is a preposterous idea that Jesus had never sung before the Last Supper and the suggestion that the Christian has no song in his heart until he has been a believer for years is completely at variance with almost all the available evidence. There is little point going into more detail because the principle behind this type of preaching is evident. The Bible was used as a kind of quarry from which illustrations could be mined to illustrate some wisdom or other which was found elsewhere. Yet Elfed heaped praise upon the volume: 'Were we asked to name the choicest half-dozen sermon volumes of the last twenty years, we would unhesitatingly place this among them.'[90] Whatever Elfed said, poetic preaching was on the whole like handwriting on a whitewashed wall. It could be very acceptable for a time, but it was a warning that Welsh preaching was losing its vigour.

To turn finally to historical preaching. We have seen several examples of this type of preaching concealed as it were within doctrinal preaching but more needs to be said. Because the influence of doctrinal preaching in Wales was so strong, there was a tendency for the historical parts of the Bible to be used as examples of some aspect or other of theology. One inevitable conclusion was that the idea of Christianity as narrative became much weaker while the concept of religion as a body of doctrine became stronger. Thus, together with the new interest in the Bible as a collection of historical documents – an interest which coincided with the development of biblical criticism – for many people the historical emphasis came like the dawning of a new truth.

Nevertheless it cannot be said that historical preaching had disappeared completely. When the realistic interpretation of historical parts of the Bible was at its strongest, preachers began to regard one event, or one character, in one part of that history as a reflection of an event or character in another part. Manna could be a figure of the Bread of Life, or Elijah could be a figure of John the Baptist. In 1885 Edward Matthews, Ewenni, was preaching at the Llanelli Calvinistic Methodist Association. He was preaching on 'that rest' which is mentioned in Hebrews 4. He referred in passing to the story in Numbers 13, about the spies who returned from Canaan bringing 'a cluster of grapes . . . between two upon a staff' together with other fruits, as proof that it was a good country. In the following account of the service Matthews describes the spies showing the grapes:

> 'Taste them!' The preacher sucked the ripe grapes with such enjoyment that Mrs E[lizabeth] Nicholas shouted, 'Wonderful!' 'Betsan's palate knows the taste of the grapes, you know. Others among you have also tried them. What kind of a country do you say that it is?' Many cried out in excitement 'A truly good country!' . . . 'Who wants to go there?' By this time scores of people in the gallery had risen to their feet and were shouting 'We shall go and occupy the country! . . .'[91]

It is impossible to make any sense of this account unless one is familiar with the biblical history that underpins it. Moreover there would be no hope for a congregation to react as the congregation did in Llanelli in 1885 were it not steeped in the same history. When Matthews said 'Betsan's palate . . . knows the taste of the grapes', he was using figurative language. The preacher was not referring to the grapes that the spies brought back; they had rotted centuries ago. He knew, however, and Betsan Nicholas knew, that her personal history, and her hope of heaven, could be linked with the history of the spies and their grapes and Israel's hope of entering Canaan. They took it for granted that the story in Numbers was to be read and understood as true history. In addition, one of Matthews's comments was omitted from the quotation above. Before he asked 'Who wants to go there?' he said, 'Ungodly men at the Association! Taste the grapes! And then you will never be heard asking for a drop of cold water to cool your tongue in hell.' Matthews not only saw this history, this true history, extending backwards, he also saw it stretching forwards. It ranges from the days of Moses, to the association meeting in 1885 in Llanelli, and onwards to eternity. The congregation who listened to him, believers and unbelievers, were part of that history and their spontaneous response proved that they knew that. One of the most fundamental changes in the minds of Welsh Christians – as in many other countries – was the loss of this understanding of biblical history.[92]

In 1893 an anonymous author made some significant comments on historical preaching. One type of sermon, he said, involves giving a brief summary of the history in the preface, and then establishing headings and preaching on them. 'This could hardly be called historical preaching'. The other kind is 'historical preaching from beginning to end'. The preacher 'does not let anything come between the history and the daily life of the listeners'.[93] A good example of this kind of sermon was by Hugh Hughes (Y Braich), on Job.[94] Although he declared in his preface that he did not intend to tackle the question whether the book of Job is history or a drama, 'since the same truths are taught in both', he took it as history and interpreted it in a realistic manner. The strength of this kind of preaching was (as we saw with Matthews and the grapes) that it taught the listener to view his or her own history as part of the history of the Bible. Thus people were convinced that the Bible portrayed a world that encompassed their own personal world and made it meaningful.

Many preachers fully realized the significance of biblical history. D. N. Jenkins spoke wisely when he said, 'The Gospel is history: and the revelation conveyed in history is understood most success-fully in the light of the circumstances in which the history is embodied.'[95] John Williams, Wrexham, tried to express the same conviction when he said, 'We must believe the facts of Christianity if we are to live the Christian life.'[96] These remarks and others similar to them echo the contemporary interest in the quest for the 'historical Jesus' and in the work of expositors such as George Adam Smith who was the means of bringing this new exegetical knowledge to the attention of many preachers.[97]

Indeed, the development of critical scholarship was beginning to shake the foundations of the type of preaching which took the biblical narrative as the framework for all other history. It became more difficult to read the historical portions of the Bible as real history. The question 'Did this really happen?' began to trouble preachers. Once these questions had been raised, revolutionary change was afoot. 'True' history was now secular history as understood by scientific historians. The biblical history had to be fitted into their history rather than fitting their history into the narrative of the Bible as before. Instead of culture being understood in the context of the Bible, there was now a demand for the Bible to be viewed within the context of culture.

For men like David Saunders, the Bible embraced everything. In his mighty sermon 'The Lord and Saviour', he held that the earth is under God's dominion, as are the 'stars, which wink in the night in their vast numbers, thousands of times more than the earth', and the spiritual world 'which is greater than the material creation'. God is Lord because he is the Saviour. 'As he reigns he completes his work as Saviour'. Thus for Saunders there was a direct link between the history of salvation, the world of nature, and the historical world because through Jesus Christ blessings pertaining to all three could be obtained. 'Not only redemption through His blood . . . and sanctification in the name of the Lord Jesus; but food and clothing, a home and the comforts of this world as well.' Thus the redeemed have a dramatic role to play on the stage of history because 'all the circumstances of the world and its times are in some way connected with the church. It is at the centre of the history of the world, as truly as the sun is at the centre of the *solar system*.'[98]

However, by the end of the century this vision of the breadth of the kingship of Christ, with its rich significance for history and culture, was under siege. From 1890 onwards preachers became more and more wary of making sweeping statements about the Kingdom of God. The Calvinistic Methodist David Lloyd Jones of Llandinam interpreted the Kingdom of God in an individualistic and pietistic way[99] and even before 1890 Edward Roberts, Pontypridd, portrayed a static if comprehensive picture of the Kingdom, contrasting starkly with Saunders's portrayal of it as a dynamic movement towards the future.[100]

By the end of the nineteenth century, preachers of the Word were facing a crisis that would undermine the convictions upon which Christianity and Welsh culture were based. Few preachers realized the extent of the danger. The tendency of the younger generation was to withdraw from the fray and preach poetic sermons which hardly got to grips with the difficulties implicit in interpreting the biblical history as parable and allegory. This path could only lead to bankruptcy. There were two other paths, however, that offered a better defence against the crashing waves of doubt. One was devotional preaching and the other was 'practical' preaching.

As has already been said, it was possible for preachers to see that the thread that held the Bible together was history and doctrine, or else the experience of the believer. The latter perspective became prominent in many kinds of sermons and especially in the poetic sermon. One obvious consequence of placing the connecting link between various parts of Christianity, or the Bible, within individual experience, was the weakening of the conviction that faith had involved anything to do with God's claim on human life and culture, and this in turn led to the idea that safeguarding intellectual consistency in doctrine was a futile task. Christianity became a private, individualistic and wholly subjective experience. These tendencies become evident in debates at the beginning of the twentieth century and where the influence of the Keswick Movement was strong, especially after the 1904–5 Revival, they had a pronounced influence on preaching. This deviation from the fullness of biblical Christianity should not however lead us to underestimate the contribution and value of devotional preaching. All the preachers take care to nourish the spiritual lives of their congregations and a host of excellent sermons were published to this end. In a powerful sermon on 'Seeking the Things that are Above', Thomas Davies of Treorchy, said:

> The world above exists. Mercifully it does. A world that is higher than the stars in heaven. A world that is more beautiful than the sun; a world of light, a world of contentment, a world of incomparable glory. And there are things that belong to that exalted world . . . The man who seeks them will be able to go up and up to its things for ever and ever; and this is the heaven for which my soul longs.[101]

The purpose of devotional preaching was to express and strengthen the various aspects of this desire, and there was a great need for it because of the powerful drive to secularize Welsh life. Sermons were preached not only on the reality of heaven but on the need for prayer, as in the discourse by John Roberts (Iolo Caernarfon) on 'The Conditions for Successful Prayer'[102] or in the sermon by J. J. Williams, Pen-y-groes, 'Asking the Father in the Name of the Son'.[103] Alternatively attention could be focused on the essential elements of the 'life of God in the soul of man'.[104] Different ways of enriching the spiritual life were examined by David John in 'A True Religious Revival'[105] and Robert Ambrose Jones (Emrys ap Iwan) in 'Spiritual Success'.[106] When the spiritual life was threatened by adverse circumstances, temptations and trials, preachers would invariably offer comfort and support.[107] In his sermon, 'Full Communion with God', Thomas Charles Williams rooted all Christian communion in the Holy Trinity.

> The love of the Spirit is the force behind all religious labours in all ages; not outward ordinances, not orthodoxy, not knowledge or enthusiasm, however valuable these things are, but faith in the Holy Spirit, and through him, and in him, full communion with God as a Trinity of persons.[108]

Of all the preachers of this period, however, Robert Ambrose Jones (Emrys ap Iwan) was the most consistent in his emphasis on nurturing the spiritual life. 'To have communion with God, you must put aside your common task, and go to your room and shut your door, in case the voices of creation should drown the voice of the Creator.'[109] He refused to believe that a devotion to worldly tasks and social activity excuses anyone from spiritual duties:

> the religious man, is a good man, a good trader, a good worker; but there is something extra as well; he is a godly man, a man with his face set towards heaven. There is an earthly vocation, and a heavenly vocation; and although the heavenly vocation encompasses the earthly vocation, the earthly vocation does not encompass the heavenly vocation.[110]

It is remarkable that the man who felt most keenly the cultural crisis that threatened the Welsh language and culture was also uncompromising in his emphasis on what many condemned as 'other-worldliness'. However Emrys ap Iwan was greatly concerned with safeguarding the completeness of Christianity and maintaining an equilibrium between its various aspects.

In a blistering piece of writing we find him complaining that Welsh preachers 'have restricted themselves too much to what is called evangelical preaching'. What he meant was the preaching of Christianity merely as a system of doctrine. The pastor's responsibility rather was to preach the whole counsel of God. 'Preaching like the preaching of Jesus', he said, 'is the true evangelical preaching; preaching that deals unceremoniously with men as they are, and not with remote teaching obscured by theological terms.' He wanted the people of Wales to walk uprightly as well as to believe rightly: 'We have had generation after generation of excellent preachers teaching us to be religious – and Pharisaic in the bargain; but when will another generation of preachers rise up and teach us to be moral?' The efforts of the preachers of Wales would not lead to true revival 'while there is so much treacle and so little salt in our preaching'.[111] To what extent were there grounds for the complaint that Wales's preachers did not pay sufficient attention to moral issues? An older generation of preachers dealt with the issue of sanctification in line with Protestant tradition, making a clear distinction between justification and sanctification.

> A common error among listeners of the Gospel is that they try to serve God in chains, they seek sanctification before forgiveness, and improve themselves before they come to the divine doctor. Only in forgiveness is it possible for sanctification to blossom; it is in the soil of justification that God grows the flowers of virtue.[112]

These are the strains of the true Protestant faith. If justification comes through faith alone, the same was not so with sanctification. Human striving had a key role in the latter. According to William Roberts, Llanrwst, God must 'turn the instincts of the soul into servants to take forward salvation in us'.[113] It is striking to note how the sermons of the younger preachers treat the moral life without recourse to the language of 'sanctification'. In *Cyflawnder Bendith* (The Fullness of Blessing) published in 1914, William Thomas of Llanrwst held forth invigoratingly on 'The Tender Virtues of Religion'; W. E. Prytherch preached on the 'pure Church'; John Williams, Brynsiencyn, on 'Conduct Worthy of the Gospel of Christ'; and it is a pleasure to read J. Puleston Jones's 'That which she did also'. In comparison with previous collections, such as *Y Pulpud Bedyddiedig* (The Baptist Pulpit, 1888), *Trydedd Jiwbili y Cyfundeb* (The Third Jubilee of the Connexion, 1893) and *Pulpud Annibynol Ceredigion* (The Independent Pulpit of Cardiganshire, 1903), this volume contains more moralistic preaching. The increase can perhaps be attributed to the call for more 'practical preaching'. Even so, the references are general and there is no

attempt to discuss specific sins. A sermon such as that of
E. Vaughan Humphreys, 'The Sin of Taking God's Name in Vain',[114]
was a rarity in the period, as was the attack on war in Josiah
Towyn Jones's sermon, 'The Great Social Change'.[115] On the whole –
at least in the printed sermons – it was not common practice to
devote an entire sermon to the discussion of a specific sin. It was not
considered acceptable to attack specific sins even occasionally, apart
from drinking or drunkenness.

The reason for this is not easy to explain. It could be argued that
the public pulpit is not a suitable place to discuss specific sins.
Certainly, it is not the place to inveigh against the moral difficulties
of individual persons. The minister's study or counselling room
would be the place to give such help, and in the Catholic tradition
and among high church Anglicans confession was an intrinsic part
of the Christian life. However the pulpit is indubitably a suitable
place to discuss moral principles and specific sins in light of the
Bible. Perhaps ministers felt that public opinion was sufficiently
influential to ensure that moral standards were kept. It may be that
the accusation that religious leaders uncritically accepted the bourgeois morality of their generation has some grounds. Whatever the
reason, the evidence of the printed sermon shows that ministers
shirked their responsibility as moral critics of their age. It would
appear, therefore, that Emrys ap Iwan's accusation can be substantiated, but he – like the firebrand R. B. Jones, Porth – was noted in
his generation for his passionate ethical stance. Not for nothing did
Emrys read Immanuel Kant:

> The old strongholds of Wales, and the insubstantial castles built in the
> air, they will have the same end. The views from the top of Snowdon,
> and the visions of the 'Sleeping Bard', will all come to an end at the
> same time. The only thing that will last is obedience, the obedience of
> love, and this will last for eternity.[116]

For Emrys ap Iwan it was only that which was moral that would
survive.[117] He realized that the preachers' silence on this matter was
a much greater danger to church members than to those who made
no religious profession at all. Their religiosity could easily stand
between them and salvation, as he explained in a discussion of
Paul's self-description as the chief of sinners.

I do not think that the apostle was merely the chief of sinners in his own sight; he was the chief of sinners in God's sight also. And I shall tell you why he was the chief of sinners – because he was the most religious sinner that ever walked the earth. He was a self-righteous sinner; a sinner who never considered himself a sinner, a sinner who presumed that he was doing God a service by persecuting His church; and a conscientious, religious sinner of this kind is the hardest sinner to save of all.[118]

What we see in the period between 1890 and 1914 is that the preaching tradition that did so much to shape modern Wales was beginning to disintegrate. There was much excellent preaching, of course, but it was no longer a formative influence on the thought, culture and morality of the nation. Doctrinal preaching maintained its pre-eminence but it was beginning to lose its vigour, either because it was turning into a weary repetition of worn-out theological truths or because it embraced opinions that dulled its spiritual force. In consequence there developed a reaction against doctrine and the undisciplined allegorization of fancy and poetic preaching began to undermine the pulpit's gravitas. Generally speaking the pulpit reneged on its responsibility to keep daily before Welsh eyes the gravity of sin and contented itself with mentioning general principles now and then. In all, there were definite signs of a crisis in the pulpit.

~ 8 ~

The Strange Story of
'the Free Church of the Welsh'

It often happens in the study of history that a local and short-lived crisis captures the atmosphere of a particular period in a dramatic way. Characters in conflict sometimes give expression to the feelings, worries, concerns and prejudices that characterized their society. The incident from which the so-called 'Free Church of the Welsh' emerged was just such a revealing crisis.

The backdrop for this drama was late nineteenth-century Liverpool. At the time it was one of the main centres of Welsh (and Welsh-speaking) life. By 1891, there were 60,819 Welsh people living in Lancashire compared with only 50,079 in Anglesey,[1] and there were at least 30,000 Welsh people living in Liverpool itself. It is hardly surprising that many thought of Liverpool as the capital city of north Wales. All the denominations had chapels there, and the Calvinistic Methodists were the most influential with a dozen churches and a membership of 5,456. During the century Liverpool had enjoyed the ministry of some of the most prominent religious leaders of the Welsh nation – William Williams, Y Wern, Henry Rees and his brother William (Gwilym Hiraethog), Owen Thomas and his brother John, among others.

In line with this tradition, the Calvinistic Methodist ministers of Liverpool at the end of the nineteenth century were men of influence. John Hughes (1850–1932) was the minister of Fitzclarence Road. He had obtained his MA from Glasgow University and was the author of the Davies Lecture in 1902. Griffith Ellis (1844–1913) was the minister of Stanley Road, Bootle. Ellis was a graduate of Balliol College, Oxford, on intimate terms with its remarkable Master, Benjamin Jowett, and a fellow student of H. H. Asquith. According to the historian Thomas Richards, he 'was the most respected man in the whole of the Methodist world; better still, he deserved total respect'.[2] Then, in Princes Road, 'the most important church in the Connexion',[3] was John Williams (1854–1921), whose aristocratic presence and mastery of the classical preaching style made the name of the village of Brynsiencyn, Anglesey, as famous in Wales as the name of Liverpool. But John Williams's popularity was hardly greater than that of Hugh Jones, DD (1830–1911), Owen Thomas's successor at Netherfield Road (subsequently Douglas Road), who served his apprenticeship as a shopkeeper with John Elias's son in Llanfechell and imbibed the virtue of the past when he slept in the former study of the 'seraph of Anglesey'.[4] Owen J. Owen was the secretary of the Liverpool Monthly Meeting in 1900, a fellow student of John Williams in Bala College and the minister of Rock Ferry since 1884.[5] He should not be confused with Owen Owens (1843–1920), who ministered at Cranmer Street from 1872 onwards and moved with the church to Anfield in 1878, a man who was, throughout his life, one of the 'foremost pillars' of the temperance movement.[6] These mighty men, and others yet to be mentioned, were to play a prominent part in this tale.

The church which will be the focus of our attention in this chapter is Chatham Street. In 1899 it had 467 members, compared with Princes Road where there were 1,051. There were six elders and an unusual collection of preachers, five in all. The minister of the church was William Owen Jones (1861–1937), the son of Pen-bryn, Chwilog, Caernarfonshire. The foundations of his education were laid in the schools of Llanystumdwy, Holt and Clynnog.[7] He subsequently attended Bala College, the University College of North Wales, Bangor, and St John's College, Cambridge, where he graduated with a second-class degree in philosophy. After his ordination in 1892, he was inducted as minister in Waunfawr near Caernarfon and in 1895 he moved to Chatham Street. By that time he was considered to be a very cultured young man of extraordinary promise.

As the demands upon him as a speaker and preacher increased, so his health began to fail. On 6 January 1899 he was on Lime Street station on his way to Wales for a short rest. Also there was John Jones, Sefton, Prestatyn, and the two men met for the first time. During their conversation, W. O. Jones mentioned that his doctor had advised him that he must rest and, indeed, had suggested that it would be beneficial for him, if possible, to go on a cruise. John Jones pricked up his ears. He was an official with a shipping company, John Glynn & Son, and he offered to arrange a cruise for the ailing young minister. The arrangements were swiftly made and on Thursday, 19 January 1899, Jones embarked on one of the company's ships, the steamer *Vito*, for the Mediterranean. There was a terrible storm on the Irish Sea and they did not reach Southampton, where they were supposed to pick up cargo, until Monday afternoon. Fortunately John Jones was there to meet the ship, since William Jones was in quite a pitiful condition after the gruelling journey. The shipping official bade him farewell and the young minister set off for the sun. The therapy was more than successful and when he returned on 17 March he had been fully restored to health. But if he had cause to be thankful for the restorative quality of the cruise, he would soon rue the day that he had ever set foot on board the ship.[8]

In April 1899, less than a month after William Jones resumed his work, a pastoral crisis arose. A church member was accused of immorality. The fellowship called upon the elders to apply the rules of the denomination and to discipline the offender. The facts of the case were considered and it was found that the case was proven. The next question was to decide what punishment would be appropriate. The minister's opinion, together with that of Eliezer Pugh and John J. Bebb, two of the elders, was that the expulsion of the offender for a fixed term would be a suitable punishment.[9] Not so, said the majority of the elders, the appropriate punishment would be to excommunicate him permanently. After weeks of dispute it was finally agreed to lay the matter before the congregation and this was done on the evening of Thursday, 13 July.[10] Following deliberation, the matter was put to the vote and the majority of the church sided with the minister and the two elders who agreed with him; the lighter of the two punishments was to be administered. The four elders who were opposed, namely John Jones (not the shipping officer who had arranged the minister's cruise), J. W. Jones, William Jones and William Williams, were exceedingly angry. On the night of Monday, 17 July, the minister was summoned to meet the elders and informed that three of the four wished to resign. Only John Jones declined to do so, although he held the most stoutly to his opinion. The minister's response was that he would also resign.[11] The following evening, 18 July, the three elders who wished to resign called upon W. O. Jones in his lodgings. After considerable discussion they succeeded in making their peace and it was agreed that everyone would keep his position and thereafter they would work together harmoniously as a team.[12] Tranquillity reigned for a short time. W. O. Jones departed on his annual summer holiday and returned at the end of August full of enthusiasm for the winter's work.

However, the minister's first meeting of the new season was one that he would remember for the rest of his life. This was the *seiat* or fellowship meeting on the evening of Thursday, 7 September 1899.[13] The following is the account of the meeting given by William Williams, the minister's most prominent critic. 'Mr W. O. Jones entered with his hair in disarray and with an unnatural gait . . .' When he rose to his feet to speak he was forced to grasp the table with both hands. 'His speech was altered and he also spoke more slowly than usual . . .' During his address he repeated some sentences unnecessarily. 'His voice was also more indistinct'.[14] There was some whispering in the congregation, said Humphrey Lloyd, and he turned to his fellow member, Richard Jones, and asked him if Mr W. O. Jones was ill.[15] At the end of the *seiat* a baptism was held. According to William Williams, the minister mistook the nurse who was presenting the baby for the mother during his prayer. At the conclusion of the meeting, Humphrey Lloyd approached William Williams, and told him that the minister smelt of drink and that he had better escort him home. 'Be careful,' said Williams, 'and do not breathe a word to anybody, it is possible that he is ill.'[16]

Immediately after the *seiat* and the baptism, the meeting of the Christian Endeavour Society was held. During that meeting, W. O. Jones sat immediately in front of William Williams, and according to the latter, when 'he wished to say something he would turn to me and my face would be near his face, and I noticed immediately that he smelt strongly of alcoholic drink, unmistakably so'.[17]

The meeting came to an end. William Williams escorted the minister to his lodgings and voiced his suspicions to him. W. O. Jones placed his hand on Williams's shoulder and said that he need not worry, that he himself was a teetotaller. 'I know, Mr Jones,' said Williams, 'your name is on the temperance book of the church, written with your own hand; but what was that smell?' Jones replied, 'I never touch a drop, you can be sure of that, only a glass of whisky sometimes on a Sunday night'.[18]

The evidence of William Williams was corroborated by

Humphrey Lloyd. The minister denied the story. He admitted that Williams had accompanied him to his lodgings for supper and that he had voiced his suspicion that the minister was drunk. After conversing on this matter, Williams acknowledged that he had made a mistake. The next thing that happened, according to the minister, was that:

> he begged me earnestly not to utter another word on the subject. I took him at his word, and I presumed that the matter had been buried for ever. What will the reader think when I say that Mr Williams had expressed his doubts to three other people on that same evening, and to another one before three days had gone by?

Clearly disconcerted by the actions of these members, W. O. Jones claimed that 'This was the beginning of the rumours about me.'[19]

These unpleasant incidents occurred on 7 September. All was quiet until Sunday, 29 October. That evening a letter, signed by the four elders who failed to get their own way in the disciplinary matter in July, enquired of the Monthly Meeting of the presbytery whether it was consistent with the rules of the denomination for a church to choose between a temporary expulsion and excommunication as a punishment for immorality. The four insisted that their colleague, J. J. Bebb, also sign the letter. He refused, saying that the matter should have been raised months previously, when the issue first came under discussion.[20]

The letter was considered by the presbytery meeting of 8 November 1899. Following discussion, a decision was reached in favour of excommunication rather than temporary expulsion. The Monthly Meeting thus justified the stand of the majority of the elders of Chatham Street, while at the same time condemning the standpoint of W. O. Jones, and the church's verdict during the meeting of 13 July. Since the Monthly Meeting had not seen fit to support him in this matter, on the Thursday after the presbytery meeting, W. O. Jones tendered his resignation to the elders. An opportunity arose for the church to discuss the matter on 20 November in a meeting which turned out to be bizarre. According to W. O. Jones:

> the officials one after another offered the highest commendation of my character and among the tributes of praise none was more fulsome than

those of Mr William Williams and Mr William Jones . . . At the end of the meeting I received a strong vote of confidence, and it was made clear that I should continue in my position.

The vote was virtually unanimous with just three or four opposed.[21]

It is quite obvious that the bulk of the church was furious with the eldership, despite the support that the elders had received from the Monthly Meeting. Some heated remarks were made in the church meeting which hurt some of the elders deeply. It was apparent by now that outside help was needed to pour oil on the waters. On Friday, 24 November 1899, Dr Hugh Jones, John Williams (Princes Road), and Hugh Jones (Trisant) came to try to restore peace. During their meeting with the elders the only issue that was discussed was that of the denomination's disciplinary rules. Not one word was mentioned concerning the accusations regarding W. O. Jones's personal conduct. When the next church meeting was held on 30 November, the minister persuaded the church to pass a vote expressing its confidence in the elders. Peace, it seemed, had been restored.

It was, however, an uneasy peace. The cauldron was still simmering and bubbling. William Williams, the church secretary, began refusing to convene elders' meetings and he arranged that communion should be administered in the minister's absence. There was little wonder that before long W. O. Jones was suffering from extreme nervous tension and lack of sleep. At the end of February the doctor advised him to take a complete break from his duties so on Friday, 2 March 1900, he offered his resignation to the elders once more. On the next day, a Saturday, his ministerial colleagues Griffith Ellis and William Jones (Balliol Road),[22] went to see W. O. Jones and pleaded with him not to resign. They succeeded in their attempt and Ellis visited all the elders of Chatham Street in turn to persuade them not to announce the minister's resignation. If there was anyone who could restore order without causing offence it was Griffith Ellis, the wise and respected minister at Bootle, and to all appearances he had succeeded in his task.

Suddenly, however, the peace was shattered. In obedience to his doctor's advice, W. O. Jones returned to Wales for a break, leaving Liverpool on Tuesday, 6 March 1900. Before he left he gave permission to Griffith Ellis, John Williams (Princes Road) and

Dr Hugh Jones to meet with the officials of Chatham Street to reconcile the different factions. It was, alas, to no avail. The elders
refused to meet them. Moreover, on Sunday, 11 March, they saw
fit to inform the church that the minister had resigned, and
announced that there would be a church meeting on the following
Thursday night, 15 March, to discuss the matter. It is obvious that
something major had occurred. According to W. O. Jones, between
2 March and 15 March 'a raging torrent of all sorts of tales about
me flowed out of somewhere'.[23] Being informed of the gravity of
the situation, he returned to Liverpool in order to be present at the
church meeting on 15 March.

One of the elders, J. W. Jones, presided over the meeting. He
informed the congregation that he, together with William
Williams, William Jones and John Jones, his fellow elders, had
decided that they could no longer work with W. O. Jones. One
member stood up and proposed that they should ask the Monthly
Meeting to hold an inquiry into the whole affair. The proposal was
seconded by W. O. Jones himself and passed unanimously. This
request was sent to the presbytery and in its next meeting, 28 March
1900, it decided to act upon the request and appointed a committee
to look into the troubles at Chatham Street.[24]

It is important to remember that the only matter under consideration was the dispute between the members of the Chatham Street
church and their elders, and between the church and the Monthly
Meeting. For all the public knew, no other subject would be discussed
by the Monthly Meeting's Committee. More importantly, this also was
what the minister presumed, which is why, of course, he was so eager
to support the decision to request an investigation committee. It would
soon transpire that the committee's remit had been changed.

The committee met for the first time on Friday, 30 March 1900,
in Chatham Street. W. O. Jones was present.[25] His critics immediately set about expanding the boundaries of the inquiry. The
church elders, J. W. Jones, William Williams and William Jones,
expressed their doubts regarding their minister's sobriety and intim-
ated that he had been drunk even in some of the church meetings.
This evidently came as a shock to W. O. Jones. This was the first
time that he had heard these accusations being made since the
evening of 7 September 1899, when William Williams had retracted
his words and apologized for mentioning them.[26]

However, there is reason to believe that W. O. Jones was incorrect in this claim and it must be borne in mind that he had not seen the minutes of the committee of investigation when he wrote his defence in the newspaper, Y Cymro, towards the end of that year. In fact, J. J. Bebb had testified to the committee that he had warned the minister in November 1899 that he should be on his guard because rumours were circulating which cast doubt on his sobriety. Bebb was a reliable witness in this regard precisely because he was strongly on the minister's side. He also testified that the real reason for the elders' request that the Monthly Meeting discuss the matter of discipline was their suspicions concerning W. O. Jones's sobriety, although this was not mentioned in their letter.[27] It was only in the first meeting of the inquiry committee that it dawned on W. O. Jones that issues other than the denomination's disciplinary rules were to be tabled.

It is difficult to understand why the chairman, Dr Hugh Jones, did not insist that the only question to be decided was whether the minister would be allowed to resign. He had, after all, tendered his resignation to the elders. The church was about to be torn apart. W. O. Jones's health was failing. It was hard to believe that there was any future for his ministry in Chatham Street. It would appear that the wisest course would have been to ensure that Jones left the church in the least painful way possible, but matters did not turn out thus. Not only did the committee consider the accusations against W. O. Jones but we have the committee's own statement that it found the accusations to be substantiated.[28] On the following day, 31 March, W. O. Jones was called to a further meeting of the committee in Crosshall Street. There is conflicting evidence about what happened there. According to W. O. Jones, 'I was informed by the president that they were in unanimous agreement that it would be better for me to abide by my resignation. They agreed that the accusations concerning drunkenness & c. did not merit further consideration.'[29] The committee, however, interpreted the situation differently. For them there was a case to answer as they were convinced that Jones was guilty of drunkenness.[30] In a later review of events, both the committee and W. O. Jones agreed that he told the committee on that Saturday that he would resign, but there was disagreement concerning the condition that he placed on his resignation. According to the minister, he agreed to resign providing that the committee placed before the church a motion declaring that the further accusations of drunkenness did not merit consideration.[31] The committee's recollection was that it would go to Chatham Street and exercise its influence to persuade the members to agree to their minister's decision to resign; and to do this publicly.[32] Whereas W. O. Jones wanted to ensure that he was able to resign and to clear his character at the same time, the committee wished to ensure that he could resign without his critics voicing their concerns about his character. Whatever happened, it is evident that the committee members were extremely careless in their failure to draw up a detailed motion and record it accurately.

The following evening, Sunday, 1 April, Dr Hugh Jones and John Williams (Princes Road), were in Chatham Street to place these issues before the congregation. Hugh Jones spoke and listed the accusations against W. O. Jones without making any comment one way or the other concerning the guilt of the accused. It is also fairly obvious that he contented himself with conveying the *substance* of the committee's decision without taking the trouble to read it out to the congregation.[33] After speaking he called upon the minister to inform the church of his resignation. W. O. Jones rose to his feet and said that he was prepared to resign on condition that he could do so without a hint of stain upon his character. To ensure this, he demanded a clearer declaration concerning his guilt than that made by Hugh Jones. Without such a declaration, it was the church's duty to refuse his resignation. When the congregation heard this, they began to applaud enthusiastically. John Williams stood up to try to restore order. 'If Mr Jones's resignation is accepted here tonight,' he said, 'he will leave here with his reputation intact.' The minister's resignation was put to a vote, but not one hand was raised in favour of accepting it. By now tempers were running high and John Williams left threatening that 'the church and the minister would regret what had been done'.[34] It was evident that W. O. Jones was still assured of the support of the vast majority of his congregation.

As the saga unfolded, the unfortunate minister had happier things to think about. On 5 April 1900, in Stanley Road chapel, Bootle, he married Ceridwen, the fourth daughter of William Jones (Balliol Road). Griffith Ellis officiated at the service, and the groom's servants were J. E. Hughes, Caernarfon, and W. L. Jones, professor of English at the University College of North Wales.[35] On Monday, 9 July, a very enjoyable meeting was held in Chatham Street to present the minister and his new wife with 'a gilded address and a purse of gold' and enthusiastic comments were made about the success of his ministry.[36]

Nevertheless, he could not long escape from the attention of the Monthly Meeting. In the meeting of 1 April, the church had rebelled against the Monthly Meeting's decision. From the denomination's point of view, the investigating committee had obviously bungled its work. Hugh Jones had presided over the committee in a very clumsy fashion and had made a complete hash of the meeting in Chatham Street. As a result, John Williams, the minister at Princes Road and a much more dangerous man to tangle with than Hugh Jones, was very angry indeed. When the presbytery next met, on 9 May, it was decided that, since the Chatham Street church had refused to accept the minister's resignation, a further investigation must be held. A second committee of investigation was appointed, its purpose being this time to discuss W. O. Jones's character and the accusations concerning his morals. Thus, on 17 May, a delegation under the leadership of Dr Hugh Jones went to convey the Monthly Meeting's decision to the congregation of Chatham Street. They were informed bluntly that W. O. Jones was no longer their minister. Three days later in a meeting of the elders, confirmed by a church meeting on 24 May, the church expressed its loyalty to the minister and passed a motion 'that we do not see sufficient reason for severing our connection with him'.

Meanwhile the second committee of investigation had begun its work. It met for the first time in the vestry of Crosshall Street chapel on Friday, 18 May 1900. All the members were present – Dr Hugh Jones in the chair, William Jones as secretary, John Williams (Princes Road) and Owen Owens, together with the lay members, William Jones (Breeze Hill), William Evans, Edward Ellis and William Patton. The committee held fifteen sittings, the last on 10 July 1900, and it submitted its report to the Monthly Meeting on 11 July. Most importantly, William Jones kept detailed and careful records of all that was said.[37]

We come now to the most unsavoury part of the story. The committee decided to scour the country for witnesses who could shed any light on W. O. Jones's private habits. The committee concentrated its attention on two subjects, namely, the doubts about his sobriety and the events during the cruise of the *Vito* in the Mediterranean.

They began with the accusation that W. O. Jones had a weakness for alcohol. A list was made of those people within the church and outside who knew about the personal habits of the accused and steps were taken to summon them before the committee to question them. The first witnesses to be questioned were the elders of Chatham Street. J. J. Bebb was not able to attend but sent a letter of apology and added, 'I must state most emphatically that during the seven years that I have known Mr Jones, I have never seen him touch or taste any intoxicating drink whatsoever nor yet, to my knowledge, under the influence of it.'[38]

This evidence was corroborated by Eliezer Pugh who believed that there was no case at all against the minister. Armed with the evidence of Humphrey Lloyd, the committee began to sift through the events of the *seiat* and the baptism and of the Christian Endeavour Meeting on 1 September 1899. Lloyd maintained that there was something about the minister that night 'that made him appear to behave differently from usual'. Lloyd confessed that he was so agitated in his mind that he was unable to lead the singing on the following Sunday 'because I was rather upset on account of what I had seen'. Under cross-examination Lloyd could not say exactly what was unusual about the minister on that evening but that he prayed in a rather more measured fashion than he generally did and that he mistook the nurse who presented the baby for its mother. He admitted that he could not smell drink on the minister's breath. Indeed, 'he could not smell anything . . . he [the minister] was eating sweets at the time'! Since the elders were being interviewed individually William Williams, who was interviewed next, did not know that he was contradicting the evidence of Humphrey Lloyd when he claimed that it was Lloyd who had told him that W. O. Jones 'smelt' of drink. He told the gathering how he had escorted the minister to his lodgings at the close of the meeting and had spoken with him. When he was asked whether he had seen signs of the minister's drunkenness on any subsequent occasion he replied that he had seen such signs on the evening of the Harvest Thanksgiving meeting, 16 October 1899, and afterwards in a prayer meeting on 26 February 1900. He also said that it was these instances that had caused the four elders to say in the church meeting of 15 March 1900 that they could no longer work together with their minister.

All of a sudden William Williams pulled a red herring across the committee's track. It had come to his attention 'recently', he claimed, that some had contended that his motive for opposing the minister was his (the minister's) courtship with Williams's daughter, Dora. The rumour was that Jones had promised to marry Dora but that he had, instead, married Ceridwen Jones. The girl had died and, according to gossip, had gone to her grave of a broken heart.[39] Williams denied that any courtship had taken place and he also denied that there was any ill feeling between himself and W. O. Jones. Dora had been ill for four years and the minister had paid her regular pastoral visits during this sad period.

The next red herring raised by William Williams concerned the relationship between himself and his son, Lloyd Williams. On Sunday, 6 May 1900, J. J. Bebb asked W. O. Jones in the presence of the elders whether he had claimed that there was a dispute between William Williams and his children, Dora and Lloyd. W. O. Jones replied that Lloyd Williams had shared his lodgings for some time following a dispute between him and his parents and that Lloyd Williams had entrusted to him the letters between himself and his parents in the hope that, as their minister, Jones could bring about a reconciliation. Williams Williams wrote to his son at once to ask what was the truth of all this. Lloyd's answer, on a postcard from Clynnog School dated 9 May 1900, stated: '1. I have never slept at W. O. Jones's lodgings. 2. I have never shown him a letter and I have only spoken of the matter once to him. Lloyd.' In response to a second letter from his father, Lloyd replied on 14 May 1900 in stronger language, saying 'W. O. Jones's claim that I have slept in his lodgings is a complete untruth'. In addition to that, the minister could not have seen William Williams's letters because he, Lloyd, had burnt them after having replied.[40] This accusation that W. O. Jones was distorting the truth was going to stick.

Williams had not finished, however. While W. O. Jones was away on his Mediterranean cruise, between January and March 1899, Williams had visited his lodgings to make some enquiries of the landlady, Miss Morris, regarding the minister. During their conversation, Miss Morris said, 'I always find, Mr Williams, that when Mr Jones does not drink spirits but confines himself to claret, his health is much better'. This suggested to Williams and to the committee that W. O. Jones had been in the habit of drinking quite heavily in the privacy of his lodgings, and this issue would be addressed in due course. The committee's task meanwhile was to proceed to hear the evidence of the Chatham Street elders. William

Jones confirmed that W. O. Jones was occasionally the worse for drink and that he, like William Williams, had received confirmation of his suspicions by speaking to Miss Morris. The last of the elders to give evidence, J. W. Jones, had little to add, apart from confirming that W. O. Jones was occasionally under the influence of drink. Having gleaned this information, the committee adjourned.

There is no doubt that the issue of drink was pivotal to the case. Later in the sittings, William Jones, the elder, said that 'the question of drinking is at the root of the whole matter'. This is what had compelled him to sign a letter to the Monthly Meeting on 29 October. This was behind the disciplinary issue and the reason for W. O. Jones's resignation as well.[41] It is no wonder that the committee made considerable efforts to gather information about this matter, and this was no easy task. To take the evidence given by W. O. Jones's landlady for instance, Miss Caroline Morris denied emphatically that she had ever mentioned the claret to William Williams. It is true that his doctor had advised W. O. Jones to take claret with his dinner and sleeping powder in whisky before going to bed but when the doctor ordered him to cease this treatment, W. O. Jones obeyed immediately.[42]

Miss Morris could not be cross-examined because her doctor forbade her to go to the committee and her evidence was given by letter. Nevertheless, it is quite clear whom she supported. There were also the maids who had been in service in the house. One of their number, Ellen Jane Edwards, mentioned carrying whisky bottles to W. O. Jones's room during her period of service between March 1899 and January 1900. She claimed that Miss Morris and he would be up late drinking and there were empty bottles around the place in the morning, but she never saw W. O. Jones drunk. She heard another maid, Elizabeth Heycock, saying of W. O. Jones that he was not fit to be a minister of the gospel.[43] Written evidence was received from Elizabeth Heycock and the only thing she had to add was that she saw W. O. Jones arriving at the house near midnight on Bank Holiday, 7 August 1899, that he was the worse for drink and that he greeted her in a manner not fitting for a minister.[44]

Realizing that the case rested too heavily on innuendo, rumour, suspicion and unproven conclusions, the committee searched for stronger evidence. W. O. Jones had attended the wedding of John Williams, the minister of Princes Road church, in Cemais,

Anglesey, in May 1899.[45] William and James Venmore were travelling with him and gave evidence that W. O. Jones was in the saloon and 'in their opinion obviously under the influence of alcohol'.[46] James Venmore was married to the daughter of David Hughes of Wylfa, Cemais, while John Williams's wife was another of David Hughes's daughters, Edith Mary.[47] James Venmore and David Hughes were elders in the church at Anfield where Owen Owens was a minister and the evidence of the brothers was obtained through Dr Hugh Jones and William Jones. However, neither was prepared to appear before the committee.[48] It seems that innuendo was being given credence once more.

The evidence of Aethwy Jones fared little better. In an interview with William Jones (Breeze Hill) he had ventured his opinion that W. O. Jones had penned his resignation 'in a drunken debauch'. When asked whether he had ever seen W. O. Jones intoxicated, he refused to answer, saying that his reply would 'get two other people' into trouble.[49] He remained silent in the committee's next meeting, although the members tried to persuade him that 'arriving at the truth was much more important than anything which might be classed as a secret'.[50] However he was betrayed in a further meeting of the committee when the Revd David Jones (Edge Lane) said that he had heard Aethwy say that 'he had seen W. O. Jones drunk and that Mr J. E. Hughes, Caernarfon, was with him in the house at the time'. He also said that Aethwy had shared another secret with him, namely that W. O. Jones claimed that 'he had done worse things than get drunk'. David Jones confessed that this information was entrusted to him as a secret but that he was of the opinion that 'there was something in this matter that was more important than concealing a secret'. The committee was exceptionally grateful to him,[51] but in the warmth of its gratitude it omitted to interrogate David Jones for solid evidence to back up the rumours, and the rumours of rumours that he submitted for its attention. Moreover, Aethwy lost his temper and accused David Jones of lying before turning to the committee and 'calling it a Court of Inquisition'. The committee, not unreasonably, considered that an attack of this kind was completely unwarranted and unfair.[52] The committee was no more successful with another highly revered Calvinistic Methodist preacher, Thomas Charles Williams. Although Dr Hugh Jones and William Evans went all the way to Anglesey to question him, he refused to say a thing.[53] The truth was that it was very difficult to come by solid evidence concerning W. O. Jones's alleged drunkenness.

Another red herring which the committee pursued more in despair than in hope was W. O. Jones's accident in Bold Street, Liverpool. One Miss Thomas, Marmion Street, gave evidence that she had seen W. O. Jones on the evening of Saturday, 6 January 1900, in Myrtle Street, 'walking aimlessly about, his hat on one side',[54] looking like a man under the influence of drink. Soon an omnibus driver was found who had witnessed the same incident. The driver was a fellow Welshman called Thomas Davies, who said how he had been driving 'one of Mason's vehicles' between seven and eight o'clock and that he had seen W. O. Jones 'crossing the bottom of Bold Street and heading in the direction of the front of the Central Station'. He was walking unsteadily and 'after reaching the front of the Station he began hitting himself against the wall like a man heavily under the influence of drink'.[55] Davies appeared again before the committee to reiterate his evidence and added that he had seen W. O. Jones in Upper Parliament Street 'some time after that'. On that occasion he was 'in an open carriage, with a cloak over him, and something on his face, and an elderly woman in the carriage with him'.[56] As a sign of their gratitude, the committee saw fit to reimburse Thomas Davies for the day's work that he had missed in order to appear before them.

The committee had spent a lot of time and energy investigating the matter of W. O. Jones's drunkenness, but the events during the cruise of the *Vito* were yet to be examined. The captain on the cruise, which lasted from January to March 1899, was Isaac Jarvis. More than a year later, on 23 May 1900, Dr Hugh Jones and John Williams, Princes Road, like a Methodist Dr Watson and Sherlock Holmes, got off the train at Prestatyn Station in order to interview Captain Jarvis. He was ill and had been ordered to remain in his bed for two months. His tongue, however, was in the best of health. He told the two ministers that he would not sit under the ministry of such a man as W. O. Jones because his behaviour was unworthy of a minister of the gospel and, more specifically, he told them of his conversations with a Mr Taylor, one of the other passengers. Captain Jarvis's opinion of him was that 'he was an immoral man' because his conversation was 'so impure and corrupt'.[57] It is easy to imagine the two reverend detectives perched on the edge of their seats in anticipation of earth-shattering revelations. 'Did it not strike you that there was something wrong with him?', they asked. 'Yes,' said Jarvis. 'I thought he was mad'. He proceeded to describe in detail the drink that he had procured for the minister. On one occasion, the captain had purchased a crate of twelve bottles of whisky for his clerical passenger. By this time, the bedroom must have been in a veritable spin as the intrepid preachers pondered upon such oceans of whisky. Their hearts, though, must have sunk at the invalid's next words: 'I cannot say that I ever saw him drunk.' He admitted however that he had seen W. O. Jones 'under the influence of intoxicating drink'. What proof did the captain have of that? 'He was speaking foolishly and behaving in a *jolly* manner.' The invalided seaman was also convinced that W. O. Jones and his companion, the shadowy Mr Taylor, had been up to no good. Their unsavoury conversation about morally dubious haunts in the different parts visited suggested as much. 'Do you believe that corrupt and impure deeds had been committed in these places?' The two visitors were insistent. Jarvis's reply was quite simply, 'Yes'.[58]

Captain Jarvis died on 2 July leaving behind him an insoluble puzzle. His evidence was a complete mystery to W. O. Jones. He was an 'exceptionally religious and cultured man although he was a bit of a "goody-goody" ', he said, and his statements made no sense at all.[59] Naturally, W. O. Jones sought evidence to disprove Jarvis's assertions. He obtained it in the form of an affidavit sworn in the presence of Gilbert Y. Tickle, JP, on 26 July 1900, by Frederick Stevens, a steward on board the SS *Vito*:

> The rev. gentleman had a small glass of whisky before retiring about 10.30 p.m. and no more during the day, and indeed many days without anything at all. At Syracuse a dozen small bottles of claret were brought on board, and he and the other passengers had a bottle between them for dinner. The Revd. W. O. Jones was never under the influence of drink during the whole voyage . . .[60]

This kind of evidence was corroborated in statements made by the first and second mate of the ship and by W. O. Jones's fellow traveller, Bernard Taylor – all under oath.

One of the strangest things about the investigation committee was W. O. Jones's absence from it. In eight sittings between 18 May and 27 June the committee gathered evidence from different individuals but the accused was not once invited to face the witnesses and he was not given any information about the accusations.[61] On 28 June he received a postcard inviting him to the next sitting which would be held that afternoon. The various pieces of evidence were read out to him. Two days later, in the tenth sitting of the committee, Jones was at last allowed to defend himself. Concerning the alleged drunkenness in Bold Street and Thomas Davies's evidence, his explanation was that he had been struck by a horse as it cut a corner. That had occurred on 23 December 1898. After the blow he succeeded in walking up Ranelagh Place until he fell down unconscious. Someone placed him in a cab and sent him home. As for the open carriage in Upper Parliament Street, that incident happened on 31 December when he was travelling in a carriage on that street with a Mrs Roberts from Ullet Road.[62] During his own cross-examination of witnesses, including the elders of the Chatham Street church, he succeeded in obtaining much evidence in his favour. Richard Jones, for instance, insisted that during the fateful *seiat* when his behaviour had caused so much talk, 'His prayer was perfect – his speech was as usual – his intonation was normal – and he stood at the table as he usually did.'[63] In the next sitting, the twelfth, on 2 July, the evidence of Captain Jarvis, John Jones, and the maids who had been in service at Huskisson Street, was read out. William Jones insisted, however, that these witnesses should be there in person and that a shorthand secretary should be obtained to record the proceedings. It is clear that this evidence had induced W. O. Jones to take the case to the civil courts.[64] The committee categorically refused to allow anyone not directly involved in the proceedings to attend the committee, not even a shorthand secretary. In response Jones refused to proceed any further with the inquiry. He admitted that there was some truth in the evidence, in fact he never once claimed that he was teetotal.[65] 'I used to drink a certain amount of wine, and also on occasions a certain amount of whisky or brandy before retiring. I never tried to conceal that from anybody, and I feel not one degree of shame . . .'[66]

By this time, and after consultation with the connexional lawyer, J. Bryn Roberts, MP from Bangor, the committee decided to bring things to an immediate conclusion.[67] On 9 July 1900, it was agreed that the report should be submitted to the Monthly Meeting the following week. The verdict was:

that we are forced to believe that the Revd W. O. Jones, BA, has been guilty on several occasions of behaviour that makes him unfit to be a minister of the gospel, and thus we come to the decision that he should not in any way hold such an important position among us.[68]

The Monthly Meeting was held on 11 July 1900 and the report of the committee of investigation was read out by its secretary, the Revd William Jones. In light of the high drama which preceded, the discussion was rather uninspired. The president, the Revd David Jones, asked if there was anyone present who wished to obtain more information before casting his vote. Eleven raised their hands. Then Hugh Roberts, Birkenhead, proposed that the report should be accepted. The Revd John Hughes seconded the proposal and it was found that 'the great majority were in favour' and only one was opposed. After the vote, W. O. Jones retired, as did Mr William Jones (Balliol Road), R. J. Williams and J. J. Bebb, and the president announced that W. O. Jones was now expelled from the ministry of the Connexion.[69]

The verdict was a great shock to W. O. Jones and he resolved to move at once to defend himself. Within five days he had asked the Monthly Meeting for all the papers of the committee of investigation, and especially for copies of any correspondence between it and 'Mr John Jones, late of Prestatyn'.[70] However, the request was denied because the Monthly Meeting had no right to do this and because showing these documents would have been 'completely contrary to the denomination's practice in such cases'.[71]

The Monthly Meeting, of course, was answerable to the association. The matter came before its meeting in Pwllheli on Wednesday, 22 August. On the previous Monday evening, W. O. Jones had posted a letter to the association giving notice that he intended to appeal, but his message did not reach Pwllheli until 6.30 on the Wednesday evening.[72] By that time the matter had been discussed and the association had endorsed the verdict and thus 'completely rejected Mr William Owen Jones as a preacher and minister in our denomination, and we trust that he should not despite this be considered as an enemy but should be prayed for.'[73]

The next step was to appeal against the verdict. W. O. Jones set about doing this immediately. On 18 October 1900, the first of his articles setting out his position appeared on the pages of the weekly newspaper, Y Cymro (The Welshman).[74] Although his critics complained that the articles were silent on points that 'reflected unfavourably' on the author,[75] it cannot be denied that he discussed the evidence fully and in a balanced manner. What is striking even today is how lacking they are in bitterness. These articles were to have a great influence on public opinion.

By this time, feelings were running high. The church at Chatham Street remained loyal to W. O. Jones and 255 of its members protested to the Liverpool Monthly Meeting against his expulsion.[76] Then on 12 January 1901, about seventy people met and decided to form a Defence Committee, as they called it, with R. O. Williams as chairman.[77] There was a general feeling that justice had not been done. This becomes obvious in the protest of his former church in Waunfawr, near Caernarfon, on 28 November 1900, when it passed a resolution that 'we are of the opinion that there is reason to fear that the way the investigation was carried out has led to injustice'.[78] Resolutions were passed on 27 January 1901 by the churches of Liscard Road, Seacombe, and Parkfield, Birkenhead, calling for W. O. Jones to be informed of the nature of the accusations against him.[79] In Liverpool printed petitions were circulated for people to sign. For instance there were 515 names on the Stanley Road petition 'entreating the Association to reopen the matter in an open Committee in accordance with the terms requested by Mr W. O. Jones'.[80]

By this time W. O. Jones had placed the matter in the hands of a solicitor. The firm acting on his behalf was Rees and Hindley[81] and in January 1901 a letter was sent to William Jones, the secretary of the Monthly Meeting, expressing the opinion that the committee of investigation had not acted lawfully. It had sought evidence from anyone who could blacken the character of W. O. Jones; the witnesses were not cross-examined; none of them were obliged to come face to face with the accused until the complaints had been formally listed 'and the committee was saturated with rumours'; W. O. Jones was asked to disprove the accusation and thus the principle that a man is innocent until proven guilty was breached; the committee acted arbitrarily in banning the presence of a short-hand secretary and the Monthly Meeting's action in passing a resolution to dismiss Jones without first hearing the evidence was against the rules of the denomination 'and the vote so taken was invalid and of no effect'.[82] The response of the Monthly Meeting's solicitor, Elwy D. Symond, on 15 January is rather un-convincing, which is hardly surprising since he had already warned the members of the Monthly Meeting that they were on precarious legal ground and they needed to be careful both in passing resolutions and in their correspondence.[83] Following that, Evan R. Davies, a solicitor from Pwllheli, had published a damning legal criticism of the work of the investigating committee, challenging their interpretation of the disciplinary rules of the denomination.[84]

The Defence Committee was working hard to win support by organizing a grand rally in the Caernarfon Pavilion to follow the robust meeting which had been held in the Town Hall, Pwllheli, on 2 January 1901.[85] It was obvious by now that the denomination needed to justify itself and the first step towards that was the publication of a fuller account of the work of the committee of investigation at the beginning of January.[86]

W. O. Jones's appeal against the verdict came before the association in Colwyn Bay on 23 April 1901. Under rule 7(1) of its constitution, it appointed a committee of appeal, containing seven members, three ministers and four laymen. In addition, the Chatham Street eldership was to name three observers, and W. O. Jones was to name three. A shorthand secretary was to be present in the sittings[87] and the committee was exhorted to follow guidelines that would safeguard it from the weaknesses found in the work of the committee of investigation.

The committee of appeal elected William James as chairman and he began his work in the chapel vestry at Princes Road on the morning of 28 May. Between then and the evening of Friday, 31 May, eleven sittings were held with four more sittings on 6 and 7 June. Eighty-nine witnesses were questioned, forty-three of them members of Chatham Street church and written evidence was also received. During these sittings, W. O. Jones and his supporters were quietly confident,[88] but their hopes were dashed when new evidence came to hand concerning what had happened during the cruise on the *Vito*. This evidence resulted from the diligent work of John Jones, Prestatyn. Initially, as has been seen, he showed considerable kindness towards W. O. Jones and organized the cruise for him, but following certain incidents about which W. O. Jones had been silent, their friendship cooled.[89] He was the source for the evidence concerning W. O. Jones's suspicious behaviour on board ship but, on the advice of his solicitors, he refused point-blank to appear before the committee of investigation unless the committee undertook to pay any legal costs that might arise if the case went to the civil courts. The committee of investigation could not promise this.[90] W. O. Jones had responded to John Jones's accusations concerning his drunkenness by means of statements taken under oath from the steward, the two mates and Bernard Taylor.[91] John Jones could not be so easily dissuaded, however. Fresh statements were obtained from the steward, the first mate and the second mate, repudiating the previous statements and making new accusations which were more serious than anything so far obtained. According to R. G. Palfrey, the first mate of the *Vito*, W. O. Jones was absent in Marseilles when the ship was ready to sail. As a result, 'The Captain had to go ashore, and seek assistance to find him, and he was found in a house of ill fame'. Again, in Valencia, he said that W. O. Jones spoke of:

> his visit to an immoral house where a number of naked women were brought before him for selection, and that he had selected one, and had intercourse with her, and that on the following day, he returned to the house, and had further intercourse with her.[92]

Thus the members of the committee of investigation (in February 1901) obtained the evidence from Jarvis, who related to them what Palfrey had said to him about a conversation with W. O. Jones concerning a night in Valencia, which had happened a year before. It was hardly immediate or direct. Moreover, this evidence was received from a man who had changed his story completely since the previous occasion when he gave evidence under oath. These witnesses were obviously of very doubtful character. Doubtful or not, W. O. Jones and his friends were convinced that this was the evidence that tipped the balance against him.

The committee of appeal submitted its report to the Association in Oswestry. On 26 June 1901, Zion chapel was full to overflowing. The Revd Evan Roberts, Dolgellau, was in the chair. When the meeting moved to the report, the public and the press were ordered to leave – except for the correspondent from the Calvinistic Methodist's weekly *Y Goleuad*. John Jones, Rock Ferry, proposed that W. O. Jones should also leave since he was not a member of the association. The president determined that this was consistent with the regulations. Then the report was read out.[93] A summary was given of the procedures of the committee, and then the verdict was announced. With regard to W. O. Jones it was found:

(1) that he was 'deficient in truth' – in other words he did not always tell the truth.
(2) that he sometimes went to 'religious meetings in his church smelling of alcohol' although there were no grounds for maintaining 'that he was under the influence of alcohol' in his ministerial work
(3) that he drank alcoholic drinks although he professed to be teetotal and that he was guilty of drinking to excess and sometimes until drunkenness
(4) that he was guilty of 'indecent and wanton conversations'; and if his own words to others are to be believed – words that were related in a credible manner to us in his presence by those persons – then he must on occasions have lived an unclean life.

William James proposed that W. O. Jones's expulsion should therefore be endorsed. He said:

> In a civil court, if there is any doubt, the benefit of the doubt is given in favour of the accused: but it happens otherwise in ecclesiastical courts – if there is any doubt, that doubt is counted against the accused because a minister is obliged to be above suspicion at all time.[94]

This speech by James was as foolish as it was ungracious. It was as if he had washed his hands of any pastoral care for the divided church or the man who had been condemned. Nevertheless, it is an interesting speech, with its ruthless moral emphasis and its overweening concern for the status of the ministry. Through his rash words he raised serious doubts in the minds of many who had guided the committee of appeal with impartiality. The proposal was seconded by Edward Griffith, Dolgellau, and was passed with only four against. Keen to turn the knife in the open wound, John Jones, Rock Ferry, asked whether W. O. Jones was still a member of Chatham Street church. T. J. Weldon proposed that he should be expelled not only from the ministry but from membership of the church as well, and this motion was passed.

An indication of W. O. Jones's hurt at the treatment he had received from his ecclesiastical colleagues can be found in his diary entry for 28 to 31 May, the time of the sittings of the committee of appeal in Princes Road. '[This has been] the most excruciating time I have ever experienced. The trial lasted this week, four days of three sittings. Went on fairly well till Friday evening when J. Jones came forward – the horrible liar.'[95] For the dates 3 to 7 June, when the committee of appeal was drawing up its report, he wrote:

> It is impossible to speak of this week. Very anxious and painful time. Nearly crushed the life out of me. In spite of all it ended fairly well. The trial was over on Friday evening and its history will be written deep in the history of Welsh Calvinistic Methodism. How wronged I have been. God knows. I know that my Redeemer liveth, and that he will stand in the end etc.

And then for Wednesday, 26 June, the day of the final expulsion in Oswestry, he wrote: 'We left Chester about 9.30 and arrived in Oswestry about 11. Stayed at a hotel there . . . Went to chapel and then the great catastrophe. They not only confirmed the old decision they also excommunicated me. Awful! What next.'[96]

The diaries show that, in W. O. Jones's opinion, John Jones, Prestatyn and John Williams, Princes Road, were his main enemies. He spoke of a man called Evans who was expelled from Princes Road 'for slandering John Williams, not one twentieth of [what] J. W. has been saying about me'.[97] He also recorded that William Edward Williams had written to Ceridwen (W. O. Jones's wife), a letter 'containing a terrible charge against J. Williams', but he did not indicate what it was.[98]

Throughout this dreadful time, W. O. Jones was awaiting his opportunity to take these accusations to the civil courts. His solicitors advised him that the actions of the denominational committees were protected by legal privilege, but this did not include anything said elsewhere. Before long, W. O. Jones's opportunity arrived. On 30 April 1902, Mr Justice Mills heard two cases of slander in St George's Hall, Liverpool. These cases had been brought against two ministers, Owen Eilian Owen and Thomas Gwynedd Roberts, by W. O. Jones. The facts of the first case were that Owen Eilian Owen, together with William Evans (a member of the investigating committee), had called on a house in Daisy Street, Liverpool. The door was answered by a Miss Winifred Williams, 19 years old, who was one of five children of a widow by the name of Mrs Anne Williams.[99] Until August 1901 she had been a member of the church at Anfield Road but the family had left that church and joined W. O. Jones's congregation. The purpose of the visit by Owen and Evans was to persuade the family to return to Anfield

Road. Eilian Owen asked Winifred Williams whether she wished to be under the ministry of a man who was in the habit of showing pictures of himself naked with young girls. That man, he said, was W. O. Jones. These words were heard by her sister, Mary, and by her mother. After the judge presented the case to the jury, they returned a verdict in favour of W. O. Jones, and awarded him compensation of £50. In the case of the second minister, T. Gwynedd Roberts had told a group of people in a train on the way home from the Flint Association, on 14 December 1901, 'that W. O. Jones was drunk, had been summoned before the church committee, and that the Free Church of the Welsh was going down'. Not one of the three statements had any foundation and before the case proceeded any further, Gwynedd Roberts withdrew his accusations, apologized to the court and it was decided that the costs should be divided.[100] As the barristers emphasized, these cases had no bearing on the accuracy or inaccuracy of the actions or verdicts of the denominational courts, but they did suggest strongly that W. O. Jones would have been able to defend his good name much more successfully in a civil court than in the ecclesiastical courts. His success in these cases explains why the accusations against him abated so swiftly.

Thus in 1901, at the age of 40, W. O. Jones's career was to all appearances in ruins and his reputation destroyed. He did, however, retain a band of enthusiastic supporters who believed unconditionally in his innocence. He was expelled from the denomination in Oswestry on Wednesday, 26 June, 1901. On the following Friday, the Committee of Defence met in the Common Hall, Hackins Hey, to consider the next step. It was decided to hold a further meeting on the following Tuesday evening, 2 July. Some 160 people attended that meeting[101] and it was decided to sever all links with the Calvinistic Methodist denomination, to look for a place to worship and to invite W. O. Jones to be their minister.[102] In a public meeting on 9 July it was agreed to begin independent worship on the following Sunday[103] and on Sunday, 14 July 1901, the first services were held in Hope Hall. A prayer meeting was held in the morning with about 600 people present. In the evening service, W. O. Jones preached for the first time in a year, to a congregation of more than 2,000, on the text 'The son of man is come to seek and to save that which was lost (Luke 19: 10)'. It is no wonder that his diary entry for that evening was 'At last a happy Sunday'.[104] The following

Sunday the congregation in the morning service had increased and in the evening Hope Hall was full to overflowing. By Sunday 28 July, 650 people had expressed their willingness to join the new church.[105] And in the evening service on that Sunday the new church was incorporated with all who wished to become members rising to their feet and W. O. Jones praying. Then William Roberts, Bootle, proposed that W. O. Jones should be called to be their pastor. William Jones, Rock Ferry, seconded this proposal and it was passed unanimously.[106]

The new church embarked on a programme of expansion by setting up Sunday schools in various places for members' convenience. On 11 August, three Sunday schools were established, one in Hope Hall with 100 pupils, one in Birkenhead, with thirteen classes, and one in Bootle.[107] By the end of the month, three more had been formed.[108] The organizational committee was in difficulties, however, for there was more work than one man could oversee and at the end of August it was decided to look for an assistant to help the pastor.[109]

Thus far the new movement had no name. In a *seiat* in Hope Hall on 4 September 1901, with 500 present, it was agreed to adopt the name, 'Eglwys Rydd y Cymry', 'the Free Church of the Welsh'.[110] The next question to be addressed was that concerning the new fellowship's creed and basic principles. The committee of organization worked diligently to try to resolve this matter and on Sunday evening, 22 September, W. O. Jones read out the declaration, or the manifesto, as the newspapers called it.

We have noticed for years the increase of the spirit of officialdom in the denomination. In very many cases we could not close our eyes to the fact that ministers and elders dominate the churches. They have succeeded, gradually and silently, in taking possession of all authority to make laws, to govern, and to judge all important cases, without consulting the members, and very often against their wishes.

Because of this, the declaration condemned the practice of electing elders for life, and making buildings the possession of the whole denomination. The new Free Church, with its seven Sunday schools and its thousand members formed 'a new religious organization, with wider freedom and with more democratic characteristics'. It was committed to a missionary spirit, to trying to exalt purity and morality and supporting social justice. Ministers and elders were to be elected for a fixed term only, although they were allowed to be re-elected if chosen, and the buildings would belong to the church that paid for them. The central court of the new denomination was to be truly representative of the churches. No confession of faith or creed had yet been drawn up but 'on every subject essential to Christianity we adhere strongly to the faith which is reckoned to be orthodox'. The declaration closed by wishing God's blessing upon the Calvinistic Methodist denomination.[111]

Because of the central location of Hope Hall, and its inconvenience for many, new chapels were swiftly opened in Garmoyle Road (25 April 1903), in Merton Road, Bootle (23–4 May 1903), in Donaldson Street, Liverpool (20–1 June 1903) and Claughton Road, Birkenhead (8–9 August 1903).[112] Noah Bevan was called as minister to assist W. O. Jones as early as 1 December 1901,[113] while Lewis Hughes was ordained on 6 March 1902[114] and David Davies on 25 October 1903.[115] Probably the best known of those who served as ministers of the Free Church was the poet David Emrys James (Dewi Emrys).[116] The old Defence Committee continued to operate as the organizing committee of the Free Church, but during March and April 1902 a new committee was elected containing three ministers and forty-six representatives. It is interesting to note that the Free Church was still heavily influenced by Presbyterianism. By July 1904, the Free Church of the Welsh had seven churches, four chapels, nine Sunday schools and four ministers.

In bringing this story to a close, what was the significance of this upheaval? One of the saddest chapters in the history of the Christian church throughout the centuries is the way in which its courts have administered judgements and punishments. When Aethwy Jones called the Monthly Meeting's investigating committee 'a Court of Inquisition' he was not speaking rashly. It is striking that whenever churches have administered the law they have leant strongly towards the tradition of Roman law rather than the tradition of common law. According to the tradition of Roman law judges themselves prosecute and look for evidence. The defendant is guilty until he succeeds in proving his innocence. The court's purpose is to discover the truth about what happened. The committee before which W. O. Jones appeared operated in this way, with the members travelling here and there – to Prestatyn, to Ffestiniog, to

Menai Bridge – rummaging around for evidence. It was W. O. Jones's responsibility to disprove this evidence and if he succeeded in doing so his accusers sought fresh evidence against him.

This has always been a characteristic of the ecclesiastical courts and was also a characteristic of the courts of privilege, such as the Star Chamber and the Court of High Commission, which the Puritans campaigned against and finally abolished. The Puritans were not alone in this opposition but were supported by the solicitors of the common law as well because, according to their tradition, the business of a court is to weigh and measure specific accusations against the defendant in light of the evidence rather than to discover the truth about what happened. The accused is innocent until it is proven through reasonable evidence that he is guilty. In light of the common law tradition, one feels instinctively that W. O. Jones was condemned on very unsatisfactory evidence. However, if the Roman tradition is also allowed its rightful place, it must be acknowledged that the arrangements made by the association for the committee of appeal were very careful and were vastly superior to those of the investigating committee elected by the Monthly Meeting.

It will not do either to suppose that the denominational authority's sole motive was to destroy W. O. Jones at any cost. It is difficult to read the papers pertaining to the case without feeling that there were some involved in the case who were completely unyielding in their decision to punish the defendant – according to W. O. Jones, John Jones, Prestatyn, was among them with John Williams, Princes Road, as a close second. However, there were less determined men on the committees who wished to uphold discipline but not at the expense of justice and they were convinced that excommunicating W. O. Jones was not an unreasonable punishment.

Nevertheless the condemnation of W. O. Jones was closely linked to the temperance movement. To be honest, it is hard to take seriously the lurid tales of the brothels of Marseille and Valencia contained in the evidence of sailors who were obvious perjurers and obtained through the dubious hands of John Jones, Prestatyn. But for Owen Owens and others like him, drinking alcohol was almost entirely unacceptable for a Christian, and certainly made a person unsuitable to be a minister. W. O. Jones admitted openly, both orally and in writing, that he was not a teetotaller. This enabled his critics to call him a liar because he had signed the temperance pledge. This is exactly what happened in the final verdict against him in Oswestry. But if every minister and member were to be expelled when, having taken a vow of temperance, they nevertheless took alcohol on medical advice or by virtue of some private conditions that they placed upon the oath, the ranks of the church would be considerably depleted.

A later generation would derive much merriment from lampooning the hypocrisy of the Victorians who would sneak through the back doors of public houses to drink after signing the temperance pledge, and they have a fair point. Every generation has its characteristic hypocrisy but the historian's task is to discover the particular hypocrisy of an age and what inspired it.

The nineteenth-century religious leaders suffered from conflicting influences with regard to drinking alcohol. On the one hand, they were aware of its devastating social effects, especially on country folk. On the other hand, they had come heavily under the influence of bourgeois middle-class habits, particularly in a large English town such as Liverpool, where the consumption of alcohol was part of the pattern of sophisticated society. The truth is that very many religious leaders in Wales followed that pattern although they were careful to restrict it to their private lives, and yet, rightly or wrongly, they felt guilty, and there was a tendency for their nervousness to turn into nastiness when this became public. This happened in the case of W. O. Jones. It is obvious that the Welsh exiles in Liverpool found it ever more difficult to walk the narrow path of the old Puritanism. It appeared that the social customs of common folk and middle-class people in a city like Liverpool undermined the traditional discipline and the guardians of the Puritan conscience became worried and edgy as a result.

The case of W. O. Jones also suggests that a crisis of leadership had come to afflict Nonconformity. As they submitted the fruit of their investigations to the Monthly Meeting and to the association, the committee adhered to the rule that it was the verdict and not the evidence that should be submitted publicly. Certainly there were valid legal reasons for behaving in this manner but the public consequences were disastrous. Since the congregation could not assess the verdict and punishment in light of the evidence, their vote was of necessity a vote of confidence in committees and leaders. A matter of opinion became a matter of loyalty. To the majority who were brought up to respect their leaders and to trust their wisdom, this did not present a problem. After all such paternalism was part of the heritage of the Victorian age[117] and as the century progressed its tendency was to develop into bureaucratic institutionalism that demanded the homage of the common members. However, a new spirit was manifesting itself among the younger generation. Thanks to social, legal and political changes, the public were beginning to partake of administration and government. The sons of common folk were swiftly penetrating the inner circles of Parliament, the commercial world, law courts and the universities. Was the world of religion to be exempt? In the Anglican Church this upsurge against paternalism gave rise to diocesan conferences and created tension between the bishop of St Asaph and his clergy. In the Nonconformist churches, the memory of their own past when the common members had a creative voice in church meetings and *seiadau* made them wary of any tendency on the part of their leaders to centralize authority. The Independents witnessed a bitter fight against these tendencies in the 'Battle of the Constitutions'. The same elements are apparent in the case of W. O. Jones. The denominational authorities felt that the events in Chatham Street were a challenge to their personal status and to the organizational authority that safeguarded that status. For William James in the Oswestry Association, the behaviour of the Chatham Street church was open rebellion against the Connexion. He spoke in the same vein when he went to Chatham Street to convey the association's verdict:

> There is no point in you trying to rebel, because whatever you do, the highest court has settled things for ever. If you are not convinced, it is your fault: and we cannot give more information concerning this. The Monthly Meeting and the Association must be in control, and if anybody does not agree, they should leave the denomination.[118]

These were harsh words, and also fearful words; they were the words of a man who felt the ground slipping under his feet and who consequently had to lean more heavily than ever on the authority of the institution. He was also facing a congregation of forty people where previously there were 400. Griffith Ellis of Bootle was a far wiser and gentler man than James, but the same note can be found in the letter which he sent on 17 August 1901 to his members in the Stanley Road church. He tried, in a restrained and gentlemanly fashion, to persuade them not to join W. O. Jones's faction, but he also asked them whether fifteen of the most responsible and wise men in the denomination could be mistaken when they agreed unanimously to condemn W. O. Jones. He could not appeal to the logic of the verdict in light of the evidence, thus he was forced to appeal to their loyalty to authority,[119] but by that time, in Liverpool at least, it was rather late in the day to depend on such an appeal. 'The doctrine of authority has unsettled us', said G. C. Rees on behalf of the rebels. They were forced to leave a denomination which had, for them, outlived its usefulness.[120] William Roberts, Orwell Road, was in agreement. Knowledgeable and respectable people can make a mistake, he said, as the Dreyfus affair had proved in France. William James had parted company with the truth 'because he has assumed that the petition and the fight to reopen the case was a rebellion. If so the rebellion must be crushed once and for all.'[121] This sentiment was echoed in the declaration of the Free Church.

The whole episode was a terrible blow to Welsh Calvinistic Methodism in Liverpool. The golden age in its history was over and it never recovered its former strength. Tension and considerable bitterness lingered long among former friends.

The Free Church of the Welsh was a short-lived affair. Why did its sun set so quickly? The historian, Thomas Richards, who was a schoolteacher in Bootle when the crisis was at its height, suggested the following reasons: 'Its membership was not rooted in the mores and traditions of the Methodists of Wales, there was no power or effective approval of its cause in rural areas, no prospective adherents from similar free churches in north Wales, no newcomers from Wales seeking membership in their midst.'[122] Each word was true, and it could also be added that the 'Free Church' had no specific doctrinal base to bind its members together. Little came of the attempts to establish the denomination on Welsh soil. For instance, in March 1902, 'Y Cysegr' (the Fellowship), a branch of the 'Free Church', was established in Carmarthen, but had little success.[123] By February 1920 the Free Church of the Welsh had begun to discuss plans to seek membership of the Quarterly Meeting of the Independents in Liverpool, Manchester and the surrounding area, and by 1921 the movement had merged with the Independents. *Llais Rhyddid* (The Voice of Freedom), the periodical established in 1902, ceased publication. W. O. Jones died on 14 May 1937 as the minister of the Independent Church, Canning Street, Liverpool, and a man greatly admired for his 'gentlemanly spirit and his culture'.[124] His right-hand man in the Free Church of the Welsh was William Albert Lewis who was ordained minister by the church in 1906. He also joined the Independents and died on 10 December 1950.[125]

~ 9 ~

The Confusion of the Intelligentsia

There are many indications that the period between 1890 and 1914 witnessed a growing uncertainty in Welsh minds. People were becoming increasingly unsure of those assumptions which had formerly motivated their lives. All such assumptions are objects of faith and when radical doubts are cast upon them, both individuals and society as a whole can be plunged into a crisis of faith.

Complaints about churches and the criticism of ministers have already been discussed. Nevertheless, the fact that people in the 1890s were generally critical of contemporary religion was more significant than the various individual complaints that they made. It is never easy for people within a closed society to make their protest against particular religious assumptions through publicly embracing a different faith from the one which that society approves. Such was the situation in Wales in the 1890s.

'It is said by many that Keri Evans is an agnostic', wrote the popular preacher Herber Evans in 1891, adding worriedly, 'is it true?'[1] The occasion was Keri Evans's appointment to the chair of philosophy at the University in Bangor. Herber Evans had been made aware of his namesake's putative scepticism by a member of the appointments committee. A Congregationalist who was a philosopher might become an Anglican without making him unsuitable to hold a chair in his subject, but to be an agnostic was a different matter entirely. The weight of public opinion forced people to express their religious doubts through complaints about wholly inconsequential matters. Like the children of Israel who carped against their leader, Moses, it could be said that 'your murmurings are not against us, but against the Lord' (Exod. 16: 8).

There is plenty of evidence for the doubt that afflicted Welsh people at this time. Garmon Roberts, Gobowen, wrote in 1901

'Our age is an age of doubt'.[2] It was clear not only that doubt was on the increase but that it concerned fundamental issues. Nine years previously the president of the Baptist Union of Wales expressed the sentiment that the nation's deepest convictions were under threat. 'Deep unease and instability exist in the religious world, almost everything is doubted and disregarded. Papism is swiftly gaining ground in our country, and at the other extreme atheism is flourishing.'[3] In an address from the chair at the Corwen Calvinistic Methodist Association in 1897, Josiah Thomas spoke of the dangers of 'the sceptical and atheistic tendencies of the age'.[4] In the same year, J. Gwili Jenkins affirmed that 'doubt' was increasing in Wales.[5] According to D. M. Phillips, one of the characteristics of the period before the 1904–5 Revival was 'uncertainty' and he linked this with the influence of 'agnosticism'. It 'spread like a hoarfrost over the life of the most faithful religious people in our churches'.[6]

It would appear, without quoting more examples, that these men used the word 'doubt' in the vaguest sense to mean almost any kind of critical enquiry. It is palpably obvious that the Christian leaders of this period had little idea how to handle doubt. They could hold forth against specific doubts with great eloquence and aplomb but they were clueless as to the difficulties between various kinds of doubt and they had little comprehension of the various influences that made people question the basic assumptions of their age. The pastoral skills that characterized Puritans such as John Bunyan or Walter Cradock and the spiritual sensitivity that characterized William Williams Pantycelyn, and other leaders of the Evangelical Revival in treating doubt, were long, long forgotten.

The description of the late Victorian age as the 'age of doubt' says much about the concerns of those who penned these words. It is hardly an objective description for the simple reason that all ages have their doubts.[7] The grouping together of unease, atheism, agnosticism and an increase in Catholicism shows how unfocused the discourse had become.

The essence of doubt is to be in two minds, which makes it wholly appropriate to describe doubt as 'uncertainty'. The most prominent characteristic of doubt is anxious questioning and as such it is a universal within the Christian experience, as anyone who has studied the hymns of Williams Pantycelyn, or Dafydd Williams, Llandeilo-fach, will know. Yet this had been forgotten to such an extent that late Victorian Christians in Wales were shocked that a man such as the renowned mid-nineteenth-century preacher Henry Rees was sometimes afflicted by doubt.[8] The tendency was to think that anxious enquiry was tantamount to unbelief and would inevitably lead to full-blown atheism. The idea that it could lead to a firm and mature faith seemed everywhere to be lacking at the time.

It seems that uncertainty spread most rapidly among the younger, university-trained preachers. William Williams (Crwys)[9] confessed in the early years of his ministry – he was ordained in February 1898 – that he felt 'a lack of conviction' concerning certain aspects of Christianity.[10] Like Tennyson, J. Gwili Jenkins inclined to the opinion that there was more faith in honest doubt than in half the creeds, a conviction which he expressed in his poem 'A Confession of Faith':

> Ond gwn, er cred anaeddfed
> Nad ofer im fu byw
> Nid ofer ymdrech galed
> Am oes i geisio Duw.

> But I know, despite an immature faith
> That I did not live in vain;
> Nor strove hard in vain
> Throughout my life to seek God.

And so with an unconsciously self-righteous touch he contrasts himself favourably with his friend who is astonished that Gwili did not have a full confession of faith.

> 'Rwy'n galw am y golau
> Bob nos yn ddinacâd
> A thithau drwy'r blynyddau
> Yn byw ar wir dy dad.[11]

> I call for the light
> Every night without fail
> And you throughout the years
> Living on the truth of your father.

The poet and academic W. J. Gruffydd felt the same dissatisfaction with creeds and confessions but in his case it was transformed into a savage attack.[12] Nevertheless, one wonders whether Gruffydd should be classed as a doubter since he was absolutely convinced that he was right: there was no room for dissent in his mind. The same might be said of the young bard Ben Bowen. He caused great consternation among his fellow Baptists with his critical views on the baptism rite and the idea of closed communion, and on 31 July 1902, his mother church of Moriah, Pentre in the Rhondda valley, excommunicated him. His opinions on the resurrection shocked an even wider circle. He argued that Christ's rising from the grave was a wholly spiritual concept and thus raised the question whether it was a historical event at all.[13]

Ben Bowen's articles do not give the impression that he was 'halting between two opinions' and thus there is little justification for calling him a doubter in the proper sense of the word. However, it is significant that at least one contemporary maintained that Bowen 'gave expression to the sentiments and unease of many young people concerning the Bible and the denomination'.[14] With his untimely death at the age of 24, Ben Bowen became a Romantic icon and a symbol of the rebellion of a new generation in their protest against the old whose soul 'had grown crooked'.[15]

T. Gwynn Jones's experiences are more interesting because he was a sceptic in a different sense from Gwili, Ben Bowen and W. J. Gruffydd. Doubt for him was not a sign of Romantic rebellion but the stuff of real agony of soul. He shared Gruffydd's conviction that conventional religious beliefs caused dissent and hypocrisy[16] but he was also acutely aware of the pain his lack of faith caused him. 'My convictions are fading one by one, so that they do not possess any force to sustain me', he lamented and he envied his friend, Silyn Roberts, because of the comfort which he (Roberts) gleaned from his faith. As for himself he could only say that 'God cares not one whit about us, children of men'.[17] There is no attempt here to romanticize doubt; on the contrary, it led to one of the bleakest couplets composed before the Great War.

> Cawn fedd fel ein gwehelyth
> Dyna ben amdani byth . . .
> Er gwychion ddychmygion mawr,
> 'Nid yw einioes ond unawr', –

Trwy ing pan fyddo'n trengi
Diau un chwedl dyn a chi[18]

We shall have a grave like our forefathers,
and nothing, nothing beyond . . .
Despite life's most splendid achievements,
'our life only lasts one hour', –
in the agony of death,
Man is no better than a dog.

This was written in June 1905, before the sound of the revival had ceased in the land.

The anxieties which afflicted sensitive and thinking people in Wales by the 1890s centred on attitudes to the Christian faith which had previously been wholly unchallenged. Wales was not unique in this respect; Christianity was under attack in many European countries. The attack on God came from many directions and took many forms. As the Industrial Revolution had an increasing impact on European life, and as the population migrated from rural areas to towns, the Christian presence disappeared from their lives. The devotional customs and the church ceremonies that had formerly shaped people's public and private lives gradually dwindled. The great tidal wave of secularization swept away the visible signs of the Christian faith and, in the wake of secularization, secularism as a philosophy that rejected the claim of religion on any part of life also flourished.

Secularization could be acceptable to Christians. Although both the movement to abolish the monasteries during the reign of Henry VIII and the campaign to disestablish the Church in Wales were inspired by a variety of motives, there were people who supported both movements for religious reasons. However, this was not the case in the secularization programmes at the beginning of the twentieth century. In December 1905 the French Parliament passed the Law of Separation of Church and State and all the property of the church was transferred to the state authorities. Secular ideology was behind the movement; it was anti-Christian as well as being anti-clerical. Five years later the same thing happened in Portugal and under harsher terms than in France.

Some of the most influential attacks were in the realm of the intellect. Although Kant was eager to preserve a strong philosophical basis for faith in God, the influence of his teaching gradually strengthened the concept of doubt. He maintained that direct knowledge of God, or of any transcendent world, was not possible but that the existence of God, the soul and eternity could be rationally maintained as the necessary foundations for our moral life. By the second half of the nineteenth century there was a growing conviction that these foundations could be dispensed with. The supernatural was not needed; the mysteries of humankind and creation could be completely solved in terms of the natural.

The Breton Ernest Renan (1823–92) for instance, felt that the supernatural was superfluous even to the biblical narrative as his celebrated, or perhaps infamous, book, *La Vie de Jesus* (The Life of Jesus, 1863), contends. The Frenchman Auguste Comte (1798–1857) had preceded him. He had lost his faith in God, but not, alas, his faith in religion. In order to ensure a united world where brotherly love would overcome selfishness, he fashioned a new religion which had humankind – the 'great Being' – as its object instead of God. The German Ernst Haeckel (1834–1919) was a scientist who taught that everything could be explained by natural causes and who denied the existence of God, the soul, free will and immortality. Consequently he came to be considered by many as the chief spokesman for materialism. One who was far more significant was Karl Marx, who died in 1883. He gave materialism unparalleled impetus by turning it into a social dynamic. He was not satisfied with shaping a doctrine to describe the world, he needed to understand it in a way which would release the social energy needed to transform it. The assumption soon spread that belief in God was nothing more than the function of a manipulative capitalist class and that part of the programme of a working class on its road to freedom was to destroy religion and render the concept of God obsolete.

One interesting aspect of the attacks on Christianity in the nineteenth century was the way in which the emphasis on man or humankind developed. Humanism took on a new guise. In the eighteenth century the Christian revelation was attacked and Christ's uniqueness was denied; the nineteenth century aimed at the heart of the matter and placed God himself under siege. Meanwhile the public were invited to embrace with religious zeal a new object of worship, namely humankind. Comte did this quite openly. In Marx, atheism and humanism joined forces to instigate revolution. Ludwig Feuerbach (1804–72) was close to the mark when he declared that 'homo homini deus' was an appropriate motto – man is the god of man. Kant, Hegel, Comte, Renan, Feuerbach, Herbert Spencer, J. S. Mill and Marx contributed to this humanistic faith in their various ways.

On the whole it was an optimistic faith which combined humanism with Darwin's theory of evolution; people became captivated by the belief in continuous development. They felt that, owing to the inexorable processes of history, the whole mighty creation was travelling homewards and that God had lost his throne. Nietzsche was not nearly so sanguine. It is true, he said, that modern men and women had murdered God, but this was not a triumph but a tragedy. 'Shall we not now wander in ineffable nothingness? Shall we not feel the wind of emptiness on our faces? Does it not become colder and colder, darker and darker?' After we have killed God, the Super-man will seize the throne. He will be the Messiah, but unlike the man of Galilee he will be beyond good and evil and utterly contemptuous of the virtues exalted in Christian morality. The tender, the merciful and the gentle will all be crushed under his weight.

Not all of these influences would reach their climax before 1914. Yet a perusal of Welsh-language journals and books at the turn of the century shows how many ideas were derived from the teaching of the continental critics, although they were often tempered by the views of English writers such as Mill, Spencer, Blatchford and T. H. Green. Not the least of the changes that occurred towards the end of Victorian age was that of swifter communications. Although common folk did not always understand the technical details of these intellectual debates, they were shaken by them. There were now members of the working class who were 'always searching blindly for the God of truth', as Bob said in Daniel Owen's epoch-making novel *Rhys Lewis*, adding, 'they know well what it is to be deeply wounded by doubt and unbelief'.[19]

When Bob expressed his doubts, his mother, Mari Lewis, insisted that they were 'some ideas you found in those old English books that have addled your head'. This brings us nearer home, and to one of the influences that contributed the most to troubling the Welsh mind. That influence was English culture. With the spread of English-medium education in elementary schools, in secondary schools after 1889 and in university colleges, Wales was increasingly influenced by English literature and culture.

Some leaders realized the implications of this. As early as 1872 William Rees (Gwilym Hiraethog) claimed that it was the desire of Satan himself to see 'the death of our ancient language, in the hope that its evangelical religion would die with it'.[20] As many liked to remark in those years, the Welsh language was a bulwark for Christian truth. John Bowen Jones could boast that the gospel had kept the literature of Wales 'so pure that there is not one book of immoral or unbelieving principles and spirit in our language'.[21] As knowledge of the English language became more prevalent in Wales, it was inevitable that ideas critical of Christianity should become more and more common. As it happened, the end of the Victorian age was a period when the cultural influence of England was particularly threatening not only to Welsh nationhood but to Welsh Christianity, indeed to British Christianity as well. The poet and critic Matthew Arnold (1822–88) in his poem 'Dover Beach' spoke of the eternal sadness that he heard in the ebb tide on that beach, and he drew this comparison:

> The Sea of Faith
> Was once, too, at the full, and round earth's shore
> Lay like the folds of a bright girdle furl'd;
> But now I only hear
> Its melancholy, long, withdrawing roar . . .

Many English people had a similar experience as the century drew to a close and it had reached Wales long before Ellis Humphrey Evans (Hedd Wyn)[22] sang of 'Duw ar drai ar orwel pell' (God ebbing on a far horizon).

According to H. N. Fairchild, the collapse of a specifically English Christian culture began in about 1870. In his view, a fairly stable synthesis, rooted in Christian morality, existed between the various elements of English culture until the middle of the Victorian age. This synthesis began to fall apart and by about 1870 Christian morality itself was losing people's allegiance. 'Psychologically speaking, the "naughty nineties" began in the seventies.'[23] Similarly, Walter E. Houghton sees the year 1870 as being significant. By that time, he said, there was a growing sentiment that it was not possible to be sure of the enduring value of any truth or standard or institution. Everything had its fleeting place in the history of humankind but before long it would be sunk into oblivion.

Thus it was futile to make a costly stand for anything, and everything was ripe for compromise. 'The basic source of this indifference was the historical relativism that began to emerge about 1870.'[24]

J. Hillis Miller also believed that historicism of this kind was significant and led to a rejection of absolute standards. Formerly, human beings were confronted by an objective creation and by an objective God but by this time God, angels and heaven were losing their objective reality. They might be important to the inner life but they were divorced from creation. There was a time when the English writer had at his disposal a wealth of symbols that linked together heaven and earth, God and humanity. 'In that old harmony man, society and language mirrored one another, like so many voices in a madrigal or fugue.' But this richness was scattered. Humankind lost its connection with the eternal and the transcendent. The world around became distant and even hostile. The only refuge was to withdraw into the depths of private experience to seek comfort and safety.[25]

In other words, while writers professed the Christian faith, there was a union between God, humankind, society and creation. The covenant celebrated on Anglican altars and Nonconformist communion tables, which was praised in hymns and sermons, was seen as a cosmic harmony. According to these scholars, however, the English people (and most especially their writers) were aware that this concord was failing and that the union was disintegrating. The Victorian age in England was 'the breaking of the circle, the untuning of the sky'.[26]

John A. Lester discusses how this led to deep despair and suggests that human beings for centuries had lived on two convictions: first that constant and unchanging truth exists beyond the varied world of daily experience and, second, that human beings have the ability through reason or revelation to discover that truth. For English writers, by about 1880 these two convictions had failed. There was no longer any harmony in creation. Humankind came face to face with a hostile, unintelligible, even meaningless, creation. Lester agreed with Hillis Miller and H. N. Fairchild that the only escape was to follow the Romantic path to the secrets of one's own heart, with tragic consequences. 'My contention is that the years from 1880 to 1914 severely jarred and shifted the bearings of man's imaginative life and left him at times bewildered as to how to recover this lost meaning and purpose.'[27]

These scholars focused mainly on literature and it does not follow, of course, that all aspects of English national life showed the same signs of disintegration. Having said that, the writers were touching upon fundamental issues and not least upon the sources of faith. It is no wonder, therefore, that the bishop of Liverpool, J. C. Ryle, complained about the people's casual attitude to beliefs, that they were unable to differentiate between different opinions and viewpoints. He said in 1884:

> Everything, forsooth, is true, and nothing is false, everything is right and nothing is wrong, everything is good and nothing is bad, if it approaches us under the garb and name of religion. You are not allowed to ask what is God's truth, but what is liberal, and generous, and kind.[28]

Thus it is reasonable to conclude that in 1870 or soon afterwards England entered a spiritual doldrum and this was the very period when its grip upon the cultural life of Wales began to tighten. Since the great ambition of the Welsh – particularly their intelligentsia – was to imitate the English in all things, it is hardly surprising that the seeds of destruction that were wreaking such a havoc in England were being sown with enthusiasm in Wales too. Although statements that are true of English literature and culture should not be applied uncritically to Wales, the connections cannot be ignored. In a sermon to the Liverpool Welsh in 1894, the Anglican G. Hartwell Jones felt that contemporary civilization showed advanced signs of decay and that it was on the route to destruction as surely as the ancient civilization of Tyre.[29]

Bearing all this in mind, we can now turn back to Wales and see how this impacted the realm of theology. One of the most striking occurrences, for good or ill, was the introduction of Romanticism into the Christian mind. 'Romanticism' is, admittedly, a rather ambiguous term which refers to a great variety of literary and artistic adherents. In so far as it expressed, in an aesthetic idiom, the experiences of the heart or pleasure in the world of nature, the Romantic movement greatly enriched contemporary culture. There were aspects of the movement, however, that contributed substantially to the undermining of the Christian faith.

According to Richard Davies (Tafolog),[30] 'The poet is the true interpreter of the deepest meaning of the scenes that are visible to all men.'[31] Poetry, he concluded, was the 'soul of religion'. John Hugh Evans (Cynfaen)[32] had the same idea when he said, not without a touch of snobbery, 'The poet . . . is the prophet of the Almighty, expressing his work to inferiors who cannot see or feel him properly with the kind of eyes and hearts that they possess'.[33] Poetry therefore was linked with truth. Rhys J. Huws put it succinctly. 'The purpose of a poem is to reveal, and try to open a closed portal so that truth may have an open field and a wide road.'[34]

The thinker who gave the most careful expression to this aesthetic was the Congregational leader David Adams. He made his stand on the philosophy of the Hegelian Idealists. God permeates the creation, he claimed, for 'the poet believes that matter and its beautiful forms are merely the realization of God's thoughts . . . The poet perceives the organic unity of the whole creation.'[35] As 'nature . . . whispers in [the poet's] ear thoughts bestowed by God who abides within [creation]'[36] it was the poet more than anyone else who possessed an innate facility for assimilating these ideas. 'Wherever the Divine *within us* comes into contact with the Divine *outside us*, pleasure is produced; and the emotion is correctly assigned to that which is called *beauty*.'[37]

Thus the focus of the poet's attention was the divine truth which indwelt creation and which harmonized with his or her own divine consciousness of the truth. It was not surprising that in other lands it was the poets who 'have been leaders of ideology on many issues in doctrine and theology' and Adams was of the opinion that Welsh poets were greatly at fault because they were not 'leaders of ideology in our country'.[38] The great exception was William Thomas (Islwyn):[39] 'we know of no other Welsh poet in this century who is so Wordsworthian in his ability to enter into the secret life of nature'[40] – 'secret' because natural objects were not the true reality. Kant had taught that individuals could not obtain knowledge of objects themselves. The scientist could only be sure of external perception of reality rather than reality itself: his science could never touch upon their essence. It was the poet's privilege to go beyond the scientist and penetrate the truth behind the appearance.

For David Adams, the 'beautiful forms of material creation' were merely 'symbols or parables, suggesting, if not explaining, the realities and principles of the moral and spiritual world'.[41] Thus the poet needed a 'prophetic or educational spirit' and must use this muse to 'draw attention to a truth that is able to inspire and sanctify the characters of those that read it'.[42] The poet's aim was not to portray natural objects in a beautiful and exquisite idiom. Rather his or her task was to express the inspiring, general and divine truth that lies beyond specific objects. Adams was quite adamant that it was not the business of a poet to fashion living images that a painter or sculptor might reproduce in paint and stone and, like many of his contemporaries, he did not think of the poet as a person who composes a poem as a beautiful and finished object.[43] This is one of the reasons for the overwhelming verbosity of so many poets of the period. If a poem, whether a sonnet or a *pryddest*,[44] were an objective creation incorporating sense, emotion and understanding in a single finished work, then the poet could write his or her composition and be done. However, if the purpose of a poem is to reveal the divine secrets of creation in order to enrich the reader's theological knowledge and heighten his or her morality, then there is no reason why the poet should ever stop.

One type of activity linked to the Romantic school reached its height in the work of the 'New Poet'. As Tecwyn Lloyd has shown, the work of the New Poet was heavily influenced by Neoplatonism, as reworked by Hegel.[45] According to T. Gwynn Jones these poets 'wanted to deify everything'.[46] J. Gwili Jenkins did this in his poem 'Beyond the veil':

> Pa le mae Horeb? Ai dim ond un berth
> A welodd Jehofa erioed yn werth
> Dyfod i'w brig yn fflamiau byw?
> Mae pob un o'r perthi yn llosgi gan Dduw! . . .
> Ai yn y Nefoedd mae Duw uwchben?
> Mae yn yr holl berthi, tu hwnt i'r llen!

> Where is Horeb? Was it only a single bush
> That Jehovah ever thought was worth
> Indwelling in living flames?
> Every bush is aflame with God! . . .
> Is God in the heavens above?
> He is in all the bushes, beyond the veil!

The echo of William Thomas (Islwyn) is unmistakable. He also expressed one of the most popular concepts of the New Poet, that visual objects are merely a cloak for reality and truth:

Damhegion, damhegion! Maent o bob tu
I'm henaid chwilfrydig, p'le bynnag y try;
Mae Duw yn llefaru, trwy'r oesau wrth ddyn
Mewn myrdd o ddamhegion, cyn dyfod ei Hun
Yn ddameg anfeidrol i'r byd . . .[47]

Parables, parables! They are on all sides
of my curious soul, wherever it turns;
God speaks throughout the ages to man
In a myriad of parables, before he himself comes
As an immortal parable to the world . . .

Could Strauss say it any better?[48] Thomas Parry's scathing assessment of the aesthetic value of the work of the New Poet is worth quoting: 'He tended to fashion blustering phrases, wax eloquent in unbridled fashion and become increasingly curious about the essence of everything until he ended up in one thick mass of unintelligible fog.'[49] A strange tribute to writers whose aim was to reveal truth! Of course, they had their critics among their contemporaries,[50] but they had their many admirers too. According to Arthur Simon Thomas (Anellydd),[51] 'The New Poet can interpret life as well as the end of man's existence in masterly fashion, and he can philosophize his subject poetically.'[52]

What was the social and ideological significance of the New Poet and his Romantic colleagues? It is difficult to read the work of these poets without gaining the impression of considerable intellectual confusion. In an age governed by strong consensus regarding the pattern and significance of existence, the poet is free to express faith confidently and to share his or her experience of the beauty and wonder of life with contemporaries. But by the mid-1890s it was clear that poets were not celebrating the ecstasy of life but were raising all sorts of questions about it. At no time before, or since, had Welsh poets used the question as a literary form so prolifically as the New Poet. They knew that they were becoming estranged from their Christian tradition and the consensus which centuries of faith had produced. Where formerly the Christian poet took creation to be an objective fact which was maintained by a gracious God, now creation had become an obscure riddle that only the privileged can solve. As a result their poetry weaves, argues, insists, protests, preaches, philosophizes and dreams fantastic dreams, as the critic Alun Llewelyn Williams has shown.[53]

There is no reason, of course, why uncertainty should not give rise to great literature; this has been the case countless times in the history of culture. But on the whole the New Poet and the Romantic were not willing to focus on a specific confusion or a particular agony and express it in polished thoughtful poetry. Since they were uncertain of the world thrust upon them, they tried to solve the problem by creating new universes and, since they operated on the assumption that the divine was implicit in human being, the stuff of these synthetic universes was within their own personalities.[54] Everything objective is ambiguous and suspect and new security must be created within the poet's subjective visions. Whereas the art of Western countries had traditionally laboured to contribute to the breadth and wealth of society's public experiences and to recreate beautiful artistic objects from the cultural heritage participated in by all, this had been replaced by introspective concentration on private experiences and individual visions.

One result of this severe subjectivism was an alienation from the Welsh literary tradition. Ioan Medi could write such an absurd sentence as this: 'Welsh literature is a comparatively recent phenomenon and up to this time its specifically Welsh sources are few.'[55] Alternatively it could mean losing sight of traditional norms, as did Arthur Simon Thomas (Anellydd) when he announced that 'Ceiriog [John Ceiriog Hughes[56]] and Elfed [Howell Elvet Lewis] have composed more beautiful lyrical and love poetry than Dafydd ap Gwilym at the height of his powers.'[57] This subjectivism also meant a distancing from social responsibility. For the Romantics the only life was the life of the soul, and they expressed this belief at the very time when Wales was being convulsed by immense social changes and economic factors were coming to the fore.

The most fascinating example of these literary tendencies was the poet who could easily be called the father of nineteenth-century Romanticism in Wales, William Thomas (Islwyn). His work demonstrated clearly the chasm between the subjective and the objective. For him, freedom lay within:

> Mae'r enaid wedi codi ynddo'i hun
> I'r uchder lle mae'r bythol haul i'r lan,
> Lle mae yn annherfynnol ddydd . . .

> The soul has arisen of itself
> To the high place where the eternal sun comes to rest
> Where it is infinite day . . .

It was Islwyn who pioneered the quest for truth through the medium of poetry but it was he, too, who first realized the dangers of this quest. Howell Elvet Lewis (Elfed) said that objectivity was an alien concept to him and that he delighted in destroying the barrier between the material and the spiritual and turning everything into one subjective whole. Afterwards, said Elfed, 'Earth, substance, rule, necessity – his imagination dissolved all these things; and out of the chaos arose the beautiful, indistinct outline of a spiritual world of pure freedom and overflowing life.' But, and here was the thrust, 'his intelligence was forced to create a world for him to live in: but no mortal intelligence can create a world as wide and as varied as that created by an Immortal Intelligence'.[58]

A review of a volume of Islwyn's sermons – by N. Cynhafal Jones perhaps – contains some revealing comments. The reviewer says that he was in the company of Islwyn in 1856 and that he had with him the manuscript of his famous epic 'Y Storm' (The Storm) but Islwyn gave him to understand that he did not intend to publish the work in its entirety.

> The reason he gave us was that, while he was writing the poem he read some German authors and that they had influenced him to such an extent that he began to cherish their ideas and partake of their spirit, but that he subsequently became convinced that the ideas of these writers were not correct, nor was their spirit right and thus he could not publish [the poem] . . .[59]

Whatever the effect of this on his later poetry, it is a tribute to his philosophical and theological perceptiveness. His pupils, however, were not as astute; they assumed that they could embrace the Hegelian philosophy and express Christianity through it without Christianity suffering as a result. We find an example of this in the young W. J. Gruffydd's views regarding hymns:

> The hymns of Williams Pantycelyn are raw emotion: and emotion is the main need of Welsh literature today . . . the shell is the insignificant convention that is always changing; and the heart of the truth is the

emotion behind them that never changes. Let this emotion be put into poetry; this is the true aim of poetry.[60]

'Raw emotion'? What is 'raw emotion'? It probably means that the emotion has an object and that the object is important. Or are we to presume that it is of no import whether Williams composed his hymn to a jam jar or to Jesus Christ? If we are to distance ourselves from the intellectual explanation of reality does this not mean bidding farewell to rationality? Moreover how can we 'make sense' of anything if we reject the very instinct in human personality that gets to grips with that task?

Without a doubt, these trends indicate that the Christian mindset in Wales was under siege. Several influential writers had embraced a theory that made the poet's consciousness a source of truth alongside the revelation in Christ. Rather than listen to God speaking to them in his Word, Welsh writers came to rely upon the richness of their own private imagination. No longer did the writer come face to face with God and confess the poverty of his spirit, rather he took pleasure in his own cultural perceptiveness. Humankind's privilege was no longer to face the meaning given by God in his Word and in an objective creation but rather to pour their own manufactured meaning into the environment. In a word, human beings were tempted to play God.[61] These trends among the Welsh-language intelligentsia during the late nineteenth century represented a kind of worship of the self.

The literary critic Tecwyn Lloyd drew the conclusion that the work of the New Poet indicated a crisis of faith.[62] He did not have a good word to say of the period: 'In truth it was a period of empty conservatism and dead institutional dignity. When the terrible horror of 1914–18 came, it collapsed like a pack of cards.' Lloyd exaggerates here because this was merely one element in an extremely complex pattern and every single New Poet in Wales in 1894 could have been contained in a very small chapel vestry. However, it is a significant element. For one thing, when there is a tendency to see a poet and writer as a mediator of enduring truths, it is a sign that a society that has for the most part been religious is becoming humanist in its orientation. Grace is beginning to yield to culture. The most obvious characteristic of the preacher-poet is that he bridges both periods.[63] Secondly, the poor aesthetic value of so much of the work of the poets of the period – and the New Poets in particular – shows how the images, the symbols and the signs which had previously expressed a unity of faith were beginning to disintegrate. As the American critic, Suzanne Langer wrote:

> If, now, the field of our unconscious symbolic orientation is suddenly plowed up by tremendous changes in the external world and in the social order, we lose our hold, our convictions, and therewith our effectual purposes . . . All old symbols are gone, and thousands of average lives offer no new materials to a creative imagination . . .[64]

She is speaking of the twentieth century but huge social and cultural changes were tearing apart the symbolism of the people of Wales at the end of the Victorian era and, in trying to combine Christianity with alien philosophies, some of the writers and thinkers of that era were paving the way for the despair that was to characterize the generation that followed.

Romanticism involved placing a fresh value on personal emotion and experience and it required that the world of nature is seen in their light. For the Romantic, the significance of history, society and religion lay in their effects upon individual experience. But when Romanticism merged with pantheistic philosophy, people were impelled to use it as a refuge from the threats posed by the objective world. As we have seen, poets and writers were retreating into the safe havens of their innermost thoughts and thus joining the great shift towards subjectivism. Why did they feel themselves to be under threat? Why had the objective world become a place of confusion which required the inspiration of poet interpreters to penetrate its veil in order to reach unadulterated truth? One answer is scientific progress. We come face to face here with a perplexing contradiction that was not only prevalent in Wales at the end of the nineteenth century, but which had existed in Europe for generations. Whereas medieval Catholicism found difficulty in reconciling nature and grace, after about 1700 the modern world found it increasingly difficult to reconcile nature and personality, or nature and freedom. In becoming more intelligible, the world, paradoxically, had become less meaningful. Step by step, from discovery to discovery, scientists were explaining the mysteries of nature and tracing the various laws that bound natural objects together. They made everything that came within the realm of the senses into a closed, if intelligible, system.

Immanuel Kant proposed a philosophy compatible with the demands of science. It was human intellect, he claimed, which organized the raw materials delivered by the senses. The product of this activity was knowledge. Raw sensory experiences were not translated into knowledge until the intellect had put them into their categories. The intellect was in no position to provide people with knowledge if they did not receive the proper materials through their senses. However, the senses had no ability to connect with the invisible, with God, with immortality or with the human soul. Thus, according to Kant, one cannot 'know' God. Nevertheless human reason, which is more wide-reaching than understanding, is forced to postulate their existence as the necessary premiss for the moral life. Kant wanted to satisfy the philosopher's need for sound foundations for scientific knowledge and, at the same time, he wished to please religious people who required justification for believing in spiritual realities. Despite the brilliance of his attempt, this philosophy soon led to fresh intellectual tensions for it taught that the world of nature is governed by rigid laws. It was a world without miracles. The spiritual realities which had hitherto made people's lives meaningful were now pushed aside. Human knowledge was confined to the world of perception, of the senses. Moreover, it was human intellect that created some order out of the sensory chaos of this world. The chasm between the world of nature and the world of personal significance was evident. Some of the most able thinkers of the century exercised their resources to the utmost, seeking to breach this divide, but an increasing number felt obliged to come to terms with it.

Charles Darwin suggested how evolution could help explain the mysteries of development including that of humankind. Was God needed at all? Darwin vacillated over this question all his life. Thomas Huxley and others deemed that God was now superfluous in his own world. In any case, Kant's teaching on the huge capabilities of the human intellect captivated people. This is what governed the world and gave knowledge its basic certainty. What need was there for miracles now? What greater proof of the remarkable abilities of human intellect, and of the accuracy of scientific learning, than the shower of blessings that issued from laboratories and factories? Yet people could not come to terms with the dogma that they were nothing more than the product of natural processes. It is no wonder that so many retreated into the world of private emotion and experience. Romanticism at least offered a more humane environment than the cold and rigid world of the scientists. There is no doubt that scientific pioneers, in lightening the burden of manual labour, had placed heavier burdens on the heart. How could these two worlds be reconciled? Was humankind now condemned to suffer the agonizing schizophrenia that was the consequence of living in the world of romance and in the world of science at the same time? It is no wonder that in 1866 Robert Louis Stevenson published his novel, *The Strange Case of Dr Jekyll and Mr Hyde*, and it is no wonder that its popularity has never waned.

In any discussion of the influence of scientific progress on the Welsh mindset towards the end of the nineteenth century, it is worth remarking that the word 'science' was used in at least three ways. Occasionally it meant the products of the new technology; at other times it meant the new facts that were continually emerging with regard to the natural world; and at others it meant the theories formulated to explain those facts. Because the word 'science' was used to mean different things, there were of course conflicting statements made about science.

Technological progress had a huge impact in the Victorian age. Invention flourished and towards the end of the nineteenth century new industries had emerged in the wake of the discovery of electricity and the perfection of the internal combustion engine. All this had a major impact on the spiritual realm, as well as on people's social and economic existence. It was not easy for a generation that remembered a Wales before the existence of trains, steamers, telephones, motor cars or anaesthetic to come to terms with this new world. On the one hand, people were generally entranced at the marvel of these new inventions. On the other hand it was difficult to get used to the displacement of the old rituals and customs that was the inevitable consequence of their use. Many felt the magic of the new 'scientific' equipment.[65] Poets composed *englynion* and poems praising inventions such as the sewing machine, the motor bike, the radio, the aeroplane, the motor car, electricity and even 'Carbide of calcium'.[66]

As the years unfolded from 1909 onwards this theme would become increasingly common. It was not often that poets attempted to tackle the tension that had developed in people's minds between the realm of nature and the realm of God. Meilir Môn did so in his *pryddest*, 'The two worlds' and followed a pattern that expressed the kind of teaching found in the work of Williams Pantycelyn,[67] but on the whole poets were eager to sing the praises of the new technological world.[68] Although it is not difficult to find references like this in contemporary journals, there were also many that expressed longing for the old world that was fast disappearing. Once again the increasing popularity of Romanticism is significant.

The Victorian age was hungry for facts. This aspect of culture is reflected in the eagerness of periodicals to publish articles explaining the secrets of the natural world. This continued until the end of the nineteenth century and beyond. For instance, in *Y Drysorfa* we find articles by David Lloyd Jones on 'the breadth of creation',[69] 'the distant suns of creation'[70] and on 'the composition of the sun'.[71] Gwilym Owen presented the fruit of contemporary research in his articles on the nature of light.[72] Nevertheless, it can hardly be claimed that the progress of factual information as such caused much mental turmoil for anyone.

It was a different story with some of the theories proposed to explain the facts. Of these the one that had the greatest impact was the theory of evolution. The intellectual atmosphere of the period was well prepared for it. Others had published the main principles of Darwin's teaching before him; his contribution was the detailed observations which were made during his voyage on the *Beagle* between 1831 and 1836 and he then set these in order to support the theory. Another reason for the popularity of his work was that he placed science within reach of the masses. Indeed it could be argued that he broadened the meaning of the word 'science'. Science had formerly been based on the mathematical and physical disciplines and no one could really claim to be a scientist without being well versed in them. Darwin, however, had no mathematical training, indeed it could hardly be said that he had received a thorough training in any discipline at all since he had been a mediocre student at university.

However, in *On the Origin of Species* he demonstrated brilliantly how science could be understood clearly even by the untrained mind. It was he, more than anyone else, who was responsible for popularizing science. People outside the restricted circle of the scientists soon realized that they could borrow his theory and apply it to other fields. Karl Marx was captivated by it and, if Darwin had allowed him, he would have dedicated *Das Kapital* formally to

him. Marx began to talk of 'scientific historicism', a clear proof of
the extension of the meaning of the word 'science'. Herbert Spencer
had adopted some of the principles of Darwin's theory before *On
the Origin of Species* was published but after reading it, he began
to apply evolution to social life in general. The theory of evolution
spilt over from the realm of biology into the realms of philosophy,
literature, ideology, sociology, theology and biblical studies.

Two Welsh authors who contributed to the discussion on evolution were David Adams and John Hughes (1850–1932). In 1893,
Adams published the essay that won him the prize at the National
Eisteddfod at Pontypridd that year, *Traethawd ar Ddatblygiad yn
ei Berthynas a'r Cwymp, yr Ymgnawdoliad, a'r Atgyfodiad*[73] (An
Essay on Evolution in its Relation to the Fall, the Incarnation, and
the Resurrection). Adams took the accuracy of the theory of evolution for granted and extended its remit from the biological world
to the world of theology. This was characteristic of the period. The
theory was so attractive that innovative thinkers did not dare to
look too closely at its workings. By 1893, it would have been un-
scientific to ask whether the theory had anything to do with fields
other than biology. Adams remained silent on a very important
aspect of Darwin's theory, namely his concept of the survival of the
fittest.[74] This, of course, was one of the ugliest doctrines which the
nineteenth century bequeathed to the twentieth century, since it
was used to justify war, racial oppression and the Nazi murder
camps. In 1893, however, Adams's interest was elsewhere, namely
the 'application' of the theory of evolution 'to all human life, physically, mentally and morally'.[75]

His chief concern was that evolutionists were using the theory to
'explain creation apart from God'. Consequently, his central question was whether the claims of Christianity could be protected
from this threat. He believed that this was possible only by basing
his argument on Hegel's philosophy.[76] Thus he argued that the
creation was the 'necessary product' of God's love and that the
varieties of plants and animals were merely 'the incarnation of
God's thoughts'. It follows that evolution was merely the loving
thoughts of God gradually coming to fruition over countless centuries. The life of plants and animals was endowed with 'divine
sanctity'.[77] Human beings were the crown of evolution and they
'partake of the mental and moral life of God Himself' since there
was 'organic union between man and God on a personal level'.[78]

The fall of humankind was to be understood as a 'step up'[79] in evolution; it was 'Man's work as he awakes from the slumber of animal life to an awareness of the divine and immortal element within him.' The clash between animal instincts and the 'eternal spirit' which dwelt within gave rise to a new synthesis, namely character.[80] Christ's incarnation was also part of this evolution. It was the result of 'the needs of God's Love as Creator, and the needs of man as a creature'.[81] God was forced to express himself in creation and he assumes a 'higher and more splendid form in the Incarnation'.[82] The incarnation was thus a completely natural phenomenon because it was an essential part of evolution. It could only be considered miraculous to the extent that every self-expression on the part of God was miraculous, whether in a flower, an animal, a human being or in Jesus Christ.[83] Similarly Jesus' death was also part of evolution. 'Justification' and a 'ransom' for sin were merely poetic imagery. In dying on the cross Jesus 'realized the highest potential of human nature' and this pleased the Father and became an example to all ages.[84] In their move towards perfection, all human beings shared in the self-sacrificing and suffering work of Jesus[85] and the climax of the evolutionary process will be immortality.[86]

This revealing book demonstrates with particular clarity the confusion that threatened to overwhelm the minds of Welsh Christians at the time. Adams was quite honest about his intentions. The faith that inspired his analysis was that of Hegel and Darwin, while Christian doctrine had to be subordinated to the demands of this faith. He continued to use Christian vocabulary but it had been bled dry of all Christian meaning.

John Hughes published his book, *Ysgol Jacob* (Jacob's Ladder), in 1899. His approach was quite different from that of Adams. He took his stand upon the Christian revelation, according to the Calvinist understanding of it. He aimed his essay at the 'common folk' and thus, unlike Adams's stilted academic style, he wrote in more idiomatic and homely Welsh. According to Hughes, 'recent ideas which are prevalent in the scientific teaching about evolution . . . tend to create a rift between God and ourselves' and his aim in the book was to 'revive our belief in God and the supernatural, and counteract the new teaching, which is like leaven in our society, consuming our religious strength, unbeknown to us'.[87] John Hughes challenged the Kantian dogma of the sovereignty of human reason and the conclusion which was being drawn from it. Science, he claimed, could only function through faith. Science could not prove that other people exist by the exercise of reason. Hughes built here upon a very significant premiss. Because faith is at the root of all human activity – including reasoning – it can be said that all human activity has its root in religion. Human beings are essentially religious. Thus when a scientist denies the existence of God, neither naked reason nor his or her work as a scientist was at the root of this but the religious inclination of the heart. Such a scientist demonstrates the inclination of the heart by creating an idol instead of God. 'If the scientist denies him as the Creator and Author of all things, he must put something in his place. He has the laws of nature, he has matter, force, energy. These are his gods.'[88]

This is what had happened to those who used the theory of evolution as the basis to undermine Christianity and God. There were religious motives at work. Without realizing it, John Hughes had chanced upon an interesting fact about Charles Darwin which is now well-known. He spent his life in spiritual turmoil and the hope that he could somehow prove that God did not exist motivated and permeated his scientific work.[89] To return to John Hughes; for him, faith governed all of humankind's cultural works. The creator intended the human personality to reflect, as if in a mirror, the unity of the reality which surrounded it, but 'man's sin has clouded the mirror'. Humankind in that condition misinterpreted that reality and heard its message incorrectly. 'The voice of the heart is faithlessness. The perversion of the heart closes the ears and blinds the eyes.'[90] This is humankind's condition under the burden of sin. If faith in Christ has been dethroned in the heart, human cultural work becomes a destructive power. 'Who would have supposed that it was possible to pervert scientific progress to make man more of a pagan and to reinforce man's unbelief through the enrichment of his civilization?' When the heart was enslaved to faithlessness or any other idol it 'is full of ungodly tendencies that pervert the intellect like an unfaithful witness'.[91] Thus it was encouraging for Christians to realize that the struggle here was not between the rational enlightenment of science and opinionated prejudice, but rather a clash between two faiths. When the heart 'is deceitful, it can place its own construction and interpretation on creation and on life'.[92]

It is important to note that John Hughes did not in any way

disparage the scientist's work nor did he deny that the analytical mind should reign supreme in its own proper sphere. Science was such a sphere and the scientist should not 'believe in a discovery or a truth that is the fruit of observation, until his reason has proved it'. Nevertheless it is not wise to let analytical reason reign supreme. It was of no avail to discuss God as if he were an object of biological research. According to Hughes, the problem with the contemporary agnostic scientist was that he confounded various aspects of reality. 'He tries to make a religion out of science and science out of religion'.[93] If his research forces him to adopt evolution as an explanation of certain biological problems, the scientist does well to adopt it. But evolution is not a theological doctrine. 'Science can be sure about facts, and quite ignorant of their causes.'[94]

Standing firmly on his biblical premisses, Hughes was able to study the theory of evolution in a measured and critical fashion. He was not tempted to sacrifice the substance of Christianity in order to effect a reconciliation with any philosophy. On the contrary, philosophy had to submit to the light of Christianity. On the other hand, there was no irresponsible condemnation such as that uttered by Jenkins, Trefdraeth, from the chair of the Baptist Union at Morriston in 1890, when he attacked Darwin, Huxley and other evolutionists, saying 'The fact of the matter is, that they are bigger monkeys, despite all their education, than their putative forefather, and we need to stand firm against their groundless assertions.'[95]

Without a doubt, scientific theories and the scientific method of dealing with questions shook people's faith. John Lloyd Williams, for instance, spoke of the doubts that troubled him when he began to study scientific subjects at Bangor Normal College, where he went as a student in 1873.[96] Evan Davies, Trefriw, said from the chair of the Pwllheli Methodist Association in 1894 that the scientific education of the colleges created an anti-religious spirit.[97] However, students and young people were not the only ones who felt the effect of the new belief in nature as a closed system. Some of the churches were accustomed to holding prayer meetings at times of drought or to entreat God to intervene directly with the weather in some other way, according to the circumstances.[98] By the 1890s the beliefs that were fundamental to this practice were waning.[99] Christian leaders had their work cut out reflecting on the implications of scientific scholarship.

John Hughes's position in *Ysgol Jacob* is particularly interesting because it is quite clearly based upon principles that would enable the creation of a rich and comprehensive doctrine of the relationship between culture in its various aspects and Christianity. His theory was not alien or novel. It was in the tradition of earlier Christian thinkers such as Thomas Jones of Denbigh, David Jones, Treborth, and Evan Evans (Ieuan Glan Geirionydd). It was strikingly similar to the one developed by the nineteenth-century Dutch Calvinists, expressed in the cultural theology of Groen van Prinsterer and Abraham Kuyper.[100]

The disastrous failure of the Evangelical Accord in Wales at the end of the nineteenth century owed much to the failure to realize the significance of the principles set out by John Hughes and others like him. Instead of embracing the affirmative, sober and biblical unity that was at the crux of this vision, the intellectual leaders of Wales embraced doctrines that blurred the edges of Christian witness in the nation's cultural and public life. The divide between religion and culture became wider and a chasm opened up in the soul of Wales.

By the end of the nineteenth century the position of Welsh Christians wavered with regard to the relationship between faith and culture. This question caused quite a stir even in the Catholic Church. A generation previously, Pope Pius IX in his encyclical *Quanta Cura* and the Syllabus of Errors, 8 December 1864, had steadfastly rejected liberalism, both secular and ecclesiastical, and had condemned the doctrine that the pope should reconcile the church with 'progress, liberalism and modern civilization'.[101] His successor, Leo XIII, had no intention of compromising on doctrinal matters but he was strongly convinced that it would do no good for the church to retreat from this fray. The church had to face the challenge of a new age and try to offer answers to the questions which people were asking. By means of a remarkable series of encyclicals, he did his best to get Christians to shoulder this task.

Part of this policy was his letter *Aeterni Patris*, 4 August 1879, recommending the teaching of St Thomas Aquinas as an excellent basis for the relationship between faith and reason – or, in other words, between Christianity and culture. Gradually, the study of Thomist philosophy succeeded in inspiring a remarkable revival among Catholic thinkers and especially among those who tried to contribute to the discussion on the nature and status of culture. However, the debate turned sour around the turn of the twentieth century due to the 'Modernist' purge. The Catholic Modernists were not completely at one in their doctrine but they shared the conviction that the Catholic Church should pay closer attention to the new trends in biblical criticism, in historical studies and in philosophy and try to present its teaching in a way that was compatible with the spirit of the age. The names of some of the leaders became very well known, such as Alfred Loisy (1857–1940), George Tyrrell (1861–1909) and Friedrich von Hügel (1852–1925) and their work had some influence on the Protestant mind. However, it was not a major movement and its influence stemmed from the fact that a number of its leaders were men of note in the academic world. Pope Pius X decided that the teaching of the Modernists could not be approved and condemned it in his encyclical *Pascendi Dominici Gregis*, 8 September 1907.[102]

In the wake of the new education system, the ease of travel and swifter communication which linked Wales more closely than ever with England, it is not surprising that Wales echoed English anxieties in cultural and theological matters. But these anxieties had a more profound impact in Wales precisely because confusion in these areas threatened the nation's language and its unique way of life.

I may conclude this part of the discussion and exemplify the depth of the crisis by looking at a volume written on the eve of the First World War and published a few weeks after it broke out. David Adams's *Yr Eglwys a Gwareiddiad Diweddar* (The Church and Recent Civilization) is a profoundly sad book. The enthusiasm of his earlier work had disappeared and he clearly felt that the church was facing a debilitating crisis of faith. By this time his belief in evolution had been tempered by the idea that decline was an undisputed part of the pattern of history. He adhered to the teaching that evolution was the only means to explain the growth of religion and civilization, but the writing is uninspired and devoid of passion. For Adams, the church's work was to influence the world around it. In the past it had been able to 'leaven the state with the spirit and teaching of Jesus'.[103] He summarized his position thus: 'The particular role of the Christian church is to emphasize the moral and religious conditions of all true success and true advance in human society'.[104] He stated frequently that the churches' work was to 'apply principles to the life of society'. He maintained that the words of Jesus Christ showed that he 'intended that the principles that he preached should be applied to the life of society in all its aspects'.[105] The personal influence of individuals would be the means of ensuring this. Thus 'The church's great mission is *to emphasize the need for moral reform in the characters of men*'.[106] The pattern was as follows; individuals come under 'the pervading influence of the principles of God's Kingdom'[107] and then through taking part in social life ensure that the moral influence of these principles 'leavens' or tempers society.

The word 'church' for Adams meant a congregation of believers – as one would expect for a Congregationalist – but its relationship with the Kingdom of God is not made clear. Yet it is of vital importance in any discussion of the relationship between Christianity and culture that this question is answered. Adams said that the Kingdom should 'include humanity in all the manifestations of its varied life'.[108] Does this mean that an institution which is not defined as part of the church (such as a theological college, for instance) can nevertheless be part of God's Kingdom? It is difficult to give a definite answer. Certainly, he said that 'nothing which is of interest and value to man should be divorced from the pervading influence of God's Kingdom',[109] by which he meant moral influence. If one asks whether the influence of Christianity involves more than moral implications, it would appear that Adams's answer was 'no'. If we ask whether the Christian faith claims that Christians see the relationship between the various sciences in a particular way, or whether it says something about the nature of aesthetics or the foundations of the law or the structure of society and the relationship of various social communities with one another, it would appear that Adams's answer was still 'no'. He had no word for these things, more than he had anything to say about the nation or the language of the people. It is true that he spoke of the family, but it is significant that he discussed it as 'a religious and sacred institution'.[110] He did not discuss whether professing Christianity binds believers to a particular concept of family structure – whether the family, for instance, should be based on marriage between one man and one woman. The aggregate of Adams's teaching on the subject of his book was that the sum total of the relationship between Christianity and culture was the moral influence of individuals. Nevertheless he came to the amazing conclusion (for a Congregationalist) that the church is the queen of civilization: 'Civilization is meant to be a servant subjected to its [the church's] divine authority'.[111]

Although *Yr Eglwys a Gwareiddiad Diweddar* is a disappointing book, it is important and revealing. It is important because it expressed the conviction about the relationship between Christianity and culture that was to govern the minds of the great majority of the Christians of Wales from that time onwards. It is revealing because it laid bare the basic confusion that killed the creative influence of Christianity upon the culture and social life of Wales. The thrust of Adams's teaching was that Christians were to retire from all responsibility for the formation of society and the pattern of its culture. Others were to be responsible for shaping these things and the churches' role was to anoint the fruit of their labours with moral influence.

What makes Adams's analysis so poignant was his real desire to see Christianity's relevance to contemporary civilization, while at the same time diluting the Christian content so thoroughly that there was very little left. He emptied the doctrines of regeneration, the incarnation, justification and the resurrection so totally of their Christian meaning that he had nothing left but vague 'principles' and 'moral influence'. Yet, it is remarkable that, within the confines of his reasoning, he inclined strongly towards the Catholic doctrine of nature and grace, where grace perfects nature rather than the Protestant ideal of grace saving nature. Not that this was of much comfort to Catholics since Adams rejected so much of what the Catholic Church has always taught about grace. However, this is an example of an unmistakable, albeit unconscious, trend among Protestant thinkers in Wales towards a standpoint that was considerably closer to Catholicism than that of their predecessors.

~ 10 ~

At the Feet of the Theologians

Between 1890 and 1914 changes occurred in the thinking of intellectuals that were to lead initially to uncertainty about the role of theology and then, later, to the disparagement of theology – at least in its traditional forms – as an entirely academic and pointless activity. It occurred something like this.

Theology is concerned with understanding the content and significance of the divine revelation. It is mainly intellectual work which is done in light of scripture as God's Word. The theologian who wishes to do his or her job properly must believe in the divine revelation and faithfully follow the light bestowed by the Bible. Anselm was not far off the mark when he stated that theology is faith seeking understanding. It follows that theology is essential to the life of the church. For a church that fully understands its responsibility, doctrine is indispensable. Among the various purposes attributed to scripture, not the least valuable is that it is 'useful for teaching' (2 Tim. 3: 16) and the importance of 'the standard of sound teaching' (2 Tim. 1: 13) is impressed upon ministers so that they may testify to the truth in the presence of people who 'will not put up with sound doctrine' (2 Tim. 4: 3, all quotations are from the NRSV). The question which must now be asked is whether Welsh Christian leaders between 1890 and 1914 were still zealous in their theology and whether their work had a creative impact upon the mind and life of the nation. When Christianity is thriving and missionary-minded, its theology underpins its vitality and shapes people's culture. Was this true of the period we are studying or did the increasingly secular culture shape theology instead?

There was no shortage of Welsh authors at the turn of the twentieth century who proclaimed the importance of theology. Perhaps not all of them were willing to go as far as R. S. Thomas when he claimed that the orthodoxy of preachers was 'as important, if not more important, than the purity of their lives'.[1] Yet the conviction that theological anarchy could not be tolerated remained strong. A. J. Parry maintained that the Baptists had safeguarded 'the evangelical nature of the ministry' and had kept the truth in an 'incorrupt and steadfast' form.[2] William Price of Holyhead agreed that his fellow religionists had kept the truth both 'in its entirety and its details'.[3] However, the liberal J. Gwili Jenkins claimed that doubt was widespread in Wales.[4] The same tension existed among the Calvinistic Methodists. The 'Monthly notes' in Y Drysorfa in 1898 proclaimed that the pulpit 'up until now . . . is very evangelical',[5] while John Hughes, Liverpool, added the 'heart of the church adhered to the sincere faith'.[6] Thomas Charles Edwards, on the contrary, was pessimistic. As early as 1888 he wrote:

> In the days of our fathers it could be assumed that the main truth of a multitude of religious laity in Wales was theological truth. But is it now thus? Is not some political or scientific theory, the focus of attention and is it not a fact that our young men by and large have no theology or appetite for it?[7]

Eight years later he was still gloomy. He believed that the outlook for Christianity in Wales was bleak, not so much because ministers generally had turned their back on the faith, but because of the laity's ignorance of theology.[8] The young William George (cousin of the later prime minister, David Lloyd George) declared quite plainly that theological uncertainty and chaos abounded in churches.[9] Some observers believed that many young people were unsure of even the basic facts and truths of Christianity.[10] It is evident that the observers did not agree with one another as they tried to read the signs of the times.

Thomas Charles Edwards was one of the few thinkers who took the Welsh theological tradition seriously. In a remarkable address to Princes Road Literary Society in Liverpool in 1870 he attempted to trace its history throughout the century.[11] His theme was that the horizons of the Welsh theologian had shrunk since the days of Thomas Jones, Denbigh,[12] and Thomas Charles of Bala.[13] They were familiar with the works of the early church Fathers, the Protestant Reformers, the theologians of the Church of England, the

Puritans and the federal theologians of the Netherlands. However, John Elias, their most popular successor, knew little of these riches because he confined himself to some of the Puritans and eighteenth-century English divines. The result, according to Edwards, was that human need was placed centre stage and that the wonder of the incarnation was barely touched upon. When Arminianism became influential in the early nineteenth century, this tendency towards humanism increased. People began to emphasize human freedom at the expense of the sovereignty of God. 'They enslaved the Creator in order to free the creature'. The worst thing, he said, was that both parties had lost sight of the doctrinal breadth of the Protestant Reformers, so that by 1870 'high Calvinist ideas' among Calvinistic Methodists 'had long since disappeared'.

He returned to this topic in 1888 in his address to the World Presbyterian Council,[14] this time insisting that the poverty of scholarship in Wales was a grievous evil. Because of this the debates of Welsh theologians had deteriorated into 'a war of empty words. Indeed theology was choking to death'.[15] Without a doubt, the churches of Wales paid dearly for the ineffectiveness of the country's theological education. It was quite appropriate for Thomas Charles Edwards to make appreciative reference to his father's work in opening the windows of Welsh theology to the world by means of the periodical Y *Traethodydd* (The Essayist). He acknowledged, however, that the new scholarship that his father helped to disseminate had created an atmosphere in which agnosticism had spread, though he was loath to believe that it would continue. What has most obviously been lost, he said, was a keen awareness of sin, indeed this was 'the great danger that faces Wales today'. Despite this, the contemporary emphasis was on Christ as a pledge of better things to come because 'we hope and pray that it may please the Great Head of the Church to endow us with the rarest and most valuable gift he possesses – a great theologian'. What is apparent in Thomas Charles Edwards's various statements is a sense of anxiety about the future, a passionate desire to safeguard the fundamentals of orthodoxy and a deep respect for the Welsh theological tradition. The most prominent aspect of his analysis was the belief that serious changes were occurring in the Welsh Calvinistic mind.

The one theological school that had made the greatest contribution to the shaping of Wales prior to 1850 was Calvinism. The least that can be said is that it had become increasingly influential from the days of Bishop Richard Davies onwards[16] – and it would not be right to forget the influence of the Augustinian tradition long before that, as Thomas Jones of Denbigh argued.[17] However, a substantial change began to occur soon after 1850, linked, as Thomas Charles Edwards suggested, with the increasing influence of Arminianism. The start of the Wesleyan mission in 1800 was a means of tempering the Calvinism of all the evangelical churches to some degree. However, Arminianism too was moving away from the teachings of John Wesley, and such Welsh pioneers as Owen Davies and John Bryan. These men were not Pelagians in any shape or form and there was no tendency to compromise on the matter of justification through faith alone or to belittle God's work in the salvation of humankind. However, as the Victorian age progressed, humanistic and rationalistic influences began to penetrate Arminianism and even the citadel of Calvinism itself.

Thus by 1870, we find Thomas Charles Edwards announcing that 'High Calvinism' had ceased to exist among the Methodists and within a year 'J.R.' (John Roberts, Conwy) was declaring that classical Calvinism was dead and that even moderate Calvinism was nothing but 'skin and bones'.[18] J.R. was himself a forceful Arminian who enjoyed riling his readers and there is no doubt that his announcement of the death of Calvinism was rather premature, as we shall see.

Nevertheless, by the time that the Disestablishment Commission was sitting, some of the witnesses confirmed what J.R. had said a generation previously. J. Rhydwen Parry, Ffestiniog, gave evidence stating that the majority of Congregational ministers were Arminians,[19] and D. Wyre Lewis agreed, adding that his own denomination, the Baptists, had by now rejected the Calvinists' doctrine of limited atonement – the doctrine that Christ died only for the elect – with both denominations inclining increasingly towards what was essentially the Wesleyan viewpoint.[20]

In light of statements like this, it is easy to understand John Humphreys's pride when he announced before the Disestablishment Commission that the theology of Wales was now the theology of the Wesleyan pioneers and that the denomination had succeeded 'in revolutionizing the theology of the inhabitants generally'.[21] Principal William Edwards, speaking on behalf of the Baptists, disagreed, claiming that his denomination's beliefs had not changed for half a century or more. Moreover, he maintained that the Baptists' theology was common to all the churches and he noted especially the agreement between them and the Calvinistic Methodists.[22]

Concerning Calvinistic Methodist theology, Lord Hugh Cecil asked John Morgan Jones (Cardiff): 'Do the Calvinistic Methodists adhere to the Calvinistic theology?' 'So I believe,' was Jones's reply. When Cecil inquired whether all the denomination affirmed its confession of faith, Jones replied unhesitatingly that they did.[23] Yet when Cecil questioned him more closely, Jones appeared to take a step backwards, finally agreeing that the teaching concerning election was an 'unintelligible mystery'. A cross-examination of another of the Calvinistic Methodist witnesses, John Owen Thomas, yielded similar results. Cecil questioned him at length about the 'Five Points' of Calvinism, but Thomas did not appear to know them, and when he was cross-examined on each one separately, it was obvious that he could not accept them.[24] The inability of these prominent leaders to agree on the precise theological convictions of their respective denominations evidently suggested that change was afoot, and that Calvinism was in decline. By 1914, one reviewer could say 'Calvin and Calvinism are familiar words in Wales. But the man himself is a stranger and his doctrine is almost unknown.'[25]

There is some evidence of disillusionment with all efforts to systematize theology. This had certainly been true of the Independents for some time. To give one example, William Davies, Llandeilo, decided to add to his library by buying a trunk full of theological books in a second-hand book shop in Newport, Gwent. After the trunk had sat unopened in his study for some considerable time, it was moved to the barn. When it was opened after his death, it was found to contain a set of the works of the Calvinistic Puritan, John Owen.[26] A brief glance through Congregational periodicals from 1870 onwards confirms the impression that interest in systematic theology was definitely on the wane.

There are indications that this was true of other denominations as well. In 1872 a ministerial fraternal in Ffestiniog decided to spend their meetings studying the *Systematic Theology* by Charles Hodge, one of the principal Calvinist leaders in that period in the United States, but according to one of their number, 'we tired of the volume before we reached the end'.[27] There is no doubt that contemporary tastes militated against the older theological systems, such as those of George Lewis and John Jenkins, Hengoed, as well as the newer ones such as those of Hodge and Shedd. Books which discussed a single theological subject, often with a practical or pastoral slant, were more to contemporary tastes. The Calvinistic Methodist Thomas Rees, Merthyr Tudful, could claim even from the chair of the general assembly in 1894 that systematic doctrine was linked with 'the chatter of pseudo-science and astrology, and as such it is repugnant to the age'.[28] Some maintained that this opposition was not confined to systematic theology but that doctrine as such was under siege.[29] Edward Anwyl echoed the same opinion ten years later when he claimed that interest in theology had been killed by fascination for politics and popular literature and he lamented this and pleaded for systematic theology to be taught in the new University of Wales.[30] But was this true? In the same year, 1896, an editorial in Y *Goleuad* claimed, 'More time is allocated in the association to discussing doctrinal and spiritual matters in these years, than several years ago.'[31] A study of books and periodicals of the era around the turn of the twentieth century confirms the view that these were years of great vitality in the history of Welsh theology.

One powerful influence on people's thinking from 1880 until the end of the 1890s was the 'New Theology' (not to be confused with the trend of the same name later linked with the name of R. J. Campbell). One of the features of this theology was a powerful emphasis on history, as a reaction against the fashionable trend to turn all the stories of the Bible into a parable of some general truths. This new school was indebted to the work of D. F. Strauss and F. C. Baur, but rejected their tendency to foist their Hegelian philosophy on to the historical facts of the Bible. On this basis, the New Theology placed a great emphasis on the central significance of Christ, highlighting the truth that he was a historical figure and together with this 'it placed particular significance on the concept that the Redeemer was seeking love towards himself among his followers more than anything else'.[32] Consistent with this was the new focus on the Fatherhood of God.

> The fruit of this awakening is the New Theology. Its most prominent element is its return to the historical Christ. It is through Him that we consider the doctrines, the sacraments, the Church, the Scriptures. What did Christ teach about God, about man, about the future? These are the questions for which answers are sought; not what the fathers

say, what the churches say, and not what the creeds teach, but what explanation does Christ give, in his person, his doctrine, his work . . .[33]

This meant shifting the emphasis from belief systems to a loving experience. Lewis Probert blamed these thinkers for undermining the authority of objective revelation through exalting religious experience. He said that it would be better for them 'not to make their feelings and their experience the criteria for truth to the extent that they do, but rather to confine themselves more to the revealed things of God, as Calvin did, and others'.[34] All things considered this 'New Theology' prepared the way for theological liberalism.

Alongside this must be placed the influence of the theory of evolution. The views of David Adams and John Hughes on the subject have already been mentioned but reference must be made also to the influence of one of the most popular books of the period, *Natural Law in the Spiritual World* (1884) by Henry Drummond. This book continues to be of interest insofar as it attempted to reconcile science and theology by the use of Hegelian presuppositions and by arguing that the same laws govern both disciplines. Drummond attempted to express Christian truths in language borrowed from the world of evolutionary science. Strangely enough, he has no chapter on the person of Christ. The truth is that he never addressed the central subject, namely whether Jesus Christ was the product of the evolutionary process. Despite this, his book was widely read and written about in Wales.[35]

There were others who did attempt to apply the theory of evolution to the doctrine of the person of Christ. The most important book in this debate was *The Place of Christ in Modern Theology* (1893) by Andrew Martin Fairbairn, the principal of Mansfield College, Oxford. In the opinion of one Welsh observer, 'there is no doubt that this will be the standard book for the new Theology'.[36] He was not far off the mark because by 1907 the book was in its thirteenth edition. Fairbairn's reputation in Wales became immense. In the fullness of time, several of his pupils would become prominent figures in the colleges and denominations. Moreover, the annual summer school held in Mansfield attracted many visitors from Wales who returned home eager to propagate the views which they had heard.

As a result of his influence, Fairbairn became the chief architect of the University of Wales's theological curriculum and later a member of the Disestablishment Commission. He was also a powerful and lucid writer. The significance of this volume lay in its portrayal of Christ as the apex of human evolution. At last it was felt that Christ and evolution could be combined. It was essential that Christ be understood as a historical figure. For over half a century, scholars had argued for the explicit historicity of Jesus of Nazareth in all the directness of his human life. Knowing him in this light, as a living person who participates in the same evolutionary process as the rest of humankind, observers would also see that he possessed a unique and crucial role in the life of the world. He was more than the saints and prophets of the Old Testament.

> He transcended them all. He was greater than Jonah, than Solomon, than Abraham. He was greater even than the most sacred institutions – the Temple, the Sabbath, the Law, and the Prophets – which He at once superseded and fulfilled. And He was not only great as regards the past, but necessary as regards the future – the one Being needful for all men everywhere and needful not simply as an official, but as a person. His very being is a condition of man's chief good.[37]

Fairbairn's sweeping vision and the eloquence of his writing gripped the imagination of many of his Welsh readers. Now the cry was 'back to Christ'. The popularity of this slogan can be measured by one observation made during the meetings of the Union of Welsh Independents in Llanelli (1899): 'Has the cry Back to Christ . . . not become rather stale by now?'[38] Stale or not, it denoted an important turning point in Welsh theology.

In the midst of these influences Thomas Charles Edwards prepared his Davies Lecture, *The God-Man* (London, 1895). Two years later it appeared in Welsh under the title, *Y Duw-Ddyn*.[39] It discussed subjects that were fundamental to the Christian faith. A year before Fairbairn's work was published, Edwards had suggested that the doctrine of Christ should be central to Christian thought.

> This doctrine is great enough and powerful enough to endow much lesser doctrines with saving efficacy, insofar as they are linked with it. This doctrine empowers doctrines which in themselves constitute merely part of the truth, until they come to possess the influence of a comprehensive theology.[40]

This suggestion was not completely original because his father, Lewis Edwards had 'placed the doctrine of Christ as the central focus of all theology and the benchmark for all other doctrines'.[41] This inclination was a foretaste of the 'christological centring' that would reach its climax in the twentieth century in the work of Karl Barth. This emphasis, like Edwards's lecture on the God-Man, also tended to raise profound questions concerning the relationship between faith and culture.

Edwards was evidently uneasy with the tendency to contrast humankind and God; he attempted to allay the tension between the human and divine by arguing that human beings are indispensable for God. This flew in the face of the classical doctrine that God, in his divine freedom and not coerced by any inward or outward necessity, had created humanity, and that humankind was not necessary, far less indispensable, to God. Edwards also claimed that the fact that God created humankind meant that human beings were of divine origin and so too were the conditions of their existence. Evolution itself issues from the divine mind and in this way it becomes possible to reconcile the concept of evolution with the theory of the supernatural, if we only realize that Christ is the mediator between both. In Christ, the concept of the supernatural becomes most closely linked with the natural and evolutionary processes that we see in the natural world. The closing sentences of his book express this conviction succinctly.

> If an ideal humanity existed necessarily and eternally in God, it became an actual humanity at the incarnation. The God-Man is not, as Hegel said, a monstrosity. A complex personality like Christ's is possible. If it be asked whether He is God or Man, the answer must be Both in One. He was in idea from eternity God-Man. He is and will be to eternity actual God-Man.[42]

In these words, he revealed the philosophical premisses of this theology. It is rooted in Hegel's teaching that everything in creation and in history stems from the Immortal. The Immortal objectifies itself in all things that exist by means of an evolutionary process. This means, basically, that humankind is an expression of God. The 'infinite qualitative difference' between God and humanity is compromised, as Kierkegaard argued in his savage attacks on Hegel. Thus Edwards argued that 'man's prototype is in God'.

Because humankind was created 'in the image of God, some of man's characteristics are already to be found in God'. These characteristics are the 'humanity of God' and in Jesus Christ they are revealed in all their glory.

The inevitable conclusion is that Christ's humanity is eternal. That which is 'highest and divinest in man' namely the 'capacity of self-abnegation and self-surrender to an Infinite Object' is 'exemplified perfectly and from eternity' in the divine son 'because He is Son, ever hearing the Father's voice'.[43] Puleston Jones maintained that this doctrine was Thomas Charles Edwards's enduring contribution to theology in Wales.[44] The question remains, however, whether it was a healthy contribution.

On the basis of this logic Thomas Charles Edwards took a step further which changed the emphasis of classical Protestant theology, and more than a little of the Catholic tradition as well, in a fundamental way. The traditional emphasis lay in the sinner's need for a Saviour as the motive for the Son of God becoming flesh, leaning heavily on Paul's words 'For you know the generous act of our Lord Jesus Christ, that though he was rich, yet for your sakes he became poor, so that by his poverty you might become rich' (2 Cor. 8: 9, NRSV). Edwards rejected this. God's revelation cannot of itself depend upon a historical – almost accidental – occurrence. On the contrary, humankind must believe 'the doctrine that the Son of God must become man, even if sin had not been permitted to enter into the world'.[45] Once again, Edwards emphasized necessity. Where theologians tried to safeguard God's freedom by speaking of his 'providences' or his 'will', Edwards rejected this vocabulary and saw all God's actions springing from the essential needs of his nature and his character.

An important aspect of classical theological teaching was that God's Son came into the world through 'grace', in other words without any compulsion or coercion. Edwards goes a considerable way towards undermining the doctrine of grace. The fact that his theology emphasized the incarnation rather than the cross demonstrates his sympathy with a Catholic doctrine that was rapidly gaining ground in this period in the Church of England. At the same time it meant changing the whole theological balance of the Evangelical Accord in Wales.

What caused the greatest stir was his doctrine of the relationship between the divinity and the humanity of Christ. He proposed a new version of the doctrine of *kenosis*. In Philippians 2: 6–7, Paul says of Jesus Christ – according to the old translation (KJV) – that he 'thought it not robbery to be equal with God: but made himself of no reputation'. The words 'of no reputation' express generally the overall concept of the incarnation, namely that the Son in taking flesh had divested himself of his heavenly glory. The New Revised Standard Version conveys more literally what is implied in the original Greek: he 'did not regard equality with God as something to be exploited, but emptied himself'. During the nineteenth century several theologians attempted to explain more fully what was implied in this 'emptying'.[46] The tendency was to claim that the Son had in some way discarded some of his attributes. In England, Charles Gore was chiefly responsible for promulgating this theory, but in Wales the influence of Fairbairn and Thomas Charles Edwards was much more significant.

In *The Place of Christ in Modern Theology* Fairbairn distinguished between 'moral' attributes and 'natural' attributes in the person of Christ. In his incarnate form, the Son of God continued to exercise his moral attributes, but he 'emptied' himself of the usual attributes of his deity, such as his omnipotence and his omniscience. By differentiating between various attributes, Fairbairn hoped to safeguard the true humanity of Christ while allowing for restrictions in his knowledge of the world, of history and of the future. Thomas Charles Edwards followed the same path and differentiated between the natural and moral attributes of God. Human beings cannot be omniscient or omnipresent, therefore it cannot be possible for them to share God's usual attributes. However, they can become like God in love, righteousness and graciousness and so there is nothing wrong in claiming that they share God's moral attributes. It was thus that the incarnation of the second person of the Trinity was possible.[47] But what about the attributes of Christ's divinity during his incarnation? According to Edwards, through 'incarnation he assumed a human personality' and at the same time it was essential that he 'continued to be God'.[48] And yet, some change did occur because he 'puts the form of God aside for a while, and takes upon himself, instead of God's form, the form of a servant'.

> The incarnation gave to a Divine Person a human personality; but He has not ceased to be a Divine Person. It is only a change of condition . . .

> All the actions of the Man are the actions of the Logos incarnate, and the actions of the Logos incarnate are the actions of the Second Person in the Trinity.[49]

The question remains, however, what happened to the usual abilities of his divinity during his incarnation? Did the person who slept in a boat on the Sea of Galilee know everything as God does? Edwards suggested that somehow he divested himself of the willingness to use these abilities. The final answer is that he did not lose these natural attributes but that they were inactive in him.[50]

This book engendered lively and interesting debate.[51] The bibliography of the debate is so lengthy as to suggest that this was one of the most important theological debates in Welsh theological history. Moreover, no one can read these articles and books without being impressed by the scholarship and skill of the contributors with the discussion being conducted, on the whole, in an excellent spirit. They knew that crucial issues were at stake and there was not much wrong with the verve, vitality and the scholarship of churches who could produce theological disputants such as these.

Thomas Charles Edwards received the support of W. Ryle Davies,[52] Ben Evans, and especially R. H. Morgan, a man whose early death was a loss to Welsh theology,[53] but, on the whole, most of his reviewers were critical. John Williams 'Brynsiencyn', T. E. Roberts, Owen Evans and D. S. Thomas insisted that the Son of God had not divested himself in any way of any of his divine attributes during the incarnation. They maintained that such a claim offended the principle that Christ's divine nature remained unchanged throughout the incarnation, as the Chalcedon definition had stated in AD 451. In their opinion, the Son emptied himself of his divine glory alone. As T. E. Roberts said, the Son 'emptied himself not of his nature or of his attributes as God, but of the glory that he shared with the Father . . . he emptied himself for his task, and for his work as a servant'.[54] Thus he retained his divine attributes intact.[55] 'I cannot believe', said Owen Evans, 'that the humanity of the Redeemer is like an eyelid over the great eye of his omniscience.'[56]

The most substantial contribution to the discussion was made by Rowland Sawil Thomas[57] with his 432-page book, *Undod Personol y Duw-Ddyn* (The Personal Unity of the God-Man). Thomas learnt his theology at Princeton at the feet of Charles Archibald Hodge, and although he did not embrace the theology of his teacher in its entirety, Calvinism had no abler defender in Wales than R. S. Thomas. He deserves a place of honour in the gallery of Welsh theologians, in the same class as George Lewis, John Jenkins of Hengoed, Thomas Jones of Denbigh, Lewis Edwards and Miall Edwards. He had all the resources of a masterly dogmatician – a catholic interest, a thorough knowledge of the field, an eagle eye to spot the weak points of his opponents' arguments, fairness of mind, a consummate ability to summarize the doctrines in question and spiritual passion as well. His Achilles heel was a leaden literary style which is the main reason why his name sank so deeply into obscurity. But for anyone wishing to become familiar with the history of the doctrine of the person of Christ throughout the centuries, R. S. Thomas's book is still an excellent handbook.

He took his stand squarely on the Chalcedonian definition, maintaining that 'it would not be possible to find a better, more measured, studious, broad and biblical explanation of the nature and constitution of the God-Man'.[58] He defended the viewpoint that the wholly unique personality of the God-Man comprises of three elements, namely, divine nature, human spiritual nature and matter and that the three elements are to be found in Jesus Christ in their perfect wholeness.[59] For him, the concept of *kenosis* violated these principles. He saw it as a 'bold attack on the completeness of the Son's deity in the area of his attributes and his personality'.[60]

In criticizing R. H. Morgan's views, he put his finger on the most significant aspect of the kenotic developments, namely that secular forces were beginning to penetrate the heart of evangelical theology. According to R. H. Morgan, 'there was a tendency in the flesh and humanity of the Lord to draw a veil over his awareness of his Deity'. In other words his humanity caused his divine nature to be eclipsed.[61] This meant that Morgan placed the human personality of Jesus Christ as the 'central focus of his life and work' and it follows inevitably from this that Jesus was really a man and 'that the Divine nature was only a kind of decorative edging' to his human nature.[62]

It was considerations such as these that caused Thomas to reject Thomas Charles Edwards's teachings as well. It is interesting, however, to note that Thomas's zeal for defending both the full humanity and divinity of Christ led him to reject an aspect of the doctrine which was generally accepted as being orthodox and sound. In order to appreciate the point, a word must be said about the background. In emphasizing the fact that Jesus Christ was both completely human and completely divine, it was very easy for Christians to give the impression that in Christ two separate entities had been joined, a form of the heresy called 'Nestorianism'. Indeed, it was felt that the Chalcedon teaching about 'two natures in one Person' threatened the unity of the person of Jesus Christ. In the sixth century, Leontius of Byzantium suggested that one way of avoiding this danger was to claim that the eternal Logos was not conjoined with a human person but that he took upon himself human 'nature' instead. This implied that human nature itself was *im*personal (*anhypostasia*) though it was made personal (*enhypostasia*) by being conjoined with the eternal Logos of God.

R. S. Thomas was very uneasy with this theory as it undermined, for him, the full, unambiguous and complete humanity of Christ. It suggested that Christ was, in some way, an *im*personal being, and if that were true, how could he have been fully a man? In accepting the *enhypostasia*, the church had committed itself to a sort of Apollinarianism and it was high time for this idea 'to be erased'.[63] R. S. Thomas expressed his viewpoint in unambiguous terms in another of his books:

> Jesus' two natures have one composite personality. The Divine and eternal self-awareness is quite aware that it has become, and continues to be, part of the human personality and the human personality is aware that it is part of the Divine personality, so as to form one composite Ego between them . . . Thus the activities carried out by the human nature, such as eating, drinking, sleeping, becoming tired and hungry, are attributed to the Divine-human Person; and the activities carried out by means of the Divine nature, such as being omnipresent, omniscient and omnipotent, are attributed to the same composite Person.[64]

One of R. S. Thomas's great admirers was John Cynddylan Jones,[65] which was not surprising since both were learned representatives of a form of Calvinism which was rapidly losing ground. Cynddylan was an apologist and a popularizer and because of this he deliberately tried to gain the attention of the ordinary church public. He possessed an enviably lucid and lively literary style. Jones rarely wrote anything which did not include something of interest. When the first volume of his major work *Cysondeb y Ffydd* (The Consistency of the Faith) appeared in 1904, it was very well received. So many classes were formed to study it in Calvinistic Methodist churches that they were forced to include it as part of the syllabus for the denomination's examinations the following year.[66] This is proof, by the way, that theological interest had not waned as completely as some melancholy observers maintained. Cynddylan Jones tackled the doctrine of the person of Christ in the second volume of *Cysondeb y Ffydd* (1907). Like R. S. Thomas he emphatically rejected the new theories of *kenosis*, saying 'this is the fruit of the popular doctrine of kenosis – the humanizing of God'.[67]

Cynddylan Jones and Thomas Charles Edwards had clashed with one another during their student days at Bala. Tension always reigned between them because of 'a basic difference in the composition of our minds'.[68] As a consequence of this, and because of his much more conservative theological convictions, Jones was not impressed with Edwards's attempt to restate the theory of the God-Man. He rejected the tendency to emphasize the similarity between God and humanity, maintaining to the contrary that 'the burden of the divine revelation is that there is an insurmountable difference between the Creator and the creation'.[69] It was very different from the emphasis on the incarnation as some kind of divine necessity. 'Such crude, extreme ideas', he claimed, 'are nothing more than a reflection of the Pantheistic doctrine of the age.'[70]

God is not dependent upon his creation in any way and so it is not possible to compromise with the teaching that sees humankind and creation as God's way of objectifying himself. 'Pantheism in its Hegelian form is the leaven that has soured the theology of the last century'.[71] Cynddylan Jones refused to accept the theory that the incarnation is such an indispensable part of the divine self-revelation and that it would have happened anyway even had there not been a fall. Thus he did not support the fashionable trend towards emphasizing not Christ's passion but his birth. He wrote that 'the incarnation as such is not the full revelation of God. It was not in the manger but on the cross, not in Bethlehem but on Calvary, that God revealed the infinity of his love.'[72] Although Jones affirmed the idea that the Logos, the second person of the Holy Trinity, was made flesh not by assuming an individual human personality but by taking human nature into himself, he felt that the discussion concerning the 'personality' of human nature was merely 'sparring with words'. None of the parties in the debate, he claimed, maintained that Jesus as God was bereft of a true, full and complete

humanity. Following the American Calvinists Charles Hodge and
W. G. T. Shedd, Cynddylan Jones maintained that the Redeemer
has one 'ego', he is one person, and he has at the same time divine
consciousness and human consciousness, 'just as the one human
person is aware at the same time of his material nature and his
spirituality'.[73]

The Wesleyans also made their contribution to the debate.
Uwch-Holwyddoryd Diwinyddol, T. J. Pritchard's translation of
William Burt Pope's *Higher Catechism of Theology* was published
in 1905.[74] It is a lengthy book which discusses a whole range of
theological topics and in the section on the person of Christ it
differs only slightly from the viewpoints of R. S. Thomas and
Cynddylan Jones. Of greater interest is the work of Owen Evans
(not to be confused with the Congregationalist of the same name),
Diwinyddiaeth Gristnogol[75] (Christian Theology). Owen Evans
was an excellent theologian with a deep and wide interest in the
work of continental thinkers. Indeed a perusal of his work gives us
a fairly clear idea of the influence of these scholars on Welsh theology
around the beginning of the twentieth century. He discussed the
doctrine of the person of Christ in his second volume, rejecting the
belief that Jesus Christ was merely a man. He argued against the
theologians who tried to place Christianity beyond the reach of
critics by declaring that the value of doctrines such as the Fatherhood of God, forgiveness, the priority of love, were completely
independent of anything that we know for sure about the history of
the One who is supposed to have expressed them, namely Jesus
Christ. Thus Evans rejected Albrecht Ritschl's separation of value
and fact. The historicity of Christianity was of fundamental
importance, and it was not possible to avoid the difficulties that it
engenders because 'if we break the connection with history, *we lose
the whole* saving force of Christianity'.[76] It follows that the identity
of Jesus Christ, what he did, his person and his work, are vital to
Christianity.

Owen Evans was very unhappy with the 'foremost trend in
recent theology' namely the definition of 'Christ's divinity in terms
of experience alone'. He did not deny that 'the divinity of Christ is
first and foremost an experiential truth' for the reason that it was
in him that the first Christians experienced salvation, but when
Ritschl declared that it is not lawful for Christians to go beyond a
declaration that Jesus Christ is 'equal with God', Evans refused to

agree. One should not differentiate between 'experiential truth' and 'objective truth'. Thus he embarked on a discussion of the person of Christ, following the same route as Cynddylan Jones and R. S. Thomas, putting great store on the virgin birth, emphasizing the humanity and divinity of Christ and expressing his adherence to the Chalcedonian definition. He formally rejected the doctrines of *kenosis*, though he inclined towards them by speaking on the 'wholly human form' of the Lord Jesus' consciousness. There is no suggestion in the gospels, he said, that Jesus had a dual consciousness. He had one consciousness which was human. 'It appears to me that Jesus did not know himself as a Son, nor did he know his Father, but to the extent that this was possible for perfect humanity . . . If there were boundaries here, they are self-appointed boundaries.'[77] From the perspective of R. S. Thomas and Cynddylan, this statement would imply an over-eagerness to restrict the divinity of the creator.

One of the most delightful books on the subject is *Person Crist* (The Person of Christ) by Richard Morris.[78] This was the second volume in a series 'Theological handbooks for the working class', a series killed off by the First World War. Once again this is a volume that combines impeccable scholarship with lucid expression. Richard Morris maintained that the greatest danger facing Christianity in the near future lay in the concept that 'Jesus was a divine man'.[79] The church had to face the question whether Jesus was the God-Man or a human being who had been deified. What should we attribute to him, divinity or godliness? Was his divine nature merely an added quality of this humanity, or was it merged with his humanity?

Morris was adamant. The Son is one of the Holy Trinity. He occupies a unique position in relation to creation because he is a 'medium' between God and creation. However, he is also a 'mediator' between God and humankind. He existed before anything was created and thus 'is the prototype of man' but of his free will and his grace he was the mediator made flesh. As such he is a 'divine-human Person', truly God and truly human. He is one person with two natures whose human nature is impersonal, though this does not make him any less of a man.

The tone of the Lord Jesus' humanity is on His entire personality. The divine nature and the human nature are not mixed but both the divine nature and the human nature infiltrate the entire personality of the Person. In other words, the divine Person has become a divine-human Person; not a divine person and a human person but a divine-human Person.[80]

Nor was Morris willing to embrace the contemporary teaching on *kenosis*. In his view, 'the Son, in taking the form of a servant, continued in the form of God. He took the form of a servant, not *instead* of the form of God, but in addition to it.'[81] Richard Morris's volume was a powerful interpretation of the evangelical viewpoint – or rather the Catholic viewpoint – which had been defended by R. S. Thomas, Cynddylan Jones and Owen Evans. The use of the word 'catholic' in this context is wholly appropriate because it reminds us that the orthodox interpretation of the person of Christ was shared by the evangelical, the Anglican and the Catholic churches, indeed all those who participated in this debate appealed to the judgement of the early ecumenical councils. Any resulting change in doctrine would affect all parties of Christians and, although the orthodox viewpoint was defended stoutly by many, the winds of change were blowing ever more strongly. Although Thomas Charles Edwards's views had veered in a liberal direction, he was, in R. S. Thomas's words, 'completely faithful to the basic truths of religion'.[82] However, it was soon felt that Edwards's views were overcautious and tame.

It was with the thought of David Miall Edwards that popular Welsh theology lurched to the left. Of all the theologians mentioned so far, he was the most prolific. He was erudite, balanced and fair and his work was imbued with a kind of refined humility. He was a first-class Welsh scholar, as one might expect perhaps from a nationalist who was encouraged to begin preaching by Michael D. Jones in Llandderfel, and through his ability to express complex subjects in a simple and clear idiom, he did more than anyone in his generation to maintain the interest of ordinary church people in theological matters. I shall now turn to his chapters on the person of Christ in his book *Crefydd a Bywyd*[83] (Religion and Life).

Miall Edwards felt deeply that the time had come to 'restate the doctrine of Christ in terms that are consistent with the best knowledge and philosophy of this age'.[84] One motive for undertaking this task was the difficulty which many felt with the classical doctrine of two natures in Christ. Miall Edwards maintained that it was not possible to define the difference between 'nature' and 'person' or to 'form an idea of the human or divine nature which does not at the same time possess a personality'.[85] Even if a satisfactory definition were possible, it would not be possible to meet the requirements of the Chalcedon definition that Jesus Christ was truly man while insisting that he had an impersonal human nature. 'What is man apart from his personality? He is nothing more than a bundle of lifeless attributes . . .'[86] If both natures were complete in themselves, how could one explain the unity between them?

One attempt at solving this dilemma was the development of the doctrine of *kenosis*. Miall Edwards rejected this doctrine outright and his comments on it are as brief as they are scathing. He rejected the emptying of the divine nature because this meant severing the 'personal continuity' between the 'Eternal Word and the Incarnate Word'. If the Word has divested himself of his supernatural attributes 'what we have in the incarnation is not a God-man but a man-man!' And how can God empty himself of his attributes? Attributes are not independent entities that can be shed like a garment without effecting the essence in any way; 'they are nothing other than a form of existence of . . . the essence itself'. And again, if the Word in this incarnation is stripped of his divine attributes, 'what would become of the government of the universe during the period of the incarnation?'[87] These were the kinds of difficulties which Miall Edwards perceived with the various attempts, both old and new, to formulate a relevant doctrine of the person of Christ.

Edwards determined to begin afresh. It is obvious, he said, that Greek philosophical thought, with its talk of 'person', 'nature', 'essence' and 'substance', had to be avoided. The need of the day was for personal and moral categories, in fact those which were found in the gospels' witness to Jesus and 'that which Christ is and has been in the spiritual and moral life of believers'.[88] Although Miall Edwards had considerable sympathy with some aspects of Hegel's teaching, he rejected the tendency of so many of his followers to regard 'Christianity as a system of essential truths rooted in the nature of things, and thus independent of historical events'.[89] Because 'God reveals himself through history', the significance of Jesus' life and teaching could not be undermined. It was not acceptable either to differentiate between 'Jesus' and 'Christ' and to say that the divine Christ is the product of the churches' piety.

'The historical Jesus and the inner Christ cannot be divorced from one another.'[90]

Equal care had to be taken when considering the facts of Christian experience. Miall Edwards relied heavily upon Schleiermacher's teaching that the essence of religion was the awareness of complete dependence upon the Eternal. But 'one must avoid the danger of relying upon self-induced experience or emotion . . . independent of the objective revelations of God'.[91] This dual emphasis on history and experience demonstrates Miall Edwards's debt to Albrecht Ritschl. One of the most prominent features of Ritschl's doctrine, however, was that religion is concerned with the value of facts to human experience. What is important is not what Jesus Christ is in himself, or in his heavenly connections, but his value to the individual believer. It is sufficient for the Christian to know that Jesus is equal to God without having to embark upon metaphysical speculations about how this could be true. Miall Edwards disagreed. The intellectual task could hardly be avoided. Christians had to attempt to 'legitimize the value of Christ as a divine power' in their life.[92]

Having established these conditions, Miall Edwards went on to propose his answer to the christological question. The key lay in Jesus Christ's awareness 'of his filial relationship with God'. God's eternal Fatherhood meant Christ's eternal Sonship because there cannot be a Father without a Son. A loving relationship or personal unity is part of who God is. The loving God is present in creation. Indeed, 'things may be graded according to their worth, may be placed lower or higher than one another according to the degrees of divinity that they possess'. God's objective in creation is to nurture 'spiritual beings who are a perfect incarnation of the filial spirit', an aim which was perfectly realized in the Son. The Word was made flesh out of love, and it is a waste of time to question whether he would have become flesh if there were no sin. We are dealing, he claimed, with facts, not conjectures. The Word could not be incarnate as a man if human beings were not 'with regard to [their] essential make-up, [children] of God'. It is 'the divine element in man and the human element in God which makes the incarnation possible'.

But what about the relationship of the divine nature and the human nature in Jesus Christ? Were we to think of both natures in static terms, as completely separate realities as taught by the classical creeds, then we are faced with insoluble questions. But if we think of them in terms of God's loving desire to give human beings their nature, and of human beings' inherent ability to coinhere with God, then the difficulties would disappear. The Word was 'from the beginning joined to Jesus in the deepest foundations of his being'. As Jesus developed his human instincts as he grew to maturity, the eternal Word 'assumed the new aspects which emerged during his human development' and at the same time 'his burgeoning humanity joined voluntarily and consciously with the new aspects of the Word'. In consequence a doctrine of *kenosis* is hardly necessary. In Jesus we see the same process as in creation as a whole; God's indwelling increased as from stone to flower, from flower to humankind, or moving from infancy to youth and from youth to maturity.[93]

It is quite obvious that Miall Edwards was willing to go much, much further than Thomas Charles Edwards. His work marks a dramatic turning point in the history of Welsh theology. What strikes the reader initially is that the literary idiom and the vocabulary he employs are quite different from those of, say, R. S. Thomas. He was convinced that he was entering a period in which the old theological terms would be dispensed with completely. To read his work is to breathe the atmosphere of the contemporary Hegelianism and Romanticism. Despite this, Miall Edwards still belongs to the school sometimes described as Evangelical Modernism. He was anxious to express the faith once given to the saints in a manner that would be meaningful for his contemporaries. He did not wish in any way to distort or truncate that faith and his personal godliness, as well as his deep reverence for the classical theologians of the church, is evident on every page he wrote. Alas, it soon became clear that, far from saving Welsh Christianity from its crisis, he helped make that crisis worse.

There were much fiercer critics than Miall Edwards already in the field. In 1907, the controversy of the 'New Theology' swept through Britain, beginning with the *Daily Mail*'s agitated coverage of R. J. Campbell's address to Congregational ministers in London. His volume *The New Theology* (1907) achieved unparalleled sales. Reginald John Campbell succeeded Joseph Parker as the minister of the City Temple, London, in 1903. The cornerstone of his doctrine was God's indwelling in creation including humankind. For Campbell, God permeated everything and thus God and humankind were essentially one.[94] In some sense everything is divine but General Booth is more divine than a crocodile because the General knew that love expressed itself through him.[95] According to this scheme, Jesus Christ was unique in his divinity and unique in his humanity since his mind was entirely governed by love. Far from being an atonement for sin or a unique means of human redemption, his death was simply an expression of this love. Sin, for Campbell, was a negation of life and the consequence of concentrating on the self rather than on the totality of creation. As a rather abstract negation, it could hardly hurt God. It followed, therefore, that the church's traditional doctrines about the Fall were obsolete.[96] In Campbell's view, the churches' declarations of faith in Christ and the doctrine of sin are simply 'unbelievable'.[97]

It is obvious that there was nothing particularly novel about this teaching. When Evan Roberts (not the revivalist) reminisced: 'I remember doing battle with that [doctrine] at the beginning of my ministry. It is nothing but Pantheism in a new guise', he was not far off the mark.[98] It was rooted in the same Hegelianism as that expounded by the earlier 'New Theology' of the period between 1885 and 1893. We should hardly be surprised that Thomas Rhondda Williams claimed that he preached Campbell's doctrine long before him.[99] What was new in Campbell's stance was his charismatic personality, his powerful turn of phrase and his willingness to destroy utterly the theological idols of the past.

This theology caused quite a stir in Wales. Campbell himself visited Cardiff in the spring of 1907[100] and, since he claimed, nonchalently, that the Labour movement was the 'true Catholic Church', it was natural that his views were heard intently in industrial areas.[101] In other circles Campbell's doctrine was regarded as blasphemy. Conwy library refused to stock *The New Theology* on its shelves but the corporation disagreed and the matter was debated in the local papers.[102] For Hugh Jones, Bangor, *The New Theology* was 'an empty and inconsistent chaos';[103] Owen Evans believed that Campbell had 'made a shipwreck of the faith'[104] and for *Seren Cymru* it was nothing but 'unhealthy nonsense'.[105] On the other hand, Josiah Thomas maintained that 'Mr Campbell says clearly what scores of preachers believe and say less clearly. Mr Campbell is so much more honest than his brethren.'[106] Years later Campbell himself claimed that Welsh Oxbridge graduates sympathized with his standpoint, but that they were afraid of falling foul of their denominations' standards and consequently hid the fact.[107] Every denominational periodical in Wales published a welter of articles about R. J. Campbell and his ideals.[108]

Since the battle was so heated, it was suggested to David Adams that he should mediate between the two factions, which he did in his *Yr Hen a'r Newydd mewn Duwinyddiaeth* (The Old and the New in Theology, 1907). 'This is not an attempt to attack the Old', claimed Adams. 'Nor is it an attempt to defend the New.' His intention rather was 'to set out the ideas of both systems as clearly as possible, and allow the reader to judge for himself'. In reality the book did nothing of the sort; rather it was an out and out declaration in favour of Campbell's position. The basis of Adams's argument was the 'immanence of God'. God permeates the whole creation and since He permeates humankind, men and women come to perceive God 'as a personal Being' because creative life could not reach its zenith in a personality without being a person itself. God and humanity, nature and supernature, are basically the same.

However, he rejected Campbell's claim that sin is a mere negation, rather it was humankind's free choice. Nor was it strictly a rebellion against God. 'From this perspective the story of Eden is far from being true to man's experience of his first sin.'[109] Turning to the person of Christ he stated that the only way Christ's humanity and divinity could be reconciled was through the concept of moral perfection. In Jesus the immanent God's centuries' long preparation to fashion a suitable body for 'a moral and spiritual personality similar to that of God himself reaches its goal'.[110]

Christ's death was to be understood, not as an atonement, propitiation or sacrifice for sin, but as an expression of the divine immanence and the moral perfection of an internalized God. All self-sacrifice, whether in the animal world or among human beings, is of divine origin. Thus there was nothing unique in Christ's death. Rather through his death Jesus Christ 'identifies with sinful mankind until he makes sins and the painful consequences of the same his own'.[111] On hearing the story of Christ's sufferings, men and women would feel ashamed of their wickedness and consequently turn to God. Such were Adams's central hypotheses and he believed that they represented a sufficient basis for reconciling the exponents of the 'old theology' and the 'new theology'. These, he insisted, were the facts and all should be free to interpret them by means of whatever doctrine they prefer.

Cofiant y Parch David Adams DD (A Biography of the Revd David Adams) by E. Keri Evans and W. Pari Huws is quite exceptional among Welsh biographies of the time because of its willingness to evaluate his teaching in a critical fashion. It emphasized that Adams's contribution to Welsh theology was 'substantial and important'[112] and, in the words of Bala–Bangor's Principal Thomas Rees, that he was 'the pioneer of the new spirit'.[113] In Keri Evans's view, Adams plainly was 'an anti-theological theologian'.[114] Although Evans and Huws were temperate and measured in their critique of Adams, occasionally their criticism becomes scathing. It certainly indicates why Adams's influence ultimately did a great disservice to the Christian mind in Wales.

Keri Evans (formerly a university professor of philosophy himself) was content for Adams to be called a 'philosopher' but only in the loosest sense.[115] Adams subordinated Christian doctrine to quasi-philosophical ideas, without being over-concerned about defining terms, and adapted Christianity accordingly. 'It is easy enough, to shout "Immanence! Immanence!" without showing *how* God "indwells creation . . ." ' he said.[116] In scholarly terms this was a damning indictment indeed. As Thomas Rees said plainly, 'he was not a theologian at all'.[117] The descriptions of orthodox and clasical theology in *Yr Hen a'r Newydd mewn Duwinyddiaeth* read like a caricature. He made very general statements about various creeds without ever saying to whom he was referring or citing any historical source.

Much of this could be forgiven had Adams's example not convinced many of his followers that to disparage the thinkers of the past was a mark of culture and erudition. Not that Adams intended to be disparaging. On the contrary, he frequently declared his reverence for the past. However, the dogma of Darwinism had such a strong influence on his mind that he inevitably believed that Christian thinkers from the apostles onwards had misunderstood Christ's teaching in quite profound ways. In order to correct this failing he embarked upon a mental subterfuge that was to have a catastrophic influence on Welsh Christianity. This subterfuge involved preserving traditional terminology such as 'justification', 'God-Man', 'miracle', 'revelation' and so on, but reinterpreting it in terms of his own ethical and quasi-Hegelian philosophy.

This method of reasoning can be studied in the two chapters he devoted to 'Jesus' miraculous conception' in *Yr Hen a'r Newydd mewn Duwinyddiaeth*. It should be borne in mind that the purpose of the book was to mediate between old and new. Do supporters of traditional orthodoxy need to cast aside their faith in the miraculous conception? No they do not, as long as they realize that it is myth and not fact. Such was Adams's logic and it created utter confusion. It is one thing to deny the miraculous conception and refuse to use the term. It is a completely different matter to continue to use the term and explain it in a way that is at complete odds with its obvious meaning. What impression would preaching based on such logic have on people who did not know the difference between Hegel and Thomas Aquinas? Before long, they would realize that their preachers spoke one language in the pulpit and a completely different language in the study. That is why Hegelianism was such a destructive influence on the Christian life of Europe and of Wales. One of the greatest tragedies in the history of ideas during the period is that David Adams, with his passionate emphasis on morality and on faithfulness to the truth, was blind to the moral deception and the casuistry which he espoused.

Not everyone was willing to follow Adams's extreme path. Other preconceptions influenced the change in people's understanding of the meaning of the death of the Lord Jesus. To those who adhered to the Evangelical Accord, the sinner's hope for salvation rested upon the unique work of the God-Man, Jesus Christ, in meeting the requirements of God's righteousness for a punishment for human sin. It was Jesus Christ himself who presented to the Father a perfect satisfaction for sin and thus made forgiveness possible without undermining the moral order. And as our sins have been reckoned to Christ, in the same way his righteousness has been reckoned to all those who believe in him. This was the theology of virtually all of Wales's best-known hymns and the basis of the 'Gospel preached by Owen Thomas, Edward Matthews and Richard Owen, Herber Evans and John Evans, Eglwys Bach'.[118] This was the teaching expounded by Thomas Charles, by George Lewis, by Thomas Jones of Denbigh, by John Jenkins and Lewis Edwards. Between 1890 and 1914 this teaching was defended by R. S. Thomas in his comprehensive volume *Yr Iawn* (The Atonement, 1903), by J. Cynddylan Jones in the third volume of *Cysondeb y Ffydd* (The Consistency of the Faith, 1912), by David Charles Davies in *Iawn ac Eiriolaeth Crist* (Christ's Atonement and Advocacy, 1899) and by H. Cernyw Williams in *Bannau Ffydd*

(Beacons of Faith, 1900) – to name just a few. These authors were not engaged in a mechanical repetition of old shibboleths; rather, they discussed their theme with the passion and fervour that it merited. Yet many still felt profoundly dissatisfied.

It was no accident that the change of emphasis could be seen in Thomas Charles Edwards's contribution to the debate. Once the teaching on the person of Christ was reformulated, the doctrine about his work would also have to be changed. Thomas Charles Edwards's article on 'The Atonement' presages the christology that was to be developed in his later book Y Duw-Ddyn.[119] For Charles Edwards, humanity already exists in God and thus 'when the God-Man offers an atonement for sin, it is man who offers the atonement'. Thus it is not appropriate to speak of 'reckoning' or 'imputing' as in the older theology. Talk of reckoning human sin to Jesus Christ smacks of immorality because the innocent cannot be punished for the sins of the guilty and speaking of transferring Christ's righteousness to sinners places a huge chasm between the two parties. Rather, the imputing occurs because Jesus Christ is both God *and* man and believers share in his righteousness because they are at one with him with regard to his humanity, so that 'his victory is a victory for us'. This involved a considerable change in emphasis. For one thing the emphasis is shifted from the cross to the incarnation. God's love towards humankind was expressed in his identification with humanity through the incarnation. The forensic implications of this older theory can be dispensed with easily. Human salvation springs from the nature of the Trinity itself. Justification is now understood not so much as a change in humankind's status before God but rather as a change in our essential humanity.

For William James, Aberdare, 'The covenantal union between Christ and his people is cast aside, for a time, to give a special place to the vital, active union that exists between the believer and Christ through personal faith in him.'[120] In a very subtle way, the doctrine which inspired such hymns as 'Cyfamod hedd, cyfamod cadarn Duw . . .' (The covenant of peace, God's strong covenant . . .) or 'Y Gŵr a fu gynt o dan hoelion . . .' (The man who once suffered under nails . . .) was being undermined.

In 1905, James Charles (a cousin of the more renowned Thomas Charles Edwards) published *Iawn a Thadolaeth* (Atonement and Fatherhood). James Charles was an interesting thinker because his work demonstrated clearly how a man of conservative inclinations could be enticed by the latest theological influences. In his critical stance towards evolutionary philosophy, and his robust opposition to every attempt to deny the biblical miracles, he was a conservative. At the same time, he felt the attraction of Harnack's concept of the Fatherhood of God. This is what provided the central theme of *Iawn a Thadolaeth*. On the other hand the most prominent feature of his book was its total rejection of legal terminology in discussing atonement theory. For instance, Charles dispensed with the teaching about the Saviour as a legal substitute for the redeemed – in other words, that God, with the voluntary consent of the Son, had punished Christ because he had agreed to take the place of sinners in face of the demands of God's righteousness. Similarly Charles does not wish to embrace the doctrine of an objective reckoning – in other words, the teaching that humankind's sins are reckoned to Christ, not in the subjective sense that he bears the stain of sin in his personality or that he suffers the guilt of sin in his conscience, but in the objective and legal sense that he has consented to be treated by God's law as if he were a sinner. For Charles the whole legal aspect of the doctrine is unacceptable and in this regard he represents one of the most dramatic developments in the Welsh Christian mindset at the beginning of the twentieth century.

The conviction that righteousness and law were part of the fundamentals of Christianity was disappearing with an astonishing rapidity. Previously, most Christians, whether they were Catholic or Protestant, had agreed that sinners could not gain salvation except on the basis of merit. The requirements of God's righteousness had to be fulfilled. In other words, it was universally accepted that salvation was something that had to be won. The controversy between Catholics and Protestants turned on the question of the relationship between a sinner's merit and the Redeemer's merit in the work of salvation. In thinkers such as James Charles we see a weakening of the conviction that legal merit was indispensable in order for sinners to be saved. For Charles the atonement stemmed from the Father's love towards sinners. It is first and foremost a revelation of God in his love and his righteousness and, since it is a revelation, it is fair to suppose that the Son would have become incarnate even had there been no sin. The atonement was the sum of Jesus Christ's perfect life and his obedience to the Father. The objective aspect of this atonement was in Christ's having satisfied the Father, not in the sense that the debt of sinners had been paid and that God's anger had been assuaged, but that God was pleased by the wonder of the Son's revelation of him. Atonement's subjective side was that it exerted a moral influence upon humankind. For Charles, the atonement was above all an expression of God's Fatherhood. Although he allowed for the righteousness of God, the emphasis is largely on the love of God. Although the whole discussion demonstrates Charles's skill and logic and is conducted in an excellent spirit, there is no doubt that he undermined the traditional doctrine in a fundamental way, and precisely because of his moderation, he enticed theological conservatives to follow the same path as him. Thus he appealed to the kind of people to whom David Adams's extremism would have been anathema.

It was quite obvious by now that the Calvinistic position was under siege. One more point needs to be said. One of the 'five points' of Calvinism was limited atonement – the doctrine that Christ died only for the elect. Even defendants of Calvinist standards – men like Lewis Probert, R. S. Thomas and Cynddylan Jones – were firmly in favour of the belief that Christ died for all.[121]

As the emphasis on God's kindness and Fatherhood increased, so the emphasis on the harsh side of Christian eschatology decreased. Reprobation and the eternal punishment of the ungodly had swiftly retreated into the background by the middle of the Victorian age. Thomas Charles Edwards confessed in 1870 that he had never heard preachers speak 'about damnation except as a punishment for man's disobedience'.[122] In other words, human actions and not God's predestination were responsible for human beings going to hell. John Jones ('Yr Hen Gloddiwr'), who died in 1879, was considered to be an oddity and throwback to the past because he made eternal punishment one of the main topics of his sermons.[123] In 1896, Griffith Roberts (Gwrtheyrn) remarked that the word 'hell' was 'swiftly disappearing from the practical vocabulary of the Welsh language'.[124] J. Gwili Jenkins struck a Romantic note when he argued that hell was the subjective condition of the heart rather than any objective situation wrought by God.[125] The same was true of the devil. Satan was now thought of as an impersonal evil influence, although there was an occasional attempt to defend the personhood of the devil.[126] More and more people were becoming uncertain about hell.[127]

This trend did not please everyone. Robert Davies of Shrewsbury, for instance, believed that the denominations were hiding their heads in the sand rather than defending stoutly the scriptural truths, but even he was forced to admit 'that orthodox doctrine has already disappeared from the pulpits of Wales'.[128] In view of this, it was inevitable that uncertainty existed concerning the fate of humankind after death. There was considerable debate on this matter in *Y Greal* between 1897 and 1902: 'If man is essentially immortal, then does his continued existence depend on his belief or his works?' The belief in the immortality of the soul was still very strong[129] but at the same time there was much uncertainty in people's minds concerning the New Testament's teaching on the resurrection. These are echoes of the fierce debates in England at the time and they are an example of the way in which English culture influenced Wales.

For Martin Luther the doctrine of justification by faith alone was the *articulus stantis vel cadentis ecclesiae* – the article the church's attitude to which determined whether it stood or fell. For Luther, this was the cornerstone of the Protestant Reformation. The most complete exposition of this doctrine in Welsh can be found in Timothy Thomas's book *Traethawd am y Wisg Wen Ddisglaer* (An Essay on the Brilliant White Garment, 1759). The 'White Garment' is Christ's righteousness. Thomas said:

> I judge that none will be saved, without being justified; and that not one sinner will be justified before God, except through Christ's righteousness alone; and that no one is justified through Christ's righteousness, but those who believe with their heart on justification . . .

For the eighteenth-century divine, justification was an objective act; it changed the legal status of a sinner, not his nature. Timothy Thomas commented further, 'And this is the only way and means by which God justifies a sinner: and not by placing righteousness within him or through him or on account of anything he could do himself'.[130] Of course no one can be a Christian without having his nature transformed. The name given by the Protestant Reformers and their disciples for this change was 'sanctification' and one feature of their doctrine was that justification and sanctification were kept logically apart.

Just as Christ's righteousness was essential for justification, so the Holy Spirit's work was essential for sanctification. The difference between the two can be demonstrated by saying that justification is by faith alone, but that sanctification is by faith and effort. Christ's righteousness is imputed to a sinner in justification, but in sanctification the work of the Holy Spirit is not reckoned to the Christian because the work is attributed to the believer in the strength of the Holy Spirit. Justification is a wholly objective work on the part of Christ; sanctification is a subjective work in the personality of the believer. Justification is a finished work because all the riches of Christ are reckoned to the one who believes in him; sanctification is a gradual growth which is not finished on this side of heaven. Through justification Christ's position in the court of God is bestowed upon a believing sinner. Sanctification is a consequence of the new position which the sinner enjoys and it does not contribute in any way towards justification.

In considering these points, the relationship between the gospel and the law becomes clear. In the matter of justification, the law comes before the gospel because God's perfect holiness cannot be satisfied except through total obedience to the law – which is secured through the work of Christ. But in sanctification the gospel comes before the law because it is only by understanding how much Christ did for them that sinners can gain strength to meet the requirements of the law. This is what Protestants had traditionally taught.

The Roman Catholic Church defined its position on justification at the sixth session of the Council of Trent, January 1547. According to the Council, it is God who justifies, though justification *makes* a sinner righteous. Thus justification means a transformation in the human person and human beings are not justified except through regeneration in Christ. Since the Fall has not taken away free will, human beings can collaborate with grace in the process of justification and thereby make their personal contribution to the process of salvation. Thus sanctification involves moving from the condition in which human beings are born as children to the first Adam to a condition of grace and adoption through the Second Adam, Jesus Christ.

Thus while Protestants differentiated clearly between justification and sanctification, for Catholics they are part of the same saving process. For the Protestant, justification comes at the start of the journey, for the Catholic it comes as the climax of a process to which every human being contributes, through grace. Protestants believe that they are justified on the basis of Christ's action and Catholics believe that they are justified on the basis of Christ's action together with their own contribution by grace.

In Welsh theology at the turn of the century we see the belief in the classical Protestant position gradually yielding to a more Catholic conception of truth. For thinkers like David Adams, the whole basis of the doctrine had been reinterpreted so radically as to nullify it totally. Indeed, wherever there were efforts to alleviate the legal aspects of the doctrine of justification, the traditional view was endangered because, in its essence, the Protestant doctrine of justification was legal. However, the threat to the Protestant truth also came from another direction. By the 1870s, the holiness movement was starting to gain ground, especially after the publication of Hannah Pearsall Smith's *The Christian's Secret of a Happy Life* in 1875.[131] She and her husband were dissatisfied with the Christian life based on faith alone. Their interest lay in salvation and for them sanctification was not a matter of gradual growth. They came to believe that sanctification could be achieved in the blink of an eye through a second act of faith. It was not enough to have faith in Christ as a sufficient atonement for sin; there must also be faith in him as a sanctifier. Thus there was a distinction between the guilt of sin and the force of sin and two separate acts of faith were necessary to gain freedom from both. Because the second act brought sanctification in an instant the movement adopted slogans such as 'instant salvation' or 'Jesus saves now'.

Thus the 'victorious life' comes through faith alone and does not involve the moral striving after the fashion of Protestant orthodoxy. It is no wonder, therefore, that this movement placed a high value on mystic quietism. It also offered its followers emotional excitement. One can see why a movement like this tended to undermine cultural or political activity by Christians. The movement became well-known in Wales through the Keswick conventions, which began in 1875, although Keswick tempered the emphasis of the holiness movements in favour of a more Reformed emphasis.

Men like Ellis W. Evans, Abergele, spoke of two types of Christians: those who have been reborn through the Holy Spirit, and those in whom the Spirit dwells 'in the full sense of the word'. In line with this concept, he spoke of exercising a two-fold faith, first to receive Christ as righteousness and secondly to receive Christ as 'sanctification'.[132]

In August 1903, the trustees of the Keswick convention organized a meeting in Llandrindod Wells 'to deepen the spiritual life'. It met on 3–7 August and F. B. Meyer, Frank and Seth Joshua, and Mrs Jessie Penn-Lewis were among the speakers.[133] The experiment was a success and an inspiring conference was held in 1904, especially on the Friday when the 'Divine power . . . was overwhelming'.[134] This emphasis on holiness was to have a profound influence on men like Keri Evans, R. B. Jones[135] and others, but it would be a mistake to suppose that everyone who longed to see a deepening in spiritual life embraced the theology of Keswick, much less the doctrine of sanctification through faith, and perfectionism. Although Seth Joshua took part in the meetings, he was uneasy with what he saw. 'My one fear', he said, 'is that many people are in danger of cultivating holiness at the expense of work.'[136] This was the voice of traditional evangelicalism which realized that one of the results of being justified by faith alone was effort, dynamism and work. Once again R. S. Thomas felt the need to defend the traditional doctrine and he published his exhaustive volume *Cyfiawnhad trwy Ffydd* (Justification through Faith) in 1894, with a second edition in 1904.

One more debate must be mentioned before drawing to a close, although this one was more of a storm in a teacup. At 10.00 on Thursday morning 23 August 1894, during the Calvinistic Methodist Association, Professor Hugh Williams addressed about 200 preachers in Pen-mount Chapel, Pwllheli, on the subject of the sacraments. He spoke rather slowly because he had forgotten his script but some of the listeners felt that they were hearing strange ideas. The following day the *Liverpool Daily Post* claimed that Williams had suggested that baptism by immersion was the biblical baptism, that infant baptism was not lawful and that regeneration came by baptism alone.[137] If the Methodists were scandalized, the Baptists were overjoyed! The Monmouthshire Baptist Association passed a motion 'greatly rejoicing' that the Methodists bore witness to the 'accuracy of our principles regarding baptism'.[138] The Baptist historian, Spinther James, wrote an unctuous letter praising Hugh Williams's scholarship.[139] In the autumn Hugh Williams's address was published as *Y Sacramentau* (The Sacraments) and went some way towards calming the excitement. Williams acknowledged that there is no mention in the New Testament of infant baptism and that this form of rite could not be a sacrament in the full sense of the word since infants cannot exercise faith. However, although he acknowledged the strength of the Baptists' position, he attempted to deliver a response to it. W. P. Williams, the editor of *Seren Cymru*, was fairly satisfied, saying, 'If there was ever a time when the Baptists could afford to be complacent this is it'.[140]

It would be a mistake, however, to disparage the debate as an impetuous reaction to a misleading report. It was a means of stimulating people to think about the issue of the sacraments – and baptism particularly.[141]

To summarize: one cannot fail to be amazed at the theological energy of the period. Whatever the prophets of woe might have said, an immense number of articles and many weighty tomes were published on theological topics and what is remarkable is how much of this belonged to the years before the 1904–5 Revival. The debates were enjoined by a succession of hugely talented people of the calibre of Lewis Probert, Thomas Charles Edwards, H. Cernyw Williams, Owen Evans (the Congregationalist), and Owen Evans (the Wesleyan), David Adams, R. S. Thomas, J. Cynddylan Jones, James Charles, Thomas Rees (Bangor) and Hugh Williams, Bala – not to mention others who will be discussed later. It is a matter of grave concern that by the second half of the twentieth century virtually all of these men had been so completely forgotten. At the same time, Wales's theological foundations were being shaken as though by an earthquake and what suffered most grievously was the Evangelical Accord. Despite the brilliance of its apologists, the traditional Calvinistic orthodoxy was being challenged and undermined by Hegelianism, by Darwinism, by vague doubts and by the cultural and social influences which stemmed from abroad. This was not a superficial shift in intellectual fashions; rather, it had to do with the fundamentals of the nation's faith and it was inevitable that in time it would influence its culture and its social life.

~ 11 ~

Cultivating the Christian Mind

One vitally important part of the church's ministry throughout the centuries has been the education of its members. Its ongoing task was to cultivate 'the mind of Christ' and 'bring all thoughts in obedience to Christ'. This responsibility gave rise to the schools, colleges and universities of Europe and also to an abundant wealth of Christian scholarship. It had been a deep conviction down the generations that Christians were to show their faithfulness to Christ by loving God with all their mind, as well as in other ways.

Throughout the centuries churches adopted numerous means of providing education. Like all worthwhile education, it was very often a consequence of belonging to a Christian society, whether it be within a congregation, a home or a district. A multitude of Welsh people imbibed their knowledge of the Christian faith by partaking of the life of a nation whose culture was enmeshed with that faith. Although the influence of a Christian upbringing could not be measured statistically, it was acknowledged to be immense.

Worship also provided a continuous source of educational influences, the effect of which would last a lifetime. In Catholic and Anglican churches the liturgy became part of the fabric of people's being and similarly, in the chapels, hymns left a deep impression on people's memories and in their turn of phrase. In chapel, it was common practice for children to 'recite a verse' during the service and thus to memorize large tracts of scripture, although there were few people who could equal the achievement of Margaret Jones, Ganllwyd, who learnt the entire New Testament by heart.[1]

Despite the importance of these methods, the churches also insisted on adopting more formal methods of instruction for their members. By the mid-nineteenth century, all denominations had their educational systems. Catholics and Anglicans and some Wesleyans relied on denominational schools. For others, interdenominational religious instruction was available in the British schools. Ministers and teachers were trained in academies, seminaries and colleges maintained by the denominations, while there were also numerous private schools which prepared students for college education.

The history of the theological colleges for the training of ministers shows that their nature changed radically when the University of Wales was founded. Up until that time, the colleges bore the mark of the Dissenting academies that were established to educate ministers after the doors of the ancient universities were closed to non-Anglicans in the seventeenth century. As a result the syllabus was broad, containing scientific and arts subjects as well as theology. The University of Wales's charter in 1893 established a Board of Theology to advise on the provision of university education in the subject. The university and its constituent colleges were prohibited from teaching theology, but there was no prohibition on examinations or setting academic standards. The arrangement therefore was that the denominational colleges were to provide the education and that the university was to supervise the examinations. Arrangements were made for a postgraduate BD degree to be available from 1896 onwards.

From then on the denominational colleges ceased to teach subjects other than those connected with the study of theology, and responsibility for other disciplines was transferred to the University of Wales. The academic standards of the colleges were improved and continental scholarship began to exert a growing influence upon the minds of ministers.

There was little change with regard to which language was used as a medium of instruction. Apart from the Congregational College at Bala under Michael D. Jones where instruction was given through the medium of Welsh, the denominational colleges taught entirely in English.[2] English was the medium of instruction for the new BD and all university examinations were conducted in English, except for the paper on the Holy Scriptures.

Considering all the talk in the 1890s about the new university being a national university, it is surprising that the BD made no provision for studying any aspect of the history or nature of religion in Wales. There is no doubt that an opportunity was missed to integrate the life of the colleges with the religious and cultural life of Wales in a positive and creative way.

A comparison of developments in Welsh-language studies with those in theology shows the unfortunate consequences of this lack. While the former pioneered the study of the nation's historical language and its literature, encouraged scholarly debate and cultivated standards of critical appraisal, the latter did nothing of the sort. Theologians' memory of their own roots became lazy and dim and a perusal of the books by men such as Miall Edwards, Thomas Rees and others could easily lead one to suppose that Wales had never had a theological tradition of its own. Were it not for the interest of certain individual historians, the widespread amnesia about its religious past that was swiftly descending upon Wales would have consigned that past to total oblivion. Certainly there is no better way of convincing a student that a subject is not significant than to banish it completely from the syllabus.

However, by far the largest educational institution that the denominations possessed was the Sunday school. The statistics given in the *Report of the Royal Commission on Disestablishment* indicate its strength (see Table).[3] Four out of ten of the population over 3 years old attended Sunday school and the average varied between 67 per cent in Cardiganshire and 27 per cent in Radnorshire, giving some indication of the size of the institution.

	Pupils	*Teachers*
Church in Wales	168,706	13,457
Baptists	143,916	12,159
Calvinistic Methodists	193,699	21,702
Congregationalists	162,621	15,818
Wesleyans	71,178	6,818
Total	740,120	69,954

As the results of the education system established in 1870 became more apparent, people began to feel the need to reform and improve the work of the Sunday schools. The quality of the teachers and the work varied considerably and schools were often badly organized. Even after the reforms, there were complaints about children's behaviour.[4] In some classes much time was spent in foolish disputes and aimless discussion.[5] The Sunday schools needed better organization. In 1884 the diocese of Bangor attempted to set up a common syllabus for all its schools and organized examinations. The first was held on August 1885, with twenty-three candidates from sixteen schools.[6]

In 1885 the centenary of the establishment of the Sunday school was celebrated and much was made of the opportunity, in Wales and elsewhere, to draw attention to its work. During the celebrations, there was talk of creating an interdenominational Sunday school union for the whole of Wales, but nothing came of the idea, and the denominations continued to work independently of one another. The Calvinistic Methodist General Assembly in Liverpool (1886) decided to establish a Union of Sabbath Schools which started work at the end of that year under the presidency of Thomas Charles Edwards.[7] The Welsh Baptist Sunday School Union was formed in 1888 and in 1890 it came directly under the wing of the Baptist Union. In 1897 an English-language Sunday School Union was formed.[8] The Union of Welsh Independents formed a Sunday School Committee during its meetings in Aberdare (1886) and annual scriptural examinations began to be held in 1890. The Sunday school was widely discussed at the Union's meetings during the following years but when the 'single syllabus' was set up in 1896 the work of reorganization began in earnest.[9] The Wesleyans included the organization of the syllabuses as part of the conference's work programme for the year, but the denomination's English-language churches in Wales followed the English system.[10]

The result of this general reform was that the work of the schools was improved. Common syllabuses were adopted and were graded according to the age of the pupils.[11] Annual examinations were held corresponding to the various syllabuses, with prizes for the best pupils. Most importantly, perhaps, was that suitable reading material for the children was now made available, including biblical commentaries for the older classes. The age of the biblical commentary dawned, with each denomination publishing one each year to accompany the syllabus.[12] These books achieved high sales, sufficient to make the authors of other books green with envy. The Calvinistic Methodists sold 30,000 of Thomas Charles Edwards's commentary on Hebrews in a few days[13] and the same number of Cynddylan Jones's two-volume commentary on the Gospel according to John, and 20,000 of Llywelyn Edwards's two-volume commentary on Luke's Gospel.[14] The Calvinistic Methodists were far ahead of the field as purchasers of commentaries. The Independents lagged behind with David Adams's commentary on Galatians selling 7,100, Thomas Rees's work on Hebrews selling 4,551 and Miall Edwards on the Epistle of James selling 6,024.[15] Taken as a whole, these commentaries reached a huge public and their influence was vast. They were studied almost word for word with innumerable classes, the length and breadth of Wales and beyond, being drilled in their content Sunday by Sunday throughout the year.

Despite the fact that not 'one aspect of religious activity received so much attention' as the Sunday school, not everyone was happy with the results. In 1902 one observer expressed the opinion that the Sunday school was in serious decline, placing the blame on the establishment of syllabuses and the learning of the Bible by rote, the competitive nature of the examinations and the fact that classes were made to read repetitive texts such as 1 and 2 Kings for terms at a time.[16] One Calvinistic Methodist agreed, commenting that 'the king who wields the sceptre of the Sabbath school now . . . is frail, weak, ugly, feeble, reactionary and petty . . . His name is "the syllabus" '. It is not surprising that this observer wished to see the syllabus abolished.[17]

A perusal of the commentaries yields some interesting insights. One of their aims was to bring the latest knowledge in biblical studies within reach of the Welsh-speaking reader. Consequently, the commentaries gave considerable attention to questions concerning date, authorship and place of composition. In the textual notes which comprised the commentaries' bulk, there were detailed discussions of the Hebrew and Greek and of the views of respected commentators. Cynddylan Jones, for instance, in *Efengyl Ioan* (The Gospel according to John) referred constantly to a host of scholars by name. On the other hand, Thomas Charles Edwards, despite his considerable erudition, was more restrained in his references to other scholars. This seems to have been the wisest course as a technical discussion about the sometimes arcane views of unknown experts would surely have meant very little to most of the people who used these books.

The Welsh word for commentary, 'esboniad', means 'explanation' and the purpose of an explanation is to explain; in other words, to make the biblical text intelligible to its readers by explaining the meaning of unfamiliar words, casting light upon the background of a book or paragraph, focusing on the historical or social background and showing the author's train of thought. Occasionally there was a tendency for these comments to be disjointed, as in Llewelyn Edwards's commentary on the Gospel according to Luke (1904, 1905), but when commentators concentrated on paraphrasing the text and making its logic clear to the reader, much entertaining writing could ensue.

William Williams, the vicar of Llangeler, in his commentary on Matthew's Gospel (1907) gave a skilful paraphrase of the gospel's content, and so too did W. O. Evans in his work on Romans (1914, 1915), which was a particularly impressive commentary.[18] However, it was difficult to achieve a smooth literary style in the kind of commentaries produced during this period because of the amount of scholarly detail which they contained. The most readable commentaries produced at this time were those by H. Elvet Lewis (Elfed), Puleston Jones, Cynddylan Jones and W. O. Evans. On the whole the commentaries produced between 1890 and 1914 were a not unsuccessful attempt to enrich Sunday school pupils' understanding of the content of the Bible. What is so remarkable about them is how ambitious they were and how highly their authors estimated the intelligence of their readers.

Nevertheless, some searching questions must be raised with regard to the commentaries as a means of education in the churches. By this time Welsh-language commentaries were beginning to follow a pattern which can be seen in England and on the continent during the same period. Discussion of the text of the Bible and discussion of the theology of the Bible were beginning to develop as two separate disciplines. This happened in college courses and can also be seen in series such as the International Critical Commentary (T. & T. Clark) which included one volume (*An Introduction to the Literature of the Old Testament* by S. R. Driver) which discussed the literary and historical questions concerning the Old Testament, and a separate volume (*The Theology of the Old Testament* by A. B. Davidson), which treated its theology. Lewis Probert's substantial commentaries on Romans and Ephesians continued to combine literary criticism and theological insight, but this tradition was now drawing to a close. This became particularly obvious in commentaries on Old Testament books, the Synoptic Gospels and Acts. It was more difficult to avoid matters of theology in exegeting the Gospel of John and the Pauline Epistles, though, of course, theological discussions did not disappear completely.

In his commentary on the Gospel of John, Cynddylan Jones had a theological field day. So too did W. O. Jones in his exegesis of Romans, and there were frequent theological observations by the Cardiff Presbyterian J. Morgan Jones in his commentary on Acts. In the work of Thomas Rees and David Adams, something different but very significant occurred, namely the introduction of specific philosophical presuppositions which coloured the engagement with the text. David Williams, the Aberystwyth scholar, complained that in Rees's work on Hebrews 'the critic in him was stronger than the commentator'. David Adams's philosophical bias was so overwhelming that in his commentary on Galatians he turned the teaching about justification through faith completely on its head. Taken as a whole, however, the commentaries did not attempt to endow their readers with a comprehensive understanding of the totality of Christian doctrine. This was not possible when Sunday school pupils, even after ten years' study, had only covered a relatively small part of the Bible.

There was an obvious tendency for the commentaries to accelerate the trend away from any kind of systematic theology. As we have already seen, there was a strong prejudice against the old 'systems' of theology during the last quarter of the nineteenth century and the commentaries did not help to alleviate this prejudice. The hope was that people would bypass all the doctrinal systems to return to the Bible alone and draw their personal conclusions on the basis of their study. That would have been a mighty task even for the most able minds in the church in any age; what happened was that the Sunday school scholars and Bible class members tended to piece together their own uncritical and private pattern of doctrine. The consequence was a weakening of the conviction that Christianity offered a system of truths, each one properly linked to the other, with the whole being relevant to all aspects of human life.

Some critics claimed that the answer to this malaise was to bring back the practice of catechizing. The Congregational scholar Owen Evans claimed that the previous fifty years had seen a serious decline and that 'important reforms with regard to our Sunday schools'[19] were needed. Evidently many felt the need to provide people with a doctrinal framework for their ideas because several catechisms were published during these years, especially for children.

Archdeacon Owen Evans, for instance, applied himself diligently to the preparation of catechisms for the children of the Church in Wales.[20] Similarly, catechisms for children in Independent churches were prepared by W. Ross Hughes and D. Silyn Evans.[21] Catechizing was still popular in many school assemblies and singing festivals, as well as at the *Cymanfa Bwnc* (Catechizing Meeting) which still flourished in the south-west.[22]

Others felt that something more substantial was needed for adults. This is what inspired the Wesleyan theologian Owen Evans to publish his two volumes, *Athrawiaeth Gristnogol* (Christian Doctrine), and Cynddylan Jones his four-volume *Cysondeb y Ffydd* (The Consistency of the Faith). Indeed, Cynddylan, who was a minister rather than a professional academic, could not resist taking a shot across the bows of those who, in his opinion, had been responsible for the failings in this area. 'The proper work of professors at our college', he said, 'is to compose a Body of Theology . . . but since they are not aware of their privilege, I have been led . . . to make an attempt to fill the gap.'[23]

Another criticism that can be made is that the commentaries themselves and the methods used to discuss them in the Sunday schools tended to fragment the Bible rather than regard it as a whole. The usual method was to progress from word to word and from verse to verse, referring to the notes of the commentary, and pupils were conditioned to think of the Bible as a huge stockpile of words and phrases. The history of human salvation was lost in a fog of detail. That the Bible was now seen as a collection of historical books, each book with its date, authorship and its particular characteristics as the work of a specific author was obviously a great benefit. This was an undoubted improvement on the idea that the Bible was merely a quarry of verses which could be used haphazardly to justify some theological scheme which had already been formulated, with no need to pay careful attention to the chronology and historical and literary context of individual verses. However, as people rediscovered the historical nature of the biblical documents, the reason why a particular collection of books had been brought together within the covers of the Bible tended to be lost from sight.

Another rather strange result of the denominations' adoption of annual syllabuses was that the children's syllabus tended to be based on the Old Testament while the New Testament became the focus of the adults' syllabus. For instance, in the syllabus of the Calvinistic Methodists, Psalms 1 to 51 were the only portion of the Old Testament studied by adult classes between 1890 and 1906.[24] Among the Independents, Owen Evans and David Adams protested against confining the 12- to 16-year-olds to the Old Testament.[25] This created the unconscious impression that the Old Testament was something for children. Generally speaking it helps to explain the decline in the influence of the Old Testament on Welsh thought in the twentieth century.

As in the early church, when the Gnostic sects rejected the Old Testament, there was a tendency to lose sight of the biblical vision of the true relationship between Christianity and culture. Any Christian theology wishing to provide a foundation which is relevant to cultural activity must take the doctrine of creation seriously, and must try to gain a Christian understanding of the significance of God's dealings with Israel. Without this, Christianity would degenerate into a form of Gnosticism, seeing the faith as an escape from the present wicked world into some ethereal spiritual realm. On the whole, the tone of the commentaries of the period was remarkably academic; there seemed to be little need to link the Bible with the needs of the contemporary world. There is no doubt that in this regard the authors were imitating the academic fashions of the day and refraining from 'corrupting' biblical scholarship by mixing it with the moral, spiritual, political or social implications of the text in question. It is a striking example of the fragmentation of the Christian vision which occurred during these years.

One exception was J. Puleston Jones's commentary on the Epistle of James, of which it has been said, without exaggeration, that it 'awoke the social conscience' in Wales.[26] In the vast majority of commentaries, readers were expected to apply the biblical text to contemporary problems without any advice from the commentator. The irony, of course, is that men who wrote these books were anxious for the Bible to become relevant once more. This was the motive behind the immense efforts to improve the Sunday school between 1890 and 1914. However, it was evident that the commentaries tended to make the Bible remote, a book full of fascinating problems to debate on a Sunday afternoon, but without any direct connection with the intellectual and social vortex that was contemporary Wales. It is no surprise, perhaps, to hear complaints such as that of David Powell, Liverpool, that the Bible was little read 'in our country's homes both individually and as families'.[27]

Other influences raised difficult questions concerning the Bible, its content and significance. By the 1890s remarkable developments had occurred in biblical studies, involving the application of the same literary and historical methods of criticism to the Bible as those used to deal with the rest of the literature of the ancient world for the purpose of discovering when a book was written, by whom and where. The name given to this kind of study was 'higher criticism' to differentiate it from 'lower criticism' which concentrated on studying the form and validity of the original texts of the books of the Bible. Higher criticism was based on the conviction that the histories chronicled in the Bible were of precisely the same material as every other history and that the world of nature in biblical times was subject to exactly the same laws as the world of nature of Newton and Darwin. Since the Victorian age was famous for the discovery of the principle of evolution, it was inevitable that biblical scholars themselves also believed that the scientific way of dealing with the Bible was to see it as an evolution from the primitive to the developed.[28]

Debates on critical questions were not foreign to Welsh thinkers. Many were roused to action by the tribulations suffered by the Lampeter theologian Rowland Williams, following his contribution to *Essays and Reviews* (1860) and the liberalism of Connop Thirlwall, the bishop of St Davids, was common knowledge.[29] In 1862, Morris Williams (Nicander) feared that the work of Bishop Colenso would undermine the Bible completely.[30] The Unitarian, Vance Smith, the principal of the Presbyterian College, Carmarthen, had voiced ideas that were very critical of traditional attitudes to the Bible.[31] Lewis Edwards, of course, was familiar with continental works in the field, and welcomed the principle of higher criticism, although he was less enthusiastic about the conclusions of critical scholars.[32] There is plenty of evidence, from articles in magazines, in the vast Welsh encyclopaedia *Y Gwyddoniadur* and in individual books, that these discussions were followed with considerable interest. However, by the 1890s the debate within Wales itself had reached something of a pitch.

In March 1893, Silas Morris of the North Wales Baptist College published an article on the 'present situation of biblical criticism' and commented with reference to the work of higher critics:

This has all turned out to be of tremendous benefit for believers. The human life of Jesus, and Paul's varied life, have been better and more fully documented in this age than ever before, outside the sphere of spirituality itself, because that sphere has been better investigated and understood. The reason is that erroneous criticism has been countered by means of more correct criticism; the unbelieving critic has been stripped of his weapons . . . and they have been used to slay his own false suppositions.[33]

This declaration is a help in understanding how, within a comparatively short time, higher criticism became acceptable in educated circles in Wales. As he looked back in 1893, Morris felt that the destructive work of critics such as Strauss and Baur[34] had been undone by 'the Cambridge triumvirate', namely Westcott, Hort and Lightfoot.[35] They had shown that it was possible to combine first-class scholarship with devout reverence for the traditional fundamentals of the churches' teaching. The truth had nothing to fear from criticism. On the contrary, this sort of criticism was a certain path to truth.

Westcott, Hort and Lightfoot's specialist field was the New Testament and there is no doubt that their theological conservatism encouraged people to be receptive to the conclusions of moderate critics with regard to the New Testament. In 1897, in his commentary on Mark's Gospel, Richard Hughes reviewed the state of play in the study of the Synoptic Gospels, and agreed with 'recent critics' that Matthew and Luke used written sources, of which Mark was one, and that a second source was in their possession, namely a collection of the sayings of the Lord Jesus Christ in Greek, possibly translated from the original Hebrew by Matthew himself.[36]

However, two subjects concerned with the New Testament were a source of controversy, the first being the authorship of John's Gospel. William Williams (Glyndyfrdwy) had criticized the opinions of Strauss, Baur and Renan, generally, and had defended the belief that John the Apostle was the author of the Gospel on the basis of Lightfoot's arguments.[37] After giving a characteristically careful outline of the critical conclusions, the Cardiff Congregationalist H. M. Hughes, proceeded in a similar vein to defend the apostolic authorship of the Gospel.[38] The other subject under debate was the relationship between Paul and Jesus. David Adams believed that the teaching of Paul should be separated from the

Gospel of Jesus Christ. But the majority at the time agreed with James Charles that setting the two against one another was 'completely unfair, of a harmful tendency, and inconsistent with the truth'.[39]

With regard to the Old Testament, by the mid-1890s the Pentateuch had become the 'main field of battle'.[40] Although attempts to analyse the sources behind the book of Genesis dated back to the work of the Frenchman, Jean Astruc (1684–1766), the most exciting period in this field began with Julius Wellhausen (1844–1918). Building on the work of his predecessors, he initially formed a theory that the Hexateuch showed traces of reliance on four literary sources, namely 'J' belonging to the ninth century before Christ, 'E' from the eighth century, material dating from King Josiah's era (640–609 BC) and found mainly in Deuteronomy, and a fourth source, with more sacerdotal overtones, from the fourth century. Wellhausen proceeded to claim that 'J' and 'E' had been one book originally, the next step being to add the Deuteronomist materials. About the time of Ezekiel the material in Leviticus 17–26 was added to 'P' and it was extended in the time of Ezra.

These documents achieved their canonical form at about 200 BC.[41] This was the literary aspect of Wellhausen's work, but in his book on the history of Israel (1878), he offered more dramatic theories. He applied the theories of evolution to the history chronicled in the Old Testament, claiming that the religion of Israel began with a primitive belief in spirits who indwelt the world of nature – animism – and that the account in Genesis about the patriarchs worshipping one god was untenable. After moving to Palestine, the Hebrew tribes began to adapt to the Canaanite methods of worship and this was a step in the direction of monotheism. But it was in the time of the prophets that monotheism developed fully and the evolutionary process of the old order reached its full maturity. One of the consequences of the prophets' teaching was the centralization of cultic worship in Jerusalem from the time of Josiah onwards. The consequence of this policy was the development of the ceremonial laws which play such a prominent part in the 'P' document. It followed that Moses had nothing to do with the ceremonial laws since they belonged to the end of the evolutionary process rather than its beginning.

The strength of Wellhausen's commentary on the history of

Israel was its clarity and its simplicity. It combined all the various elements of Old Testament literature in one tidy pattern. Most importantly, its plan harmonized perfectly with the spirit of the age. The response of religious leaders in Wales in 1890 to this situation will be discussed shortly.[42]

Higher criticism had its unbending critics. According to the president of the Baptist Assembly of Arfon, in 1898, higher criticism destroyed religious enthusiasm; was it not the 'product of pride and faithlessness? To my mind it is a jelly fish type of Gospel.'[43] Thomas Rees (Merthyr Tudful) called higher criticism an 'ugly fantasy'; his opinion was that it was 'starting to take over Wales, and had had too much opportunity to leaven our denomination', as he said to the general assembly in 1894.[44] William Williams (Swansea) commented in 1893 that higher criticism 'made a great deal of noise, and caused not a little unease in the minds of many', and he proceeded to critique it in a lively and very skilful manner.[45] R. S. Thomas protested against the appointment of Llewellyn Ioan Evans as a professor at Bala College, 'in the face of his leanings towards Higher Criticism'.[46]

There is no doubt that religious leaders were preoccupied with these subjects in the 1890s. One visitor to the Union of Welsh Independents' assembly in Llanelli (1899) remarked that he was fed up of hearing about higher criticism. 'It was like salt on the table at every meal, until in the end it became insipid and tasteless'.[47] 'Gildas' did not mince his words about the new trends, claiming in 1898 that 'all false criticism, all poisonous doctrine, philosophy and empty deception, are being carried under the name of "Higher Criticism" to the pulpits of Wales'.[48]

Although some contented themselves with attacking the new critical methods with rash remarks, it was not easy to leave the debate at that. For one thing, young people, especially those with a college education, were posing honest questions about the significance of the critics' conclusions. It was not easy either for ministers to have to face the accusation that they were 'far behind the times with regard to Scriptural criticism'.[49] At least they should be able to explain and debate the critics' conclusions. This is what induced D. D. Hopkins, Pontarddulais, and many others to call upon preachers to familiarize themselves with biblical criticism.[50] If there was substance in their suspicion 'that the Armageddon of divine revelation is to be fought on the field of the Old Testament, and that the battle is nigh',[51] then there was sense in Josiah Thomas's warning from the Chair of the Calvinistic Methodist Association meeting at Corwen that people should refrain from 'speaking mockingly of criticism and higher criticism' and that they should bear in mind that faith in God is not inextricably linked 'to the idea that Moses wrote every word of the Pentateuch as they have come down to us'.[52]

The problem was that many could not distinguish between the critical method and the conclusions of the critics. Cynddylan Jones took a markedly conservative standpoint in these matters and yet we find him declaring that 'the wild accusation that orthodox theologians are hostile to biblical criticism is wholly without foundation'. 'There is no difference of opinion regarding the principles of criticism, but with regard to the practical application of the principles.'[53] Admittedly there is some oversimplification here, because there was some difference of opinion even concerning some of the principles. For example, Cynddylan rejected the principle adopted by Kuenen and Wellhausen that supernatural elements should be outlawed from the Bible.

However, even orthodox scholars were becoming increasingly sympathetic to the use of criticism as an appropriate tool for biblical exposition. Some like Owen Evans soon adopted a position where they counted S. R. Driver and George Adam Smith as 'moderate higher critics' and were prepared, as a result, to accept many of their conclusions.[54] Among others there was great enthusiasm for higher criticism. J. Lloyd Williams maintained that the contribution of higher criticism added to the value of the Bible and showed 'how the Book is the word of God',[55] while Iona M. Williams could not understand why some people claimed that it led to doubt and unbelief.[56] The Brecon theologian, Thomas Lewis, clearly shared this difficulty because he claimed that 'Biblical Criticism today is completely devout. It is not an attack on the Bible, rather a defence of it.'[57] His fellow professor at the Congregational Memorial College, Thomas Rees, succeeded in persuading many in the meetings of the Union of Welsh Independents in Caernarfon (1902) that there was no need to worry about the effect of criticism on the Bible because its authority depended not on the conclusions of scholars but on the evidence of the experience of Christians of its worth.[58]

Robert Ambrose Jones (Emrys ap Iwan) had no doubt in his

mind that the future success of Christianity in Wales depended on an acceptance of higher criticism, although he disliked the term, preferring the phrase 'Historical Criticism' instead. If human reason and conscience were ignored, the consequence would be the 'loss of our most enlightened members and listeners, as has happened many other countries'. He accepted the ideas of Réville, Kuenen and Wellhausen to the extent that Robertson Smith recommended them.[59]

Among books on the subject, *Llawlyfr Uwchfeirnidaeth Ysgrythurol* (A Handbook of Scriptural Higher Criticism, 1897) by Evan Cynffig Davies exuded enthusiasm on every page. He felt that there was an 'unusual magic' in Wellhausen's analysis of the history of Israel. D. E. Jenkins was eager to familiarize Welsh-speaking readers with these new opinions – but in their most moderate guise – and he translated *Yr Hen Destament a'i Gynnwys* (The Old Testament and its Contents, 1897) by James Robertson in Glasgow, M'Clymont's *Y Testament Newydd a'i Ysgrifenwyr* (The New Testament and its Writers, 1897), as well as W. F. Adeney's book, *Pa Fodd i Ddarllen y Beibl* (How to Read the Bible, 1898).

Robert Williams, Llanllechid, was a fine Hebrew scholar, and he adopted a conservative standpoint in his book *Craig yr Oesau* (The Rock of Ages, 1899).[60] T. Witton Davies's *Ysgrythyrau yr Hen Destament* (The Scriptures of the Old Testament, 1900) was much more radical and John Morgan Jones, Cardiff, regretted that it had been published because it could 'only shake the faith of some, and abase the Scriptures in the eyes of all those who put their faith in them'.[61]

J. Gwili Jenkins also took a radical view in *Llin ar Lin* (Flax on Flax, 1909),[62] as did Robert Roberts, Trefnant, in *Yr Hen Destament a'i Genadwri* (The Old Testament and its Message, 1909). Indeed, Roberts believed that the Pentateuch derived from as many as fourteen sources and he maintained that Jeremiah was the first to declare the doctrine of monotheism. Spinther James disagreed, as he demonstrated in *Yr Ymosodiadau ar y Beibl yn Cael eu Beirniadu* (A Critique of the Attacks on the Bible, 1909).

Llestri'r Trysor (The Vessels of the Treasure) edited by D. Tecwyn Evans and E. Tegla Davies[63] was a much more substantial book, the publication of which caused some controversy. A number of Wesleyan ministers came together to contribute essays to a book on higher criticism but when Hugh Jones saw the manuscript, he declared that if its content were true then he would never preach again. This declaration was the catalyst for a heated debate on the subject in the Ordination Assembly at Llanrhaeadr-ym-Mochnant in 1913. The denomination refused to publish the book and so the editors published it independently. The first edition sold out within a very short time and a second edition was prepared, but there was no demand for it, and much of the stock had to be destroyed.[64]

The various contributors represented a wide spectrum of opinion but they were all in agreement that the critics' work had strengthened the foundations of the Christian faith, although this involved acknowledging that the Bible was fallible in details and abandoning a belief in its verbal inspiration. Tegla tended towards a radical position, abolishing the predictive element in the prophecies of the Old Testament and tending strongly towards excluding the supernatural elements by interpreting them as symbolic of human actions or moral truths. It is easy to understand why a conservative such as Hugh Jones was so resolutely opposed to the whole tone of the book.

In evaluating the influence of higher criticism on contemporary thinking, there is no doubt that it had a profound effect on many people, and that its influence was on the increase. The debate between the supporters of higher criticism and their opponents tended to be a debate between two generations. The older generation on the whole were suspicious of it – people like John Morris (Brecon), David Rowlands (Dewi Môn), John Morgan Jones (Cardiff), James Spinther James, Charles Davies, Lewis Probert, Hugh Jones (Bangor), John Cynddylan Jones and Thomas Rees (Merthyr Tudful), to name some of them. On the other hand its most vociferous support came from among the younger generation – people such as J. Gwili Jenkins, Thomas Rees (Bangor), John Puleston Jones, Edward Anwyl, John Morgan Jones (Bangor), Silas Morris, Thomas Lewis (Brecon) and D. E. Jenkins. This boundary should not be drawn too strictly because Thomas Charles Edwards, Cynffig Davies, Robert Ambrose Jones (Emrys ap Iwan) and R. S. Thomas were obvious exceptions to the categorization according to age, and in any case, the opposition to higher criticism did not disappear. It continued not only among those who campaigned openly against it such as the proto-fundamentalist R. B. Jones of Porth, and the members of the evangelical 'Mission

Halls', but among a whole host of individuals in all denominations who refused to endorse the conclusions of the higher critics.

Nevertheless, the advent of higher criticism made a difference to everyone who took an intelligent interest in the Bible. A distinction was made between criticism as a method of studying the literature of the Bible and criticism as the sum of the conclusions reached by critics who adopted these methods. Conservatives and orthodox believers had come to acknowledge that there was no way of avoiding criticism as a means of shedding greater light upon the various books of the Bible, their authors, their date, their vocabulary and their historical and literary characteristics and so on.[65] From their standpoint, it was a matter of urgency to respond to perfectly legitimate questions raised by critics concerning apparent inconsistencies in the Bible and regarding the overall challenge to the authenticity of biblical history. If the critics' analysis was unacceptable, the only way to answer it was to offer a more correct and scholarly analysis. Many believed that the measured criticism based on painstaking scholarship affirmed the Bible's historicity and accuracy.[66] For these reasons, the advent of higher criticism influenced biblical studies among conservatives for the better.

The adoption of the new critical methods, therefore, did not mean necessarily the adoption of particular conclusions about the Bible itself: it was, in fact, a matter of presuppositions. Every critical method is based on presuppositions. One of the weaknesses of the period, among conservatives and modernists alike, was a failure to realize how important it was to take scholars' presuppositions into account.[67] At the time, belief in the unbiased sovereignty of human reason was very strong, and few realized that this was an article of faith, not the fruit of any rational analysis. Reasoning has to rely on faith in reasoning. Because of this, the debaters were not sufficiently perceptive in their criticism, for instance of Wellhausen's work which took evolution as a fact, and squeezed the biblical evidence relentlessly into that restrictive and unproven framework.

The critical method should not be confused with the fruit of any specific piece of research. The higher critics themselves were at fault in this, tending to trumpet the 'indisputable conclusions' of criticism when they were really talking about theories. Before long they would take a further step and vilify those who did not accept the theories derived from their logic. The unassailable confidence of a scholar does not transform his or her theories into facts. The Didache certainly existed because it was discovered in 1889, but no one had ever seen 'Q' or 'P'. At the beginning of the twentieth century it came to be realized that this must be taken into account in any discussion of their work. Robert Williams argued in every bit as scholarly a fashion – if not more so – than Robert Roberts, Trefnant, but his conclusions were radically different.

A brief perusal of the situation leads to the conclusion that, on the whole, the radical higher critics made little headway in Wales during the period up until 1914. The weight of opinion in Wales sided with the moderates. Nevertheless supporters of higher criticism were gaining ground in the colleges, and when their influence upon ministers reached its peak, the tide turned very rapidly against conservative opinion from 1914 onwards.

People's attitude towards biblical criticism is a convenient yardstick for distinguishing between theological liberalism and theological conservatism. Conservatives complained that biblical criticism corrupted the content of the faith because of its philosophical presuppositions. Their complaint was valid because to a very large extent this critical work was inspired not by scholarship as such but by the desire to legitimize liberal theology.[68] It took a long time for liberal critics to realize how much truth there was in the conservatives' complaint because they were so convinced of the immense benefits that came from dealing with the books of the Bible as historical documents. However, they tended to be blind to the inconsistency between their philosophical premises and the biblical foundation of the gospel. On the other hand, the conservatives believed that in their campaigns against the critics, they were defending the Bible, and the gospel, against vicious enemies, without realizing how often they were attempting to defend rationalist and scholastic theology whose roots were not in the Bible but rather in the philosophical presuppositions of the eighteenth century.[69] Cynddylan Jones had grasped this point when he wrote that the debate 'between Orthodoxy and Higher Criticism' was a debate 'about the historical truth of the Bible' and added stridently, 'the order of salvation is a system of facts, and not a system of ideas, as the Hegelians tend to think'.[70]

The work of the higher critics shook the faith of many. Wellhausen himself confessed before the end of his life that his research had driven him to total scepticism concerning the authority of the Old Testament.[71] Was the influence of his work on the thinkers of Wales to give rise to the same consequence? What was people's attitude towards the Bible's authority between 1890 and 1914? One anonymous writer in 1891 insisted that 'the traditional theories of inspiration are being discounted', and that we must know what criteria to use to separate true from false elements in the Bible itself. Previously the Bible was considered to be true in its entirety but now such a view seemed untenable. It followed that the standard for differentiating between truth and falsehood within the Bible should be the same as the standard which operated outside the Bible. However, no satisfactory definition of the standard was given.[72] 'The Bible is a supernatural book, and we had better not define the nature and method of its inspiration.'[73] Owen Evans (at that time at Llangefni) gave essentially the same answer. The Bible was not infallible in all its details but it must be remembered that its purpose was salvation and 'there is no need to make a shibboleth of any one theory concerning its inspiration'.

The Welsh American theologian, Joseph Roberts, Minneapolis, refused to accept this compromise as a retreat, as it were, from the fray. In a thoughtful article he attacked the premises of Wellhausen and Baur. They claimed impartiality, but he disputed this rather dubious claim. 'Their entire method of biblical criticism is coloured and corrupted by their belief.' It was useless for them to argue that they used a scientific method 'to examine the literature of the divine-human book, while at the same time believing in a philosophical theory that rejects the belief in miracles'. For Roberts, this was not a battle between faith and science but between two competing faiths. Wellhausen's agnosticism was not the only possible foundation for biblical criticism. A sound doctrine of biblical inspiration was one of the indispensable foundations for a sound theory of biblical criticism. It was not the Christian preacher's principal task to declare that the Bible is divinely inspired but rather to present the gospel, the biblical message of salvation in Christ. The one who believes the message does so because he or she has been completely convinced that what the biblical writers say is true, and it is on exactly the same basis that 'we must accept its teaching about inspiration'. It is true that 'Christianity does not rest on the doctrine of the inspiration of the scriptures', but the person who believed the biblical evidence concerning the Redeemer was obliged to take seriously his teaching about his own relationship with God, in other words, his teaching about inspiration. 'If we do not accept the Bible's own teaching on this, why do we bother accepting its teaching on anything else?'[74]

What concerned many was the question of the infallibility of the Bible. Were there errors in the Bible? If there were, as the critics claimed, did this not undermine its authority as a book inspired by God? Llewellyn Ioan Evans remarked that he did not know of one revered critic who still claimed that the Bible was inerrant from cover to cover,[75] but the classical standpoint, as expressed by A. A. Hodge and B. B. Warfield, was:

> that all the affirmations of Scripture of all kinds whether of spiritual doctrine or duty, or of physical or historical fact, or of psychological or philosophical principle, are without any error, when the *ipsissima verba* of the original autographs are ascertained and interpreted in their natural and intended sense.[76]

For Griffith Ellis it was no longer possible to accept this belief in the infallibility of the Bible and he discussed whether it was possible therefore to safeguard belief in the divine inspiration of the Bible while allowing that it contained errors. He inclined towards the suggestion of the scholar C. A. Briggs that the Bible's central purpose was to convey to humankind knowledge of God and his gracious purposes in offering salvation to men. In this area the divine inspiration of the Bible was beyond doubt and its message was infallible. It may have been true that it contained errors in relation to scientific and historical matters but they were nothing but motes of dust in a sunbeam.[77]

Ellis differentiated between religious and factual elements in the Bible and this was indicative of the trend of the time. The question was whether this dualism was possible or not. As Cynddylan Jones said, the validity of the Christian faith depended on historical events. If God did not call Abraham and Moses, then it was futile to quote his dealings with them as a model to show how he intervened in the lives of people in 1900.

Some felt that it was better to consider some portions of the Bible as infallible rather than to attribute infallibility to a certain aspect of it which would be difficult to define. The infallible part was the witness of Jesus Christ himself. This conviction was expressed usually by saying that Jesus Christ was the Lord of scripture, a statement which would offend no one though it presupposed that the New Testament's portrayal of Christ was historically accurate. This viewpoint was expressed clearly by H. M. Hughes, minister of Ebenezer church, Cardiff, when he argued that final authority could not rest in the church, or in human reason, or in the Bible as a whole, but in a faith inspired by the appropriation of the biblical message itself. Having believed in Christ, the believer was free to judge the Bible in the light of Christ.[78] This view depended on the belief that criticism, when directed towards the New Testament, could not undermine people's confidence in its accuracy. But the further development of criticism was already shaking that belief even when Hughes's article appeared. In any case, if it was right to believe in the infallibility of the New Testament, or the Synoptic Gospels, was it not necessary to accept Jesus' views on the author-ity and accuracy of the Old Testament as well? If Jesus was the highest authority for Christians in matters concerned with their relationship with God, could they reasonably reject Jesus' belief in the relationship between the Old Testament and God?

In the face of questions such as these, some thinkers came to con-sider the Bible as a record of individuals' religious experiences or moral codes, all a means of circumventing this critical problem. The view of the Bible as a compendium of morality was connected particularly with the influence of Albrecht Ritschl.[79] Lewis Williams of Bangor, in his review of the progress of theology in Wales, deemed that Ritschl had been a major influence. For the Ritschlian school the *value* of a fact became of central significance; the important thing was the meaning of a fact in the spiritual and moral experience of the believer. However, it was very easy to lose sight of factuality altogether and to maintain that it was of no import provided that it inspired the reader and gave him or her an uplifting experience. Was there ever an exodus from Egypt? Did the transfiguration on Mount Tabor actually happen? If it could be proved that such events had never occurred as historical facts, then it would not be of great concern because the moral and spiritual value of these accounts would remain.[80] But those who ducked the critics' challenge in this manner paid a tremendous price – nothing less than the emptying of the Christian faith of its historical content and turning it into a theoretical system of values or ideas.

In the face of such manifold difficulties, many embraced a creed not unlike the Quakers' 'Inner Light'. The most complete attempt to present such a theory was that of J. Puleston Jones in the 1909 Davies Lecture published under the title, *Until the Day Dawns*. For him, authority was enshrined within the spiritual experience of the mature Christian. The Bible provides men and women with a revelation through the medium of history but, although the history is valuable, this was not the ultimate revelation. It is the voice of the Spirit within which gives the Bible its authority. 'The revelation within is our final warrant for believing in the truth of the revelation from without. Christ dwelling by faith in the heart is the final ground of assurance – Christ speaking with the voice of reason and of conscience'.[81] For Puleston Jones, the Spirit does more than enlighten the mind to grasp the divine revelation, it produces another revelation which is superior to the 'historical revelation'. Does this mean that the Christian believer has been afforded a more excellent revelation than that of Jesus of Nazareth and, if so, can such a revelation be attributed to the Holy Spirit whose work is directed specifically towards illuminating the historical Jesus to the mind? Puleston Jones's theory is a clear example of the flight into subjectivity seen in the same period in the work of the Romantic poets and it is linked very closely with the growing popularity of subjective theology – the theology of experience – and the call of Thomas Rees, the principal of Bala–Bangor College, for theology to be rebuilt on the basis of Jesus' experience of God's Fatherhood.[82]

The debate on the authority of the Bible during this period showed which way the wind was blowing. The objective authority of the Bible was being eroded. An authoritative scripture was ceasing to be the foundation for the life and thinking of Christians for the whole of their lives. If the Bible's authority in historical, physical and scientific matters was to be denied, was there any point in using it to search for guidance on the relationship of faith and culture? If its claims concerning the history of the past could be ignored, then it could hardly be expected to shed light on God's dealings with the Welsh people in their church in 1900 either. If it was a book which dealt solely with spiritual experiences and personal values, then the Christian faith had become a completely private matter, and if people desired guidance in political and cultural matters, they would be forced to search for wisdom elsewhere. That is precisely what happened from 1890 onwards. The Christian life in Wales lost its biblical wholeness, it became fragmented and compartmentalized and Christians were obliged to share the control over their lives with powers other than the realities of the Christian thinking as presented in God's word.

Let us move now from the doctrine of scripture to the development of public education in Wales. The aim of the 1870 Education Act was to place elementary education within the reach of every child. Under this Act denominational schools were permitted to continue their work but where such voluntary efforts were unable to meet the demand, elected local councils, called 'school boards', were to be set up to fulfil this task and make good any deficiency. The denominational schools were free to provide religious education in accordance with their beliefs and the school boards were free to organize religious education in their schools in accordance with the wishes of the majority of the members of the board or, of course, to choose not to provide religious education at all.

The sentiment in favour of wholly secular education was stronger in Wales than in England. In 1886, there were 1,800 school boards in England, but only six of them provided wholly secular education. In Wales, however, 49 school boards out of 332 had banished religious education from their schools – thirteen in Carmarthenshire, eleven in Cardiganshire, ten in Pembrokeshire, nine in Glamorgan, two in Breconshire, and one each in Anglesey, Caernarfonshire, Merioneth and Monmouthshire.[83] In other words, about 85 per cent of the school boards provided for religious worship and instruction but the provision was ineffective as a means of raising the standard of children's biblical knowledge and it soon became evident that the Sunday schools could not make good this deficiency.

The new educational system meant that churches had less influence on the development of children's thinking while the state's influence on their education increased. In every school, denominational schools and board schools alike, religion was relegated to the periphery, compared with the 'Three Rs' and 'specific subjects' such as history, geography, Latin and French that the pupils were allowed to take in standards IV, V and VI. It is worth dwelling on this point a little to underline the significance of the change that was afoot. This was an example of the great divide in European culture that was to become a chasm as the generations progressed, and was a result of the thinking developed by Descartes, Locke and especially Kant. On the one hand, there was the natural world, the world of science and fact, and on the other there was the world of faith, morality, values and religion. The tension between these two worlds had a myriad of often tragic consequences in the thinking, art and religion of Europe.

In 1870 in Wales the task of immersing children in the mysteries of this duality began. To begin with, secular subjects were given pride of place and religion was marginalized. Moreover, the 1870 Education Act had started a fundamental revolution in Welsh thinking. To understand it, we must cast our minds back again to philosophical influences of the past, to the influence of John Locke. Locke taught that the human mind was like a sheet of unmarked paper, receiving information from the world around it, its physical sensations moulded by the intrinsic processes of the mind into ideas. During the eighteenth-century Enlightenment, Locke's teaching was used in ways that he would not have approved. One aspect of the Enlightenment was its continuing warring with the past. Tradition, whether Calvinistic, Scholastic, ecclesiastical or patriotic, was deemed an enemy to those who wished to live under the government of Reason and so everything traditional had to be rooted out. Since the human mind in its infancy had been completely pure of all traditional influences, education could provide humankind with a fresh start. A new 'brotherhood' could be formed on the basis of enlightened reason and free from the fetters of tradition. Thus the idea was born of a radical revolution which was realized in France in the 1789 Revolution, whose ambition was to erase the past completely.

In the 1870 Education Act, these ideas were applied (albeit unconsciously) to the children of Wales. They were to be weaned from their traditional background, their language, their history, their nationality and their religion. The convictions that were to govern children's minds were those given to them in schools. The aim was to serve the 'scientific state', so-called because it undertook to mould the life of society in accordance with plans which result from a scientific study of the problems that need to be resolved. Thus rationalist politics were deemed a concomitant of the scientific state. This kind of state developed very gradually but there is little doubt that it made particularly significant progress between 1870 and 1912 and few things were more important in people's preparation for it than the 1870 Education Act.

The Act was part of the mechanism created to instruct people to take their place in the service of the scientific, centralized and democratic state. By serving this state, people could feel that they were helping to create history and fashion the society of the future. For Welsh people that meant accepting the uniformity that characterized the state which governed them, uniformity in language, culture and political philosophy. And the scientific state was not a new state but the historical English state and the 1870 educational system was devised in Wales to serve its interminable uniformity.

As the century drew to a close, it became clear that the Conservative government was intending to amend the 1870 Act in favour of denominational schools. This brought joy to Anglicans, and infuriated Nonconformists no end. When the government introduced its Education Bill in 1896, a campaign was launched against it, with the Anglesey and Arfon Joint Education Committee in the vanguard, interviewing Members of Parliament and calling the country as a whole to battle.[84] However, nothing came of this Bill or of the one introduced in 1901.

On 24 March 1902, Arthur James Balfour rose in the House of Commons to introduce the Education Bill which was to cause a terrible uproar.[85] The Bill set out that the school boards were to be abolished and their work transferred to the county councils, which would act as the local education authorities. They would be responsible for the old board schools (the 'provided schools' in the new parlance) and for secular education in the denominational schools (the 'non-provided schools'). Although the costs of building and maintaining the denominational school buildings were to be borne by the voluntary bodies which owned them, all other costs were to be paid out of taxes. Although the local education authorities contributed towards maintaining the denominational schools, they were not allowed to appoint more than a third of the governors or to forbid the appointment of a teacher except on purely educational grounds. The religious education in these schools would be the governors' responsibility. Religious education could be provided in other schools on condition that it did not conform with any denominational catechism. A fierce battle was waged against the Bill inside and outside Parliament but it became law on 18 December 1902.

Opposition to the Act developed in Wales in a completely different way from the opposition in England. In England preparations were made to organize personal protests by means of 'passive resistance' – in other words, people refused to pay the portion of the tax that went towards denominational education and were punished in the courts.[86] This happened to a certain extent in Wales too but the protest throughout most of the country was different. Of the county councils, eleven expressed their intention not to implement the Act. On 17 January 1903, Lloyd George announced a different scheme. He recognized that the councils' policy 'appealed to the sentiment of hatred towards the Act and its provisions' but he argued that it would be better to 'take possession of the enemy's cannons, and turn his own guns against him'. Therefore, 'Our purpose . . . should be to labour for total self-government in educational matters in Wales'. With that purpose in sight, the councils should implement the Act but as strictly as possible with regard to denominational schools. The education authorities should ensure that these schools meet the requirements of the Act in full before agreeing to support them. They were to give an undertaking 'that no teachers would be tested as to their beliefs before being appointed' and that the financial side of the schools would be under public control. If the governors of denominational schools could show 'that they were inclined to accept these conditions, then they should be given ample opportunity to teach the Church's doctrines to the children of Anglicans within the schools'.

Lloyd George believed that 'the 1902 Education Act has extended to Wales its greatest political opportunity' to ensure national unity.[87] It was a brilliant proposal. Lloyd George gained the support of his fellow Liberals and representatives of the county councils agreed in Llandrindod Wells, 27 February 1903,[88] to invite the authorities of denominational schools to discuss the possibility of agreement. The bishop of St Asaph responded positively to the new policy[89] but there was no support for it among Anglicans generally. Bishop John Owen was truly doubtful of the policy and feared that the church could lose its schools and everything for which it had fought.[90] Thus, when further meetings were held, on 24 March 1903, to discuss the terms of an agreement between the education authorities, only the representatives of St Asaph and the Roman Catholic Francis Mostyn, bishop of Menevia were present.[91] Although in his autobiography the bishop of St Asaph gave the impression that he had been pleased by the meeting, he was in an irritable mood when the education board of his diocese met in Chester on 14 April. He did not mince his words; he hoped that the whole scheme would fail, and diocesan leaders drew up terms that made any agreement impossible.[92] This was the real turning point.

Despite the warm talk of agreement – the 'concordat' – there was no hope for it to succeed.

So, as Lloyd George had said, there was no option but war. This was his message to the county council representatives in the education conference held in Swansea on 19 May.[93] In a second conference on education, held in Cardiff on 3 June, the Swansea policy was endorsed, namely that a recommendation be given to county councils to refuse to maintain denominational schools unless they were given full control over them.[94] However, there was not a total consensus in Wales regarding support for the policy. Carmarthenshire County Council refused to support it, under the leadership of D. E. Jones, tutor in the Presbyterian College, Carmarthen.[95] It was only under pressure from Lloyd George and his friends that the council decided to withhold the tax in the case of denominational schools on 22 July 1903.[96] In Brecon and Radnorshire a Conservative majority ensured that both counties rejected the policy of the Cardiff Conference. In the mean time the 1902 Act had not been implemented in the rebellious counties.

County council elections were held in March 1904. Education became the sole topic of the campaign and the Liberals gained a huge victory with every county returning a majority in favour of Lloyd George's policy. Throughout Wales, 640 Liberals and 156 Conservatives had gained seats.[97] Lloyd George reckoned it to be one of the greatest victories in centuries[98] and others spoke of a 'national awakening' and of the resurrection of the ideals of Cymru Fydd.[99] The government could do nothing now but bring a Bill before Parliament that would enable the Board of Education to wrest control from any rebellious education authority and implement the Act directly. There was ferocious debate in the House of Commons concerning the Education (Local Authority Default) Bill and scenes of disorder reigned. But despite all opposition the 'coercion bill' or the 'bill of oppression', its nickname, became law on 15 August 1904.[100]

Since Lloyd George's attempt to secure some kind of concordat in the spring of 1903 had made a favourable impression on the bishop of St Asaph, he made a fresh attempt to bridge the gap between the two parties by proposing a measure – the Education (Transferred Schools) Bill – in the House of Lords. It was given a second reading in May 1904, but it pleased no one and promptly died.[101]

The uproar in Wales was still increasing. It reached its climax in the summit conference in Cardiff, 6 October 1904, to discuss the coercion bill. Herbert Lewis proposed a resolution saying that if the Board of Education were to implement the coercion bill, the local authority would 'immediately declare its inability to fulfil the duties laid upon it by the Education Act of 1902'.[102] This was passed and an opportunity soon arose to measure the strength of the policy in Merioneth. The intention was for Nonconformist parents, who had children in the denominational schools, to arrange for them to be educated elsewhere through voluntary means. Merioneth Council withheld £2,000 worth of grants to the denominational schools. On 1 April 1905, it was notified that it had violated the Act of 1902 and so, in accordance with the Coercion Act, the same amount was withheld from its grants. A summit conference was held in Bala on 2 May, and it was agreed that Nonconformists should be asked to remove their children from church schools. At the same time fund-raising began to pay for voluntary education for them. The parents responded, and the first 'rebellion school' was opened in the Calvinistic Methodist chapel in Maentwrog, with twenty-three children. Soon afterwards a school was opened for the children of Llandecwyn in the Wesleyan chapel there, and for the children of Carrog in the Baptist vestry.[103] Merioneth was not the only transgressor because grants to Barry, Glamorgan, Montgomeryshire and Mountain Ash were curtailed for the same reason.

The whole affair came to an end very suddenly with the fall of the Conservative government on 4 December 1905, which meant that the Coercion Act ceased to be implemented from that time. However, although the Liberals won one of their biggest victories in the general election that followed, nothing was done to resolve Nonconformist grievances. Some agitation continued, but the 1902 Act worked better than the Nonconformists feared. They saw the number of denominational schools decreasing from year to year.[104] The Anglicans for their part were not unhappy with public control because it worked more fairly than they had supposed.

What was the significance of this 'Welsh rebellion'? The issues in question stirred up strong emotions. This was apparent partly in the 'passive resistance' campaign to withhold payment of the education tax. On 27 July 1903, eight townspeople from Carmarthen were the first to appear before the magistrates' bench for non-payment. In their midst were the ministers Edward Davies, E. Ungoed Thomas, W. W. Lewis and W. S. Jones.[105] They were followed by others in

Breconshire and Liverpool, including Thomas Rees (Merthyr Tudful), Peter Price, Owen Owens, David Powell, O. L. Roberts, John Hughes, Owen Evans, Griffith Ellis, Hugh Jones (Liverpool) and more.[106] Of course, because of the councils' rebellion there was less opportunity in Wales to protest in this way than in England. By making the protest through the county councils, Lloyd George made the battle one between the different government departments, between central government and local government. This strengthened the protest and at the same time it gave people who were uncomfortable with breaking the law the opportunity to show their colours in a lawful manner.[107]

Despite the perseverance of individual protestors, some radicals became very critical of the struggle. W. J. Gruffydd had been critical of it in 1903 and he was still critical in 1951.[108] In his view, passive resistance had been a great mistake. Similarly, Thomas Rees, the principal of Bala–Bangor College, argued in a remarkable article that it was the voluntary tradition which had safeguarded the true Christian perspective on education. He believed that religious education should have a place of honour in the educational system and that means should be devised for secularists and Catholics to have their own schools. Thomas Rees himself took part in the campaign of passive resistance but he came to believe that acting in this way had been a mistake and that his former teacher, D. E. Jones, was correct when he argued in favour of implementing the 1902 Act.[109] This, in fact, was the crux of the matter. The viewpoint of classical Nonconformists such as the mid-Victorian radical Evan Jones (Ieuan Gwynedd) was that all education was rooted in faith. Ieuan Gwynedd set out his conviction thus:

> What is education? Is it learning the ABC, spelling, reading and arithmetic? No; these things are merely the means of education – no knowledge is involved in being able to read books, but in understanding the tasks and duties of life. The main aim of education is to make a man a useful member of society, and this is secured by teaching him that which will make him useful, respectable, and contented . . . The knowledge mentioned must be moral. Religion is the basis of morality, and education must include knowledge of God, before it can be called moral . . .[110]

Anglicans and Catholics would agree with the substance of such a declaration. He merely stated the classical Christian belief that faith gave unity and wholeness to education, in its moral and social aspects, and also in its function as an opportunity to summarize factual information. For various reasons, Nonconformists abandoned the standpoint of Ieuan Gwynedd and others like him and supported the effort to secure an educational system which was largely secular and funded by the state. During the years after 1902 some of the most radical Nonconformists campaigned that religion should have no place at all in public schools. They wanted the councils to take over all the schools in order to banish religion from them,[111] but this meant embracing a concept of education which was diametrically opposed to the standpoint of their radical predecessors, and the tensions increased during the struggle against the 1902 Act.

In 1905, the Calvinistic Methodist General Assembly passed a motion in favour of religious education in schools. Even before then, a Baptist as prominent as William Morris, Treorchy, had warned of the adverse effects of exiling the Bible from schools and had persuaded the Rhondda school board to adopt a joint syllabus for religious education.[112] Among Independents, people like James Charles, Cynffig Davies and D. E. Jones were adamantly opposed to the secular viewpoint.[113] During the campaign, Nonconformists tended to emphasize public control while Anglicans emphasized the safeguarding of religious education. The question was whether these two views were mutually exclusive. Some Anglicans (such as Frank Edwards) were in favour of complete public control, and some Nonconformists (such as Lloyd George) were in favour of effective religious education. Compromise was possible, as Lloyd George and the bishop of St Asaph both saw. Part of the tragedy which ensued was that they failed to carry their followers with them in their attempts to reach a viable compromise.

The end of the story by 1914 was that both sides had won part of the argument but had lost substantially more. An opportunity to strengthen Christian thinking in Wales by means of effective religious instruction in day schools was squandered. The door was opened ever wider to the process of secularizing the Welsh mind. Religious education in schools will not necessarily breed Christians, but it can at least ensure that children brought up in a Christian nation appreciate the culture shaped by their hereditary faith. And there is no surer way of undermining respect for a subject – whether the Welsh language or the Christian faith – than by relegating it to the sidelines or ignoring it completely. This, alas, is what occurred.

~ 12 ~

Heavenly Fire

The 1904–5 Revival was one of the most remarkable events in twentieth-century Welsh history. A 'religious revival' involves a spiritual 'awakening' or 'revitalization' within churches or within an area which contrasts with the smooth flow of daily life. From the Christian perspective, it should be understood as the specific activity of the Holy Spirit deepening people's commitment to God and intensifying their concern about their eternal destiny. Individuals are converted often in large numbers, churches are re-vitalized and the excitement spreads to surrounding localities. These newly converted or revival Christians become infused with missionary spirit and dedicate themselves to a holy life and not infrequently to cultural and social service.

A revival of this kind can be either locally focused or very widespread; the validity of a revival does not depend on its geographical distribution. It can be quiet and intense or exuberant and exciting, since a revival should not be defined merely in terms of its emotional fervour. It can be short-lived or long lasting because a revival cannot be measured in terms of its temporal span. A revival can lead to unusual and abnormal behaviour because no phenomenon on earth has been exempt from abuse by unstable minds or evil hearts.

The great yearning for a revival at the turn of the century has already been discussed and when the awakening eventually came, some leaders were not surprised. 'There has been a great longing for the break of dawn', said Charles Davies, minister at the Tabernacle church in Cardiff,[1] and his fellow Baptist Cernyw Williams agreed, commenting that 'many of us have been expecting a revival for some time'.[2] This expectancy went hand in hand with concern for the spiritual condition of Wales. The work of the

Holy Spirit was a frequent topic of discussion at conferences and there was much prayer for an outpouring from above which illustrated the concern of the time. Despite all the churches' activity, an increasing number of leaders were convinced that only divine intervention could save Wales from a terrible spiritual collapse. 'The situation of our country,' declared the editorial of *Y Dysgedydd* at the end of 1901, 'politically, socially, commercially and religiously, cries out for submission and fasting before God.' 'We do not recall a time of more insolent and unbridled ungodliness.'[3] In the same vein, Peter Roberts of St Asaph called upon the Calvinistic Methodists to join in a week of fasting from 27 October to 3 November 1901 to 'counter worldliness and luxury' and to cultivate a 'spirit of faith and prayer'.[4] It is not surprising that there was a general yearning in the churches for God to show his power in revival.[5]

However it was a statement on the issue by David Howell (Llawdden) that attracted the most attention. As the foremost leader of the evangelical wing of the Church in Wales, Dean Howell was in complete accord with the longing for divine intervention. His declaration, 'The Great Need of Wales', was published widely in the month of his death, January 1903, and was regarded as his spiritual will and testament. The only remedy for the nation's ills, he claimed was:

> Spiritual revitalization! . . . Not a local disturbance . . . but a kind of spiritual saturation, that overflows into the country as a whole, that would immerse all classes with the Baptism of the Holy Spirit . . . If God's word contains any truth at all it is without doubt that GOD'S SPIRIT is the only source of spiritual life; that it is not possible to produce or revive religious life by any means apart from the instrumentality of the Spirit – 'Not by might, nor by power, but by my spirit saith the Lord of hosts'.[6]

This eloquent and powerful statement made a deep impression on the nation and the longing for revival became more intense than ever. Throughout the country fervent prayer meetings were held – in the valleys of the south as well as the quarry areas in the north.[7] The Keswick Movement contributed to the fervour with its August conference in Llandrindod.

Prominent among the religious bodies which were concerned

about spiritual decline was the Cardiganshire Monthly Meeting of the Calvinistic Methodist Church. In May 1892, Joseph Jenkins was inducted into the pastorate at New Quay and two years later his nephew John Thickens became the minister of Tabernacle chapel, Aberaeron.[8] The two had frequent heart-to-heart discussions on the spiritual condition of the area, and in the summer of 1903[9] they came into contact with people who had been under the influence of the Keswick Movement.

Sometime during October 1903, Jenkins began to feel that they needed to break through the veneer of formality that was stifling church meetings. He wanted the kind of meeting where those present would be expected to pray, sing, read or speak according to the inspiration of the moment. The trial was a success and the 'first signs of sunrise from on high were seen'. One young girl prayed in such a manner as to penetrate one elder's composure. He came forward with tears running down his face saying, 'It is alright. I know him. He is the Holy Spirit.'[10]

At the Abermeurig Monthly Meeting in the same month, Jenkins spoke with extraordinary power concerning the wretched condition of the churches of the land, and called earnestly on all present to join in an effort to awaken them from their slumber.[11] Jenkins himself had had remarkable spiritual experiences. Although he had been converted years previously, it was not until 1903 that he came to understand that God was giving him 'the present assurance of full salvation'. A friend of his, Ceredig Evans, had been weeping and praying with him and Jenkins heard a voice within him ordering him to 'fulfil his ministry'. One night in his study he saw a vision of the cross which filled his soul 'with joy and peace'.[12]

The Monthly Meeting had organized a series of meetings to be held on 31 December 1903 and New Year's Day 1904. The meetings were led by W. W. Lewis, Carmarthen,[13] and J. M. Saunders and his wife.[14] Lewis's preaching inspired scenes of great emotion.[15] Since shortly before Christmas 1903, Jenkins had been holding meetings of the Christian Endeavour movement, exactly as John Thickens was doing in Aberaeron; this was a foretaste of the crucial role which young people would play in the story of the revival.[16] The spiritual temperature was rising and as he preached in early February[17] Jenkins felt strange forces moving within him. That night a young girl came hesitantly to his door in spiritual torment. After talking to her, Jenkins told her 'to accept Jesus as her

Saviour, and not only as her Saviour but as Lord.'[18] In the young people's meeting on the following Sunday morning[19] Jenkins urged them to share their spiritual experiences. One of the girls, Florrie Evans (who was subsequently to have a key role in the revival) stood up and said simply, 'O! I love Jesus with all my heart'.[20] With that the floodgates opened.[21]

The young people of New Quay now set out like an army to evangelize the surrounding areas.[22] It was thus that Joseph Jenkins reckoned February 1904 to be the date when the revival began and according to him its effect on the inhabitants of New Quay was evident; the church was revitalized, people's morals improved, and Bible reading and family prayer became not the exception but the norm.[23] In the mean time there were similar stirrings in other places. By the end of 1903, the Congregational church of Saron, Maesteg, had come heavily under the influence of the revival and in the final communion of the year seventy-two new members were received, while sixty were welcomed back into the fold in the first communion of 1904.[24]

At about the same time a mighty revival began among the Baptists at Heolyfelin, Aberdare. Ever since the minister, W. Cynog Williams, had arrived in December 1903 there had been baptisms every month, about 110 in all by November 1904.[25] There were similar occurrences in Pisgah, Pyle, in Pen-prysg, Pencoed, and Rhos, Mountain Ash, where there were thirty-five converts in April 1904.[26] In Merioneth the Wesleyans held their Regional Meeting in Tywyn at the beginning of May 1904. The subject of the theological conference was 'The Holy Spirit and His work', and when Richard Jones, Blaenau Ffestiniog, described his conversion, someone began to sing the hymn, 'O! anfon Di yr Ysbryd Glân . . .' ('O! send Thou the Holy Spirit . . .'). The place ignited and the meeting continued with people rejoicing until ten o'clock at night.[27]

By the summer of 1904, there were stirrings in several places. In Cardiganshire M. P. Morgan had joined enthusiastically in the revival and in his chapel in Blaenannerch a second revival conference was held under the auspices of the Monthly Meeting, similar to the one held in New Quay some time before. The same spiritual fervour became evident again.[28] The thrill of revival could be felt in the Rhondda valley when the jubilation at the Baptist Singing Festival in Treorchy, 23 May 1904, was such that the organizers were obliged to extend it for another day. E. Gwynhefin Thomas of Pen-prysg, and R. B. Jones, Porth, were invited to give an address and members of the congregation contributed freely to the service exactly as happened with Joseph Jenkins at New Quay.[29] For months afterwards the same anointing was felt throughout the Treorchy churches.[30]

By this time there was fresh excitement in north Wales. On 19 and 20 June, 'unforgettable meetings were held' at Seion, Ponciau, when J. R. Jones, Pontypridd, and Thomas Shankland were officiating at the preaching meetings. By the evening services on Monday, 20 June, 'the influence was overwhelming'. The services continued throughout the week and the fervour reached its climax in a baptismal service on Sunday, 26 June. This was followed by more preaching meetings led by Charles Davies, Cardiff, and J. R. Jones, which continued until the first week in July.[31] By that week revival had broken out in Noddfa, Caerau, in Glamorgan. Here as in Treorchy, people could not refrain from singing and when thirty converts were received into membership, on Sunday night, 31 July, the service ended with the singing of the hymn which would later become one of the favourites of the revival, 'Cerdd ymlaen, nefol dân . . .' ('Walk on, heavenly fire . . .').[32] At the same time prayer meetings full of fervour and inspiration were held in Nant Peris in Gwynedd.[33]

It would not be true to say that meetings everywhere were necessarily charged with emotion. The minister of Hebron, Dowlais, W. Ceinfryn Thomas, bore witness that his people 'had felt the outpouring of the Spirit during the last week in August' but it happened very quietly. Nevertheless, the blessing continued until the revival swept through the country as a whole.[34]

Individual evangelists gave similar reports. Of 1903, Rosina Davies said that 'the tide was rising everywhere, and there was a spiritual awakening that made it easy and pleasant to preach and sing the Gospel'.[35] In Maesteg and Ferndale in February she felt that people's thirst for the Holy Spirit was on the increase and during her campaign at Moreia chapel, Llangefni, she received help from a group of young men in recording the names of inquirers. By the beginning of 1904 she was sure that the churches were awakening, 'especially in north Wales'.[36]

Seth Joshua reported similar scenes. His biographer claims that 1903 was the most remarkable year of his life. Every meeting he held produced conversions and in one meeting as many as fifty people came under conviction.[37] In January 1904, he began his work as the official evangelist of the Calvinistic Methodists and in his frequent travels from one end of Wales to the other he saw signs of spiritual stirring.[38] Not everyone was aware of this; as late as July 1904 one correspondent complained about the lukewarmness of the churches and declared that they were in need of revival.[39] One remarkably prophetic correspondent saw in the longing for revival in America, in England, in Switzerland and in Wales a hopeful sign of things to come. The stirrings that had happened as a result of the evangelistic missions of Gypsy Smith, William Booth, F. B. Meyer, Pearson Dowie, Torrey and Alexander, were 'but "like a man's hand" saying that a greater excitement will soon come'.[40] The editor of Y Goleuad expressed the conviction of thousands when he wrote in July 1904 that 'the signs of revival' could be seen 'in many places'.[41]

By this time Joseph Jenkins was one of the most influential figures in the south-west. On 30 October 1904, the effect of his preaching at Bethany chapel, Ammanford, was quite extraordinary. Already emboldened in spirit, by Tuesday night, 1 November, 'the floodgates opened'.[42] Some took offence at the emotional excitement and the lengthy meetings. One minister rose to his feet and said publicly that he did not approve of keeping young people in chapel until unearthly hours, but the congregation was quick to express its disapproval not of the revival but of its critic.[43]

Jenkins's young people at New Quay were also spreading the fire. People flocked in droves to the meetings from distances of fifteen miles or more and carried the enthusiasm home with them. The young people of New Quay held many meetings in the surrounding area, which were invariably well-attended with the enthusiasm increasing into the autumn months.[44] At Trinity chapel, for instance, on 4 November, 'sometimes a young woman would rise to her feet to read out a hymn, and the congregation would sing; then another would start to pray in his seat. Afterwards, another would rise to her feet to give her testimony in simple and effective language and style ...' All this happened in the midst of emotional excitement with much weeping.[45]

There were similar scenes at Clos-y-graig on 8 November when Jenkins spoke to the young people of his intention to make an evangelical onslaught on the Cardigan fair. On Thursday, 10 November, the town's winter fair was turned into a religious festival with street preaching and a service following at Tabernacle chapel.[46] The revival was spreading swiftly through south Cardiganshire and adjacent areas of Carmarthenshire.

During the same period the revival was reaching its climax in Rhosllannerchrugog, north-east Wales. On 8 November, one of the most prominent leaders of the revival, R. B. Jones of Porth, arrived in the village to hold meetings at the Penuel Baptist chapel.[47] For a week he directed his sermons at church members, and then, during the second week, he turned to address the public generally. The chapel was full to overflowing for each meeting and the preacher 'swept the people off their feet with his exhortations'.[48] The climax came on the last day of his campaign, Friday 18 November. At five o'clock in the afternoon the congregation marched from Penuel to the Methodist Capel Mawr and after a brief sermon, R. B. Jones opened the meeting to the floor and numerous individuals contributed to the service with prayers, testimonies and hymns. Jones, meanwhile, preached to the hundreds who had failed to gain entry to the chapel. It was a great night in the history of Rhos and a significant milestone in the history of the revival.[49]

In the mean time, in September 1904, mighty revivals were occurring in Baptist churches of the East Glamorgan association, in Tabernacle chapel, Merthyr, Gwawr, Aberaman, Elim, Penydarren, and others.[50] In Cardiff and the surrounding districts the American evangelistic tradition made its contribution to the occasion. By Sunday, 23 October 1904, Torrey and Alexander were beginning the last leg of a four-week campaign there with two or three thousand people in the afternoon meetings and between five and seven thousand in the evenings.[51] Weeks previously the passion of the revival had reached London through one of the New Quay girls who worked there.[52]

In New Quay, Cardiganshire, the birthplace of the revival, the enthusiasm continued unabated. On Saturday, 17 September 1904, Seth Joshua arrived to hold a campaign and by Friday, 23 September, he counted that forty had been converted. He noted in his diary two characteristics of the revival generally. First, it was mainly young people who came under the influence of the Spirit. 'They devote themselves to prayer, praise, witnessing and exhortation in a remarkable manner.' The second characteristic was that it was not drunkards or public sinners who received the greatest blessing 'but members of the visible church, who had not been grafted into the True Vine . . . or baptized into the same spirit'.[53]

Joshua moved on to Newcastle Emlyn on 24 September. He could not speak of the events in New Quay without breaking down but his fervour did not succeed in melting people as he had hoped. Although he was rather disappointed with the work of the campaign, nevertheless there were some twenty converts and in their midst Sidney Evans, a man who would soon take a prominent part in the revival.[54]

Early on the morning of Thursday, 29 September, Joshua was on his way from Newcastle Emlyn to Blaenannerch. He was the main speaker at the third conference organized by Joseph Jenkins and his friends for the deepening of the spiritual life. In one of the meetings Joshua used the plea 'Humble us, O Lord!' during his prayer and this had a dramatic effect on one young man present.[55] He fell like a stone with his arms draped over the seat in front of him while the sweat ran in rivulets down his face and he sighed 'Humble me! humble me!' The young man's name was Evan Roberts.

Evan Roberts was born in Loughor, Glamorgan, on 8 June 1878, of very ordinary though pious parents. His father was a coal miner and Evan followed him down the mines in Loughor, Blaengarw and Mountain Ash until September 1902 when he was apprenticed to Evan Edwards, his mother's brother, who was a blacksmith in Pontarddulais. However, he had his heart set on the ministry. He left Pontarddulais on 17 December 1903 and delivered his first sermon on the following day. After meeting the requirements of his denomination, the Calvinistic Methodists, he was accepted as a candidate for the ministry by the West Glamorgan Monthly Meeting in May 1904, and the way was clear for him to attend one of the preparatory schools.[56]

Evan Roberts was a typical product of the Welsh-speaking industrial areas towards the end of the nineteenth century. He was brought up as a monoglot Welsh-speaker, and delighted in composing hymns, poetry and *englynion*, competing occasionally in local eisteddfodau.[57] He was interested in singing and spent six months studying tonic sol-fa and taught himself to play the harmonium. He was not widely read, but he had received a solid grounding in Thomas Charles's biblical dictionary, the Welsh translation of A. A. Hodges's *Systematic Theology*, the Sunday School Testament and the popular Welsh encyclopaedia of the time *Y Gwyddoniadur*. His reading had awoken in him a passionate desire for more knowledge.[58] Of even greater importance was that

290

his upbringing and his reading had cultivated in him a passionate interest in Christianity and a deep concern about its future in Wales.

He was an ardent chapel-goer and began to serve as a Sunday school teacher at the age of 15 by which time he had already been a church member for two years. As the years passed, he developed an extraordinary spiritual life. From an early age he put great emphasis upon prayer and even as a child he spent hours daily in devotion.[59] When he began to preach, his devotional life became very unsettled, for he was torn between the desire to give himself to Christian work and the need to educate himself for the ministry. After enrolling, according to denominational procedure, at John Phillips's preparatory school in Newcastle Emlyn, his spiritual agitation worsened. He could not concentrate on his lessons and he became convinced that the Holy Spirit would allow him to read the Bible alone.[60] His spiritual unease continued to deepen. He later confessed that for thirteen years he had pleaded for the Spirit and with the passage of time he began to pray more specifically to receive the Spirit immediately. He had been praying for over ten years for a revival in Wales.[61]

By the spring of 1904 he had been granted ecstatic experiences in prayer. One night he felt himself being snatched up by God into a great vastness beyond time and space.[62] This happened night after night. He would wake up about one o'clock in the morning and he would enjoy close, warm fellowship with God until about five o'clock. But although these experiences afforded him deep contentment, a certain amount of tension continued. His biographer, D. M. Phillips listed twenty such mystical visions, fourteen of which occurred at Newcastle Emlyn between 13 September and 31 October 1904.[63] For his part, Roberts considered that they were direct messages from God. He related one experience thus:

> I experienced a vision last Thursday morning. Near me I saw a candle burning and casting light. Far in the distance I saw a Sun rising. And O! What a sight it was. Not the Winter or Autumn Sun, or the Spring Sun, but the Sun of a Summer's morning. Well, there was something divine in it. Its rays were like long arms reaching out over the whole heavens. What is the meaning of this? It is simple enough. Day is nigh. This is the start of revival. But O! The great Sun of the revival is nearby.[64]

Several times during his visions, he claimed to have seen a person stretching out his hand from the midst of a shining mist and in it there was a paper with the number 100,000 written down. His explanation was that one hundred thousand would be converted in the coming revival.[65] It is evident that by 1904 Evan Roberts displayed all the characteristics of a charismatic prophet, enjoying direct contact with God, and thus receiving supernatural guidance independent of any medium apart from his own psychological processes. Such mystical enthusiasm was to have a profound influence on that aspect of the revival which became linked with his name. This too was the psychological and spiritual background of his collapse in Blaenannerch. Although he felt the Spirit's hand upon him and believed that the visions were the work of the Spirit, he was eager for a fuller baptism. 'The altar has been built, and the wood is placed on it, and the sacrifice is ready', and so there was nothing for it, he claimed, 'but to wait for the fire to descend'.[66] Roberts believed that this is what happened on 29 September at Blaenannerch: 'After being humbled, a wave of peace filled my bosom. . . . After this the salvation of souls weighed heavily upon me. I felt on fire to go through the length and breadth of Wales to tell people about the Saviour.'[67]

The tension, depression and nervousness that had characterized his public work up to that point disappeared.[68] With his friends he began to organize a mission throughout the whole of Wales. One of the methods he used to seek the guidance of the Holy Spirit was to write questions on a piece of paper which he would then place on the two Bibles in the bedroom and leave the room for a while. Then he would return to check whether the Spirit had written something on the paper.[69] This was not the first time that the desire of Evan Roberts and his friends for the direct guidance of the Holy Spirit had led to that which bordered on fanaticism and superstition.

What did his experience at Blaenannerch mean to Evan Roberts? If we can answer this question, it will be a help to understand how Roberts valued similar experiences in other people's lives, and will also be an aid to understand the aim of his revival campaigns. Certainly he was not converted at Blaenannerch. He believed that he had already been 'born again' although he could not put a date on this.[70] We have the testimony of his minister, David Jones, that Roberts believed that he had 'been saved' when he was accepted as a full member at the age of 13, but that he did not have the 'awareness of God's love burnt into his heart'.[71] Occasionally Evan Roberts suggested that it is possible to be a Christian without having received the Holy Spirit. Indeed he himself believed that he had been 'saved' at a young age and he had prayed for thirteen years to 'receive the Spirit'.[72] He referred to two things that characterized those who had not received the Spirit. First, they did not express the joy that is appropriate for Christians. In a long and revealing letter to his sister Mary, he exhorted the family at home 'Shake off that graveyard seriousness, and be joyful, always joyful'.[73] Secondly, they do not possess the 'blessed assurance of salvation'.[74] Because of these deficiencies Christ is not appropriately glorified, but he will be glorified when revival comes.[75] In a discussion of the assurance of salvation he quoted Isaiah, 'The Lord hath laid on him the iniquity of us all', and added, 'Now, if the Lord has laid *all our sins* upon Jesus, not one sin remains to be placed upon us.'[76]

What we have here is the Protestant doctrine of justification by faith alone on the basis of Christ's objective work taking upon himself the sins of the world, and such an unambiguous expression of this doctrine occurred very rarely during Evan Roberts's career. In this early period he gave the distinct impression that he was differentiating between justification and the outpouring of the Holy Spirit. A person could be freed from the guilt of sin through faith alone, but the outpouring of the Spirit was the result of obedience, the individual's spiritual efforts and the fruit of his or her self-discipline. In a letter to his brother Dan, Evan Roberts wrote, 'I know that you have peace, but ask for joy. And if you want to possess it, you must be ready to do what the Spirit says.'[77]

We shall see shortly how this belief influenced his evangelistic methods. However, it is a striking deviation from the traditional belief that the saving work of Christ ensured not only a peaceful conscience and reconciliation with God, but the presence of the Holy Spirit. It should also be noted that Roberts was already explaining the presence of the Spirit in emotional terms (such as joy) or as direct guidance for individuals. He made little reference to the Spirit as the one who illuminates the scriptures and the believer's understanding. This differs quite considerably from the doctrine in which Evans Roberts was brought up,[78] but it must be borne in mind that Evan Roberts was not always consistent with himself.

For instance he stated publicly, 'I was for years a faithful member of the church, a zealous worker and a generous contributor. But I discovered recently that I was not a Christian and there are thousands like me.'[79] Taken at face value, this means that he considered the Blaenannerch experience to be the occasion of his conversion, but it is probably not very fair to analyse Evan Roberts's statements in such a precise manner. He made such statements in the midst of great emotional intensity and he did not possess detailed theological knowledge. Despite this his ideas – clear or unclear – would soon influence the revival, as we shall see. Nevertheless, there can be no doubt about his heavy emphasis on the Holy Spirit or on the influence that the Blaenannerch experience had upon him. He described it as the 'most terrible and the most wonderful day of my life'.[80]

During the following month he contributed to the revival meetings organized by Joseph Jenkins and spoke to his friends about his plans. They were very worried about him because a physician had suggested that it would be a sensible idea for Evan Phillips's daughters to keep an eye on him. According to Rachel Phillips, they were afraid 'that he was starting to turn into a religious maniac'.[81] Roberts was waiting for a definite command from God to begin his public work. In a service on 30 October, while the Calvinistic Methodist patriarch Evan Phillips was preaching, he heard a voice saying 'You must go'.[82] He believed that the call had come and he said to Sidney Evans 'I am going home tomorrow to work for a week with the young people of Moriah'.[83] He caught the quarter-to-eleven train on the morning of Monday, 31 October, to return to Loughor to begin his campaign in Moriah chapel, the church where he had been brought up.

That evening, after the usual prayer meeting had finished, eighteen stayed behind for the young people's prayer meeting.[84] Evan Roberts broke with the usual order by urging everyone present to 'confess Christ publicly', which they did. The following evening, during the meeting at Pisgah, Bwlchmynydd, as well as exhorting those present to confess Christ, Evan Roberts declared his doctrine of the Holy Spirit. In order for people to be filled with the Spirit, they must obey his promptings, confess Christ publicly and rid their lives of everything questionable. By Wednesday evening these suggestions had developed into the 'four conditions for revival'.

Roberts held two meetings that night, one in Libanus, Gorseinon, and the other in Moriah. By this time there was revival in the air at Libanus but the atmosphere in Moriah was frigid when Evan Roberts arrived to hold the meeting there. He began to list the 'conditions for revival', namely (1) to confess sin openly before God; (2) for Christians to remove anything doubtful from their lives; (3) to obey at once the Holy Spirit's promptings and (4) to confess Christ publicly. He admitted to Sidney Evans that these conditions were part of 'the plan that the Holy Spirit revealed to me' for holding meetings.[85] On Thursday night, 3 November, in the *seiat* (fellowship meeting) at Moriah, he revealed more of the Spirit's secret messages to him. He had received a message from the Spirit, he said, that the children were to learn the prayer, 'Send the Spirit to Moriah for Jesus Christ's sake.' Another of his evangelistic methods emerged in this meeting in that he urged people to confess Christ publicly. Ten came forward, but he was not content. He began to pray saying, 'O, Lord, make another ten confess you, as well as the ten who have done so'. Ten more came forward.[86]

Some of Evan Roberts's most prominent characteristics as a revivalist were already evident during the first week, and there were more to come. On the evening of Sunday, 6 November, the meeting was starting to lose its warmth by ten o'clock and Roberts told the congregation that they 'must get the blessing' and to get it they must 'fight heaven'. By this time he had changed the prayer that he taught the children on Thursday night. He said that 'the Spirit wanted everyone to pray' and that this was the prayer, 'Send the Spirit now, for Jesus Christ's sake'. Moreover everyone in the congregation was to pray these words. The prayer went from person to person, until a young man called David Jones began to sob. He confessed to Roberts that he was experiencing strange feelings as if his heart was bursting within his chest. Roberts said to him 'You have received the Holy Spirit'.[87] then he asked the congregation to pray again, varying the words and saying, 'Send the Spirit more powerfully, for Jesus Christ's sake'. Before the prayer had done the rounds of the congregation, two women were crying out; 'I never heard such shouting,' said Roberts.[88] However, by this time people were starting to be alarmed and the meeting was brought to a close.

Roberts, whose own words have been quoted above, was quite sure that these methods were completely legitimate. 'Remember,' he said, 'I am doing all this under the guidance of the Holy Spirit, thanks be to him.' This hugely confident assertion was in itself very influential at the time; who indeed would dare doubt the wisdom of the Holy Spirit? This mechanical means of intensifying emotion by the repetition of a short sentence over and over again was vindicated by the thrilling emotional effects. Indeed, the meetings became more impassioned with every day that passed. By the evening of Monday, 7 November, people not only were shouting out but were writhing in agony. On that evening for the first time in the meetings people sang the hymn 'Dyma gariad fel y moroedd . . .' ('Here is love, vast as the oceans . . .'), which soon became the most popular hymn of the revival.

By this time, talk of the meetings was spreading and people were flocking to them from far and wide. On the evening of Thursday, 10 November, Roberts was at Bryn-teg chapel, Gorseinon, and there was a newspaper correspondent in the congregation. On the following day brief reports appeared in the *Western Mail* and the *South Wales Daily News*. This introduced an element the like of which had not been seen in any previous revival in Wales, namely the interest of the media. The revival became international news and the newspapers soon decided that Evan Roberts was both its creator and hero. Although the reports in the newspapers provide a mine of detailed information about the meetings, they also contributed towards creating a completely unbalanced and distorted picture of its nature and progress. For instance, the *Western Mail* announced, 'it is absolutely incorrect to say that there was a revival movement in Wales prior to the meetings which Mr Roberts and his friends held at Loughor'.[89] As we have already seen this was not true. It may have been that Evan Roberts was the best known product of the revival, but he was certainly not its instigator. Moreover, the reports in the papers were a means of introducing a malign element into the meetings by attracting people eager to satisfy their desire for emotional extremes. On 11 November, the night that the first reports appeared in the two main south Wales newspapers, there was an obvious increase in emotionalism with 'some falling helplessly under the mighty influence, and others crying out so loudly that they could be heard from a distance'.[90] Not that this worried Evan Roberts. His response was 'The world is coming to us from far and wide. We are thankful that Christ through the Holy Spirit is drawing people to him.'[91]

The *Western Mail* report led to the next step in Evan Roberts's career. The preacher for Sunday, 13 November, at Bryn Seion, Aberdare, was unable to fulfil his engagement and after reading the report in the paper, they sent a message to David Jones, Evan

Roberts's minister, to ask whether the young revivalist could fill in. Evan Roberts agreed. Sidney Evans came home from Newcastle Emlyn to help in the meetings at Loughor on the Saturday night which became famous for two reasons: parts of the service were led by women – this was a novel development – and one of the most famous singers of the revival, Sam Jenkins, was heard for the first time.[92]

So on the morning of Sunday, 13 November, Evan Roberts travelled by train from Swansea to Aberdare. The members of Bryn Seion chapel were incensed when they saw that he had five young women with him,[93] and there was no blessing on the services on that Sunday. Nevertheless he was persuaded to stay on in the area and services were arranged for him on the Monday and Tuesday night at Ebeneser, Trecynon.[94] There was a chilly response until the Tuesday evening when similar scenes to the enthusiasm of Loughor occurred.

Evan Roberts had been the instigator of the revival in Loughor, Gorseinon and Trecynon, but from then onwards it was the revival which preceded him. In Pontycymer, the next place he visited, 'the place was alive with excitement' when he arrived. The South Wales Women's Temperance Movement was holding its half yearly meetings in the Tabernacle and it was decided after the conference began that it would be a good idea to ask Evan Roberts to give an address. The Revd Mardy Davies went over to Trecynon with the invitation and Roberts agreed to attend the meeting on Wednesday, 16 November.[95] When he arrived at Bethel chapel, Pontycymer, the congregation was truly representative of the area. In the gallery to the right sat the coal miners with their faces shining and looking smart in their best clothes. There were women of all ages and classes there – wives and daughters of miners, shop assistants, maids and teachers. The 'big seat' surrounding the pulpit was occupied by the local ministers.[96] The revivalist walked into the midst of an expectant warmth. He explained the four conditions of revival and emphasized that the Holy Spirit would guide them and that everyone was to take part as the Spirit prompted. The following day, 17 November, saw scenes of great excitement. Roberts was at the pit head at five-thirty in the morning inviting the miners to the prayer meeting at seven-thirty. Roberts was deeply hurt because two of the miners mocked him. In the ten o'clock meeting Roberts mentioned the two scoffers and asked people to pray for them. The effect was electric:

Near us someone falls on his face on the floor of the *sedd fawr*. People are in a wild commotion, some are on their feet, some seated, some on their knees, others at the foot of their seats weeping helplessly and unable to draw breath. When we sat down we saw the young evangelist prostrate on the floor of the *sedd fawr*, in a torment of agony, and his face streaked with his copious tears. He tried to gather himself together as best he could by holding on to the seats as he walked out, and crying with hands uplifted to the heavens, 'O Lord, hold back your hand, or we will die; I shall die, this is too much for me to bear'.[97]

Weeping copiously, he went to the house of one of the two sceptics and brought him to conviction. By this time there was no difficulty in getting people to take part and among those who took part for the first time were Annie Davies and her sister Maggie, both of whom were brought up locally and whose singing would become an integral part of the revival. During the same visit Evan Roberts appointed the Revd Mardy Davies as his secretary to deal with the large volume of mail he was receiving.[98]

This was the beginning of Evan Roberts's first campaign beyond the immediate vicinity of his home. It began (as we have seen) in Trecynon on Sunday, 13 November, and went on for almost six weeks. He returned home on 24 December for a short rest. It seems hardly credible that a preacher who had left in order to take someone's place on a Sunday morning should have taken so long! He visited the valleys of Aberdare, Rhondda Fawr, Rhondda Fach, Merthyr and the Vale of Glamorgan, delivering ninety-three addresses and everywhere he experienced the same thrilling atmosphere as in Pontycymer.

Evan Roberts was at his peak during this campaign. His youth – he was only 26 – won the sympathy of the congregations and because he was a stranger he excited their curiosity. 'His smile lights up his face. He has a pleasant face, rather boyish, perhaps, long and thin and clean-shaven, and topped with wavy brown hair.'[99] He would slip quietly into services without drawing attention to himself and sit quietly in the pulpit watching the scenes of excitement before him or praying. According to H. Elvet Lewis (Elfed), he was a very quiet and measured speaker, not fluent by any means though thoroughly sincere.[100] Sometimes he would give a long sermon, up to an hour. But to all appearances the extremes of emotional agitation were not the direct result of his preaching.[101]

On the whole people listened quietly and intently to him and only after he ceased to speak did the congregation erupt. Quite early on in the campaign people began to romanticize about his eyes. Even a sober individual like William Morris, Treorchy, commented, 'We were struck from the outset that in his expression there was a natural perceptive ability far beyond that of ordinary people. His eyes seem to penetrate into the condition of people's souls and search them.'[102]

His rejection of the normal order of service, the unfamiliar presence of young women as fellow workers, his willingness to yield to emotionalism which was wildly excessive at times, and his undisputed ability to tailor his 'plan' to ensure lively services – all this enthralled people. His message was serious and yet tender. He succeeded in causing thousands to agonize over their relationship with God and he warned people of the dire consequences of refusing Christ. As he said to the people of Blaen-cwm, Rhondda, 'Mark these words, friends, if someone here continues to reject Christ, and reject him until the end, the thief upon the cross will rise up on the day of Judgement as a witness against you.'[103] On the other hand he could strike a comforting and confident note as he did in Hafod when he said,

> If you place your hand on a child of God, God's hand will crush you . . . how much did it cost God to make us his children? The cost was to place his hand on his own Son. Woe to anyone who touches the children of God. He is touching the apple of God's eye.[104]

All things considered, it is no wonder that the young man from Loughor took centre stage at the revival.

Despite these dramatic events in Glamorgan and the amount of attention paid to Evan Roberts, it must be remembered that this was just one element in a much wider movement. To gain a more balanced picture of the revival in its entirety, the evidence from Welsh-language newspapers and journals must be studied as well as the reports from the *Western Mail*, the *South Wales Daily News*, the London papers and D. M. Phillips's book on Evan Roberts. Thus it is appropriate to reprise the progress of the revival in other parts of Wales. In Rhosllannerchrugog the passionate enthusiasm continued unabated. One of its characteristics was that the sermon did not lose its importance and a host of well-known preachers were invited to preach in the various chapels. On 12 December, General William Booth, looking 'wonderfully patriarchal', came to preach in Capel Mawr[105] and by Christmas the number of new converts in Rhos was 743.[106]

Bethesda, Caernarfonshire, was another industrial area where the revival reached its climax in November. The Free Church Council arranged for Hugh Hughes (Y Braich) to hold a series of preaching meetings and he started on his campaign on the evening of Monday, 21 November, at Jerusalem chapel.[107] These meetings were full of heavenly blessing, yet the women's prayer meeting at half past two in the afternoon was no less remarkable, with some 500 gathering for what was an exceedingly fervent meeting.[108] As in Rhosllannerchrugog, the people of Bethesda insisted on safeguarding the place of the sermon in the meetings and the enthusiasm continued unabated. 'Crowds in and crowds out; the largest congregations ever seen in the chapels of Bethesda.'[109] For J. T. Job, who wrote this description, the most memorable part was the visit of Joseph Jenkins, with the young women of New Quay, Maud Davies and Florrie Evans, and the young women of Tal-y-sarn assisting him. The women's prayer meeting, on the afternoon of Thursday, 22 December, had been more remarkable than usual. First there was talk of 'singing in the air' when one mother gave evidence that her 18-year-old son had heard sweet music very late each night outside the house with no obvious source.

'Well,' said J. T. Job,

> Thursday night came. And this was the great night of the storm! When I look back on that night I cannot but describe it as the hurricane of the Holy Spirit! I know one thing: Thursday evening, 22 December, will be carved in letters of fire on my heart for ever . . . I saw Jesus Christ and my nature melted at his feet . . .

He was not the only one brought low that night. The atmosphere at the service was electric and then Joseph Jenkins rose to his feet to preach on 'Work out your own salvation . . . because it is God which worketh in you' and the thrust of the message was 'it is all God – every step from the rebirth to the glorification' and the will is enslaved to serve him. This memorable service reached its climax when the congregation sang, 'Y Gŵr a fu gynt o dan hoelion . . .' ('The Man who once suffered under nails . . .').[110]

On the following day Jenkins travelled to Tal-y-sarn and he was followed in Bethesda by J. Gwili Jenkins who preached to the accompaniment of the ecstatic utterances of William Hughes, Cae Star, the most well-known of the local 'rejoicers' during the revival.[111] Before the end of November the breezes of the revival had touched Llanfairfechan and on 2 December the young workers at the quarry at Penmaenmawr insisted on holding prayer meetings during their lunch break. Apart from these dramatic meetings, the area soon saw an improvement in morals. One correspondent said:

> It is a beautiful sight to see the workers getting their wages on a Saturday, waiting at the works office until everyone has been paid, and then marching the two miles from the office to their homes while singing hymns with the intention of keeping the weaker brothers from calling in at the public house.[112]

Rosina Davies helped to ignite the flame on the north Wales coast. She was already well-known through her campaigns in the area in 1903 and her visits continued at the beginning of 1904, but towards the end of the year it became evident that the flame was well alight. In Holywell, the Independents organized evangelistic meetings for her, beginning on 4 December, but the first meeting became a revival meeting and there was great enthusiasm in the town.[113] It was the same story when she moved from there to Colwyn Bay to hold meetings under the auspices of Salem and Engedi chapels. There was 'great blessing' on her ministry and the 'young people were crying out for mercy and making public professions of faith'.[114] Not far from Colwyn Bay in the little village of Betws, the revival was in full swing before the end of November[115] and in Llandudno the mission of Seth and Frank Joshua between 29 October and 4 November soon fired up the town. However when they travelled to Rhyl to evangelize between the 5 and 15 November they had a chilly reception – according to Seth Joshua 'it was difficult to preach, difficult to pray, and difficult to refrain from speaking out against the unspiritual condition of the church'.[116]

The revival began in Bangor on 22 November 1904, in the Baptist Schoolroom in Kyffin Square.[117] According to Ellis Jones, the minister of Ebeneser, it was Morgan Jones, one of the students at the Baptist College, who brought the fire with him from south Wales. The revival sprang from prayer meetings held jointly between the Baptist College students and students of Bala–Bangor College.[118] In Dyffryn Nantlle the revival broke out in a meeting of the Good Templars at about the end of November. It was decided to invite Joseph Jenkins to the valley to hold a mission which he launched in Baladeulyn chapel on Sunday, 18 December, with Maud Davies and Florrie Evans helping. He stayed there all week, apart from his remarkable visit to Bethesda. There was the same emotional intensity in the confession and the prayers as in other places, although the singing of 'Iesu, Iesu, gwrando lais fy nghri . . .' ('Jesus, Jesus, hear the voice of my cry . . .') about twenty times was an example of extraordinary musical enthusiasm.[119]

After Jenkins returned home, Samuel Glannedd Bowen[120] took over as leader and the area raised up its own revivalist evangelists, such as Maggie Parry, Tal-y-sarn, and John Hughes, Tan-rallt.[121] The revival reached Sardis, Dinorwig, on 11 December[122] and before the end of the year interdenominational revival meetings were being held in the Town Hall at Penygroes.[123]

On the Llŷn peninsula an increase in spiritual fervour had been noticed in Sarn and Bryn-mawr ever since the Thanksgiving meetings on the third Monday in October, but the power of the revival was first felt in Dinas during November and it spread from there to Garnfadryn and Penllech, where not only young people, but children led the services.[124] In Pwllheli, 'extraordinary meetings' had been held since mid-November and the 'air was gradually becoming more rarified'. These prayer meetings consisted of spontaneous contributions from all present. On Saturday evenings there were temperance meetings and the congregation would march through the town.[125]

Before the end of 1904, the first rains had reached Eifionydd in places like Cricieth, Porthmadog, Tremadog, Chwilog and Beddgelert.[126] At Ebeneser, Four Crosses, the ground had been prepared for the revival in an unusual way. When the minister, William Jones, was a student in Edinburgh, he had come under the influence of Sankey and Moody's revival and the imprint of that experience was on his preaching. During the first week of December 1904, two special prayer meetings were held and after the meeting of 9 December William Jones wrote the word 'jubilation' in his diary and from then on there was a meeting every night.[127] Almost at the same time the revival broke out among their Baptist neighbours at Tyddyn-Siôn, with meetings going on until midnight and as many as thirty taking part.[128]

In Merioneth, the revival first took hold in Barmouth, on about 21 November,[129] among the young people at Ebeneser, the Wesleyan chapel, and at Caersalem and when the Free Church Council organized a week of prayer at the beginning of December the town was set ablaze. As they attended these meetings and read an account of the revival in other parts of Wales in Y *Goleuad* the inhabitants of Llwyngwril were inspired.[130] The Ffestiniog area gives a good example of the long preparation for revival. Sunday morning prayer meetings had been set up for the young men of Bethel, Tanygrisiau, as early as 1895. There was nothing unusual in this because it was part of the churches' way of preparing young people to take part in public worship. But during the summer of 1903 there was a sharp rise in numbers at the prayer meetings at Bethel and at the same time a fresh blessing. The fervour continued to deepen during the following months and on 4 December the officials of the church were asked to arrange special prayer meetings. This was done and in the service on Sunday morning, 11 December, the 'early rain' came as the hymn 'O gofio ei riddfanau yn yr ardd . . .' ('Remembering his groans in the garden . . .') was sung with overwhelming intensity. During the following week it was evident that the full power of the revival had arrived. Its power, but not unruly disorder, was initially the most prominent characteristic of the revival in Tanygrisiau; its gravity was evident in the meeting on Monday night, 12 December:

> Before a quarter of an hour had passed everyone was weeping. One person recited the hymn 'Ai am fy meiau i . . .' ('Was it for my sins . . .') in a quavering broken-hearted voice . . . As the verse progressed from line to line, and from idea to idea, people began to weep bitterly, and sigh deeply. No one could think of singing the verse – but four or five other verses were recited at the same time, amidst many tears.[131]

By the evening of Saturday, 17 December, however, the intensity had turned to jubilation.

As in Barmouth, Tanygrisiau and many other places, the revival in Llan Ffestiniog began with the young people. Since the beginning of winter there had been a particular blessing on the young people's prayer meeting at Peniel and on the class that was studying the dotrine of atonement and this new warmth spread to the church's general prayer meeting and *seiat* by 21 November. By Sunday,

5 December, it was obvious that the revival had arrived.[132] The revival can scarcely be claimed to have started in Blaenau Ffestiniog before Christmas although the warmth of some services was a foretaste of greater things to come.[133]

By the beginning of December, Siloam, Llanfrothen, was enjoying lengthy and impassioned services[134] and over at Dinas Mawddwy the warmth of the united meetings became red-hot when three young men returned from the south to spend Christmas at home and brought the passion of the south Wales revival with them.[135] By 14 December, the fire had touched upon Abergynolwyn and Tywyn[136] and before long every soul in Llanfihangel valley – the valley which Mary Jones had left to procure a Bible from Thomas Charles a century before – had joined a church.[137] In Llanegryn, the spiritual excitement broke out among the Wesleyans on 6 December and in the united prayer meetings which began on 15 December as many as two dozen brothers and sisters of all ages would take part together and 'dozens of other people in every part of the building would sing, others would give their testimony, and the whole congregation would be in floods of tears.'[138] At the beginning of December the revival reached Bala, Dolgellau and Trawsfynydd.[139]

There was one place in Merioneth which attracted international attention and that was the little chapel at Egryn in the Vale of Ardudwy. A branch of Dyffryn chapel worshipped there and they held a small prayer meeting throughout the summer led by Mary Jones, Islaw'r Ffordd. Over the summer the numbers in attendance gradually increased and the atmosphere became more intense. What made Mary Jones and the area famous however, was the 'Light of Egryn'. E. W. Jones, a church elder from Dolgellau, went to find out the facts for himself, and this is part of his report:

> On the way to the chapel [one evening] she [Mrs Jones] saw a light in the sky, and she said that this light guided her about whom to pray for . . . The light was seen by neighbours . . . I obtained the names of about eighteen respectable, learned men who are adamant that they have seen the light – sometimes on their own, sometimes in the company of one another. What is its form? 'Three columns about a yard wide', was one description I received. 'A column of fire, the brightest light I ever saw' was another.[140]

Another who insisted on studying these claims for himself was the journalist Beriah Gwynfe Evans. Mary Jones told him that during December 1904 she had seen Jesus in shining robes and that he had appeared with a retinue of angels around him. On another occasion she had seen a cluster of tiny stars around a cross. A local poet told Evans that he was crossing the fields one day in broad daylight when he was threatened by wild animals but that a person in white robes had come to save him. He found himself on the bank of a river in a foreign country where multitudes in shining robes were playing on the bank opposite 'and their sweet songs reached him like a whisper over the waters' and indeed, during his research Evans himself claimed to have had similar experiences. On one occasion on 31 January 1905, he saw a 'shining star' leaping on the mountains and coming towards him.[141] Mrs Jones's visions were not restricted to the Egryn area because she had similar experiences in Ynys-y-bwl, Glamorgan, and in the Rhondda valley and she was not the only one who saw a mysterious light.[142] However one interprets this evidence, Mary Jones was the means of bringing forty of her neighbours to conviction in the week before Christmas 1904.[143]

The people of Llanfairpwll claimed that it was there that the revival first broke out in Anglesey[144] and by 3 January 1905, thirty-three had been converted.[145] But there was a foretaste of it in Brynsiencyn under the ministry of Roger Williams, Dyffryn Ardudwy, on Sunday, 27 November.[146] There was a feeling of great expectancy for a revival in Anglesey and the island came alive when the news spread about the stirring scenes during the meetings of the Good Templars in Dwyran, on Saturday, 10 December. The meeting was inspired by the preaching of J. H. Williams, the minister of Moriah, Llangefni, who, early on, had come under the influence of the revival.[147] The hymn 'Golchwyd Magdalen yn ddisglair . . .' ('Magdalen was washed shining white . . .') was sung many times on the Saturday night but the following evening during the preaching of J. H. Williams 'the floodgates opened'.[148] Proof of the eager expectancy on the island was the united prayer meeting which was held at Hyfrydle chapel, Holyhead, on 15 December 1904. This meeting, held for the churches of west Anglesey under the leadership of John Williams, the minister of Hyfrydle chapel, was a meeting 'the like of which had not been seen for many years'. As in Cardiganshire, Bethesda and Dyffryn Nantlle, Joseph Jenkins contributed to the enthusiasm by preaching at the evening meeting.[149]

On the following day Jenkins and J. H. Williams were addressing a conference for the deepening of the spiritual life – another
means of preparation for revival – in Llannerch-y-medd.[150] Three
days later, on Sunday, 18 December, the revival began during the
young people's prayer meeting at the Calvinistic Methodist chapel
at Menai Bridge.

The blessing began as those present listened to an account of
events in the south Wales and the flame was fanned by George
Williams. These events were not surprising because, after a bout of
illness in 1902 and 1903, the Calvinistic Methodist leader from
Menai Bridge, Thomas Charles Williams, had become convinced
that when he resumed his work his mission would be to prophesy
that 'a great light was about to break upon Wales'.[151] The village
began to hold united prayer meetings and 'among the most electrifying things' in them 'were the prayers of the children'[152] and by the
end of the year over thirty people had been converted.[153] A taste of
the 'heavenly influences' was felt in Llangefni at about the beginning of December and in Amlwch before the New Year.[154]

We have already seen how important Rhosllannerchrugog was in
the history of the revival in Clwyd. On 19 November, crowds sang
on the streets as a result of R. B. Jones's preaching, and from there
the fire spread to Salem, Pen-y-cae, and by 28 November it had
reached Tabernacle chapel, Brymbo, where E. K. Jones baptized
twenty-two on Christmas Day.[155] The revival broke out among the
Baptists of Froncysyllte too before 11 December.[156] Some of the
inhabitants of Wrexham were quite downhearted when they heard
this news because they believed that God was 'angry with the town
because the prophets Walter Cradock, Morgan Llwyd of Gwynedd
and others had been forced to flee' from there.[157] But the truth was
that a quiet revival had begun among the Baptists of Pen-y-bryn as
early as the last week in October.[158] Rosina Davies was the catalyst
for the revival in Gwersyllt[159] but it spread from Rhos to places like
Bwlch-gwyn, Coed-poeth, Tan-y-fron, Llangollen, Ruabon and
Cefn-mawr.[160]

In Powys, the revival was not widespread before the end of
1904. The first stirrings happened in Llanfyllin on 28 November
in Pen-dre chapel[161] and the fervour there caused the young people
of Llanrhaeadr to start praying every day for a revival in the village.
Their entreaties were answered on Saturday, 10 December, with a
great procession through the village and a fervent prayer meeting

that lasted into the small hours.[162] In Trefeglwys where there had been a powerful revival over ten years previously, the return of a number of young men from the south to spend the holidays at home was the catalyst for the revival on 27 December.[163]

In Ystradgynlais the preaching of Hugh Hughes (Y Braich), brought down the blessing,[164] but the most remarkable meeting there began in an unexpected way. On 27 November, Eleazar Davies, a member of Ainon Baptist chapel, was on his way home from a prayer meeting when a man began to mock him. Davies immediately began to pray for him and a crowd gathered around. Soon they went to Sardis chapel and an unforgettable meeting lasted until two o'clock in the morning with thirty converted.[165] One of the main leaders of the revival there was the Anglican, E. L. D. Glanly, who led united meetings in the parish church and the chapels.[166] Not far from Ystradgynlais lies Cwm-twrch where the revival broke out on 19 November and where the Baptists of Beulah had a memorable service on 18 December when forty-seven converts were baptized.[167] It is a comfort to know that the Holy Spirit could descend even during a college lecture, as happened in Trefecca during a lecture by the principal, Owen Prys, on the atonement.[168]

Cardiganshire was the cradle of the revival and the South Cardigan Monthly Meeting was its foster father. It is not surprising that on the occasion of its meeting in Aberaeron, on 8 December 1904, 'elders and ministers, elderly and white-haired, wept like children in the *sedd fawr* and around it.'[169] John Evans had written press reports at the time of the 1859 Revival and he marvelled that he had lived long enough to do the same during the 1904 Revival in the Abermeurig area. 'Bwlchyllan is moving', he said, 'Llanddewibrefi is in great excitement, Tregaron is on fire and Blaenpennal is following on. From Pontsaeson and Pennant down to the southernmost part of the county much of the revival has been carrying on for some time.'[170] By the end of November it had reached Llangeitho,[171] the most famous of all the centres of the Evangelical Revival in Wales. In the north of the county, in Aberystwyth, the reviving breezes were felt by the beginning of December and soon they touched all the churches.[172] T. A. Levi said, 'Indeed, there is no commotion . . . every meeting is quiet, peaceful and measured, and every event is led by the spirit. But all other meetings, cultural, political and entertainment have had to yield their place to it.'[173] Another commentator rejoiced when he saw that the 'MAs had participated so thoroughly' in the revival, 'together with a number of the students at the main college'.[174] By the first week in December the revival had reached the Calvinistic Methodists in Pen-llwyn and Pontrhydfendigaid, the Independents of Tal-y-bont and the Baptists of Swyddffynnon and Pontrhydfendigaid.[175]

It was comparatively quiet in Pembrokeshire, with only certain portions of the county affected thus far. The people of Newport and Haverfordwest knew of the revival before the end of November[176] and by mid-December there were 'many anointed prayer meetings' in the Baptist churches but it was acknowledged at the same time 'that the revival had not yet broken out in all its power in the land of Dyfed'.[177] Within a fortnight reports came from among the Independents that St Dogmaels, St Davids and Newport were 'on fire', and there were scenes of brokenness of spirit and jubilation in Fishguard and Llandysilio.[178]

In Carmarthenshire, Nantlais Williams had been influenced by the revival in its early days and his church, Bethany, Ammanford, was an influential centre. Nantlais decided to forgo travelling the country and concentrated on the pastoral work at his church in order to turn the initial emotionalism into spiritual discipline.[179] On 19 November 1904, Seth Joshua arrived in the town to hold a mission and on the following day, a Sunday, he wrote in his diary:

> This has been one of the most remarkable days of my life . . . In the afternoon the blessing fell upon scores of young people . . . at seven o'clock a surging mass filled the [Congregational church, the] Christian Temple, with crowds unable to gain entrance. The Holy Spirit was indeed among the people . . .[180]

Their enthusiasm did not cool despite the carpet of snow on the ground, but the cold brought Seth Joshua low. He travelled with a group from Ammanford to evangelize in Llandeilo and after marching through the streets, he caught a dreadful cold and was forced to stay at home for three weeks.[181] One correspondent wrote that the days of heavy snow between 20 and 24 November[182] created an extraordinary scene: 'The hot air, rising from the ventilators of the chapels, is condensed immediately on contact with the outer atmosphere, and spreads heavenwards in half a dozen pillars of cloud.'[183] This happened in Cilfynydd, but the revival was ablaze in the Amman valley too. The journalist Anthony Davies wrote at the time: '4 December. Bi-annual meeting of Bethel Newydd, Amman Valley. Two preachers invited there, but no one wanted to listen to them. The place was ablaze with revival. Praying, weeping, singing: such a thing was never heard before in the valley.'[184] J. Towyn Jones added his testimony that the public houses were empty, playing cards had been burnt, all sorts of plays and sports had ceased and family worship was held in every home.[185] By February 1905 there were 1,200 converts in the Amman valley.[186]

It was mid-December before the revival took a grip on the town of Carmarthen. A conference was held for the deepening of the spiritual life, on 23 to 25 November, with R. B. Jones and Jessie Penn-Lewis as the main speakers, and W. W. Lewis, Keri Evans and W. S. Jones assisting them. A further conference was organized in the town, 20 November to 1 December, under the auspices of the Calvinistic Methodists.[187] Although the conferences enthralled individuals and inspired a thousand people to march through the town, it was not a direct means of reviving the churches.[188] Rather the outpouring came on 11 December.[189] Two days previously the same thing had happened in Kidwelly after a fortnight of importunate prayer.[190] In Carmarthenshire, as in other counties, one characteristic of the preparation for revival was the weeks of pleading for it in prayer meetings. In Burry Port and Pembrey, for instance, such meetings were held every night for five weeks.[191] Even at the end of December, according to the correspondents, there was little excitement in the north of the county, apart from Llandovery where the revival had arrived by Christmas.

Although Llanelli was only on the other side of the river from Loughor, the revival did not take hold immediately. In the words of Anthony Davies, 'Sidney [Evans] was in charge of Llanelli, Swansea and Cardiff while Evan set the Cymer, Cynon and Rhondda valleys ablaze'.[192] According to this arrangement, Sidney Evans launched a campaign in Trinity chapel, Llanelli, with Mary Roberts, Evan's sister, helping him.[193] Although the meetings did not create the fervour that people expected, some maintained that the revival had reached the town before the campaign began.[194] The opinion of the campaigners, however, was that 'Llanelli proved to be difficult ground to work'.[195]

We now return to Glamorgan. As has already been said, in many places the revival preceded the visits of Evan Roberts. In Treharris, for instance, meetings were held which reached a climax of jubilation on the evening of Saturday, 10 December.[196] It was no wonder that over 900 were converted in the town by 18 January,[197] a fortnight before Evan Roberts visited the place. Although D. M. Phillips wrote so much about the revival, he was not tempted to draw attention to his own considerable contribution to it. In Tylorstown, where he was a minister, the revival had broken out a whole month before Evan Roberts's visit and also in nearby Maerdy.[198] It was the same story in Morriston, at the other end of the county. Sidney Evans had a highly successful campaign there over the weekend of 27 November[199] and some 500 new members joined the churches. By 14 December the revival had come in all its might. By the time Evan Roberts arrived at the end of the month, there were over 1,300 new converts in Morriston and fervent meetings were held in places in Glamorgan and Monmouthshire that Evan Roberts did not visit at all.[200]

On 28 November, for instance, the revival began at Ebenezer Baptist church, Abertillery. By the third week in January over 400 new converts had joined the churches and the Sunday school had increased from 600 to 840.[201] In Cardiff, H. M. Hughes, the minister of Ebenezer Congregational chapel, announced on 20 November that there would be a prayer meeting every night the following week and by the end of the week the revival had broken out.[202] From then onwards revival meetings were held for the women every afternoon and for the public every night.[203] On Sunday, 27 November, young men from Tylorstown hurried to carry the revival to the Calvinistic Methodist church in the dockland area – and succeeded in their mission.[204]

One of the keenest supporters of the revival was Charles Davies, the minister of Tabernacle Baptist church in the Hayes. By the end of December he was holding never-ending meetings twenty-four hours a day, with the young people fetching strangers off the streets to join them, with dramatic consequences.[205] By January, Tabernacle had welcomed 503 converts into the church.[206]

By the end of December 1904, the revival had inspired the nation. Although not every parish in the country had yet been touched, what was true was that all kinds of areas in every county in Wales had experienced revivalist zeal. And already the characteristics of this revival were quite clear. The meetings were full of excitement. Everyone was urged to take part as the Spirit prompted and without worrying about a set order. People responded with perfect freedom, praying, reciting verses of scripture or hymns, and giving a word of testimony. From the beginning singing became an integral and memorable part of the activities and the congregational singing was punctuated by singers such as Annie Davies or Sam Jenkins. The revival was preceded in many places by prayer meetings pleading for the baptism of fire – those meetings would sometimes go on for many weeks. The revival would usually come suddenly, and people could name the day and the hour that this happened. Idioms such as 'the floodgates opened', 'the fire came down', 'the baptism happened' and others were part of the excitement. It was a young people's revival, some of its practitioners being very small children. They took the reins without being prompted and contributed to the worship as if they had been born to the work. Control was wrested very often from the hands of the traditional leaders and to all appearances thus far, they were more than content to see this happen. This is one reason why the revival produced such a wealth of personalities. On the one hand, there were the itinerant leaders – people like Hugh Hughes, Rosina Davies, Seth Joshua, D. M. Phillips, Frank Joshua, R. B. Jones, Joseph Jenkins, Sidney Evans, Evan Roberts and his brother Dan. On the other hand, there were many scores of local leaders – people like Keri Evans, Nantlais Williams, Charles Davies, Ceinfryn Thomas (Hebron, Dowlais), Pumpsaint Jones and David Phillips (Treharris), W. S. Jones, H. M. Hughes, E. L. D. Glanly, J. H. Williams (Llangefni). But there is little point in listing names, since there were a multitude of people in every part of the country who became charismatic leaders in their own localities.

And this was just the beginning.

~ 13 ~

A Year of Rejoicing

Evan Roberts launched his second campaign on 28 December 1904 in Clydach in the Swansea valley, and travelled from there to Morriston and Swansea and the surrounding area. He then moved on to the vicinity of Neath, starting in Skewen on 10 January and reaching Resolven by 17 January. He travelled up the Vale of Neath and crossed over to the Vale of Merthyr. He was in Dowlais on 22 January and he preached in several chapels in the valley until he reached Treharris on 2 February. The campaign ceased abruptly there, although his travel organizer, Mardy Davies, had arranged visits to villages in the vicinity of Pentyrch. People tried earnestly to persuade Evan Roberts to visit Cardiff but he refused to go because, he said, the Holy Spirit forbade him.[1] It is quite possible that the excitement of the meetings was starting to take its toll and it is not surprising that he insisted on taking a rest from 3 to 8 February. However, in the mean time Evan Roberts had become the focus of a particularly ferocious debate.

On 31 January 1905, a letter appeared in the *Western Mail* under the heading 'Double revival in Wales. A strange attack on Mr. Evan Roberts.' The letter was signed 'Peter Price (BA Hons), Mental and Moral Sciences Tripos, Cambridge (late of Queen's College, Cambridge), Minister of Bethania Congregational Church, Dowlais, South Wales.'[2] Peter Price himself was a minister who worked 'in accordance with the revival'[3] and who had seen the membership of his church increase by three hundred between his arrival in July 1904 and January 1905 by which time there were over a thousand members.[4] However, he turned savagely upon Evan Roberts in his letter to the *Western Mail*.

The crux of his argument was that there were two revivals in the land. One was from God and had been anticipated for two years.

It was the result of earnest preaching on the substitutionary atonement of Christ for the sins of the world and the particular emphasis of certain preachers on the person and work of the Holy Spirit. The other, however, was a 'sham revival, a mockery, a blasphemous travesty of the real thing' and its most prominent figure was Evan Roberts, a man who used language 'inconsistent with the character of anyone except of a person endowed with the attributes of a Divine Being'.

Price was in attendance at a meeting held by Evan Roberts at Bethania chapel, Dowlais, on Monday evening, 23 January. During Roberts's address he said that 'there were two in the *sedd fawr* [diaconal pew] who were extinguishing the Spirit'.[5] Basing his remarks on what he had observed during the meeting, Price said that Roberts's language implied that he had some kind of control over the Holy Spirit. The revival was aflame in Bethania six months before Evan Roberts's arrival and all he had done was to light a strange fire, 'by means of threats, complaints, and incantations, which reminded me of the prophets of Baal'. It would be of great benefit to the true revival if Evan Roberts 'and his girl-companions' were to return home.[6]

There was a spirited response to the attack. For days the *Western Mail* published letters on the topic, the majority in support of Evan Roberts. What is astonishing about so many of these letters is they were so very vitriolic and tasteless and wholly inconsistent with the spirit that one would expect in people determined to defend a revival. Having said this, Price had behaved in a puerile fashion in drawing attention to his Cambridge degree and in a manner unworthy of a defender of true revival in the way in which he cast scorn upon Evan Roberts's intellectual ability. Concerning the theory that there were two revivals, the *Western Mail* editorial for 31 January 1905 insisted that there was not a scrap of evidence for this and on the whole the public shared this opinion.[7]

What set the debate alight, however, was the personal attack on Evan Roberts. Several ministers entered the fray to defend him, such as the Congregationalists Keri Evans, C. E. Morgan and J. T. Rhys, G. S. Railton, Commissioner of the Salvation Army, F. B. Meyer and others. In north Wales the students' committee of Bala–Bangor College passed a vote of censure on Price.[8] On the other hand, Price had his defenders such as the Anglican Vyrnwy Morgan, J. Gari Phillips, a Congregationalist from Tredegar, and J. Morris-Evans, a Baptist from Builth Wells,[9] while his own church, Bethania, came out strongly in support of him.[10] There were a few who soon recognized the signs of the 'false revival' in their own experience. For instance when some young people took charge of a meeting in Taffs Well because Evan Roberts had not arrived, E. J. Phillips, Gwaelod-y-garth, saw in their behaviour the 'sham revival' of which Price had spoken.[11]

Evan Roberts himself refused to be drawn into the argument. The only public statement he made was 'I am content; I am on the rock'.[12] Indeed, he said to John Morgan Jones, Cardiff, that Price's attack had hardly crossed his mind.[13] He said this on 7 February, when he was coming to the end of a few days' rest and it is possible that the break had given him an opportunity to compose his thoughts. Certainly, during the previous week he had mentioned 'on more than one occasion' that the work 'was taking on a new aspect that was becoming too much for him', and in the final meeting of his second campaign, on 2 February in Treharris, 'he suffered extreme agony of mind'.[14]

After resting, Evan Roberts set out on his third, and brief, campaign. He began in Nant-y-moel on 8 February. After visiting Ogmore Vale two days later, he spent a week in the Maesteg area, finishing in Cwmafan on 21 February. He was supposed to be in Briton Ferry on Wednesday, 22 February, but while in his lodgings in Godre'r Coed, Neath, getting ready to depart, he was overcome by spiritual torment and announced that he did not intend to keep his engagement. Moreover, he said that he wished to spend a week without speaking at all and through the kindness of his host, Rhys Jones, he was able to spend a week in his bedroom without communicating with anyone but Annie Davies.[15] This was the 'Week of Silence' that attracted as much public fascination as any sermon he had ever preached. He left Godre'r Coed on 5 March and returned home to Loughor.[16]

By this time Evan Roberts had attracted international attention. People from many countries came to see him and to partake of the ferment of excitement. On 12 January, while the congregation at Nazareth chapel, Tonna, was awaiting Roberts's arrival, Cadot de Chauney, a minister of the Reformed Church of France in Aisne, prayed in English and French. The consequence of focusing attention on Evan Roberts in this way was that people from other countries lost sight of the fact that the revival was burning white-hot throughout the whole of Wales, and the numerous other leaders in every part of the country were completely disregarded.

Moreover, Roberts's own behaviour coloured people's impressions of the revival. Many noticed that there was a change in his spirit and approach during his second and third campaigns. He began to show a rather ill-disposed and harsh side to his personal mission. One or two examples of this will suffice. When he arrived at Tabernacle chapel, Morriston, on 30 December, the great auditorium was packed to the rafters and the large courtyard around it was full of people, all singing enthusiastically. Evan Roberts immediately stopped the singing, saying that it was not singing that was needed but praying and that there was too little of the spirit of prayer there.[17] At the beginning of December, however, he had rebuked those who called for less singing in the revival, and had explained that there were two stages in a revival, first the singing, and then the praying. The praying would come in good time.[18]

Soon, stopping the meetings became part of his mode of operation. This happened in Soar, Neath, on Sunday afternoon, 15 January. Before Roberts arrived the crowd were so tumultuous that a policeman tried to calm them down, whereupon they shouted at him 'There is no order when the Holy Spirit speaks!' Order had been restored by the time the revivalist had arrived. As soon as Roberts appeared, the entire congregation spontaneously began to sing a hymn. He climbed into the pulpit and sat for some time with his head in his hands. Then he rose to his feet and said 'The Spirit of God is not here'. He rebuked the congregation for singing continually and commanded that everyone should pray.[19] Similarly in Bethesda chapel, Merthyr, he stopped the jubilant singing, saying 'Things are too awesome for us to sing'.[20]

Naturally enough, these abrupt changes of direction in meetings were very confusing for people, and yet whetted their curiosity about this strange leader. This practice was sometimes accompanied by Roberts's desire to 'discern the spirits'. In Pontmorlais, Merthyr, on 29 January, he halted the meeting, saying that the Holy Spirit was displeased because there were two people present who had quarrelled with each other and that this was an obstacle to any further worship. This caused an uproar with many praying for the obstacle to be removed. Roberts kept them in suspense for some time before announcing that the offenders had repented, that the blockage had been removed and that the service could proceed.[21]

These interruptions and prophecies created unbearable tension in congregations. The most alarming example of this occurred in Cwmafan. During the service at Seion chapel, on the evening of Monday, 20 February, Evan Roberts himself was seemingly in an irritable mood. He stopped the service and said that there were several people who were disobeying the Spirit's prompting and that the meeting could not proceed until they had confessed and repented. Some stood up and did so, but Evan Roberts was not content. Others stood up, but he was still not satisfied. Only after this had happened several times did he allow the service to proceed.[22]

The following night at Tabernacle chapel he behaved very harshly. By seven o'clock, before he arrived, the chapel was so full that people were suffocating and they started breaking the windows.[23] Evan Roberts arrived and ordered people to stop breaking the windows. One of the young women began to sing a hymn. While she was still singing Roberts interrupted her and asked, 'Where is the person who smiled or laughed when the young girl was singing?' At once his body began to twist and contort. When this ceased, he told the people that he had a message of the gravest import to convey to them. He fell to his knees in the pulpit and the congregation was shaken by the volubility of his sobs. Then he said, with great emotion, 'There is a lost soul here!' In the midst of his pitiful sighs he explained that this soul was lost because someone had disobeyed the promptings of the Holy Spirit. Roberts then cried out 'Too late! Too late!', and cried out again and again, 'O! Forgive! Lord! Forgive!' saying to the congregation 'Dear people, it is too late, too late – a soul has gone!' The weeping and lamenting spread throughout the congregation with some falling prostrate to the ground and others shouting out loud.[24] Such was the pitch of woeful emotion that characterized Evan Roberts's ministry at its most extreme.

By this time it was becoming clear that Evan Roberts was guiding the revival in a new and unnerving direction. In one of his first interviews he said, 'I preach nothing but Christ's love'[25] and this was attested by many observers during his first campaign. However, in Cwmafan he announced that he knew whether individuals were saved or lost. Vyrnwy Morgan observed this change in emphasis:

> During his first appearance he was a man of charming gentleness, unassuming, brotherly and unconscious of his power to draw and to sway.

A man of unquestionable wealth of heart. But he developed the austere and the turbulent. His voice became peremptory without being convincing . . .[26]

Since Vyrnwy Morgan became one of the most merciless critics of Evan Roberts's character and work, perhaps we should not give his words too much credence. However, H. Elvet Lewis (Elfed), the gentlest of critics, and one who made a major contribution to the revival, concurred:

His general methods were becoming more sharply marked, his clairvoyant expressions more definite and more frequent. He was more and more given to locate hindrances at his meetings, and almost to name the hinderer. It was the growth of these practices that led to some most unhappy incidents . . .[27]

Serious questions were being raised about the claims he made concerning people in his congregations and concerning the work of the Holy Spirit. People wanted to know whether he was claiming that he was in God's confidence in a unique way and on what basis he could know the ultimate secrets of human hearts. On 9 January 1905, he wrote a fascinating letter to D. M. Phillips, which contained these words, 'This, for me, is a meaningless sentence – "Forgive my sins". I do everything he asks of me. I have been moved from darkness to Light.'[28] Did he mean that he had attained sinless perfection? Did he believe that his obedience gave him knowledge about the intentions of the Holy Spirit that was unavailable to others?

With the English-medium press focusing its attention on Evan Roberts, and his words and actions raising doubts and questions about the nature of the revival, it is nevertheless important to remember that the awakening was spreading over vast parts of Wales like the bloom of springtime. There was fervour and emotionalism, of course, but on the whole people experienced the same virtue as their parents and grandparents had felt in the revivals that had done so much to mould the life of modern Wales. It was an inspiration to many hundreds of ministers of the Word and 1905 stayed in the memories of tens of thousands of people as a year of rejoicing. As has already been seen, the fire of the revival spread over large parts of Wales during the final weeks of 1904 but in many places the great wave of fervour came during the first weeks of 1905.

In Anglesey R. B. Jones, Porth, held a campaign throughout the month of January. Until 12 January, he held meetings at Hebron chapel, Holyhead, while at the same time David Lloyd and R. R. Hughes held meetings at the Old Station.[29] According to his usual practice, R. B. Jones concentrated first on the churches and their need for repentance and renewal and his labours were not in vain because by 10 February over 200 new members had joined the churches.[30] From 13 to 18 January, he was based at Llanfachraeth and the village witnessed a manifestation of the great rejoicing that characterized the revival at its most fervent.[31]

Jones was rather downcast at the chillier reception at Llannerch-y-medd where he stayed until 21 January[32] but the atmosphere warmed up when students from Bangor arrived to help, and indeed, to 'storm the place'.[33] It is appropriate to acknowledge that the atmosphere was decidedly frosty at the Bangor Baptist College, and threats were made to curtail the grants of six of the students for being absent from their lectures.[34] Despite the disapproval of college authorities, 112 were converted within three days after the students' arrival.[35] However, R. B. Jones was disappointed with the results of his own work and when he moved to Amlwch at the end of the month it seemed 'as if he was sulking'.[36] One obvious reason why there were not as many converts as he had expected was the great success of Joseph Jenkins's campaign a few days previously, when forty joined the churches, in addition to the sixty who had been converted during the New Year meetings. However, R. B. Jones's enthusiasm returned in the wake of the inspired meetings that he held at Amlwch and Llaneilian.[37]

By the third week in January, Y Cloriannydd declared that 'the old county is under divine influences almost from one end to the other'.[38] This was quite true. In the first fortnight of the year, there was great excitement at Caergeiliog, Valley and Beaumaris.[39] In Brynsiencyn, 'the floodgates opened' at nine o'clock in the morning on New Year's Day 1905.[40] Two days afterwards, revival broke out during the young people's meeting in Newborough and women's meetings were started every afternoon on the pattern of Bethesda, and meetings every night in the village church.[41] It was the same story throughout the island. It was no wonder that H. Elvet Lewis (Elfed) could announce before the end of March that 'Anglesey almost belongs to Christ'.[42]

The story of the revival in the town of Caernarfon was remarkable because its growth was more like the coming of spring than the rush of a mighty wind. The day after Christmas 1904 the ministers and deacons began to join in a daily prayer meeting and at the end of five weeks it was as 'sweet and blessed' as ever. At the same time, there was 'an uncommon gravity and fervour' in the women's prayer meetings during the afternoons. There was a similar increase in the usual church meetings with at least 200 converts during the first month.[43] During the same period a powerful revival broke out in places like Felinheli, Penmachno and Waunfawr.[44]

By the end of February there was a 'general revival' in Llŷn.[45] The most memorable night in Pwllheli was on Thursday, 12 January. D. M. Phillips, Tylorstown, was to lead the meeting but he was unable to return in time from Edern and Simon G. Evans, at that time a student at Bala College, took over. He invited the congregation to march with him through the town and they did so, holding prayer meetings here and there and singing as they marched. After arriving back at Salem chapel a young man from Llithfaen began to plead for the Spirit to be given 'now – now – now!' The congregation joined him 'and at that moment God answered'. The whole congregation began to rejoice with 'some standing on the benches, others walking around with their hands in the air, and others sitting quietly'. But before long 'some fell into a swoon, and others continued to groan upon the floor'.[46]

In Blaenau Ffestiniog, the first breath of the revival was felt in services at Jerusalem chapel about mid-December and at about the same time, on 17 December, the united prayer meeting was established on Saturday afternoons. A spiritual gravity overtook the town. All swearing ceased among the inhabitants, the public houses were deserted, and every break time at the quarries became an opportunity for prayer. Prayer meetings were begun in the chapels to strengthen the revival. We gain a very personal glimpse of the progress of the revival in Tabernacle chapel through the diary of the minister, R. R. Morris.[47] He kept a list of the converts and the first name on it is 'Wm. John Jones Devon Terr.' for 11 December 1904. But for R. R. Morris, the finest hour came at the end of January.

Thursday 26 – an unforgettable night at Tabernacle – the evening on which great rejoicing broke out. *Eternal thanks.*

The chapel has probably never held so many hundreds. People packed in in their hundreds especially after rejoicing broke out.

Eternal thanks. Great rejoicing continued from about 9.40 until 10 o'clock – and there was great enthusiasm until 10.35 when the chapel meeting was brought to a close and the Meeting was held in the Vestry.

This happened during the campaign of D. M. Phillips, after he had been speaking for an hour. Daily prayer meetings continued to be held until June 1905 with a procession every day through the town for much of this period. Strangely enough, the *seiat* was not held for the nine weeks preceding 8 March, since members preferred to enjoy their experiences rather than discuss them. Phillips's visit to Blaenau Ffestiniog was a means of bringing a 'more generous out-pouring' to all the churches.[48]

Although the revival was slow to reach Dolgellau, when it happened it came in all its power. The same characteristics were in evidence as in other places – united prayer meetings with the congregation participating spontaneously, and fervent emotion. One beautiful expression of the anointing was the prayer meetings organized independently by the children. Mary Jones, Egryn, was one who lit the flame in Bont-ddu, and early in 1905 there were inspiring meetings in Llanelltud, Arthog and Islaw'r-dre.[49]

The same situation prevailed throughout Wales, as a perusal of the local papers and particularly the Welsh-language papers for the first months of 1905 indicates. In order to gain a balanced picture of the revival in its entirety, we need to remember this widespread and fervent activity over the country as we turn back to follow Evan Roberts's progress again.

At the close of his 'Week of Silence' at Godre'r Coed, Neath, Evan Roberts spent a few days in Loughor. But he wished to visit Neath and the surrounding area again and he remained there from 10 to 23 March. His main aim was to rest but he occasionally attended meetings. During an afternoon meeting in Blaenannerch, on 14 March, there was a further example of the behaviour that was causing concern at the time and confusion subsequently. Roberts told the congregation that there was a youth present who was mocking him. Three rose to their feet to confess but the revivalist was not satisfied. He raised the same matter in another guise in the evening meeting, announcing that someone present was denying the divine inspiration of the Bible and asking that person to stand up and confess publicly. Dozens rose to their feet and '[Roberts] said that God had revealed to him that the denier was

standing up' but no one confessed. There were many sighs throughout the congregation. Suddenly Roberts cried out 'The man's name
is T—— W——, twenty-three years old'. The congregation began
to sing with joy, 'Praise the Lord'. After they had quietened down,
Roberts said that the offender did not need to confess since he had
changed his views.[50]

Evan Roberts set out to hold his fourth campaign in Liverpool
on 28 March 1905, with his sister Mary, Annie Davies, and
D. M. Phillips keeping him company on the train from Cardiff.
This campaign was a new step forward in his career. Up until this
time he had worked independently but his meetings in Liverpool
had been arranged by the Welsh Free Church Council in the city,
and the most influential of the organizers was the Revd John
Williams, formerly of Brynsiencyn, Anglesey, but by then minister
of the Calvinistic Methodists' most renowned charge at Liverpool's
Princes Road. Indeed, he had led a deputation to Dowlais to invite
Evan Roberts to lead the campaign.[51] Detailed arrangements were
made for the visit. Every home in Liverpool was canvassed, which
unearthed 30,000 Welsh-speakers, 4,000 of whom had no connection with a church. Tickets were printed for the meetings so that
everyone who so wished could have a fair chance to see Evan
Roberts. One hundred and ninety seven meetings were arranged for
him in various places.

The campaign opened in Princes Road chapel on the evening of
Wednesday, 29 March. The huge chapel, which held 1,800, was
full. Evan Roberts arrived at seven o'clock and sat silently in the
pulpit for an hour and a half. He eventually intervened with a
rebuke when the congregation were singing a hymn. He claimed
that hundreds of them had been disobeying the Spirit. 'The lesson
of ready obedience to the Spirit must be learnt, whatever the cost'.
The atmosphere of the meeting became a little warmer after this,
with people more willing to take part, but Roberts was not satisfied and he rose to administer the same rebuke within an hour.
When John Williams 'tested' the meeting at ten o'clock there were
about a dozen converts. People were disappointed with this first
meeting because they did not find the warmth of emotion they had
anticipated. However, at the following night's meeting at Anfield,
there was fervour equal to anything experienced in the Rhondda
valley.

Nevertheless there was considerable tension in the meetings in

Liverpool and on Merseyside. The crisis of the 'Free Church of the Welsh' (discussed in chapter 8 above) had left scars and Evan Roberts knew this well. This emerged during his third meeting, on 31 March, in Birkenhead. He halted the meeting and said the place 'must be cleansed' because there were some present who could not forgive those who had trespassed against them. One of the young leaders of the 'Free Church of the Welsh' rose to his feet and prayed earnestly that God would humble people to work together in brotherly love. However, Evan Roberts insisted that there were some present who were resisting the Holy Spirit and were refusing to forgive one another.

Although those who had previously attended Evan Roberts's meetings were familiar with the unexpected swings of emotion that could occur, the extremes in Liverpool were astonishing even to them. At a meeting at Shaw Street, 1 April, Evan Roberts suddenly announced that the Spirit had withdrawn and that there were five people present, three of them ministers, who were envious because the work of salvation was being accomplished there. The congregation became very agitated and considerable tension developed between the chairman, John Williams, who wished to draw the meeting to a close, and Evan Roberts who forbade this.

There were, however, meetings which were remarkable for their joy and spiritual ease, such as the meeting in Everton Brow, on 5 April, and the one in Stanley Road on the following day. Despite this, a story was put about that the meetings were unsuccessful and John Williams and Thomas Charles Williams issued a statement to the effect that they had brought great blessing.

The 6 and 7 of April were strange days. On the first of these two days Evan Roberts was involved in an accident when his carriage overturned on the beach at Hilbre Island when something frightened the horse.[52] Fortunately he was uninjured. On the following afternoon a reception was held in his honour by the lord mayor of Liverpool, John Lea, at the Mansion House. In the evening he was to address a meeting at the Sun Hall in Kensington, which could seat 6,000 people. From the outset of the meeting Evan Roberts was restless and ill at ease and his face was distorted in agony. After the introductory parts of the service, the prayers arose like a cloud from the congregation. Evan Roberts interrupted the petitions and said in English, 'There is an English friend in this meeting and he is trying to hypnotize me this very moment. Will you leave the building at once or ask the Lord to forgive you?' The congregation of thousands was astounded and all leapt to their feet as one, while hundreds offered prayer. Roberts was trembling from head to toe and collapsed helplessly into his chair laying his head on his arms on the table in front of him. After the congregation had sung a hymn, Roberts rose to his feet and said 'Some of you are praying to the Lord to save this person. I cannot do this. I can pray for him to be removed from the face of the earth, but I cannot ask the Lord to save him . . .'

From then on the meeting went well, but there was another storm on the horizon. John Williams 'tested' the meeting by asking everyone who believed in the Lord Jesus Christ to raise their hands. This happened so many times that some people complained. Evan Roberts came to hear of this and having remarked that Jesus did not complain when he stretched out his arms on the cross, he asked the complainants to ask for forgiveness so that the meeting could proceed. Nothing happened. Roberts said that the Holy Spirit had given him a message ordering the complainant to stand up and confess. There was an uneasy pause. Then Roberts said that he had a further message from the Spirit, 'If you do not confess, do not be surprised if you are not able to lift up your arm after tonight. Then you will have to carry this sign to your grave.'[53] Roberts collapsed on to his chair once more in dreadful physical agony. Then he informed the congregation that the offender was a minister.

In the ensuing uproar, Hugh R. Roberts, the minister of Edge Lane Baptist church, asked Roberts to name the offender. He was backed up by O. L. Roberts, the minister of Tabernacle Congregational chapel, and a member of the deputation that had visited Dowlais to invite Evan Roberts to Liverpool. His voice was drowned out by the congregation shouting 'Shame! Shame!' John Williams attempted to calm the storm by saying that he did not believe that Evan Roberts had occult powers, 'but it is remarkable how they are proved correct every time'. By this time, Evan Roberts and the young women assistants had slipped out through the back entrance and the meeting was brought to a close. On the following day, Dr Walford Hodie, a well-known hypnotist and entertainer who was performing in the Lyric Theatre at the time, admitted that he had sent a member of his staff to the Sun Hall to try to hypnotize Evan Roberts. The following services went well.

Another storm arose during the meeting at Mynydd Seion

(Mount Zion) chapel, on the evening of Tuesday, 11 April. On this occasion following one of his most extreme paroxysms, Evan Roberts made a statement to this effect: 'God gave me this message . . . The message is concerned with the "Free Church of the Welsh". It is a direct message from God – "This church is not founded on the Rock". That is the message.' This caused a great uproar. When W. O. Jones was interviewed by members of the press, he said that D. M. Phillips (who was staying at the same lodgings as Evan Roberts in Liverpool) had assured him that the revivalist's wish was that the members of the 'Free Church of the Welsh' should take part in the meetings. This was hardly a surprise since the revival in Liverpool had begun in one of their churches. W. O. Jones had been to listen to Evan Roberts in Swansea and was sufficiently impressed to announce that 'no explanation can be given for him and for his work, except that it is supernatural. It must be that he is an instrument in the hand of God's Spirit.'[54] However, he changed his tune after the attack in Mynydd Seion and began to criticize him harshly, declaring that Evan Roberts did not possess any supernatural abilities, and that he himself in all his reading had not come across any example of 'occultism being used for the propagation of the Christian religion'.[55]

This was not the end of the matter. A men's meeting was organized in the chapel at Chatham Street where the whole issue of the 'Free Church' had arisen. Evan Roberts remained silent throughout the meeting but at about a quarter past nine a minister stood up in the *sedd fawr* and asked him publicly, 'Were you reconciled with your brother before coming to the meeting tonight? Why are you playing around with holy matters like this?' This minister was Daniel Hughes, Chester, and he was referring to the relationship between Evan Roberts and W. O. Jones.[56] Later on, H. M. Roberts, the minister of the Calvinistic Methodist church at Rhydlydan, stood up and said, 'This is not the work of the Holy Spirit but the work of man. Everything that happened here tonight is counterfeit.' The revivalist entered into a heated argument with the ministers in the *sedd fawr* and also tried to address the congregation but his words were drowned out by the shouting, 'Throw him out!'

In the *Liverpool Courier* on the following day a furious letter was published from Daniel Hughes suggesting that Evan Roberts's public work was a sham and that his methods indicated a mastery of hypnotism and the art of mind reading.[57] Indeed, Daniel Hughes threatened to follow Evan Roberts everywhere and lecture on the subject 'Evan Roberts explained and exposed'.

By now the public had so many doubts concerning Evan Roberts's psychological stability that he was persuaded to undergo a medical examination. The certificate issued by the four specialists who examined him is an important document concerning Evan Roberts's mental and physiological state. 'We find him mentally and physically quite sound', they concluded. 'He is suffering from the effects of overwork, and we consider it advisable that he should have a period of rest.'[58]

The visit to Liverpool was a stormy one. According to R. R. Hughes, the biographer of John Williams, it was a mistake to arrange large meetings 'where people of all kinds gathered together' and especially the reception by the lord mayor for which Williams was chiefly responsible. As a result, 'John Williams played a large part in shifting the attention from the revival to the revivalist . . . and the message of the revival was forgotten as people chased after the miracle worker. John Williams was more responsible for this than anyone else.'[59]

This was an exaggeration. It was the newspapers, particularly the *Western Mail* and the *South Wales Daily News* that were responsible for the change in emphasis. John Williams followed their lead, and he was not the only one by a long way. One of the correspondents of *Y Goleuad* was so overjoyed at the contribution of the newspapers to the revival that he made up a new verse 'Blessed be the *Western Mail*'[60] and the East Glamorgan Baptist Association passed a motion thanking the two south Wales papers 'for the prominent place they give the revival in their columns'.[61] However, it is only fair to note that many meetings during the Liverpool campaign were smooth and edifying, as H. Elvet Lewis (Elfed) said, although he declared 'I have very little faith in the usefulness of his telepathic exercises'.[62]

Evan Roberts decided to follow the doctors' advice and take a rest. He spent the great part of a month – from 19 April to 16 May – resting at the Royal Hotel, Capel Curig, in the heart of Snowdonia[63] before beginning his fifth campaign. A delegation from Anglesey had been down to Nant-y-moel in south-east Wales on 9 February to invite him to the island.[64] The revivalist made a great impression on the visitors. As he shook hands with him, Hugh Williams said, 'I felt something moving from him over my whole body and soul'.[65] Roberts agreed to visit Anglesey under the auspices of the Monthly Meeting and his journey there was arranged by John Williams, minister of Liverpool's Princes Road church.[66]

He left Capel Curig on 16 May and travelled by train from Betws-y-Coed to Rhos-goch, where a horse and trap awaited to convey him to his lodgings at Cemais, the home of John Williams's father-in-law.[67] He received a princely welcome with hundreds lining the narrow roads while he bowed to the right and left to acknowledge their tumultuous applause. He opened his mission in Bethesda chapel, Amlwch, on Tuesday night, 6 June 1905, and finished in Llanfairpwll, on the evening of Monday, 3 July. He was present in twenty-eight meetings which were attended by between 90,000 and 100,000 people.

During this mission Evan Roberts was seen at his best. The clouds that hovered over the Liverpool mission had cleared and he was in a more equable frame of mind following his break at Capel Curig. It is true that he was overcome on several occasions by the spiritual agonies that characterized him and that some of the meetings experienced a Pentecostal exuberance equal to anything that the revival had produced in any part of Wales. Having said that, the Christians of Anglesey were very familiar with such stirrings. If it is appropriate to speak of a Pentecostal 'tradition', such a term could be applied to the religion of Anglesey, with its great open-air assemblies and its churches which knew how to combine passionate emotion with doctrinal and moral discipline.

Although Roberts was honoured everywhere as a well-known religious leader, he was welcomed not as some miraculous wonder but rather as a man who had a contribution to make to a ministry that stretched back into the past through a mighty succession. The ministers and other leaders of the island's life stood like a retinue around him,[68] and the campaign was well blessed. The weather was particularly fine during June 1905 and one remarkable proof of this was that at Brynsiencyn on 25 June, the police provided vats of water to quench the thirst of those worshipping in the heat.[69] H. Elvet Lewis (Elfed) captured the pleasant scenes of the mission when he wrote:

> Here in the brightness of June days and the golden stillness of June evenings, sometimes within sight of the sea, oftener still within sight of the heights of Snowdon, thousands upon thousands gathered, and

made the open field sacred ground with prayers and psalms, with confessions and conversions.[70]

The Anglesey campaign provided Evan Roberts with new experiences. It was at Cemais on 9 June that he addressed a congregation in the open air for the first time ever. He was rather hesitant at first because he believed that he could only do full justice to his message in an indoor setting. However, he soon became accustomed to the unusual location. Indeed, at Llannerch-y-medd, on 12 June, when tickets for the chapel services were being sold to visitors at extortionate prices, he put an end to this unseemly practice by ordering that the service should be held in the open air.[71]

It is also clear that his doctrinal emphasis was changing. In Amlwch, on 8 June, he said, 'Shouting is not essential to salvation'. The condition of having 'Jesus as a brother' was 'doing the Father's will'.[72] In Bryn-du on 16 June, when the meeting was starting to lose its warmth, he said 'I am afraid that some member is idle. Go out into the crowd, friends, and offer Jesus to them.' Thomas Charles Williams and Annie Davies obeyed at once.[73] It is evident that what he meant here was the duty of worshippers to use the service as an opportunity for evangelism.

These ideas were not new, although possibly he emphasized them more heavily in Anglesey than before. However, it appears that by this time he was concerned about excesses of emotionalism in the meetings. In Moriah, Llangefni, on 19 June, a young man stood up in the gallery and said that he had come all the way from Durham but that he was disappointed because he could not feel passionately about Christ. 'Feel!' said Evan Roberts harshly, 'you don't need to feel, but to believe. Emotions can lead you astray. Do not put your trust in emotion.' Sidney Evans approached the young man and urged him to accept Christ 'in cold blood' – a very unexpected expression at the time from one of Evan Roberts's assistants.[74] Owen Parry said that Evan Roberts did not 'support excitement or any extremes with the revival'.[75] This can only mean that Evan Roberts was having increasing doubts concerning extreme emotionalism.

Certainly there was quite extraordinary exuberance in some meetings. It is true that Evan Roberts was not the instigator of the great rejoicing on Cae Dinas, in the shadow of John Elias's old chapel in Llangefni, on 19 June. There was no excitement when he

327

spoke but when J. H. Williams, the minister of Moriah, addressed the crowd a 'strange influence' descended.[76] At least a thousand people began to pray all at once. Others wept and sighed, many of the women fainted and hundreds waved hats and pocket handkerchiefs shouting, 'Jesus Christ for ever!' This intense emotion lasted for some ten minutes.[77] According to R. P. Williams, Holyhead, 'Anglesey has not experienced as much of what can be called rejoicing as was experienced in this meeting since the 1859 Revival.'[78]

However, it was Evan Roberts's own remarks that brought a tumultuous reaction during his last meeting in Holyhead, on 23 June. A crowd of ten thousand or more, according to eyewitnesses, had gathered together in Ucheldre and in their midst 'man-of-wars men' – an Anglesey expression meaning the crew of a warship – who were making a noise at the edge of the crowd. Roberts became very agitated and rebuked the congregation because it had not yet become a 'flaming conflagration' and because the 'powers of darkness were fighting against us'. He was overcome by agonizing paroxysms and with tears streaming down his cheeks he pleaded, 'Humble them, O! Lord!' The crowd began to join him in prayers of supplication with their arms raised heavenward like a huge forest. Suddenly Roberts rose to his feet saying 'Glory to God, we can sing now, and laugh, and be joyful, because we have been given the victory. Christ is conqueror, and the devil has been conquered' whereupon the crowd erupted into rejoicing.[79]

All things considered, the campaign in Anglesey can be reckoned as the most blessed and most tranquil of all Evan Roberts's journeys. As a footnote to this campaign, he crossed the Menai Straits on 3 July to hold two large meetings in the Caernarfon pavilion.[80] From there he travelled to Bala, giving the college students a simple, unpretentious but significant address on 5 July.[81] He said that God must be known as love but that they must realize that the devil was at work and that it was becoming more difficult to differentiate between his voice and the voice of God. This was a foretaste which he would elaborate on in his later books *Gwasanaeth a Milwriaeth Ysbrydol* (Spiritual Service and Warfare, 1912) and *War on the Saints* (1912). He also said that only after long preparation could one hope for the 'baptism of the Holy Spirit' and when it came 'too much emphasis should not be placed on feeling . . . it is not feelings that are needed but believing'. It is evident that his ideas had changed and that he was moving towards the view (which he would later hold) that the self should be obliterated and that all emotionalism should be rejected.[82] He concluded his visit to north Wales when he addressed a large congregation on the green at Bala on 6 July before returning home to Loughor.[83]

By the summer of 1905, Evan Roberts was inclining towards the convictions that were presently to remove him from the public stage altogether. These convictions appeared to intensify during the following months. The revival continued to thrill the country, although its fervour was not to endure. Roberts had a quiet summer but in the autumn he confessed that there was a conflict in his heart between the call of his public work and the desire to rest from his activity.[84] He attended a Calvinistic Methodist singing festival at Mountain Ash on 26 October and spoke there.[85] However, as the anniversary of the commencement of his public work was approaching, Mardy Davies urged him to visit Pontycymer, where the revival was still burning bright. 'I am in a quandary,' he said. 'What shall I do? Shall I go or stay? I fear the element of curiosity.'[86]

In the end he went, arriving at Bethel, Pontycymer, by eight o'clock, on Wednesday evening, 15 November.[87] The congregation was very small but the chapel gradually filled up and he spoke for half an hour emphasizing the characteristics of true worship and warning the people to be on their guard against the enemy, the Prince of Darkness. There was a taste of the old rejoicing and the meeting concluded with song.[88] He remained there until Saturday, 18 November, and by that time he had begun to speak of those 'who were freed last year and who have returned to slavery'.[89] Afterwards he visited Bridgend, Pencoed, Kenfig Hill, Tylorstown, Trecynon, finishing on 2 December in Bristol. His sixth campaign was thus very brief.

He commenced his seventh and last campaign on 5 December 1905 in the town hall, Pwllheli. He confined himself to Caernarfonshire during this trip, although he did not travel further north than Deiniolen, Waunfawr and Caernarfon town. Huge crowds came to hear him, 'gentry and poor folk, drunkards and sober people, refined and rough'.[90] The campaign received great attention in the press and Y Genedl Gymreig published a special 'supplement' entitled 'Mr Evan Roberts's mission'. This journey left mixed impressions. His silence during the opening meeting at Pwllheli disappointed many people but on the whole he spoke for longer during this campaign than his custom had previously been. In Bethel, Penygroes, he spoke for almost two hours[91] and he addressed the congregation at the Caernarfon pavilion for almost one hour on 28 December.[92]

He was not so eager now to use the exciting methods that had characterized his previous meetings, but at Caernarfon on 26 December, he halted the singing because there was too much disobedience to the Spirit's promptings. He was once more overwhelmed by agonizing torments in Trefor on 11 December.[93] On the other hand, there were many blessed and memorable services, such as at Llanllyfni on 15 December, in Clynnog on the following evening and the series in Porthmadog between 19 and 21 December.[94]

One striking thing about this campaign was the shift in emphasis towards Christ's saving work on the cross. Previously the substance of his message had been the person and work of the Holy Spirit and the four conditions for securing the blessing. He still made reference to the importance of obedience to the promptings of the Spirit but the four conditions had disappeared and instead of focusing attention on the spiritual condition of the worshippers, he urged them to concentrate on the sufferings of the Redeemer. This pattern can be seen in his remarks at Tabernacle chapel, Porthmadog, on 21 January. He asked the congregation to sing 'Gwaed dy groes sy'n codi i fyny . . .' ('The blood of your cross raises up . . .') and as he announced the hymn he said:

and sing [the hymn] remembering that we can do nothing without the blood of the cross. Without the shedding of blood there is no forgiveness. If we gain a glimpse of the blood, it will be too divine a sight to keep it to ourselves. When the Spirit works here tonight, let him work. Let us sing asking the Spirit to lead us to Calvary.[95]

There were very few converts at these meetings for the simple reason that there were so few left to be converted. He was told in Penygroes that in the whole village there were only twenty-six who were totally indifferent to religion and only a hundred or more 'adherents' or regular non-communicant worshippers.[96] The revival had done its work.

By this time political stirrings had begun to capture people's attention. The Welsh Members of Parliament were organizing a national meeting in Caernarfon for 2 January 1906. When D. Stanley

Jones, the chairman of the Caernarfon Free Churches, sent a letter to say that a meeting at that time would clash with Evan Roberts's campaign, Lloyd George postponed the meeting, saying that he did not wish to interrupt the campaign 'which I consider to be much more important than any political conference'.[97] However, if a conference could be postponed for the sake of the campaign, a general election could not. Wales was to vote between 19 and 26 January 1906 and the country had been in a ferment since the beginning of December, 'See two spirits meeting! The spirit of the revival and the spirit of the election! Will one overwhelm the other?'[98]

Some succeeded in combining both, such as Rhys J. Huws, who spoke at the meetings of the North Wales Quarrymen's Union and who was a member of the deputation which asked Evan Roberts to visit Bethesda.[99] However, the majority were unable to summon up enough enthusiasm for two separate matters in this way. The organizers of Evan Roberts's journey acknowledged this by announcing that the meetings arranged for him would not be held between 8 and 18 January 1906, and Y Cymro announced on 4 January that the revivalist 'had brought his mission in Caernarfonshire to a close'.[100]

This was Evan Roberts's seventh and last campaign. He continued to appear in public and made statements that clearly indicated his maturing ideas. He attended a preaching meeting at Llanlluan, Carmarthenshire, in February where there was unparalleled enthusiasm[101] but he had a warning for the congregation. 'It is a dangerous thing', he said,

> to rest upon feeling instead of faith . . . It is faith that endures. Emotion will pass; faith will remain. Emotion will be certain to decline if you do not pay attention to prayer and the word of God . . . simple faith in God in the true spirit of revival . . . And I believe that there is too much singing in meetings.[102]

On 17 April Roberts attended a conference in Bangor under the auspices of the Keswick Convention for the deepening of the spiritual life, but he did not speak there.[103]

At the end of March 1906 he was invited by Mrs Jessie Penn-Lewis to go for a holiday to her home – Woodlands, Great Glen, Leicester – to regain his strength, and from there he travelled to his preaching engagements in 1906. He attended the Keswick Convention[104] and also the fourth conference at Llandrindod Wells which began under the auspices of Keswick on 6 August 1906. On the morning of Tuesday, 9 August, there was a ministers' breakfast and Mrs Penn-Lewis told the assembled company that the cross had not been given its rightful place in Welsh preaching. Several influential Christian leaders denied this and Evan Roberts was impelled to contribute to the debate. He said:

> It is true that I have preached about the Cross, but self had the upper hand. Although I received the Holy Spirit, self was there too. But, thank God, it is otherwise now. During the last three months the Cross of Christ has been revealed to me in a way that has never happened before. The veil has been drawn back and now Christ and his Cross fill my horizons. I felt its power crushing the self that had adhered so long to me, and if I am spared, my only goal will be to preach Christ crucified – not as a theory – but as a living truth.[105]

These words show that Roberts was a man on a pilgrimage and one who could also look critically at himself and at his work. On Sunday, 12 August 1906, he began a series of meetings at Llandrindod Wells which continued until the following Friday. The revivalist spoke in a careful and organized fashion and he was aided by various speakers from many countries. Although the meetings were fervent there was no evidence of the excesses of emotionalism that had characterized his meetings a year before.[106]

With this Evan Roberts had held his final mission. He was about to slip into obscurity at the age of 28. Jessie Penn-Lewis's home at Leicester was now his home. Rumours began to circulate that he had become to all intents and purposes the prisoner of a powerful and domineering woman. He did not answer his mail or else replies to letters were signed by Mrs Penn-Lewis.[107] So secure was his retreat that even his father and his brother Dan were refused access to him, despite their travelling all the way from south Wales.[108] It was a curious end to a glittering, if strange, career.

Evan Roberts joined in Mrs Penn-Lewis's activities. In January 1909, the first issue of her magazine, *The Overcomer*, appeared containing a hymn and short article by Evan Roberts.[109] In 1912, he published two essays in the booklet *Gwasanaeth a Milwriaeth Ysbrydol* (Spiritual Service and Warfare).[110] He made it clear that he had devoted himself wholly to intercession and that he was 'gathering the whole world under the wings of my prayers'. He discussed the causes of the decline in the revival and his conclusion was that the 'main causes were that life was pent up within believers'. By this he meant 'the spirit becomes closed up and there is an experience of hardness'. 'Life must pass outwards, and to another, and for the sake of another, and outwards in prayer and work.'[111] In the essay 'Spiritual Warfare' he argued that 'neither conversion nor rebirth nor the baptism of the Holy Spirit can ensure total freedom from the deceit of evil spirits'. Christians had to battle tirelessly against Satan and his kingdom. He had an astonishing confession to make about the influence of demons on the revival. He said:

> With the waves of revival that came during the past seven years, there came also malign spirits, deceiving those who had received the baptism of the Holy Spirit; and although they received spiritual awareness, yet this was not enough to keep them from the wiles of the enemy, they needed spiritual understanding.[112]

This astonishing declaration goes far towards acknowledging the accuracy of Peter Price's theory of two revivals, though the men explained their standpoints in different ways. Evan Roberts saw the churches as having fallen prey to the deception of demons and he saw himself as a man who had withdrawn from the bustle of daily life to fight the demons in prayer just as the early monks retreated to the deserts of Egypt and Syria to do the same thing. His calling was to wage spiritual warfare 'in order to encourage the salvation of the saints under the oppression of the horn' referring to Daniel 7: 19–22. If the battle could be won, 'a more powerful revival than those seen recently will be seen again'. The booklet also throws unexpected light on Evan Roberts's Welshness. Disconcerted by the apocalyptic symbolism of Revelation 12: 3, 4, 7–12, he insisted that Wales should replace the Red Dragon with a more appropriate national emblem.

Evan Roberts gave a much fuller expression to his incipient demonology in the substantial book that he published jointly with Mrs Penn-Lewis, *War on the Saints* (1912). He was obviously being drawn into a twilight world populated by spirits and demons. The world was coming to an end, he claimed, and nations and individuals would be led astray 'on such a vast scale that the deceiver will practically have the whole earth under his control'. Theosophy, the New Theology, Mary Baker Eddy's Christian Science, spiritualism and the non-Christian religions were all 'demonic doctrines', while the Welsh revival showed that even God's most powerful works provided an opportunity for Satan to intervene for his own ends. Many who were saved in the revival were now enslaved to the master of deception. Through the baptism of the Holy Spirit, people came into contact with a previously foreign supernatural world populated not only by angels but by demons as well. It was his mission to oppose these demons in prayer and intercede for those who had been deceived and possessed by demons during the revival.[113] Christians were charged with praying that those free from such influences would lead the next revival and ensure its purity. What had corrupted the previous revival was that converts, under the influence of the powers of darkness, turned inwards and focused on themselves. If human beings in revival are self-centred 'or [are] occupied in any degree with an inward experience, the outflow of the Holy Spirit is hindered'.[114]

This sad and wholly unbalanced book leaves the reader with the impression that nothing much more terrible can happen to a person than to be baptized with the Holy Spirit. But in the midst of these fanciful imaginings are penetrating observations on the revival and its effects which are unlikely to be given their due because of their context in an erroneous theology which does scant justice to the biblical conviction that in Christ the powers of darkness have been overcome. Without a doubt, the book shows that Evan Roberts and Jessie Penn-Lewis were in a terrible spiritual impasse after the revival and it is easy to see how the former revivalist came to react so sharply against the extremes of emotionalism and to see them as the product of demonic influence. In short, he came to share Jessie Penn-Lewis's conviction that Pentecostalism was thoroughly evil.[115]

Evan Roberts returned to Wales in 1925 and Jessie Penn-Lewis died on 15 August 1927.[116] The revivalist occasionally attended services and eisteddfodau but he was no longer a public figure. He died at Hillside Nursing Home, Pen-y-Lan, Cardiff, on 29 January 1951, and his remains were buried in his parents' grave at Moriah chapel, Loughor.[117]

It would be incorrect to suppose that the revival was extinguished like a candle in the mighty winds of the 1906 general election. Generally, the emotional extremes subsided and the atmosphere in the services became cooler. One could hardly expect anything else.

Despite this, in some places the flame was occasionally lit. For instance, a revivalist spirit was felt, on Sunday 11 March 1906, during the annual preaching meetings at Bethania, Cymer, when J. H. Howard and D. M. Phillips, Tylorstown, took services there,[118] and there were scenes of great exuberance at Cross Hands in the month of April.[119] But such sporadic stirrings were soon felt to be no longer newsworthy.

There were some unusual exceptions. By mid-April 1906, the papers were speaking of 'The New Revival' with reference to stirrings in Carmarthenshire and particularly in the Penygroes area. At the centre of the ferment was Sarah Jones, Gors-fach, Carmel. When Evan Roberts was at the Llanlluan preaching meeting on 25 April, he stayed at her home at Gors-fach and laid hands on her. Before long she herself was transmitting the Holy Spirit and his gifts in the same way to other people.[120] She would often fall into a trance which, according to eyewitness descriptions, was not unlike the trances which overcame some mystics. At the beginning of April – before she had met Evan Roberts – her devotions were so intense that she would lose consciousness, much to the consternation of Daniel, her husband. At other times she would interrupt chapel services.

> Sometimes she would walk slowly, slowly back and forth along the chapel aisle in the manner of a mother nursing her baby. She gave the congregation the impression of the Blessed Virgin Mary nursing Jesus. She would speak to him in the tone of a mother speaking to her beloved little firstborn. She would sing quietly to him, and call him 'Beloved of the Father', 'The Rose of Sharon', 'the Lily of the Valley', 'the Lord's Anointed'.[121]

Sarah Jones would frequently address the congregation in an unintelligible language – an early Welsh example of the phenomenon of 'speaking in tongues'. She began to attend meetings in various places; on the evening of Tuesday, 17 April 1906, she was present at meetings at Ty'n-gors farm and Maespica farm, Cwm-twrch, where there was much excitement. In Maespica people were speaking, praying, weeping and having fainting fits. Sarah Jones threw herself on the table in agonies crying 'I love you'. By the time she began to speak men and women could be seen making all sorts of grimaces, 'gesticulating, shouting, praying and laughing . . . with shouts, wild and ear-piercing shrieks and the thumping of tables and chairs'.[122]

Healing powers were attributed to Sarah Jones and people flocked in their hundreds to see her. She held meetings outside her native area where people jumped and danced.[123] Sarah Jones was linked – incorrectly – to Pastor R. Howton[124] who held missions in Carmarthen, Llanelli and Gowerton in April 1906. He caused quite a stir by claiming that he had raised a young man from the dead and he maintained that he had the ability to cast out demons and to heal the sick.[125] Although some believed such claims, there were many more who were profoundly sceptical.

Seth Joshua launched a bitter attack on Howton at a meeting in Swansea on 24 April. 'The devil', he said, 'is raising a counterfeit revival . . . It is a mixture of spiritualism and mesmerism, and it will need a strong hand to keep it down and a strong voice to denounce it.' However, he spoke favourably of Sarah Jones, and expressed the hope that she would be safeguarded from all perils.[126] Nevertheless Sarah Jones also had some very harsh critics.[127] W. E. Prytherch, minister at Trinity Calvinistic Methodist church, Swansea, described the 'New Revival' as 'rubbish' and 'heathenism'.[128] This is indicative of the sharp reaction against extreme claims and overt emotionalism which would characterize Welsh religion after 1905.

And so the revival ended.

~ 14 ~
Fool's Gold or the Real Thing?

Before assessing the influence of the 1904–5 Revival on Welsh life, we must consider a few more of its direct results. For one thing, the revival inaugurated a spiritual reawakening that encircled the globe. Previous attempts to 'explain' and evaluate the revival have been inadequate because historians did not consider the fact that the revival was not confined to Wales. It would be sensible, therefore, to outline this aspect of its history.[1]

It is well known that the revival touched Welsh people living in England. Some of the events which occurred in Liverpool have already been discussed and similar scenes were witnessed in other Welsh-speaking communities in England. Before the end of 1904 the revival had reached Prescot in Lancashire,[2] in January 1905 it touched the Wesleyans of Manchester and Ashton-in-Makerfield,[3] and soon afterwards the Baptists of Manchester came under its influence.[4] In London, the revival quickly took hold, mainly through church members' personal links with places like New Quay.[5] By the middle of December 1904 hundreds were flocking to prayer meetings at the new hall at Jewin Calvinistic Methodist chapel in London and the attendance at Sunday services was higher than for the previous twenty years.[6]

By the beginning of 1905, the revival was starting to take hold in earnest and New Year prayer meetings were extended until the beginning of February. The literary meetings held jointly between King's Cross Welsh Congregational chapel and Castle Street Welsh Baptist chapel were transformed into prayer meetings and although they were not so well attended as prayer meetings in Wales, they were marked by the same freedom and spiritual verve.[7]

The revival also spread to English-language churches. Since the awakening had begun to touch London, the National Free Church

Council decided to hold a service, led by F. B. Meyer, in Christ Church, Westminster Bridge Road, on 31 December 1904.[8] The church was packed. At the same time the revival affected St Paul's, Westbourne Grove, where the Welshman Robert Roberts was the minister, and daily prayer meetings were arranged.[9] On 22 January 1905, Torrey and Alexander brought their mission in Liverpool to a close with a huge meeting attended by 25,000 and on 4 February they launched a similar mission at the Albert Hall, London.[10] Of course, it is reasonable to ask whether these types of campaigns should be included in the history of the revival but, if the campaigns of R. B. Jones in Anglesey or Joseph Jenkins in Dyffryn Nantlle formed part of the story of the revival (and hardly anyone would dispute this) then it is only right that campaigns such as those of Torrey and Alexander should be noted. Of course, there was a significant difference in their methods, with the Americans relying upon careful advance organization. The arrangements in London cost about £17,000, with a purpose-built hall being erected for the meetings in Brixton. A committee, supervised by the London Evangelistic Council, was charged with overseeing the work and a choir of 3,000 was trained for the campaign.[11] Moreover, as one correspondent remarked, 'Dr Torrey is well versed in the maintenance of order and discipline in his meetings, and it is unlikely that he would permit . . . untimely interruptions.'[12]

For some reason (which remains unclear) religious people in Wales developed a strong prejudice against these American methods and criticized them as attempts to 'work up a revival'. Nevertheless this kind of pattern was adopted during Evan Roberts's visits to Liverpool and to Anglesey. For his part, Alexander said that he had learnt much from the revival in Wales and the effects of that revival were evident during his meetings. By the end of the mission on 29 March it was announced that 7,000 had been converted.[13] There was a different kind of activity at the Baptist church at Lambeth Road, London, where a young woman from Cardiganshire had gathered together a group to spread the revival. By the end of January, the group had grown to seventy members.[14]

It is evident that the spread of the revival was directly associated with Welsh influences. In Newcastle upon Tyne an evangelistic campaign was opened in the Westgate Hall by Illtyd Jones, Mrs C. K. Evans (Eglwys-bach) and Miss Annie M. Rees. This was the beginning of a series of 'amazing' meetings and all three were present when Dr W. E. Geil was welcomed by a huge crowd at the Exhibition Hall at St Mary's Place.[15] Geil placed a great emphasis on Bible study and by Saturday night, 11 February, 3,000 had gathered in the Exhibition Hall to take part in a Bible class.[16] Annie Rees was present until the end of the campaign on 26 February and by that time a total of 120,000 had attended the meetings and 3,500 were converted.[17]

On 2 January 1905, the Baptist church at Knighton Public Hall, Leicester, began to hold revival prayer meetings following a visit to Wales by the minister.[18] Enthusiasm soon grew and by the middle of February at least a dozen of the town's churches had come under the influence of the revival and arrangements had been made for John McNeill to hold a fortnight's campaign there.[19] Evangelistic campaigns also had some effect among the intelligentsia, with Alexander opening a mission in Cambridge on the evening of Saturday, 28 January, under the auspices of the University Christian Union. On the following night, thirty-five professed conversion.[20] Clearly evangelistic campaigns were popular in England during this period and they were the means of numerous conversions. This was true, for instance, of Gypsy Smith's campaign in Islington during February 1905, which was promoted by thirty-five local Free Churches.[21] During the same month at Hereford, over 2,000 claimed to be converted during George Clarke's mission at the Drill Hall.[22]

In Derbyshire, the missionaries were the Wesleyan, R. B. Woodward, and the Baptist, W. Owen, the centre of the revival being in Sadlincote. From there it spread to Woodville, Newhall and Church Gresley, where the miners held an underground prayer meeting at 6 o'clock each morning.[23] T. D. Roberts, a Wesleyan evangelist in St Just in Cornwall – the land of many previous awakenings – held a mission there which succeeded in lighting the fire of revival and by the middle of February over 200 had been converted.[24] The same number were won over during the first week of the mission at the Metropolitan Tabernacle in London's East End, which began on 13 March 1905 led by six Welsh students from Spurgeon's Pastor's College.[25]

A revival had been in progress at the Primitive Methodist church at Westgate Buildings in Bath since November 1904 and by the following April the membership had increased by 130. The revival spread to the Baptist church at Oldfield Park as a result of a mission under the leadership of Miss Kitty Mathias of Tredegarville chapel in Cardiff.[26] In Sidcup, south London, H. Elvet Lewis (Elfed) held a mission week at the beginning of April 1905 and for months the churches held united prayer meetings that had a profound influence on young people and the working class.[27] In the first quarter of 1905, the revival came to St Albans by means of evangelical campaigns led by George Hunter, the minister of Lower Edmonton Congregational church and by the beginning of May some 350 had been converted.[28]

The revival in England was not restricted to specific areas or to any particular social class. There were reports of revival stirrings among the Wesleyans at Oxford Place, Leeds,[29] and at Kingswood, Bristol, where as many as 700 were converted in the space of three weeks.[30] The revival spread to Mevagissey and the surrounding area,[31] and by the end of March there was a 'great spiritual revival' in north Devon, with its centres in Barnstaple and Torrington where 'a multitude joined the churches'.[32] Similar events occurred in the north of England, for instance among the Wesleyans at Lancaster and Harpushey, Manchester. Indeed when the National Free Church Council met at Manchester,[33] a particularly blessed meeting was held at the Free Trade Hall at midnight on 8 March.[34]

Although folklore maintains that the Welsh are more emotional than the English, there were scenes in England that were as emotionally charged as anything ever witnessed in Wales. In the village of Ellenborough in Cumberland, for instance, there were scenes of great emotion at meetings led by the Revd W. Crewdson, with 200 converted, public houses deserted and sports such as football, pigeon racing and hare coursing completely abandoned. There was evidence of the same passionate intensity among the Wesleyans of Cockermouth and the Primitive Methodists of Aspatria. There was so much interest that a conference was organized in Appleby where clergymen and ministers could discuss the revival.[35]

In light of all this activity it is not surprising that Campbell Morgan declared in a Free Church conference at Westminster Bridge Road chapel in London, on 23 February 1905, that 'there are quiet but certain signs on all sides that a great revival is coming'.[36] It is clear from the evidence that the English Methodist churches benefited most from the revival but the awakening was not confined to them. In March 1905, the archbishop of Canterbury held a conference for clergymen and won their unanimous support for his favourable stance on the revival,[37] and in his Whitsun sermon he appealed for people generally to pray for an outpouring of the Holy Spirit on the whole United Kingdom.[38]

Since the beginning of 1905, the Anglican clergy had shown an increasing interest in the revival. On 27 January, the *Record*, the paper of the evangelical wing of the Church published an editorial, 'England and the Revival', and within a fortnight thirty bishops had gathered in a conference to discuss the revival,[39] some of whom were extremely enthusiastic. The bishop of London made a particularly successful evangelistic journey through the churches of the West End[40] and when a letter written by the bishop of Dorking to his former parishioners in Barrow-in-Furness was read out, revival broke out there.[41] As might be expected, others were critical. Francis Paget, the bishop of Oxford, informed his clergymen that all things necessary for salvation were to be found in the Church of England, the one true church, and that they should not take part in interdenominational revival meetings.[42] The dean of Manchester did not approve of sudden conversions, and declared curtly, 'swift to ripen, swift to rot'.[43] Nevertheless, the negative reaction of these prelates proves that the revival was at work in the Church of England.

The truth is that every single one of the attributes of the revival in Wales emerged somewhere or other in England. There were congregations of 5,000 'like a raging fire' in Wigan and the Methodists of Hull spoke of the place as a 'furnace of revival', while as many as 2,000 gathered for prayer meetings in Bradford.[44] There was unusual fervour in Nuneaton and R. M. Redward filled the Prince's Theatre every Sunday night with a congregation of 1,500. The meetings were so popular that the railway companies found that it was worth their while to run cheap trains to transport the worshippers there.[45] As a result of the revival, there was an increase of 800 in the membership of the Free Churches, with the Baptists benefiting the most with an increase of 20 per cent. It is easy to understand why the editor of the Wesleyan *Methodist Magazine* wrote: 'Happily there is no longer any need to use the comparatively restricted phrase "the Revival in Wales". There is spiritual movement in the churches all along the line . . . London, the Midlands, the North and West'.[46] The revival was not confined to England. By the end of January revival had broken out on the Isle of Man, especially amongst the Wesleyans.[47] There were direct links between the revival in Scotland and Wales. Even before the revival came in all its intensity, Seth Joshua led an evangelistic mission in Glasgow between 19 January and 3 February 1904,[48] and by the end of the year the Scottish papers carried lengthy reports of the revival in Wales which created a desire for a similar blessing in Scotland. This is what compelled a merchant from Glasgow to pay the expenses of a party from Wales to travel there to hold revival meetings. In response to the request, J. J. Thomas, Maesteg, travelled with Miss Kitty Mathias and Miss Sutton to hold a campaign in the city.[49] Their work was not in vain because the revival soon spread in Glasgow and both the inner-city halls and suburban churches were packed with people.[50]

J. J. Thomas was also the medium for an outbreak of spiritual enthusiasm in Motherwell and a powerful revival was soon under way in Cambuslang, a place already famous for its revivals.[51] The fire spread from Glasgow to the country round about. Maggie Condie from Dowlais held a month-long campaign at Govanhill and meetings there were noted for their fervent emotion.[52] Reports were received of similar stirrings at Dumbarton and Clydebank,[53] Paisley and Leith.[54] J. J. Thomas was also the link between Wales and the revival to the south of Edinburgh, as well as Aberdeen.[55] In the city of Edinburgh, the revival in Charlotte chapel broke out following the visit of the minister, Joseph Kemp, to Wales. He adopted the methods popular in Wales to encourage the revival, including marching through the streets.[56] The revival spread through the Highlands to Thurso and to Orkney. This revival was not so powerful in Scotland as the 1859 awakening, but nevertheless thousands more members were added to the churches.

Seth Joshua ensured that the revival spread to Northern Ireland when he visited the General Assembly of the Irish Presbyterians to speak about events in Wales. There were local revivals in all the counties of Northern Ireland, particularly in the market towns, and the revival also spread among the Protestant congregations of the rest of Ireland, especially in the area around Dublin.[57]

One of the most remarkable features of the revival was the way in which it spread among the Welsh-speaking communities in every part of the world and even in the mission fields where Welsh people worked. One example was the Calvinistic Methodist mission in the Khasia hills in India. The local people's desire for revival was inspired by reading the history of the exciting events in Wales on the pages of *Nongialam Khristan*, the monthly periodical edited by

J. Ceredig Evans and John Roberts. When the annual assembly was held in Cherra in February 1905, this desire was strongly expressed and during the following month a powerful outpouring of the Holy Spirit was received during the eldership meetings at Pariong. One of the delegates returned home to Cherra with his soul on fire. There was a blessing at the preparation service on the last Saturday night in March but on the following day, at the close of the communion service, the floodgates opened.

> A young girl called Ka Simai, suddenly rose to her feet and began to say a few words of testimony then she began to pray, and then as she prayed she began to weep . . . Emotions began to deepen, and then suddenly five or six young girls, who had been weeping silently for some time, began to cry out loudly . . . The women on one side of the chapel cried out loudly and in less time than it takes to write these words, the flame had crossed to the other side of the chapel, and suddenly the whole congregation was ablaze . . . finally it broke out in confession and praise, and there we remained for about four hours, singing hymns of praise about the love of God in Christ Jesus our Lord.[58]

In other words, exactly the same scenes were witnessed there as had been seen in Loughor or Treorchy or Ffestiniog.[59]

Similar events occurred on the island of Madagascar where missionaries from Wales had contributed so much to the spread of Christianity. After hearing the story of the Welsh revival, meetings began to be held to plead for an outpouring of the Holy Spirit and, as in Wales, the passion of revival was first manifested among young people. At the end of a meeting in Ambohimandroso on 6 May 1905, some of the students remained behind to pray and sing and confess sins. At the end of the month the annual meetings at Ambohimandroso were redolent with revival. 'People broke down and confessed their sins; and many trembled as if they had been overcome by malaria.' One of the striking features of this visitation was that so many people experienced dreams and visions.[60] Within two months, some 1,290 had applied for membership, including 200 children and their parents, and about half this total had come 'directly from paganism'.[61]

After these meetings in May, the revival spread far and wide throughout the churches, creating a fresh desire among members to hear biblical preaching and exposition, and the services were full of passion and zeal. 'Many were in agony of soul; some fell to the ground, completely overcome; others struggled in prayer before God on behalf of relatives and friends' who were still pagans.[62] But 'the great characteristic of the awakening is the service of women. In speaking, praying, visiting and winning souls, women are at the forefront.'[63] Once again, it is remarkable how many of the characteristics of the revival in Wales were manifested in the revival in Madagascar.

Turning from the mission fields for a brief glance at the Welsh of the United States, we find ourselves in a country where revivals had featured prominently and a country that had witnessed remarkable charismatic stirrings just before the start of the revival in Wales.[64] In December 1904, H. P. Roberts, the minister of Parish Street Congregational church, Wilkes-Barre, Pennsylvania, was thrilled by the reports on the revival in *Seren Cymru* and read some of them out to his congregation. Before the end of the service revival had broken out there too.[65] It would seem that this was the first link between the 1904 revival in Wales and the United States of America.

By the following March the Welsh-language churches were holding revival meetings on the 'Heights' in Wilkes-Barre[66] and the revival was beginning to spread throughout the country. Ellinor Williams went on an evangelistic tour of the Welsh churches in the States[67] and she witnessed scenes not unlike those which characterized the revival in Wales. For instance, she said of the people of West Pawlet that 'they had experienced one of the most powerful revivals found anywhere. Almost all the Welsh people, old and young, had come to religion.'[68] When the United Assembly of the Congregationalists and Baptists of Pennsylvania met in September 1905 in Minersville, Luzerne county, there was so much revival enthusiasm in the meetings that Charles A. Jones was obliged to postpone his sermon and allow the congregation the freedom to rejoice.[69] In brief, there was no doubt about the fervour of the revival in the Welsh churches in America.[70]

Furthermore, this was not confined to the Welsh-language churches. The churches of America had set aside 15 April 1905 as a day of prayer for world-wide revival and Campbell Morgan had arranged for similar meetings to be held simultaneously in Westminster Chapel, London.[71] Even before this date the revival was spreading in Pennsylvania and other parts of the country. Ten thousand were said to have been converted in Philadelphia in the spring of 1905 and in Atlantic City, New Jersey, only a handful of the population of over 60,000 were not brought to conviction. In Calvary Episcopal Methodist Church, in New York City, the congregations numbered over 2,000 and on 2 February 1905 a grand total of 364 new members were received into the church. The revival spread throughout the eastern states and before the end of March the southern states were under its influence. In Louisville, Kentucky, 'everywhere in shop and store, in the mill and on the streets, the only topic of conversation is salvation'. Similar reports were obtained from other places, from Florida, Texas, South Carolina, Michigan, Ohio, Indiana, Iowa, Minnesota, Illinois and California and in many areas the frequent reports in the papers about events in Wales heightened people's enthusiasm. To take one example out of many, the Baptist journal, the *Michigan Christian Herald*, allocated the front page to Evan Roberts and articles on the revival, including Campbell Morgan's article, 'Lessons from the Welsh Revival'. This publicity was the impetus for a revival that caused 2,575 to seek baptism, more than at any time for over ten years.[72]

The revival's influence was seen in countries in every part of the world. There is such a wealth of evidence distributed throughout so many countries and expressed in such a variety of languages that a single individual could scarcely be expected to summarize a thousandth part of it. We must be content with a selection of examples. According to the *Western Mail* one of the most prominent features of the revival was the fact that other countries took such an interest in it,[73] and none more so than France. Some French newspapers published detailed descriptions of Evan Roberts's meetings as well as supplements which told his story. Furthermore, visitors from France came to Wales to see the revival for themselves. To give one example, in the Sunday night service at the Calvinistic Methodist chapel at Llannerch-y-medd, Anglesey, on 11 June 1905, a Frenchwoman prayed fervently in French.[74] In a meeting at Tabernacle chapel, Cardiff, in January 1905, Principal William Edwards read out a letter from a friend in Paris saying that the revival had broken out in the city.[75]

A report was published in the periodical *L'Eglise Libre* concerning an address delivered on the revival in Wales by Professor Henri Bois, the author of the volume, *Le Réveil au Pays de Galles* (The Welsh Revival), where he had pleaded for emotion to be given a more central place in worship. Before he had stopped speaking, people were rejoicing, some praying spontaneously with 'freedom, simplicity and power'.[76] Another scholar who came under the influence of the revival was Paul Passy, a philologist and professor at the Sorbonne. He wrote to Evan Roberts urging him to start a mission in Brittany and suggested the establishment of something similar to a Welsh-language missionary colony somewhere on the coast.[77] Ambassador Sir Robert Bruce Lockhart paints an unusual picture of Passy in his autobiography:

> When first I saw him he was under the influence of Evan Roberts, the Welsh evangelist, and for the only time in my varied career I had the strange experience of appearing on the platform and singing Welsh revivalist hymns in French before a Paris slum audience. Passy said the prayers and played the harmonium with three fingers, while I sang the solos supported by a chorus of three trembling English students.[78]

Another man who contributed to the revival in France was Reuben Saillens who visited Wales and returned with fire in his heart which he shared in meetings in every part of the country. The heat of the revival was felt even in Cannes! The revival was a means of healing the divisions which existed among French Protestants and one consequence was the establishment of the 1907 Federation which encompassed the vast majority of the country's evangelical Christians.[79]

Norway experienced a powerful revival in 1905 as a result of the ministry of Albert Gustav Lunde. Although there was a tendency to compare Lunde with Evan Roberts, their methods were quite different and Norway did not experience the extremes of emotion which characterized the revival in Wales. Through Lunde's ministry the awakening spread to Sweden, touching the aristocracy, including King Gustav Adolf, as well as the common folk. The revival, under the leadership of Frans Hannula, spread also to those parts of Finland where Swedish was spoken.[80]

The link between Wales and Denmark was more direct. In the spring of 1905, P. M. S. Jensin, together with ten other ministers, wrote to Evan Roberts urging him to ask the churches of Wales to pray for a revival in Denmark.[81] The history of the awakening in Wales was followed with growing interest and by the autumn a revival was spreading in Denmark where it continued powerfully throughout the winter. Indeed the fervour persisted in some parts of the country until 1908. However, in the Scandinavian countries the Lutheran Church was opposed to the emotional side of the revival and thus – with the exception of Denmark – less of the characteristics of the Welsh revival were manifested in these countries than in America or France.

In Germany, however, the pietistic tradition ensured that news from Wales was welcomed. In 1902, Jakob Vetter had established the German Tent Mission to hold evangelistic campaigns. In 1905, he visited Wales and upon his return he joined Ernst Modersohn to campaign in western Germany. The revival first began in Mülheim, in the Ruhr, and before long there were similar revivals in Hanover and Breslau between March and September 1905. Berlin witnessed scenes of rejoicing not unlike those seen in Wales and this is how some Welsh hymns came to be included in German hymn books. It is no wonder that an eager audience in Marburg in 1909 listened to T. Jones Parry, a former student of Bala College, describing the revival in Wales – he did so, according to Thomas Witton Davies (latterly professor of Hebrew in Bangor) who was present, in fluent German.[82]

Because the revival spread among the Czech and Slovak peoples, translations of Welsh hymns were found in their languages too. There was not such a direct link between Wales and the awakening in Silesia, Hungary, Latvia and Bulgaria. However, a mighty revival was experienced among Russian Baptists in 1909, and the link with Wales in this case was William Fetler, a student from Latvia educated in London who had himself felt the blessing of the revival in Cardiff.[83]

The Dutch papers gave considerable space to descriptions of the Welsh revival and they made a deliberate attempt to imitate the Welsh meetings in the *conferenties à la Wales*. Prayer meetings became more frequent and enthusiastic and lasted for hours. This period of activity corresponded with Abraham Kuyper's term in office as the country's prime minister – Kuyper also being a famous minister and Calvinist theologian. The revival had an immense influence on some parts of the country – Friesland for instance – and spread over the border to the Protestants of Belgium.

It would take too long to tell of the spread of the revival to other countries of the world. In South America, not only Patagonia was affected, since one of the consequences of the outpouring was a substantial increase in the number of Pentecostalists in Brazil and the number of evangelical churches in Chile. The West Indies enjoyed a powerful revival and in St Kitts the meetings manifested exactly the same characteristics as in Wales. The revival also spread through Africa, and to eastern countries, particularly Korea and Australia.

Evan Roberts prophesied that the revival would spread throughout the world and this prophecy was realized. He also prophesied that 100,000 would be converted to Christ through the revival; in that respect he was inaccurate because many more than that professed to having experienced salvation. In any discussion of the revival and its value, the proper weight must be given to its dissemination throughout the world. It is evident that the Welsh revival was the starting point of an immense spiritual movement. Were it appropriate to speak of the revival as one nation's gift to another, it could be said that this awakening was one of the most inspiring gifts given by Wales to the twentieth-century church. Nevertheless, certain vexing questions regarding the 1904–5 Revival remain, and it is to those questions that I must now turn.

The first point to make is the reticence of many historians even to mention the revival. Perhaps it is not surprising that it is not included in such wide-ranging volumes as *Christianity in a Revolutionary Age* by K. S. Latourette or *The Church in an Age of Revolution* by Alec R. Vidler. But the fact that David Williams does not discuss it in *Modern Wales* does demonstrate the way in which the judgement of historians can be distorted by deep preconceptions and prejudices. Before 1904, there was a general yearning for revival but many subsequently became very critical indeed. The Anglican theologian D. R. Davies was one of those who began preaching under its influence, and his sister, Annie, was one of the best-known among Evan Roberts's band of singers. But Davies describes the revival in his autobiography as the 'swan-song of the old religious tradition in Wales . . . the Revival was certainly a remarkable phenomenon, the consumptive flush of death'.[84]

Donald Gee, a Welshman and one of the most respected leaders of the Pentecostal movement, speaks of the revival as a disaster: 'the Revival disappeared, and has made those valleys in Wales almost inaccessible to any further divine visitation'.[85] Over the years there has been further writing of a critical – and even malicious – nature to the same effect.[86] How can this be explained?

Certainly many were disappointed by the revival and there was a tendency to vindicate this attitude by attacking the awakening in its entirety. This feeling was given bitter expression in J. Vyrnwy Morgan's book, *The Welsh Religious Revival* (1909), with its vicious attack on Evan Roberts. Admittedly Evan Roberts himself gave his critics some ammunition because he too had been disillusioned by the revival. In his opinion something major had gone wrong. Even in the midst of the excitement, he believed that malevolent spirits were interfering in the revival and he came to embrace a complex doctrine of demonic activity. By 1912, he had reached the conclusion that the activity of the Holy Spirit during the revival had angered these demons.[87] Naturally, the fact that the foremost leader of the movement believed that the powers of darkness had harmed the revival influenced many people's attitudes. Consequently, we must look closely at the questions that arose in the revival's wake: its causes, its nature and its consequences.

Before going any further, we must face squarely the undeniable fact that many thousands of people were wholly convinced that the chief author of the revival was God. Of course, those who played a prominent role in the movement believed this, people like Joseph Jenkins, R. B. Jones, John Williams (Brynsiencyn), W. W. Lewis, Keri Evans, H. Elvet Lewis (Elfed), D. M. Phillips, Thomas Charles Williams and D. Tecwyn Evans. Theological conservatives believed this, men like Lewis Probert, Charles Davies, Cynddylan Jones and Mardy Davies. Liberals such as Thomas Rees, David Adams and J. Gwili Jenkins were of this opinion as well. It was inevitable that evangelists such as Seth Joshua and his brother Frank, Rosina Davies and Hugh Hughes (Y Braich), shared this belief, not to mention the thousands upon whom the revival left a permanent impression. The short-story writer D. J. Williams believed throughout his life that the Holy Spirit acted powerfully during the revival and that 'Evan Roberts was a man of God'.[88] Prominent Anglicans also shared this conviction. 'I believe that this movement is from God', said the bishop of Llandaff, and the bishop of St Davids and the archbishop of Canterbury agreed. It would be foolish to ignore such an array of witnesses.

With regard to the historical causes of the revival, Basil Hall emphasized those influences that touched the heart of Wales at the beginning of the twentieth century, such as the struggle for education after 1902 and the fight for Disestablishment.[89] The sociologist

C. R. Williams placed considerable emphasis on the state of Nonconformity at the beginning of the twentieth century, with church membership dwindling, the chasm between ministers and members widening, and the influence of the denominations on morals and customs becoming weaker. The crisis was worsening because religious leaders were indifferent to the social struggles of the workers. R. J. Campbell's 'New Theology' challenged traditional orthodoxy while new-fangled sports and social customs undermined Nonconformist traditions.[90] The Baptist historian T. M. Bassett agrees partly with C. R. Williams but he gives the argument a Marxist slant by claiming that the revival was an 'expression of mass rejoicing in a society which was being torn apart by class quarrels' as it heard the love of Christ powerfully proclaimed. It was a protest against sinful standards and disillusionment with voluntary and amateurish efforts to solve the problems of industrial society and thus it can be said that 'the revival has its roots in the crisis of meaning in contemporary society'.[91] All of these suggestions are certainly relevant because they remind us of the tension that affected the course of the revival, but they fall short of being a satisfactory analysis of the historical milieu.

Campbell's 'New Theology' came to prominence not before the revival but after it, while it is difficult to see how the revival could have its roots in a sense of meaninglessness of any kind. From a Christian standpoint, what is now called 'the crisis of meaning' is linked with humankind's attempts to deal with the human condition without considering how God addresses it in his Word.[92] The Welsh mindset in 1904 was quite different from this. The revival was much more closely linked to a crisis of conscience than to a crisis of meaning, although the two were not unconnected. The analyses of Basil Hall and C. R. Williams are inadequate. Two and two and two make six, but the struggle for education, the increase in immorality and the dwindling numbers attending chapel do not make a revival. There is some essential element missing in the analysis. Space must be allowed for some powerful dynamic that could shake a nation to its foundations. These analyses are also deficient because they are based on too narrow an inspection of the facts. Assuming that social tension gave rise to a revival in Wales, what caused the revival in Norway, Madagascar and Russia?

It is evident that too parochial an analysis will not suffice. We must search for more common denominators and observers from other countries attempted to do just this. One of the countries which took the most interest in the revival in Wales was France. Among those who wrote on the subject, there are two authors whose comments merit consideration, J. Rogues de Fursac and Henri Bois. De Fursac was a psychiatrist who was commissioned in 1906 by the French Home Affairs Minister to visit Wales and 'study the influence of mysticism on the development of mental disorders'. His report to the government is contained in the book *Un movement mystique contemporain: Le reveil religieux du Pays de Galles 1904–5* (1907). De Fursac was an atheist and he did not believe in 'the need for Grace to explain conversion, more than the god Jupiter is needed to explain a thunderbolt'.[93] As a matter of conscience therefore he felt obliged, in terms of his work as a psychiatrist, to discover a natural explanation for the revival.

De Fursac based his explanation on an analysis of the phenomenon of conversion. Having spoken at length with a coal miner from Pontypridd about his spiritual pilgrimage, he concluded that there were three elements in conversion. First, the Welsh were a race which was 'essentially religious, a race of periodic revivals'. Secondly the Welsh person's entire cultural instruction steeped him or her in the Bible and disciplined him or her in the standards and values of the chapel. Each of these influences inculcated in the individual an ideal to which he or she should strive. However, people can betray this ideal and act in a way which is contrary to it. As a result, the ideal, together with its standards and values, is thrust into the subconscious, but it does not disappear; it is always there. Then, while hearing an inspiring sermon or reading the history of the revival in the newspaper, the ideal ego takes control of the personality. This was the third element in conversion, the conviction that restores the ideal personality to its throne and since this happens with explosive suddenness this process appears to be miraculous.[94]

De Fursac applied the analysis to Wales as a whole. Welsh people are religious by nature – 'perhaps the most religious of all the people of the civilized world'.[95] This instinct is strengthened by a culture which is thoroughly Christian. The Sunday schools were 'flourishing' and their influence immeasurable, while the Welsh language was the medium for this culture and 'isolates the nation completely', although English was the language of business. It was the Welsh-speakers who were more or less monolingual who came under the influence of the revival. The Anglicized people, the *bourgeoisie riche*, and the professional people were not affected by the revival nor were the inhabitants of the large towns.

The Welsh nation had tended to betray the ideal set before it by its Christian culture. By the end of the nineteenth century, faith had become feeble, practical religion was at a low ebb, chapels were emptying, while their former members had gone on to embrace lawful and unlawful pleasures. Nevertheless, Christian culture left such a deep impression on the nation's personality that, when prophets such as Dean Howell, Joseph Jenkins and Evan Roberts came to unmask their unfaithfulness, the religious nation wrested control from the hands of the faithless nation, in an unparalleled storm of emotion. 'The Revival is not the work of one revivalist but the work of a revived nation' ('n'est pas l'œuvre d'un Revivalist, mais de la population revivalisée').[96] But why did the intrinsic mysticism of the Welsh take the form of an explosive crisis? To be fair to de Fursac, he was completely honest; he did not know the answer ('je suis très embarrassé pour y répondre').[97]

The strength of de Fursac's analysis is that he attempted to provide a psychological mechanism that offered a generic pattern suitable for the study of revivals generally. At the same time, he suggested a way of relating the experience of individuals in revival to the experience of society in revival and he allowed for the social conflict which was so important for the analysis of Hall, Williams and Bassett. He also had a strong grasp of the positive influences, such as culture and the Bible, that contributed to the revival. Nevertheless, he acknowledged that his analysis did not account completely for the phenomenon of personal crisis and it is a tribute to his scrupulous scholarship that he left the question unanswered. Nevertheless, the question is crucial.

Henri Bois attempted to give a more comprehensive analysis. Bois was a professor in the Faculty of Protestant Theology at Montauban in the south of France. He stood therefore in the Calvinistic tradition of the Reformed Church of France and he sympathized, albeit critically, with the revival. He came to Wales over Easter 1905, visiting places such as Cardiff, Aberdare, Rhosllannerchrugog and Liverpool, where he insisted on interviewing all kinds of people. However, unlike de Fursac, he did not have an opportunity to speak to Evan Roberts. The fruit of his visit was a hefty 613-page tome, entitled *Le Réveil au Pays de Galles*

(undated but the preface was completed in December 1905).
Taking all things into consideration, this is the best volume ever
written on the revival, although almost a century has passed since
it appeared. Henri Bois also published another volume summarizing
his doctrine of the psychology of revivals, *Quelques réflexions sur
la psychologie des réveils* (1906), in which Wales once again
received considerable attention.

Bois, like de Fursac, maintained that 'every country has its
national character with individuals partaking of it to greater or
lesser degrees'.[98] The character of the Welsh has been shaped by
their religious culture. The people had been 'steeped in sermons'.[99]
They had dedicated ministers, Sunday schools, singing festivals and
prayer meetings. 'These things pioneered the way for the Revival in
Wales'.[100] Without this cultural immersion there would be no
revival. That is why the movement had little impact in other
European countries.[101] Wales is not France and a French revival
would need to be different from a Welsh revival because the quality
of the culture and national identity of the French is different.

> The Revival in Norway is the direct result of the Revival in Wales. It
> was the practice to use *seiadau* (*les after-meetings*) to gather together
> new converts, meetings were held without a leader and there was a
> deliberate attempt to steer young people towards a conviction of sin –
> in short the methods of the Methodist movement were adopted.[102]

Henri Bois claimed that desire for revival was an intrinsic part
of the Welsh religious tradition and he linked this desire with the
itinerant preaching that contributed so much to the growth of
Methodism. Itinerant preaching, he said, gave a sense of urgency
(*un caractère d'urgence*) to the work of the ministry because the
preacher had to bring people to a conviction of sin within a short
time before continuing his journey. The ideal therefore was 'a sudden conversion for individuals and a revival for the churches'.[103]
Henri Bois did not approve of this emphasis. He tried to distinguish
between 'revival' and 'revitalization'[104] and cited approvingly the
famous declaration in 1903 by David Howell (Llawdden), claiming
that 'revitalization' involves the Holy Spirit blessing the churches'
usual labours with a revitalizing spirit, rather than revivals which
are 'passionate, wild, dramatic, religious crises'.[105] This is the
authentic voice of the Reformed tradition in all its sobriety, the

same tradition as that found among the 'Dry Dissenters' before the Evangelical Revival pushed them into the Methodist mould.

Henri Bois was of the opinion that there was a close link between the revival and Wales's national identity. He said that secular and religious historians were in agreement that 'the succession of various religious revivals in Wales have always been' a revitalization of the spirit 'of the nation as a nation'.[106] Thus the 1904 revival was, according to Henri Bois, in debt to the previous work of the churches and to the national characteristics of the people. However the nation began to think more deeply during the battle against the 1902 Education Act. 'Wales, which is Nonconformist through and through and a renowned defender of freedom, was a stronghold of the opposition to an unjust Education Act.' The struggle caused people to concentrate in an extraordinary way on religious matters and at the same time a revitalization of the national spirit occurred, 'which in Wales has always been inextricably linked to religious revival'. This intensity turned into a conflagration under people like Evan Roberts who felt that something more exciting was needed even than saving a soul.[107]

These French scholars made a substantial contribution to the debate. As we shall see, de Fursac had a better grasp of the significance of psychology while Henri Bois had a better grasp of the historical background. Of course they were children of their age. Had they been writing in 1981 they would not have dreamt of describing Wales as a nation with an intrinsic religious instinct, while the fine points of their psychological analyses are not so compatible with more recent theories. Nevertheless their emphasis on Welsh Christian culture as a creative contribution to the revival is valuable and their belief that the revival indicated a crisis of Welsh identity is striking. De Fursac glimpsed the idea, which became commonplace later, that religious revivals occurred when closed societies attempted to wrestle with cultural and social changes that were both rapid and threatening as they were overtaken by the modern world.[108]

Nevertheless, there have been revivals in many countries apart from Wales and we need an analysis that is at the same time Christian (or at least takes Christian convictions seriously) and that also does justice to historical, psychological and social considerations. In his weighty volume on the Holy Spirit, *Nerth y Goruchaf* (The Strength of the Almighty, 1906), Lewis Probert, the principal of Bala–Bangor College, claimed that Christians had been commanded to practise the means of grace ordained by God to ensure the success of the church, the preaching of the Word, pastoring the flock, administering the sacraments and so on. However, there is nothing mechanical about the means of grace and they do not produce revival mechanically. Christians were also commanded to pray for blessing on their labours. 'We should labour as if the work was entirely our responsibility; and we should pray, also as if our efforts were completely worthless.'[109] Our hope is that God will not be deaf to our prayers.

However God, in his divine freedom, also sees fit to permit the churches a particular revival, or an extraordinary blessing, and does this occasionally even when the churches do not pray for it. There is an unpredictable element of this kind in every revival. But whatever the quality of the revival may be, the same Spirit is at work and his influence bears the same fruit in a quiet period as in a period of great excitement. The reason for emphasizing this uniformity in the work of the Holy Spirit is that there was a tendency among many to confine the Spirit's influence to revival and to act as if he had completely withheld his influence during the lifeless period which preceded it.

Thus one common element in revivals in various countries is the presence of the Holy Spirit. Another element is Christian doctrine and the teaching and culture which derive from it. The human heart must also be considered. Henri Bois said that the same Holy Spirit works in all places and at all times but that he adapts his actions to meet the requirements of various circumstances in different countries and different periods. A particular set of cultural, social, political and psychological circumstances existed in Wales and the Holy Spirit worked on people who were in the midst of these circumstances. To understand what was pricking people's consciences, and what was of concern to them, we must also understand their environment.

The German sociologist, Max Weber, in a discourse on conversion, emphasized the importance of taking people's 'world views' into account in order to understand their response to the gospel. The image that people have of the world in which they live, and of their place in it, is a great help in understanding what they wish to be saved from, and for what they can be saved.[110] An exceptionally important part of the 'world image' of the Lutherans of Norway, the Calvinists of France, the Wesleyans of England, the Congregationalists of Madagascar and the Methodists of the Hills of Khasia was the Bible. However, their social and political circumstances were widely disparate.

No doubt wide-ranging and detailed research in the countries where revival has been experienced would reveal common elements but this research is hitherto far from complete. The Welsh responded to their responsibility before God through the medium of their Welsh-language Christian culture. Did they continue to be obedient and faithful to God? In their case, the revival raised a thorny question concerning their allegiance to Wales's historical culture through which their forefathers had expressed their responsibility before God. This allegiance was not in question in Norway or in Korea. However, since circumstances in Wales were threatening historical Christianity, and since the faithlessness of individuals was part of the threat, it was at this point that the Holy Spirit met his people. This is what makes the 1904–5 Revival a critical turning point in the history of twentieth-century Wales.

Generalization is unhelpful in any discussion of the 1904–5 Revival. For instance, it has been said incessantly that preaching was completely eclipsed during the revival, yet H. Elvet Lewis (Elfed) maintained that forgoing the preaching of a sermon was an exceptional occurrence in the revival in north Wales, although it was common in the south.[111] Yet again, others emphasized, along with Henri Bois, that God's love had pride of place among the messages of the revival. It was not a crisis of terror, said Bois, but a crisis of love ('une crise d'amour').[112] 'There is no *dies irae* to terrify people,' said Elfed, 'but a *dies caritatis* who wends his way like summer through an expectant forest.'[113] Yet the fact is that the sermons of Joseph Jenkins and R. B. Jones consistently stressed holiness and the harsh requirements of the divine law. When Evan Roberts was in Caerphilly, people rose from their beds and ran in terror in their night clothes to confess their sins in chapel.[114] There can be no doubt that, for thousands, the revival was a day of judgement as well as a day of grace.

Nevertheless, the revival offered a refuge from judgement and its meetings were characterized by great joy expressed through constant singing. There have been many attempts to compare and contrast the revivals of 1859 and 1904. John Stephens, Bryn-teg, Gorseinon, maintained that they were 'as alike as two gold sovereigns',[115] but there were major differences as well. One of them was that singing supplanted rejoicing during the services. 'Rejoicing' (*gorfoleddu*) involved reciting verses from scripture or from hymns under the influence of fervent emotion, and occasionally to the accompaniment of handclapping or even dancing.[116] There was believed to be a biblical precedent for this activity in the Magnificat, the Song of Simeon and many of the Psalms. Indeed, singing had been linked to previous revivals. The publication of Williams Pantycelyn's volume *Caniadau y rhai sydd ar y Môr o Wydr* (The Songs of those who are on the Sea of Glass) was the means of igniting revival in Llangeitho in 1762 and, in his diary for 27 August 1763, John Wesley refers to the constant singing in Wales. By the end of the Victorian age, however, singing began to be used as a deliberate means of whipping up congregational fervour. American evangelists such as Sankey and Moody were probably responsible for this. In 1904, congregational singing was used constantly to *excite* emotions as well as to *express* them.

However, the most prominent feature of the 1904–5 Revival was the 'spontaneous' meetings, as they were called. Evan Roberts placed great emphasis on people's unquestioning obedience to the Holy Spirit and that they should speak, pray or sing as the Spirit prompted. As a result, many people, occasionally scores of people, would take part at the same time. For Seth Joshua, this freedom in worship represented 'the apostolic order'.[117] It was generally believed that this disorder in itself proved that the Spirit was indeed in control of the meeting. Or to put it another way, it was believed that this was proof that the revival 'came from the common people, and disregarded the positions and officialdom of the church'.[118] On this basis it was said that there had 'never been a religious revival in Wales which was more free from that which is called organization'.[119] However, this is only part of the truth.

As we have already seen, apart from Evan Roberts's first campaign, considerable organization lay behind the meetings, and Roberts's visits to Liverpool and Anglesey were arranged very carefully. Moreover, all the various revivalists' activity took the churches' organization for granted. On the other hand, in the midst of their powerful yearning for revival the public were in a mood to make full use of this organization and to enjoy their freedom in meetings. But because of the belief that there had been no preparation for the revival, and that congregations were happy to take the reins into their own hands, in some quarters ministers were judged harshly. Some said that the ministry 'had rejected the Spirit through failing to fulfil the necessary conditions – through neglecting to prepare themselves to receive him; in consequence, was it not thus the church's duty to reject the ministry?'[120] One critic in Anglesey claimed that the ministers were 'the coldest class of any' in Evan Roberts's meetings in the county.[121] These observations were very far from the truth. All the evidence points to the fact that the revival's wisest, most fervent support came, in the main, from the ministers.

On the whole, this was a 'young people's revival',[122] and perhaps it is always young people who are affected most deeply by revival. A huge host of them subsequently became leaders in the churches. One interesting aspect of the ferment of excitement was that small children spontaneously formed processions, held meetings and evangelized.[123] Evangelism was another characteristic of those affected by the revival. People would go canvassing from house to house and form processions which visited public houses and clubs to persuade people to attend services.

Above all, Wales was swept by a huge emotional tempest in 1904 and 1905. This period witnessed singing, weeping, shouting, falling in terrible physical agonies, fainting fits, visions, seeing lights, hearing voices and heavenly singing and speaking in tongues. And extremes of emotion bring a reaction. After the revival many began to feel embarrassed by their behaviour and tried to forget it or hide their discomfort by telling funny stories about the foolish things they had said under the weight of fervent emotion. If there is any truth in the Christian conviction that humankind's fate is of eternal importance, there would be something gravely wrong if the gospel never stirred the emotions. A faith that never excites the emotional side of one's personality is a crippled faith. On the other hand, if there is any truth in the Christian conviction that the heart is deceitful above all things, it would be surprising if the emotional aspect of the Holy Spirit's work did not provide some people with an excuse for yielding to emotionalism in order to feed the lust of the flesh.

The Methodist pioneer Williams Pantycelyn uttered true and sober words on this subject many generations previously. In his opinion, it was no wonder that there was 'a mixture of grace and nature, of good and bad . . . in churches upon whom God shines his face'. The 'sound of the wind' touches hypocrites and incites their 'natural passions' and then 'they are like a ship before the wind, without any ballast but with their sails fully unfurled, and in danger of being shattered by the rocks, or driven into narrow coves'.[124] Thus it was in 1904–5. Some leaders were guilty of deliberately whipping up emotions. At the outset Evan Roberts was party to this offence in that he adopted the methods first popularized by the American Charles Finney, such as public confession of sins by individuals, lengthy meetings and special meetings for those in spiritual torment, while encouraging the belief that if specific instructions were followed then the Holy Spirit's presence could be ensured.[125] But after the problems experienced in Liverpool, Evan Roberts was more circumspect in his attitude towards emotionalism, as when he said publicly to a young man from Durham who had travelled to Anglesey to partake of the emotional excitement, 'Feel! You don't need to feel, but to believe'.[126]

Many leaders were concerned with the overemphasis on feelings. O. L. Roberts, Liverpool, said that there was 'a strong case for fearing that fleshly emotion and passions were the only standards by which some judged the value of the present Revival'.[127] In the same spirit W. W. Lewis and Keri Evans – 'the Carmarthen fire-brigade', according to Nantlais Williams – placed a ban on 'fainting fits and pangs of sighing or weeping'.[128] Newspaper reports did much damage by giving excessive coverage of extraordinary events. H. Elvet Lewis (Elfed) believed that the meetings where quiet and deep emotion was experienced had a more lasting influence than the meetings where there was great excitement.[129] Half a century later, R. R. Hughes could not but agree.[130] All this is true, but it would be foolish to dismiss the passion and emotional excitement of the revival simply because the psychological excesses of wicked people were mingled with the sincerity of true converts.

As for Evan Roberts himself, he was the subject of more international debate than any other Welshman ever, except perhaps for Lloyd George and King Arthur! Many questions concerning Evan Roberts have remained unanswered. He was a young man – 26 years old – when he threw himself into the work of the revival, thus placing a responsibility on his shoulders that would have weighed down a much more experienced person. He was also a private man, keeping everyone at arm's length except his family, Sidney Evans and the young women in his evangelistic team. His loneliness was exacerbated by his quite unique concept of the Holy Spirit's guidance. The concept of the communion of the saints meant little to him and he did not understand the value of consulting friends on any guidance he received. He had no particular theological mission. The ambiguity of his theological standpoint caused heated debate in Germany. P. Glage in *Wittenberg oder Wales* (1906) argued that his tenets were contrary to the standards of the Reformation but in a booklet entitled *Wittenberg und Wales* (1906) R. Mummsen responded that Roberts was consistent with the teaching of evangelicals in Germany.

Evan Roberts did not attempt to establish a new sect and he did not create any organization to encourage the revival or to nurture new converts. The truth was that he was a loner and an individualist. He was not a 'great preacher' in the accepted sense: his style was to speak quietly. There can be no doubt about his charismatic personality. He might remain completely silent in a meeting, yet his presence was sufficient to set the place ablaze. Many spoke of his penetrating gaze and others – such as John Williams, Brynsiencyn – of the energy that passed through them when he shook their hands. Indeed, people cultivated quite superstitious ideas concerning his abilities. He possessed an unusual psychological make-up, with his visions, his pangs of agony and his unswerving belief that he was being directly guided by the Holy Spirit. Henri Bois believed that he had a quite unusual sensitivity to the emotional temperature of a congregation and that he responded to them with physical contortions and sighs which made an electrifying impression upon his hearers. 'These have a telepathic significance certainly' ('une signification télépathique'), said Bois.[131] And if a person has a telepathic gift, is it less appropriate for him to use it to evangelize than to speak in public?

However, it must be admitted that Roberts was occasionally tempted to misuse his gifts. His behaviour at Cwmafan on 21 February 1905, when he announced that there was a damned soul in the chapel, was quite inexcusable. For de Fursac, this was delirium.[132] Also, during the first months of 1905 Roberts used his telepathic ability to pinpoint enquirers within a congregation so accurately that it raised doubts about the validity of his gift. This is what caused Daniel Hughes and W. O. Jones to declare in Liverpool that there was something of the 'occult' about his methods.

Another point of contention, ever since the time of the revival itself, has been Evan Roberts's relationship with women. Henri

Bois was offended by the sight of Roberts in the pulpit with two young women; he explained to his French readers that the Welsh were much more tolerant of contact between the sexes than the French![133] In fact Roberts's relationship with his five female companions caused offence not only to the Frenchman Bois but to very many Welsh people as well. Indeed the philologist Paul Passy told Bois that Roberts had been severely criticized by his friends for allowing the women to accompany him.[134] It did nothing for Roberts's reputation when the newspapers announced in July 1905 that he and Annie Davies were engaged and then subsequently denied the truth of the story. Evan Roberts was very unwise in this matter and this lack of wisdom did his reputation much harm.

For Peter Price and J. Vyrnwy Morgan, Evan Roberts was the man who led the revival astray and, taking their cue from this, many people tended to confuse the man with the revival itself.[135] Henri Bois commented, accurately, 'The *Western Mail* increasingly, and in a rather extreme fashion, came to identify the Revival in Wales with Evan Roberts.' The *Western Mail* denied the existence of any revival in Wales until the appearance of Evan Roberts. In fact it is high time that Evan Roberts's limited, though important, role in the movement be recognized. Of the tens of thousands of meetings held between 1904 and 1906, Roberts was only present in about 250. Nor is it appropriate, given the limited part that he played, to portray him (as Vyrnwy Morgan did) as the man who poisoned the revival. The truth is that 'Evan Roberts's Revival' was the creation of the newspapers, and it is their biased portrayal that has remained most firmly in people's memories.

However, Evan Roberts must be given his due. This young man made mistakes and he was unwise in many things but his work was a means of grace to thousands. In any appraisal of Roberts's contribution, the evidence of E. Morgan Humphreys should not be disregarded. At the time he was a young reporter who proved his brilliance at his craft with his reports in Y *Genedl Gymreig* (The Welsh Nation). Initially he was strongly prejudiced against Evan Roberts, but he changed his opinion 'radically'. He continued:

> The more I saw of him, the deeper my love for him and my respect for him became. It was impossible not to respect his mental ability; some of his addresses were brilliant; they did not contain a trace of superficial

appeal to sentiment, and it is a great mistake to presume that Evan Roberts was a religious spell-binder . . . it was unfortunate for him that many people were afraid of him . . . He was completely natural, he was jovial in company and at the same time he possessed a simple and wholly natural dignity which made it impossible for anyone to take advantage of him . . . he did not make any appeal to the emotions . . . It would not be far off the mark were I to say that his appeal was almost invariably to the mind and the conscience . . . Whatever my ideas are about the Revival – those are mixed – I have only one opinion of Evan Roberts.[136]

No one would find it easy to pull the wool over William George's eyes, but in his old age he bore witness to Evan Roberts's natural amiability and humour.[137] And in the words of these judicious witnesses it is appropriate for us to take our leave of one of the best-known Welshmen of the twentieth century.

To turn to the consequences of the revival: a revival presents a new opportunity. It gives the churches new energy to continue with their daily work, and this was true of the 1904–5 Revival in Wales. It enabled the churches to face the terrible crisis of the Great War and the social upheaval of the Depression that followed. It is true that the churches did not take full advantage of this opportunity but through the revival a huge phalanx of church leaders emerged who continued to make a substantial contribution to Christian life in every part of the country until the outbreak of the Second World War. In particular, it enabled the churches to introduce a new category of workers, namely women, into their public work.[138] This was providential. It is true that the revival did not promote women into the ranks of the ministry or to high positions within the denominations, but the day was not far off when many congregations would depend more on women than on men.

One result of the revival was an increase in church membership. In 1903, for instance, the combined membership of the Congregationalists, Baptists and Calvinistic Methodists was 429,486. After the revival it was 509,269, an increase of 79,683 or 18.6 per cent. There was an unhealthy obsession with the numbers of converts during the revival, not least because Evan Roberts had prophesied at the outset that they would number 100,000. The statistics published regularly by the *Western Mail* can hardly be relied upon.[139] To start with, it is difficult to know how many of the converts were already church members and how many were from 'the world', and it is also difficult to find out how many of the converts 'from the world' had joined churches.

H. Eynon Lewis, the Congregationalists' statistician, raised this question in 1906. In 1904, he said, the increase in membership of Congregational churches as a result of the revival was 11,443 while the total increase was 12,688. In 1905 however the increase through the revival was 17,726 while the increase in church membership was only 9,013, leaving unaccounted some 8,713.[140] Many converts fell away during 1905 and 1906. Among the Calvinistic Methodists there were on average 2,631 backsliders every year between 1897 and 1900. The number rose to 5,492 in 1905 and to 5,437 in 1907.[141] Among the Baptists an average of about 2,639 left 'without a ticket' every year before 1902. The number rose to 5,941 in 1906 and 5,489 in 1907. The Baptists also kept an account of those who were excommunicated every year. Before 1903 there was an annual average of 1,243 in this category. The number rose to 2,417 in 1906 and to 2,457 in 1907.

Throughout the country as a whole the pattern was very uneven. The English Presbytery of the Calvinistic Methodists of Glamorgan lost 10 per cent of their 1905 membership in 1906, while the Baptists of Anglesey and Arfon lost the same percentage of their membership in 1907. The Congregationalists in Monmouthshire lost 11 per cent of their 1905 membership in 1906. Nevertheless, it is clear that the greatest percentage of backsliders were in Gwent and Glamorgan. Only about a quarter of the converts were successfully retained between 1904 and 1912. In north-west Wales in the same period one out of three proved faithful. In south-west Wales, on the other hand, almost six out of every ten converts remained faithful. Indeed the Calvinistic Methodists in that region were particularly successful in retaining converts. In Carmarthenshire, for instance, after a drop of 100 in membership in 1906, there was an increase so that the total number in 1912, namely 11,625, was greater than at the climax of the revival when it was 11,103. Despite this, the total of those who fell back from 1905 to 1909 inclusive was 1,159. The fall out in the years from 1897 to 1903 was 122 on average and if this trend had continued, the fall out between 1905 and 1909 should have been about 610. On the whole, therefore, the Calvinistic Methodist churches were winning more than they were losing. Strangely enough the Congregationalists in Dyfed were not as successful, retaining only about 40 per cent of those converted during the revival, while the Baptists retained about 30 per cent. In Gwynedd, moreover, the Calvinistic Methodists only succeeded in retaining about 20 per cent of those converted. If we look at the whole of Wales, we will see that church membership was 10 per cent higher in 1912 than in 1903. What statistics show is that the numbers of those falling away varied greatly in different parts of the country, that Gwent and Glamorgan suffered the most, that it was the south-west that was most successful in safeguarding the fruit of the revival, with Gwynedd somewhere in the middle between the two extremes. Generally speaking, the revival meant an obvious increase in members of the churches.

It is certain that many churches were overwhelmed by the influx of converts. For instance, there was an astonishing increase in some Baptist churches. Membership increased by 400 in the space of six weeks at Ebenezer chapel, Abertillery, and the Sunday school increased by 600 to 800; there was an increase of 66 in a month in Bethania, Cwm-bach in the Rhondda; 153 in two months in Adulam, Felin-foel, Llanelli; 219 in five weeks in Zion, Morriston, and the membership of Trinity, the Calvinistic Methodist church in Tonypandy, increased from 115 to 750 in four years while the Sunday school increased from 150 to 1,900.[142] It was a very difficult task for these churches to instruct and prepare people to partake of the responsibilities of congregational life.

Moreover, the custom in all the denominations was to accept those converted during the revival without any preparation. On the basis of intense experience they were received into full membership more or less at once.[143] This was a serious weakness and a costly mistake that would create immense problems in the future. The old practice of instructing potential members carefully and keeping them on probation for a considerable time had long ceased to exist. During nineteenth-century revivals the ministers would not have dreamt of receiving people into membership solely on the basis of their jubilant emotions in a single service. According to the old system new converts were encouraged to apply for membership to the *seiat* (in the case of the Methodists) or to the church meeting (in the case of the Congregationalists and Baptists) and this gave them an opportunity to discover whether their conviction was genuine or spurious. As a result, far fewer fell away than in 1905. In 1850, the practice of 'hauling in the net' became popular, that is, people were encouraged to choose Christ publicly at the end of an emotional service.[144] A difference soon became apparent. It was claimed that not a single convert fell away after the 1811 Revival,[145] but there was quite considerable backsliding in 1861.[146]

One of the unfortunate effects of the 1904 Revival, therefore, was that standards of church membership were lowered. There was a heavy price to pay for this because many people were received as members on the basis of their feelings and not because they were really converted to Christ. It also showed that a theology of experience had triumphed over a proper understanding of the principles of the faith. This in turn led to a growing emphasis on turning adherents into full members and little by little the category of 'adherents' disappeared. 'Adherents are now few in number in any congregation,' said Thomas Charles Williams as he related the history of the cause in Anglesey in 1907.[147] Chapel attendance became synonymous with membership of the church; the service was deprived of its function as a public meeting for anyone who wished to attend and became a private meeting for members alone. It was a very significant turning point in the history of the churches themselves as well as in their relationship to the public life of the nation.

The revival had a great impact on the consumption of alcohol. Abstention from drink became a particular focus in the services and one of the first blessings brought by the revival was that thousands of families were set free from the fear and the deprivation that resulted from the head of the household's heavy drinking. In this regard, according to de Fursac, the effect of the revival was 'indisputably favourable'.[148] The statistics received from the authorities at the time showed that the improvement tended to vary from area to area according to the strength of the revival. In 1903, 10,881 cases of drunkenness were dealt with in the courts of Glamorgan, 10,686 in 1904 and 8,422 in 1905. There was also a reduction of 6 per cent in other crimes in the county during the period of the revival. However, there was no difference recorded in Swansea, while in Cardiff there was an increase in the cases of drunkenness.[149]

There was strong evidence throughout the country of the beneficial effect of the revival on people's morals. There were no cases of drunkenness at the petty courts at Wrexham[150] and the courts of Rhayader, Aber-carn and Llandysul had very little work to do.[151] There was a great reduction in the cases before the courts in Tredegar, Abertillery and the Rhymney valley.[152] The average number of cases dealt with by justices of the peace at Bridgend dropped from ninety to twenty.[153] Sir Marchant Williams joined Judge Gwilym Williams and the chief constable of Flintshire in attributing the reduction in crime to the revival.[154] Perhaps such improvements could hardly be expected to continue. Drunkenness had increased by 1908[155] but there was a permanent change in the attitude of religious people to the consumption of alcohol. The refusal of alcohol became part of the personal discipline of thousands and the decision to restrict the sale of alcohol and to reduce the number of public houses was strengthened.[156]

A belief existed in some circles that there was a great increase in adultery as a result of the revival. One observer said, 'there is room to fear that there have been many instances of this sin being committed during the Revival and that by prominent persons from the Revival meetings'.[157] This criticism was corroborated by Gwilym Davies in his article 'The Moral Condition of Wales'.[158] He noted that the statistics of the General Registrar in 1906, the year 'in which the effects of the Revival should have been chiefly felt', show that there were 2,421 illegitimate births in Wales and that Denbigh, Anglesey and Merioneth were the three 'most immoral counties in the Kingdom'. The conclusion was that the revival did nothing to remedy the evil, to say the least.

The truth is that there was a reduction in the proportion of illegitimate births in Wales in 1906. In 1905, 54.6 of every thousand births were illegitimate and in 1906 it was 51.8, in 1907 it was 53.6 and in 1908 it was 53.5. The trend throughout England and Wales during this period was for a decrease in illegitimate births – between 1870 and 1908 there was a reduction of 50.5 per cent in Monmouthshire, 76.1 per cent in Montgomeryshire and 52.9 per cent in Anglesey. Davies also confused the 'most immoral counties'. Anglesey was indeed at the top of the list with 85 illegitimate births for every thousand, followed by Merioneth (80), Cardiganshire (71), Montgomeryshire (69), Radnorshire (65), Caernarfonshire (63), Pembrokeshire (58), and Denbighshire in eighth place (50). Over such an issue statisticians should make sure of their facts!

What did all this have to do with proving that the revival encouraged immorality? Davies took it for granted that the statistics for illegitimate births are an accurate reflection of the true moral condition of the country when they are, in fact, nothing of the sort. What statistics show is how many illegitimate children were born; they do not cast any light upon how much adultery existed and they tell us nothing whatsoever about the connection between the parents of these infants and the revival. This is a false trail, and one pursued energetically by those glad of any excuse to cast aspersions upon the revival. On the other hand, this does not mean that people, as Williams Pantycelyn said, were not tempted in the heat of passion to satisfy the lusts of the flesh.[159]

When we turn to other aspects of the social impact of the revival, we see a mixed picture. It was a means of reconciling old enemies,[160] improving morals,[161] and getting people to settle old debts. John Morris Jones, professor of Welsh at the University in Bangor, declared that 'the revival was essentially a moral movement' and gave as one example the fresh concern of the young men of Llanfair-pwll for the old and poor.[162] There were many other aspects to its social influence. Many football clubs were disbanded either because people did not go to watch the games or because the players refused to have anything more to do with the sport.[163] Drama companies were forced to disband,[164] but in the Aberdare Theatre people broke into rejoicing as they watched a performance of 'Saints and Sinners' by Henry Arthur Jones.[165] In places like Llansanffraid, Wrexham, Llandudno and Blaenau Ffestiniog, eisteddfodau had to be cancelled,[166] and at the National Eisteddfod at Mountain Ash the pavilion was half-empty.[167]

All these occurrences were an indication that people's interest had turned away from entertainment but there was also a puritan reaction against new customs and even against cultural activities as such. Nantlais Williams turned against competition and writing poetry and the revival destroyed the immense literary talent of Eluned Morgan.[168] Here we see the influence of a kind of pietism at work, coupled with unbiblical convictions concerning the nature of the relationship between faith and culture.

The revival had a profound influence in industrial areas. At the Grovesend steelworks, for instance, the workers sounded the hooter to announce a prayer meeting, and despite the protests of the overseers, they prayed for three-quarters of an hour.[169] Prayer meetings became a daily occurrence at Nantyffyllon colliery and in many other coal mines.[170] Similarly prayer meetings were held daily at Glynceiriog and Llanddulas quarries,[171] and the workers at the Town Hall in Merthyr Tudful decided to begin their working day with prayer.[172] In Neath, the Union of Steel Founders asked for alcohol to be banned from their recreation rooms.[173] At the Newport steelworks services were held at breakfast time as a result of Sidney Evans's mission and over at Pembroke Dock hundreds gathered together every morning by the gates to listen to Herbert John preaching.[174]

In an address to a union meeting at Elim chapel, Kenfig Hill, Thomas Richards MP, the general secretary of the Union of South Wales Coal Workers, declared his belief that the revival would strengthen the trade unions. A good sign of this, he said, was that they had received permission for the first time to hold their meeting in a chapel.[175]

Was his desire realized? J. H. Howard maintained that the revival restricted the churches' interest in the social implications of the gospel and that it strengthened the influence of the Keswick emphasis on personal perfection.[176] This certainly happened in many circles and devotional preaching once more came to prominence. Having said that, these two things are not necessarily in conflict. There was a clear tendency within perfectionist movements – as in America with the emancipation of slaves – to encourage social activity. There is a very close link between aiming for personal holiness and the sanctification of society and there is room to believe that social interest was heightened rather than diminished by the revival.[177]

The revival also brought new churches into existence. Some of the offspring of the revival formed independent churches, the 'Gospel Halls', the majority of them holding their services in English. However, the movement linked with the name of R. B. Jones and his friends was not a new movement but rather a network created to safeguard the evangelical witness and later on to establish a college and to evangelize through its periodical *Yr Efengylydd* (The Evangelist), and through meetings and conferences.[178] One movement better-known in the outside world is the Apostolic Church with its headquarters at Penygroes, Llanelli.[179] The Elim Four Square church was also to all intents and purposes a product of the revival in Wales.[180]

After the revival came the decline. Indeed before 1905 was out, it was announced that the 'fire had ebbed' – rather a mixed metaphor! – but the question of most import was how to retain the new converts.[181] According to one observer, ten years went by after the revival 'with hardly any converts throughout the whole of Wales'.[182] Indeed as early as 1907, one person announced that the church was blighted by a surge of backsliding[183] and a few even claimed during the previous year that they had witnessed a great decline.[184] According to another observer in 1907, 'there are many churches that are no better at this moment than when the revival broke out, and some are worse',[185] with quarrelling increasing and tolerance failing. It is not difficult to gather evidence to show people's disillusionment during the years following 1905. This is when, in some circles, the tide of opinion began to turn against the revival.[186] However, it is difficult to evaluate these statements fairly. Some writers give the impression that they expected revival to break out every year while others seem unable to differentiate between the insignificant aspects of the revival story, the foolish actions and mistakes which came in its wake and the pure gold found through it.

It is evident also that the theological confusion that was on the increase throughout Wales influenced people's ability to assess the revival and its significance correctly and to see it as a new opportunity. Because of an inadequate grasp of the scriptures, people came to think of revival as a divine outpouring which did away with the need for ministers and preachers and the need to study the Bible and build up church life. They did not realize that the Holy Spirit does not revoke or undermine the very means laid down by Christ in his church to enable it to glorify God through ministering to the salvation of people and strengthening their cultural work.

This analysis has been confined to the revival in Wales. It would take a very thick volume indeed to analyse the consequences of the 1904–5 Revival in their entirety throughout the various countries of the world. Taking a broad view, it is clear that it was an extremely fruitful blessing. Although Wales would soon turn its back on the God who gave it such a thrilling opportunity in 1904–5, the historian must note that the revival was, on the whole, a hugely significant event. It remains one of the most remarkable occurrences in the history of modern Wales.

~ 15 ~
Grappling with the World

In the Wales of 1890, Christianity impinged on every social class. Whereas the Anglicized aristocratic families tended to belong to the Church of England, the coal miners of the Rhondda valley were to be found in the chapels. There may have been educated intellectuals among the Methodists, but the Catholic Church was the home of poor Irish immigrants. Certainly some congregations tended more towards one class than others, but there were many which brought together a full cross-section of society. After the First World War, some religious leaders became irritated by the accusation that the churches were middle-class institutions. In 1926, M. H. Jones complained that the Labour Party had made an example of the Methodists to prove the point that 'the chapels of Wales are siding with the Middle and Wealthy Classes, the Tories, &c.'[1] The Calvinistic Methodist layman, Henry Lewis, struck the same note in 1922:

> What reason can be given that the middle class in Welsh society are so eager to be Methodists? A friend of mine reckoned . . . that, some fifteen years ago, 90 per cent of the chief drapers in the towns of North Wales were Methodists. Hitherto they are far more numerous among merchants and the learned professions than any other denomination.[2]

Before the War, people were untroubled by considerations such as these. Robert Thomas of Landore, Swansea, spoke in 1908 of the complaint heard often in England 'that the churches are failing to reach the working class'. It was not so in Wales, he said, 'because in our case this class forms the main bulk of the church'.[3] The chairman of the Disestablishment Commission concurred with the evidence that chapel-goers were by and large members of the working class.[4] Nevertheless there was an undeniable trend within the chapels towards the cultivation of virtues which came to be thought of as 'middle class' or 'bourgeois'.[5] These were sometimes social courtesies, as when J. Bowen Jones commented that there was a need for: 'a greater study and practice of the rules and rituals of courtesy and good manners . . . we are not as accomplished as we should be in what our [English] neighbours call *politeness* and *good breeding*'.[6] Nine years earlier, as he cast a glance back over sixty years, John Thomas, the Congregational patriarch, was of the opinion 'that our churches by and large have increased in politeness and good manners'.[7] Many ministers and clergymen, not to mention elders and deacons, were disposed to imitate the upper-class customs of the English-speaking towns. In Caernarfon, the Congregational minister Herber Evans used to travel to services in considerable style in his carriage, a dignified figure in his silk hat and tailcoat – and there were others like him. By the end of the nineteenth century ministers, like clergymen, could be recognized by their dress, and were greeted as 'The Reverend', although some ministers, such as John Thomas and the Baptists generally, continued to use 'Mister' or 'Brother', as a more seemly greeting.

Michael D. Jones was swimming against the tide in his protests against the ostentation of his clerical contemporaries. He insisted upon wearing a suit of homespun cloth – but did consent to wear a tall, white hat.[8] At the end of the nineteenth century ministers delighted in their social status. The 'ministry of the Gospel had become fashionable' and the 'social status of ministers had become comparatively respectable', according to Josiah Jones.[9] Some of them indeed were quite comfortably off. The biographer of John Williams, Brynsiencyn, said of him, 'There had never been a Nonconformist minister in the county surrounded by so many worldly comforts' and he would set out early in the morning 'with his gun on his shoulder to shoot in the mountains, or to fish in the sea'.[10] In short, John Williams was a gentleman.

Having said this, very few ministers and clergymen could afford to be gentlemen – after all, 105 Welsh Independent ministers in 1915 earned less than £80 a year. All the denominations had their capitalists and landowners, and starving workers who were desperate for employment were tempted to curry favour with their employer by attending his chapel or church. This did the Christian cause much harm and it is easy to see why class consciousness was intensified wherever such unfortunate behaviour occurred. However, the pattern was not uniform even in rural areas. D. Lleufer Thomas testified that there was no obvious difference between farmers and farmhands in rural Wales, except for the Vale of Clwyd and Anglesey where 'there appears . . . a greater tendency to caste, giving rise to a distinct peasant class separate from the farmer class'.[11] In the towns too, slovenly and neat worshippers were sometimes deliberately kept apart, either by building mission halls in the slums, or even (as with the Rechabite Hall in Bangor) by hanging a curtain across the middle of the hall and placing slatternly worshippers behind it, out of sight of the more respectable members of the congregation.

The churches had a profound influence on people's moral customs and on their social ambition. Virtues such as thrift, temperance, refined speech, self-control, marriage, motherhood, reading, reciting, composing poetry and singing were taught. To bundle these together as 'bourgeois' virtues would be misleading. Victorian Wales saw the emergence of a class of common folk who prized kindness, upright behaviour and culture.[12] No generation is free of hypocrisy, and there were plenty of people who counterfeited these virtues without really making them their own. One reason for this was the emphasis which was placed on 'bettering oneself' or 'getting on in the world'. William Williams (Crwys) recalled that 'becoming famous was the main goal of education and of life; each one of us was expected either to discover a continent, or to locate a new star'.[13] If a person failed to achieve fame in these directions, it was easy to compromise and content oneself with amassing money, buying comfortable furniture, filling the house with fripperies, or adopting the social niceties of the well-off.[14] And in the same easy atmosphere philistinism could flourish – as it did in Wales.

However, these developments brought the churches face to face with a basic danger familiar to all established churches. The more they were accepted by society and expected to give leadership and guidance, the less they became congregations of believers covenanted together in unquestioning obedience to their Redeemer, in opposition to the standards and temptations of the world. For such congregations, the foremost consideration should be the example of Christ and the law of God with the world and its pomp treated with disdain. By the end of the nineteenth century, however, the churches served not the elect but the Welsh nation as a whole and, without realizing it, their mental and moral preconceptions changed. Their function had now become to furnish the population at large with standards, values and religious resources. The prime consideration was what was likely to be expedient and acceptable to society, or at least the majority in society. It no longer paid to be uncompromising.

The conditions for church membership were lowered and people were allowed to join more or less on their own, or at least on very favourable, terms. 'Confirmation' and 'being received into full membership' became social rituals, part of the process of growing up. The requirements of the Christian ethic were softened and the previously clear distinction between world and church became blurred. Trivia became confused with principles because people were expected to display their Christianity in the clothes they wore, in their hairstyles, in their quality of speech and in their ritual courtesies. Christian moral practice was simplified so that it might appeal to more people. It could be summed up in the painless principles of a 'grade A Lifestyle' (*Buchedd A*), namely, attendance at services, Sabbath observance and teetotalism.[15] When the nation needed guidance on political and national matters, this compromise came into conflict with the attempt to safeguard the old immutable standards and created tension and confusion. By the beginning of the twentieth century, sects born from protest against worldly standards had grown into denominations,[16] which tried hard to influence the world but which found themselves in danger of becoming enslaved to it. One example of this was the campaign to disestablish the Church of England in Wales.

The Disestablishment campaign was a sad affair, which bore all the hallmarks of a Greek tragedy. There were, on both sides, sincere individuals obeying their consciences and acting on lofty principles, but it gave rise to hatred and cruelty which left deep scars on the spiritual life of the nation.

Like all such great battles, the Disestablishment campaign had many facets, social and political as well as religious. It was in essence a conflict between two differing Christian visions concerning the nature of the world and the church. The Anglican Church in Wales was part of the Church of England, the established church the basis for whose belief and constitution had been set out in Tudor times, and which provided the religious dimension in national life. Its basic principle was expressed by Richard Hooker

(1554?–1600), when he said 'Church and State are one society, and this society is called the State because it lives under secular law . . . and Church because it possesses the spiritual law of Jesus Christ.'[17] According to this teaching, the Welsh dioceses were one aspect of the national unity that encompassed both England and Wales. How was this doctrine to be reconciled with the powerful increase in Welsh national consciousness in the 1880s? The man who tried to answer this question was Henry Thomas Edwards, dean of Bangor from 1876 until 1884, who applied Hooker's philosophy to Wales.[18]

According to Edwards, the church represented the spiritual aspect of the Welsh nation. Unfortunately, it had become enslaved to English politicians who were determined to destroy the nation and eradicate the Welsh language. It was this policy which undermined the church's ability to claim the loyalty of the Welsh people and which gave Nonconformity the opportunity to gain ground. The common people had turned their back on the church not so much because they rejected its doctrines and sacraments but because the Anglicized clergy insulted them and their culture. Edwards believed that social harmony and national uniformity could be restored by reforming the church and bringing the various denominations together, and that the Church in Wales was the natural historical focus for this unity.[19] Although Edwards's historical analysis was shaky in many respects, the brilliance of his argument cannot be disputed. However, it was too late in the day to try to apply Hooker's teaching to meet the needs of Wales.

For their part, the Nonconformists' understanding of the relationship between the church and world was unacceptable to Hooker and his disciples. To the extent that they were indebted to the Calvinistic tradition, Nonconformists saw the nation not as a seamless union between church and state but as a society of societies. The state is a comprehensive form of society because it serves all its members. Its proper characteristic is that it is responsible for upholding order in obedience to the righteousness expressed in public law. However, its citizens vary greatly in their interests and in their religious and political convictions. Every citizen is loyal to a host of communities besides the state and it is no use the state trying to inflate its own authority if at the same time it destroys the citizen's loyalty to those other communities. The citizen is a member of a family, he or she lives in a particular area and may be a manual worker or a maid, he or she may be a school teacher or a member of a sports team or belong to a local club or a local church. It is not sufficient that a citizen as an individual has freedom to speak and meet and write; the sovereignty of the various societies to which he or she belongs needs also to be upheld.

This philosophy was implicit in the 'voluntary principle' so widely promulgated by Nonconformists during the Victorian age. The essence of this vision is that the modern nation is a heterogeneous, rather than a uniform society. On the basis of these presuppositions, Nonconformists insisted on breaking the bond between one particular denomination and the state. Their view was that the state expresses its obedience to God's ordinances by restricting itself to its proper field, in other words, to the maintenance of a righteous order. In trying to do the work of a church it confuses God's ordinances and forces the norms of a single, privileged denomination on all its citizens. The ideal, for many of the Nonconformists, was a secular, though righteous, state.

During the Disestablishment campaign these motives had become seriously blurred. Anglicans were naturally jealous of the legal privileges and the social pre-eminence which they enjoyed as members of an established church. Moreover, the maintenance of the buildings and the ministry was a matter for constant concern and this intensified in the face of a threat to the church's financial resources. On the other hand, the balance of Welsh religious life had been completely transformed by the massive growth in Nonconformity during the nineteenth century. The Anglican Church became a minority church within Wales and this undermined the strength of its argument that it was the national church. Moreover, the Nonconformist majority were reluctant to contribute financially to support a church whose ministry they did not benefit from and whose authority they did not wish to recognize. During the economic hardship which affected rural areas in the 1880s, tensions developed into heated protests during the Tithe Wars. Despite the passing of a Bill, on 22 March 1891, making the payment of tithes the responsibility of the landlord rather than the tenant, the conflict continued.[20]

In the wake of the increase in Nonconformity's political strength and the rise of the Liberal Party in Wales, it became possible to launch a strong parliamentary campaign in favour of the disestablishment of the church. By 1892, thirty-one Welsh MPs supported such a measure, with three expressing their opposition. And although the disestablishment issue had been simmering for half a century, around 1890 a new vehemence entered the campaign, with former leaders, people such as Henry Richard, Lewis Llewellyn Dillwyn, George Osborne Morgan and Stuart Rendel, withdrawing one by one, while a new generation of young leaders, such as Thomas Edward Ellis, Lloyd George and Herbert Lewis, took control.

In May 1890, the Calvinistic Methodist General Assembly passed a motion in favour of disestablishment,[21] and the Union of Welsh Independents and the Baptist Union passed similar motions, as did the Wesleyan regional meetings. At the same time the campaign to defend the church's interests underwent a radical transformation. Here too new leaders entered the fray. The most prominent among them were Alfred George Edwards and John Owen. Edwards was an Anglican of illustrious pedigree, originating from a family which had contributed at least twenty-five clergymen to the Anglican Church since 1825. John Owen was the son of Griffith Owen, a weaver and farmer from the Llŷn peninsula in north Wales, who was an elder in the Calvinistic Methodist chapel in Bwlch. During his time as a student in Oxford, John Owen had become an Anglican. Edwards was consecrated bishop of St Asaph on 25 March 1889, and he appointed Owen as dean, but he moved in 1891 to be the principal of St David's College, Lampeter, and in 1897 to become the bishop of St Davids.[22] They enjoyed a very close partnership, although personally they were very different indeed. Edwards was forceful, wholly indifferent to the feelings of others and in his element in the political fray, while Owen was a more sensitive soul. They were wholly united in their aim – to defend to the utmost all the privileges and resources of the church against all attacks. In their opinion, Wales and England were not two separate nations but one, and the Welsh dioceses were an integral part of the established church of the realm.

A. G. Edwards's vision was diametrically opposed to that of his brother Dean Henry T. Edwards. A. G. Edwards had not a shred of sympathy with the concept of a separate Welsh identity[23] while the younger patriots – now being dubbed 'Welsh Nationalists' – were very disappointed in John Owen's attitude towards Welsh issues.[24] There were some patriotic Welsh Anglicans who were sorely critical towards Edwards and Owen and their plans to defend the church. For Hartwell Jones (admittedly a biased witness),

Edwards, Owen and their supporters were 'a knot of ambitious clerics, with their headquarters at Lampeter and Llandovery, but little known outside College walls'.[25] Edwards insisted on unquestioning loyalty to his policy and he behaved very harshly towards the traditional defenders of the church, as shown by the treatment he meted out to David Howell (Llawdden), the patriotic archdeacon of St Asaph.[26]

On 26 January 1890, Howell was preaching at St Margaret's church, Westminster, as part of the effort to establish a Welshlanguage church for the London Welsh. He launched a scathing attack upon the Church in Wales for neglecting these Welsh people.[27] The bishop was furious and tried to abolish the post of archdeacon (which was created by his predecessor for Howell), but he discovered that it was legally impossible to do so.[28] Relations between them hardly improved when Howell sent a copy of the Nonconformist plan for Disestablishment to a friend of his. The bishop, incandescent with rage, accused him of treachery against the church. Howell vigorously denied the accusation.

> I am not in favour of disestablishment, but I am not deterred by my convictions on this question from criticizing the administrative policy that has prevailed in the Welsh church for the last 180 years: on the contrary, those convictions require that I should do so, as a reversal of that policy is imperatively demanded if the Church, established or disestablished, is ever to recover the allegiance of the people of Wales.[29]

Howell evidently had considerable sympathy with H. T. Edwards's ideas but the bishop did not wish to give them any credence at all. The dispute between the bishop and his archdeacon demonstrates the fact that there was no serious attempt on the part of religious leaders to try to agree on a policy which would be acceptable to church and chapel without recourse to the politicians. Rather they agreed to let the politicians settle the matter in their stead.

By this time there was no alternative to open war. There were two campaigns; the first lasted from 1890 to 1895 and the second from 1906 until the Disestablishment Act was passed.

The annual decision in favour of disestablishing the church was on the House of Commons' programme for 20 February 1891 and, to the surprise of many, Gladstone announced that he intended to vote for it. In his disappointment, John Owen demanded an interview with the prime minister and he asked him what effect, in his opinion, disestablishment would have on the Church in Wales. To this he replied: 'Death, Mr Dean, and then, resurrection!' Although he listened patiently to Owen's arguments, Gladstone voted in favour of the motion,[30] which was only defeated by a majority of thirty. Both parties were now vigorously engaged in making disestablishment an issue in English politics. The question was on what grounds could the disestablishment of that part of the Anglican Church in Wales be justified, without the disestablishment of the Church of England as well? The answer was that it could be justified on the grounds that Wales was a nation and that its national wishes should be respected when they differed from those of England. In the meetings of the Liberal Federation in Newcastle, on 1 and 2 October 1891, the principle was accepted that disestablishment was a Welsh issue and that, from then on, the Liberal Party should incorporate it into its policies. Stuart Rendel had already argued that the 'question of the disestablishment of the Church in Wales was inextricably linked to the principle of Welsh national identity'[31] and when Asquith came to speak in the second reading of the Disestablishment Bill in March 1895 he made the point in one of the most important clauses of his argument when he said, 'We assert that the Welsh people are a nation, whether you look at the test of race, religion, literature, temperament and genius, or national memories and traditions.'[32]

The supporters of disestablishment might have gained allies on the other side of Offa's Dyke, but so also had the defence. Osborne Morgan claimed that the turning point came during the Anglican Congress in Rhyl in October 1891 when a new policy was adopted calling for the assistance of 'a body of foreign auxiliaries' – a rather inappropriate reference since the disestablishmentarians had done the same![33] The archbishop of Canterbury responded with the declaration, 'I come from the steps of the chair of Augustine, your younger ally to tell you that, by the benediction of God, we will not quietly see you disinherited.'[34]

Gladstone became prime minister for the fourth time on 18 August 1892 and deemed that he had to give priority within the legislative programme to a suitable bill. On 31 January 1893 he informed Asquith that he intended to meet Welsh demands and with this intention the Suspensory Bill was drawn up which would prevent the creation of any 'new vested interests in the Welsh dioceses by the exercise of patronage'.[35] It passed its first reading, 23 February 1893, by 301 votes to 245. However, there was no second reading and the Bill was formally buried on 18 September. This Bill caused many Anglican leaders considerable anxiety, but there were some in the church who responded differently.[36] We gain a fascinating insight into events in a rural parish in the lively diary written by David Griffith (1841–1910), the curate of Pentraeth. His entry for 18 March 1893 reads:

> 'The sound of battle' – our Rector astir with the *Suspensory Bill Petition* – Would to God were he so active and enthusiastic anent the Spiritualities as he is now-a-days about the *Temporalities* of the *Church in Wales*. Felt sorry for such an *Erastian* zeal for the *Church* of *England*. Felt almost glad our strength was unequal to the task of 'hunting out' signatories for the Petition. Two Llanbedr youths, one a *Churchman* and the other a Chapel-man, relieved us entirely of the arduous task of *canvassing* the *Parish* . . .

Then there comes a cry from the heart: ' "Be spiritual, be spiritual" is the best *Church-Defence-Work*. "Above all things be spiritual." '[37]

This petition was one consequence of the wholesale overhaul of the organization of the anti-disestablishment campaign. On 4 March 1893, in a meeting organized by Archbishop Benson, Lord Salisbury pressed for a large-scale, organized, militant campaign, throughout the kingdom.[38] The Central Church Committee was formed in London to be the headquarters of the campaign and in 1896 the Church Defence Institution was merged with it. As a result of this enthusiasm mass meetings were held in Swansea, Caernarfon, Carmarthen and other places, culminating in a rally in the Albert Hall, London, on 16 May 1893.[39]

By this time, the supporters of disestablishment in Parliament and in the churches had become very frustrated. In Aberdare, on 14 August 1893, the Liberal Council of South Wales called on Members of Parliament to form an independent political party unless disestablishment was placed at the top of the legislative programme for the following session.[40] The MPs agreed, with the exception of Bryn Roberts. The critical turning point came in their meeting on 1 September. David Randell, a Calvinistic Methodist and the member for Gower, wanted to form an independent Welsh party immediately and D. A. Thomas wanted to form one if a firm promise was not obtained for a bill for the following session of Parliament. However, the motion proposed by Lloyd George and T. E. Ellis was carried, namely to maintain the status quo but that the policy should be reconsidered if it became clear that the government would not give a guarantee that the Disestablishment Bill would be passed before the end of the following session.[41] All this did was postpone the outburst for a few weeks.

There was a threatening tone at the meetings of the North Wales Liberal League in Newtown on 8 February 1894. Within a month, however, on 3 March, Gladstone had retired and Lord Rosebery was prime minister. What would his attitude be? The majority of Welsh MPs were willing to trust him on the matter of disestablishment but a minority were sceptical and in mid-April rebellion broke out when Lloyd George, Frank Edwards, D. A. Thomas and David Randell informed their party whip that he could no longer rely on their vote in the house. On 14 April, amid scenes of great enthusiasm, Lloyd George explained to his electors in Caernarfon why he had decided that 'the Welsh party should form an independent party'.[42] By the middle of May, J. Herbert Lewis had joined the rebels and meetings were held in various places to explain their position.[43] The government responded by introducing a Disestablishment Bill,[44] stating that the church was to be disestablished on New Year's Day, 1896, but hopes were dashed once more. By 18 July it became known that there would not be a second reading.

On 25 February 1895, H. H. Asquith introduced his second Disestablishment Bill,[45] which was effectively the same as the first.[46] It passed its second reading on 1 April and went to committee, where it soon got into difficulties because Lloyd George and D. A. Thomas wanted to amend it against the government's wishes. Lloyd George wanted the money received from the disendowment of the church to be administered not by commissioners as the government insisted, but by a council elected by the county councils of Wales.[47] According to Lloyd George, his intention in proposing this was to move a step closer to self-government for Wales.[48] Whatever his motives, it was only to be expected that the Conservatives would take advantage of dissension among the Liberals. They insisted on voting on the amendment and it was only by voting against his own amendment that Lloyd George was able to save the administration. The Bill suffered increasing difficulties and when the House was unexpectedly divided, the government was defeated and forced to resign and the second Disestablishment Bill perished. This, the first act in the play, was gripping not only because the House had been forced to focus its attention on an issue of Welsh interest and because an independent Welsh party, albeit short-lived, had appeared on the political stage, but because the 'Nonconformist Conscience', as it came to be known during these years, had had an opportunity to show its political muscle.[49]

With a Conservative victory in the subsequent election, the subject of disestablishment was set to one side and 'the partisans of the Establishment said that it was as dead as Queen Anne'.[50] This was not completely true since the fierce battle against the 1902 Education Act was in reality another aspect of the same issue. But there was no hope for any kind of legislation on disestablishment for ten years.

With the landslide Liberal victory in 1906 when all the Welsh seats were seized by Liberals, the second act of the play began. The disestablishmentarians were hoping to see rapid progress, but so many topics were competing for attention that there was nothing for it but to be patient. The government, and Lloyd George particularly, wanted to settle the matter as quietly as possible and were even willing to compromise. As a result, Lloyd George suggested that a Royal Commission be appointed to inquire into the contribution of the various churches to the spiritual life of Wales.[51] The Commission was authorized on 21 June 1906. Its chairman was Judge Roland Lomax Bowdler Vaughan-Williams,[52] and the members were Hugh Cecil, Sir John Williams, Frank Edwards, Archdeacon Owen Evans, S. T. Evans, A. M. Fairbairn, the principal of Mansfield College, Oxford, John Ernest Greaves, Criccieth, and Henry Jones, the philosopher.

The appointment of the Commission caused general bewilderment. The Anglicans were genuinely suspicious of it and the Nonconformists could not see the need for it since the Welsh had left no doubt as to their opinion on the subject in the general election. The religious bodies vacillated between hope and impatience and 1907 was a year when patience was wearing seriously thin. One example of the rising dissatisfaction was the detailed and scathing report presented to the Union of Welsh Independents. Like the other denominations, it had appointed a committee in 1906 to prepare evidence for the Royal Commission. That committee submitted a report to the Union conference in Neath on 25 June 1907, three days after Campbell-Bannerman announced in the House of Commons that there would be no Disestablishment Bill in 1907. The committee complained bitterly about the Royal Commission, about its lack of courtesy in the way it treated witnesses and the chairman's prejudice in rejecting relevant evidence. The committee's opinion was that the Commission's labours would lead to 'a superficial and ineffective investigation'. Indeed, its dilatoriness suggested that there would be no Disestablishment Bill in the near future.

The committee threatened not to give evidence at all to the Commission, and it was only after the chairman promised changes that the committee members were mollified. However, there was no improvement and so the committee urged the Union 'in the present serious crisis' to insist that all the denominations 'take stronger, more emphatic and effective' measures to secure a Bill to disestablish the church. The blame for the delay can be placed first on MPs, secondly on the government and thirdly on Nonconformists themselves because of their reluctance to speak out. The Union accepted the report and passed two motions, one castigating the Royal Commission and MPs, the other calling for a more militant battle in the country and for a promise from the prime minister that a Bill would be passed 'during the present Parliament'.[53]

A fortnight previously in Llandeilo, the Calvinistic Methodist General Assembly had passed a more moderate motion but had informed MPs that any further delay would mean deliberately ignoring the wishes of the Welsh people.[54] There is no doubt that all the religious bodies throughout Wales were hopping mad during the summer of 1907 and there was every sign that they were becoming seriously disillusioned. The purpose of the mass national conference in Cardiff on 10 October was to express their general bitterness and give the MPs a fright, but it did not turn out thus. Lloyd George made careful preparations in advance to pacify the leaders and the flames of rebellion were extinguished by his sweeping rhetoric.[55] The results were soon evident. In September, the Baptist Union was still 'breathing out threats'. By the middle of October even Principal William Edwards, one of the main leaders of the Disestablishment campaign, was keeping a low profile and Y Greal was hailing Lloyd George as a 'man of the nation'. In an even more bizarre turn of events, the Baptist Union of Wales honoured Lloyd George by electing him president.[56]

The critics in Wales may have been disarmed but the government could not ignore them for ever. When H. H. Asquith became prime minister in April 1908 and Lloyd George was promoted to chancellor of the exchequer, the prospects for disestablishment began to look rosier. On 21 April 1909, Asquith introduced a Disestablishment Bill into the House of Commons but nothing came of it. As always, Westminster's interest in any topic directly concerning Wales was brief and fickle and the turmoil caused by Lloyd George's financial bills swept all other bills into oblivion. On 15 June it was announced that there were no plans to proceed with the Disestablishment Bill.

The Royal Commission continued to sit, lurching from crisis to crisis. Whatever Vaughan-Williams's talents were, chairing a commission was not one of them. He insisted on putting the narrowest possible interpretation on the guidance given to the Commission. He was abrupt with witnesses, interrupting them and arbitrarily cutting short their evidence, and he was harsh to the point of rudeness when the members of the Commission tried to question witnesses. Everyone, whatever their religious allegiance, became completely disenchanted with him. By April 1907, three Nonconformist members of the Commission had resigned, namely S. T. Evans, Henry Jones and A. M. Fairbairn. J. H. Davies, Brynmor Jones and J. Morgan Gibbon were appointed to take their place. The report was finally published, dated 1 November 1910. It was a meagre volume, a mere seventy-seven pages and the Chairman and J. E. Greaves were the only ones who agreed with every word in it. However, the other members insisted on including six additional treatises, comprising more than 315 pages, offering their observations on the evidence collected. It was all very confused and completely irrelevant to the ongoing political battle. The best that can be said about the eight volumes of the report is that they are a fount of invaluable information to those who wish to familiarize themselves with Welsh religion during this period.

The rest of the story can be summarized in a few sentences. The Disestablishment Bill was introduced once again on 23 April 1912 by Reginald McKenna. It received its second reading from 13 to 16 May and was passed by 348 votes to 267. As it happened, the 250th Jubilee of the 'Great Ejection' fell in 1912 and the Nonconformists set about celebrating with great enthusiasm. Mass meetings were held in Swansea and Caernarfon in July to praise the great men of the past and to encourage the struggle for disestablishment,[57] and appropriate pamphlets were published to mark the occasion. On 4 February 1913, the Disestablishment Bill passed its third reading and 'Hen Wlad fy Nhadau' was sung in the House.[58] As might be expected, it was rejected by the House of Lords on 13 February 1913 by 252 votes to 51. According to the provisions of Parliamentary Law, it had to be passed three times by the House of Commons before the House of Lords was obliged to pass it. This process was complied with and on 18 September 1914 the Bill received royal assent. Because War had broken out, implementation of the Act was postponed until its conclusion and the Church in Wales came into being as an independent province within the Anglican communion on 1 April 1920. Its former endowments – those it had received before 1662 and which were worth about four million pounds – were secularized by sharing them between the county councils, the University of Wales and the National Library.

The achievement of disestablishment was probably the last victory for old radicalism. It was an expression of the conviction that there were defined limits to state authority and that it should not interfere in the religious life of its subjects. Yet during this period, as we shall see, the state was extending its authority to new areas and even interfering more and more powerfully in the beliefs of its subjects (albeit not their religious beliefs) through the new educational system. Gradually the descendants of traditional radicalism abandoned their previous doubts over the influence of the state and began to view it rather as a valuable tool for securing social reforms. The truth is that they were very confused about the concept of the state. In any debate on its relationship with the churches, they could see the way ahead quite clearly. However, when we begin to examine the attitude of Welsh Christians to their own national identity their indecision becomes evident.

Initially many believed that the differences between England and Wales were to be safeguarded. Henry Richard for instance said 'We do not wish for Wales to be swallowed up by England', yet he had little concept of Welsh national identity as an entity which needed to be expressed by particular political institutions.[59] For the young nationalists, Richard could never be the O'Connell or Parnell of Wales because 'his spirit was not sufficiently Welsh'.[60] Traditional radicalism, then, held that the chief aim of politics was to secure for the Welsh people the same privileges and the same freedom from oppression as the English enjoyed. Their 'national characteristics' were their own affair. Men such as A. G. Edwards and John Thomas, Liverpool, took a closely related position. In his sermon on 'True Patriotism', Thomas took it for granted that there was no real difference between the Welsh and the English and claimed that 'the true patriot is the man who consecrates himself to the moral and religious service of his country'.[61] It did not cross his mind that one's attitude towards language and nationality could be a moral issue. John Thomas believed of Wales and England 'that we are one great British nation'.[62] Henry Jones, the philosopher, went as far as to make nationality a wholly subjective concept. It is the 'Patriotic Spirit', he said, that binds 'people as one body, that makes the Welsh people into a nation'.[63] Once this idea had taken hold, it was easy to devalue the objective elements that constitute a nation and make such dubious claims as 'Our nationality does not depend on our language.'[64] This kind of reasoning led to some remarkable confusion. J. Glyn Davies of Newport, for instance, wrote that the Welsh language was not necessary to the 'Welsh spirit' and that religion was more important than language, while at the same time expressing his support for nationalism.[65] His topic was English-language churches in Wales and it was very fashionable in that context to say that safeguarding religion was more important than safeguarding language. Were it a matter of placing a list of values in order of priority, no Christian would disagree. The strange thing is that this argument was used invariably *against* the Welsh language and never against English. People were extremely sensitive in case the state abused its power in the life of the church, believing that its powers in this respect must be curtailed. However, they were ambivalent at best when considering the right of the English state to overrule the ancient language of the people of Wales. If the state angered God by favouring one religious creed over another, did it please God by favouring one language at the expense of the other?

If we are to understand the mindset of the period, it is important to realize that these questions hardly occurred to the majority of Christian leaders in Wales. Admittedly there were certain individuals, such as Kilsby Jones and John Roberts (J.R.), who believed that the demise of Welsh would be a good thing, usually for wholly commercial reasons. There were other people, some of them fervent supporters of Welsh, who wanted the best of both worlds.

They wanted the language to have a more prominent place in schools, for instance, but they also believed that Wales should send more of her children 'to rule and civilize the colonies'.[66] According to John Hugh Edwards, the Welsh were supposed to make their major contribution not at home in Wales but out in the world, like the Scots.[67] Such ambition meant that it was natural to argue that 'we are first and foremost British' and that 'we are not a nation at all in a political sense' and that we should not be a nation in this sense either.[68] Thus it is worth remembering that many people who called themselves 'nationalists' in 1895 or thereabouts were far removed from being everything that this word would mean by the middle of the twentieth century. They were Romantics who cultivated a 'Welsh spirit' – no more than that – and they had little grasp of the nation as an objective form of society and no concept whatsoever of the significance of either its culture or its history.

On the other hand, there were thinkers who were true nationalists. This could involve taking a very critical attitude towards England, as in the address by David James (Dewi o Ddyfed) which has already been quoted, when he said in 1859, 'The English government's policy towards the Welsh people is to eradicate them'.[69] It could also mean declaring forthrightly that Wales was a nation and that political self-government was one of the essentials of national life.[70] Among the religious leaders, Michael D. Jones occupies a unique position in the history of the development of modern Welsh nationalism. For one thing, the roots of his teaching are unmistakably Christian. He insisted that God is sovereign over society in exactly the same way as he is sovereign over each individual, and that his moral law binds societies as surely as it binds individuals.

> When the moral law says, 'Do not steal', people believe that the government is free to steal lands and kingdoms as much as it can, while boasting of the courage, the arrogance and the skill shown in doing this. For my part I believe that everyone is subject to the same moral rule, individuals as well as any number of people who have covenanted together and governments are bound by exactly the same rule as persons.[71]

Thus he fiercely rejected any attempt to justify immorality merely because the state authorizes it. He wrote, quite provocatively, that if a man wished to kill and then avoid punishment, he should 'kill to order, and in the name of Government, and after that not only will he escape censure, but he will be well-paid for killing, especially if he kills thousands in war'.[72] People criticized Parnell for his adultery with Mrs O'Shea but how many of these protested against Gladstone's actions in 'firebombing' Alexandria? 'Now then, was corrupting one woman, and wrecking one family through adultery the greater sin, or shooting thousands of patriotic people down for defending their rights and their homes?'[73] Michael D. Jones based his tireless polemic against English imperialism on this emphasis on the social requirements of the moral law. The way the English and the Germans spoke of spreading the gospel by means of their imperialist conquests angered him deeply. 'The only difference between the English and the Germans is that the English are more deceitful and more learned in the art of cunning than the German, but both of them are well-versed in the bloody art of the gun.'[74] All empires were wicked because 'the Great Babylon of the Bible is a conquering government, with which all the kings of the earth fornicated' and, as a result, the British Empire was not something to be proud of but something deeply to be regretted.[75]

Implicit in these convictions was his Christian humanism. The creator gave human beings a task when he created them and that task is to produce culture. In the course of history the human family, as it attempted to fulfil this task, has developed into nations. It is a kind of blasphemy on the part of one of these nations to presume that the creator entrusted the cultural task to itself and not to other nations. The English were deeply entrenched in this blasphemy because they 'have never taken heed of the Bible's teaching, that man, and not the Englishman, is Lord of creation'.[76] Every nation had its part to play in this general task and as individuals were supposed to respect one another, in accordance with moral law, so too were nations.

> The English have assumed that it is their prerogative to govern the earth, and that their language is to be the only language of the world . . . But the gospel of our Lord Jesus Christ has declared love and righteousness as the great law of the human family . . .[77]

From such principles, Michael D. Jones developed a strong notion of Wales's uniqueness as a nation. His departure from the individualism of the old radicalism is evident. Humankind is a family of nations and in order for Wales to contribute to that family's life it must have its own government because 'if self-government is valuable to the Englishman, is self-government not equally valuable to the Welshman?'[78] The fact that the Irish, the Scots and the Welsh were represented in the London Parliament was of no value because they only had 'representation to have what the majority in England choose to have for themselves, or what that majority in its grace and mercy would choose to give to us'.[79] Despite this, Michael D. Jones placed the emphasis on freedom, rather than on independence. The human family is one and it is a form of disrespect for other nations to wish to be completely independent of them. As for the relationship between Wales and England, he said, 'For my part, I am very eager to continue the union', but on Wales's terms.[80]

Although Michael D. Jones expressed his ideas in a flood of articles rather than in books, there is no denying the powerful consistency of his Christian vision. Michael D. Jones takes a place of honour among those European thinkers who have argued for a pluralist, multicentric social pattern – people like Althusius, Lammenais, Groen van Prinsterer and Abraham Kuyper – but the bias towards the common people is more evident in his work. Taking his thought as a whole, it can be seen that it cuts across the conventional divisions between Liberals, Tories and radicals. This is possibly why few of his contemporaries understood properly what he meant.

One who supported Michael D. Jones's position was Robert Ambrose Jones (Emrys ap Iwan). Michael D. Jones assumed that his younger compatriot had, to some extent, come under his influence,[81] but whether this was true or not, there were great similarities between the conceptual framework of both men. Emrys ap Iwan also rejected every attempt to centralize authority and it is significant that he was censured by the Calvinistic Methodist Association because 'his ideas on the nature and organization of the church lead to Congregationalism'.[82] The weave of his doctrine was also unmistakably Christian. Like Michael D. Jones, he emphasized the responsibility placed by God on the whole of humankind. As he said in his sermon, 'The New and the Old Learning': 'Remember first of all that you are *men*, of the same blood as the English, the Boers, the Kaffirs and the Chinese; therefore, be prepared to grant them the privileges that you wish for yourselves.' God is the Creator, Sustainer and Governor and human history shows the mark of his handiwork. Thus Emrys ap Iwan urged his readers, 'Remember in the second place, that you are a nation by God's ordinance; therefore do what you can to keep the nation inviolate, by nurturing its language and every other valuable thing that belongs to it.'[83]

One prominent aspect of his moral passion was his anger against the Welsh for neglecting their nationality:

> By now, most of the nation's idolatry runs along two channels – Love of Money and Worshipping the English! Instead of sharing their heart as before between many gods, the Welsh have now concentrated all their love on two calves – the golden calf and the English calf.[84]

Grovelling in this way showed a lack of dignity. He tried to convince people how much they had to be proud of in their national heritage and, especially, in their language. For him, it was pure folly to suppose that Welsh nationality could be safeguarded without the language, even if self-government were obtained.

> Remember that the God who made men also ordained nations; and the destruction of a nation is a disaster second only to the destruction of humankind, and the destruction of a nation's language is a disaster second only to the destruction of the nation, because a nation ceases to be a nation not long after it loses its language.[85]

Moreover, Emrys ap Iwan's nationalism was political nationalism. A national parliament was needed and it was needed urgently. Wales, he said, 'under the present disadvantages is becoming daily more Anglicized with regard to its language, its character and its practices; and what benefit would self-government be to it were it to lose its national attributes?' Local councils and free education were part of the deception practised by the conquerors in order to hide the fact that the nation was being destroyed politically and culturally.[86] However, he argued for a federal system, rather than full independence and he was not optimistic that self-government could be obtained by fair means. 'Our freedom was stolen from us by violent means, and there is room to fear that it is by violent means that it will be regained.'[87] Nevertheless, the first step was to reject the pattern of English nationalism. Wales must prepare to fight not against specific parties but 'against a whole nation', namely England, and 'there should be two political parties in Wales, namely a Welsh party and an Anti-Welsh party'.[88]

What influence did Michael D. Jones and Emrys ap Iwan's ideas have on their contemporaries? Both faced vicious criticism during their lifetimes but their influence could be seen on individuals in many circles. Their contribution certainly strengthened the national consciousness. Michael D. Jones was the father of one of the most remarkable national experiments during the century, the Welsh colony in Patagonia. His influence was also evident on the Cymru Fydd (Young Wales) Movement and its attempt to seize the reins of power from the Welsh Liberal Party,[89] but this campaign fell apart in the midst of the conflict between Lloyd George and D. A. Thomas, a man 'to whom nationalism meant little'.[90]

Michael D. Jones and Emrys ap Iwan also influenced the cultural wing of the national movement, organizations such as Cymdeithas yr Iaith Gymraeg (the Welsh Language Society), and many individuals such as O. M. Edwards, Beriah Gwynfe Evans, Keinion Thomas, Miall Edwards, J. E. Lloyd, Llewelyn Williams, T. E. Ellis, John Morris Jones, Puleston Jones, T. Gwynn Jones and others. Very few people, however, realized the significance of Michael D. Jones's comprehensive Christian philosophy as an attempt to meet all facets of the challenge that was looming before Wales. Both he and Emrys ap Iwan had realized that the Welsh were rapidly becoming a people with divided minds and thus were developing a dichotomy in their souls. They wanted to be both Welsh and English, or 'British' as they described it at the time, and there were considerable differences of opinion among them concerning how much of either they wanted. Both Michael D. Jones and Emrys ap Iwan realized the importance of making the nation's mindset whole again.

This dichotomy of thinking can be seen in people's attitude towards the Welsh language. There was a total of 898,914 Welsh-speakers in 1891 and 929,183 in 1911. The number of Welsh-speakers therefore was continuing to increase at the beginning of the twentieth century. It was only afterwards that it began to decrease. The danger was that the proportion of Welsh-speakers in the whole population was decreasing. It was truly a crucial time.

Some welcomed the decline. Daniel Lewis, the rector of Merthyr Tudful, told the Royal Commission on Education that no effort should be made to teach Welsh in schools: 'the language is a spoken one; it really has no body of literature of its own'.[91] Such a comment showed appalling ignorance, which was a direct result of the deficiencies in his own education. As well as ideas like this, there existed the belief that the decline of the language was inevitable.[92] Many agreed with the Baptist David Powell, Liverpool, when he said, regarding the language's decline, 'it should not be hurried, and it should not be delayed'.[93] This belief rested on two tenets, first, the *laissez-faire* philosophy of traditional radicalism, that languages, like goods, had to compete together on the free market and that Welsh had no hope in this regard against English, and secondly, on Darwinism, the belief in the survival of the fittest and that the English language was more suited than Welsh to the modern world. The Welsh were told countless times that they needed English to 'get on in the world' and when this incentive was combined with the two beliefs already mentioned, a powerful conviction was fostered in Welsh minds that the bulk of the Welsh nation could not enjoy the privileges and advantages of the modern world while it continued to be monoglot Welsh. The fact that the intelligentsia believed this put paid to any serious attempt to make Welsh an effective means of transmitting the riches of education to the Welsh people and it completely deterred any effort on the part of the government and local authorities to make Welsh a medium of administration. This bundle of superstitions was like a deadly cancer in Welsh thinking.

This shows once again how this basic dichotomy in Welsh minds caused a split in the life of the nation. William Rees (Gwilym Hiraethog), for instance, could warn that one of Satan's wiles was to deprive the Welsh people of their language,[94] and yet he corresponded in English with his daughters and even composed English prayers for pupils in their school in Porthmadog.[95] Many such examples could be given,[96] although as a rule Anglican priests were more eager than Nonconformist ministers to speak and correspond with one another in English.[97]

Bilingualism became very popular as a solution to the language problem. Dan Isaac Davies was the main spokesman for the campaign with his slogan, 'Three million bilingual Welsh people in a hundred years.'[98] But this was not bilingualism in the sense that Welsh and English should be given equal status. What it involved, in reality, was an attempt to identify some particular domains within national life where a place for Welsh could be secured. It is true that there are many instances of protests where the Welsh language had been denigrated by public officials and by the courts of law, but there was no general call for Welsh to be given status in public life. Indeed the National Eisteddfod from time to time was in danger of turning completely to English, as when the twelve presidents at the Brecon Eisteddfod (1889) gave their address in that language.[99]

Ironically, one sphere that witnessed a slight softening in attitude was education. The 1870 Education Act had not made any provision for teaching the Welsh language or Welsh history but by the time the new system had become established some had come to realize how perilous this situation was. Even Beriah Gwynfe Evans forbade the children at his school in Gwynfe to speak Welsh, until a small boy arrived late and was unable to explain to the teacher in his sketchy English that the reason for this was that he had been sick on the way. 'That, I think, was the last time I ever enforced the rule that Welsh should be excluded from my school', he said in his evidence to the Royal Commission for Education in April 1887.[100]

Beriah Evans made generous recompense for this by devoting his long life to the service of the language. In August 1885, he became the first secretary of the Welsh Language Society formed during the Aberdare National Eisteddfod on 19 September 1885. Papers published by David Jones Davies, the rector of North Benfleet, Essex, and Professor Thomas Powell, Cardiff, in *Y Cymmrodor* (1882) provided a spur for Henry Tobit Evans to ask Dan Isaac Davies to convene the meeting, and 'The Society for the Utilization of the Welsh Language' was formed, with Archdeacon John Griffiths as president.[101]

Small changes gradually came about in the education system. In 1886 inspectors were permitted to test children's intelligence through the medium of Welsh. In 1890, the Education Board's instructions permitted schools to teach the language as a 'special subject' in standards 5, 6, and 7 and four shillings were received for every pupil who was successful in the examination.[102] All this meant was that Welsh was treated in the same way as foreign languages. Then in 1893, Arthur Hart Dyke Acland (who knew a little Welsh) agreed to make it a class subject.[103] The Welsh language had a consistently inferior status. It is no wonder that O. M. Edwards said that 'day schools kill the Welsh language.'[104] The problem was that teaching the language was optional for local authorities and for teachers. Llywelyn Williams argued that 'the children of English people should be forced to learn Welsh in the bilingual regions of Wales',[105] and Michael D. Jones and Emrys ap Iwan took it for granted that this should be the case, but few agreed with them. There is considerable evidence that it was the local education authorities and the teachers who were dragging their feet rather than the parents raising objections. When a questionnaire was organized in Cardiff on the issue in 1897, 81 per cent of the parents wanted their children to study Welsh in schools.[106] Yet, according to H. M. Hughes, a minister in Cardiff, 'the teachers succeeded in turning the effort into a failure within two years'.[107] They did not get their own way, for the campaign recommenced and by 1907 there were 14,000 children learning the language in the city's schools.[108] However, the situation was still very unsatisfactory. The Board of Education reported in 1899 that the language was only taught as a subject in twenty-eight elementary and secondary schools out of 1,419. The situation was woeful in Carmarthenshire, for instance. Of the 149 schools in the country in 1903, as many as 111 of them taught no Welsh at all.[109]

On the whole, the religious bodies lent their enthusiastic support to the new developments. The Union of Welsh Independents set up an Education Sub-Committee to observe the activity of the school boards and encourage pressure to be placed on those of them that neglected their opportunities[110] and in 1904 the Union passed a motion calling on Welsh to be made 'an essential part of the regular education course provided in every educational institution'.[111] There was fierce criticism of the anti-Welsh attitude of some of the school inspectors[112] and there was an occasional heartfelt cry, like the one for a 'wholesale change, a change which will be tantamount to a revolution' in education by teaching children in Welsh instead of English from the commencement of their education.[113] Admittedly only a minority in the Church in Wales shared the enthusiasm of Archdeacon John Griffiths. Dean Shadrach Pryce, St Asaph, maintained that 'teaching Welsh as an independent subject . . . was not in harmony with the feelings and wishes of the Welsh'.[114] Indeed one Anglican maintained that 'the true patriots of Wales are the men who gave and who give their influence, their money and their time to teach English to the common folk of Wales'.[115] This attitude is reflected in the Anglican schools in Carmarthenshire; out of fifty-one in the county in 1903 only one taught the language.

If there was a willingness to allow the Welsh language a toehold in the elementary schools this was scarcely true of other organizations. Of the ninety secondary schools in Wales in 1906, forty-two of them taught no Welsh at all and of the 10,000 pupils, 2,000 received instruction in Welsh and only 500 sat the examinations.[116] The situation was very unsatisfactory in the teacher training colleges as well. J. Lloyd Williams commented that during his time in the Normal College, Bangor, 'I did not officially hear one word about Wales, or about the Welsh language, or about one Welsh melody'.[117] The University of Wales was little better. It is true that departments taught Welsh as a subject, but through the medium of English alone. When the issue of teaching Welsh history as a subject was raised, no one was more implacably opposed to this than the teaching staff themselves.[118] This raises an issue which is hard to fathom. When the University of Wales was formed on the basis of the university colleges of Aberystwyth, Bangor and Cardiff, it was widely touted as a national university. According to Thomas Charles Edwards: 'If we are not a nation, the reason is that we have neither colleges nor a university to create and develop our cultural life. With a National University, we will make ourselves into a nation.'[119]

It is true that Aberystwyth particularly raised up men who were inspired to give excellent service to Wales, men such as O. M. Edwards, J. E. Lloyd, T. F. Roberts, T. E. Ellis and others. Despite the general situation, at least some of the students showed enthusiasm for nationalism. On this basis W. Llywelyn Williams argued that the new university should give a privileged place to the Welsh language and its literature in its course of studies[120] and with the passage of time the Welsh departments did accomplish invaluable work. However, the University of Wales and its constituent colleges was a completely Anglicized institution from the outset. When H. M. Hughes said of the university, 'It is far too foreign as it is and it needs a breeze of Welshness',[121] his comments were not without foundation. One writer claimed that the staff of the colleges of Aberystwyth, Bangor and Cardiff wanted to 'exile everything Welsh from the institution and Anglicize or Continentalize everything concerned with education'. Neither David Adams nor Silyn Roberts were prepared to acknowledge this, but they offered a lame defence.[122] Y Faner did publish a letter under the heading 'The English College, Bangor', but Thomas Gee, the editor at the time, was goaded by his concern over the appointment of English people rather than for the position of the Welsh language within the college.[123] All things considered, the architects of the University of Wales had a strange concept of what a national university should be.

The issue of the Welsh language in the churches must now be considered. One of the providential workings in the history of the language was that Nonconformist churches had committed themselves to accomplish by far the largest part of their work through the medium of Welsh and that the Church in Wales also held innumerable Welsh-language services. The denominations were large corporations and the work of their courts and committees was conducted entirely through the medium of Welsh. Whatever the leaders' abstract ideas about the language, the fact was that church life, for the thousands who participated in it, was a great continent of Welshness, not to mention, of course, the great sum of Welsh literature produced consistently by the churches, both books and periodicals.

Despite this, Nonconformist churches did not escape some upheavals with regard to the language. In the 'Battle of the Constitutions', which tore the Independents asunder between 1879 and 1892, one cause of dissension among many was the attitude of both parties to the Welsh language. The general of the 'Old Constitution Party', Michael D. Jones, insisted that one of the objectives of his main opponent, John Thomas, Liverpool, the leader of the 'Party of the New Constitution', was the Anglicization of the Welsh-language Independents and the 'Liverpoolization' of Wales. He was particularly scathing about the support of the New Constitution for the movement for the establishment of English-language chapels. According to Michael D. Jones, they tried to destroy Welsh national identity 'by evicting our language from the pulpits of Wales, under the guise of evangelizing English people and establishing English causes but in reality they make Wales less Welsh'.[124] When he heard that Disraeli wanted to make English the official language of Cyprus, he suggested that the island would be an excellent field for the Anglicizing wing of the Union of Welsh Independents![125] The history of the 'English Cause' among the Calvinistic Methodists was similar if more dramatic because it led to the decision to refuse to approve Emrys ap Iwan's ordination to the ministry in 1881. He had already published scintillating articles criticizing the establishment of English-language churches and had provoked the foremost leader of the movement, Lewis Edwards, to order churches not to invite him to preach. Although Owen

Thomas tried assiduously in a lengthy cross-examination before the association to persuade Emrys ap Iwan to keep silent on the matter of the English-language causes, he failed to achieve his aim.[126] It should be pointed out that Michael D. Jones and Emrys ap Iwan were not objecting to the English providing chapels for themselves, but they were complaining vociferously because the Welsh were doing the work for them and even sending their own church members to form the nucleus of an English-language congregation. By the turn of the century a much more complex difficulty was facing the Welsh denominations, namely the Anglicization of Welsh-language congregations through the loss of the language. This issue increasingly became a topic for debate and there were attempts to draft suitable measures to increase knowledge of the language. In 1902, for instance, the Cardiff Union of Welsh Sabbath Schools was very concerned about the ability of its pupils to sit their examinations through the medium of Welsh.[127] In 1914, the East Glamorgan Monthly Meeting insisted on holding an investigation into the situation of Welsh in the churches[128] and the following year the Eastern Assembly of the Glamorgan Baptists published the results of their research into the same subject.[129] In an attempt to resolve the same problem the Liverpool Union of Sabbath Schools published a handbook for learning Welsh.[130] There was no clear vision on the subject and the tendency was merely to encourage parents to safeguard the language in the home.

The Catholic Church had no experience of this particular problem because the mass was celebrated in Latin and there were very few Welsh-speaking Catholics. Nevertheless they undertook to publish a few handbooks in Welsh, mainly with a missionary bias.[131]

The Church in Wales was a bilingual church with regard to its laws and constitution and in this respect it was not concerned by the 'language problem'. However, by the turn of the century the anti-Welsh attitude of some of its leaders infuriated many rank-and-file Welsh Anglicans. In 1886, for instance, the following words, which have already been quoted, were written about the diocese of St Asaph, 'very little that is popular and concerned with the *Welsh language* or *culture* goes on in the Annual Conference . . . all *the work* is carried on in English'.[132] Only eight years later Robert Williams, Dolwyddelan, complained vociferously about the Anglicization of the Bangor diocesan conference.[133]

No one pleaded more fervently for the church to change its ways than T. Edwin Jones, the vicar of St Mary's, Bangor. He lamented that there was not a single Welsh-language service in any of the four cathedrals, apart from the parish services in Bangor and St Davids.[134] In his St David's Day sermon in Manchester in 1894, he said, 'We would like to see our cathedrals made truly national, with a cathedral service in the Welsh language being held in every one of them.'[135] In 1898 there was a harsh attack on Bishop John Owen – 'the national party in the Church has nothing to expect from Bishop Owen'[136] – but on Trinity Sunday 1901 he held an ordination service in Welsh and one correspondent believed that this was the first time that this had ever happened.[137] On the whole, however, the Welsh language suffered within the Anglican Church because so many of the leaders were indifferent towards, or disparaging of, it.[138]

Ever since New Testament times, the church reckoned that its disciplinary system was a valuable tool to protect its boundary with the world outside. By the end of the nineteenth century in Wales this system had declined in all the churches. Over generations the courts of the Church of England had lost their cutting edge and the sight of offenders making public penance in churches in a white garment and a candle in their hand belonged to the distant past. The Puritans were scathing of the church for its disciplinary weakness but since they themselves had now abandoned their sectarian characteristics and become denominations, they were also treading the path of tolerance. This wholesale change occurred during the Victorian age. In 1850 the Methodists of Rehoboth, Corris, could excommunicate Jane, the mother of John Roberts, the famous missionary in India, for marrying a man 'who did not profess faith',[139] but when a similar motion was placed before the *seiat* of Engedi, Caernarfon, less than fifty years later, it was rejected.[140]

By this time, crimes of immorality and drunkenness received the most attention. The North Wales Association heard in 1899 in relation to Merioneth, 'The two sins that devastate the church are drunkenness and wantonness, the latter more than the former'.[141] In 1889, the Merioneth Calvinistic Methodists had excommunicated 2.5 per cent of their members in the Vale of Ardudwy, 2 per cent in Dolgellau and 1.6 per cent in Ffestiniog, almost all for immorality.[142] These disciplinary measures did not stem from puritan sexual fantasies; the situation was dire in some places. For instance, one in seven children in the parish of Llanfihangel-y-traethau was illegitimate.[143]

At the same time, religious leaders were increasingly realizing that poor social conditions were an invitation to immorality. In the large towns prostitution was a cause for concern. For instance, in 1897 seventy-three Welsh women were summoned before the magistrates in Liverpool for offering their services as prostitutes on the streets.[144] Religious people were no longer content merely to condemn but searched for ways to help these women. Mrs William Edwards, the wife of the principal of Cardiff Baptist College, made strenuous efforts to rehabilitate girls who had become prostitutes.[145] A strictly moralistic attitude continued to be prevalent with calls for the harsher application of the punishment laws against those convicted of sexual offences, for instance by the Calvinistic Methodist General Assembly in 1911,[146] yet at the same time there was an increasing appreciation among religious leaders that social circumstances affected moral behaviour and that these had to be improved.

Regarding drunkenness, this had been well understood for years. Although moral condemnation of this evil was still quite common, temperance movements offered alcoholics interests other than those afforded by the public houses. The temperance movement reached its peak in the early part of the twentieth century[147] but it had been gaining strength ever since the 1830s. To those who knew it in the years of its weakness and decline, it is difficult to believe that it was once a very popular movement, with very innovative means of communication and giving pleasure to thousands. In many churches the 'Band of Hope' became the usual name for the children's meeting. On the whole, it was a cheerful and lively movement and there were occasional complaints that temperance meetings consisted of entertainment only.[148] Of course the movement had its fanatics, people of whom it could be said that 'temperance was their religion',[149] but many more enjoyed themselves immensely in the movement's activities and there is no doubt that it was a means of freeing thousands from the clutches of alcohol.

The movement gave people the opportunity to come together, to partake of dignified ceremonies, to wear colourful robes and revel in pompous titles. At the same time, they were able to save money because of the work of movements such as the Rechabites and the Good Templars. By the beginning of the twentieth century the Rechabites had overtaken other thrift societies and were growing rapidly. By 1894, the Gwent and East Glamorgan district, with 6,000 members, was the largest in the world, except for Victoria, Australia.[150] The Good Templars came a close second. The Welsh Higher Temple was established in 1871 and its annual meetings with their processions and conferences were important events.[151] According to Henry Jones Williams (Plenydd), one of the best-known leaders of the temperance movement, it was Good Templarship which fostered interest in the legislative aspect of temperance and inspired campaigns to reduce drinking hours and ensure better public control over the drinks trade.[152] The temperance movement was not just for men. The North Wales Women's Temperance Union was formed in May 1892,[153] and the South Wales Union in March 1901.[154]

On the whole the Nonconformist denominations were rather slow to take an active role in the temperance movement. A Temperance Society was formed under the auspices of the Baptist Union in Llangefni in 1879 at a time when the subject was not particularly popular.[155] By 1902 its membership included 395 ministers.[156] During their general assembly in Liverpool in 1896 the Calvinistic Methodists formed a temperance movement[157] and in 1899 the Union of Welsh Independents formed its own temperance society.[158] Although temperance, like teetotalism, was not so influential among Anglicans the temperance movement had some fervent supporters among the rank and file of the church.[159] There was a faction within the temperance movement that campaigned to make abstinence a condition of church membership.[160] Among the Calvinistic Methodists the rule was adopted in some parts of the country that church officials should not drink alcohol[161] but this was not extended to the membership as a whole, and the denominations generally did not insist upon this since there was no biblical basis for making it a condition of church membership. The campaign to use non-alcoholic wine at communion was more successful.[162] The Union of Welsh Independents passed a motion in favour of the principle but within two years less than a quarter of the churches had adopted the practice.[163] However, the practice gradually spread throughout the Nonconformist churches.

Reading through the wealth of literature produced by the temperance movement during the early years of the twentieth century, one of its most interesting aspects is the way its supporters became more aware of the involvement of psychological and social factors in the problem of alcoholism. As a result there was a need to broaden the movement's horizons. There was some truth in the claim made by D. J. Lewis, Tumble, in 1913, 'that the social movement . . . in Wales . . . has its roots in the temperance movement'.[164] For very many church people at least, it was a bridge between personal and individualistic action and the public and social activity that was gaining ground at the time.

By 1890, the strength of Britain's economy was being challenged by international competition and Welsh people were becoming sceptical of the capitalist system. The bosses' solution to the business crisis, more often than not, was to cut workers' wages. Indeed, the vast majority of strikes at that time were attempting to stop wages being reduced rather than battles to raise them. These struggles served to increase the appeal of the trade unions and the conviction was growing that world conditions could be improved if only people had the will to achieve this. The workers were no longer content to accept low wages, long working hours, poor housing and unpleasant working conditions as inevitable circumstances of life. Rather they were becoming 'problems', in other words, difficulties to be resolved by means of determined action. As the crisis of capitalism deepened, the churches were drawn into the social and economic debate.

During this period Pope Leo XIII (1875–1903) gave new direction to the Catholic Church's teaching by means of the dozen encyclicals which he published on social issues.[165] The most famous of them, *Rerum Novarum*, 'On the condition of the working classes', was published on 15 May 1891 and expressed concerns that were spreading generally among Christians. It included guiding principles for politicians and sociologists in relation to the nature of society, 'for a solution must soon be found for the wretchedness and misery that oppress the vast majority of the working classes'. Welsh people were encouraged by their religious leaders to take more interest in social matters.[166] Although one might question whether this was necessary since Welsh people had for years taken a deep interest in politics, it must be remembered that pietism remained influential. The proper task of the church, according to some, was 'saving the individual' and not 'improving society'.[167] John Williams, Brynsiencyn, took the same line. 'Improving the existing situation a little was the limit of his vision . . . religion was supposed to influence everything, but it was not to revolutionize anything.'[168]

But should the church as such devote itself to social work? The Salvation Army had already made a notable contribution in this way. Should it be imitated? Some believed that it should. For instance, in 1902 the Calvinistic Methodists opened a home for orphaned children in Bontnewydd, Caernarfon, the Treborth Home for young women in Grangetown, Cardiff, in 1905 and the Kingswood-Treborth House in Canton, Cardiff, in May 1908.[169] Individual churches made humanitarian efforts too, such as the 'Cup of Cold Water League' in the Wesleyan church in Roath Road, Cardiff, which put families in the church in touch with poor families in the slums so that they could help them out with food.[170]

The Church in Wales also had many humanitarian institutions, such as the St Margaret's House of Mercy in Cardiff for the rehabilitation of prostitutes which was run by the East Grinstead Sisters.[171] All the churches gave support to many humanitarian movements by means of regular collections. However, the conviction was increasing that social evils were too great for voluntary movements to be able to make much of an impression on them. And in any case, zealous individuals were by now insisting that what was needed was not to mitigate the ills of the present social order but to change it completely.

Church leaders soon came to believe social ills must be studied in a much more orderly and scientific fashion and that practical improvements had to be proposed. In its meetings in Mountain Ash in 1911 the Baptist Union established the Welsh Baptist Social Service League with William Morris, Treorchy, as president. During the same year the Union of Welsh Independents decided to set up a Social Service Department and to appoint Lleufer Thomas, Miall Edwards and R. E. Peregrine to draft a constitution for it. During that summer, Lleufer Thomas, Miall Edwards and Gwilym Davies met and agreed to organize a summer school in Llandrindod Wells in September. The response was disappointing with only a handful of Congregationalists and Baptists present.

However, it was decided to set up a wider committee and representatives from ten bodies were invited to join it, with Canon Buckley, Llandaff, as chairman. This was the beginning of the Welsh School of Social Service.[172] Enthusiasm for the venture was soon fostered and the practical focus of its interest can be seen in its first manifesto on a 'Living Wage'. The same emphasis was evident in the annual summer schools where subjects such as

'Housing', 'Leisure Hours', 'The Worker's Wife' and 'the Minimum Wage' were discussed.[173] Through this institution and denominational organizations, the churches of Wales contributed to the overwhelming interest in social matters which was spreading throughout Christian countries and which reached its zenith in the Conference on Christian Politics, Economics and Citizenship (COPEC) held in Birmingham in 1924[174] and the International Conference on Life and Work, held in Stockholm in 1925.[175]

The attitude of religious leaders to trade unionism was mixed. By the end of the century opposition to the principle of trade unionism, such as that mounted by John Roberts (J.R.), Conwy, on the grounds that it was a monopoly and prevented free trade in labour, was rapidly disappearing.[176] People came to feel instead that if the capitalist system was to work fairly, then trade unions were necessary to ensure market freedom against the owners' monopoly. The conclusion subsequently reached by some thinkers was that it was not the churches' business to interfere at all in battles between unionists and capitalists. This was the standpoint of John Owen, Ffestiniog, at the time, as he wrote about 'Christianity and Society'.[177] The church is 'the employer's church just as much as the worker's church', and Owen drew the unexpected conclusion from this truth that 'interfering in commercial disputes is not part of its mission'. The church has no 'bias towards one social organization over another' since its proper task is to impress 'divine influences' upon human hearts and to bring 'the light of eternity to shine on all the travails of the world'. There is a basic confusion in these remarks. Owen instinctively conceived of a 'church' as a congregation of believers engaged in worship. This is all well and good. The church as a worshipping congregation is not a trade union or a political party or a sociological college. However, when we think of the church as a congregation of Christians who are also trade unionists and politicians and sociology students, is it consistent with Christianity to claim that the 'light of eternity' shining on their own field of interest cannot lead them to particular political and social convictions? And could the church (in Ffestiniog of all places) be completely indifferent to the nature of the 'social order'? Would Owen have been prepared to apply the same rationale to family life, for instance, and say that the 'social order' of marriage and the family is neither here nor there? His denomination, however, was willing to go a step or two further by encouraging the churches to 'conduct honest and impartial research into the social questions that are relevant to its sphere', with the 'aim of applying the Christian belief to daily life' but keeping 'completely clear of the influence of a political or industrial party'.[178] It is significant, however, that when the church's general assembly announced this, it gave no suggestions as to how exactly it should be applied.

Despite this, there were obvious links between trade unionism and the churches and, if people like John Owen wished to distance themselves as much as possible from the problems of manual workers, there were others, no less devout, who strode into the eye of the storm. The story of the quarrymen of Bethesda, after they formed their union, taking their hats off to sing 'O Arglwydd Dduw Rhagluniaeth . . .' ('O Lord God of Providence . . .') was to warm the hearts of religious people for many years.[179] Similarly, the leadership among the miners of William Abraham (Mabon) succeeded in winning sympathy for his union in the denominational papers. For that matter, it was not unusual for him to start a union meeting with a word of prayer.[180] He believed that the capitalist and the worker had their proper place in the social order and that it was his work as a labour leader to reconcile the two factions as far as possible. The practical manifestation of this attitude was the 'sliding scale' which linked the miner's wage to the fluctuations in the price of coal on the market. Mabon was the president of the scale committee and it was primarily his influence that ensured that this system had continued to work from 1875 to 1902. It is not surprising, then, that Mabon was hailed as a 'responsible leader' both in religious and Liberal circles.[181]

In Bethesda too there was a close relationship between the union leaders and the chapels. The North Wales Quarrymen's Union was formed in 1874[182] and peace reigned during the lifetime of Lord Penrhyn, Edward Gordon Douglas (1880–6), the 'Old Lord', but when he died, his son Sholto Douglas took the title and through his overbearing recalcitrance he created increasing tensions which reached their height in the Great Strike of 1900–3.[183] The first president of the quarrymen, Robert Parry, was a chief elder in Jerusalem Calvinistic Methodist chapel and a man of noble Christian character.[184] The quarrymen's secretary, Griffith Edwards, was a deacon with the Independents in Bethesda chapel, and 'his heart was in the chapel, and the chapel was the heart of his life'.[185] Robert Arthur Griffith (Elphin) claimed that 'the Welsh Pulpit gave scarcely any help to the brave quarrymen of Bethesda', indeed they sided with the owners.[186]

Of course there was a difference of opinion among ministers, as among the public generally, over this particular strike. There were many – the majority, if Elphin was correct – who did not wish to express an opinion, but there were also ministers who were only too keen to speak on behalf of the quarrymen. To go back a few years to 7 May 1892 when the first quarry workers' Labour Festival was held in Caernarfon, it is interesting to note that ministers such as Bryniog Roberts, R. D. Rowlands, W. O. Jones, Tecwyn Parry and Lewis Williams were among the 'influential gentry' on the Pavilion stage.[187] In the case of the Bethesda quarry workers the sympathy of many religious leaders was gained through the services of William John Parry who, according to Ernest Roberts, was the 'most able man and the worker with the most multifaceted abilities and talents ever raised in Bethesda'.[188] He was also the quarry workers' main adviser for many years, and his home, Coetmor Hall, was not only the 'headquarters of North Wales Liberalism in that period' but also gave a hospitable welcome to both prominent and minor preachers over many years.[189]

There were many places besides Bethesda and the Rhondda valleys where the close links between trade union leaders and the churches were exemplified, and where some ministers were indifferent towards the unions while others were enthusiastic in their support. The climate changed with the emergence of more militant unionism, under the leadership of men like William Brace. He and his supporters in the coal mines insisted on a fixed wage and shorter working hours and were very critical of Mabon's 'sliding scale'. It is true that some prominent religious people welcomed the new spirit[190] but for other radicals, 'Brace and his fellow Englishmen' were foreign interlopers and no good could be expected from them 'because Jack the Englishman never changes'.[191] There was so much respect for Mabon that there was a tendency to support the activities of his union, the Cambrian Union, when it came into conflict with others.[192] But although Mabon became the president of the South Wales Miners' Federation, formed on 11 October 1898, and his own union joined it, observers in the churches were not so easy in their minds.

Indeed, from 1902 onwards, Mabon's influence tended to wane and he was unable to share his younger colleagues' enthusiasm for action which he reckoned to be too militant.[193] W. J. Parry met a similar fate. With the emergence of a more militant spirit in the unions from 1904 onwards, his contribution to labour politics ceased. His career shows how the gap was gradually opening up between the radical politics of the old middle-class leaders and the new and militant zeal of the leaders who sprang from the working class.[194] This was not merely a matter of transferring the reins of leadership from the hands of one social class to another, but a matter of a fundamental change in ideology. And this brings us to Socialism.

The emergence of Socialism opened up a new period in the history of the relationship between the churches and social issues. The word 'Socialism' was not new to Wales; as early as 1839, Evan Davies (Eta Delta) had complained bitterly that ' "Socialism" was the worst kind of faithlessness, flourishing in England'.[195] In 1884, the Fabian Society was formed to promote socialist principles as an ideology and in 1893 Keir Hardie formed the Independent Labour Party (ILP) to promote Socialism as a political programme. On 27 February 1900, the Labour Party was formed as a merger of both societies and the trade unions.[196] The first Member of Parliament to represent the new party in Wales was Keir Hardie who was elected for Merthyr Tudful in 1900 and by 1906 the representation had risen to six members. This rapid increase caused Liberals much alarm and thus it is no surprise that a substantial part of the opposition to 'Socialism' among religious people was based on loyalty to Liberalism – and to Lloyd George in particular. Despite this, the conviction was increasing that workers should be given a greater representation in council and Parliament and the hope was that this new trend could be kept within the confines of the Liberal Party.

However, socialists had been pioneering the way for some years. The Progressive Labour League was formed in Cardiff in 1892.[197] The following year the Fabians won 3,000 votes in the city's school board election but failed to gain a seat; apparently there was not a single Fabian in Wales two years previously.[198] By 1898, the ILP had thirty-one branches in south Wales, mainly in Merthyr Tudful and the Rhondda valleys.[199] Later on the movement spread in north Wales. Soon afterwards a branch of the Independent Labour Party was founded in Rhosllannerchrugog, and one was established in March 1908 in Blaenau Ffestiniog, for which R. Silyn Roberts, the Methodist minister in Tanygrisiau, was the main instigator.

During the same month the first socialist meeting was held in Caernarfon under the presidency of E. Morgan Humphreys and David Thomas was among the speakers. In April a branch of the Independent Labour Party was also formed in the town.[200]

Men like Silyn Roberts and David Thomas worked untiringly during this period to explain and promote socialist ideas in the press. In this respect they were continuing the pioneering work of Robert Jones Derfel (1824–1905) who began to publish his ideas on the nature of society in *Y Cymro* (17 March 1892) in what became a long series of articles.[201] He argued in favour of rejection of the capitalist system rather than reform. Property should be in the hands of the centralized state as the representative of the people, and this change would lead to social morality – 'cymundebaeth' (communionism) – which would correspond to the organic and united society where the individual could reach his or her full potential. Some of the Fabian pamphlets appeared in Welsh. Evan Pan Jones, the Independent minister at Mostyn, translated the first of them and T. Hudson Williams (the secretary of the Fabian Society founded in 1900 in the University College of North Wales, Bangor) translated the pamphlet written by the prominent Baptist John Clifford which bore the title *Sosialaeth a Dysgeidiaeth Crist* (Socialism and the Teaching of Christ, 1897). Another of Clifford's pamphlets was translated by David Thomas in 1909, *Sosialaeth a'r Eglwysi* (Socialism and the Churches, 1908). In 1909 also J. R. Jones's pamphlet appeared, *Sosialaeth yng ngoleuni'r Beibl* (Socialism in the Light of the Bible). However the most substantial and the most brilliant of these attempts to present Socialism was David Thomas's book, *Y Werin a'i Theyrnas* (The People and their Kingdom, 1910). Of course, periodicals published a constant stream of articles on the subject, particularly *Y Genedl Gymreig* (The Welsh Nation) under the editorship of William Eames, and *Llais Llafur* (The Labour Voice). If 'the political arm of the Labour movement was weak' during these years,[202] it possessed enough mental and literary vigour to ensure that people could not avoid the subject.

To turn now to the reaction of religious leaders to this activity, it is clear that it was very mixed.[203] To start with, it is fair to say that they were genuinely concerned for the hardship suffered by the working class, as has already been shown. This was why some of the old radicals (like E. Pan Jones) and the young ministers (like

Silyn Roberts and T. E. Nicholas) became enthusiastically involved with the new movement. There were others, like H. M. Hughes, Cardiff, who criticized Socialism harshly, but on the basis of detailed knowledge and careful reasoning.[204] After the 1906 election and the increasing scepticism over the Liberal Party's willingness to take workers' complaints seriously, both parties' attitudes became more entrenched. With Lloyd George as the president of the Baptist Union, it was inevitable, perhaps, that *Seren Cymru* would be scolded for its constant invectives against Socialism and the Labour Party[205] but, to be fair, it had published a series of favourable articles in the same year by 'Alcwyn', namely D. Tudwal Evans, the minister of the Temple, Newport.[206]

The tendency among church leaders, however, was to turn against the socialist movement. One observer claimed in 1910, in a critical but not unkind article, that the leaders were still supporting Liberalism and workers were turning their backs on the churches. Generally speaking, he said, the pulpit was an implacable enemy of the Labour Party.[207] In 1911, one correspondent claimed that the ILP 'to all intents and purposes was being driven out of the churches'.[208] These statements should be taken with a pinch of salt, of course. New enthusiastic movements are always impatient and over-react to any kind of criticism and when they come into conflict with old movements which are oversensitive towards their younger critics there is no end to the accusations. However, there is evidence that tempers were becoming heated in many congregations, as, for instance, in Carmel, Gwaun-cae-gurwen, where a neighbouring minister, Edryd Jones, was refused permission to lecture on a socialist topic.[209]

Before this, in Mountain Ash, George Neighbour had been sacked from his church for supporting Socialism and R. J. Campbell's New Theology, and he and his supporters formed a 'Brotherhood Church'.[210] It was evident that a split was opening up in many places between supporters of Socialism and church leaders. 'Recent discussions in south Wales', said one Labour supporter, 'have drawn attention to the increasing separation between the Labour movement and the churches.' The attitude of the leaders, he said, was to compromise reluctantly. 'They are afraid of the Labour Movement, and they do not dare to oppose it: they want to work hesitantly with it, but they do not dare to lead it.'[211] However, there was no consensus among religious leaders about Socialism. In

October 1912 in the Llandaff Diocesan Conference, a motion was proposed rejoicing that Socialism was not anti-religious and urging Anglicans generally to study social issues in order to ensure 'that the near future will see the more equitable distribution of wealth'. It was not passed, but it was significant that it was proposed at all.[212] Similar events occurred in Nonconformist denominations. On 5 January 1912, a ministers' conference was held in Cardiff to discuss 'The minister's relationship with social issues'. The conference was opened by John Morgan Jones, Pembroke Terrace, and he took the attitude that 'the gospels do not support any social theory or propaganda'. Indeed, he claimed that 'the gospel evidence is either negative or neutral' with regard to all social issues. However, several of the ministers present disagreed furiously with him and the meeting was somewhat tumultuous.[213]

Socialism had some keen supporters among ministers and preachers, several of whom have already been mentioned. There is certainly some truth in the statement by one Labour supporter that 'the majority of Welsh Socialists are Christians'[214] and although one correspondent in *Llais Llafur* claimed heatedly that the Labour movement was not indebted at all to the 'reactionary pulpit', there was no real foundation for his remarks.[215] The Wesleyans and their ministers contributed to the growth of Labour ideology in the Rhondda,[216] while the Revd G. W. Hockley, Hawarden, was one of the first Anglicans to press for 'the just and moral production, distribution, possession and utilization of wealth . . . by all' in accordance with socialist teaching.[217] There was no lack of support as, before long, a Socialist Society was founded for Anglicans,[218] and no one made a more zealous contribution to the debate than the Methodist J. H. Howard. He published his book, *Cristionogaeth a Chymdeithas* (Christianity and Society), in 1914 – a lively book, full of vigour, pleading the case for 'Christian Socialism' to eradicate poverty and exploitation in society.

We have come a long way from the kind of reasoning that characterized the work of men such as Michael D. Jones and Emrys ap Iwan. Whatever the strength or weakness of their ideology, their aim was to move from biblical foundations to practical conclusions. The Labour movement, on the other hand, adopted and nurtured a sophisticated philosophy of human nature and society and of moral standards. It is true that many (like Mabon) had joined the movement because of their sympathy with its humanitarian ideals while rejecting the underlying socialist philosophy, but it is not possible to ignore the power of that philosophy. To people who accepted it, it was, in the basic meaning of the word, a 'faith'. It involved total – and often costly – personal consecration. But for people who embraced this faith, the socialist philosophy also provided a yardstick by which all other doctrines could be measured – including Christian doctrine. Thus classical Christian reasoning is turned on its head. Instead of drawing social conclusions on the basis of biblical revelation, the aim now was to reach conclusions about the Bible on the basis of socialist philosophy. Socialism was the true revelation and Christian doctrine had to be pruned to respond to its requirements. This is what is meant today by the 'politicization of the Christian faith' and this process was very much in evidence at the beginning of the twentieth century.

On a Sunday afternoon in May 1912, Keir Hardie gave an address at the Ystalyfera Playhouse on 'Socialism and religion'. His theme was Jesus Christ, the carpenter's son and a carpenter himself, who worked among common folk and campaigned to undermine the oppression and militarism of the Roman Empire. He called upon people to set aside mammon and to dedicate themselves to the service of God and one another. 'Christ's Kingdom was not something to save souls for some mythological heaven after death: its purpose was to create heaven here on earth in accordance with Christ's teaching.' 'Christ was a rebel, a revolutionary rebel, executed by the authorities because of this, condemned by the church, killed by the state because he defended the poor and condemned their oppressors.'[219]

It is easy to understand the appeal of Hardie's eloquence and to appreciate how his passion and the desire of his listeners for better living conditions blinded them to the ruthless distortion of biblical evidence. The beguiling simplicity of his exposition gave freshness and relevance to Christian teaching. It is not surprising that socialists subsequently became intolerant of church doctrine and disparaged it as being 'without any practical value at all' and, indeed, as obscuring the 'practical doctrines preached and practised by the Nazarene a long time ago'.[220] R. J. Campbell's New Theology became very popular among socialists. Campbell himself had claimed that this was the theology of the Labour movement, whether it knew it or not.[221] Many eagerly adopted its tenets of faith – the belief that humankind and God are essentially the same; that sin is merely an error; that the orthodox teaching on the person of Christ is 'un-believable', for he is divine and human solely because his mind is completely under the governance of love; that his purpose in dying was to reveal the true quality of that love, and that the churches' work is to 'make the world into God's kingdom, and fill it with love'. In 1907, Campbell formed the 'Progressive Theology League' to promote these ideas. Under the auspices of this body we find T. Rhondda Williams, for instance, lecturing in Mountain Ash on 'Christianity and Socialism',[222] explaining that what the Bible gives us is a body of moral principles to be applied to society and thus to put an end to the class war.

In a word, this is the 'social gospel'.[223] Its aims were to strip Christianity of its 'supernatural' elements, humanize God and deify society, turn heaven into a myth to be exchanged for earthly utopia, erase God's righteousness in favour of exalting his love and make salvation the fruit of social and political activity. Theology is cast aside as irrelevant scholasticism and socialist studies are enthroned, with their new scholasticism, in its place. The church is condemned as a reactionary body except to the extent that it helps in practical terms to promote the political campaign. This is an extreme example of the politicization of the Christian faith. If there is a clash between Socialism and Christianity, Christianity must be curtailed, rather than Socialism modified. It would be misleading to claim that a large section of the Labour movement had embraced this teaching in its entirety, but it was very influential. It went some way towards alleviating the difficulties of certain young people at that time. Many, like David Thomas, were in a spiritual impasse concerning their attitude towards traditional theology and yet they felt a warmth towards their religious background. For such people the social gospel justified their continued allegiance to the chapel although almost everything they heard there had to be modified by the application of this doctrine. Thus, as David Thomas confessed, he was able to continue his church membership 'on his own terms', an odd arrangement considering that he would be the last to allow anyone to belong to the Labour Party and embrace, for instance, Tory convictions.[224] The desire to link religious tradition with socialist campaigning, the passionate desire to provide a religious justification for the political battle, was a powerful motive for many young people. For James Griffiths, one of Silyn Roberts's great contributions as an apostle of Socialism was this: 'He was a minister and a Socialist . . . he linked the South Wales of Evan Roberts to the South Wales of Keir Hardie'.[225] Nevertheless, these developments laid bare the crisis that was closing in on the Welsh Christian mindset in the social arena. They had mislaid the key that would open the door to a social doctrine that would be derived from the Bible and that would simultaneously get to grips with the complexities of contemporary society. The result was a descent into a sterile pietism, or conversely, into anaemic modernism. Socialism stepped into the gap and offered a holistic doctrine of life, and Welsh Christian thinkers did not really know how to criticize it creatively while accepting what was valuable in it and rejecting those elements which were false. And since that doctrine – despite an occasional gesture in a different direction – combined high humanitarian ideals with a stubborn allegiance to the belief that Wales's national identity was not of any great political import, the bankruptcy of the Welsh Christian mind in this impasse was also a terrible disaster for the nation.

Conclusions

Clearly the years between 1890 and 1914 were complex and turbulent in the history of Welsh Christianity. During that time, a crisis emerged both for the nation and for the Christian faith as well, and it is no exaggeration to say that all the elements that were to rock the foundations of Welsh Christianity after 1914 were already present a quarter of a century previously.

For many centuries, Christianity had been inextricably linked with Welsh culture and the relationship between them was still close in 1890. Being Welsh was almost the same as being a Christian, at least in name, and it was difficult to describe Wales's national characteristics without referring to its Christianity.

Between 1890 and 1914, however, this union came under increasing strain. Welsh was no longer the language of the majority of the population. For many, this was not a cause for concern, since the general sentiment was that the substance of Christianity could be transmitted just as well in English as in Welsh. This was a great error of judgement, for when people lose their language, they lose the vital link with their own past. Familiarity with a Christian past is insufficient, of course, to create Christians, but it still acts both as a witness and a challenge which only the uncivilized could ignore. Wales's Christian past, expressed in Welsh in Siôn Cent's poetry, William Morgan's Bible, Morgan Llwyd's prose, Charles Edwards's writing, Ellis Wynne's compositions, and in hymns by Williams Pantycelyn and Ann Griffiths, is as much a witness as the voice of a contemporary evangelist, and they demand a thoughtful response. However, if the language is lost, the evidence of the cultural and Christian forces which created the society that nurtured the non-Welsh-speaking Welshman is also lost. This is not merely a question of losing touch with the religious past; it also means losing one's national identity.

A brief glance at the situation in Wales at the time demonstrates this. How many Welsh schools in 1900 gave non-Welsh-speakers lessons on *Llyfr y Tri Aderyn* (The Book of the Three Birds) or Morgan Rhys's hymns, or Howell Harris's life and work? The fact is that in 1900 – and afterwards – losing the language meant virtual exile from Welsh society because there was no real difference between education in Anglesey and that in Sussex. For Welsh-speakers, on the other hand, church services, Sunday schools, concerts and periodicals formed a link between them and their national and Christian past.

The danger in this, however, was that the Welsh-language churches were forced to shoulder the responsibility for safeguarding the national tradition and culture which is not the primary responsibility of any Christian church. Day schools, colleges, government and all the public media have their role to play in maintaining national culture, with the churches making an appropriate contribution to the task. But a meek acceptance of an order which viewed Welsh as a sacred language – the language of poets, preachers and prophets – and English as the language of everything else was a certain route to extinction for the nation and the churches alike. Gradually, fervent Welsh people began to attend Welsh-language services not because they were Christian but because they were in Welsh. By failing to secure a thoroughly Welsh-language educational system and by not insisting that Welsh should have priority as the public language of government, church leaders were hastening the day when the Welsh-language churches would become cultural societies which people would frequent for the sake of the language rather than for the sake of Jesus Christ.

Historians have long emphasized the mass migration from the countryside to the towns, from an agricultural environment to industrial areas, as the social process which weakened Christianity. This theory should not be applied to Wales until almost the end of the period under review. The churches reached their statistical apex in 1907 and up to that year, to all appearances, they had been remarkably successful in attracting industrial workers throughout Wales. Only in very large towns, such as Cardiff, was there any evidence of urbanization giving rise to alienation from the churches.

From about 1900 onwards tensions emerged between some keen supporters of the Labour movement and the churches. Many trade union leaders were church members, but this did not always mean that they acknowledged their debt to the churches for the training they had received in organizing meetings and public speaking. A change came when unionists were urged towards more militant action on behalf of workers' demands. Although the churches did not favour such action, the accusations by some fervent Labour supporters that they were completely reactionary bodies should not be given too much credence. After all, workers were the backbone of the valley chapels until 1914. The 'social gospel' and the evident need for social improvements stung the conscience of church leaders and led them to realize that there was a need for a new Christian perspective on the problems created by capitalism. However, it was inevitable that those people who dedicated themselves to socialist political activity became impatient with religious institutions and ultimately that they abandoned them.

One influence, the significance of which was not fully realized by Christian thinkers of the period, was the growth of the scientific state. Indeed, it was a brand-new phenomenon. Between 1870 and 1900 it was taking its first unsteady steps and half a century would go by before it attained its full stature. It gradually extended its grasp until it touched the whole of life. As it grew, people did not realize that it had its own particular philosophy, morals and pre-conceptions. Above all they did not realize its power. The socialist ideology was an exception because it enthusiastically embraced Rousseau's philosophy that only the state had sufficient power to break the bonds of oppression and to overturn the traditional social patterns that enslaved the common people. Thus, according to socialist philosophy, the state was the medium of social salvation. Strengthening its authority was tantamount to moving towards a better future, while limiting its authority was to be in favour of reaction.

For the scientific state, which deals with millions of people, administrative effectiveness is vital, or otherwise its bureaucratic processes become impeded and it cannot cope with minor differences in language, customs, belief and culture. For this reason some socialist pioneers came to the conclusion that Wales should have its own scientific state, which is why self-government was occasionally included in their programme. But the scientific state, when it reached maturity, would not be a new state, but the historical English state and, as a result, Wales's unique national identity was a hindrance. Thus, as the influence of this state increased in Wales, it gradually suffocated Welsh identity and as this occurred the scope for the Welsh-language churches to make a contribution gradually decreased.

The 1890s were anxious years for church leaders. It is a complete misconception to think of the people of the Victorian age as smug and self-satisfied. Of course, there were some people like this, but, on the whole, church leaders were worried about the future. In spite of their anxieties, the churches were overflowing with vitality, each church a hive of industry, yet there was a very strong feeling that all this activity concealed a decline. Somehow it was not directed towards the highest ends. Church discipline, which had formerly been strict, became lax. Receiving people into membership became a formality. Although the great variety of meetings gave pleasure to tens of thousands, they did not seem to help them to grow to maturity as Christians. There were many excellent preachers throughout the country, but the temptation to please their listeners meant that their sermons had little substance, which in turn undermined the moral authority of the pulpit.

Religious leaders were in general agreement that there was a lack of blessing on the nation's spiritual life. There was a general longing for revival, and there was much evangelism and prayer in support of this. The answer came with the 1904–5 Revival, when the nation was faced with the challenge of the gospel in a very personal way, creating an unparalleled emotional response. Mixed in with this response was much sterile emotionalism and not a little hysteria and superstition, but this was merely the dross. Basically, the revival was a dramatic crossroads in the nation's history. Did the Welsh wish to profess the God of their fathers, or turn their back on him? Many did turn their backs on him, and one form of this abandonment, particularly among the intelligentsia, was to attribute the entire revival to natural or social causes and to deny completely any divine involvement at all.

To many thousands of others, the revival was the most creative turning point of their life and for over two generations these people remained a force within the churches. Yet even they felt that the revival had yielded a disappointing harvest; Wales had been given a great opportunity of which it had failed to take advantage, despite the fact that the revival in many other parts of the world had brought forth fruit a hundredfold. One of the reasons for this was the gradual change in people's thinking.

During the period between 1890 and 1914 theology, at least in its systematic form, was slowly falling into disrepute. The burning desire to safeguard the wholeness and balance of Christian truth was gradually disappearing. In the first part of this period, there was much discussion of many aspects of theology but it was clear that a fundamental change was under way. The Evangelical Accord suffered the most because of this change and, in many ways, the crisis faced by the accord was the same as the crisis which emerged in succeeding years in Welsh thought generally.

Doubt grew over the Bible's authority and since people were looking elsewhere for guidance on social and cultural matters, the classical Protestant emphasis on *sola scriptura*, scripture alone, was effectively losing ground. Similarly, *sola fide*, justification by faith alone, was being undermined by the belief that salvation was attainable by some other means than simple faith. Naturally, these two developments did not concern the Catholics, Roman or Anglican, but they were a grievous blow to the Evangelical Accord. Similarly the emphasis on the Fatherhood of God at the expense of his holiness led to the belief that Christ had not offered himself as an atonement for sin but rather had died as a demonstration of God's love to humankind. And once doubt concerning the uniqueness of his sacrifice had arisen, it was inevitable that doubts about the uniqueness of his person would follow. These tendencies were seen in their rawest form in R. J. Campbell's 'New Theology'. It would be a mistake to claim that the vast majority of Welsh Christians had embraced these various deviations from orthodoxy, but it would not be incorrect to say that a great many of them were becoming increasingly indifferent to the importance of doctrine and tended to embrace any teaching that happened to be in vogue at the time.

One reason for the lack of enthusiasm for the defence of orthodoxy was the sterility of its traditional form. Welsh-speaking Christians could not make up their minds during this period. In some areas the influence of their Christian instruction was very strong, particularly in moral and personal issues and in matters concerned with church life. But with regard to education or politics or culture, their guidance came from other places, the influence of thinkers who had either distorted Christianity – men like Kant and Hegel and Ristchl – or who had abandoned Christianity – men like Rousseau, Bentham, Darwin, Mill, Marx and Spencer. Once the

Bible and theology came to be considered as the source for private principles or standards or values, it was inevitable that people would come under the sway of ideas which would sooner or later completely destroy the Christian way of thinking. Between 1890 and 1914, a chasm was opening up in the souls of Christians in Wales.

They no longer strove to 'bring all thoughts into obedience to Christ' but rather resigned themselves to the hope that they could temper their ever more secularized thoughts with a little godliness. After the First World War the tragic consequences of this would become plain for all to see.

It is appropriate to close this discussion with an attempt to explain why the various difficulties which emerged between 1890 and 1914 gave rise eventually to a crisis of faith. Throughout the centuries, great cultural problems have challenged faith. In periods when faith was vibrant and vigorous it could face the challenge successfully. So it was during the first three centuries of Christianity, and when the Roman Empire crumbled, and also at the close of the medieval period. During these great crises, faith had the power to restore unity and balance and harmony in the midst of disarray.

The subject of this study has been the Christian faith and we must do it justice in order to appreciate the magnitude of the challenge it faced during the period in question. For Christianity, the universe is the product of the work of a wise creator, and thus an orderly and meaningful system can be perceived therein. If human beings are in harmony with the creator, they will see the glory of the creator reflected in creation. Every aspect of their lives, spiritual and material, economic and scientific, individual and social, natural and supernatural, forms a pattern of rich diversity which centres upon God. The eighth Psalm expresses this amazing variety with unique power; the creator is not an abstract principle or impersonal energy. Rather in the fullness of time he revealed himself in Jesus Christ, the eternal Son. What is more, he is related in a unique way to the creation and everything there is: 'All things came into being through him' (John 1: 3) or, as Paul expressed the vision, 'for in him all things in heaven and on earth were created, things visible and invisible, whether thrones or dominions or rulers or powers' (Col. 1: 16).

Thus, in principle, there is nothing in creation that is not linked to Christ and that does not derive its meaning from him. In him the loving essence which gives everything meaning is revealed. This is not a static order but rather one which expands and develops and grows. But there is a dark side to the story. Sin came to damage and defy this order and destructive forces were unleashed to corrupt this harmony. Human beings lost sight of the relationship between creation and creator. Their consciences were seared by guilt and their spirits were overwhelmed by terror as they sensed the order of their life falling apart and the death of meaning, with the inevitable result that they tried to fashion a new order of their own invention, based upon themselves or on some aspect of the creation around them. Men and women 'by their wickedness suppress the truth', by exchanging 'the glory of the immortal God for images resembling a mortal human being' (Rom. 1: 18, 23). This temptation comes in all its might when great and unexpected changes occur in a person's own life or in the pattern of society or in the economic order – when a nation's existence is being threatened, when a language is under siege, when there is migration on a large scale or an industrial revolution, or when people are faced with an influx of new ideas or foreign practices. The answers once given to old questions cannot easily be applied to new ones and if the former answers reflected God's place at the centre of this meaningfulness, it is easy in the face of a crisis to run towards explanations which dethrone him.

Instead of seeing the meaning of life and of creation as issuing from God the Creator and Father, human beings take one aspect of creation and try to see value and meaning in its light, whether it be science, history, sociology, politics or philosophy, or even the individual's spiritual life and emotional experiences. Men and women express, in these various ways, their demonic reliance upon themselves – demonic because they thrust God to one side. The fashionable term for this process is 'secularization'. Plenty of evidence has been given in this work to indicate how this process was becoming evident in Welsh life at the beginning of the twentieth century. It had tragic consequences because the change meant that Welsh people began to buckle under the temptation to share the highest place in their hearts between Christ and many other faiths, and especially faith in the human ability to give meaning to life and to creation without God and without Christ. Trying to serve God and mammon provokes a serious crisis for the Christian, and this was beginning to happen in the period studied above.

However, if we allow Christianity to speak for itself, it has more to say. Christianity is also concerned with proclaiming a way of redemption. Christ is not merely a concept, but the Redeemer of the world. The Creator is also God the Saviour. Through preaching, sacraments, services, pastoral work and education the churches beckon people from their confusion into the 'marvellous light' that is the mark of the Kingdom of God. Doubtless the churches have often failed in this task, and we have seen examples of this, but it would be folly to claim that the flame on their altars has been wholly extinguished. In them and through them God saw fit to allow the Welsh people a mighty renewal in the midst of the period we have been studying. And in the years between that time and the present day the vision persists that the people of Wales can still find harmony and unity and joy and meaning in Christ.

And where there is vision, the people will not perish.

Notes

1. Wales, 1890

1 For Siôn Cent (1400–c. 1445), see *Gwaith Sion Cent*, ed. T. Matthews (Llanuwchllyn, 1914). The 'cywydd' is a poem or song in 'strict metre . . . composed of rhyming couplets . . . consisting of lines of seven syllables': see *GPC*, I, 837.

2 For Edmund Prys (1544–1623), archdeacon of Merioneth and poet, see J. E. Lloyd and R. T. Jenkins (eds), *Dictionary of Welsh Biography down to 1940* (London, 1959) (hereafter *DWB*).

3 For Charles Edwards (1628?–91), Puritan author, see *DWB*.

4 For William Williams, Pantycelyn (1717–91), Methodist cleric, author and hymn-writer, see *DWB*.

5 For Thomas Jones, Denbigh (1756–1820), Calvinistic Methodist minister and author, see *DWB*.

6 For Robert Ambrose Jones (Emrys ap Iwan) (1851–1906), Calvinistic Methodist minister and author, see *DWB*.

7 For H. Elvet Lewis (Elfed) (1860–1953), Congregational minister, hymn-writer and poet, see E. D. Jones and Brynley F. Roberts (eds), *Y Bywgraffiadur Cymreig, 1951–1970* (London, 1997) (hereafter *Bywg.* (1951–70)).

8 D. Gwenallt Jones, *Gwreiddiau* (Aberystwyth, 1959), p. 9.

9 *Diwygiwr* (1901), 6. For Lewis Jones (1842–1928), the minister at Ty'n y Coed, Abercraf, see *Tyst* (23 August 1928), 9; *Dysgedydd* (1928), 296, 311–14, 342–6.

10 *Celt* (28 December 1900). For Rees (1869–1926), professor at the Memorial College, 1899–1909, and principal of the Bala–Bangor College 1909–26, see *DWB*; Robert Pope, *Seeking God's Kingdom: The Nonconformist Social Gospel in Wales 1906–1939* (Cardiff, 1999), pp. 56–67.

11 Cf. W. E. Powell and G. W. Brewer, *Cristnogaeth a Chrefydd* (Abercynon, 1967); E. L. Mascall, *The Secularization of Christianity* (London, 1965); Arnold E. Loen, *Secularization: Science without God* (London, 1967); Kenneth Hamilton, *What's New in Religion?* (Exeter,

1968), pp. 65–123; Martin E. Marty, *The Modern Schism* (London, 1969). For an alternative thesis, see Callum G. Brown, *The Death of Christian Britain* (London, 2001).

[12] 'Gair o'r Gair: Neu Son am Swn', in *Gweithiau Morgan Llwyd o Wynedd*, II, ed. J. H. Davies (Bangor, 1908), pp. 129–205; *The Poems of Matthew Arnold*, ed. Kenneth Allott (London, 1965), p. 242. For Morgan Llwyd (1619–59), poet and mystic, see *DWB*.

[13] Karl Rahner, *The Shape of the Church to Come* (London, 1974), p. 184.

[14] B. B. Thomas, *Braslun o Hanes Economaidd Cymru* (Cardiff, 1941), p. 184.

[15] Ibid., pp. 164–5.

[16] Ibid., pp. 160–1.

[17] Kenneth O. Morgan, *Wales in British Politics, 1868–1922* (Cardiff, 1991), p. 315.

[18] 'Bywyd cymdeithasol yn mharthau gwledig Cymru', in *Y Geninen* (1897), 209–13. For T. E. Ellis (1859–99), MP for Merioneth, see *DWB*.

[19] T. G. Thomas, *Y Parch W. Thomas, Gwynfe* (Carmarthen, 1903), p. 31.

[20] *Drysorfa* (1898), 166.

[21] *Census of England and Wales*, III (London, 1893), 550–2.

[22] *Drysorfa* (1895), 29.

[23] *Royal Commission on Land . . . Report* (London, 1896), *Appendices*, appendix E, p. 292.

[24] D. Lleufer Thomas, 'The Agricultural Labourer in Wales', *Young Wales* (1898), 184–5, 197–202; *Tyst* (28 March 1890), 11.

[25] D. Tecwyn Lloyd, *Safle'r Gerbydres* (Llandysul, 1970), pp. 120–1.

[26] See Daniel Halévy, *Essai sur l'accélération de l'histoire* (Paris, 1948), *passim*.

[27] *Geninen* (1901), 20.

2. Church and Chapel

[1] General statistics can be found in the *Report of the Royal Commission on Disestablishment* (London, 1910), I, 1–77, but various analyses are made by some of the Commissioners at 165–76, 200–18, 225–32, 262–74, 301–95. Although there was considerable argument at the time over the statistics, the detailed analysis throws valuable light on individual areas. The statistics pertaining to the Church in Wales are found in volume V and those for the Nonconformists in volume VI.

[2] For the purpose of analysis, the commissioners ignored children below 3 years old. The population of Wales in 1901 was 2,012,876, and after ignoring children under 3, it was 1,864,696. If children under 5 are ignored, it was 1,767,645.

3   *Report of the Royal Commission on Disestablishment*, I, 20. The size
of the different denominations by proportion of the population was
Church in Wales, 10.3; Congregationalists, 9.4; Calvinistic Methodists,
9.1; Baptists 7.7; Wesleyans, 2.2; the remainder, 1.0.

4   For full tables ibid., I, 302–95.

5   Quoted in K. S. Inglis, *Churches and the Working Classes in Victorian
England* (London, 1963), p. 3. For Winnington-Ingram (1858–1946),
see *DNB*. There was a big rise in the number of communicants at
Bethnal Green as a result of his work there.

6   *Tyst* (6 July 1894), 11; (13 July 1894), 7.

7   The councils under observation were Valley, Aethwy, Dwyran,
Gwyrfai, Llŷn, Glaslyn, Ynyscynhaearn, Deudraeth, Dolgellau, Tywyn
(borough), Aberystwyth (rural), Aberaeron (rural), Cardigan (rural)
and Llandudoch. Haverfordwest District Council was not included
because it belonged to the pattern of the 'second corridor'. The statistics come from the *Report of the Royal Commission on
Disestablishment*, I, 302–95.

8   The statistics of the population in the following councils: Holywell,
Wrexham (rural), Llanfyllin (rural), Newtown and Llanidloes (rural),
Builth Wells, Brecon, Glyncorrwg and Maesteg (urban), Margam and
Bridgend (rural).

9   The statistics of population in the following councils: Hawarden,
Overton, Y Waun, Fforden, Trefyclo, Maesyfed (New Radnor), Lampeter
Castell-paun, Y Gelli, Abergavenny, Pembroke (rural and urban).

10 Apart from the Wesleyans and the Baptists. The first did not present statistics and the Baptists included their students with the assistant preachers. See
Report of the Royal Commission on Disestablishment, I, 22.

11 Statistics were not sent about them from Denbighshire. Ibid., I, 217–18.

12 Ibid., VI, 442, for the full list, leaving out the Jews and the YMCA.

13 For Clynnog (*c*.1525–81), Robert (*c*.1552–*c*.1610) and Lewis (1533–95),
see *DWB*, and E. Gwynne Jones, *Cymru a'r Hen Ffydd* (Cardiff,
1951), ch. 1.

14 The three were hanged, drawn and quartered, Gwyn in Wrexham, 17
October 1584, Davies in Beaumares Castle, 21 July 1593, and Roberts
at Tyburn in London, 10 December 1610, see T. P. Ellis, *The Catholic
Martyrs of Wales, 1535–1680* (London, 1933), p. 25.

15 On the evidence of Charles Walmesley (1722–97), a monk of the
Order of St Benedict, according to David Attwater, *The Catholic
Church in Modern Wales* (London, 1935), p. 25.

16 For the main facts in this paragraph, ibid., pp. 26–65.

17 John Hickey, *Urban Catholics* (Louvain, 1967), pp. 61–2.

18 Evidence of the vicar apostolic, Peter Augustine Baines, according to
Attwater, *Catholic Church in Modern Wales*, p. 75. But, according

to G. E. Beck, *The English Catholics, 1850–1950* (London, 1950), p. 202, n. 25, there were only 5,000 Catholics in Wales and Hereford in 1840.

[19] For this able man see Beck, *English Catholics*, pp. 73–4. The vicar apostolic, the pope's vicar, was bishop in name without a geographical diocese or cathedral or a chapter of canons.

[20] For the history of the restoration, see Beck, *English Catholics*, ch. 3. The apostolic letter in English can be found at pp. 107–15.

[21] Attwater, *Catholic Church in Modern Wales*, pp. 99–100.

[22] For Hedley (1837–1915), see Beck, *English Catholics*, pp. 220–1, and Attwater, *Catholic Church in Modern Wales*, pp. 1–13.

[23] For Francis Edward Mostyn, see *DWB*.

[24] It becomes clear how close the connection was between the life of Cardiff's Catholic churches and Irish culture in John Hickey's excellent study, *Urban Catholics*, chs 5 and 6.

[25] In an interview with the *Western Mail* (a newspaper which was inaugurated by a Catholic, the marquess of Bute, in 1869), Attwater, *Catholic Church in Modern Wales*, p. 125.

[26] *Report of the Royal Commission on Disestablishment*, I, 42, and appendix I, 127–9.

[27] W. Eilir Evans, *Geninen* (1906), 209. The quotation is translated from *Y Geninen* and not taken from the original.

[28] *Haul* (1899), 321. Cf. the sad picture by 'Hynafgwr', 'Atgofion tri ugain mlynedd', *Haul* (1860), 107–9.

[29] For the change in general, see articles by E. T. Davies and Owain W. Jones in David Walker (ed.), *A History of the Church in Wales* (Penarth, 1976), pp. 121–63; J. W. James, *A Church History of Wales* (Ilfracombe, 1945), ch. 14. Although their work was disappointing at the time, valuable points are made in older books like D. Ambrose Jones, *A History of the Church in Wales* (Carmarthen, 1926), pp. 253–69; the last chapters in A. G. Edwards, *Landmarks in the History of the Welsh Church* (London, 1927) and his autobiography, *Memories* (London, 1927); his brother's book is much more provocative, H. T. Edwards, *Wales and the Welsh Church* (London, 1889); J. Myfenydd Morgan's chapter is not bad in J. Morgan Jones (ed.), *Trem ar y Ganrif* (Dolgellau, 1902), pp. 79–113; there are a number of good passages in J. Vyrnwy Morgan, *The Church in Wales* (London, 1918), and good chapters on churchmen in the volume edited by Morgan, *Welsh Religious Leaders in the Victorian Era* (London, 1905).

[30] James, *Church History of Wales*, pp. 173–6.

[31] Ibid., p. 74.

[32] For the history of St David's College, see D. T. W. Price, *A History of Saint David's University College Lampeter* (Cardiff, 1990), 2 vols.

[33] *Haul* (1886), 95–6. James (1827–86) ended up as rector of Letterston and Llanfihangel Nant-y-gof.

[34] For an alternative treatment, see Roger L. Brown, *The Welsh Evangelicals* (Cardiff, 1986).

[35] *Llan* (17 October 1952), 2, in the first of his articles, 'Trem ar Efengyliaeth a Chatholigiaeth yng Nghymru yn y bedwaredd ganrif ar bymtheg.'

[36] Llandaff Church Extension Society: see the thorough study by Wilton D. Wills, 'The Established Church in the Diocese of Llandaff, 1850–70: a Study of the Evangelical Movement in the South-Wales Coalfield', *Welsh History Review*, IV (1968–9), 235–67. For Alfred Ollivant (1798–1882), see *DWB*.

[37] For Bruce (1815–95), see *DWB*, and J. Vyrnwy Morgan, *Welsh Political and Educational Leaders in the Victorian Era* (London, 1908). Richards (1741–1867) was a solicitor and the manager of the Bute estates.

[38] Wills, 'Established Church in Llandaff', p. 246.

[39] Ibid., pp. 249–50.

[40] The reasons for the ebb are discussed ibid., pp. 265–7.

[41] *Report of the Royal Commission on Disestablishment*, II, 184, questions 5295–5300. Lewis was the means of building fourteen new churches and six mission rooms, ibid., question 5964; also see William Morris, Treorchy (Rhosynog), 'Rhai o'm hatgofion am y Canon Lewis', *Geninen* (1922), 104–6.

[42] *Llan* (31 October 1952), 3.

[43] For the family, see *DWB*, Richard Thomas (1754–1837). A splendid description of Richard Richards is given by Mary Ellis in *Haul* (spring 1976), 15–20.

[44] *Cymru* (1893), 123. For Hughes (1787–1860), see *DWB*.

[45] D. Eifion Evans, *Llan* (24 October 1952), 2; (31 October 1952), 3. For more details, see O. W. Jones, *Isaac Williams and his Circle* (London, 1971), pp. 97–100. Hughes's printed sermon buffets the 'Puseyites' fairly plainly, *Haul* (1842), 45.

[46] For Parry (1794–1877), see *DWB*.

[47] See Walter T. Morgan, 'The Diocese of St David's in the Nineteenth Century: the Unreformed Church (II)', *Journal of the Historical Society of the Church in Wales*, 22 (1972), 43–4. For Herbert (1762–1835), see *DWB*, and David Evans, *Adgofion yr Hybarch David Evans* (Lampeter, 1904) for witty stories about him.

[48] Wills, 'Established Church in Llandaff', p. 252.

[49] For Griffiths (1820–97), see *DWB*, and Morgan, *Welsh Religious Leaders*, pp. 86–103, which includes a picture.

[50] Morgan, *Church in Wales*, pp. 156–7.

[51] For Evans (1823–1900), see *Un o Gymry Duw, sef cofeb fechan am William Evans* (Lampeter, 1904); *Geninen* (1904), 42; *DWB*. He was editor of *Y Cyfaill Eglwysig* from 1866 to 1893.

[52] For Thomas (1844–1911), see Morgan, *Church in Wales*, pp. 160–4; D. Eifion Evans, *Llan* (17 October 1952), 2; for the rest of the names see Wills, 'Established Church in Llandaff', pp. 251–2.

[53] O. W. Jones, *Isaac Williams*, p. 104.

[54] It was said that Gladstone regretted appointing Hughes when he discovered that he was not a graduate of one of the universities. G. Hartwell Jones, *A Celt Looks at the World* (Cardiff, 1946), p. 51.

[55] For Hughes (1807–89) and Wynne (1667–1743), see *DWB*.

[56] For Robert Williams (1814–1902) and Eleazar Williams, see B. R. Hughes, 'Biographical Epitome of the Bishops and Clergy of the Diocese of Bangor', VII, 1208 and IX, 14; *Geninen Gwî yl Dewi* (1905), 28–9.

[57] Morgan, *Welsh Religious Leaders*, p. 106. For Howell, see Roger L. Brown, *David Howell, A Pool of Spirituality: A Life of David Howell (Llawdden)* (Denbigh, 1998).

[58] *Haul* (Spring 1971), 32.

[59] *Celt* (24 April 1896), 1. For his career see *DWB*; Morgan, *Welsh Religious Leaders*, pp. 104–26; idem, *Church in Wales*, pp. 158–60.

[60] *Geninen Gwî yl Dewi* (1905), 29.

[61] A full and scholarly history of the movement is given by D. Eifion Evans in his articles 'Dylanwad Mudiad Rhydychen yng Nghymru', *Journal of the Historical Society of the Church in Wales*, IV (1954), VI (1956), VII (1957), X (1960). See also A. Tudno Williams, *Mudiad Rhydychen a Chymru* (Denbigh, 1983). For a lyrical description of a visit to Hursley, John Keble's parish, see T. Llechid Jones in *Haul* (1910), 70–6. For the liturgical principles of the movement, see J. Edwin Davies, 'Defodaeth', *Haul* (1899), 167–73; Walker (ed.), *History of the Church in Wales*, pp. 149–54.

[62] Jones, *Isaac Williams*, p. 5; for Williams (1802–65), see also *DWB*. Matthew Williams, Cwmcynfelin, died in 1860.

[63] D. Eifion Evans, *Llan* (17 October 1952), 2. Tractarian teaching should not be confused with the renewal in ritual. One of the clearest and most succinct descriptions of the development of high church-manship is the evidence of Randall Davidson, archbishop of Canterbury, to the Royal Commission on Ecclesiastical Discipline (*Minutes of Evidence, Royal Commission on Ecclesiastical Discipline* II, (London: Wyman & Sons Ltd., 1906), pp. 340–74) and he said, for example, that Keble 'was never in the modern sense a "ritualist" . . . [he] never himself adopted vestments or other ritual usages of the kind' (ibid., p. 341). To him and his friends, the movement was a doctrinal revival rather than a ritualistic one.

[64] Jones, *Isaac Williams*, pp. 92–3.

[65] D. Eifion Evans, *Journal of the Historical Society of the Church in Wales*, VI (1956), 92.

[66] For Robert Isaac Jones (Alltud Eifion) (1814–1905), see Mary Ellis, *Haul* (Summer 1975), 16–21; for Robert Roberts (Y Sgolor Mawr) (1834–85), see J. H. Davies, *The Life and Opinions of Robert Roberts* (Cardiff, 1923), and *DWB*.

[67] For Alltud Eifion's reminiscences about the society, and its minutes, see *Haul* (1896), 15–17, 196–7, 304–5, 335–6, and for an address to it by Glasynys in 1856 see *Haul* (1897), 11–12.

[68] For *Baner y Groes*, see D. Eifion Evans, *Journal of the Historical Society of the Church in Wales*, VII (1957), and Saunders Lewis's introduction to *Straeon Glasynys* (Denbigh, 1943). John Williams (Ab Ithel) (1811–62) was the editor and Owen Wynne Jones (Glasynys) (1828–70) was the principal contributor. The journal was resurrected to serve the Sunday schools, 1870–3.

[69] For Williams (1808–74), see *DWB*, and Mary Ellis, 'Portread o Nicander', *Haul* (Summer 1973), 29–38.

[70] For Lewis (1818–1901), see *DWB*, and *Geninen Gŵyl Dewi* (1902, 1903); D. Eifion Evans, *Journal of the Historical Society of the Church in Wales*, VI (1956), 94–5.

[71] See G. A. Jones and J. W. Doran, *Hyfforddwr ar y Gân Eglwysig i'r Côr a'r Gynulleidfa* (Oxford, 1884).

[72] For Ellis (1822–1900), see *DWB*.

[73] D. Eifion Evans, *Journal of the Historical Society of the Church in Wales*, VI (1956), 95–7.

[74] For Jones (1827–1906), see *DWB*, and John Wollaston Ward, *Father Jones of Cardiff* (London, 1907).

[75] *Father Jones of Cardiff*, pp. 15–16.

[76] Ibid., p. 65, in an address in the Llandaff Diocesan Conference.

[77] Others who contributed to the revival were E. Osborne Williams (Pwllheli), D. Watkin Davies (Llanrhyddlad), D. Walters Thomas (Holyhead), J. Crawley Vincent (Caernarfon), Richard Jones (Llandyfrydog), William Hughes (Llanfechell: for Hughes, 1827–88, see *Haul* (1914), 16–21), John Pryce (1828–1903), dean of Bangor, and his two brothers, Hugh Lewis Pryce (1826–95) and Shadrach Pryce (1833–1914) – see *Haul* (1902), 56–7; (1914), 17; *Geninen* (1904), 160–4 – Thomas Davies (Trawsfynydd and Llanwrin) and Griffith Roberts (1845–1943).

[78] In his evidence, *Report of the Royal Commission on Disestablishment*, IV, 504, question 47844.

[79] For How (1823–97), see *DNB*.

[80] For Foulkes (1815–86), see *DWB*, and *Haul* (1886), 83–4, and D. Eifion Evans, *Journal of the Historical Society of the Church in Wales*, XII (1958), 83–4.

81 For Pughe (1812–60) see Evans, *Adgofion*, pp. 49, 108.

82 For Lloyd (1820–91), see *DWB*.

83 D. Eifion Evans, *Journal of the Historical Society of the Church in Wales*, XII (1958), 82–9; George Lerry, *Alfred George Edwards* (Oswestry, 1940?), pp. 111–12; for Ellis, see R. O. Roberts, 'Rowland Ellis – esgob Aberdeen', *Haul* (Spring, Summer 1975).

84 D. Eifion Evans, *Journal of the Historical Society of the Church in Wales*, XII (1958), 90–1. For Lyne (1837–1908), see *DNB*. Perhaps the best rendering of 'gorsedd' here would be either 'court' or 'gathering'. See *GPC*, II, p. 1495.

85 For Talbot (1803–90) and his daughters, Olivia Emma (d. 1894) and Emily Charlotte (d. 1918), see *DWB*.

86 Edwards, *Wales and the Welsh Church*, p. 162. For Edwards (1837–84), see the biography at the beginning of the book; R. O. Roberts in *Haul* (Autumn 1976), 8–15, and his MA dissertation on him, University of Wales, 1978.

87 Edwards, *Wales and the Welsh Church*, p. 168.

88 Ibid., pp. 215, 217.

89 Ibid., p. 267.

90 Bedwyr Lewis Jones in *Yr Hen Bersoniaid Llengar* (Penarth, 1963). For John Jenkins (Ifor Ceri) (1770–1829), Richard Davies (Dewi Silin) (1783–1926), William Jenkin Rees (1772–1855) and Burgess (1756–1837), see *DWB* and Thomas Parry, *Hanes Llenyddiaeth Gymraeg hyd 1900* (Cardiff, 1953), pp. 243–8.

91 For Walter Davies (Gwallter Mechain) (1761–1849), Daniel Evans (Daniel Ddu), (1792–1844), see *DWB*. For Evan Evans (Glan Geirionydd) (1795–1855), see *DWB*, and W. J. Roberts, *Geirionydd* (Rhuthin, 1862); for John Blackwell (Alun) (1797–1840), see *DWB* and *Ceinion Alun* (Rhuthin, 1851).

92 Parry, *Hanes Llenyddiaeth Gymraeg*, p. 261.

93 For Price (1788–1848), see *DWB*, and Mary Ellis in *Haul* (Winter 1974), 32–40.

94 For Evans (1818–1903), see *DWB*.

95 This subject is explored in Roger L. Brown, 'In Pursuit of a Welsh Episcopate', in Robert Pope (ed.), *Religion and National Identity: Wales and Scotland c.1700–2000* (Cardiff, 2000), pp. 84–102.

96 For the debates about abolishing the Court of Great Session, see *Cymro* (1830), 60–1, 75, 108–9 (third reading in the Commons, 18 June 1830), 146; (1831), 26–7, 87, 108; (1833), 1–3; *Gwladgarwr* (1837), 151–3, 176–9, 203–7. Thirlwell refused to place Richard Lewis (later bishop of Llandaff) in the living of Llanddewi Efelffre in 1851 because his Welsh was not good enough, but he was forced to do it in the end by the archbishop of Canterbury, see Francis Jones, 'A Victorian

Bishop of Llandaff', *National Library of Wales Journal*, XIX (1975–6), 33–7.

[97] For Hughes (1803–63), D. James (Dewi o Ddyfed) (1803–71) and his brother T. James (Llallawg) (1817–79), see *DWB*.

[98] *Geninen* (1903), 209.

[99] *Haul* (1886), 287.

[100] *Geninen* (1893), 15–18.

[101] *Haul* (1896), 314–16.

[102] *Young Wales*, III (1897), 260; cf. *Tyst* (18 December 1930), 9, for an attack on Edwards's anti-Welshness.

[103] *Young Wales*, IV (1898), 7.

[104] For the change in general, see J. Wheldon Griffith, for the Llŷn deanery, *Haul* (1909), 65–71; D. Jones, Newborough, for the diocese of Bangor, *Haul* (1886), 358–9; for the Glyn Aeron deanery, *Haul* (1908), 177–83; for the diocese of St Davids, evidence of the bishop, *Report of the Royal Commission on Disestablishment*, V, 216–21; for St Asaph, evidence of the bishop, ibid., IV, 504; for Llandaff, bishop in *Haul* (1894), 254; for Rhondda, Canon William Lewis, *Report of the Royal Commission on Disestablishment*, II, 184, 196; also *Haul* (1914), 17; *Geninen* (1904), 269–70; (1906), 209–15.

[105] Census of Great Britain, 1851, published in *Religious Worship: England and Wales* (London, 1853), p. cxciv. The census was taken on Sunday, 30 March 1851. For further details, see I. G. Jones and D. Williams (eds), *The Religious Census of 1851: A Calendar of Returns Relating to Wales*, I *South Wales* (Cardiff, 1976).

[106] *Report of the Royal Commission on Disestablishment*, VII, 89. The largest church was at Trebanos in the Swansea valley, with 195 members. Second largest was Pantydefaid Cardiganshire, with 172.

[107] Ibid., I, 40, but 302 members were put in ibid., VI, 442. According to the lists, ibid., VI, 264, 274, 428, 430, these were their meeting houses in Maesyfed, Llanbadarn-fawr (20 members), Llandegla (30), Llandrindod (64), Llanyre (17) and in Glamorgan, Cardiff (80) and Swansea (50).

[108] D. Bogue and J. Bennett, *History of Dissenters*, IV (London, 1812), p. 328.

[109] Comparing 1851 Census, *Religious Worship*, pp. lvii and cxciv.

[110] *Report of the Royal Commission on Disestablishment*, VII, 16.

[111] Ibid., I, 20. It must be remembered that many more attended the services in 1905 than the total of members.

[112] Bogue and Bennett, *History of Dissenters*, IV, p. 328.

[113] J. M. Davies, 'Y Bedyddwyr', in Jones (ed.), *Trem ar y Ganrif*, p. 194. See also T. M. Bassett, *The Welsh Baptists* (Swansea, 1977).

[114] *Report of the Royal Commission on Disestablishment*, VII, 3 –

143,835 was the membership of the Particular Baptists without the two small denominations.

[115] Ibid., I, 20; VII, 6, which gives the statistics for every five years from 1855. In the analysis the membership figures that were accepted by the Disestablishment Commission are used.

[116] Ibid., I, 40.

[117] A. H. Williams, *Welsh Wesleyan Methodism 1800–1858* (Bangor, 1935), p. 45. Also see Hugh Jones, *Hanes Wesleyaeth Gymreig*, 4 vols (Bangor, 1911–13).

[118] Williams, *Welsh Wesleyan Methodism*, p. 45, correcting figures in the *Report of the Royal Commission on Disestablishment*, VII, 157.

[119] According to A. H. Williams, *Welsh Wesleyan Methodism*, p. 346, the Welsh Wesleyans had 293 chapels, 64 ministers and 11,839 members. According to the 1851 Census, the Wesleyans in Wales had 659 worship places.

[120] *Report of the Royal Commission on Disestablishment*, I, 20–2. The Commission corrected the denomination's statistics as they are given ibid., VII, 158–9.

[121] Ibid., VII, 89. For J. R. Jones (1765–1822), see J. Idwal Jones, *J. R. Jones, Ramoth, a'i Amserau* (Llandysul, 1966) and David Williams, *Cofiant J. R. Jones, Ramoth* (Carmarthen, 1913). Further information can be found in Brian Talbot, 'Unity and Disunity: the Scotch Baptists, 1765–1842', in Pope (ed.), *Religion and National Identity*, pp. 221–241.

[122] *Report of the Royal Commission on Disestablishment*, VII, 3 and I, 126, for William George's memorandum on the denomination; for its teaching, see W. George, *Richard Lloyd, Criccieth* (Cardiff, 1934), ch. 2.

[123] For further information, see F. L. Cross (ed.), *Oxford Dictionary of the Christian Church* (3rd edn Oxford, 1997), articles on 'Bible Christians', 'Methodist New Connexion' and 'United Methodist Free Churches'.

[124] *Report of the Royal Commission on Disestablishment*, I, 41, and VII, 166–9 for a list of their churches.

[125] Ibid., I, 41.

[126] Ibid.

[127] For the story, see Williams, *Welsh Wesleyan Methodism*, ch. 7.

[128] For the movement, see *Oxford Dictionary of the Christian Church*, articles on 'Primitive Methodist Church'; H. B. Kendall, *The Origin and History of the Primitive Methodist Church* (London, 1905); W. J. Townsend and H. B. Workman, *A New History of Methodism*, I (London, 1909), pp. 555–98.

[129] *Report of the Royal Commission on Disestablishment*, VII, 76, for

the details see also Cynffig Davies, 'Brawdoliaeth Plymouth ym Môn', *Geninen* (1909), 61–2; and *Oxford Dictionary of the Christian Church*, article on 'Plymouth Brethren'.

[130] The rest were the Catholic Apostolics, the Christadelphians, the Christian Brothers, the Church of Christ, the Free Church of the Welsh, the Free Gospellers, the Moravians, New Thought, the Norwegian Lutheran Church, the Reformed Church of England, the Scandinavian Church, the Seventh Day Adventists, the Swedenborgians. A full list is given in the *Report of the Royal Commission on Disestablishment*.

[131] The figure is given in the totals for the different counties ibid., VI.

[132] R. Tudur Jones, *Yr Undeb* (Swansea, 1975).

[133] T. Jones-Humphreys, *Methodistiaeth Wesleyaidd Gymreig* (Holywell, 1900), p. 163.

[134] For Michael D. Jones's attitude towards the Union of Welsh Independents, see *Celt* (22 May 1885), 8; (31 August 1888), 1.

[135] For the 'Battle of the Constitutions', see R. G. Owen, 'Brwydr y Ddau Gyfansoddiad, 1877–1885', MA dissertation, University of Wales, 1941; Iorwerth C. Peate, 'Helynt y Cyfansoddiadau', *Llenor*, XII (1933), 1–10, 231–41; XIII (1934), 163–70; XV (1936), 209–14.

[136] This subject is discussed in Alun Tudur, 'O'r Sect i'r Enwad: Datblygiad Enwadau Ymneilltuol Cymru, 1840–1870', unpublished Ph.D. thesis, University of Wales, 1992.

[137] The Plymouth Brethren in Ammanford, the Salvation Army in Betws, the Evangelical Hall in Llanelli, and the Wern, Pencarreg, were minuted as 'non-denominational chapels'. *Report of the Royal Commission on Disestablishment*, VI, 72,82.

[138] For Finney (1792–1875), see G. Frederick Wright, *Charles Grandison Finney* (Boston and New York, 1891); Sydney E. Ahlstrom, *A Religious History of the American People* (London, 1972), pp. 459–61; *Yr Efengylydd* (1927), 76, 100, 126.

[139] For the transformation in Anglesey, see R. Tudur Jones, *John Elias: Pregethwr a Phendefig* (Bridgend, 1975), pp. 36–40.

[140] These men are all found in *DWB*. See also the detailed study by Iorwerth Jones, *David Rees, Y Cynhyrfwr* (Swansea, 1971) and T. M. Jones, *Cofiant y Parch Roger Edwards* (Wrexham, 1908), chs 10 and 12.

[141] For the attempt to analyse services according to language, see *Report of the Royal Commission on Disestablishment*, I, 295–6.

[142] *Celt* (22 May 1885), 8.

3. Stoking the Denominational Fires

[1] The words 'enwadaeth' and 'enwadyddiaeth' can be translated either as 'denominationalism' or 'sectarianism'. In this chapter, Tudor Jones uses both, the latter usually having a pejorative meaning. As a result, 'denominationalism' has been used for 'enwadaeth' and, when the meaning is pejorative, 'denominational sectarianism' has been used. The issue is compounded by Dr Tudur's use of 'sectyddiaeth' translated here as 'sectarianism'.

[2] For John Thomas (Eifionydd) (1848–1922), see *DWB*. For William Richard Jones (1840–98), see *DWB* and Alafon, *Gweithiau Llenyddol Goleufryn* (Caernarfon, 1904).

[3] *Geninen* (1887), 43, and *Gweithiau Llenyddol Goleufryn*, pp. 225–304.

[4] *Geninen* (1890), 33.

[5] Catterick in Yorkshire was the scene of a battle between the Celtic Brythons and the Saxons recorded in the sixth-century poetry of the bard Aneirin.

[6] *Tyst* (7 March 1890), 3 – 'Ymylon y ffordd', by Lladmerydd (Dr John Thomas, Liverpool).

[7] A letter supporting 'Siluriad' can be found in *Tyst* (14 March 1890), 13–14.

[8] R. Gwylfa Roberts, *Cofiant y Parch William Davies, Llandeilo* (Llanelli, 1925), p. 140.

[9] Cf. Gildas, 'Y meginau enwadol', *Geninen* (1894), 49–53, for a skit on the blarney found in denominational papers.

[10] *Greal* (1903), 168.

[11] *Drysorfa* (1898), 233.

[12] *Celt* (12 June 1896), 4.

[13] James Williams, *Give Me Yesterday* (Llandysul, 1971), pp. 18–19.

[14] Juno, 'Rhagfarn enwadol Cymru', *Geninen* (1892), 224.

[15] *Geninen* (1893), 188.

[16] Ibid., p. 78.

[17] *Tyst* (21 February 1890), 3. C. A. H. Green (1864–1944), the vicar of Aberdare and the bishop of Monmouth and Bangor after that, admitted to the Disestablishment Commission, 15 February 1907, that he had never been inside a Nonconformist chapel, *Report of the Royal Commission on Disestablishment*, II, 257.

[18] For Davies (d. 12 November 1884, aged 63), see *Celt* (21 November 1884), 1; (28 November 1884), 10; (12 December 1898), 1. His daughter, Catherine, was married to Sir Francis (Frank) Edwards (1852–1927), see the article on him in *DWB*. For H. T. Edwards's marriage to Mary

(she died in 1871), see H. T. Edwards, *Wales and the Welsh Church* (London, 1889), p. 22. It is fair to say that A. G. Edwards was present at David Davies's funeral!

[19] *Young Wales*, IV (1898), 5 – 'a bitter rivalry among sects'. *Report of the Royal Commission on Disestablishment*, II, 516, question 1746.

[20] *Report of the Baptist Union of Wales*, Carmarthen (1891), p. 30. There is a memorial article about Jenkyn in *Geninen* (1893), 235–8.

[21] *Drysorfa* (1900), 88. Years before, churchmen were equally as defamatory towards the Methodists, describing the *Goleuad* as 'the lowest and impolite paper' ('y papuryn iselwael ac anfoneddigaidd'), *Dywysogaeth* (14 May 1870), 1.

[22] *Drysorfa* (1899), 30. On the other hand, in a scathing piece of cross-examination in the Disestablishment Commission, S. T. Evans got Canon William Lewis, Ystradyfodwg, to admit that he had never read any of the literary output of his neighbours Dr William Morris, Noddfa, David Bowen, Ben Bowen, Dr Waldo James, D. M. Phillips or even the work of Lewis Probert who lived for years within a hundred yards of him in Pentre. *Report of the Royal Commission on Disestablishment*, II, 194, questions 5823–70.

[23] *Geninen* (1898), 227–8; cf. Iwan Jenkyn, *Report of the Baptist Union of Wales*, Carmarthen (1891), p. 28.

[24] Professor Ian Henderson wrote strongly on this point. 'Denominationalism, the courageous abandonment of the nightmare dogma of the One Church . . . is the conviction that if you cannot agree with your fellow Christians, it is better to live with them than to kill them', *Power Without Glory* (London, 1967), pp. 12–13.

[25] *Report of the Union of Welsh Independents*, Ferndale (1892), pp. 260–7, 'Peryglon cystadleuaeth enwadol'.

[26] *Tyst* (18 April 1890), 9.

[27] Llythyr, 'Undeb crefyddol', *Faner* (30 April 1890), 3.

[28] *Report of the Union of Welsh Independents*, Wrexham (1891), p. 102.

[29] W. A. Visser 't Hooft, article 'Ecumenical Movement', in *Twentieth Century Encyclopaedia of Religious Knowledge* (1955); Carl F. H. Henry, *Evangelicals at the Brink of Crisis* (Waco, TX, 1968), pp. 83–4; Ruth Rouse and S. C. Neill, *A History of the Ecumenical Movement, 1517–1948* (London, 1954), pp. 309–17.

[30] The story is reported briefly on Rouse and Neill, *History of Ecumenical Movement*, pp. 318–24; see also Henry Richards's comments in *Memoirs of Joseph Sturge* (London, 1863), pp. 373–83.

[31] *Tyst* (11 April 1890), 9.

[32] Ibid; and, strangely enough, the same words by Rouse and Neill, *History of Ecumenical Movement*, p. 334 – 'no question of the union of Churches can be profitably discussed except on the basis of

complete equality of civil rights between the religious bodies concerned'.

33 *Report of the Union of Welsh Independents*, Beaufort (1890), pp. 35–66.

34 The declaration was based on the one adopted by the General Assembly of the Protestant Episcopal Church of the United States in Chicago in 1886; see Rouse and Neill, *History of Ecumenical Movement*, pp. 264–5.

35 'Rhagolygon Undeb Cristionogol', *Geninen* (1910), 164–7.

36 *Haul* (1894), 55, 57.

37 *Haul* (1920), 128–9, 'Catholigrwydd yr Eglwys'.

38 H. T. Edwards, *Wales and the Welsh Church*, pp. 229–30.

39 D. J. Davies (Llanddeusant, Carmarthenshire), 'Undeb yr Eglwys', *Haul* (1893), 205 – from a series of articles on the subject.

40 *Report of the Royal Commission on Disestablishment*, IV, 536, questions 48496–8; 541, questions 48602–8.

41 Ibid., II, 482, question 16296; cf. ibid., III, 75–6, questions 20471–88 – evidence from the vicar of Brymbo; for the tension in Denbigh, see ibid., IV, 130, question 38357.

42 *Haul* (1894), 242.

43 *Report of the Royal Commission on Disestablishment*, III, 115–16, question 21923 – evidence from Howell Roberts.

44 Ibid., II, 110.

45 Ibid., III, 137, also in Raglan, ibid., II, 376.

46 Ibid., II, 44.

47 MS Bangor 1668. Griffith's dates were 1841–1910.

48 *Llan* (9 February 1900), 5.

49 *Haul* (1902), 219–23; cf. pp. 291–4, 466–7.

50 *Geninen* (1908), 73–83; response by John Owen, Bowydd, pp. 152–9; also 'Un Eglwys i Gymru', *Geninen* (1909), 43–8, and the response by Griffith Evans, Bangor, pp. 183–6.

51 For example, M. J. Hughes, rector of Prestatyn, 'Y gwyliwr, beth am y bore?', *Geninen* (1909), 228–33.

52 *Haul* (1891), 344.

53 James Owen, Swansea, in T. Stephens (ed.), *Cymru Heddiw ac Yforu* (Cardiff, 1908), p. 6.

54 D. Jones, vicar of Aber-erch, 'Methodistiaeth Galfinaidd a'r Eglwys yng Nghymru', *Geninen* (1898), 122–6.

55 *Haul* (1892), 172.

56 Dean John Owen in *Geninen* (1890), 145; *Report of the Royal Commission on Disestablishment*, IV, 425, question 46089 for more details, and ibid., I, 121.

57 Rouse and Neill, *History of Ecumenical Movement*, pp. 266–8; *Geninen* (1892), 138–41.

58 The growth of the idea, and the details of arrangements, can be found in 'The Reunion Party at Grindelwald', *Review of the Churches*, I (1891–2), 322–4, and Henry Lunn, 'A "Reunion" Trip to Norway', *Review of the Churches*, I (1891–2), 143–4, 182–3; see also D. P. Hughes, *The Life of Hugh Price Hughes* (London, 1904), ch. 15 for a lively description of the conferences. The Church in Wales's response can be found in 'Grindelwald', *Haul* (1893), 23–6, and the Congregationalists, Thomas Williams (Merthyr) and Joseph Williams (publisher of *Y Tyst*) were present. *Tyst* (10 August 1894), 3, but the editor's response was barbed (H. M. Hughes), *Tyst* (18 October 1895), 8–9.

59 *Haul* (1894), 46–50, 124–5.

60 *Geninen* (1887), 38.

61 *Geninen* (1893), 139.

62 *Report of the Union of Welsh Independents*, Holyhead (1893), 351–66, 'Enwadaeth Cristionogol'.

63 *Drysorfa* (1894), 309.

64 For example, E. E. Jones, Rhos-y-bol, in *Greal* (1898), 57–60.

65 *Report of the Union of Welsh Independents*, Neath (1907), p. 333. See further D. Jones, Aber-erch, in *Geninen* (1898), 125–6; Hugh Edwards, 'Undeb enwadol', *Drysorfa* (1900), 347–52.

66 The entry on him in *DWB* is inadequate.

67 *Faner* (30 April 1890), 9; *Geninen* (1890), 154–5.

68 *Faner* (30 April 1890), 3.

69 *Faner* (14 May 1890), 3.

70 *Faner* (30 April 1890), 3.

71 *Faner* (4 November 1891), 9; *Goleuad* (5 November 1891), 8–9. For Saunders (1831–92), the minister of Trinity, Swansea, see W. James and J. M. Jones, *Cofiant a Phregethau D. Saunders DD* (Swansea, 1894) – his wife was Llawdden's sister; for Davies (1823–98), minister of Siloa, Llanelli, see *Diwygiwr* (1898), 133–42, and *Congregational Year Book* (1899), 169–70. For Freeman, one-time mayor of Swansea and deacon in Siloh, Landore, see *Dysgedydd* (1902), 449. According to his grand memorial in the cemetery at Bethel, Sketty, he was born 17 August 1842 and died 16 August 1902.

72 For the details, see R. Tudur Jones, *Congregationalism in England, 1662–1962* (London, 1962), pp. 331–3; also E. K. H. Jordan, *Free Church Unity* (London, 1956); *Eurgrawn Wesleaidd* (1899), 125.

73 *Report of the Royal Commission on Disestablishment*, I, 75; T. Roberts, 'Cynghrair Gogledd Cymru' (established in Rhyl, 1897), *Dysgedydd* (1901), 212–14.

74 *Seren Gomer* (1901), 55.

75 *Greal* (1899), 220.

[76] *Report of the Baptist Union of Wales*, Rhymney (1899), 6; the correspondence can be found on pp. 9–10. See also H. Harris, Treherbert, 'Y Bedyddwyr a'r Eglwysi Rhyddion', *Geninen* (1904), 95–7; James Evans, 'Cyngor yr Eglwysi Rhyddion a'r Bedyddwyr', *Geninen* (1907), 210–13.

[77] *Report of the Baptist Union of Wales*, Bangor (1900), p. 17; *Seren Cymru* (15 March 1901), editorial.

[78] *Geninen* (1907), 211.

[79] *Report of the Union of Welsh Independents*, Bridgend (1896), p. 56; (Liverpool, 1897), p. 212; (Maesteg, 1901), p. 73; *Drysorfa* (1898), 379.

[80] *Drysorfa* (1901), 129, 172; *Dysgedydd* (1901), 121, 145–50.

[81] Full details can be found in *Report of the Royal Commission on Disestablishment*, I 2, 'Appendix T', 159–61.

[82] For the Bridgend programme, ibid., 164–5, 'Appendix U'.

[83] *Report of the Royal Commission on Disestablishment*, IV, 369, question 44857.

[84] 'Arthur', 'Sectyddiaeth ynte Cristionogaeth?', *Geninen* (1907), 200–3.

[85] 'Annibynwr', 'Y Methodistiaid a'r Annibynwyr', *Geninen* (1907), 271–3; E. Ungoed Thomas, '"Un Bedydd" ac uniad yr enwadau', *Geninen* (1909), 245–6; Deon Griffith Roberts, Bangor, 'Yr Eglwys Anglicanaidd ac yndeb Cristionogol', *Geninen* (1910), 14–17, and 'Rhagolygon undeb Cristionogol', pp. 164–7. A more cynical view of the subject can be found in T. Gwynn Jones 'Credoau [sic] a chyffesion enwadol; ai rhaid wrthynt?', *Geninen* (1903), 228–34.

[86] Griffith Ellis proposed, in the CM General Assembly in 1910 that a copy of the report of the conference should be placed in every library belonging to Methodist chapels. *Blwyddiadur y Methodistiaid Calfinaidd* (1911), 49.

[87] *Report of the Union of Welsh Independents*, Rhyl (1914), p. 818.

[88] 'Enwadaeth', *Beirniad* (Summer 1913), 73–85.

[89] *Beirniad* (Winter 1913), 254–8.

[90] *Beirniad* (Spring 1914), 39–46.

[91] For Herbert Morgan (1875–1946), see Robert Pope, *Seeking God's Kingdom: The Nonconformist Social Gospel in Wales 1906–1939* (Cardiff, 1999), pp. 82–90.

[92] *Beirniad* (Autumn 1914), 176–82; (Winter 1914), 257–65; for Tecwyn's response, see *Beirniad* (Spring 1915), 33–46.

[93] *Report of the Royal Commission on Disestablishment*, I, 74.

4. Anxieties

[1] David Griffith, *Cofiant y Parchedig David Roberts, DD, Wrecsam* (Dolgellau, 1899), pp. 195–7.

[2] *Celt* (17 April 1885), 1.

[3] *Greal* (1901), 55.

[4] *Cenad Hedd* (1901), 80.

[5] Griffith Ellis, *Victoria: Ei Bywyd Hardd fel Gwraig, Mam a Brenhines* (Wrexham, 1901), p. 192.

[6] A selection of them can be found in J. A. Hammerton (ed.), *The Passing of Victoria* (London, 1901).

[7] Samuel Hynes, *The Edwardian Turn of Mind* (Princeton, 1968), p. 15, n.

[8] 25 January 1901, *Hansard*, 89, cols 19–20.

[9] I tried to say something about the age's attitude towards children and women in 'Darganfod plant bach', in J. E. Caerwyn Williams (ed.), *Ysgrifau Beirniadol VII* (Denbigh, 1974), pp. 160–204; and *Coroni'r Fam Frenhines* (Llandysul, 1977).

[10] C. B. Cox and A. E. Dyson, *The Twentieth-Century Mind*, I (London, 1972), p. 54.

[11] *Drysorfa* (1892), 46–7.

[12] *Drysorfa* (1888), 282. Some of these words are repeated by him in *Geninen* (1896), 225.

[13] *Tyst* (14 November 1890), 9.

[14] *Haul* (1894), 196.

[15] *Tyst* (15 August 1890), 9; (11 September 1891), 9.

[16] *Tyst* (16 May 1890), 3–4.

[17] *Tyst* (17 November 1890), 10.

[18] *Report of the Baptist Union of Wales*, Morriston (1894), p. 10.

[19] *Drysorfa* (1894), 269–73.

[20] 'Yr Hen Gorff' (literally 'The old (dear) body') is a colloquial and affectionate way of referring to the Calvinistic Methodists, now the Presbyterian Church of Wales.

[21] *Drysorfa* (1899), 179.

[22] Thus H. N. Fairchild, *Religious Trends in English Poetry*, IV (New York, 957), pp. 538, 540, and Walter E. Houghton, *The Victorian Frame of Mind* (New Haven, 1957), p. 179. An alternative view can be found in Callum G. Brown, *The Death of Christian Britain* (London, 2001).

[23] *Drysorfa* (1900), 101.

[24] *Report of the Union of Welsh Independents*, Llanelli (1899), p. 492. For Davies (1852–1912), ironmonger in Pentre, see *Tyst* (4 August 1915) and R. Tudur Jones, *Yr Undeb* (Swansea, 1975), p. 274.

[25] D. Myrddin Lloyd (ed.), *Detholiad o Erthyglau a Llythyrau Emrys ap*

Iwan (Clwb Llyfrau Cymreig, 1937), p. 44, from the article 'Wele dy dduwiau, O Walia!'
26 J. Morris Jones, *Caniadau* (Oxford, 1907), p. 87.
27 *Greal* (1900), 171.
28 *Geninen* (1898), 229 – anonymous author.
29 *Drysorfa* (1898), 121.
30 *Report of the Union of Welsh Independents*, Holyhead (1893), pp. 416–25.
31 *Report of the Union of Welsh Independents*, Carmarthen (1872), p. 33.
32 E. Parry, *Llawlyfr ar hanes y diwygiadau crefyddol yng Nghymru* (Corwen, 1898).
33 'Criticus', in *Seren Gomer* (1899), 131.
34 *Drysorfa* (1897), 321.
35 *Celt* (28 December 1900), 4.
36 *Geninen* (1901), 200.
37 Ibid., p. 199.
38 *Diwygiwr* (1901), 6.
39 For example, *Report of the Baptist Union of Wales*, Swansea (1890), J. Thomas, 'Dyledswydd yr eglwys yn ngwyneb chwareuon yr oes'; *Report of the Union of Welsh Independents*, Bridgend (1896), H. Elvet Lewis, 'Yr eglwys a phobl ieuinc yr oes'.
40 For example, deacons' meeting at the CM Association, Tregaron, 13 August 1890, *Drysorfa* (1891), 152; Cil-y-cwm Association, June 1891, ibid., p. 32; Rhuthun Association, April 1896, *Drysorfa* (1896), 280–1; Arfon Baptist Assembly, 23 June 1898, *Greal* (1898), 195.
41 *Report of the Union of Welsh Independents*, Holyhead (1893), p. 402. For Morris (1845–1900), see *Dysgedydd* (1900), 476.
42 *Report of the Union of Welsh Independents*, Beaufort (1890), p. 86. An extensive quotation from his attack can be found in R. Tudur Jones, *Yr Undeb*, p. 116. For Davies (1846–1918), the minister of Bethlehem, see *Dysgedydd* (1918), 329–30.
43 *Celt* (1 December 1899).
44 *Dysgedydd* (1901), 230.
45 *Drysorfa* (1896), 280–1: Rhuthun, April 1896.
46 *Greal* (1898), 195.
47 Thus Rees Rees, *Report of the Union of Welsh Independents*, Holyhead (1893), pp. 417–18; cf., Blaenau Ffestiniog (1883), p. 85. For Rees (1852–1910), minister at Allt-wen, see *Congregational Year Book* (1912), 164–6.
48 *Report of the Union of Welsh Independents*, Blaenau Ffestiniog (1883). For David Roberts, Dewi Ogwen (1818–97), see D. Griffith, *Cofiant y Parchedig David Roberts*, and *DWB*.

49 *Report of the Union of Welsh Independents*, Llanelli (1899), p. 621. For Owen (1859–1916), see 'Hanes Coleg Bala-Bangor', MS.
50 *Tyst* (2 November 1894), 11.
51 *Drysorfa* (1897), 37; ibid., p. 81, for the comparable decision in the Wrexham Association, November 1896. For Megan Watts Hughes (1842–1907), composer of the tune 'Wilton Square', see *DWB*.
52 O. Llew Owain, *Hanes y Ddrama yng Nghymru 1850–1943* (Liverpool, 1948), p. 78.
53 *Tyst* (4 April 1890), 3.
54 J. R. Williams and G. Williams, *History of Caersalem, Dowlais* (Llandysul, 1967), p. 47.
55 T. Hudson Williams, *Atgofion am Gaernarfon* (Aberystwyth, 1950), p. 47.
56 Owain, *Hanes y Ddrama*, pp. 82–4.
57 Hudson Williams, *Atgofion am Gaernarfon*, pp. 47–9.
58 *Drysorfa* (1891), 289–92.
59 T. Stephens (ed.), *Cymru: Heddiw ac Yforu* (Cardiff, 1908), p. 6.
60 *Drysorfa* (1891), 311. A decision was reached on the same subject at the CM general assembly, Morriston, June 1891, ibid., p. 393.
61 *Tyst* (18 October 1889), 3–4.
62 Ap Iorwerth, 'Chwaraeon yr oes', *Dysgedydd* (1901), 229.
63 J. T. Evans, 'Pa fodd i ymddwyn yn Nhy Dduw', *Haul* (1894), 209–10.
64 See J. G. Davies, *The Secular Use of Church Buildings* (London, 1968).
65 For example, E. W. Davies, *Spirit and Sports, Church and Cheer, or the Attitude of the Christian Church towards the Sports, the Amusements, and the Recreations of the Age* (London, 1902).
66 *Drysorfa* (1892), 415.
67 'Arferion yr oes a dyledswydd yr eglwys', *Seren Gomer* (1901), 181–8.
68 *Report of the Union of Welsh Independents*, Bridgend (1896), pp. 123–7.
69 Iolo Caernarfon, 'Yr angen am yr Ysbryd Glân i wrthweithio cynydd llygredigaeth yr oes', *Drysorfa* (1893), 82–90. For John Roberts (Iolo Caernarfon) (1840–1914), minister of Tabernacl, Porthmadog, see T. R. Jones, *Y Parchedig J. J. Roberts (Iolo Caernarfon)* (Caernarfon, 1915?), *DWB*.
70 *Young Wales*, II (1896), 257.
71 For example, *Drysorfa* (1893), 189–92, Oswestry Association, April 1893; *Drysorfa* (1898), 322–3, Pontycymer Association, May 1898.
72 *Report of the Union of Welsh Independents*, Beaufort (1890), p. 99, and John Thomas, Liverpool, in almost the same words, *Tyst* (16 May 1890), 4, and T. E. Thomas, *Report of the Union of Welsh Independents*, Ferndale (1892), p. 233. For Thomas Ellis Thomas (1858–1951), Congregational minister at Coed-poeth, see *Blwyddiadur yr Annibynwyr* (1953), 153.
73 *Drysorfa* (1891), 311.

74 *Tyst* (19 September 1890), 3.

75 A long list of them can be found by W. Davies, Ton Pentre, in 'Y deffroad presennol gyda golwg ar le yr Ysbryd Glân yn llwyddiant yr Efengyl', *Greal* (1896), 33–7.

76 As in *Seren Gomer* (1896), 125–9.

77 As in *Drysorfa* (1897), 390–9; *Greal* (1898), 309–13; also pp. 123–8.

78 As in *Drysorfa* (1894), 7–9.

79 Gordon was minister of Clarendon Road Baptist Church, Boston, MA. He died on 2 February 1895. A good review of his book can be found in *Greal* (1896), 76, and information about his career ibid., pp. 1–4.

80 For further information, see Alan Richardson (ed.), *Dictionary of Christian Theology* (5th impression, London, 1977), p. 322.

81 Minutes of Corwen Association, April 1897, *Drysorfa* (1897), 281.

82 Jonathan Edwards, *Works*, III (London, 1843), pp. 427–508.

83 See Rouse and Neill, *A History of the Ecumenical Movement 1517–1948* (London, 1954), pp. 228, 345–6.

84 *Gwyliedydd* (15 November 1893), 1.

85 *Greal* (1900), 221.

86 Ibid., p. 305.

87 *Drysorfa* (1900), 370.

88 For Richard Owen (1839–87), see W. Pritchard, *Cofiant y Parch Richard Owen, y Diwygiwr* (Amlwch, 1889) and *DWB*.

89 For John Roberts (Ieuan Gwyllt) (1822–77), see *DWB*.

90 John Price Roberts and Thomas Hughes, *Cofiant y Parch John Evans Eglwysbach* (Bangor, 1903), p. 461. For Evans (1840–97), see also *DWB*.

91 R. Gwylfa Roberts, *Cofiant William Davies, Llandeilo* (Llanelli, 1925), p. 134.

92 Parry, *Llawlyfr ar hanes y diwygiadau crefyddol yng Nghymru* – and this book is itself a sign of the times.

93 *Gwyliedydd* (1 March 1893), 6; (15 March 1893), 6; (6 September 1893), 3.

94 *Tyst* (15 June 1894), 12. Rosina Davies (d. 18 October 1949) took part in the services, see her autobiography *The Story of My Life* (Llandysul, 1942), p. 155.

95 Roberts, *Cofiant William Davies*, p. 136.

96 *Drysorfa* (1898), 327.

97 *Drysorfa* (1899), 564.

98 *Traethodydd* (1922), 180.

99 *Eurgrawn Wesleaidd* (1935), 452.

100 For his preaching style, see Roberts and Hughes, *Cofiant*, p. 307.

101 *Eurgrawn Wesleaidd* (1935), 612; for his successful campaign in Bangor, see pp. 458–9.

102 For an analysis of the things which caused the failure of the

NOTES

experiment, see *Eurgrawn Wesleaidd* (1940), 258–62, 304–6. See also E. Berwyn Roberts, 'Dyddiau olaf John Evans', ibid., 311–16.

[103] For Davies (d. 1 January 1898), only son of David Davies (1818–90), Llandinam, see *Drysorfa* (1898), 66–8; his death is described as 'one of the heaviest blows which the Methodist Connexion has suffered for a quarter of a century'.

[104] For Prys (1857–1934), see *DWB*.

[105] J. M. Jones and Abraham Morris, *Hanes Symudiad Ymosodol y Methodistiaid Calfinaidd* (Caernarfon, 1931) and Mrs W. Watkin Williams, *Atgofion am John Pugh* (Llandysul, 1944), and Pugh's reports in *Drysorfa*.

[106] For Seth Joshua (1858–1925) and his brother Frank (1861–1920), see T. Mardy Rees, *Seth Joshua and Frank Joshua: The Renowned Evangelists* (Wrexham, 1926). Their brother, Caleb Joshua (1851–1923) was a Baptist minister.

[107] Further information about the Forward Movement can be found in the *Report of the Royal Commission on Disestablishment*, I, 68–70.

[108] For example, Llangynwyd, 4–14 October 1902, *Haul* (1902), 490–1.

[109] J. W. Ward, *Father Jones of Cardiff* (London, 1907), pp. 55–6.

[110] *Report of the Baptist Union of Wales*, Rhyl (1895), p. 5; Merthyr Tudful (1902), pp. 36–40; Liverpool (1903), pp. 95–7; Maesteg (1904), pp. 108–9; Abercarn (1905), pp. 95–8.

[111] For more details see R. Tudur Jones, *Yr Undeb*, pp. 152–9.

[112] G. E. Beck (ed.), *The English Catholics 1850–1950* (London, 1950), p. 117.

[113] 'Passionists', namely the Congregation of the Barefooted Clerics of the Most Holy Cross and Passion of our Lord Jesus Christ, established by St Paul of the Cross (1694–1775) in 1720 in Italy.

[114] In the Caernarfon Association, August 1896, it was decided to form a committee to consider the Catholic efforts to win ground, *Drysorfa* (1896), 472, and its activity can be followed in the minutes of association meetings from that time. The Methodists maintained four 'anti-Catholic' schools in Flintshire at Rhuallt, Gronant, Carmel and Ffynnongroyw. There was quite a lot of worried and fierce writing against Catholicism in periodicals of the time, for example, *Geninen* (1889), 22–4; *Tyst* (16 March 1894), R. H. Morgan, 'Y Jesuitiaid', *Drysorfa* (1897), 97–105; T. M. Jones, 'Pa fodd i gyfarfod Pabyddiaeth?', ibid., pp. 202–5; Owen Davies, 'Cymru a'r Babaeth', *Greal* (1907), 319–23. Regular attacks were made in *Y Faner* and almost every edition of *Cenad Hedd* (1901) attacks Catholicism.

[115] For Hughes (1833–87), see *DWB*; *Menevia Record*, I (1953), 21–2; J. H. Matthews, *A Sketch of the Life and Labours of Father Hughes*

440

(1890); D. Attwater, *The Catholic Church in Modern Wales* (London, 1935), pp. 114–21.

[116] P. E. Hook died on 7 March 1933 at the age of 61. Attwater, *Catholic Church in Modern Wales*, pp. 131–5.

[117] For J. H. Jones (1843–1910), see *DWB* – he hailed from Bala and was a grandson of Dafydd Cadwaladr.

[118] It was published in 1889. There is a review in *Cymru*, II (1892), 252 by O. M. Edwards. For J. H. Matthews (1858–1914), see *DWB*. He translated *Ffordd y Groes* into Welsh and edited *Emynau Catholig*.

[119] A clear outline of the above developments is given in Attwater, *Catholic Church in Modern Wales*, pp. 110–14, and there are a number of pertinent articles in *Menevia Record* from 1953.

[120] Much information about his activity is given in *Y Gad-lef*.

[121] Davies, *Story of My Life*, p. 167.

[122] *Eurgrawn Wesleaidd* (1933), 237; T. Jones-Humphreys said the same thing at p. 244.

[123] Ibid., p. 241. See also *Gwyliedydd Newydd* (11 May 1933), 8; (23 May 1933), 6; (1 June 1933), 7; memorial verses by Glanystwyth, *Goleuad* (10 May 1933), 6; *Dysgedydd* (1904), 213 for a review of his book, *Y Ddau Oleuni*.

5. 'And Here are the Announcements!'

[1] Literally, 'big seat', refers to the diaconal pew, often quite ornate, which was located at the bottom of the pulpit and in which the elders or deacons sat. Customarily, they would stand, turn and face the congregation when singing hymns and kneel during the prayers.

[2] *Report of the Royal Commission on Disestablishment*, VI, 2–13.

[3] For these movements, see *Oxford Dictionary of the Christian Church*.

[4] *Report of the Royal Commission on Disestablishment*, VI, 451.

[5] Ibid., pp. 445–71.

[6] Ibid., pp. 473–7, for the churches' response: the names of the churches can be found on pp. 270–4.

[7] *Gwyliedydd* (20 January 1902), 2.

[8] *Herald Cymraeg* (20 January 1903), 5.

[9] Ibid., p. 7.

[10] *Herald Cymraeg* (13 January 1903), 5.

[11] *Gwyliedydd* (26 February 1902), 2.

[12] *Tyst* (1 November 1895), 10.

[13] *Herald Cymraeg* (20 January 1903), 7.

[14] *Tyst* (25 January 1895), 10.

[15] *Tyst* (27 December 1895), 7.

[16] The phrase used, 'cyfrif llyfrithen', refers to the fact that a charm was to be repeated very quickly. It means that someone talks quickly and at length. See *GPC*, p. 716.

[17] Kate Roberts, *Y Lôn Wen* (Denbigh, 1960), pp. 46–7. The chapter 'Diwylliant a'r capel' is a very lively picture of the activity that is under discussion here.

[18] *Llan* (13 February 1903), 6.

[19] See also William George's description of similar occasions in Llanystumdwy school, *Atgof a Myfyr* (Wrexham, 1948), pp. 15–18, and for his brother's protest when Sir Hugh Ellis Nanney visited the school. See also H. du Parcq, *Life of David Lloyd George*, I (London, 1912), p. 17.

[20] *Llan* (13 March 1903), 3.

[21] *Llan* (6 March 1903), 7.

[22] *Llan* (20 February 1903), 7.

[23] *Llan* (13 February 1903), 7.

[24] *Llan* (20 February 1903), 6.

[25] *Llan* (6 March 1903), 6.

[26] *Llan* (13 February 1903), 7; (20 February 1903), 1.

[27] *Herald Cymraeg* (13 January 1903), 5.

[28] According to J. R. Williams and G. Williams, *History of Caersalem, Dowlais* (Llandysul, 1967), from about 1914 to the early 1920s it was most popular in that church.

[29] *Llan* (20 February 1903), 3.

[30] Ibid., p. 7.

[31] Ibid.

[32] *Llan* (13 February 1903), 7.

[33] Ibid.

[34] Ibid. D. Parry-Jones, *Welsh Country Upbringing* (London, 1949), p. 76, gives a description of a tea party in the squire's grange.

[35] *Haul* (1886), 49–50.

[36] See John Hickey, *Urban Catholics* (Louvain, 1967) and *idem*, 'The Origin and Growth of the Irish Community in Cardiff', MA dissertation, University of Wales, 1959.

[37] G. E. Beck (ed.), *The English Catholics 1850–1950* (London, 1950), pp. 276–7.

[38] In his valuable article, 'Diwylliant Gwerin', in *Diwylliant Gwerin ac Ysgrifau Eraill* (Llandysul, 1972), pp. 7–84.

[39] T. Eirug Davies (ed.), *Ffrwythiau Dethol* (Llandysul, 1938), p. 46. The volume offers an outline of Ben Davies's career (1864–1937) including 'Darn o hunangofiant' – a revealing document! 'Hwyl' was the 'characteristic musical intonation or sing-song cadence formerly much in vogue in the perorations of the Welsh pulpit', *GPC*, p. 1937.

[40] W. C. Elvet Thomas, *Tyfu'n Gymro* (Llandysul, 1972), pp. 92–3.

[41] Alun Llewelyn-Williams gives a description of this transformation during his adolescence in Cardiff in *Gwanwyn yn y Ddinas* (Denbigh, 1975), p. 21. James Williams, *Give Me Yesterday* (Llandysul, 1971), is more disparaging of his upbringing in the chapel.

[42] The *Report of the Royal Commission on Disestablishment* only gives details on this subject for Glamorgan, VI, 445–77. The number of week meetings is given for Monmouthshire and Anglesey.

[43] In the *Report of the Royal Commission on Disestablishment*, VI, 445–77, there is a column with the heading 'Church Meetings'. Some churches appear to have one each week, others every fortnight or every month and Bethlehem (Independent), Pentyrch, three per year. It is clear that there is confusion here between the Methodist *seiat*, usually a devotional meeting, and the Congregational and Baptist 'church meeting', namely the main legal and governing authority in the congregation.

[44] For the background to the liturgical history, see C. W. Dugmore, 'Canonical Hours', in J. G. Davies (ed.), *A Dictionary of Liturgy and Worship* (London, 1972) and E. C. Ratcliff, 'The Choir Offices', in W. K. Lowther Clarke (ed.), *Liturgy and Worship* (London, 1932), pp. 257–95.

[45] *Report of the Royal Commission on Disestablishment*, IV, 523, question 48199–208.

[46] Ibid., I, 22, but 25 is in ibid., V, 92–100.

[47] Ibid., I, 22, 26.

[48] Ibid., IV, 98, question 36938.

[49] Ibid., III, 98, question 21391.

[50] Ibid., IV, 431, question 46220.

[51] C. W. Arthur, *Haul* (Autumn 1964), 13.

[52] See *Geninen* (1906), 208, for a description by Edward Thomas (Cochfarf) (1853–1912) of the host of candles he recalled being used at the 5 a.m. 'Plygain' service on Christmas Day.

[53] The reports in *Llan* for this period each year give a rich picture of the devotional busy-ness of the churches.

[54] *Tyst* (10 January 1890), 6.

[55] *Tyst* (11 April 1890), 3.

[56] Cf. Iorwerth C. Peate, *Diwylliant Gwerin Cymru* (Liverpool, 1942), pp. 88–92.

[57] See Leslie F. Church, *More about the Early Methodist People* (London, 1949), pp. 242–5. John Thomas, Liverpool, condemned the practice, *Tyst* (12 January 1872), 2. There are numerous descriptions of them in *Gwyliedydd* for January of each year.

[58] Owen Thomas, *Cofiant y Parchedig Henry Rees* (Wrexham, 1890),

p. 584. For the Alliance see the article 'Evangelical Alliance', in *Encyclopaedia of Religion and Ethics* (New York, 1925), and in Philip Schaff (ed.), *A Religious Encyclopaedia* (New York, 1883), I, pp. 60–2.

[59] *Haul* (1896), 284–5.

[60] Ibid., p. 285.

[61] For a simple description of it, with pictures, see J. E. Duce, *The Parish Church* (London, 1962), pp. 18–22.

[62] See Glyn Simon's cutting comments from the president's chair, *Archaeologia Cambrensis*, CXV (1966), 1–10.

[63] *Haul* (1891), 343.

[64] *Haul* (1895), 18–9.

[65] For Owen (1796–1881), 'Dr Owen, Siamber Wen', a teacher in Beaumares school, 1819, and headmaster in 1830, see R. R. Hughes, 'Biographical Epitome of Bangor Clergy', VI, 1842–3; for Brown (d. 1878), ibid., I, p. 52.

[66] *Haul* (1901), 523.

[67] *Report of the Royal Commission on Ecclesiastical Discipline* (London, 1906): Minutes of Evidence I, 354, question 5410. There is a letter to the Commission by Williamson, 16 November 1904, recognizing the accuracy of the evidence. For the background to the Commission, see G. K. A. Bell, *Randall Davidson*, I (London, 1935), ch. 25. The Commission received similar testimony about the following churches in Cardiff: St Agnes, St Ann, St Dyfrig, St Francis, St Garmon, St Margaret (Roath), the church of Mary and St Saviour. And for the church of John the Baptist, Newport, church of Mary, Aberafan, and St Theodore, Port Talbot.

[68] 'Defodaeth yng Nghymru', *Eurgrawn Wesleaidd* (1899), 45–7.

[69] *Traethodydd* (1899), 25–6. His statistics were based on the *Tourist's Church Guide* (London, 1898) published by the English Church Union.

[70] For example, John Hughes in *Drysorfa* (1899), 52.

[71] *Dysgedydd* (1890), 476; (1891), 18–22.

[72] D. A. Jones, *A History of the Church in Wales* (Carmarthen, 1926), p. 151.

[73] *Dysegdydd* (1899), 304; (1890), 104–8.

[74] *Traethodydd* (1899), 27.

[75] *Dysgedydd* (1899), 304.

[76] Ibid., p. 104. Churchmen, at times, shared the feeling. Because Hartwell Jones turned to the east after preaching in Holyhead, Thomas Briscoe accused him of being addicted to 'popish pranks', *A Celt Looks at the World* (Cardiff, 1946), p. 79.

[77] *Drysorfa* (1899), 275. See also J. Rhydderch, 'Peryglon presenol ein gwlad oddiwrth Babyddiaeth a defodaeth', *Dysgedydd* (1899), 62–7; 'Eglwys Rhufain heddiw', *Faner* (24 May 1899), 3–4; (31 May 1899), 3 and the series of articles at the same period on 'Y Gyffesgell'; 'Y

Catholiciaid yn yr Eglwys Sefydledig', *Gwyliedydd* (15 March 1899), 1; 'Y Pab yn obeithiol am Brydain', editorial in *Goleuad* (22 February 1899).

[78] There is an excellent description in Bell, *Randall Davidson*, I, chs 17 and 25, but it can be followed also in the Welsh journals, for example, *Dysgedydd* (1899), 119; *Faner* (8 February 1899), 3.

[79] This is the date by Ieuan Gwyllt in *Cerddor* (July 1873). W. James and J. M. Jones give 10 January in *Cofiant a Phregethau D. Saunders DD* (Swansea, 1894), p. xliv.

[80] For the story, see R. D. Griffiith, *Hanes Canu Cynulleidfaol Cymru* (Cardiff, 1948), with a review by O. Llew Owain in *Faner* (1 December 1948) adding greatly to the bibliography; the testimony of Thomas Thomas, Cardiff, *Report of the Royal Commission on Disestablishment*, VII, 120–3; testimony of M. O. Jones, ibid., 139–144; J. Meirion Evans, *The Musical Festivals of North Montgomeryshire* (1924); Ben Davies, *Hanes Cymanfaoedd Canu Cylch Glandwr* (1926); Eos Llechid, 'Byr hanes cerddoriaeth gysegredig', *Haul* (1880), 266–8; 'Sylwedydd', 'Hanes cerddoriaeth y cysegr yn Nghymru', *Haul* (1902), 58–64; J. Lloyd Williams, 'Y Cyfnod cyn David Jenkins', in J. H. Jones (ed.), *Er cof am yr Athro David Jenkins* (Liverpool, 1935), pp. 12–23.

[81] For a lively description of a Cymanfa, see Evan Evans, 'John Thomas ddydd y gymanfa ganu', in *Cofiant John Thomas, Llanwrtyd* (Caernarfon, 1926), pp. 189–93.

[82] *Celt* (20 January 1893), 7. For the arrangements, see his letter in *Celt* (14 July 1893), 8. For the development of the organization, see R. D. Griffith, *Hanes Canu Cynulleidfaol Cymru* (Cardiff, 1948), pp. 85–9.

[83] M. O. Jones, 'Meithriniad cerddoriaeth ymhlith gwerin Cymru', in T. Stephens (ed.), *Cymru: Heddiw ac Yfory* (Cardiff, 1908), pp. 337–40.

[84] *Report of the Royal Commission on Disestablishment* VII, 142, footnote.

[85] Ibid., 123 – without counting England's assemblies.

[86] For Ieuan Gwyllt's class preparing for the Aberdare assembly, see J. T. Rees in Evan Evans, *Cofiant John Thomas, Llanwrtyd*, pp. 198–9.

[87] Ibid., pp. 194–206. J. T. Rees, 'Yr Arweinydd'; for David Jenkins's similar method, see J. H. Jones (ed.), *Er Cof am yr Athro David Jenkins*, pp. 95–103.

[88] 'Singing festivals' is the Archdeacon A. O. Evans's name for them in his testimony, *Report of the Royal Commission on Disestablishment*, IV, 98, question 36946.

[89] The bishop of Bangor ibid., IV, 534, questions 48462–9.

[90] Ibid., VII, 142. There were some severe critics. One letter-writer held that the singing festivals caused 'more harm than good' and they 'had lost their religious characteristics', 'Asaph', *Faner* (14 June 1899), 5.

The opinion of the Catholic, Henry Hughes, was, 'to all appearances, the whole religion of this land is tonic sol-fa and I believe that Wales will be saved sooner through singing than through preaching', Attwater, *The Catholic Church in Modern Wales*, p. 118.

[91] William Hughes, *Recollections of Bangor Cathedral* (Bala, 1904), p. 85.

[92] Thus A. O. Evans, *Report of the Royal Commission on Disestablishment*, IV, 98, question 36946. For John Owen (Owain Alaw) (1821–83), and Owen Humphrey Davies (Eos Llechid) (1828–98), see *DWB*.

[93] *Haul* (1886), 28.

[94] *Haul* (1885), 246.

[95] *Haul* (1886), 253.

[96] For example, *The Choral Union of the Bangor and Anglesey Archdeaconry: The book of the children's choral festival, 1906, arranged by T. Westlake Morgan*. Morgan was the organist at Bangor cathedral.

[97] Bishop of Bangor, *Report of the Royal Commission on Disestablishment*, IV, 534, questions 48464–9.

[98] The Revd T. B Walters, Carmarthen, who was present in 1866, ibid., II, 71, question 1558.

[99] Ibid., questions 1553–5.

[100] J. J. Morgan, *A Welais ac a Glywais* (Liverpool, 1948), p. 120.

[101] According to *Seren Cymru* (2 May 1902), 7, in Tabernacl chapel, Brymbo, 'over twenty years ago' the first one was held in the north.

[102] *Report of the Royal Commission on Disestablishment*, VII, 143; see also J. Morgan, 'A ydyw yn briodol defnyddio offerynau cerdd yn nghaniadaeth y cysegr?', *Celt* (28 August 1896), 13.

[103] Thomas Levi in *Dysgedydd* (1898), 438 – and a definition, by the way, of the word 'gorfoleddu'.

[104] *Haul* (1897), 232.

[105] See R. D. Griffith, *Hanes Canu Cynulleidfaol Cymru*, ch. 5 and the appendix; T. Levi, 'Llyfrau Hymnau Methodistiaid y De', *Drysorfa* (1898), 436–9, 486–9; T. M. Jones, *Cofiant y Parch Roger Edwards*, Yr Wyddgrug (Wrexham, 1908), pp. 235–7; *Geninen* (1887), 29; *Report of the Royal Commission on Disestablishment*, VII, 104 (Baptists), 120–3 (CM), 139–44 (Congregationalists); T. Thomas, 'Canu cynulleidfaol y ganrif', in J. M. Jones (ed.), *Trem ar y Ganrif* (Dolgellau, 1902), pp. 273–301; M. O. Jones, 'Caniadaeth y ganrif', *Diwygiwr* (1901), 21–5.

[106] William Hughes said that it was used in Bangor cathedral until 1864, *Recollections*, p. 29.

[107] Wilton D. Willias, *Welsh History Review*, IV (1968–9), 252. For Rees (1793–1857), see *DWB*.

[108] The 1885 edition included a tonic sol-fa appendix.

[109] According to Canon William Lewis, Ystradyfodwg, this was used in the Welsh services of the churches in the Rhondda, and *Hymns Ancient and Modern* was used in the English services, *Report of the Royal Commission on Disestablishment*, II, 195, questions 5893–4.

[110] For Lloyd (1843–99), see *DWB*. R. D. Griffith said that the *Emyniadur* was published in 1895, but *Emyniadur . . . Adran yr Ysgol Sul* was published that year and the foreword says that the hope was to publish the full book 'early next year'.

[111] Edward Jones, *Y Gymdeithasfa* (Caernarfon, 1891), p. 430.

[112] For the difficulties encountered by the committee and David Charles and Roger Edwards sulking, see *Drysorfa* (1899), 99–102.

[113] Further editions were published in 1870, 1873, 1875 from Gwasg Gee, then in 1880, 1882, 1886, 1887, 1890, 1891, 1894 from Hughes & Son. It says in *Trysorfa y Plant* (1891), 343, that Dafydd Morris was the first 'to put the name "Emynau" and not "Hymnau" on his compositions' in his book *Cân y Pererinion* (Carmarthen, 1773). But the word 'emynau' is found in its singular form in the thirteenth century, and in the plural form in the fifteenth century according to *GPC*.

[114] See *Drysorfa* (1899), 102, and minutes of the General Assembly, 1869, *Drysorfa* (1869), 245.

[115] For this book, see R. W. Jones, *John Puleston Jones MA, DD* (Caernarfon, 1929), pp. 136–8, relative to the debate between Puleston and Dyfed in *Traethodydd* (1899–1900); for the debate in Bridgend Association, November 1894, see *Drysorfa* (1894), 465; (1895), 39; also (1895), 369; (1897), 312–13.

[116] For the details, see R. Tudur Jones, *Yr Undeb* (Swansea, 1975), pp. 146–50.

[117] For W. E. Jones (1841–1914), minister of Tabernacl, Morriston, see T. Lloyd Evans, *Y Cathedral Anghydffurfiol Cymraeg* (Swansea, 1972), pp. 76–95; for Evans (1843–1913), see *DWB* and the biography by his brother E. Keri Evans; for Lewis (1845–1920), see *DWB*; for M. O. Jones (1842–1908), see *DWB* and *Tyst* (10 July 1941), 6–7. For all those named, see Huw Williams, *Tonau a'u Hawduron* (Caernarfon, 1967) and *idem*, *Rhagor am Donau a'u Hawduron* (Caernarfon, 1969).

[118] For Rowlands (1836–1907), principal of the Memorial College, Brecon, see *DWB* and the biography (1910) by H. Elvet Lewis (Elfed); for Elfed (1860–1953), see Emlyn G. Jenkins, *Cofiant Elfed* (Aberystwyth, 1957) and Dafydd Owen, *Elfed a'i Waith* (Swansea, 1963): for David Adams (Hawen, 1845–1922), see *DWB*, correcting his date of death to 5 July 1922, and the biography by E. Keri Evans and W. Parri Huws (1924).

[119] For John Richards (Isalaw) (1843–1901), see *DWB*.
[120] See D. G. Jones and H. M. Hughes, *Cofiant Glanystwyth: Sef bywyd y diweddar Barch. John Hughes, D.D.* [1842–1902], (Bangor, 1904), pp. 121–2.
[121] Nine impressions of the 1880 *Llawlyfr Moliant* had been published by 1886. It contained 422 hymns and 125 tunes. In the new book in 1890 there were 1,082 hymns and 294 tunes.

6. *The Demise of the Great Preacher*

[1] 'Philos', 'Pregethu Cymdeithasfa Caernarfon', *Traethodydd* (1908), 418.
[2] *Dysgedydd* (1914), 13–14.
[3] This was an 'assembly for catechising and discussing prepared portions of scripture'. See *GPC*, p. 755.
[4] Owen Thomas, *Cofiant y Parchedig John Jones, Talsarn; mewn cysylltiad a hanes duwinyddiaeth a phregethu Cymru* (Wrexham, 1874), p. 968. For Owen Thomas (1812–91), see D. Ben Rees, *The Life and Work of Owen Thomas, 1812–1891: A Welsh Preacher in Liverpool* (Lampeter, 1991).
[5] Cf. for example, *Hynodion hen bregethwyr Cymru gyda hanesion difyrus amdanynt* (Wrexham, n.d.), by an anonymous author, and Benjamin Thomas (Myfyr Emlyn), *Cofiant Dafydd Evans, Ffynnonhenri* (Carmarthen, 1870). Other books which closely relate to this tradition are J. J. Morgan, *A Welais ac a Glywais*, I (Caernarfon, 1948), II (Caernarfon, 1949); Robert Ellis, *Doniau a Daniwyd* (Llandybïe, n.d., 1956?); Owen Jones, *Some of the Great Preachers of Wales* (London, 1885); O. Jones and R. Thomas, *Cofiant y diweddar Dafydd Rolant y Bala* (Wrexham, 1863).
[6] See the series by John Thomas, Liverpool, 'Lletydai Cymru' in *Dysgedydd* (1890) and references in his series 'Fy adgofion', *Tyst*, for example (5 November), 6, (19 November), 6, (3 December) 7.
[7] R. Tudur Jones, *Yr Undeb* (Swansea, 1975), pp. 71–2.
[8] *Dysgedydd* (1890), 219.
[9] See W. P. Griffith, ' "Preaching Second to No Other under the Sun": Edward Matthews, the Nonconformist Pulpit and Welsh Identity during the Mid-Nineteenth Century', in Robert Pope (ed.), *Religion and National Identity: Wales and Scotland c. 1700–2000* (Cardiff, 2001), pp. 61–83.
[10] There is the sound of disapproval in Nantlais's observation, 'There was something in his voice like the howling of a dog', W. Nantlais Williams, *O Gopa Bryn Nebo* (Llandysul, 1967), pp. 58–9. Rheinallt

Nantlais Williams told me that he believed it was John Williams, Brynsiencyn, who first made the observation in a conversation with Nantlais.

11 For David Owen (Brutus) (1795–1866), see *DWB*.

12 For Matthews, see J. J. Morgan, *Cofiant Edward Matthews Ewenni* (Denbigh, 1922); Evan Evans in *Drysorfa* (1898), 389–97; *Geninen* (1893), 192–7; *DWB*.

13 For Christmas Evans (1766–1838), see *DWB*; D. Densil Morgan, *Christmas Evans a'r Ymneilltuaeth Newydd* (Llandysul, 1991); Tim Shenton, *Christmas Evans: The Life and Times of the One-Eyed Preacher of Wales* (Darlington, 2001).

14 For R. D. Roberts (1820–93), see Charles Davies in *Geninen* (1893), 278–83; Waldo James in *Geninen Gwî yl Dewi* (1894), 45–9; Roberts's own reminiscences in *Greal* between 1889 and 1892; *DWB*.

15 J. Williams, *Cofiant a Phregethau y Parch John Hughes, D.D.* (Liverpool, 1899), p. lxxvi.

16 R. R. Hughes, *John Williams, Brynsiencyn* (Caernarfon, 1929), p. 124.

17 T. Hudson-Williams, *Atgofion am Gaernarfon* (Aberystwyth, 1950), p. 32.

18 As well as the biography (1899) by J. Williams, Brynsiencyn, see *Geninen Gwî yl Dewi* (1894), 37–45, and *DWB*. He convinced John Williams of the importance of preaching doctrine. Hughes, *John Williams, Brynsiencyn*, p. 125.

19 For Davies (1826–91), see E. W. Parry, *Cofiant a phregethau y diweddar Barch. David Charles Davies* (Wrexham, 1896); J. J. Morgan, *A Welais ac a Glywais*, I, pp. 93–100; *DWB*.

20 Peter Williams, in J. Vyrnwy Morgan (ed.), *Welsh Religious Leaders in the Victorian Era* (London, 1905), p. 98.

21 For Griffiths (1820–97), see *Geninen Gwî yl Dewi* (1898), 36–9; *Geninen* (1898), 233–5; *DWB*.

22 For Jones (1832–93), see *Geninen Gwî yl Dewi* (1894), 63–6; T. Rees, *Hanes Eglwlsyi Annibynol Cymru*, III, (Liverpool, 1893), pp. 419–20.

23 Thomas Hughes and J. P. Roberts, *Cofiant y Parch. John Evans, Eglwysbach: (yn cynnwys ei 'adgofion')* (Bangor, 1903), p. 307.

24 But without lasting success, *Eurgrawn Wesleaidd* (1940), 259–60.

25 John Evans's 'Adgofion' in *Cofiant*, pp. 9–195 are important. See also *Eurgrawn* (1934), 275–8; (1935), 403–11; (1940), 258–62; Robert Ellis, *Doniau a daniwyd*, pp. 14–19.

26 Ellis, *Doniau a daniwyd*, p. 17.

27 So Dyfnallt, a former student of his in Bala–Bangor College, *Tyst* (12 February 1942), 2, and Puleston Jones, 'The Welsh Pulpit during the Victorian Era', *Young Wales*, III (1897), 178.

28 *Tyst* (12 February 1942), 2.

29 *Tyst* (18 February 1937), 9.

[30] For Evans (1836–96), see H. Elvet Lewis, *Cofiant y Parch E. Herber Evans, D.D. Caernarfon* (Wrexham, 1901), especially chs 17 and 19; *Geninen* (1897), 82–6; 155–60; *Tyst* (22 October 1942), 3; (3 November 1942), 5; *DWB*.

[31] 'Troedigaeth y diweddar Brifathraw T. Charles Edwards, D.D.', *Deonglwr*, IV (1906), 71–5, 116.

[32] For Edwards (1837–1900), see D. D. Williams, *Thomas Charles Edwards* (Liverpool, 1921) and the review of it in *Cymro* (5 October 1921), 8–9; J. Lloyd Humphreys, 'Thomas Charles Edwards: ei fisoedd olaf', *Traethodydd* (1943), 114–20; J. E. Caerwyn Williams, 'T. C. Edwards a'i gyfraniad i ddiwinyddiaeth Cymru', *Diwinyddiaeth*, XXV (1974), 8–28.

[33] Eifionydd (1848–1922) was educated, 1872–4, in the Memorial College, Brecon. See *DWB*.

[34] 'Pregethu Cymru: pa un ai cryfhau ai gwanhau y mae ei ddylanwad?', *Geninen* (1892), 196. For Charles Davies (1849–1927), see J. Williams Hughes (ed.), *Charles Davies, Caerdydd* (Cardiff, 1933); *DWB*.

[35] *Geninen* (1893), 'Un o'r bobl' writing on the subject was Charles Davies.

[36] For Richard Mills (Rhydderch Hael) (1809–44), see *DWB*.

[37] *Geninen* (1896), 99–105.

[38] *Geninen* (1894), 122. The article is anonymous.

[39] *Drysorfa* (1894), 307–8.

[40] *Tyst* (28 June 1895), 8.

[41] 'Henadur', 'Pwlpud y Bedyddwyr Cymreig', *Seren Gomer* (1897), 54–60.

[42] *Dysgedydd* (1901), 258.

[43] In the Tredegar Association, October 1898, *Drysorfa* (1898), 515.

[44] D. D. Williams, *Thomas Charles Edwards*, p. 109.

[45] Anonymous, 'Diffygion a rhagoriaethau y Pwlpud Bedyddiedig yn Nghymru', *Geninen* (1893), 25–9.

[46] *Dysgedydd* (1901), 147.

[47] Dewi Môn, *Geninen* (1898), 66.

[48] *Geninen* (1897), 25.

[49] *Dysgedydd* (1910), 407.

[50] R. H. Evans, *David Williams, 1877–1927* (Caernarfon, 1970), pp. 96, 97.

[51] For David Emrys James (Dewi Emrys) (1881–1952), see *Bywg.* (1951–70), also Eluned Phillips, *Dewi Emrys* (Llandysul, 1971).

[52] W. Anthony Davies, *Berw Bywyd* (Llandysul, 1968), p. 54, 24 May 1913, preaching meeting, Minny Street, Cardiff.

[53] 'Athraw', *Geninen* (1897), 119.

[54] Huw Roberts (ed.), *Atgofion am E. T. Jones* (Llandysul, 1967), p. 107.

[55] There are many examples in J. J. Morgan's book: *A Welais ac a*

Glywais and *Cofiant Evan Phillips Castellnewydd Emlyn* (Liverpool, 1930), pp. 115, 175, 179.

⁵⁶ Nantlais, *O Gopa Bryn Nebo*, p. 126.

⁵⁷ J. Lloyd Williams, *Atgofion Tri Chwarter Canrif*, IV (Aberystwyth, 1945), p. 104; J. H. Howard, *Winding Lanes* (Caernarfon, 1938), p. 110. Even in 1879 the Revd J. H. Davies, Bethel, Llandovery, was wandering through the land with his lecture 'Imitation of some of the major renowned figures of the Independent pulpit', *Tyst* (28 March 1879), 9.

⁵⁸ J. J. Morgan, *Evan Phillips*, p. 146.

⁵⁹ *Cymro* (5 July 1897).

⁶⁰ See *Brython* (19 December 1907), 4.

⁶¹ R. H. Evans, *David Williams*, p. 97.

⁶² According to *Goleuad* (26 September 1894), 1; see also pp. 10, 11; (10 October 1894), 11. In *DWB* Robert Arthur Griffith (Elphin) (1860–1936) is spoken of as joint author. For Ap Ffarmwr (John Owen Jones, 1860–90), see *DWB*.

⁶³ *The Welsh Pulpit*, p. 43.

⁶⁴ Ibid., pp. 74–7.

⁶⁵ Ibid., p. 49.

⁶⁶ Ibid., p. 108.

⁶⁷ For example, *Tyst* (13 July 1894), 3; *Drysorfa* (1894), 338. For the authors' protest against calling it an 'atheist book', see *Goleuad* (10 October 1894), 11.

⁶⁸ J. Evans, Pontarddulais, 'Ffugchwedleuaeth a'r pulpud', *Drysorfa* (1897), 260–2.

⁶⁹ W. A. Jones, Seion, Merthyr Tudful, 'Pregethu effeithiol', *Greal* (1903), 10.

⁷⁰ 'Rhagoriaethau a diffygion y pulpud Eglwysig yn Nghymru', *Geninen* (1895), 93.

⁷¹ *Brython* (19 September 1907), 4.

⁷² *Greal* (1900), 172.

⁷³ *Geninen* (1893), 25–9.

⁷⁴ *Atgofion am Gaernarfon*, pp. 31–2.

⁷⁵ *Genedl Gymreig* (5 April 1904), 7.

⁷⁶ 'Pulpud Cymru heddyw', *Brython* (12 September 1907), 1; for Tecwyn Evans's response, see *Brython* (26 September 1907), 5.

⁷⁷ 'Caledfwlch', in *Geninen* (1908), 62.

⁷⁸ For David Rowlands (Dewi Môn) (1836–1907), see *DWB*.

⁷⁹ *Geninen* (1898), 65, where it also says that there was 'endless complaining about the quality of preaching'; William Phillips, Bangor, 'Pregethu yng Nghymru yn ôl y cyfnodolion', *Traethodydd* (1961), 129–41.

⁸⁰ *Blwyddiadur y Methodistiaid Calfinaidd* (1911), p. 120. The same

contrast between 'preaching' and 'sermons' can be found in John
Williams, Brynsiencyn, *Beirniad* (Summer 1912), 140.

[81] *Dysgedydd* (1901), 258.

7. *The Word Once Spoken*

[1] These are rough figures based on an analysis of 800 printed sermons
from the period.

[2] John Calvin, *Institutes of the Christian Religion*, I, ed. J. T. McNeill,
tr. F. L. Battles (London, 1960), p. 72.

[3] For George Lewis (1763–1822), see *DWB*.

[4] W. James and J. M. Jones, *Cofiant a Phregethau y Parchedig
D. Saunders, DD* (Swansea, 1894), p. 115.

[5] *Pregethau, damegion, ac areithiau: ar wahanol byngciau
athrawiaethol ac ymarferol gwir grefydd*, II (Wrexham, 1883), pp.
346–63.

[6] Charles Edwards, *Y Ffydd Ddi-ffuant* (Dolgellau, 1811 ed.), pp. 221–2.

[7] *Pregethau*, pp. 194–9, on the text Exod. 24: 6–7.

[8] Ibid., pp. 22–8 on 1 Cor. 8: 6.

[9] J. Williams (ed.), *Cofiant a Phregethau y Parch. John Hughes*
(Liverpool, 1899), pp. 163–9 on 2 Sam. 23: 5.

[10] James and Jones, *Cofiant D. Saunders*, p. 92.

[11] In his book *Peri Archon*, 4. 2. 45, Origen holds that there are three
meanings to the scriptures, namely the literal meaning, the moral
meaning and the spiritual meaning. On occasion he was content to
speak of the two meanings, literal and spiritual. See R. P. C. Hanson,
Allegory and Event (London, 1959), ch. 9. The vast majority of Welsh
sermons accepted this theory unwittingly, especially in discussing the
difficult subjects in the Old Testament.

[12] *Dysgedydd* (1899), 220, 222.

[13] 'Y pregethwr a'i bregeth', *Greal* (1907), 304–5. Owen Evans outlines
the pinnacles of the evangelical faith in the same way, *Dysgedydd*
(1909), 444–5.

[14] J. A. Morris and T. E. Williams, *Y Pulpud Bedyddiedig* (Aberystwyth,
1888), pp. 27–34.

[15] Ibid., p. 95.

[16] As by William Morris in 'Unoedd y drefn gyfiawnhaol', *Pwlpud
Noddfa* (Treorchy, 1905), pp. 278–93.

[17] William Evans, *Cyfrol o Bregethau* (Merthyr Tudful, 1893), p. 68.

[18] Williams (ed.), *Cofiant John Hughes*, pp. 308–22.

[19] Hugh Ellis (ed.), *Cyfrol Goffa, yn cynwys pregethau a draddodwyd
gan chwech ar hugain o weinidogion y Methodistiaid Calfinaidd*

perthynol i Gyrfarfod Misol Gorllewin Meirionydd (Dolgellau, 1903), pp. 68–78.

[20] E. Wynne Parry, *Cofiant a Phregethau y diweddar Barch. David Charles Davies* (Wrexham, 1896), pp. 225–36. The same subject is discussed by William Thomas, Llanrwst, in 'Duw yn caledu calon dyn', in John Jones (ed.), *Pregethau . . . Sasiwn Pwllheli* (1903), pp. 12–21, and by W. Evans, Aberaeron, in 'Ni all Duw fod yn awdur pechod', *Cyfrol o Bregethau*, pp. 43–9.

[21] W. O. Evans (ed.), *Cyfrol goffa y Parchedig D. O. Jones: Yn cynnwys ei gofiant a nifer o'i bregethau* (Bangor, 1904), pp. 123–35.

[22] B. Davies, *Pyrth Sion* (Dolgellau, 1899), pp. 69–83.

[23] T. T. Jones (ed.), *Yr Angel Mawr a'r Llyfr Bychan: Pregethau William Jones, Abergwaen* (Llangollen, 1899), pp. 264–76. W. Jones died on 24 March 1895.

[24] D. M. Phillips, *Cofiant a Phregethau . . . David Jones, Llaneurwg (1836–89)* (Cardiff, 1895), pp. 176–83.

[25] Cf. J. Cynddylan Jones, *Pregethau* (Caernarfon, 1901), pp. 9–22; J. Mostyn Jones (1840–1911), 'Perchenogaeth y saint', in Evan Davies (ed.), *Cofiant a phregethau . . . John Mostyn Jones, Bangor* (Dolgellau, 1913), pp. 299–307; D. Stanley Jones (1860–1919), 'Rhoddion Iesu Grist i ddynion', in Ben Davies, *Stanley a'i Bulpud* (1920), pp. 161–70.

[26] Evans, *Cyfrol o Bregethau*, p. 131.

[27] James and Jones, *Cofiant D. Saunders*, pp. 248–60, 'Yr angenrheidrwydd am ail-enedigaeth'; cf. Owen Evans, 'Adenedigaeth', *Dysgedydd* (1909), 394–402.

[28] David Oliver (1842–1924), 'Undeb y saint â Christ', in O. L. Roberts (ed.), *Y Pregethwr a'i Bregeth* (Merthyr Tudful, 1912), pp. 444–55.

[29] Ibid., pp. 126–41. William Parri Huws (1853–1936), 'Cymod yn y gwaed'; Francis Jones (1834–1913), 'Lladd gelyniaeth pechadur at Dduw', in D. Ward Williams, *Cofiant a Phregethau y Parchedig Francis Jones, Abergele (1834–1913)* (Caernarfon, 1927), pp. 180–7; Thomas Charles Williams (1868–1927), 'Cymundeb llawn â Duw', in John Owen (ed.), *Anchwiliadwy Olud Crist* (Caernarfon, 1928), pp. 128–37.

[30] T. Richards (d. 1895), Aberafan, 'Sicrwydd cadwedigaeth y credadyn', in Morris and Williams (eds), *Y Pulpud Bedyddiedig*, pp. 177–81.

[31] Robert Jones (1806–96), Llanllyfni, ibid., pp. 41–5; W. James (1833–1905), 'Prynedigaeth a maddeuant', in Lewis Ellis (ed.), *Cofiant a rhai o Bregethau y Parchedig William James, BA, DD, Manchester* (Caernarfon, 1910), pp. 163–72.

[32] David Saunders, 'Crist yn gadael tangnefedd i'w ddisgyblion', in James and Jones, *Cofiant D. Saunders*, pp. 18–35.

[33] Ibid., pp. 261–73, 'Dyddanwch Duw'.

[34] T. C. Edwards, 'Gwaed y Crist yn puro', *Pregethau* (Bala, 1900), pp. 105–22.

[35] Ibid., pp. 149–59.

[36] D. M. Davies, 'Gwasanaeth gobaith ym mywyd y Cristion', in J. T. Parry (ed.), *Pulpud Annibynol Ceredigion* (Pencader, 1903), pp. 105–22.

[37] David Jones, Liverpool, 'Llawenydd gwastadol', in *Gair a Glybuwyd* (Wrexham, 1900), pp. 184–200.

[38] D. D. Walters, 'Y bywyd helaethach', *Pulpud Annibynol Ceredigion*, pp. 115–21; H. Parry Thomas, 'Bywyd yn helaethach', in O. L. Roberts (ed.), *Lloffion Grawnwin: Sef cyfrol-goffa y Parchedigion William Roberts, William Nicholson, D. M. Jenkins, Hugh Jones, David John, H. Parry Thomas, o gyfundeb Anibynwyr Cymreig Lerpwl, Manchester, a'r amgylchoedd* (Liverpool, 1907), pp. 159–76.

[39] Robert Ambrose Jones, *Homiliau*, II (Denbigh, 1909), p. 34. Cf. D. Lloyd Jones (1843–1905), in E. Jones, J. Williams and T. C. Williams (eds), *Cofiant a Phregethau y diweddar barch. David Lloyd Jones, MA, Llandinam* (Wrexham, 1908), pp. 154–64.

[40] *Pulpud y Beirdd*, I (Morriston, 1904), pp. 91–5.

[41] The same proximity to Sabellianism can be found in the sermon by Hugh Roberts, Rhyd-y-main, 'Lleferydd Duw yn y dyn', in Hugh Ellis (ed.), *Cyfrol Goffa . . . Gorllewin Meirionydd*, pp. 98–9.

[42] O. L. Roberts (ed.), *Y Pregethwr a'i Bregeth* (Merthyr Tudful, 1912), pp. 92–103.

[43] Ibid., pp. 187–8.

[44] W. Lewis (ed.), *Trydydd Jiwbili y Cyfundeb* (Lampeter, 1903), pp. 72–84.

[45] S. T. Jones, *Er mwyn Iesu* (Liverpool, n.d.), pp. 14–15; also 'Y cyfoethog yn dlawd', pp. 33–41; 'Y gyfatebiaeth rhwng Crist a dynion a rhwng dynion a Christ', pp. 71–83.

[46] *Pwlpud Noddfa*, pp. 244–5.

[47] Thomas Charles Williams, *Anchwiliadwy olud Crist, a phregethau eraill*, p. 86.

[48] Ibid., and the sermon 'Tair gwedd ar yr Ymgnawdoliad', pp. 178–89.

[49] Hughes, *John Williams, Brynsiencyn*, pp. 113–15.

[50] A good example of this view can be found in 'Crist yn datguddio yn raddol. Pam?', in *Y Gair a Glybuwyd*, pp. 165–83.

[51] William Davies, Llanegryn, in *Cyfrol Goffa*, p. 6; cf. S. T. Jones, 'Iesu'n unig', in *Er Mwyn Iesu*, pp. 159–70.

[52] Ben Davies, *Stanley a'i Bulpud*, pp. 108–17, 'Derbyniad teilwng i Grist'.

[53] Roberts, *Y Pregethwr a'i Bregeth*, pp. 14–29.

[54] R. E. Jones, Tal-y-bont, 'Dyfodiad Crist a'i neges', on John 10: 10, in *Pulpud Annibynol Ceredigion*, pp. 101–9; Dan Evans, Hawen, 'Cwyn yr Iesu', on John 5: 40, pp. 110–14.

NOTES

[55] Evan Davies, *Cofiant a Phregethau y diweddar Barch. William Roberts, Llanrwst* (Dolgellau, 1896), pp. 185–6.

[56] Roberts, *Y Pregethwr a'i Bregeth*, pp. 460–74, 'Y ffordd i fyw a'r ffordd i farw'.

[57] Robert Ambrose Jones, *Homiliau*, II, pp. 46–7, 'Pa fodd i fod yn ieuangc?'

[58] Ibid., p. 268. Ll. Bryniog Roberts is delightful on the same subject in 'Y ddau gartref', Roberts, *Y Pregethwr a'i Bregeth*, pp. 274–88; cf. J. Pickering, 'Ceisio bywyd tragwyddol', *Greal* (1902), 40–3; Robert Ambrose Jones, 'Gwir drysori, trysori i Dduw', *Homiliau*, II, pp. 165–82; W. E. Prytherch, 'Gogoniant ein cartref tragwyddol', in D. M. Phillips (ed.), *Hau a Medi, sef cyfrol o bregethau . . . W. E. Prytherch* (Cardiff, 1910), pp. 267–78.

[59] D. Mardy Davies (ed.), *Cyflawnder Bendith* (Dolgellau, 1914), p. 134.

[60] Roberts, *Y Pregethwr a'i Bregeth*, p. 118.

[61] John Owen (ed.), *Pregethau'r Diweddar Barch John Williams* (Caernarfon, 1922), p. 281.

[62] T. R. Jones, *J. J. Roberts (Iolo Caernarfon)* (Caernarfon, n.d.), p. 199.

[63] W. O. Evans (ed.), *Cyfrol Goffa y Parch D. O. Jones* (Bangor, 1904), p. 204.

[64] For John Jones (1821–79), see W. Trefor Jones, *J. Jones (Yr Hen Gloddiwr)*, Cyfres y Bedyddwyr Ieuainc, IV (Cardiff, 1924). There are two sermons by him, one on heaven and the other on hell, pp. 99–119. See also J. Spinther James, *Hanes y Bedyddwyr yn Nghymru*, IV (Carmarthen, 1907), p. 330.

[65] See, for example, Evans, *Cyfrol o Bregethau*, pp. 324–48; Phillips (ed.), *Hau a Medi*, pp. 227–78.

[66] *Seren Cymru* (20 October 1905), 7. For Rhys Bevan Jones, see B. P. Jones, *The King's Champions* (Redhill, 1968).

[67] J. H. Howard (ed.), *Perarogl Crist: Cofiant a Phregethau y Parch. William Jones, Treforis* (Bala, 1932), p. 138. Before this sermon there is a description by W. Llywelyn Lloyd of the stunning effects that followed its delivery in the Anglesey Association by Jones (1851–1931).

[68] *Dysgedydd* (1910), 22–6.

[69] Robert Ambrose Jones, *Homiliau*, II, p. 155.

[70] D. Mardy Davies (ed.), *Cyflawnder bendith*, pp. 136–46. See also Hugh Ellis (ed.), *Cyfrol Goffa . . . Gorllewin Meirionydd*, pp. 30–40, for the sermon by David Jones, Garreg-ddu, 'Amynedd i feddianu yr enaid'.

[71] W. Lewis (ed.), *Trydedd Jiwbili y Cyfundeb*, pp. 115–28. 'Hyder dydd y farn'. It is interesting to note how limp a scholar like Griffith Ellis, Bootle, was in his sermon on the Day of Judgement, 'Datguddiad meibion Duw', John Owen (ed.), *Cofiant y Parch. Griffith Ellis, Bootle (1844–1913)* (Liverpool, 1923), pp. 167–76.

72 As, for example, by John Hughes, Liverpool, in 'Gobaith Israel', in Y *Gair a Glybuwyd*, p. 107.
73 Hugh Ellis (ed.), *Cyfrol Goffa* (Dolgellau, 1903), pp. 41–53.
74 E. Ll. Williams (ed.), *Cofiant . . . Robert Williams, Glanconwy* (1921), p. 66.
75 W. A. Jones, Merthyr, 'Pregethu effeithiol', *Greal* (1903), 7–10.
76 E. W. Parry, *Cofiant a Phregethau y diweddar Barch David Charles Davies* (Wrexham, 1896), pp. lxii-lxviii.
77 *Dysgedydd* (1914), 5–9, on Eph. 3: 8.
78 'An epigrammatic stanza . . . (now always a quatrain) composed in the "strict" metres according to certain specific rules', see *GPC*, p. 1182.
79 Ellis (ed.), *Cyfrol Goffa*, pp. 185–95.
80 John Owen (ed.), *Anchwiliadwy Olud Crist*, pp. 21–32. For the attack by Michael D. Jones on 'fancy headings' in his preaching class in the Independent College, Bala, see *Celt* (26 January 1900), 1.
81 H. Elvet Lewis (Elfed), *Planu Coed a phregethau eraill* (Bala, 1898), pp. 9–24.
82 For John Davies (Sion Gymro) (1804–84), see *DWB*.
83 For the attack by Sion Gymro on 'Pregethu dychmygion', see *Dysgedydd* for February 1850 and E. Pan Jones, *Cofiant y Tri Brawd* (Bala, 1892), pp. 254–8.
84 T. T. Jones (ed.), *Yr Angel Mawr a'r Llyfr Bychan* (Llangollen, 1899), p. 17.
85 Vol. I (1904) vol. II (1906).
86 *Pwlpud Noddfa*, pp. 59–71.
87 *Pwlpud y Beirdd*, I, pp. 183–91.
88 T. T. Phillips, *Angel y Nos* (Bala, 1903), p. 46.
89 Ibid., pp. 79–86.
90 Review in the *British Weekly* according to O. L. Roberts, Y *Pregethwr a'i Bregeth*, p. 306.
91 J. J. Morgan, *Cofiant Edward Matthews, Ewenni* (Denbigh, 1923), p. 236.
92 This development is analysed masterfully by W. Frei, *The Eclipse of Biblical Narrative* (London, 1974).
93 *Geninen* (1893), 248–9.
94 Hugh Hughes, Y *ddau oleuni* (Bangor, 1903), pp. 18–45.
95 *Report of the Union of Welsh Independents*, Bridgend (1896), p. 84. The same emphasis can be found in a sermon by Jenkins, 'Efengyl Paul', *Dysgedydd* (1899), 85, and in Roberts (ed.), *Lloffion Grawnwin*, pp. 107–13, where he describes the Judgement as an event within the boundaries of history in the future.
96 Ellis, *Cyfrol Goffa*, p. 169; cf. the sermon by J. B. Jones, Dowlais, 'Yr Efengyl mewn Hanes', *Greal* (1902), 320–2.
97 Elfed acknowledges his debt to the commentaries by George Adam

Smith on Isaiah, *Planu Coed*, 'Rhagymadrodd'; for a similar debt belonging to E. T. Jones, Llanelli, see Huw Roberts, *Atgofion am E. T. Jones* (Llandysul, 1967), p. 112.

[98] James and Jones, *Cofiant D. Saunders*, pp. 175–89. Although it was published in 1894, the sermon was composed around 1860–2 and so it expresses the comprehensive vision which held the field prior to being corrupted by the doubts of the Victorian age.

[99] John Jones (ed.), *Pregethau Sasiwn Pwllheli* (1903), pp. 22–3, 'Crist y Brenin'.

[100] Morris and Williams, *Y Pulpud Bedyddiedig*, pp. 8–14, 'Crist yn cynal pob peth trwy air ei nerth'. J. P. Williams, Rhymney, pp. 218–23, 'Cymeriad brenhinol Crist', discusses the matter well, but he does not suggest that there are cultural or historical implications to the mediatory kingship.

[101] W. Lewis (ed.), *Pwlpud Methodistaidd Dwyrain Morganwg* (Manchester, 1893), pp. 147–59; John Davies, Pandy, has a sermon on the same text in D. Mardy Davies (ed.), *Cyflawnder Bendith*, pp. 62–74.

[102] *Cyfiawnder Bendith*, pp. 82–91.

[103] *Greal* (1903), 230–4.

[104] As J. Griffiths, Llanfairfechan, 'Bywyd crefyddol' in Morris and Williams, *Y Pulpud Bedyddiedig*, pp. 208–13; and D. C. Davies, Resolven, on the same subject, *Greal* (1903), 98–101.

[105] Roberts (ed.), *Lloffion Grawnwin*, pp. 133–40.

[106] Robert Ambrose Jones, *Homiliau*, II, pp. 70–86.

[107] As did J. Griffiths, Llanfairfechan, in 'Goruwchwyliaethau dyrys', *Greal* (1902), 197–202, and Robert Jones, Aberdyfi, 'Cysuron yr Efengyl' in D. Mardy Davies, *Cyflawnder Bendith* (Dolgellau, 1914), pp. 75–81 – the comfort which the two offer is that God supervises all circumstances.

[108] J. Owen (ed.), *Anchwiliadwy Olud Crist*, p. 137; the sermon was dated 16 November 1903.

[109] Robert Ambrose Jones, *Homiliau*, I, p. 236, from the sermon, 'Y ddwy alwedigaeth'.

[110] Ibid., p. 237. For other examples of Emrys's intense preaching on the devotional life, see *Homiliau*, II (1909), 'Y ddau orphwysdra', pp. 87–103; 'Llwyddiant ysprydol', pp. 70–86; 'Y tair ewyllys', pp. 104–17.

[111] Robert Ambrose Jones, *Homiliau*, I, pp. 301–3, 'Cymru gelwyddog'.

[112] Morris and Williams, *Y Pulpud Bedyddiedig*, p. 196; J. Thomas, Carmarthen, 'Cadwedigaeth trwy ras yn gymhelliad i sancteiddrwydd'.

[113] Evan Davies (ed.), *Cofiant*, pp. 286–92.

[114] Ellis, *Cyfrol Goffa*, pp. 155–68.

[115] *Dysgedydd* (1901), 96–100, 180–5.

[116] Robert Ambrose Jones, *Homiliau*, II, p. 211.

[117] For the connection between the moral and the gospel, see 'Pwy yw fy nghymydog?', Robert Ambrose Jones, *Homiliau*, II, pp. 150–64.

[118] Ibid., p. 302.

8. *The Strange Story of 'the Free Church of the Welsh'*

[1] *Census of England and Wales* (London, 1893), III, 550; *Preliminary Report* (London, 1891), p. 2.

[2] Thomas Richards, *Rhagor o atgofion Cardi* (Cymdeithas Llyfrau Ceredigion, 1963), p. 33.

[3] R. R. Hughes, *John Williams, Brynsiencyn* (Caernarfon, 1922), p. 146.

[4] For Jones, see *Blwyddiadur y Methodistiaid Calfinaidd* (1912), 314–5.

[5] Hughes, *John Williams, Brynsiencyn*, p. 53. For Owen J. Owens (1851–1925), see *Blwyddiadur y Methodistiaid Calfinaidd* (1927), 269.

[6] *Blywddiadur y Methodistiaid Calfinaidd* (1921), 168–9.

[7] For Ysgol Clynnog, see William Morris (ed.), *Ysgolion a Cholegau y Methodistiaid Calfinaidd* (Caernarfon, 1973), pp. 47–80.

[8] W. O. Jones, Letter IV, *Cymro* (8 November 1900), 6.

[9] *Cymro* (25 October 1900), 6.

[10] Ibid., and Gaianydd MS, UWB, 36, letter from J. J. Bebb, 9 June 1900.

[11] According to W. O. Jones, *Cymro* (25 October 1900), 6.

[12] For the agreement, see J. J. Bebb's letter, 9 June 1900, Gaianydd MS, 36.

[13] The date of 17 September is a mistake in the evidence of William Williams (9 Verulam Street) to the Committee of the Monthly Meeting, 21 May 1900, Gaianydd MS, 36; 17 September was a Sunday. As the committee's minutes, which are part of the Gaianydd collection, are unnumbered, they are quoted according to the number of the sitting when the evidence was received.

[14] Gaianydd MS, 36; evidence to the Committee of the Monthly Meeting, Second Sitting, 21 May 1900.

[15] Ibid., Humphrey Lloyd's evidence.

[16] Ibid., William Williams's evidence.

[17] Ibid.

[18] Ibid.

[19] *Cymro* (25 October 1900), 6.

[20] Gaianydd MS, 36, Committee of the Monthly Meeting, Fourth Sitting, 8 June 1900, J. J. Bebb's evidence. According to W. O. Jones, John Jones refused to sign and Eliezer Pugh's signature was obtained through deception.

[21] *Cymro* (25 October 1900), 6.

22 For Jones (1841–1919), the minister of David Street, see *Blwyddiadur y Methodistiaid Calfinaidd* (1920), 15.

23 *Cymro* (25 October 1900), 6.

24 Its members were Dr Hugh Jones, Owen Owens, William Jones and John Williams, from the ministers; and from the lay people, Edward Ellis (Princes Road), William Evans (Anfield Road), William Jones (Breeze Hill) and William Patton (Newham Park).

25 *Cymro* (25 October 1900), 6.

26 Ibid.

27 Gaianydd MS, 36, Committee of the Monthly Meeting, Fourth Sitting, 8 June 1900, J. J. Bebb's evidence (41 Old Hall Street, Liverpool).

28 *Cymro* (10 January 1901), 5, 'Datganiad y Pwyllgor', as a response to W. O. Jones's articles in Y *Cymro*.

29 *Cymro* (25 October 1900), 6.

30 *Cymro* (10 January 1901), 5, 'Datganiad y Pwyllgor'.

31 *Cymro* (25 October 1900), 6.

32 *Cymro* (10 January 1901), 5, 'Datganiad y Pwyllgor'.

33 See W. O. Jones's analysis in *Cymro* (17 January 1901), 5, and the letters of his solicitors Messers Rees and Hindley, *Faner* (16 January 1901), 1, referring to this.

34 W. O. Jones's evidence, *Cymro* (25 October 1900), 6 and the evidence of the Committee (10 January 1901), 5.

35 John Evan Hughes (1865–1932), the minister of Seilo, Caernarfon, from 1894 to 1926, a graduate of the university of London and St John's College, Cambridge. He was married to Lily, the sister of Principal J. H. Davies, Aberystwyth, and Mrs T. E. Ellis. Hughes and William Lewis Jones (1866–1922) were fellow students with W. O. Jones in Cambridge.

36 *Cymro* (12 July 1900), 8.

37 They have been secured as part of the Gaianydd MS 36 in UWB.

38 Gaianydd MS 36: minutes of the (second) Committee of the Monthly Meeting, Second Sitting, 21 May 1900.

39 Dora Williams died at the beginning of March 1899, see *Goleuad* (21 March 1899), 4; *Cymro* (8 March 1899), 8.

40 The two cards are in Gaianydd MS, 36.

41 Gaianydd MS, 36: Committee of the Monthly Meeting, Ninth Sitting, 28 June 1900.

42 Ibid., Fifth Sitting, May [*sic*=June], 16.

43 Ibid., paragraph IV.

44 Ibid., but the paper has been put into the minutes.

45 Hughes, *John Williams, Brynsiencyn*, p. 163; Gaianydd MS, 36, Committee of the Monthly Meeting, Fourth Sitting, 8 June 1900, paragraph V.

46 This was on the train, ibid., Seventh Sitting, VI.

47 For William Venmore (1844–1920), and his brother James (1850–1920), see *Brython* (16 December 1920), 2. For their funeral, see *Brython* (23 December 1920), 4. The brothers died on the same evening of the 11–12 December 1920.

48 Gaianydd MS, 36: Committee of the Monthly Meeting, Seventh Sitting, 27 June 1900, VI and VII; Fifth Sitting, 16 May [= June], VI.

49 Ibid., Fourth Sitting, 8 June, III.

50 Ibid., Fifth Sitting, 16 June, VII.

51 Ibid., VIII.

52 Ibid., Fourth Sitting, 5 June, IV.

53 Ibid.

54 Ibid., VI.

55 Ibid., Fifth Sitting, X.

56 Ibid., Seventh Sitting, 27 June, IV.

57 Ibid., Third Sitting, 25 May, III.

58 Ibid.

59 *Cymro* (18 October 1900), 6.

60 Ibid.

61 Ibid., and the minutes of the Committee confirm W. O. Jones's words in the article.

62 Gaianydd MS, 36, Tenth Sitting, 30 June, V.

63 Ibid., Eleventh Sitting, 2 July, III–IV.

64 This is confirmed in the minutes of the Committee, Twelfth Sitting, 2 July, see also *Cymro* (10 January 1901), 5, The Committee's Decision.

65 Gaianydd MS, 36, Twelfth Sitting, II and IV.

66 *Cymro* (18 October 1900), 6.

67 Gaianydd MS, 36, Thirteenth Sitting, 3 July, III.

68 Ibid., Fourteenth Sitting, 9 July. The Fifteenth Sitting was held on 10 July in order that John Williams, Princes Road, could sign the decision. He was absent from the Thirteenth Sitting. In Gaianydd MS, 39, there is a paper with the heading 'Pwyllgor a benodwyd gan Gyfarfod Misol Lerpwl, Mai 9, 1900 . . .' After making the above decision, it lists the accusations. It is a stunning document. Every accusation is listed that was made by anyone against W. O. Jones, with this opening sentence, 'Behold, following are the accusations that we consider that he has failed to disprove . . .' That is, W. O. Jones was guilty until he had proven his innocence – a completely contrary principle to that of the civil courts.

69 In Gaianydd MS, 36, there is a twelve-page document, 'Crynodeb o'r ymddiddan yn y Cwrdd Misol . . . Gorff. 11, 1900 . . .' which was prepared on the basis of shorthand minutes by J. H. Morris. The official minutes of the meeting can be found in *Goleuad* (15 July 1900), 5. For

Rowland J. Williams, a wood merchant, see *Llais Rhyddid*, III (1904), 73–4. He was married to the daughter of William Jones, Balliol Road, and so he was the brother-in-law of W. O. Jones.

70 Gaianydd MS, 38, a letter in English, 16 July 1900, from 9 Montpellier Terrace.

71 Ibid., a letter from Owen J. Owens, 8 August 1900, from 11 Well Lane, Rock Ferry.

72 *Goleuad* (29 August 1900), 9, letter by W. O. Jones; *Cymro* (6 September 1900), 3.

73 *Drysorfa* (1900), 515; *Goleuad* (29 August 1900), 4; *Cymro* (30 August 1900), 3.

74 There are eleven articles in the first series. After the Committee's response, *Cymro* (10 January, 1901), 5, 8, Jones got to grips again with his defence.

75 Gaianydd MS, 38, a paper of fourteen pages, 'Achos Mr W. O. Jones, B. A.', 10.

76 *Cymro* (6 December 1900), 6.

77 *Cymro* (17 January 1901), 8. According to this report, R. W. Thomas, Coltart Street, was the treasurer and J. S. Wynne, Walton Park, was the secretary. But according to a letter by R. O. Williams, 99 Botanic Road, to William Jones, the secretary of the Monthly Meeting, 28 February 1901, the secretary was W. A. Lewis.

78 *Cymro* (6 December 1900), 6.

79 Gaianydd MS, 37.

80 Ibid., the secretary was sent to the Monthly Meeting, 26 February 1901.

81 G. C. Rees from this firm was one of W. O. Jones's main supporters. He became a prominent leader after this among the Free Church of the Welsh, with his mother and sister, in Claughton Street, Birkenhead. There is a picture of him in *Llais Rhyddid*, I (1902–3), 33. For the marriage of his sister, Gwladys, to W. Augustus Phillips, see p. 96.

82 Gaianydd MS, 38.

83 Ibid. See also his letter to William Jones, 11 January 1901. In the bundle there are also letters from the solicitors from around 11 to 28 January 1901.

84 *Cymro* (10 January 1901), 6; (17 January), 7.

85 *Cymro* (10 January 1901), 6.

86 *Goleuad* (9 January 1901), 2–3; *Cymro* (10 January 1901), 5–6.

87 The members of the Committee of Appeal were William James, DD, Manchester; T. Gwynedd Roberts, Conwy; John Owen, Gerlan; Mr Peter Roberts, St Asaph; Mr Richard Williams, Newtown; Dr Roger Hughes, Bala and Mr O. Robyns-Owen, Pwllheli. The solicitors, John Herbert Lewis and John Bryn Roberts, refused to serve – Roberts

because the Committee of Investigation had already sought his counsel, *Faner* (1 May 1901), 9, *Cymro* (25 April 1901), 8. E. James Jones, Caernarfon, was named secretary, and E. W. Evans, Dolgellau, shorthand secretary. The observers for the Liverpool presbytery were Dr Hugh Jones, William Jones (David Street) and Mr William Evans (Elm Bank); and for W. O. Jones, Rowland J. Williams, J. J. Bebb and E. R. Davies, a solicitor from Pwllheli, see *Blwyddiadur y Methodistiaid Calfinaidd* (1902), 194–8, and for the Colwyn Bay Association, *Drysorfa* (1901), 274–5.

88 As R. J. Williams said in the Oswestry Association, *Cymro* (4 July 1901), 5.

89 W. O. Jones in *Cymro* (8 November 1900), 6; John Jones paid the costs of the journey on the *Vito* according to the minutes of the Committee of Appeal, sitting at 6 p.m., 31 May.

90 Gaianydd MS, 36, and minutes of the committee of inquiry, Third Sitting, 25 May 1900, II.

91 W. O. Jones announced them in his letter in *Cymro* (18 October 1900).

92 Gaianydd MS, 39. There is a letter by E. James Jones, dated 28 February 1901, to William Jones, the secretary of the Liverpool Monthly Meeting, organizing men to get the evidence of S. S. Jerret (c/o Goodyear & Co., 31 St James Street, Liverpool) in the vestry of Crosshall Street, because he would be out of the country at the time of the Committee of Appeal. The date should be noted – 23 April that committee was convened.

93 It can be found in full in *Blwyddiadur y Methodistiaid Calfinaidd* (1902), 194–8; *Goleuad* (3 July 1901), 2–4; *Cymro* (4 July 1901), 5, 8.

94 The report in *Cymro* (4 July 1901), 5, was wrong and that was admitted in the edition on 11 July, p. 5. E. W. Evans. *Goleuad*, was the only reporter allowed to remain in the chapel, but complaints were made in *Cymro* (18 July 1901), 8, that his report in *Goleuad* (3 July), 2–4, showed traces of his bias against W. O. Jones. William James corrected the report in *Cymro* (11 July 1901), 5.

95 NLW, W. O. Jones Collection, Diary for 1901, which is complete.

96 Ibid.

97 Ibid., 17 December.

98 Ibid., 2 July.

99 For Winifred, who died on 26 August 1902, aged 22, see *Llais Rhyddid*, IV, 160–1. For her mother, Anne Williams (1849–1905), the widow of David Williams, see pp. 184–6. Annie (1874–97), Winifred's sister, was a missionary in Shillong, see J. H. Morris, *Hanes Cenhadaeth Dramor y Methodistiaid Calfinaidd* (Salford, 1907), p. 441.

[100] *Cymro* (1 May 1902), 5, 8. This case proved to be expensive for Eilian Owen. He did not have the means to pay the £169 asked for, between the compensation and the costs. He was disappointed by friends who promised to help him if he brought the case to court. He was taken before the Debtors Court and was judged to be a defaulter. The Monthly Meeting established a committee to consider whether he should be excommunicated on the basis of some of his confessions when being cross-examined in court. He was declared innocent. 'Adroddiad pwyllgor yn achos y Parch O. Eilian Owen', which was presented to the Monthly Meeting, can be found in Gaianydd MS, 39. The court order against Owen was cancelled by the court, 22 May 1903, see *Faner* (27 May 1903), 10. For Owen (1865–1938), see *Blwyddiadur y Methodistiaid Calfinaidd* (1939). For T. Gwynedd Roberts (1840–1920), see *Blwyddiadur y Methodistiaid Calfinaidd* (1922), 177.

[101] NLW, W. O. Jones diary for 2 July. 'Monday' in *Llais Rhyddid*, I (1902–3), 11, is a mistake.

[102] *Cymro* (4 July 1901), 8.

[103] The meeting was in City Hall, Eberle Street, *Llais Rhyddid*, I (1902–3), 11.

[104] The sermon was published in *Cymro* (18 and 25 July 1901), and in W. O. Jones, *Pwlpud Hope Hall* (Liverpool, 1902), pp. 5–18, along with other sermons.

[105] *Cymro* (25 July 1901), 8.

[106] *Cymro* (1 August 1901), 5.

[107] *Cymro* (15 August 1901), 8.

[108] *Cymro* (22 August 1901), 8; (29 August), 5.

[109] *Cymro* (29 August 1901), 5.

[110] *Cymro* (12 September 1901), 5; *Llais Rhyddid*, I (1902–3), 11.

[111] *Cymro* (26 September 1901), 5. The decision was signed by the Chairman of the Arrangements Committee, G. C. Rees, and by the Secretary, W. A. Lewis.

[112] There are histories and pictures of the chapels in *Llais Rhyddid*.

[113] *Llais Rhyddid*, I (1902–3), 11.

[114] *Cymro* (13 March 1902); *Llais Rhyddid*, I (1902–3), 14–15. A call was extended to Hughes, 27 October 1901. For Hughes, see *Llais Rhyddid*, III (1904), 1–2.

[115] *Llais Rhyddid*, II (1903), 121–5; for Davies, see III (1904), pp. 49–50.

[116] Eluned Phillips, *Dewi Emrys* (Llandysul, 1971), pp. 52–3.

[117] See David Roberts, *Paternalism in Early Victorian England* (London, 1979).

[118] *Cymro* (1 August 1901), 5.

[119] For this letter in full, see *Cymro* (22 August 1901), 5.

[120] *Cymro* (1 August 1901), 5.

[121] *Cymro* (25 July 1901), 6. Roberts was originally from Pistyll, Nefyn, and was a wood merchant in Liverpool, *Llais Rhyddid*, III (1904), 97–9.

[122] *Rhagor o Atgofion Cardi*, p. 49.

[123] *Llais Rhyddid*, II (1903), 61–2; III (1904), 123–7, 188–9.

[124] *Tyst* (3 June 1937), 9; *Congregational Year Book* (1938), 681.

[125] For Lewis (1871–1950), see *Tyst* (4 January 1951), 9; (11 January), 7, and 'Oriel', *Tywysydd y Plant* (1938).

9. *The Confusion of the Intelligentsia*

[1] Letter to W. J. Parry, Bethesda, 12 December 1891, Bangor MS, Coetmor A.

[2] *Dysgedydd* (1901), 257.

[3] *Report of the Baptist Union of Wales*, Caernarfon (1892), p. 12.

[4] *Goleuad* (12 May 1897), 12.

[5] *Seren Gomer* (1897), 31–7.

[6] *Goleuad* (2 December 1904), 3.

[7] For doubts in the previous age, see R. S. Williams, *Cydymaeth yr Ysgol Sabbothol*, I (1884–5), 82; Griffith Parry, 'Rhai o agweddau amheuaeth ddiweddar', *Geninen* (1888), 85–96, which discusses philosophers; Robert Davies, Shrewsbury, 'Yr amser presenol', *Geninen* (1886), 46–52, which says that Christian doctrine was under attack.

[8] *Geninen* (1906), 85.

[9] W. Williams (Crwys), *Pedair Pennod* (Aberystwyth, 1950), p. 66.

[10] For William Williams (Crwys) (1875–1968), see *Bywg.* (1951–70).

[11] E. Cefni Jones, *Gwili: Cofiant a Phregethau* (Llandysul, 1937), pp. 76–7.

[12] 'Goeru awen, gwirionedd', *Geninen* (1903), 67–9.

[13] For Bowen (1878–1903) and the whole affair, see David Bowen, *Cofiant a Barddoniaeth Ben Bowen* (Treorchy, 1904), pp. lviii–lxxix.

[14] *Seren Cymru* (1 August 1902), 10–11; see (8 August), 10; (22 August), 11.

[15] W. J. Gruffydd, 'Yr ieuainc wrth yr hen', *Ynys yr Hud* (Cardiff, 1923), pp. 44–5. This poem was composed at the time of the armistice.

[16] 'Creodau [*sic*] a chyffesion enwadol: ai rhaid wrthynt?', *Geninen* (1903), 228–34; answered by John Owen, Ffestiniog, *Geninen* (1904), 88–91; David Jenkins, *T. Gwynn Jones* (Denbigh, 1973), pp. 140–1.

[17] Jenkins, *T. Gwynn Jones*, pp. 162, 169–70.

[18] T. Gwynn Jones, *Manion* (Wrexham, 1932), p. 32.

[19] Daniel Owen, *Rhys Lewis* (first published, Wrexham, 1885), p. 184.

[20] *Report of the Union of Welsh Independents*, Carmarthen (1872), p. 16.

[21] Ibid., p. 36. For J. B. Jones (1829–1905), see *DWB*.

[22] For Ellis Humphrey Evans (Hedd Wyn) (1887–1917), see *DWB*.

23 Hoxie Neale Fairchild, *Religious Trends in English Poetry*, IV (1830–80) (New York, 1957), pp. 538, 540.

24 W. E. Houghton, *The Victorian Frame of Mind 1830–1870* (New Haven, 1957), p. 179.

25 J. Hillis Miller, *The Disappearance of God* (Cambridge, MA, 1963), p. 5.

26 See M. H. Nicolson, *The Breaking of the Circle* (New York, 1950); A. O. Lovejoy, *The Great Chain of Being: A Study in the History of an Idea* (Cambridge, MA, 1936); John Hollander, *The Untuning of the Sky: Ideas of Music in English Poetry 1500–1700* (Princeton, NJ, 1961).

27 John A. Lester, *Journey through Despair* (Princeton, NJ, 1968), pp. xx–xxi; cf. J. H. Buckley, *The Victorian Temper* (Cambridge, MA, 1951; London, 1966), pp. 9–10. Raymond Williams argued that the 'Victorian age' was over by the 1870s, *The English Novel from Dickens to Lawrence* (London, 1970), as does Malcolm Bradbury, *The Social Context of Modern English Literature* (Oxford, 1971), pp. xxxi–xxxii. C. B. Cox and A. E. Dyson favour 1870 as the key year of change and they place more importance than the others on the economic decline in England, *The Twentieth Century Mind*, I (London, 1972), p. 54.

28 J. C. Ryle, *Principles for Churchmen* (London, 1884), p. xix.

29 G. Hartwell Jones, *Religious Eclipse and National Decline* (Liverpool, 1894).

30 For Richard Davies (Tafolog) (1830–1904), see *DWB*.

31 *Geninen* (1884), 51.

32 For John Hugh Evans (Cynfaen) (1833–86), a Wesleyan minister, see *DWB*.

33 *Geninen* (1893), 67.

34 *Geninen* (1896), 10. For Rhys Jones Huws (1862–1917), Congregational minister, see *DWB*.

35 *Geninen* (1886), 40.

36 *Geninen* (1887), 19.

37 *Geninen* (1888), 20.

38 *Geninen* (1887), 18.

39 For William Thomas (Islwyn) (1832–78), see *DWB*.

40 *Geninen* (1887), 18.

41 *Geninen* (1904), 86.

42 *Geninen* (1906), 150.

43 *Geninen* (1888), 21.

44 A 'pryddest' is a 'fairly long poem in free metre, sometimes with "cynghanedd", for which the crown is offered at the National Eisteddfod'. See *GPC*, p. 2919.

45 D. Tecwyn Lloyd, 'Y Bardd Newydd', in J. E. Caerwyn Williams (ed.), *Ysgrifau Beirniadol*, III (Denbigh, 1967), pp. 71–85.

[46] *Geninen* (1908), 14.

[47] J. Gwili Jenkins, *Tu Hwnt i'r Llen* (Llanelli, 1897), pp. 17, 16. He placed as a motto on the first page, 'All visible things are emblems'.

[48] Strauss (1808–74) held to a mythological explanation of Jesus. Myth, he said, is that activity which expresses religious ideas as clothing for historical people and events. Jesus was a historical person and because of their admiration for him his disciples attributed ideal characteristics to him and crowned the work by making of him a divine figure.

[49] Thomas Parry, *Hanes Llenyddiaeth Gymraeg hyd 1900* (Cardiff, 1944), p. 284.

[50] For example, Elphin, *Geninen* (1895), 262–8; (1896), 67–8, and R. Abbey Williams's satire in *Geninen Eisteddfodol* (1907), 15, and T. Gwynn Jones, *Welsh Outlook*, I (1914), 21.

[51] For Arthur Simon Thomas (Anellydd) (1865–1935), see *DWB*.

[52] Anellydd, *Haul* (1901), 534. The New Poet was defended by Rhys J. Huws in *Geninen* (1896), 9–11, and Tafolog in *Geninen* (1897), 112–15. See also David Adams, 'Tafolog', *Geninen* (1904), 83–7, and the review of Iolo Caernarfon's *Ymsonau* in *Drysorfa* (1895), 262–4.

[53] Alun Llewelyn Williams, *Y Nos, y Niwl a'r Ynys* (Cardiff, 1960).

[54] 'The new type of man is the romantic artist, the man who in the absence of a given world, must create his own.' J. Hillis Miller, *The Disappearance of God* (Cambridge, MA, 1963), p. 14.

[55] *Geninen* (1884), 69.

[56] For John Ceiriog Hughes (1832–87), see *DWB*.

[57] *Haul* (1901), 534.

[58] *Geninen* (1888), 242.

[59] *Drysorfa* (1896), 511–12.

[60] *Geninen* (1903), 68.

[61] See Kenneth Hamilton, *God is Dead: The Anatomy of a Slogan* (Grand Rapids, MI, 1966), pp. 28, 73.

[62] Lloyd, 'Y Bardd Newydd', in Williams (ed.), *Ysgrifau Beirniadol*, III, p. 85.

[63] Raymond Williams's suggestion in *The Long Revolution* (London, 1961), p. 12.

[64] Suzanne K. Langer, *Philosophy in a New Key: A Study in the Symbolism of Reason, Rite and Art* (Cambridge, MA, 1942), pp. 291–2.

[65] For example, David Griffith in *Geninen* (1901), 9–20.

[66] The knitting machine, *Geninen Eisteddfodol* (1909), 53; electricity, *Geninen* (1898), 213; *Geninen Eisteddfodol* (1899), 7; (1908), 21; (1909), 5, 26; motor bike, *Geninen* (1910), 46; wireless, *Geninen Eisteddfodol* (1908), 32; aeroplane, *Geninen Eisteddfodol* (1907), 58; (1909), 14, 31; (1910), 52; motor car, *Geninen Eisteddfodol* (1898), 46; (1908), 13, 37; (1910), 15, 20; carbide, *Geninen Eisteddfodol* (1909), 5.

[67] *Geninen Eisteddfodol* (1898), 7–11.

[68] An *englyn* to Edison by Trebor Aled, *Geninen Eisteddfodol* (1898), 37. Notice how he uses the word 'gwyddonydd' (scientist).

[69] *Drysorfa* (1893), 51–3, 102–4, 130–4, 171–5.

[70] *Drysorfa* (1893), 257–60, 336–43.

[71] *Drysorfa* (1895), 156–61, 302–7, 399–404, 448–55.

[72] For Gwilym Owen (1880–1940), professor of physics in the University of Wales, Aberystwyth, 1919–36, see *DWB*.

[73] Ebenezer Griffith-Jones (1860–1942), later principal of the Yorkshire United Theological College (Congregational), Bradford, was a joint winner with Adams.

[74] Later in his life, Adams severely attacked this doctrine as a 'barbaric idea', *Yr Eglwys a Gwareiddiad Diweddar* (Merthyr Tudful, 1914), p. 153.

[75] David Adams, *Traethawd ar Ddatblygiad yn ei Berthynas a'r Cwymp, yr Ymgnawdoliad, a'r Atgyfodiad* (Caernarfon, 1893), p. 12.

[76] Ibid., p. 29.

[77] Ibid., pp. 70–1.

[78] Ibid., p. 56.

[79] Ibid., p. 64.

[80] Ibid., pp. 41–8.

[81] Ibid., p. 77.

[82] Ibid., p. 82.

[83] Ibid., p. 73.

[84] Ibid., p. 94.

[85] Ibid., pp. 94–6.

[86] Ibid., pp. 116–28.

[87] 'At y darllenydd'.

[88] John Hughes, *Ysgol Jacob: Breuddwyd ac Ymchwil am Dduw* (Wrexham, 1899), p. 108.

[89] For Darwin's gradual move towards atheism, see R. E. D. Clark, *Darwin: Before and After* (London, 1948), pp. 80–90. A thinker's motivation does not necessarily nullify his thinking, but if he sees a theological aim to his work, it is fair for the theologian to take note of it.

[90] *Ysgol Jacob*, p. 109.

[91] Ibid.

[92] Ibid., p. 110.

[93] Ibid., p. 98.

[94] Ibid., p. 92.

[95] *Report of the Baptist Union of Wales*, Swansea (1890), pp. 13–14.

[96] J. Lloyd Williams, *Atgofion Tri Chwarter Canrif* (Aberystwyth, 1944), pp. 127–9.

[97] *Drysorfa* (1894), 380.

[98] For example, *Drysorfa* (1893), 316 – by order of Mold Association, June 1893.

[99] For example, Rhys Morgan, 'Duw a'r tywydd', *Drysorfa* (1893), 326–30.

[100] For Guillaume Groen van Prinsterer (1801–76), Dutch historian, politician and educationalist, and Abraham Kuyper (1837–1920), Dutch theologian, politician and prime minister, see E. L. Hebden Taylor, *The Christian Philosophy of Law, Politics and the State* (Nutley, NJ, 1966), pp. 28–63, and the bibliography.

[101] Anne Freemantle, *The Papal Encyclicals* (New York, 1956),pp. 143–52.

[102] Ibid., pp. 197–201, for parts of it. For the movement in general, see A. R. Vidler, *The Modernist Movement in the Roman Church* (Cambridge, 1934); H. Daniel-Rops, *A Fight for God* (London and New York, 1966), ch. 6. The key documents are in B. M. G. Reardon (ed.), *A Roman Catholic Modernism* (Stanford, CA, 1970), with an excellent historical foreword.

[103] David Adams, *Yr Eglwys a Gwareiddiad Diweddar*, p. 11.

[104] Ibid., p. 182.

[105] Ibid., pp. 169–70.

[106] Ibid., p. 101.

[107] Ibid., p. 60.

[108] Ibid.

[109] Ibid.

[110] Ibid., p. 190.

[111] Ibid., p. 80.

10. At the Feet of the Theologians

[1] *Goleuad* (6 October 1897), 9.

[2] *Report of the Baptist Union of Wales*, Pontypridd (1896), p. 17.

[3] *Llythyr cymanfaoedd Bedwyddwyr Môn ac Arfon . . .* (1895), p. 4.

[4] *Seren Gomer* (1899), 41–7.

[5] *Drysorfa* (1898), 121.

[6] *Drysorfa* (1900), 100.

[7] *Drysorfa* (1888), 287–8.

[8] *Geninen* (1896), 225–7.

[9] *Young Wales*, III (1897), 116–17.

[10] So E. Garmon Roberts, Gobowen, 'Dynion ieuainc a'r eglwysi', *Dysgedydd* (1901), 257.

[11] 'Effeithiau Ymneilltuaeth yng Nghymru'. It is quoted extensively in D. D. Williams, *Thomas Charles Edwards* (Liverpool, 1921), ch. 6.

[12] For Thomas Jones (Denbigh) (1754–1820), Calvinistic Methodist minister and author, see *DWB*.

[13] For Thomas Charles (1755–1814), Methodist cleric involved in the first Methodist ordinations in Wales in 1811, see *DWB*.

[14] 'Religious Thought in Wales', in D. D. Williams, *Thomas Charles Edwards*, pp. 103–12.

[15] 'Theology, in fact, was dying of asphyxia', ibid., p. 106.

[16] For Richard Davies (1501?–81), bishop and Bible translator, see *DWB*.

[17] See 'Rhyddiaith Grefyddol y Bedwaredd Ganrif ar Bymtheg', in Geraint Bowen (ed.), *Y Traddodiad Rhyddiaeth* (Llandysul, 1970), pp. 318–53. See also R. M. Jones, *Llên Cymru a Chrefydd* (Swansea, 1977), which is the most comprehensive study to date of the influence of the Augustinian and Calvinist traditions on Wales's literary culture.

[18] *Cronicl* (1871), 153, 242. There was quite considerable criticism of Calvinism in *Y Cronicl*; see, for example (1867), 325–6; (1868), 183, 253–4; (1870), 215–17; (1872), 177–8, where mention is made of 'the dark territories "the slough of despair" of soul-destroying Calvinism'. For the difference between Arminianism and Calvinism see the clear and concise article on it in *Beirniad*, XII (1871), 281–92.

[19] *Report of the Committee on Disestablishment*, II, 521, question 17619.

[20] Ibid., III, 85, questions 20862–75.

[21] Ibid., 314, question 27370.

[22] Ibid., 291, question 26710; 301, question 26964.

[23] Ibid., 418, question 13854; 419, question 13860.

[24] Ibid., 170–1, questions 23621–34. For the Five Points, see D. N. Steele and C. C. Thomas, *The Five Points of Calvinism: Defined, Defended and Documented* (Philadelphia, 1963).

[25] *Welsh Outlook* (1914), 327.

[26] R. Gwylfa Roberts, *Cofiant y Parch. William Davies, Llandeilo* (Llanelli, 1925), pp. 163–4.

[27] W. James, *Cofiant a Phregethau y Parch. Robert Thomas, Glandŵr* (Cardiff, 1913), p. 31.

[28] *Drysorfa* (1894), 308.

[29] *Geninen* (1886), 46–52.

[30] *Dysgedydd* (1896), 89, 92.

[31] *Goleuad* (13 May 1896), 8–9.

[32] R. S. Williams, Bethesda, 'Y ddiwinyddiaeth ddiweddaraf', *Cydymaith yr Ysgol Sabbothol* (1883–4), 82.

[33] Llenfab, 'Y Dduwinyddiaeth Newydd', *Y Gwyliedydd* (29 March 1893), 2; this is the best explanation of the subject.

[34] Lewis Probert, *Esboniad elfenol ac eglurhaol ar yr epistol at yr Rhufeiniaid yn nghyda rhagdraeth ac attodiad* (Wrexham, 1890), p. 342; see also his comments in *Traethodydd* (1891), 421.

[35] See Griffith Ellis's detailed review, 'Deddfau natur yn y byd ysbrydol', *Traethodydd* (1886), 85–105; Ishmael Evans, 'Perthynas damcaniaeth

Datblygiad a chrefydd', *Eurgrawn Wesleaidd* (1896), 13–21; T. Gwynn Thomas, 'Henry Drummond', *Diwygiwr* (1897), 158–60; D. Powell, 'Llyfr y Proffeswr Drummond ar *Egyniad Dyn*', *Seren Gomer* (1894), 212–19, and W. O. Jones, 'Esgyniad Dyn', *Traethodydd* (1894), 288–300.

[36] Llenfab, *Gwyliedydd* (29 March 1893), 2.

[37] A. M. Fairbairn, *The Place of Christ in Modern Theology* (13th edn, London, 1907), p. 369. For Fairbairn, see W. B. Selbie, *The Life of Andrew Martin Fairbairn* (London, 1914).

[38] *Dysgedydd* (1899), 279.

[39] It also appeared in the *Expositor*, 'The God-Man' (5th series, II, August 1895), 241–61.

[40] *Drysorfa* (1888), 289.

[41] Trebor Lloyd Evans, *Lewis Edwards: Ei Fywyd a'i Waith* (Swansea, 1967), p. 236.

[42] Thomas Charles Edwards, *The God-Man* (London, 1895), pp. 153–4.

[43] Ibid., pp. 16–17.

[44] In J. Vyrnwy Morgan, *Welsh Religious Leaders in the Victorian Age* (London, 1908), p. 368.

[45] *The God-Man*, p. 79.

[46] T. C. Edwards believed that his father had embraced a form of the recent kenotic theories when he wrote *Athrawiaeth yr Iawn* but that he had later rejected it; *Y Duw-Ddyn*, pp. 146–8.

[47] *The God-Man*, pp. 25–6, 122–5.

[48] Ibid., p. 128.

[49] Ibid., p. 151.

[50] Ibid., pp. 133–4.

[51] See William Evans, *Monthly Treasury* (1895), 217–19; T. E. Roberts, Aberystwyth, *Traethodydd* (1896), 206–15; W. O. Jones, ibid., pp. 216–35, 361–78; R. S. Thomas, ibid., pp. 277–88, and *Drysorfa* (1896), 193–201; Owen Evans, *Dysgedydd* (1896), 5–10, 49–53; B. Evans, ibid., pp. 305–10; D. S. Thomas, *Dysgedydd* (1897), 317–24, and also in *Diwygiwr* (1897), 305–10; John Williams, *Traethodydd* (1896), 43–55; R. H. Morgan, *Drysorfa* (1896), 436–9; O. B. Jones and R. H. Morgan, ibid., pp. 253–7.

[52] For Davies, see R. Humphreys, *William Ryle Davies* (Caernarfon, 1904).

[53] For Morgan (1850–99), the son of Edward Morgan, Dyffryn, see *DWB*; *Drysorfa* (1899), 234; *Blwyddiadur y Methodistiaid Calfinaidd* (1900), 183; *Trysorfa y Plant* (1899), 169–71.

[54] *Traethodydd* (1896), 211–12. For a bibliography, see note 51.

[55] This is the *extra Calvinisticum* that the Lutherans attacked, claiming that it led to Nestorianism. Calvin's judgement on the subject can be found in *Institutes*, II, 132–14. Karl Barth, in discussing the *kenosis* is

very clearly against the kind of standpoint embraced by T. C. Edwards, see *Church Dogmatics* IV/1 (Edinburgh, 1956), pp. 180–3.

56 *Dysgedydd* (1896), 8.

57 For R. S. Thomas (d. 3 June 1923, aged 79), see *Blwyddiadur y Methodistiaid Calfinaidd* (1924), 238. Cynddylan Jones said of him, 'I do not wish to say that Mr Thomas was the greatest thinker in the Methodist Connexion, but I will say boldly that he possessed the widest and most detailed knowledge of theology of anyone I knew'. Cf. D. Densil Morgan, 'Wales, Princeton and a Nineteenth Century Battle for the Bible', *Journal of Welsh Religious History*, new series, II (2002), 51–81.

58 R. S. Thomas, *Undod Personol y Duw-Ddyn* (Merthyr Tudful, 1900), p. 294. His translation of the Definition can be found on pp. 295–6.

59 Ibid., pp. 284–6.

60 Ibid., p. 287.

61 Ibid., p. 315. Morgan's standpoint can be found in *Drysorfa* (1897), 8.

62 Ibid., pp. 287–90.

63 Ibid., pp. 328–40. According to Apollinarius the divine Logos had taken the place of the mind (*nous*) in Jesus' human nature, and this meant (said his critics) that Jesus was not fully human.

64 R. S. Thomas, *Atebion i ddwy gyfres holiadau, y diweddar Dr Lewis Edwards ar Berson Christ* (Bala, 1908), pp. 74–5.

65 For John Cynddylan Jones (1840–1930), see *DWB*.

66 *Report of the Royal Commission on Disestablishment*, III, 554; VII, 119.

67 J. Cynddylan Jones, *Cysondeb y Ffydd*, II (Cardiff, 1907), p. 307.

68 J. Cynddylan Jones, *Athrylith a Gras* (Caernarfon, 1925), p. 18.

69 Jones, *Cysondeb y Ffydd*, II, p. 271.

70 Ibid., pp. 271–2.

71 Ibid., p. 259.

72 Ibid., p. 116.

73 Ibid., pp. 79, 95, 341, 343.

74 Fror T. J. Pritchard (d. 21 January 1918, aged 65), see *Eurgrawn Wesleaidd* (1918), 78–9, and for Pope (1822–1903), a professor at Didsbury College, see *DNB*.

75 Vol. I (Bangor, 1906), Vol. II (Bangor, 1911). Owen Evans died on 7 February 1945, aged 91, see *Minutes of the Methodist Conference* (1945), 130.

76 Owen Evans, *Diwinyddiaeth Gristnogol*, p. 41.

77 Ibid., p. 89.

78 1st impression, 1911; 2nd impression, 1912. For Morris (1869–1940), see *Blwyddiadur y Methodistiaid Calfinaidd* (1942), 119–20.

79 See also his article, 'Was Jesus a "Divine Man" and Nothing More?', *Hibbert Journal* (April 1908), 621–31. Its substance was embodied in *Person Crist*.

[80] R. H. Morris, *Person Crist* (Wrexham, 1911), p. 80.

[81] Ibid., p. 107.

[82] *Traethodydd* (1896), 279.

[83] (Dolgellau, 1915). The first materials appeared in *Dysgedydd* (1910). For David Miall Edwards (1873–1941), professor in the Memorial College, Brecon, 1909–34, see *Bywg.* (1941–50); Robert Pope, *Seeking God's Kingdom: The Nonconformist Social Gospel in Wales, 1906–1939* (Cardiff, 1999), pp. 38–55.

[84] D. Miall Edwards, *Crefydd a Bywyd* (Dolgellau 1915), p. 137.

[85] Ibid., p. 159.

[86] Ibid., p. 161.

[87] Ibid., pp. 172–6.

[88] Ibid., p. 138.

[89] Ibid., p. 143.

[90] Ibid., p. 140.

[91] Ibid., pp. 146–7.

[92] Ibid., p. 182.

[93] Ibid., pp. 177–200.

[94] R. J. Campbell, *The New Theology* (London, 1907), p. 74. For Campbell (1867–1950), see *Encyclopaedia Britannica (Britannica Book of the Year 1957*, article, 'Obituaries'). For a description by Campbell of the debate, see his book *My Spiritual Pilgrimage* (London, 1916), pp. 184–249. For a detailed analysis of the debate, see John W. Grant, *Free Churchmanship in England 1870–1940* (London, 1955), pp. 132–42; Keith W. Clements, *Lovers of Discord: Twentieth Century Theological Controversies in England* (London, 1980), pp. 19–48; Keith Robbins, 'The Spiritual Pilgrimage of the Rev. R. J. Campbell', *Journal of Ecclesiastical History*, XX/2 (1979), 261–76.

[95] *New Theology*, p. 75.

[96] Ibid., pp. 52, 73.

[97] Ibid., p. 73.

[98] J. J. Morgan, *Cofiant Evan Phillips, Castellnewydd Emlyn* (Liverpool, 1930), p. 177.

[99] T. Rhondda Williams, *How I Found My Faith* (London, 1938), pp. 69–71, 92–7, and his book *The New Theology* (London, 1907). For Williams (1860–1945), see *Congregational Year Book* (1946), 456.

[100] *Gwyliedydd* (4 April 1907), 4.

[101] Ibid.

[102] *Goleuad* (17 April 1907), 4.

[103] See his measured article in *Eurgrawn Wesleaidd* (1908), 135–7, 178–81, 249–52.

[104] *Dysgedydd* (1907), 75–9.

[105] *Seren Cymru* (20 March 1907), 'Arwr y Ddiwinyddiaeth (?) Newydd yn Caerdydd'.

[106] *Dysgedydd* (1907), 218. For Thomas (1845–1913), the son of John Thomas, Liverpool, a 'marine surveyor' by trade and the owner of *Y Tyst*, see *Dysgeydd* (1913), 530–1, 533–4.

[107] *Dysgedydd* (1910), 321.

[108] Here is a selection: *Gwyliedydd*, series from 4 April 1907 onwards; D. Adams, *Geninen* (1907), 73–8; E. Griffith-Jones, ibid., pp. 233–6; 'Rhywun', *Geninen* (1908), 143–7; J. Lewis Williams, ibid., pp. 146–51; D. Powell, *Greal* (1908), 57–60; *Goleuad* (23 January 1907), 3, 8–9, and regularly after that for weeks. The New Theology was criticized in W. T. Ellis's series, 'Y Bod o Dduw', *Goleuad* (1907), 27 March onwards; *Seren Cymru* (5 April 1907), 1, 7; (10 May), 10 and letters from 24 May onwards; Owen Evans, *Dysgedydd* (1907), 233–6; J. Lewis Wiliams, ibid., pp. 264–70; 'Aleph', *Diwygiwr* (1907), 160–2; J. Young Evans, in T. Stephens (ed.), *Cymru Heddyw ac Yforu* (Cardiff, 1908), pp. 28–31.

[109] David Adams, *Yr Hen a'r Newydd mewn Duwinyddiaeth* (Dolgellau, 1907), p. 40.

[110] Ibid., pp. 62–3.

[111] Ibid., p. 129.

[112] E. Keri Evans and W. Pari Huws, *Cofiant y Parch David Adams DD* (Liverpool, 1924), p. 178.

[113] Ibid., p. 183.

[114] Ibid., p. 145, in relation to *Yr Hen a'r Newydd mewn Duwinyddiaeth*.

[115] Evans and Huws, *Cofiant y Parch David Adams*, p. 171.

[116] Ibid., p. 172.

[117] Ibid., p. 183.

[118] Lewis Williams, Bangor, *Traethodydd* (1927), 205. For the subject in general, see R. Gele Williams, 'Athrawiaeth yr Iawn yng Nghymru yn y bedwaredd ganrif ar bymtheg', MA dissertation, University of Wales, 1939.

[119] *Traethodydd* (1893), 148–52.

[120] *Goleuad* (20 May 1896), 11; see also David Adams, 'Iesu ei Hun yw'r Iawn', *Dysgedydd* (1900), 453–7.

[121] R. S. Thomas, *Yr Iawn*, pp. 489–518; J. Cynddylan Jones, *Athrylith a Gras*, pp. 197–208.

[122] D. D. Williams, *Thomas Charles Edwards*, p. 74.

[123] For Jones (1821–79), see W. Trefor Jones, *John Jones (Yr Hen Gloddiwr)* (1923).

[124] *Geninen* (1896), 191. For Gwrtheyrn (Griffith Roberts, 1846–1915), see *DWB*.

[125] *Geninen* (1897), 121–4.

126 For example, E. Pritchard, *Greal* (1899), 181–6.

127 *Young Wales*, III (1897), 116–17.

128 *Geninen* (1886), 47.

129 See James Charles, 'Anfarwoldeb naturiol yr enaid', *Dysgedydd* (1899), 21–7.

130 Timothy Thomas, *Traethawd am y Wisg Wen Ddisglaer* (Dolgellau, c.1805), pp. 221–2, 133. For Timothy Thomas (1720–68), see *DWB*.

131 For Hannah Smith (1832–1911), see her autobiography, *My Spiritual Autobiography* (New York, 1903) and *New International Dictionary of the Christian Church* (Exeter, 1974). For a discussion of her teaching and that of her husband, see B. B. Warfield, *Perfectionism* (New York, 1971), pp. 216–311. For their predecessor, William Edward Boardman (1810–86), see the biography by his wife, *The Life and Labours of W. E. Boardman* (New York, 1886).

132 *Drysorfa* (1897), 390–7. For a view of the doctrine in a light more congenial to the Calvinistic Methodists' Confession of Faith, see David Roberts, Rhiw, in *Drysorfa* (1898), 10–14.

133 *Goleuad* (21 August 1903), 9.

134 *Seren Cymru* (9 September 1904), 6; see also D. Wynne Evans, *Geninen* (1906), 225–9 and M. H. Jones, *Goleuad* (12 August 1904), 8–9.

135 For the influence of the Llandrindod Convention on R. B. Jones, see B. P. Jones, *The King's Champions* (Redhill, 1968), 48–9.

136 *Seren Cymru* (21 September 1894), 12.

137 It can be found in *Faner* (5 September 1894), 5, *Y Genedl Gymreig* (28 August 1894), 3, with summaries in *Goleuad* (5 September 1894), 4 and *Seren Cymru* (17 September 1894), 9.

138 *Seren Cymru* (14 September 1894), 11.

139 *Seren Cymru* (21 September 1894), 12.

140 Ibid., p. 11.

141 W. Morris Lewis, *Araeth a draddodwyd o gadair Cymdeithasfa y Methodistiaid Calfinaidd yn neheudir Cymru, a gynhaliwyd yn Nhrefdraeth, Sir Benfro, Hydref 2, 3, 4, 1893* (Dolgellau, 1894); J. Gwyddno Williams, 'Y Sacramentau': Adolygiad ar lyfr y Parch. Hugh Williams, M.A., Bala* (Llangollen, 1895); J. G. Jones, *Bedydd 'Sacramentau' y Parch. Hugh Williams, M.A., Bala: Beth ydyw* (Carmarthen, 1895); D. G. Jones, *Llyfr ar fedydd: Sef detholiad o'r llithiau a ymddangosasant ar faes y Darian, gan Taenellwr, yn yr hwn lyfr y ceir barn a meddwl dynion dysgedicaf yr oesau ar y pwnc* (Treherbert, 1882); Griffith Parry, *Y Sacramentau: Bedydd a Swper yr Arglwydd* (Denbigh, 1896), and the sharp response by David Evans, Blaenconin, *Olion y Gwyriad* (Tonypandy, 1898, 2nd edn, 1899) and the Davies Lecture by William James, Manchester, *Yr Eglwys: Ei Sacramentau, a'i Gweinidogaeth* (Wrexham, 1898).

11. Cultivating the Christian Mind

[1] This was in 1821, *Dysgedydd* (1821), 344. For other examples, see *Trysorfa y Plant* (1883), 20–1; (1895), 49; *Y Winllan* (1888), 119.

[2] For A. J. Parry's attack on the Anglophone emphasis of these colleges, see *Report of the Welsh Baptist Union*, Pontypridd (1896), p. 30.

[3] *Report of the Royal Commission on Disestablishment*, I, 59, 67. In a memorandum by Owen Evans and Hugh Cecil, 728, 792 is given as the total pupils with 404, 418 of them under 15 years of age. Ibid., p. 133.

[4] *Seren Gomer* (1904), 315.

[5] J. Lloyd Williams, *Atgofion Tri Chwarter Canrif*, IV (Aberystwyth, 1944), pp. 265–7.

[6] A. O. Evans, *Haul* (1911), 255. For Archdeacon Albert Owen Evans (1864–1937), see *DWB*.

[7] D. D. Williams, *Llawlyfr Hanes Cyfundeb y Methodistiaid Calfinaidd* (Caernarfon, 1927), p. 231.

[8] David Powell, *Report of the Royal Commission on Disestablishment*, III, 278, question 26330.

[9] R. Tudur Jones, *Yr Undeb* (Swansea, 1975), pp. 122, 131–2.

[10] *Report of the Royal Commission on Disestablishment*, I, 64.

[11] For the details, see ibid., pp. 58–66; III, pp. 181, 195–6.

[12] For those of the Calvinistic Methodists, the handbooks for those unsure of Welsh, ibid., III, p. 184, and the commentaries for adults, 1891–1905, ibid., pp. 116–19; for the Baptists, 1890–1905, ibid., p. 279; VII, p. 104; for the Wesleyans, ibid., VII, p. 39; and for the Independents, see Jones, *Yr Undeb*, pp. 133–6.

[13] *Drysorfa* (1896), 359.

[14] *Report of the Royal Commission on Disestablishment*, III, 185.

[15] Jones, *Yr Undeb*, p. 135.

[16] *Greal* (1903), 1; *Cymro* (29 May 1902), 2.

[17] *Faner* (8 August 1903), 14; for a response to it (26 August), 5.

[18] This deserves a more appreciative review than that given by Maurice Jones in *Beirniad*, VI/1 (Spring 1916), 67–8.

[19] *Dysgedydd* (1909), 322.

[20] *Gofyniadau ac atebion i blant yr Eglwys ar fywyd Samuel* (1909); *Gofyniadau ac atebion . . . Credo'r Apostolion* (1909); *Hawl ac ateb . . . Y greadigaeth a chwymp dyn* (3rd impression, 1909).

[21] W. Ross Hughes, *Camrau'r Iesu* (3rd impression, Pwllheli, 1909); D. Silyn Evans, *Eiddo'r Plant* (Dolgellau, 1909).

[22] For its origin, see R. Tudur Jones, *Hanes Annibynwyr Cymru* (Swansea, 1966), p. 67; for a lively description of it today, see D. J. Roberts, 'Y Pwnc', *Cardigan and Tivy-side Advertiser* (4 June 1973).

[23] J. Cynddylan Jones, *Cysondeb y Ffydd*, IV (Cardiff, 1916), 'Introduction'.

[24] *Report of the Royal Commission on Disestablishment*, III, 181.

[25] D. Adams, *Yr Ysgol Sabbothol: llawlyfr ymarferol i'r athrawon* (Aberdare, 1908), p. 43; O. Evans, *Dysgedydd* (1909), 322–3.

[26] R. W. Jones, *Y Parch John Puleston Jones, MA DD* (Caernarfon, 1929), p. 288.

[27] *Greal* (1900), 175.

[28] The standpoint of the higher critics at the turn of the twentieth century can be seen in C. A. Briggs, *General Introduction to the Study of Holy Scripture* ([n.pl.], 1899), chs 11, 12, 21. For the pioneers of the movement, see T. K. Cheyne, *Founders of Old Testament Criticism* (London, 1893).

[29] For his view, see J. Connop Thirlwall, Jr., *Connop Thirlwall: Historian and Theologian* (London, 1936), pp. 256–7. Thirlwall (1797–1875) was bishop of St Davids from 1840 to 1874.

[30] Myrddin Fardd, *Adgof uwch anghof: Llythyrau lluaws o Brif Enwogion Cymru: hen a diweddar* (Pen y Groes, 1883), pp. 256–7. I outlined the development of biblical criticism in Wales up to 1890 in 'Astudio'r Hen Destament yng Nghymru, 1860–1890', in Gwilym H. Jones (ed.), *Efrydiau Beiblaidd Bangor*, II (Swansea, 1977); and 'Esbonio'r Testament Newydd yng Nghymru, 1860–1890', in Owen E. Evans (ed.), *Efrydiau Beiblaidd Bangor*, III (Swansea, 1978).

[31] George Vance Smith, *The Bible and its Theology as Popularly Taught* (London, 1871; new impression, 1892).

[32] T. Lloyd Evans, *Lewis Edwards: Ei Fywyd a'i Waith* (Swansea, 1967), pp. 216–23.

[33] *Traethodydd* (1893), 105–13. For Morris (1862–1923), professor (1886–96) and principal of the Baptist College, Bangor, see *DWB*.

[34] For their work, see J. Young Evans, 'Bannau beirniadaeth y Testament Newydd', in *Geninen* (1898), 249–53.

[35] For Fenton John Anthony Hort (1828–92), Joseph Barber Lightfoot (1828–89), bishop of Durham, and his successor in the see, Brooke Foss Wescott (1825–1901), see *DNB*.

[36] By his own admission, Hughes relied heavily on H. J. Holtzmann (1832–92), *Die synoptischen Evangelien* (Leipzig, 1863). From this stemmed the idea of 'Q'. For the origin of 'Q' as the name of a source, see Stephen Neill, *The Interpretation of the New Testament, 1861–1961* (London, 1964), p. 119, n. 2; pp. 110–11 for Holtzmann.

[37] *Drysorfa* (1892), 161–5.

[38] *Dysgedydd* (1892), 5–10, 45–9, 100–5.

[39] *Dysgedydd* (1896), 252.

[40] *Traethodydd* (1894), 119.

[41] The analysis was published in J. Wellhausen, *Die Komposition des Hexateuchs* (1877).

⁴² See Griffith Ellis, 'Duwinyddiaeth yr H. D. yng ngoleuni beirniadaeth ddiweddar', *Traethodydd* (1895), 37–48. It is heavily dependent on S. R. Driver, *Introduction to the Literature of the Old Testament* (Edinburgh, 1891).

⁴³ *Mynegiad Cymanfa Bedyddwyr Arfon* . . . (1897–8). The president was Mr John Rees, Caernarfon.

⁴⁴ *Drysorfa* (1894), 309.

⁴⁵ *Drysorfa* (1893), 248–53.

⁴⁶ *Goleuad* (6 October 1897), 9. For Evans (1833–92) and his unusual career, see *DWB*. He died before he could begin his work in Bala. See also D. Densil Morgan, 'Wales, the Princeton Theology and a Nineteenth Century Battle for the Bible', *Journal of Welsh Religious History*, new series, II (2002), 51–81.

⁴⁷ *Dysgedydd* (1899), 279.

⁴⁸ *Geninen* (1898), 212.

⁴⁹ 'Athraw', *Geninen* (1897), 119.

⁵⁰ *Seren Gomer* (1899), pp. 49–52, 118–23.

⁵¹ *Goleuad* (20 May 1896), 12.

⁵² *Goleuad* (12 May 1897), 10.

⁵³ *Drysorfa* (1898), 97.

⁵⁴ *Dysgedydd* (1909), 323–5.

⁵⁵ *Report of the Union of Welsh Independents*, Lampeter (1910), p. 1242.

⁵⁶ *Diwygiwr* (1906), 33–6.

⁵⁷ T. Stephens (ed.), *Cymru, Heddyw ac Yforu* (Cardiff, 1908), p. 26.

⁵⁸ *Report of the Union of Welsh Independents*, Caernarfon (1902), pp. 299–306.

⁵⁹ *Geninen* (1898), 145–151.

⁶⁰ For Williams (1857–1919), see E. Ll. Williams, *Cofiant* (1921).

⁶¹ *Drysorfa* (1900), 470.

⁶² For J. Gwili Jenkins (1872–1936), see E. Cefni Jones, *Gwili: Cofiant a Phregethau* (Llandysul, 1937). For *Llin ar Lin*, ibid., pp. 148–51.

⁶³ First impression with the preface dated 22 September 1914.

⁶⁴ E. Tegla Davies, *Gyda'r Blynyddoedd* (Liverpool, 1952), pp. 143–4.

⁶⁵ As J. Cynddylan Jones realized, for example, in his address to the Calvinistic Methodist General Assembly (1902), 'Diwinyddiaeth y Cyfundeb', *Athrylith a Gras* (Caernarfon, 1925), p. 155.

⁶⁶ For example, D. Tecwyn Evans and E. Tegla Davies, *Llestri'r Trysor: Y Beibl yng ngoleuni beirniadaeth ddiweddar* (Bangor, 1914), pp. 11–12.

⁶⁷ Cf. W. E. Houghton, *The Victorian Frame of Mind, 1830–1870* (New Haven, 1957), p. 150, which holds that those who rejected the infallible Bible lay on dogmatism 'founded . . . on the possession of an infallible

power of insight: either reason or intuition'. The one, he says, came from the rationalism of the eighteenth century and the other from the Romanticism of the nineteenth century.

[68] See R. M. Grant, *A Short History of the Interpretation of the Bible* (2nd edn, London, 1963), p. 132. 'The nineteenth century critical movement was not simply a movement in the history of interpretation, but . . . had its own theological axes to grind. It stood for liberalism in theology.'

[69] Cf. Kenneth Hamilton, *Revolt against Heaven: An Enquiry into Anti-Supernaturalism* (Grand Rapids, MI, 1965), pp. 85–6.

[70] Cynddylan Jones, *Athrylith a Gras*, pp. 155, 156.

[71] Harrison, *Introduction to the Old Testament*, p. 26. A Welsh example can be found in the book *Australia Revisited in 1889, and Excursions in Egypt, Tasmania* (London, 1891). Its author was Josiah Hughes, the owner of an ironmongers on the High Street, Bangor. In the book, we see 'A sketch of the author's life' where he recognizes that the discussions on the sources of Genesis turned him into an atheist.

[72] *Eurgrawn Wesleaidd* (1891), 110–13.

[73] *Eurgrawn Wesleaidd* (1892), 322–6; cf. R. Lloyd Jones, 'Ysbrydoliaeth y Beibl', *Eurgrawn Wesleaidd* (1894), 90–6, 140–5, 176–85.

[74] *Traethodydd* (1894), 113–24.

[75] *Inspiration and Inerrancy* (London, 1891), p. 155.

[76] A. A. Hodge and B. B. Warfield, 'Inspiration', *Prebsyterian Review*, VI (April 1881), 238.

[77] *Geninen* (1897), 214–20, 'Golygiadau diweddar ar ysbrydoliaeth y Beibl'.

[78] 'Beth yw'r awdurdod uchaf mewn Cristnogaeth?', *Dysgedydd* (1909), 213–18, 295–300.

[79] For the interest in Ritschl (1822–89), see 'Ritschlaeth', *Seren Gomer* (1896), 97–105, 145–53, 193–202, 241–9; (1897), 1–5.

[80] *Traethodydd* (1927), 203; (1928), 23.

[81] J. Puleston Jones, *Until the Day Dawn: The New Testament Basis for a Doctrine of Inspiration* (London, 1913), pp. 310, 311, 314, 328–30.

[82] *Dysgedydd* (1906), 61.

[83] As the annual reports of the Council's Education Committee did not refer to religious education, the information was gained through asking questions in the House of Commons. Statistics were published in this way for 1875, 1876, 1879, 1883 (in the House of Lords) and 1886. See also Daniel Rowlands, 'Addysg grefyddol yn yr ysgolion dyddiol', *Traethodydd* (1886), 431–53.

[84] *Faner* (16 April 1902), 3; *Celt* (17 April 1896), 4; (24 April), 1; (4 May), 2; (24 July), 1; *Drysorfa* (1896), 472.

[85] For the developments between 1902 and 1906, see Kenneth O. Morgan, *Wales in British Politics* (Cardiff, 1991), pp. 184–98.

[86] For the opposition in England, see R. Tudur Jones, *Congregationalism*

in *England, 1662–1962* (London, 1962), pp. 336–42. Cf. David W. Bebbington, *The Nonconformist Conscience: Chapel and Politics 1870–1914* (London, 1982).

[87] *Faner* (21 January 1903), 6.

[88] *Faner* (4 March 1903), 5. Kenneth Morgan gives the wrong impression that they had gathered to meet the representatives of the diocese of St Asaph in the person of Lord Kenyon.

[89] A. G. Edwards, *Memories* (London, 1927), pp. 191–2.

[90] Eluned Owen, *The Later Life of Bishop Owen* (Llandysul, 1961), pp. 38–40.

[91] Ibid., pp. 41–2; Edwards, *Memories*, pp. 192–4; *Faner* (25 March 1903), 8.

[92] Eluned Owen, *Later Life of Bishop Owen*, pp. 43–4; *Faner* (22 April 1903), 3–4.

[93] *Faner* (27 May 1903), 7.

[94] *Faner* (19 June 1903).

[95] *Faner* (24 June 1903), 3, 5, 9; (1 July), 3–4. For David Eleazar Jones (1840–1913), see *Dysgedydd* (1913), 387, and *Congregational Year Book* (1914), 182–3.

[96] *Faner* (29 July 1903), 5 – a useful summary; *Faner* (5 August 1903), 9.

[97] *Faner* (9 March 1904), 5, 9.

[98] *Faner* (16 March 1904), 9.

[99] *Faner* (27 April 1904), 3.

[100] First reading, *Parliamentary Debates*, ser. VI, vol. CXXXIII, col. 1203 and forward, and the second reading, vol. CXXXIX, col. 1220 and forward.

[101] *Goleuad* (13 May 1904), 3.

[102] *Faner* (12 October 1904), 6–7.

[103] *Seren Cymru* (1 September 1905), 9; (23 September), 4.

[104] The annual statistics can be found in *Blwyddiadur y Methodistiaid Calfinaidd*.

[105] *Faner* (5 August 1903), 5.

[106] *Seren Cymru* gave particular attention to the opponents, see (16 October 1903), 3; (22 January 1904), 7; (29 January), 12; (12 February), 5 and so on.

[107] It can be reasoned that Brynmor Jones in the Cardiff Conference, 3 June 1903, had taken this from the pages of Calvin, that revolution can be justified if it is led by a constitutional authority, *Faner* (10 June 1903).

[108] *Llenor* (1951), 2–3.

[109] 'Diwylliant ysbrydol trwy addysg', *Beirniad*, VIII/4 (1920), 197–210; *Dysgedydd* (1925), 271.

[110] Brinley Rees (ed.), *Ieuan Gwynedd: Detholiad o'i Ryddiaith* (Cardiff, 1957), pp. 50–1.

[111] This standpoint is expressed, for example, by the Baptist Evan Kenffig Jones (1863–1950), in *Seren Cymru* (27 May 1904), 8–9.

[112] *Report of the Welsh Baptist Union*, Bangor (1900), p. 36; W. R. Watkin, *Cofiant y diweddar Barch. William Morris, D.D. (Rhosynnog), gweinidog Noddfa, Treorci, 1869–1922* (Aberdare, 1957), pp. 75–7.

[113] *Tyst* (27 July 1894), 7, 10.

12. Heavenly Fire

[1] *Geninen* (1905), 156.

[2] *British Weekly* (12 January 1905), 376; so also David Griffith, Bethel, in *Geninen* (1905), 73, and Evan Davies, Morriston, *Geninen* (1904), 81.

[3] *Dysgedydd* (1901), 495.

[4] *Drysorfa* (1901), 505–6.

[5] John Thomas, Merthyr, in *British Weekly* (15 December 1904), 276.

[6] *Dysgedydd* (1903), 16–19; *Seren Cymru* (13 January 1903), 9, and many other places.

[7] *Geninen* (1905), 114; *Tyst* (21 and 28 September 1904), 5, (12 October and 19 October).

[8] For Jenkins (1861–1929), see *DWB* and Robert Ellis, *Doniau a Daniwyd* (Llandybïe, 1957), pp. 41–5. For Thickens (1865–1952), see *Blwyddiadur y Methodistiaid Calfinaidd* (1954), 232–3.

[9] According to Jenkins himself in an address, November 1904, *South Wales Daily News* (hereafter *SWDN*) (16 November 1904), 6.

[10] Ibid.

[11] *Y Diwygiad a'r Diwygwyr: Hanes toriad gwawr diwygiad 1904–1905* (Dolgellau, 1906), p. 51.

[12] According to Jenkins, *SWDN* (16 November 1904), 6. In Sidney Evans and Gomer M. Roberts (eds), *Cyfrol Goffa Diwygiad 1904–1905* (Caernarfon, 1954), p. 35, he is said to have felt a flame taking hold of him and filling him with great strength. It is difficult to date these experiences in any detail.

[13] For W. W. Lewis (1856–1938), see *Blwyddiadur y Methodistiaid Calfinaidd* (1939), 210.

[14] For J. M. Saunders (1862–1919), see *Blwyddiadur y Methodistiaid Calfinaidd* (1921), 172.

[15] *SWDN* (16 November 1904), 6.

[16] For the beginning of the meetings, see Jenkins's letter to Evan Phillips in J. J. Morgan, *Cofiant Evan Phillips Castellnewydd Emlyn* (Liverpool, 1930), pp. 331–2. For the events of this period, see Eliseus Howells in

Evans and Roberts, *Cyfrol Goffa Diwygiad 1904–1905*, pp. 25–38, and Eifion Evans, *The Welsh Revival of 1904* (London, 1969), chs 2 and 4.

[17] So *Cyfrol Goffa Diwygiad 1904–1905*, p. 35, but the end of February on p. 53.

[18] *SWDN* (16 November 1904), 6.

[19] So D. M. Phillips, *Evan Roberts the Great Welsh Revivalist and his Work* (3rd edn, London, 1906), p. 113; and *Cyfrol Goffa Diwygiad 1904–1905*, p. 35. It was on Sunday evening according to J. Vyrnwy Morgan, *The Welsh Religious Revival 1904–1905: A Retrospect and a Criticism* (London, 1909), p. 118, but this is incorrect.

[20] *SWDN* (10 November 1904), 6. Jenkins does not say that it was the same girl that visited him but historians have taken this for granted.

[21] *Y Diwygiad a'r Diwygwyr*, p. 53; there is a portrait of Florrie and her friends, May Phillips and Maud Davies ibid., pp. 52, 54.

[22] *SWDN* (10 November 1904), 6.

[23] In his letter, *British Weekly* (22 December 1904), 308.

[24] *British Weekly* (15 December 1904).

[25] *Seren Cymru* (16 December 1904), 4.

[26] *Seren Cymru* (23 December 1904), 4; (17 March 1905), 5.

[27] O. Madoc Roberts, *Cofiant y Parch Hugh Jones, DD* (Bangor, 1934), pp. 128–30.

[28] Evans and Roberts (eds), *Cyfrol Goffa Diwygiad 1904–1905*, p. 36; for M. P. Morgan (d. 27 December 1964), see *Blwyddiadur y Methodistiaid Calfinaidd* (1966), 300–1.

[29] W. R. Watkin, *Cofiant y Diweddar Barch William Morris, DD, (Rhosynnog), gweinidog Noddfa, Treorci, 1869–1922* (Aberdare, 1957), pp. 151–2.

[30] *Goleuad* (9 December 1904), 10.

[31] *Seren Cymru* (15 July 1904), 4; *Y Diwygiad a'r Diwygwyr*, p. 346.

[32] *Seren Cymru* (19 August 1904), 6.

[33] Dyfnallt in *Tyst* (20 March 1930), 1.

[34] *British Weekly* (29 December 1904), 332; *SWDN* (15 November 1904), 6.

[35] Rosina Davies, *The Story of My Life* (Llandysul, 1942), p. 180.

[36] Ibid., pp. 178, 179, 185; *Y Diwygiad a'r Diwygwyr*, p. 346.

[37] T. Mardy Rees, *Seth Joshua and Frank Joshua: The Renowned Evangelists: the Story of their Wonderful Work* (Wrexham, 1926), p. 61.

[38] Note his diaries, ibid., pp. 62–70.

[39] *Faner* (27 July 1904), 12.

[40] *Faner* (3 August 1904), 7. For 'Gypsy' Rodney Smith (1860–1947), see Harold Murray, *Gypsy Smith: An Intimate Memoir* (Exeter, 1947). For William Booth (1829–1912), see Harold Begbie, *The Life of William Booth*, 2 vols (New York, 1920). For Reuben Archer Torrey

(1856–1928) and Charles McCallon Alexander (1867–1920), see *New International Dictionary of the Christian Church* (Exeter, 1974). For Frederick Brotherton Meyer (1847–1929), ibid., also *DNB, Baptist Handbook* (1930), 324, E. H. Jeffs, *Princes of the Modern Pulpit* (London, 1931), pp. 109–24. For Person Dowie, see *Faner* (4 May 1904), 15.

41 *Goleuad* (22 July 1904), 9.
42 W. Nantlais Williams, *O Gopa Bryn Nebo* (Llandysul, 1967), pp. 61–76.
43 *SWDN* (15 November 1904), 6.
44 Jenkins in *SWDN* (14 November 1904), 5.
45 *Faner* (9 November 1904), 14.
46 *Faner* (16 November 1904), 4, 7.
47 For Rhys Bevan Jones (1869–1933), see B. P. Jones, *The King's Champions* (Redhill, 1968).
48 *British Weekly* (24 November 1904), 165 – the first article in the *British Weekly* about the Revival.
49 *Y Diwygiad a'r Diwygwyr*, pp. 347–9.
50 *Seren Cymru* (16 December 1904), 3–4; (20 January 1905), 3.
51 *Faner* (2 November 1904), 7; *British Weekly* (27 October 1904), 61. Nantlais believed that the campaign was a substantial contribution to the Revival. See Nantlais Williams, *O Gopa Bryn Nebo*, p. 79.
52 *Faner* (23 November 1904), 4.
53 T. Mardy Rees, *Seth Joshua and Frank Joshua*, pp. 72–3; J. V. Morgan, *Welsh Religious Revival*, pp. 121–2.
54 Morgan, *Welsh Religious Revival*, p. 123.
55 According to D. M. Phillips, *Evan Roberts, the Great Welsh Revivalist*, p. 124, this was a meeting at nine o'clock in the morning. According to Evans and Roberts (eds), *Cyfrol Goffa Diwygiad 1904–1905*, p. 37, it was an afternoon meeting.
56 For this part of his career, see D. M. Phillips, *Evan Roberts a'i Waith* (Dolgellau, 1912), pp. 42–58, 117–27, and Eifion Evans, *Welsh Revival of 1904*, ch. 5.
57 Despite their interest as historical documents, the selection made by Dyfed for *Evan Roberts a'i Waith*, pp. 400–56, do not justify the excessive praise of D. M. Phillips, ibid., ch. 10.
58 Ibid., pp. 63–71.
59 Ibid., pp. 59–62, 92, 110.
60 Ibid., pp. 130–2.
61 Ibid., pp. 151–2.
62 Ibid., pp. 154–5.
63 Ibid., pp. 212–21.
64 Ibid., pp. 292–3, letter to Evans, 5 November 1904.
65 Ibid., p. 218.

66 Ibid., p. 158.
67 Ibid., pp. 160–1.
68 Ibid., pp. 162–3.
69 Ibid., pp. 173–4.
70 Ibid., p. 91.
71 Ibid., p. 92.
72 Ibid., p. 151.
73 Ibid., p. 201, letter 28 October 1904.
74 Ibid.
75 Ibid., p. 181, letter to J. H. Hughes, 10 October 1904.
76 Ibid., p. 201, letter to his sister, Mary.
77 Ibid., p. 181.
78 D. M. Phillips differentiates between 'Baptism in the Holy Spirit', which comes with being 'born again', and 'filled with the Holy Spirit' which occurs later. This is a form of the Pentecostal teaching about the 'Second Blessing'. He also differentiates between the 'general filling' with the Spirit and the 'particular filling' which occurs later. He applies the second process of the two definitions to Roberts's experience at Blaenannerch. But this is Phillips's gloss. It is not clear if Roberts himself accepted the explanation.
79 In Ebeneser, Trecynon, 14 November 1904, D. M. Phillips, *Evan Roberts the Great Welsh Revivalist*, p. 253.
80 Phillips, *Evan Roberts a'i Waith*, p. 176 – letter to his sister.
81 Ibid., p. 192.
82 Ibid., pp. 223–4. The story of the service is given in Roberts's letter to Florrie Evans, 31 October 1904.
83 Phillips, *Evan Roberts a'i Waith*, p. 205. For Sidney Evans (1883–1960), see *Blwyddiadur y Methodistiaid Calfinaidd* (1961), 303–4; *Goleuad* (16 November 1960), 4.
84 Phillips, *Evan Roberts a'i Waith*, p. 289. Evan Roberts himself gave the figure.
85 Ibid., p. 293.
86 Ibid., pp. 291–2, 265.
87 Ibid., p. 296.
88 Ibid., p. 297.
89 *Western Mail* (31 January 1905), 4.
90 Phillips, *Evan Roberts a'i Waith*, pp. 280–1.
91 Ibid., p. 317, in a letter of the following day, 12 November.
92 Sam Jenkins, d. 3 August 1953. He kept a guest house in London for many years.
93 Namely Priscilla Watkins, Mary Davies, Lininia Hooker, Annie M. Rees and Mary Davies, all from Gorseinon, Phillips, *Evan Roberts the Great Welsh Revivalist*, p. 249.

[94] *SWDN* (15 November 1904), 6; Phillips, *Evan Roberts the Great Welsh Revivalist*, pp. 255–6.

[95] *SWDN* (17 November 1904), 6.

[96] *SWDN* (18 November 1904), 6.

[97] David Hughes's words in *Dysgedydd* (1906), 521.

[98] Ibid., p. 522; *SWDN* (21 November 1904), 6.

[99] *SWDN* (18 November 1904), 220.

[100] *British Weekly* (8 December 1904), 220.

[101] So *SWDN* (18 November 1904), 6.

[102] Phillips, *Evan Roberts the Great Welsh Revivalist*, p. 283. 'Rhys Gethin' mentions them as 'hawk's eyes', *Seren Cymru* (23 December 1904), 9.

[103] Phillips, *Evan Roberts the Great Welsh Revivalist*, p. 278.

[104] Ibid., p. 318.

[105] *Faner* (21 December 1904), 7, 11.

[106] *Faner* (28 December 1904), 6.

[107] *Genedl Gymreig* (29 November 1904), 5.

[108] *Faner* (30 November 1904), 7; *Goleuad* (2 December 1904), 13; *Diwygiad a'r Diwygwyr*, p. 144.

[109] *Goleuad* (9 December 1904); *Diwygiad a'r Diwygwyr*, p. 145.

[110] The author was one of the local heroes, Hugh Derfel Hughes (1816–90), see *DWB*.

[111] *Goleuad* (6 January 1905), 12. For the conversion of William Hughes, see H. Elvet Lewis, *With Christ among the Miners* (London, 1906), pp. 122–6.

[112] *Seren Cymru* (6 January 1905), 4–5.

[113] *Tyst* (14 December 1904), 5; *Goleuad* (16 December 1904), 6.

[114] *Cloriannydd* (18 December 1904), 3; *Goleuad* (16 December 1904), 1.

[115] *Faner* (3 December 1904), 7; *Goleuad* (16 December 1904), 6.

[116] Rees, *Seth Joshua and Frank Joshua*, pp. 75–6.

[117] John Roberts, *Seren Cymru* (17 November 1905), 3.

[118] Letter to *SWDN* (2 December 1904), 5; also *SWDN* (25 November), 6. For Ellis Jones (1861–1954), the minister of Ebeneser, Bangor, 1891–1931, see R. Tudur Jones, *Undeb yr Annibynwyr Cymraeg, Llawlyfr Undeb Bangor* (Swansea, 1975), p. 15.

[119] *British Weekly* (5 January 1905), 352.

[120] For Bowen (d. 29 May 1923), minister of Penuel and Ebeneser (Baptist), Dyfed, 1897–1923, see *Mynegiad Coleg y Bedyddwyr, Bangor* (1950–51), 7.

[121] *Goleuad* (6 January 1905), 10–11.

[122] *Seren Cymru* (13 January 1905), 4.

[123] *Seren Cymru* (30 December 1904), 7.

[124] *Goleuad* (27 January 1905), 12.

[125] *Goleuad* (16 December 1904), 6.

[126] *Genedl Gymreig* (27 December 1904); (29 November 1904), 5.

[127] W. H. Pritchard, *Canmlwyddiant Eglwys Ebeneser (M.C.) Fourcrosses: Hanes yr Achos* (1962), pp. 40–1. For William Jones (1846–1925), see pp. 31–3. His wife was Ceridwen Peris (d. 17 April 1943), see pp. 33–5.

[128] *Seren Cymru* (30 December 1904), 4.

[129] *SWDN* (6 December 1904), 6.

[130] *Goleuad* (16 December 1904), 6.

[131] *Y Diwygiad a'r Diwygwyr*, p. 318.

[132] *Goleuad* (13 January 1905), 7.

[133] *Goleuad* (16 December 1904), 6.

[134] *Goleuad* (30 December 1904), 12.

[135] *Goleuad* (13 January 1905), 13.

[136] *Faner* (14 December 1904), 12.

[137] *Goleuad* (20 January 1905), 6.

[138] *Gwyliedydd* (12 January 1905), 6; *Goleuad* (13 January 1905), 10.

[139] *Goleuad* (23 December 1904), 10.

[140] *Goleuad* (6 January 1905), 6.

[141] 'Merionethshire Mysteries', *Occult Review* (March 1905), 113–20; 'Lights in the Heavens', *SWDN* (3 February 1905), 6; W. Morris Jones, 'Ymweliad â Mrs Jones, Egryn', *Cymro* (2 March 1905), 7; series by Garret Roberts, 'Y goleuadau rhyfedd ym Meirionydd', beginning in *Gwyliedydd* (16 February 1905), 5; Elvet Lewis, *With Christ among the Miners*, pp. 236–9.

[142] A. T. Fryer, 'Psychological Aspects of the Welsh Revival, 1904–5', *Proceedings of the Society for Psychical Research*, LI/19 (December 1905), 80–161.

[143] *British Weekly* (29 December 1904), 332; *Goleuad* (6 January 1905), 6.

[144] *Herald Cymraeg* (4 July 1905), 8.

[145] *Herald Cymraeg* (10 January 1905), 6.

[146] *Tyst* (7 December 1904), 12.

[147] For John Henry Williams (d. 25 February 1938, aged 68), see *Blwyddiadur y Methodistiaid Calfinaidd* (1939), 217–18.

[148] *Genedl Gymreig* (13 December 1904), 5. E. Morgan Humphreys was the author of these articles about the Revival in Anglesey. See his book, *Gwŷr Enwog Gynt: Argraffiadau ac Atgofion Personol*, II (Aberystwyth, 1953), p. 100.

[149] *Genedl Gymreig* (20 December 1904), 5.

[150] *Cloriannydd* (22 December 1904), 4.

[151] H. Ll. Williams, *Thomas Charles Williams* (Caernarfon, 1964), p. 60. For T. C. Williams (1868–1927), see also *DWB*. For George Williams (d. 7 January 1935), see *Mynegiad Coleg y Bedyddwyr, Bangor* (1950–1), 9.

[152] According to T. C. Williams, *Goleuad* (13 January 1905), 5.

[153] *Herald Cymraeg* (10 January 1905), 6.

[154] *Cloriannydd* (5 January 1905), 3; *Herald Cymraeg* (10 January 1905), 6.

[155] *Seren Cymru* (9 December 1904), 7; (16 December), 3; (13 January 1905), 3.

[156] *Seren Cymru* (23 December 1904), 4–5.

[157] *Tyst* (21 December 1904), 5.

[158] *Seren Cymru* (13 January 1905), 4.

[159] *Tyst* (7 December 1904), 12.

[160] *Faner* (21 December 1904), 7; *Goleuad* (20 December 1904), 12.

[161] *Tyst* (14 December 1904), 5.

[162] *Goleuad* (30 December 1904), 10.

[163] *Goleuad* (27 January 1905), 13.

[164] *SWDN* (1 November 1904), 6.

[165] *Faner* (7 December 1904), 6; *Tyst* (7 December 1904), 12. By 7 December there were fifty-seven converts in Ainon alone, *Seren Cymru* (16 December 1904), 4.

[166] *Faner* (28 December 1904), 6.

[167] *Seren Cymru* (6 January 1905), 3.

[168] *SWDN* (29 November 1904), 6.

[169] *Goleuad* (23 December 1904), 6.

[170] Ibid., p. 9. He had been in Bwlch-y-gwynt, Tregaron, since 23 November, *Faner* (7 December 1904), 7.

[171] *Faner* (7 December 1904), 6.

[172] *Genedl Gymreig* (6 December 1904), 5.

[173] *British Weekly* (15 December 1904), 276.

[174] *Goleuad* (16 December 1904), 7.

[175] Ibid.; *Tyst* (21 December 1904), 4; *Seren Cymru* (13 January 1905), 3.

[176] *SWDN* (2 December 1904), 6.

[177] *Seren Cymru* (16 December 1904), 7.

[178] *Tyst* (28 December 1904), 5.

[179] For Nantlais Williams (d. 18 June 1959), see *Blwyddiadur y Methodistiaid Calfinaidd* (1960), 275–6.

[180] Rees, *Seth Joshua and Frank Joshua*, pp. 77–8.

[181] Ibid., p. 78.

[182] *British Weekly* (24 November 1904) – and the Moelfre lifeboat showed great valour in a storm.

[183] *SWDN* (28 November 1904), 6.

[184] Anthony Davies, *Berw Bywyd*, ed. J. Ellis Williams (Llandysul, 1968), p. 17.

[185] *British Weekly* (5 January 1905), 352.

[186] Towyn Jones in *Western Mail* (11 February 1905), 7.

[187] See *The Welshman* (25 November, 2 and 9 December 1904).

[188] *Tyst* (7 December 1940), 12; (14 December), 6; B. P. Jones, *The King's Champions*, pp. 38–41; *Faner* (2 December 1904), 12. For Keri Evans (1860–1941), see *Bywg*. (1941–50); and *My Spiritual Pilgrimage from Philosophy to Faith* (London, 1961); for W. S. Jones (d. September 1933), see *Seren Gomer* (1935), 97–101.

[189] *Tyst* (14 December 1904), 4.

[190] Ibid.

[191] *Faner* (28 December 1904), 3, 5, 6.

[192] Anthony Davies, *Berw Bywyd*, p. 19 – from his diary for 1904.

[193] Sidney Evans later married Mary, Evan Roberts's sister.

[194] For conflicting reports, see *Tyst* (21 December 1904), 5.

[195] *Faner* (28 December 1904), 2.

[196] *Goleuad* (6 January 1905), 12; *British Weekly* (29 December 1904), 332.

[197] *Goleuad* (27 January 1905), 13.

[198] *British Weekly* (22 December 1904), 308.

[199] *SWDN* (29 November 1904), 6.

[200] Phillips, *Evan Roberts the Great Welsh Revivalist*, p. 331; T. Lloyd Evans, *Y Cathedral Anghydffurfiol Cymraeg* (Swansea, 1972), p. 35. There were 219 converts in Seion, Morriston, in five weeks, *Seren Cymru* (13 January 1905), 3.

[201] *Seren Cymru* (27 January 1905), 4.

[202] *SWDN* (21 November 1904), 6; (26 November), 6.

[203] *Faner* (30 November 1904), 9.

[204] *Goleuad* (9 December 1904), 11.

[205] H. Elvet Lewis in *British Weekly* (29 December 1904), 344.

[206] *SWDN* (6 February 1905), 5.

13. A Year of Rejoicing

[1] D. M. Phillips, *Evan Roberts the Great Welsh Revivalist and his Work* (3rd edn, London, 1906), p. 356.

[2] For Peter Price (1864–1940), see D. J. Roberts, *Cofiant Peter Price* (Swansea, 1970).

[3] They are listed as such by H. Elvet Lewis in *British Weekly* (7 December 1905), 275.

[4] *The Rev. Peter Price and Evan Roberts: Controversy on the Welsh Revival* (London, 1905), p. 32.

[5] 'Constant reader' said in *Western Mail* (3 February 1905), 5, that Roberts was repeating what he had said to him on the way to the meeting. R. M. Richards confirmed that he said the words, *Rev. Peter Price and Evan Roberts*, p. 5, although the *Western Mail*'s report was

silent on the subject – see n. 16 for details of these reports – Awstin, *The Religious Revival in Wales* (no. 3), pp. 23–4.

6   The *Western Mail* republished the letter with a selection of the correspondence that followed in *Rev. Peter Price and Evan Roberts*. A number of letters which were sent personally to Peter Price can be found in J. V. Morgan, *The Welsh Religious Revival 1904–1905* (London, 1909), pp. 141–62. The affair is discussed objectively by D. J. Roberts in *Peter Price*, pp. 90–109.

7   The *London Welshman* (11 February 1905), 8–9, went as far as to say that Price's idea was 'a complete absurdity'.

8   *Herald Cymraeg* (7 February 1905), 6.

9   See J. Vyrnwy Morgan, *Welsh Religious Revival*, pp. 155–62. For Morgan (1861–1925), see *Western Mail* (11 August 1925), and E. G. Millward, 'John Vyrnwy Morgan', *National Library of Wales Journal*, XII (1961–2), 198–200.

10 *SWDN* (6 February 1905), 5; *Rev. Peter Price and Evan Roberts*, pp. 30–1; D. J. Roberts, *Peter Price*, pp. 105–7.

11 *SWDN* (10 February 1905), 6.

12 *Rev. Peter Price and Evan Roberts*, p. 32.

13 *Western Mail* (8 February 1905), 5.

14 *SWDN* (4 February 1905), 5.

15 His letters to Mr and Mrs Rhys Jones can be found in *Herald Cymraeg* (14 March 1905), 8.

16 The daily reports of the *Western Mail* were published as pamphlets at the end of every month, edited by 'Awstin' (Tom Davies), under the title *The Religious Revival in Wales*. Evan Roberts's second and third campaigns can be found in pamphlet 2 (9 to 31 December), 3 (1 to 31 January) and 4 (2 to 28 February).

17 T. Lloyd Evans, *Y Cathedral Anghydffurfiol Cymraeg* (Swansea, 1972), pp. 35–6; D. M. Phillips, *Evan Roberts the Great Welsh Revivalist*, p. 331.

18 In Caerphilly, 5 December, ibid., p. 290.

19 J. V. Morgan, *Welsh Religious Revival*, p. 53.

20 Awstin, *Religious Revival in Wales* (3), p. 18. Phillips is silent on the subject, *Evan Roberts the Great Welsh Revivalist*, p. 347.

21 Awstin, *Religious Revival in Wales* (3), p. 28.

22 Ibid., pp. 28–9. The same thing occurred in Salem, Heolygerrig, three days previously. Ibid., p. 27.

23 This also occurred in Hebron, Dowlais, on 24 January, at the behest of the minister, Ceinfryn Thomas. See Awstin, *Religious Revival in Wales* (3), p. 24.

24 Ibid., pp. 24–5. Phillips does not mention the lost soul, *Evan Roberts the Great Welsh Revivalist*, pp. 262–3.

[25] *SWDN* (18 November 1904), 6.

[26] Morgan, *Welsh Religious Revival 1904–1905*, p. 62.

[27] H. Elvet Lewis, *With Christ among the Miners* (London, 1906), p. 148.

[28] D. M. Phillips, *Evan Roberts a'i Waith* (Dolgellau, 1912), p. 333.

[29] For David Lloyd (1870–1927), see *Seren Cymru* (11 February 1927) and the following issues. For R. R. Hughes (1871–1957), see *Blwyddiadur y Methodistiaid Calfinaidd* (1958), 249–50.

[30] *Herald Cymraeg* (17 January 1905), 6.

[31] *Seren Cymru* (10 February 1905), 3.

[32] B. P. Jones, *The King's Champions* (Redhill, 1968), p. 70.

[33] D. Tecwyn Evans's words, *Seren Cymru* (17 March 1905), 6.

[34] The minutes of the North Wales Baptist College, vol. XII, July 1904 to 3 July 1912. The first threat came as early as 23 November 1904.

[35] *Herald Cymraeg* (31 January 1905), 2.

[36] *Cloriannydd* (2 February 1905), 3.

[37] *Herald Cymraeg* (31 January 1905), 2.

[38] *Cloriannydd* (19 January 1905), 2.

[39] *Herald Cymraeg* (31 January 1905), 2.

[40] *Cymro* (12 January 1905), 8.

[41] *Cloriannydd* (12 January 1905), 3; *Goleuad* (27 January 1905), 10.

[42] *Cymro* (2 March 1905), 8.

[43] *Goleuad* (27 January 1905), 10.

[44] *Y Diwygiad a'r Diwygwyr: hanes toriad gwawr diwygiad 1904–1905* (Dolgellau, 1906), pp. 244, 316, 322.

[45] *Seren Cymru* (3 March 1905), 4.

[46] *Goleuad* (20 January 1905), 10.

[47] MS Bangor 9870A. For R. R. Morris (1852–1935), see *Blwyddiadur y Methodistiaid Calfinaidd* (1936), 202–3.

[48] *Seren Cymru* (17 March 1905), 6. R. R. Morris in J. W. Jones, 'Tro trwy'r hen adroddiadau blynyddol', *Goleuad* (18 April 1951), 7.

[49] *Goleuad* (27 January 1905), 10.

[50] *Cymro* (23 March 1905), 7.

[51] R. R. Hughes, *John Williams, Brynsiencyn* (Caernarfon, 1929), p. 157. Gwilym Hughes republished his reports in *SWDN* as a pamphlet, *Evan Roberts, Revivalist: Story of the Liverpool Mission* (Dolgellau, 1905).

[52] Gwestai Jones, the keeper of the telegraph office at Hilbre Island, said that it was Evan Roberts but 'the story was pure lies from start to finish' according to Lewis Jones, *Atgofion Ynyswr* (Liverpool, 1939), p. 61. It is recounted as a valid story by D. M. Phillips, *Evan Roberts the Great Revivalist*, pp. 385–6.

[53] *Cymro* (13 April 1905), 2–3, 5.

[54] *Llais Rhyddid*, III (1904), pp. 245, 263.

[55] Gwilym Hughes, *Story of the Liverpool Mission*, pp. 74–5; *Llais Rhyddid*, IV (1905), pp. 30–7, 49–56.

[56] *Cymro* (20 April 1905), 3.

[57] The whole letter can be found in Gwilym Hughes, *Story of the Liverpool Mission*, pp. 85–7. For H. M. Roberts (1870–1937), see *Blwyddiadur y Methodistiaid Calfinaidd* (1938), 209–10.

[58] The doctors were James Barr, MD, FRCP; William Williams, MD, MRCP; Thomas H. Bickerton, MRCS; William McAfee, MD.

[59] Hughes, *John Williams, Brynsiencyn*, pp. 157–8.

[60] *Goleuad* (18 November 1904), 7.

[61] *Seren Cymru* (10 February 1905), 11; cf. the similar commendation in *Diwygiwr* (1905), 11, 28.

[62] *British Weekly* (7 November 1905), 277. See also the critical conclusion drawn by David Powell, *Cymro* (20 April 1905), 5, and Pedrog's incisive questions, *Cymro* (27 April 1905), 3. In comparing D. M. Phillips's reports, *Evan Roberts the Great Welsh Revivalist*, pp. 379–89, and contemporary reports in the newspapers about the Liverpool meetings, his tendency to slip past any unfavourable events to concentrate on his hero was painfully clear.

[63] *British Weekly* (27 April 1905), 60.

[64] The story can be found in *Y Diwygiad a'r Diwygwyr*, pp. 331–45. The members were John Williams (Holyhead), John Evans (Holyhead), Llywelyn Lloyd (Bethel), and Hugh Williams (Amlwch).

[65] Ibid., p. 340; so also *Cymro* (23 February 1905), 3. The same impact can be found in John Williams when he was with the deputation from Liverpool, Hughes, *John Williams Brynsiencyn*, p. 157.

[66] Hugh Owen, *Hanes Methodistiaeth Calfinaidd Môn*, p. 50; *Cymro* (1 June 1905), 8.

[67] *British Weekly* (25 May 1905), 163; Hughes, *John Williams Brynsiencyn*, pp. 163, 188.

[68] Although one reporter spoke of the ministers as 'the coldest class' in the meetings, *Cloriannydd* (3 August 1905), 3, the evidence suggests that it was they who led the meetings.

[69] *Cymro* (29 June 1905), 5.

[70] H. Elvet Lewis, *With Christ among the Miners*, p. 152.

[71] *Cloriannydd* (15 June 1905), 3; *Herald Cymraeg* (13 June 1905), 8.

[72] Ibid.

[73] *Herald Cymraeg* (20 June 1905), 5; *Cymro* (22 June 1905), 5.

[74] *Cymro* (22 June 1905), 9.

[75] *Cloriannydd* (17 August 1905), 3.

[76] *Cymro* (22 June 1905), 5.

[77] *Herald Cymraeg* (20 June 1905), 8; *Cymro* (22 June 1905), 5.

[78] *Tyst* (28 June 1905), 9.

[79] *Cymro* (29 June 1905), 5. R. R. Hughes's reminiscences over more than half a century later can be found in *Goleuad* (13 March 1957), 6. But the harsh editorials on the first two of the four meetings in Holyhead should be noted, *Gwyliedydd* (29 March 1905), 3.

[80] The two addresses can be found in Phillips, *Evan Roberts a'i Waith*, pp. 342–7.

[81] 'June' is a mistake by Phillips, ibid., p. 348. For the address, see pp. 348–55. For the revivalist activity of the students, half a year previously, see J. T. Alun Jones, 'The Revival amongst Bala Students', *British Weekly* (29 December 1904), 332.

[82] As H. Elvet Lewis noted in *With Christ among the Miners*, pp. 160–1.

[83] D. M. Phillips, *Evan Roberts a'i Waith*, pp. 356–60; *Herald Cymraeg* (11 July 1905), 7.

[84] Phillips, *Evan Roberts a'i Waith*, pp. 362–3.

[85] *SWDN* (27 October 1905), 6. Phillips, *Evan Roberts a'i Waith*, p. 365, dates it incorrectly on 27 October.

[86] *SWDN* (15 November 1905), 4.

[87] Not 16 October as in Phillips, *Evan Roberts a'i Waith*, p. 366.

[88] *SWDN* (16 November 1905), 5.

[89] *SWDN* (17 November 1905), 6.

[90] *Genedl Gymraeg* (2 January 1906), 5.

[91] *Herald Cymraeg* (19 December 1905), 8.

[92] 'Atodlen', *Genedl Gymreig* (2 January 1906), 1.

[93] *Herald Cymraeg* (12 December 1905), 8.

[94] *Herald Cymraeg* (19 December 1905), 8; (26 December), 8.

[95] *Herald Cymraeg* (26 December 1905), 8.

[96] *Herald Cymraeg* (19 December 1905), 8.

[97] Ibid.; for the happy association between Evan Roberts and Lloyd George, and with his brother, see William George, *Atgof a Myfyr* (Wrexham, 1948), pp. 121–31.

[98] *Herald Cymraeg* (12 December 1905), 8.

[99] Both items in *Herald Cymraeg* (19 December 1905), 5. For the North Wales Quarrymen's Union, see R. Merfyn Jones, *The North Wales Quarrymen, 1874–1922* (Cardiff, 1981).

[100] *Cymro* (4 January 1906), 6.

[101] 'indescribable enthusiasm', *SWDN* (27 February 1906), 6.

[102] *SWDN* (28 February 1906), 5.

[103] *SWDN* (19 April 1906), 5.

[104] *Goleuad* (1 August 1906), 10.

[105] *SWDN* (10 August 1906), 6.

[106] A full report in *Goleuad* (29 August 1906), 10–11.

[107] Examples of such letters can be found in the appendix to J. V. Morgan, *Welsh Religious Revival 1905–1906*.

[108] These things are discussed by David Matthews in his book, *I Saw the Welsh Revival* (Chicago, 1951). Matthews also failed to see Roberts.

[109] It was published by H. M. Reade, Bible Booklet House, 118 Evington Road, Leicester. For something of its history, see M. N. Garrard, *Mrs Penn-Lewis: A Memoir* (London, 1931), pp. 234–5.

[110] From the Overcomer Office, Toller Road, Leicester.

[111] Evan Roberts, *Gwasanaeth a Milwriaeth Ysbrydol* (Leicester, 1912), p. 7.

[112] Ibid., p. 16.

[113] Jessie Penn-Lewis with Evan Roberts, *War on the Saints* (London, 1912), p. 283.

[114] Ibid., p. 287.

[115] See M. N. Garrard, *Mrs Penn-Lewis*, pp. 227–8. In the autumn of 1905, Brynmor Thomas heard the revivalist chastize a congregation in Carmarthen for its over-emotionalism and saying 'that the whole lot was nothing more than the devil churning trivial feelings and physical emotion', G. Brynmor Thomas, *Llwybrau Llafur* (2nd edn, Swansea, 1970), p. 55.

[116] After developing a cold in the Llandrindod Conference, the first time that she had been there since 1911, Garrard, *Mrs Penn-Lewis*, p. 238. The memorial service is described in *SWDN* (16 April 1906), 6.

[117] Sidney Evans, 'Marw a chladdu Evan Roberts', *Goleuad* (21 March 1951), 2. He spent his final years living at 61 Beulah Road, Rhiwbina, Cardiff.

[118] *SWDN* (15 March 1906), 5.

[119] *SWDN* (12 April 1906), 5.

[120] Brynmor Thomas, *Llwybrau Llafur*, p. 96. Sarah Jones died in November 1918 at the age of 48. I am grateful to her grandson, the Revd A. Walford Jones, Capel Newydd, Llandeilo, for giving me information about her. A picture of her with her husband can be found in *SWDN* (16 April 1906), 6.

[121] Brynmor Thomas, *Llwybrau Llafur*, p. 96; *SWDN* (13 April 1906), 6.

[122] *SWDN* (18 April 1906), 6 – 'Revival pandemonium'.

[123] In Hermon, Pont-y-gwaith, 25 April, *SWDN* (26 April 1906), 6. There are further reports about her in *SWDN* (12 April 1906), 5; (13 April), 6; (14 April), 6; (16 April), 6; (17 April), 6; (25 April), 6.

[124] The connection is denied in *SWDN* (14 April 1906), 6, but she had been in his meetings; see also *SWDN* (13 April), 6, which denies incorrect claims about her.

[125] *SWDN* (30 April 1906), 6; (1 May), 6.

[126] *SWDN* (25 April 1906), 6 – it said, 'she has evidently been in the hands of a district [*sic.* destructive?] power, but, thank God, she is coming through'.

[127] For example, W. D. Griffiths who was present in Maespica: he gave a critical description of the events there, *SWDN* (21 April 1906), 5.

[128] *SWDN* (5 May 1906), 5.

14. *Fool's Gold or the Real Thing?*

[1] The international spread of the revival is traced fully in J. Edwin Orr, *The Flaming Tongue* (Chicago, 1973), and there is a comprehensive bibliography on pp. 231–7.

[2] *Faner* (28 December 1904), 13.

[3] *Gwyliedydd* (26 January 1905), 6; (2 February), 2.

[4] *Seren Cymru* (30 June 1905), 3.

[5] *London Welshman* (14 January 1905), 3; (4 February), 2.

[6] *British Weekly* (22 December 1904), 309.

[7] H. Elvet Lewis, 'The Welsh Revival in London', *British Weekly* (2 February 1905), 448.

[8] *British Weekly* (5 January 1905), 359.

[9] Ibid., p. 353.

[10] *British Weekly* (26 January 1905), 424; (9 February), 472.

[11] *British Weekly* (19 January 1905), 407; *Seren Cymru* (17 February 1905), 13.

[12] *British Weekly* (19 January 1905), 407.

[13] *British Weekly* (2 February 1905), 455; (6 April), 667.

[14] *British Weekly* (26 January 1905), 424.

[15] Ibid.; and *British Weekly* (2 February), 448.

[16] *British Weekly* (16 February 1905), 496.

[17] *British Weekly* (2 March 1905); (27 April), 61.

[18] *British Weekly* (2 February 1905), 448.

[19] *British Weekly* (16 February 1905), 496. For McNeill (1854–1933), see *Who Was Who, 1929–1940*.

[20] *British Weekly* (2 February 1905), 448.

[21] Ibid., p. 449. For Smith's contribution to the revival in Pontypridd, see W. T. Stead, *The Coming Revival* (London, n.d.), pp. 23–9.

[22] *British Weekly* (16 February 1905), 496.

[23] *British Weekly* (23 February 1905), 520.

[24] Ibid.

[25] *British Weekly* (23 March 1905), 626.

[26] *British Weekly* (13 April 1905), 4.

[27] Ibid., p. 5.

[28] *British Weekly* (11 May 1905), 106.

[29] *British Weekly* (9 February 1905), 476; (16 February), 496; (23 February), 520.

30 *British Weekly* (16 Feburary 1905), 496; (9 March), 571. One of Evan Roberts's closest friends in Bristol was T. Ferrier Hulme, DD. There is a letter from him to Roberts, dated Christmas Day 1931, in NLW, CM Archives, 25, 701.
31 *British Weekly* (23 February 1905), 520.
32 *British Weekly* (6 April 1905), 668.
33 *British Weekly* (2 February 1905), 448; (9 February), 476.
34 *British Weekly* (16 March 1905), 599.
35 *British Weekly* (16 February 1905), 496.
36 *British Weekly* (2 March 1905), 544.
37 *The English Churchman* (16 March 1905).
38 *The Record* (16 June 1905).
39 *The Witness* (17 February 1905).
40 *The Record* (17 March 1905).
41 *The Record* (10 March 1905).
42 S. Paget and J. M. Crum, *Francis Paget* (London, 1912), pp. 221–3.
43 *The Witness* (3 March 1905).
44 *Methodist Times* (26 January, 2 March, 26 March, and 6 April 1905).
45 *Methodist Times* (26 January, 16 February and 18 May 1905); *Methodist Recorder* (19 and 26 January); *Christian Herald* (23 March).
46 *Methodist Magazine* (1905), 129.
47 *British Weekly* (3 February 1905), 448.
48 T. Mardy Rees, *Seth Joshua and Frank Joshua: The Renowned Evangelists: the Story of their Wonderful Work* (Wrexham, 1926), pp. 63–4.
49 *Herald Cymraeg* (28 March 1905); *British Weekly* (30 March 1905), 640.
50 *Missionary Herald* (1905), 114; *British Weekly* (30 March 1905), 640.
51 *Missionary Record* (1905), 213.
52 *Scottish Baptist Magazine* (1905), 87.
53 *Missionary Record* (1905), 213.
54 *Methodist Times* (20 April 1905); *Missionary Record* (1905), 112.
55 *Scottish Baptist Magazine* (1905), 66, 86.
56 W. Kemp, *Joseph W. Kemp: The Record of a Spirit-Filled Life* (London and Edinburgh, 1934), ch. 5.
57 For the revival in Scotland and Ireland, see Orr, *Flaming Tongue*, ch. 4.
58 R. J. Williams, *Y Parch John Roberts DD Khasia* (Caernarfon, 1923), pp. 243–4; Eifion Evans, *The Welsh Revival of 1904* (Bridgend, 1969), pp. 153–60.
59 S. M. Roberts, *The Revival in the Khasia Hills* (Newport, 1907).
60 Report by Mrs L. Rowlands, Ambohimandroso, *Dysgedydd* (1905), 523–5; and *Diwygiwr* (1905); *Cronicl Cenhadol* (Autumn 1905).
61 *Dysgedydd* (1906), 141.
62 Ibid., pp. 239–40.

63   Ibid., p. 241.
64   The modern Pentecostal movement began with the work of Charles F. Parham in Topeka, Kansas, in 1901. For an exhaustive study of the movement see Walter J. Hollenweger, *The Pentecostals* (London, 1972).
65   *Seren Cymru* (3 March 1905), 9; Orr, *Flaming Tongue*, p. 70. For the Parish Street church, see David Jones, *Memorial Volume of Welsh Congregationalists in Pennsylvania* (Utica, 1934), pp. 110–11. For Henry P. Roberts (b. Aber-erch, 1857; d. Wilkes-barre, 7 October 1905), ibid., pp. 317–18.
66   *Seren Cymru* (9 March 1905), 571.
67   *British Weekly* (9 March 1905), 571, said that she went out 'eighteen months ago'. She was a sister to Robert Williams (B), Llangollen.
68   *Y Drych* (8 February 1906), 2.
69   David Jones, *Memorial Volume*, p. 167.
70   See, for example, William J. Williams, 'Adgofion am flwyddyn y Diwygiad, 1905, yn Middle Granville a'r cylch', *Y Cyfaill* (Utica, March 1906), 124–7.
71   *British Weekly* (13 April 1905), 5.
72   This paragraph is a summary of Orr, *Flaming Tongue*, chs 10 and 11.
73   *Western Mail* (6 February 1905), 6 – 'Foreigners and the Revival'.
74   *Herald Cymraeg* (13 June 1905), 8.
75   *British Weekly* (26 January 1905), 424.
76   *British Weekly* (11 May 1905), 111.
77   *British Weekly* (6 April 1905), 665.
78   Robert Bruce Lockhart, *Memoirs of a British Agent* (Harmondsworth, 1950), p. 13.
79   See Orr, *Flaming Tongue*, ch. 7.
80   Ibid. for further details.
81   *British Weekly* (27 April 1905), 60.
82   *Seren Cymru* (13 August 1909), 10.
83   For some of the history, see *Seren Cymru* (31 December 1909), 5.
84   D. R. Davies, *In Search of Myself* (London, 1961), p. 37.
85   Hollenweger, *The Pentecostals*, p. 183.
86   It reached its climax with Tom Davies's series in the *Western Mail* in Spring 1974. This was basically an attack on Evan Roberts and shows only superficial knowledge of the revival.
87   E. Roberts, *Gwasanaeth a Milwriaeth Ysbrydol* (Leicester, 1912), p. 16. Together with Jessie Penn-Lewis he published a 'handbook' on the subject, *War on the Saints* (Leicester, 1912).
88   D. J. Williams, *Yn Chwech ar Hugain Oed* (Aberystwyth, 1959), pp. 158, 160.
89   'The Welsh Religious Revival of 1904–5: a Critique', in G. J. Cuming and Derek Baker (eds), *Popular Belief and Practice* (London, 1972), pp. 293–4.

[90] C. R. Williams, 'The Welsh Religious Revival, 1904–05', *British Journal of Sociology*, III (1952), 245–51.

[91] T. M. Bassett, *Bedyddwyr Cymru* (Swansea, 1977), pp. 361–2.

[92] See Kenneth Hamilton's perceptive discussion in his chapter, 'The Theology of Meaningfulness', in *Revolt Against Heaven* (Grand Rapids, MI, 1965), pp. 1–26.

[93] J. Rogues de Fursac, *Un movement mystique contemporain: Le réveil religieux du Pays de Galles 1904–5* (Paris, 1907), p. 68.

[94] Ibid., p. 70.

[95] Ibid., p. 180.

[96] Ibid., p. 176.

[97] Ibid., pp. 175–82.

[98] Henri Bois, *Quelques réflexions sur la psychologie des réveils* (Paris, 1906), pp. 10–11.

[99] Henri Bois, *Le Réveil au Pays de Galles* (Toulouse, 1905), p. 53.

[100] Bois, *Quelques réflexions*, p. 19.

[101] Ibid., pp. 17n., 19.

[102] Ibid., p. 42.

[103] Ibid., p. 23.

[104] It should be explained that French does not differentiate between 'awakening' and 'revival'. Bois used 'réveil' for 'awakening' and 'Réveil' (capital 'R') or more often 'réveil revivaliste' for 'revival'.

[105] Ibid., p. 19; cf. pp. 14–15, 22–3.

[106] Ibid., p. 72. See also his chapter on previous revivals in *Le Réveil au Pays de Galles*, pp. 28–49.

[107] Ibid., pp. 53, 73.

[108] See Vittorio Lanternari, *The Religions of the Oppressed: A Study of Modern Messianic Cults*, tr. L. Sergio (London, 1963); Paul Albrecht, *The Churches and Rapid Social Change* (London, 1961), E. A. Nida, *Customs, Culture and Christianity* (London, 1963).

[109] Lewis Probert, *Nerth y Goruchaf* (Wrexham, 1906), p. 25.

[110] H. H. Gerth and C. Wright Mills, *From Max Weber: Essays in Sociology* (New York, 1946), p. 280.

[111] *British Weekly* (16 March 1905), 595.

[112] Bois, *Quelques réflexions*, p. 58.

[113] *British Weekly* (2 February 1905), 445; cf. *Cymro* (22 December 1904), 5 and *Seren Gomer* (1905), 63.

[114] *British Weekly* (15 December 1904), 274.

[115] *Diwygiwr* (1905), 25–6. For a balanced evaluation, see H. Cernyw Williams, *Geninen* (1905), 69–71, cf. pp. 94–9.

[116] A full description by D. Davies, Ton-Pentre, can be found in *Geninen* (1905), 95–6.

[117] T. Stephens (ed.), *Cymru Heddyw ac Yforu* (Cardiff, 1908), pp. 56–8.

[118] W. R. James, India, *Seren Cymru* (9 December 1904), 4.

[119] John Davies, Pandy, *Goleuad* (16 December 1904), 8.

[120] 'Thesbiad', 'Y Diwygiad a'r Weinidogaeth', *Geninen* (1906), 127–32.

[121] *Cloriannydd* (3 August 1905), p. 3.

[122] *Seren Cymru* (23 December 1904), p. 11.

[123] In the north, *British Weekly* (26 January 1905), 424; in Conwy (9 March), 571; in Newport (2 March), 544; in Bangor (2 March), 544; in Barmouth (9 February), 476 and *Seren Cymru* (3 February 1905), 6.

[124] 'Ateb Philo-Evangelius', in Garfield H. Hughes (ed.), *Gweithiau William Williams Pantycelyn*, II (Cardiff, 1967), pp. 13–15.

[125] See C. G. Finney, *Darlithiau ar Adfywiadau Crefyddol*, tr. Evan Griffith (Swansea, 1839), pp. 32–41, 102, 119, 242. These were the 'new measures' that were criticized by B. B. Warfield, *Perfectionism* (New York, 1931), pp. 30–5. For the 1827 Revival, he says in relation to the 'new measures', 'They were . . . the natural and inevitable effect of the doctrine on which the revival was based . . . This was a Pelagian revival.' See also W. D. Evans (Carroll, Nebraska), 'Evan Roberts a Charles G. Finney: y tebygrwydd rhyngddynt a rhwng y ddau ddiwygiad', *Drych* (6 April 1905), 1.

[126] *Cymro* (22 June 1905), 5.

[127] *Report of the Union of Welsh Independents*, Tredegar (1905), p. 846.

[128] W. Nantlais Williams, *O Gopa Bryn Nebo* (Llandysul, 1967), p. 134.

[129] *Mundesley Bible Conference* (London, 1915), report, p. 113. This series of five lectures, 'Studies in Revival', by H. Elvet Lewis, is an excellent study.

[130] *Goleuad* (13 March 1957), 6.

[131] Bois, *Le Réveil au Pays de Galles*, pp. 415–16. His long chapter 'Evan Roberts', ibid., pp. 395–557, is particularly balanced and interesting.

[132] 'Il est difficile de donner à cela un autre nom que celui de délire', de Fursac, *Un movement mystique contemporain*, p. 98. Bois discusses the event in *Le Réveil au Pays de Galles*, pp. 435–6. The picture given by D. M. Phillips, *Evan Roberts, the Great Welsh Revivalist and his Work* (3rd edn, London, 1906), pp. 362–3, is completely misleading. See also J. Vyrnwy Morgan, *The Welsh Religious Revival 1904–1905: A Retrospect and a Criticism* (London, 1909), pp. 150–1.

[133] Bois, *Le Réveil au Pays de Galles*, p. 330.

[134] Ibid., p. 332.

[135] Ibid., p. 418.

[136] E. Morgan Humphreys, *Gwŷr Enwog Gynt*, II (Aberystwyth, 1953), pp. 100–9.

[137] William George, *Atgof a Myfyr* (Wrexham, 1948), pp. 121–31.

[138] *Cymro* (22 December 1904), 5; *Seren Cymru* (28 April 1905), 3.

[139] It is summarized by D. M. Phillips, *Evan Roberts the Great Welsh Revivalist*, pp. 455–62. The total was 80,936 by the end of February 1905.

[140] *Report of the Union of Welsh Independents*, Ffestiniog (1906), p. 104.

[141] Statistics can be found in *Blwyddiadur y Methodistiaid Calfinaidd* and the Baptists' *Dyddiadur*.

[142] *Seren Cymru* (27 January 1905), 4; (6 January), 4, 5; (13 January), 5; *British Weekly* (30 March 1905), 640. Slightly different figures for Abertillery can be found in W. R. Watkin, *Cofiant y Diweddar Barch. William Morris, DD, (Rhosynnog), gweinidog Noddfa, Treorci, 1869–1922* (Aberdare, 1957), p. 159. The fiery David Collier (d. 1931) was minister there.

[143] De Fursac mentions this, *Un movement mystique contemporain*, p. 62.

[144] *Drysorfa* (1896), 23.

[145] *Geninen* (1905), 7.

[146] Statistics can be found by E. K. Jones in *Seren Gomer* (1905), 113–19.

[147] *Goleuad* (10 July 1907), 9.

[148] De Fursac, *Un movement mystique contemporain*, p. 125.

[149] Ibid., pp. 126–8.

[150] *British Weekly* (26 January 1905), 242.

[151] *British Weekly* (16 February), 469; (2 March), 544.

[152] *British Weekly* (2 February 1905), 448; (9 February), 476.

[153] *British Weekly* (8 December 1904), 220.

[154] *British Weekly* (9 February 1905), 476; (23 February), 520; (9 March), 571.

[155] Statistics can be found in *Geninen* (1909), 207–8.

[156] C. R. Williams, 'The Welsh Religious Revival, 1904–05', p. 251.

[157] *Geninen* (1906), 193–4; mention is made of a boy and girl having sexual intercourse at the end of a service by 'Native-born Cymro' in *The Times* (4 February 1905), 9.

[158] *Geninen* (1909), 201–8.

[159] The statistics can be found in *Annual Report of the Registrar-General of Births, Deaths and Marriages in England and Wales* from year to year. On figures on extra-marital births, Alwyn D. Rees said that they are 'valueless for comparing the extra-marital sexual life of urban and rural communities', *Life in a Welsh Countryside* (Cardiff, 1950), pp. 47–8.

[160] *Geninen* (1905), 115; for Bethesda, see *British Weekly* (6 April 1905), 664.

[161] 'tremendous moral cleansing', *British Weekly* (8 January 1905), 352.

[162] *SWDN* (3 February 1905), 5; cf. Rhosynog in *Geninen* (1905), 115.

[163] *British Weekly* (26 January 1905), 424; (12 January), 376; *Diwygiwr* (1905), 27.

[164] *Tyst* (30 November 1904), 4–5.

[165] *SWDN* (28 December 1905), 6.

[166] *British Weekly* (26 January 1905), 424; (23 February), 520.

[167] *Geninen* (1905), 274.

[168] Dafydd Evans, *Tyred Drosodd: Gohebiaeth Eluned Morgan a Nantlais* (Bridgend, 1977); R. Bryn Williams, *Eluned Morgan* (Aberystwyth, 1948), p. 34.

[169] *SWDN* (18 November 1904), 6.

[170] *British Weekly* (12 January 1905), 376; cf. (29 December 1904), 332; (2 February), 448; *Seren Cymru* (6 January 1905), 4.

[171] *British Weekly* (9 February 1905), 476; (2 March), 544.

[172] *British Weekly* (16 February 1905), 496.

[173] Ibid.

[174] *British Weekly* (2 February 1905), 448; (26 January), 424.

[175] *British Weekly* (19 January 1905), 403. J. H. Howard described Richards as 'a deeply religious man, a deacon in his church at Beaufort, and later at Cardiff, a lifelong total abstainer', *Winding Lanes: A Book of Impression and Recollections* (Caernarfon, 1938), p. 54.

[176] Ibid., p. 98.

[177] As in Merthyr, according to *Seren Cymru* (23 December 1904), 9.

[178] See B. P. Jones, *The King's Champions* (Redhill, 1968), chs 7 and 8.

[179] For the Apostolic Church, see *Souvenir Exhibiting the Movements of God in the Apostolic Church: Issued in Commemoration of the opening of the Apostolic Temple, Penygroes* (6 August 1933); T. N. Turnbull, *What God hath Wrought: A Short History of the Apostolic Church* (Bradford, 1959).

[180] See Noel Brooks, *Fight for the Faith and Freedom* (London, 1946), which gives the history of George Jeffreys, who was raised in Siloh, Maesteg, and Stephen, his brother; B. R. Wilson, *Sects and Society* (London, 1961). The Elim movement was founded by Jeffreys in Monaghan, Ireland, in January 1915.

[181] *Deonglwr*, III (1905), 171–3.

[182] *Eurgrawn Wesleaidd* (1922), 376.

[183] *Greal* (1907), 205.

[184] *Geninen* (1906), 193–4.

[185] *Gwyliedydd* (3 January 1907), 1.

[186] See, for example, the harsh words by John Williams, Waun-wen, Swansea, in *Dysgedydd* (1906), 507.

15. *Grappling with the World*

1 Bangor MS 5054, 37, letter to D. D. Williams.
2 Bangor MS 5054, 48, letter to D. D. Williams, 6 June 1922.
3 *Report of the Union of Welsh Independents*, Rhos (1908), pp. 695–6.
4 *Report of the Royal Commission on Disestablishment*, IV, 127, questions 37784–90.
5 For the variety of meanings which are implicit in the word 'bourgeois', see Raymond Williams, *Keywords: A Vocabulary of Culture and Society* (rev. edn, London, 1983), pp. 37–40. For the word 'class', ibid., pp. 51–9. There is such difficulty now with their exact meaning, and the readiness to use them as swear words, that they are dubious weapons in historical analysis.
6 *Report of the Union of Welsh Independents*, Carmarthen (1872), p. 39.
7 *Dysgedydd* (1881), 81.
8 *Celt* (15 February 1884), 8.
9 *Report of the Union of Welsh Independents*, Ferndale (1892), p. 208.
10 R. R. Hughes, *Y Parchedig John Williams, DD, Brynsiencyn* (Caernarfon, 1929), pp. 188–9, 190–1.
11 *Royal Commission on Labour* (London, 1893), *The Agricultural Labourer*, II, p. 6.
12 For the way in which the Clynnog area was enriched by the social and cultural activity of the churches between 1861 and 1907, see the evidence of Howell Roberts, *Report of the Royal Commission on Distestablishment*, III, 121–2, questions 22131, 22175–89.
13 W. Williams (Crwys), *Pedair Pennod* (Aberystwyth, 1950), p. 30. For a quite unpleasant expression of the ethic of 'getting along in the world', see Henry Richard, 'Llwyddiant mewn bywyd', *Dysgedydd* (1882), 113–17.
14 R. P. Williams, 'Adfywiad masnachol: ei fanteision a'i beryglon', *Report of the Union of Welsh Independents*, Beaufort (1890), pp. 92–9. Cf. *Report* (Dowlais, 1903), pp. 504–8. 'All levels of bourgeois society exercised their acquisitive powers at leisure moments in amassing great stores of bric-a-brac, wax flowers, ormolu candelabras, porcelain vases', J. H. Buckley, *The Victorian Temper: A Study in Literary Culture* (London, 1966), p. 131.
15 For 'grade A lifestyle' (*Buchedd A*), see Elwyn Davies and Alwyn D. Rees (eds), *Welsh Rural Communities* (Cardiff, 1960), pp. 13–14, 42. For a criticism of the idea, see Isabel Emmett, *A North Wales Village* (London, 1964), pp. 112–14.
16 See Alun Tudur, 'O'r Sect i'r Enwad: Datblygiad Enwadau Ymneilltuol Cymru, 1840–1870', unpublished Ph.D. thesis, University of Wales, 1992.

[17] John Keble (ed.), *The Works of that Learned and Judicious Divine, Mr. Richard Hooker, Laws of Ecclesiastical Polity*, VIII/1 (Oxford, 1874), p. 4.

[18] Edwards died in 1884 and a collection of his work was published with a biography in 1889 under the title *Wales and the Welsh Church* (London, 1889).

[19] Ibid., pp. 151, 183, 282–3.

[20] For the Tithe Wars, see T. Gwynn Jones, *Cofiant Thomas Gee* (Denbigh, 1913), pp. 449–93; K. O. Morgan, *Wales in British Politics, 1868–1922* (Cardiff, 1991), pp. 84–90; A. G. Edwards, *Memories* (London, 1927), pp. 123–43. The main argument in the dispute about the tithe can be found in the debate between Gee and John Owen on the pages of *Faner* from August 1890 onwards.

[21] E. Jones, *Y Gymdeithasfa* (Caernarfon, 1891), p. 362. A tentative decision was reached in 1873 and a stronger one by the North Wales Association in 1883, ibid., p. 445.

[22] Edwards (1854–1926) became Wales's first archbishop in 1920 and he retired in 1934. John Owen (1854–1926) was bishop of St Davids from 1897 until his death.

[23] *Young Wales*, III (1897), 260.

[24] *Young Wales*, IV (1898), 7.

[25] G. Hartwell Jones, *A Celt Looks at the World* (Cardiff, 1946), p. 69.

[26] See Roger L. Brown, *David Howell: A Pool of Spirituality: A Life of David Howell (Llawdden)* (Denbigh, 1995), pp. 157–86.

[27] *Faner* (12 March 1890), 3; (19 March), 3–4, for the sermon.

[28] Edwards himself admitted this in a letter to Llawdden, 13 February 1893, which was published in *News of the Week* (15 July 1893), 7.

[29] Letter to the bishop, 13 February 1893, ibid. For the squabble, see also George Lerry, *Alfred George Edwards* (Oswestry, n.d.), pp. 37–42.

[30] Eluned Owen, *Early Life of Bishop Owen* (Llandysul, 1958), pp. 113–65.

[31] S. Rendel, *Mr Stuart Rendel MP and Disestablishment in Wales* (Oswestry, 1892), pp. 5–6.

[32] *SWDN* (22 March 1895), 5–6.

[33] G. Osborne Morgan, *The Church of England and the People of Wales* (2nd edn, London, 1895), p. 7.

[34] J. H. Slater, *The Established Church in Wales* (The Anti-Liberation Society, n.d.), pp. 81–8.

[35] P. M. H. Bell, *Disestablishment in Ireland and Wales* (London, 1969), p. 231; Morgan, *Wales in British Politics*, pp. 136–7.

[36] For John Owen's response, see E. Owen, *Early Life*, p. 148.

[37] Bangor MS 1668; the rector was Joseph W. Griffith. See further about the diarist Gwynfryn Richards, 'Dyddlyfrau cynnar David Griffith, Y Bontnewydd', *Ar Lawer Trywydd* (Swansea, 1973), pp. 11–22.

[38] G. K. A. Bell, *Randall Davidson*, I (London, 1935), p. 225; E. Owen, *Early Life*, p. 148.

[39] E. Owen, *Early Life*, pp. 149–53.

[40] *SWDN* (15 August 1893).

[41] *Faner* (6 September 1893).

[42] *Faner* (18 April 1893), 4.

[43] *Faner* (23 May 1894), 4.

[44] *Faner* (2 May 1894), 3–4, 5, 6–7; (9 May), 3, 6–7; Morgan, *Wales in British Politics*, pp. 145–6, for the content of the measure.

[45] *Faner* (27 December 1895), 5; (6 March), 3.

[46] Parliamentary Debates (4th series), XXX, 1487 a.y.

[47] Ibid., XXXIII, 1615 a.y.

[48] Ibid., 1637.

[49] See David W. Bebbington, *The Nonconformist Conscience* (London, 1982).

[50] *Seren Cymru* (22 September 1905), 9.

[51] Bell, *Randall Davidson*, I, p. 504.

[52] For Vaughan Williams (1838–1916), see *DWB*, Williams, John (1757–1810), and *DNB*.

[53] *Report of the Union of Welsh Independents*, Neath (1907), pp. 346–57.

[54] *Blwyddiadur y Methodistiaid Calfinaidd* (1908), 44.

[55] The story can be found in *Faner* (16 October 1907).

[56] *Greal* (1907), 318; (1908), 276; the vice-president, J. R. Jones, Pontypridd, died before reaching the chair and so this was a rushed election.

[57] The addresses can be found in James Evans (ed.), *Dylanwad Ymneilltuaeth ar Fywyd y Genedl* (Llanelli, 1913).

[58] W. Anthony Davies, *Berw Bywyd* (Llandysul, 1968), p. 53.

[59] H. Richard, 'Perthynas Cymru a Lloegr', *Geninen* (1888), 253–8.

[60] *Cronicl* (1888), 290.

[61] *Report of the Union of Welsh Independents*, Aberystwyth (1885), pp. 22–3.

[62] John Edwards, 'Edwards Castellnedd' (Llandysul, 1935), p. 52.

[63] 'Anghenion Cymru', *Geninen* (1889), 210.

[64] *Transactions of the Liverpool National Eisteddfod* (1884), 52.

[65] T. Stephens (ed.), *Cymru Heddyw ac Yforu* (Cardiff, 1908), p. 54.

[66] *Cymru*, XIV (1898), 35.

[67] Stephens (ed.), *Cymru Heddyw ac Yforu*, p. 103.

[68] David Richards, St Davids, *Geninen* (1890), 253, 256.

[69] *Geninen* (1903), 209.

[70] As Edward Roberts, Pontypridd, does in 'Y Cymry a'r genedl', *Geninen* (1889), 201–6.

[71] *Celt* (25 July 1890), 7.

[72] *Celt* (11 May 1890), 7.

[73] *Celt* (5 December 1890), 7.

[74] *Celt* (30 May 1890), 1.

[75] *Celt* (27 March 1885), 8.

[76] Ibid.

[77] *Celt* (9 September 1892), 1.

[78] *Celt* (8 October 1888), 6.

[79] *Celt* (11 November 1887), 2.

[80] *Geninen* (1893), 241; cf. *Geninen* (1894), 92–4.

[81] T. Gwynn Jones, *Emrys ap Iwan* (Caernarfon, 1912), p. 192.

[82] D. Myrddin Lloyd, 'Rhagymadrodd', *Detholiad o Erthyglau a Llythyrau Emrys ap Iwan*, I (Clwb Llyfrau Cymraeg, 1937), p. xv.

[83] Robert Ambrose Jones (Emrys ap Iwan), *Homiliau* (Denbigh, 1907), pp. 41–56. The translation used here was by R. Tudur Jones and can be found in his book *The Desire of Nations* (Llandybïe, 1974), pp. 181–2.

[84] 'Wele, dy dduwiau, O Walia!', D. Myrddin Lloyd, *Detholiad o Erthyglau*, p. 43.

[85] *Homiliau*, p. 50.

[86] 'Cymru i'r Cymry', *Geninen* (1886), 156, 158.

[87] Ibid., pp. 155–62.

[88] D. Myrddin Lloyd, *Detholiad o Erthyglau*, pp. 32, 40.

[89] For the Young Wales Movement, see Gwynfor Evans, *Aros Mae* (Swansea, 1971), pp. 284–91; Morgan, *Wales in British Politics*, pp. 104–6, 160–5; William George, *Cymru Fydd: Hanes y Mudiad Cenedlaethol Cyntaf* (Liverpool, 1945).

[90] *D. A. Thomas, Viscount Rhondda, by his Daughter and Others* (London, 1921), p. 31.

[91] J. E. Southall, *Bi-lingual Teaching in Welsh Elementary Schools* (Newport, 1888), p. 43.

[92] For example, R. E. Peregrine, *Report of the Union of Welsh Independents*, Carmarthen (1872), p. 16.

[93] *Greal* (1900), 176.

[94] *Report of the Union of Welsh Independents*, Carmarthen (1872), p. 16.

[95] T. Roberts and D. Roberts, *Cofiant y Parch. W. Rees, DD (Gwilym Hiraethog)* (Dolgellau, 1893), pp. 385–90.

[96] For a list of the names of ministers who were killing the language like this, see *Celt* (13 January 1893), 2.

[97] For a protest against public Welsh and private English, see 'Y Saesneg', *Goleuad* (23 May 1890), 9.

[98] The title of a pamphlet by him. For Davies (1839–87) and an excellent outline of the movement, see J. V. Morgan (ed.), *Welsh Political and Educational Leaders in the Victorian Era* (London, 1908), pp. 437–93.

[99] *Geninen* (1889), 36; cf., O. M. Edwards, *Cymru*, III (1892), 160.

[100] Southall, *Bi-lingual Teaching*, p. 6.
[101] The story is told in J. V. Morgan, *Welsh Leaders*, pp. 437–93.
[102] The evidence is analysed carefully by B. G. Evans in *Tyst* (11 April 1890), 5.
[103] *Celt* (7 April 1893), 3; *Cymru*, V (1893), 133; *Tyst* (31 March 1893), 3.
[104] *Cymru*, V (1893), 100.
[105] *Geninen* (1893), 206.
[106] *Young Wales*, III (1897), 213–15.
[107] *Report of the Union of Welsh Independents*, Ffestiniog (1906), p. 232.
[108] *Geninen* (1907), 219–20.
[109] Minutes of the County Council (1903), 974–96.
[110] For example, *Report of the Union of Welsh Independents*, Liverpool (1897), p. 196; (London, 1898), p. 318.
[111] *Report of the Union of Welsh Independents*, Bangor (1904), p. 666.
[112] As in *Gwyliedydd* (28 November 1899), 5.
[113] *Drysorfa* (1901), 32.
[114] *Haul* (1899), 328–30.
[115] *Haul* (1894), 16.
[116] According to H. M. Hughes, *Report of the Union of Welsh Independents*, Ffestiniog (1906), pp. 231–2.
[117] J. Lloyd Williams, *Atgofion Tri Chwarter Canrif*, IV (Aberystwyth, 1945), p. 75.
[118] *Drysorfa* (1901), 32.
[119] *Young Wales*, II (1896), 139 – translation.
[120] Ibid., p. 146; Beriah Gwynfe Evans, 'Tom Ellis a'r deffroad Cymreig', *Geninen* (1899), 145–7.
[121] *Report of the Union of Welsh Independents*, Ffestiniog (1906), p. 233.
[122] *Geninen* (1909), 41, 119–28; cf. *Geninen* (1895), 16–22.
[123] *Faner* (11 July 1894), 5; also (7 February 1894), 3; (21 February), 3; (28 February), 3; (7 March), 3; (14 March), 3.
[124] *Celt* (22 May 1885), 3.
[125] *Celt* (23 August 1878), 8.
[126] For the story and background see T. Gwynn Jones, *Emrys ap Iwan*, chs 5, 6, 7; Frank Price Jones, 'Yr Achosion Saesneg', *Journal of the Historical Society of the Calvinistic Methodists*, XLVII/2 (October 1972), 66–80; XLVIII/1 (March 1973), 2–11.
[127] *Seren Cymru* (16 May 1902), 3.
[128] *Welsh Outlook*, I (1914), 247.
[129] *Cwestiwn yr Iaith Gymraeg: Sef ymchwil yn egluro dwys gyfyngder y cyfnod parthed anwybodaeth y plant a'n hieuenctyd o'r iaith Gymraeg, yn bennaf yn eu perthynas a'r gwasanaeth crefyddol* (Aberdare, 1915).
[130] O. Eilian Owen, *Gomerydd y Plant* (Liverpool, 1911), a successor to *Llawlyfr Cymraeg* (1887).

[131] In one of the products of St Teilo Catholic Society, *Llyfr Gweddi: Yn cynnwys yr offeren yn Lladin a Chymraeg: Ynghyd a defosiynau ereill yr Eglwys Gatholig yng Nghymru* (1899), the main editor, Father J. H. Jones, Caernarfon, said in his preface that one Catholic book was published in Welsh in the nineteenth century. This is too low. In 1903 J. H. Jones also published *Epistolau ac Efengylau yr holl Suliau a'r gwyliau pennaf o'r Flwyddyn Gatholig.*

[132] *Haul* (1886), 287.

[133] *Haul* (1894), 220.

[134] *Geninen* (1893), 15–18, but the same complaint can be found in *Haul* (1909), 265–7.

[135] *Haul* (1894), 135.

[136] *Young Wales*, IV (1898), 7.

[137] *Haul* (1901), 248.

[138] See further Eilir Evans, 'Yr Eglwys a'r Iaith Gymraeg', *Geninen* (1910), 281–2; David Jones, *The Welsh Church and Welsh Nationality* (London, 1893); *Llan* (8 May 1903), 3; *Young Wales*, III (1897), 260, where the favourable attitude of Dean Vaughan, Llandaff, is mentioned.

[139] R. J. Williams, *Y Parch John Roberts, DD, Khasia* (Caernarfon, 1923), pp. 10–11.

[140] T. Hudson Wiliams, *Atgofion am Gaernarfon* (Llandysul, 1950), pp. 46–7.

[141] *Drysorfa* (1899), 82; a similar point is made about Anglesey, *Drysorfa* (1899), 276.

[142] See *Royal Commission on Labour* (London, 1893), *The Agricultural Labourer*, II, p. 107.

[143] Ibid., pp. 40, 151–2.

[144] *Drysorfa* (1898), 23.

[145] W. Anthony Davies, *Berw Bywyd* (Llandysul, 1968), pp. 43–4; on the subject in general, see Keith Nield, *Prostitution in the Victorian Age* (Farnborough, 1973) and Kellow Chesney, *The Victorian Underworld* (Newton Abbot, 1970).

[146] *Blwyddiadur y Methodistiaid Calfinaidd* (1912), 77.

[147] For the background, see W. R. Lambert, 'Drink and Sobriety in Wales, 1835–95', unpublished Ph.D. thesis, University of Wales, 1970.

[148] *Report of the Union of Welsh Independents*, Tredegar (1905), p. 791; see also Hudson Williams's description of the Band of Hope in Engedi, Caernarfon, *Atgofion am Gaernarfon*, pp. 28–9.

[149] *Report of the Union of Welsh Independents*, Tredegar (1905), p. 794.

[150] *Tyst* (16 March 1894), 10. For the speed of the growth, *Tyst* (25 October 1895), 3; Lleufer Thomas, *Young Wales*, IV (1898), 199–200; *Royal Commission on Labour* (1893), *The Agricultural Labourer*, II,

p. 28; David Griffith, *Geninen* (1902), 6–7.

[151] *Temlyddiaeth Dda yng Nghymru* (1923). Annual reports can be found in the newspapers. For the English Higher Temple, see *Tyst* (5 October 1894), 11.

[152] *Geninen* (1910), 250–1. For Plenydd (Henry Jones Williams, 1844–1926), see J. Lloyd Jones a Phedrog, *Plenydd (H. J. Williams): Yr areithydd dirwestol enwog: hanes ei fywyd a detholiad o'i weithiau* (Caernarfon, 1929).

[153] *Y Gymraes* (1896), 24–7.

[154] *Y Gymraes* (1901), 114.

[155] *Report of the Royal Commission on Disestablishment*, VII, 107; W. R. Watkin, *Cofiant y diweddar Barch. William Morris, DD (Rhosynnog), gweinidog Noddfa, Treorci, 1869–1922* (Aberdare, 1957), pp. 111–12.

[156] *Seren Cymru* (8 August 1902), 10.

[157] *Drysorfa* (1896), 328; (1901), 502–6; *Report of the Royal Commission on Disestablishment*, VII, Appendix 28, 123–5.

[158] *Report of the Union of Welsh Independents*, Llanelli (1899), pp. 514–15.

[159] John Owen, 'Yr Eglwys a dirwest', *Haul* (1896), 50–2; S. Jones, 'Yr Eglwys a'r Mudiad Dirwestol', *Haul* (1896), 366–8.

[160] *Drysorfa* (1897), 506–11; *Report of the Union of Welsh Independents*, Tredegar (1905), p. 798; Ffestiniog (1906), pp. 34, 70.

[161] Resolution of the Association in the North, *Drysorfa* (1900), 276–7.

[162] Resolution in support by Pembrokeshire Baptists, *Seren Gomer* (1901), 110; for Tabernacl, Cardiff, rejecting it, see *Seren Cymru* (20 December 1901), 9.

[163] *Report of the Union of Welsh Independents*, Caernarfon (1902), p. 281; (Bangor, 1904), p. 661.

[164] *Report of the Union of Welsh Independents*, Swansea (1913), pp. 548–9.

[165] They can be found, with an introduction and notes, in Etienne Gilson (ed.), *The Church Speaks to the Modern World: The Social Teachings of Leo XII* (Garden City, NY, 1954).

[166] For example, William Roberts, Llanrwst, *Drysorfa* (1892), 414.

[167] D. J. Lewis, Tymbl, *Report of the Union of Welsh Independents*, Swansea (1913), p. 549.

[168] Hughes, *John Williams, Brynsiencyn*, p. 225.

[169] *Blwyddiadur y Methodistiaid Calfinaidd* from year to year.

[170] *Report of the Royal Commission on Disestablishment*, II, 437, questions 14565–6.

[171] Ibid., II, 426, question 14116, and 430, question 14311.

[172] *Welsh Outlook*, I (1914), 43; Gwilym Davies, *Welsh School of Social*

Service, 1911–1925 (1926). See also, Robert Pope, *Building Jerusalem: Nonconformity, Labour and the Social Question in Wales 1906–1939* (Cardiff, 1998), pp. 133–8, 189–95.

173 The papers from the Summer School of 1913 can be found in Gwilym Davies (ed.), *Social Problems in Wales* (Swansea, 1913), and the other programmes can be found in Davies, *Welsh School of Social Service*.

174 B. B. Thomas, *Cenadwri Copec* (Wrexham, 1924).

175 R. Rouse and S. C. Neill, *A History of the Ecumenical Movement, 1517–1948* (London, 1954), pp. 540–56.

176 For J.R.'s arguments see *Cronicl* (1875), 102, 128–32, 188–91; the same standpoint can be found in *Yr Adolygydd* (1852), 247–50.

177 *Traethodydd* (1908), 408–17. Owen Prys, on the basis of the doctrine of 'General Grace', defined the relationship between the world and the church in a more penetrating way, when addressing the Calvinistic Methodist General Assembly in 1911, *Blwyddiadur y Methodistiaid Calfinaidd* (1912), 122.

178 General Assembly 1913, *Blwyddiadur y Methodistiaid Calfinaidd* (1914), 119–20.

179 *Tyst* (10 October 1890), 4.

180 E. W. Evans, *Mabon (William Abrahams, 1842–1922): A Study in Trade Union Leadership* (Cardiff, 1959), p. 143.

181 'Ap y Freni Fach', *Celt* (18 August 1893), 5.

182 See R. Merfyn Jones, *The North Wales Quarrymen, 1874–1922* (Cardiff, 1981).

183 For the story, see Ernest Roberts, *Bargen Bywyd fy Nhaid* (Llandybïe, 1963).

184 For the exceptional testimony by Thomas Roberts, his minister, to him on the day of his funeral, see Roberts, *Bargen Bywyd fy Nhaid*, p. 17. Parry died on 2 January 1896, *Cymro* (9 January 1896), 5.

185 Roberts, *Bargen Bywyd fy Nhaid*, p. 13. He was the author's grandfather.

186 *Geninen* (1905), 125.

187 *Celt* (13 May 1892), 3; *Cymru*, II (1892), 257–60.

188 Ernest Roberts, *Ar Lwybrau'r Gwynt* (Caernarfon, 1965), p. 35; W. J. Parry, *Chwareli a Chwarelwyr* (Caernarfon, 1897). For Parry (1842–1927), see *DWB* and J. Roose Williams, *Quarryman's Champion* (Denbigh, 1978).

189 Roberts, *Ar Lwybrau'r Gwynt*, p. 34.

190 For example, *Celt* (29 September 1893), 9.

191 *Celt* (6 October 1893), 4.

192 *Tyst* gave some attention to the industrial disputes in 1893, for example (28 August), 6, 8–9; (1 September), 8–9; (15 September), 9.

193 For further details, see E. W. Evans, *Mabon*, p. 66; Ness Edwards, *History of the South Wales Miners* (London, 1926).

[194] Cyril Parry discusses the 'embourgeoisiement' of the Liberal Party in *The Radical Tradition in Welsh Politics* (Hull, 1970), pp. 15–17.

[195] *Dysgedydd* (1839), 174.

[196] Francis Williams, *Fifty Years' March* (London, 1950), chs 1–3.

[197] *Celt* (29 July 1892), 4.

[198] *Celt* (27 January 1893), 8.

[199] Evans, *Mabon*, p. 76.

[200] David Thomas, *Silyn* (Liverpool, 1956), pp. 74–5; Parry, *Radical Tradition*, pp. 30–3.

[201] They can be found also in *Llais Llafur* (1899–1900), and *Y Cymro* (1902–3). For R. J. Derfel (1824–1905), see 'Rhagymadrodd', D. Gwenallt Jones (ed.), *Detholiad o Ryddiaeth Gymraeg R. J. Derfel* (Denbigh, 1945), and Islwyn ap Nicholas, *R. J. Derfel* (London, 1945).

[202] K. O. Morgan, *Journal of the National Library of Wales*, XVII (1971–2), 367.

[203] See Pope, *Building Jerusalem*, ch. 3.

[204] *Dysgedydd* (1908), 32–8, 256–61, 346–51, 556–61, 'Sosialaeth a Christionogaeth'; cf. W. F. Phillips, 'Sosialaeth a chrefydd', *Y Ddraig Goch ynte'r Faner Goch?* (Cardiff, 1913), pp. 119–24.

[205] *Seren Cymru* (19 November 1909), 11.

[206] *Seren Cymru* (12 February 1909) to (7 May); see also his book *Sosialaeth* (Barmouth, 1911).

[207] 'Gwerinwr', *Geninen* (1910), 258–61.

[208] *Llais Llafur* (13 May 1911), 5.

[209] *Llais Llafur* (22 April 1911), 2. For a peevish response to the socialists' criticism, see W. F. Phillips, 'Sosialaeth a chrefydd', pp. 119–24.

[210] *Aberdare Leader* (23 January 1909), 8.

[211] *Llais Llafur* (13 January 1912), 7; Vernon Hartshorne agreed, 'Politics and the Pulpit', *Llais Llafur* (9 September 1911), 4.

[212] *Llais Llafur* (12 October 1912), 4.

[213] *Llais Llafur* (6 January 1912), 2; cf. J. M. Jones, 'Was Jesus a Socialist?', *Monthly Democrat* (1912), 33–5.

[214] *Llais Llafur* (22 July 1911), 4.

[215] *Llais Llafur* (17 June 1911), 4.

[216] C. E. Gwyther, 'Methodism and Syndicalism in the Rhondda Valley, 1906 to 1926', unpublished MA dissertation, University of Nottingham.

[217] *Haul* (1896), 26–8, to (1897), 54–6.

[218] *Llais Llafur* (10 June 1911), 1.

[219] *Llais Llafur* (11 May 1912), 6.

[220] John Edwards, Pontardawe, on the Calvinistic Methodist Confession of Faith, *Llais Llafur* (25 May 1912), 4.

[221] R. J. Campbell, *The New Theology* (London, 1907), p. 255.

[222] *Aberdare Leader* (9 January 1909), 4. For Rhondda Williams (1860–1945), see his autobiography, *How I Found My Faith* (London, 1938), and *Congregational Year Book* (1946), 456. There was a split in 'Bethlehem Congregational Church, Abercwmboi' and a branch of the Progressive League was established with Roderick Rhydderch as president, *Aberdare Leader* (23 January 1909), 8.

[223] For the 'Social Gospel', see *New International Dictionary of the Christian Church* (Exeter, 1974), articles on 'Social Gospel' and 'Walter Rauschenbusch (1861–1918)'. Also see Robert Pope, *Seeking God's Kingdom: The Nonconformist Social Gospel in Wales, 1906–1939* (Cardiff, 1999).

[224] David Thomas, *Diolch am Gael Byw* (Liverpool, 1968), pp. 27–31 – a revealing and honest chapter on 'Religion'.

[225] Quoted by David Thomas, *Silyn*, p. 77.

Index

INDEX